Koren Talmud Bavli

THE NOÉ EDITION

KETUBOT

Steinsaltz Center

KOREN

תלמוד בבלי

KOREN TALMUD BAVLI

THE NOÉ EDITION

כתובות

KETUBOT

Daf 29a through Daf 41b

COMMENTARY BY

Rabbi Adin Even-Israel Steinsaltz

EDITOR-IN-CHIEF

Rabbi Dr Tzvi Hersh Weinreb

SENIOR CONTENT EDITOR

Rabbi Dr Shalom Z Berger

EXECUTIVE EDITOR

Rabbi Joshua Schreier

STEINSALTZ CENTER

KOREN PUBLISHERS JERUSALEM

Supported by the Matanel Foundation

Koren Talmud Bavli, The Noe Edition
Vol. 15c: Tractate Ketubot, Daf 29a through Daf 41b
Paperback, ISBN, 978-965-7765-73-9

First Hebrew/English paperback edition, 2021

Koren Publishers Jerusalem Ltd.
PO Box 4044, Jerusalem 91040, ISRAEL
PO Box 8531, New Milford, CT 06776, USA
www.korenpub.com

Steinsaltz Center

Steinsaltz Center is the parent organization of institutions established by Rabbi Adin Even-Israel Steinsaltz

PO Box 45187, Jerusalem 91450 ISRAEL
Telephone: +972 2 646 0900, Fax +972 2 624 9454
www.steinsaltz-center.org

הִנֵּה יָמִים בָּאִים, נְאֻם אֲדֹנָי יֱהוִה, וְהִשְׁלַחְתִּי רָעָב בָּאָרֶץ,
לֹא־רָעָב לַלֶּחֶם וְלֹא־צָמָא לַמַּיִם, כִּי אִם־לִשְׁמֹעַ אֵת דִּבְרֵי יהוה.

Behold, days are coming – says the Lord God – I will send a hunger to the land, not a hunger for bread nor a thirst for water, but to hear the words of the Lord. (AMOS 8:11)

The Noé edition of the Koren Talmud Bavli
with the commentary of Rabbi Adin Even-Israel Steinsaltz
is dedicated to all those who open its covers
to quench their thirst for Jewish Knowledge,
in our generation of Torah renaissance.

This beautiful edition is for the young, the aged,
the novice and the savant alike,
as it unites the depth of Torah knowledge
with the best of academic scholarship.

Within its exquisite and vibrant pages,
words become worlds.

It will claim its place in the library of classics,
in the bookcases of the Beit Midrash,
the classrooms of our schools,
and in the offices of professionals and business people
who carve out precious time to grapple with its timeless wisdom.

For the Student and the Scholar

DEDICATED BY LEO AND SUE NOÉ

Steinsaltz Center

Executive Director, Steinsaltz Center

Rabbi Meni Even-Israel

Managing Editor

Rabbi Jason Rappoport

Senior Content Editor

Rabbi Dr. Shalom Z. Berger

Editors

Rabbi Joshua Amaru, *Coordinating Editor*
Rabbi Avishai Magence, *Content Curator*
Rabbi Alan Haber
Gila Hoch
Stephen Lauber
Eli Ozarowski
Avi Steinhart
Rabbi David Strauss
Rabbi Abe Y. Weschler

Copy Editors

Aliza Israel, *Coordinator*
Bracha Hermon
Ita Olesker
Debbie Ismailoff
Shira Finson
Ilana Sobel
Deena Nataf
Eliana Kurlantzick Yorav
Erica Hirsch Edvi
Nava Wieder

Language Consultants

Dr. Stephanie E. Binder, *Greek & Latin*
Rabbi Yaakov Hoffman, *Arabic*
Dr. Shai Secunda, *Persian*
Shira Shmidman, *Aramaic*

KOREN

Design & Typesetting

Dena Landowne Bailey, *Typesetting*
Tani Bayer, *Jacket Design*
Raphaël Freeman, *Design & Typography*

Images

Eliahu Misgav, *Illustration & Image Acquisition*

Introduction by the Publisher

The Talmud has sustained and inspired Jews for thousands of years. Throughout Jewish history, an elite cadre of scholars has absorbed its learning and passed it on to succeeding generations. The Talmud has been the fundamental text of our people.

Beginning in the 1960s, Rabbi Adin Even-Israel Steinsaltz שליט״א created a revolution in the history of Talmud study. His translation of the Talmud, first into modern Hebrew and then into other languages, as well the practical learning aids he added to the text, have enabled millions of people around the world to access and master the complexity and context of the world of Talmud.

It is thus a privilege to present the *Koren Talmud Bavli*, an English translation of the talmudic text with the brilliant elucidation of Rabbi Steinsaltz. The depth and breadth of his knowledge are unique in our time. His rootedness in the tradition and his reach into the world beyond it are inspirational.

Working with Rabbi Steinsaltz on this remarkable project has been not only an honor, but a great pleasure. Never shy to express an opinion, with wisdom and humor, Rabbi Steinsaltz sparkles in conversation, demonstrating his knowledge (both sacred and worldly), sharing his wide-ranging interests, and, above all, radiating his passion. I am grateful for the unique opportunity to work closely with him, and I wish him many more years of writing and teaching.

Our intentions in publishing this new edition of the Talmud are threefold. First, we seek to fully clarify the talmudic page to the reader – textually, intellectually, and graphically. Second, we seek to utilize today's most sophisticated technologies, both in print and electronic formats, to provide the reader with a comprehensive set of study tools. And third, we seek to help readers advance in their process of Talmud study.

To achieve these goals, the *Koren Talmud Bavli* is unique in a number of ways:

- The classic *tzurat hadaf* of Vilna, used by scholars since the 1800s, has been reset for great clarity, and opens from the Hebrew "front" of the book. Full *nikkud* has been added to both the talmudic text and Rashi's commentary, allowing for a more fluent reading with the correct pronunciation; the commentaries of *Tosafot* have been punctuated. Upon the advice of many English-speaking teachers of Talmud, we have separated these core pages from the translation, thereby enabling the advanced student to approach the text without the distraction of the translation. This also reduces the number of volumes in the set. At the bottom of each *daf*, there is a reference to the corresponding English pages. In addition, the Vilna edition was read against other manuscripts and older print editions, so that texts which had been removed by non-Jewish censors have been restored to their rightful place.
- The English translation, which starts on the English "front" of the book, reproduces the *menukad* Talmud text alongside the English translation (in bold) and commentary and explanation (in a lighter font). The Hebrew and Aramaic text is presented in logical paragraphs. This allows for a fluent reading of the text for the non-Hebrew or non-Aramaic reader. It also allows for the Hebrew reader to refer easily to the text alongside. Where the original text features dialogue or poetry, the English text is laid out in a manner appropriate to the genre. Each page refers to the relevant *daf*.

- Critical contextual tools surround the text and translation: personality notes, providing short biographies of the Sages; language notes, explaining foreign terms borrowed from Greek, Latin, Persian, or Arabic; and background notes, giving information essential to the understanding of the text, including history, geography, botany, archaeology, zoology, astronomy, and aspects of daily life in the talmudic era.
- Halakhic summaries provide references to the authoritative legal decisions made over the centuries by the rabbis. They explain the reasons behind each halakhic decision as well as the ruling's close connection to the Talmud and its various interpreters.
- Photographs, drawings, and other illustrations have been added throughout the text – in full color in the Standard and Electronic editions, and in black and white in the Daf Yomi edition – to visually elucidate the text.

This is not an exhaustive list of features of this edition, it merely presents an overview for the English-speaking reader who may not be familiar with the "total approach" to Talmud pioneered by Rabbi Steinsaltz.

Several professionals have helped bring this vast collaborative project to fruition. My many colleagues are noted on the Acknowledgments page, and the leadership of this project has been exceptional.

RABBI MENACHEM EVEN-ISRAEL, DIRECTOR OF THE STEINSALTZ CENTER, was the driving force behind this enterprise. With enthusiasm and energy, he formed the happy alliance with Koren and established close relationships among all involved in the work.

RABBI DR. TZVI HERSH WEINREB שליט״א, EDITOR-IN-CHIEF, brought to this project his profound knowledge of Torah, intellectual literacy of Talmud, and erudition of Western literature. It is to him that the text owes its very high standard, both in form and content, and the logical manner in which the beauty of the Talmud is presented.

RABBI JOSHUA SCHREIER, EXECUTIVE EDITOR, assembled an outstanding group of scholars, translators, editors, and proofreaders, whose standards and discipline enabled this project to proceed in a timely and highly professional manner.

RABBI MEIR HANEGBI, EDITOR OF THE HEBREW EDITION OF THE STEINSALTZ TALMUD, lent his invaluable assistance throughout the work process, supervising the reproduction of the Vilna pages.

RAPHAËL FREEMAN, EXECUTIVE EDITOR OF KOREN, created this Talmud's unique typographic design which, true to the Koren approach, is both elegant and user friendly.

It has been an enriching experience for all of us at Koren Publishers Jerusalem to work with the Steinsaltz Center to develop and produce the *Koren Talmud Bavli*. We pray that this publication will be a source of great learning and, ultimately, greater *avodat Hashem* for all Jews.

Matthew Miller, Publisher
Koren Publishers Jerusalem
Jerusalem 5772

Contents

Ketubot 163

Image Credits 234

For the vocalized Vilna Shas layout, please open as a Hebrew book.

Introduction to **Perek III**

And if a man seduce a virgin who was not betrothed, and lies with her, he shall pay a dowry for her to be a wife to him. If her father refuses to give her to him, he shall weigh money like the dowry of the virgins.

(Exodus 22:15–16)

If a man finds a young woman who is a virgin who was not betrothed, and lay hold on her, and lie with her, and they be found; and the man who lay with her shall give to the father of the young woman fifty shekels of silver, and to him she shall be as a wife, because he tormented her; he may not put her away all his days.

(Deuteronomy 22:28–29)

The *halakhot* of the seducer and the rapist are explicit in the Torah; however, since they are written succinctly, many questions remain that demand practical halakhic resolution.

One of the primary questions relates to the attitude toward the language of the verses: Do the *halakhot* of the seducer and the rapist apply only in the cases delineated in the verse; or does the verse merely cite a specific case in order to illustrate the *halakha*, which applies in other cases as well? This question relates to several details. Does this apply only to a young woman who is a virgin or does it apply to a minor girl and a grown woman as well? Does this apply only to a young woman whose father is alive, or even to an orphan? Is the right of refusal for the marriage of the victim exclusively that of the father and is it applicable only in the case of seduction?

Another related fundamental problem is: What is the *halakha* when there is an additional prohibition associated with this intercourse beyond the seduction and the rape? It could be that the woman is forbidden to the rapist by rabbinic law, due to a positive mitzva, due to a prohibition, or even due to a prohibition punishable by death. Is the perpetrator required to marry his victim in all these cases? Is he obligated to pay the fine? Does he receive only one punishment, or is he is subject to both punishments? These questions require a comprehensive analysis of the general principles of punishment: What is the *halakha* when there is more than one punishment for violating a single prohibition?

Another basic question involves the nature of the payment paid by the seducer and the rapist. Is the sum mentioned in the Torah the total compensation to the victim or is it merely a special fine paid in addition to other payments of compensation like those paid to any other victim of violence? If there are additional payments, how are they assessed and to whom are they paid?

These problems and others that emerge from their resolution constitute the focus of this chapter.

מתני׳ אֵלּוּ נְעָרוֹת שֶׁיֵּשׁ לָהֶן קְנָס: הַבָּא עַל הַמַּמְזֶרֶת, וְעַל הַנְּתִינָה, וְעַל הַכּוּתִית. הַבָּא עַל הַגִּיּוֹרֶת, וְעַל הַשְּׁבוּיָה. וְעַל הַשִּׁפְחָה שֶׁנִּפְדּוּ וְשֶׁנִּתְגַּיְּירוּ וְשֶׁנִּשְׁתַּחְרְרוּ פְּחוּתוֹת מִבְּנוֹת שָׁלֹשׁ שָׁנִים וְיוֹם אֶחָד.

MISHNA **These**[N] are the cases of **young women**[HB] **for whom there is a fine**[N] paid to their fathers by one who rapes them: **One who engages in intercourse with a** ***mamzeret*****,**[N] **or with a Gibeonite woman** [***netina***]**,**[N] who are given [*netunim*] to the service of the people and the altar (see Joshua 9:27), **or with a Samaritan woman** [***kutit***]**.**[N] In addition, the same applies to **one who engages in intercourse with a female convert,**[NH] **or with a captive woman, or with a maidservant,** provided **that** the captives **were ransomed,** or that the converts **converted, or that** the maidservants **were liberated** when they were **less than three years and one day old,** as only in that case do they maintain the presumptive status of a virgin.

NOTES

These – **אֵלּוּ**: There was a variant version of the text before the early commentaries that read: And these are the young women. The Rosh justifies the version that appears in the mishna, as the phrase: And these, indicates continuation, and a new topic is addressed in this chapter. However, in the *Shita Mekubbetzet*, the version: And these, is explained. After the women who receive marriage contracts of one hundred or two hundred dinar were enumerated in the earlier chapters, the *tanna* cites an additional list comprised of women for whom there is a fine for rape. In the *Melekhet Shlomo*, support for that contention is cited, as that accounts for the fact that the *tanna* included only young women who are of flawed lineage or otherwise unfit in this list. In addition to the women of unflawed lineage mentioned in the previous chapters, these women, too, are entitled to the fine.

For whom there is a fine – **שֶׁיֵּשׁ לָהֶן קְנָס**: In addition to the fine, the rapist pays compensation for humiliation and degradation as well. However, the *tanna* did not mention those payments here, as he based himself on the verse, which mentions only the fine in the context of a young woman who was raped (*Shita Mekubbetzet*).

One who engages in intercourse with a ***mamzeret*** – **הַבָּא עַל הַמַּמְזֶרֶת**: In the *Shita Mekubbetzet*, the reason that the mishna is formulated in terms of the rapist: One who engages in intercourse with, instead of simply: These are the young women…a *mamzeret*, a Gibeonite, etc., is addressed. The explanation supports Rabbi Yoḥanan's opinion cited later that the mishna is referring to a case where the rapist was not forewarned. The formulation: One who engages in intercourse with a *mamzeret*, indicates that there was no forewarning.

Gibeonite woman – **נְתִינָה**: The halakhic status of the descendants of the Gibeonites is addressed in several places in the Talmud, primarily in tractates *Yevamot* and *Kiddushin*. Nevertheless, several fundamental questions are not completely resolved and are addressed by the early and later commentaries. From Rashi's commentary here, it appears that the prohibition against the Gibeonites entering the congregation of Israel is not by Torah law but by rabbinic law in the broadest sense of the term, as everyone agrees that it is an early decree dating back to the time of Moses or King David. *Tosafot*, based on the context here and other sources, explain at length that this cannot be the case, and they assert that the prohibition is in fact by Torah law. There are also different opinions with regard to the nature of the prohibition. Some claim that the decree was that the Gibeonites were to be slaves and as such may not marry Jews. That is problematic, because if the legal status of a Gibeonite woman were that of a slave, she would not be entitled to a fine at all. In the Jerusalem Talmud it is explained that the Sages prohibited the Gibeonites from entering the congregation due to concerns about their flawed lineage, although they are still considered Jews. Others explain that the decree accords them the halakhic status of slaves, although fundamentally, they are not actual slaves. Most commentaries contend that Gibeonites are Canaanites, to whom the prohibition "You shall not marry them" (Deuteronomy 7:3) takes effect only after they converted.

Some early commentaries suggest an intermediate opinion. They contend that the first generation of Gibeonites was forbidden by the Torah prohibition: "You shall not marry them"; however, that prohibition did not apply to their children. The extension of the prohibition to their descendants is a decree issued by Joshua or King David (*Talmid HaRa'ah*). *Talmidei Rabbeinu Yona* state, in the name of *Tosefot Rabbi Shimshon of Saens*, that the *tanna* lists a Gibeonite together with a *mamzeret* because they appear together in other contexts, much as a divorcée and a *ḥalutza* are enumerated together as women forbidden to a priest. In both cases, one is prohibited by Torah law, i.e., the *mamzeret* and the divorcée, and one is prohibited by rabbinic law, i.e., the Gibeonite and the *ḥalutza*. The Ritva responds that although there is similarity that would justify listing a divorcée and a *ḥalutza* together, there is no similarity between a *mamzeret* and a Gibeonite. The only justification for listing them together is if they are both prohibited by Torah law.

Samaritan woman – **כּוּתִית**: The status of Samaritans is also subject to a dispute between *tanna'im*. There are two aspects to this matter. First, with regard to their status: Are they considered Jews at all? Second, how does one relate to them in practice? Some *tanna'im* hold that Samaritans are converts coerced by lions (see II Kings, chapter 17), whose conversion never took effect, and they are therefore full-fledged gentiles. The fact that they practice certain mitzvot of the Written Torah does not render them part of the congregation of Israel. Others maintain that they are actual converts. Although they did not initially convert with sincere motives, they later accepted Judaism. According to this opinion, they are full-fledged Jews, despite the fact that their practices deviate from normative *halakha*. Yet even those Sages who deem them Jews disagree with regard to the attitude toward them. Some contend that due to their treatment of the Jewish people, their idolatrous practices, and other reasons, they were penalized to the extent that not only are they kept at a distance, but they are treated as though they are not Jews at all, in the same manner as Jewish apostates. Others assert that it is prohibited to marry them due to concern about their lineage in terms of *mamzerim*, resulting from their lack of observance of *halakha*.

Tosafot, who discuss various aspects of this issue, maintain contrary to the opinion of Rashi that the *tanna* of this mishna holds in accordance with the opinion of Rabbi Meir that the Samaritans were genuine converts. Although Rabbi Meir himself holds that sanctions were imposed upon them with regard to certain monetary matters, he concedes that the fine for rape remains in place, so that the sinner would not profit from his wrongdoing. In the Jerusalem Talmud it is explicitly stated that the mishna is in accordance with the opinion of Rabbi Meir.

One who engages in intercourse with a female convert, etc. – **הַבָּא עַל הַגִּיּוֹרֶת וכו׳**: The Rashash asks why the *tanna* did not list those women forbidden by a standard prohibition, e.g., a *mamzeret*, first, followed by those forbidden by a prohibition punishable by *karet*, e.g., one's sister. Why did he insert the convert between them? The Rashash explains that the *tanna* did so to underscore that although the lineage of a *mamzeret*, a Gibeonite, etc., is flawed, her status is unlike that of a convert or a woman taken captive, whose circumstances rob them of their presumptive status as a virgin.

HALAKHA

These are the cases of young women, etc. – **אֵלּוּ נְעָרוֹת וכו׳**: With regard to one who rapes or seduces a virgin who was forbidden to him by a standard Torah prohibition or by a prohibition punishable by *karet*, if he was forewarned he is flogged and does not pay the fine. If he was not forewarned, he is not flogged, and he pays the fine (Rambam *Sefer Nashim, Hilkhot Na'ara Betula* 1:11; *Tur, Even HaEzer* 177).

One who engages in intercourse with a female convert, etc. – **הַבָּא עַל הַגִּיּוֹרֶת וכו׳**: If a gentile converted, a woman taken captive was redeemed, or a maidservant was freed when they were three years old or less, they are entitled to the fine for rape (Rambam *Sefer Nashim, Hilkhot Na'ara Betula* 1:10; *Tur, Even HaEzer* 177).

BACKGROUND

A young woman – **נַעֲרָה**: The *halakha* recognizes three distinct stages in the development of a woman from childhood to adulthood.

A female minor is a girl who has not yet reached puberty, which takes place at or about age twelve. As a minor, her father has the right to sell her to be a Hebrew maidservant or to betroth her to a man. If he does so, the result is a full-fledged betrothal in every sense. The father also receives his minor daughter's marriage contract and has the exclusive right to accept a bill of divorce on her behalf.

Once she reaches puberty, her legal status is that of a young woman. Although she is no longer a minor, she is not yet a full-fledged adult. Accordingly, her father retains certain authority over her.

Six months later, her legal status is that of a grown woman. From that point on, she is a fully independent adult, and her father no longer has any authority to make decisions on her behalf.

הַבָּא עַל אֲחוֹתוֹ וְעַל אֲחוֹת אָבִיו וְעַל אֲחוֹת אִמּוֹ וְעַל אֲחוֹת אִשְׁתּוֹ וְעַל אֵשֶׁת אָחִיו וְעַל אֵשֶׁת אֲחִי אָבִיו וְעַל הַנִּדָּה – יֵשׁ לָהֶם קְנָס, אַף עַל פִּי שֶׁהֵן בְּהִכָּרֵת – אֵין בָּהֶן מִיתַת בֵּית דִּין.

Similarly, **one who engages in intercourse with his sister,** i.e., he rapes her, **or with his father's sister, or with his mother's sister, or with his wife's sister, or with his brother's wife,**[N] **or with his father's brother's wife** after they divorced, **or with a menstruating woman, there is a fine** paid. **Although there is *karet*** for engaging in relations with any of the women enumerated in this list, one is liable to pay the fine because **there is no court**-imposed **capital punishment.** In cases where there is a court-imposed death penalty, the rapist would be exempt from paying the fine.

גמ׳ הָנֵי נְעָרוֹת פְּסוּלוֹת – אִית לְהוּ קְנָס, כְּשֵׁירוֹת – לָא?! הָכִי קָאָמַר: אֵלּוּ נְעָרוֹת פְּסוּלוֹת שֶׁיֵּשׁ לָהֶם קְנָס: הַבָּא עַל הַמַּמְזֶרֶת וְעַל הַנְּתִינָה וְעַל הַכּוּתִית.

GEMARA

The Gemara wonders: Is it **these young women** with **flawed** lineage[N] listed in the mishna, **for whom there is a fine** paid if they are raped, while for young women with **unflawed** lineage, **no,** there is no fine? The Gemara explains that **this** is what the *tanna* **is saying: These are** the **young women** with **flawed** lineage **for whom there is a fine** paid if they are raped. This is not a comprehensive list; rather, the *tanna* enumerates those young women for whom a fine is paid despite their flawed lineage: **One who has relations with a *mamzeret,* or with a Gibeonite woman, or with a Samaritan woman.**

נַעֲרָה – אִין, קְטַנָּה – לָא, מַאן תַּנָּא?

The mishna teaches the *halakha* with regard to a young woman, from which the Gemara infers: With regard to **a young woman, yes,** one is liable to pay the fine if he rapes her, but with regard to **a minor, no,**[N] one is not liable to pay the fine. **Who is the *tanna***[N] who maintains that one is liable for raping a young woman but not a minor?

NOTES

Or with his brother's wife, etc. – וְעַל אֵשֶׁת אָחִיו וכו׳: The early commentaries note that the women listed in the mishna as the wife of his brother or of his father's brother are either widowed or divorced, as one who has relations with a married woman is liable to receive the death penalty. Furthermore, they must have been widowed or divorced when they were betrothed, not married, as the fine is imposed only on one who raped or seduced a virgin young woman. A married woman can no longer be considered a virgin young woman even if she did not engage in conjugal relations. That is the understanding that emerges from a careful reading of Rashi. In the Jerusalem Talmud the following question is raised: The wife of one's childless deceased brother is a *yevama*, with regard to whom there is neither prohibition nor fine, as it is a mitzva to have relations with her. They explain that the reference is to the widow of a brother who had children with another woman. Therefore, there is no mitzva of levirate marriage, and the prohibition against relations with one's brother's wife remains intact. Rashi resolves this difficulty by explaining that she is a divorcée, with regard to whom there is no mitzva of levirate marriage.

These young women with flawed lineage, etc. – הָנֵי נְעָרוֹת פְּסוּלוֹת וכו׳: The Ritva reinforces this question, as he explains that the term: These, is typically exclusionary, meaning: These and not others. Other early commentaries, however, contend that the term does not always bear that connotation, especially in this case, where there is another list in the next mishna. See also previous note, with regard to the textual variant: And these. A different problem, raised by the Ramban, is that not all of these young women are unfit for marriage; converts, for example, are certainly not barred from entering the congregation of Israel. Therefore, some commentaries explain unfit in this context as referring to women whose lineage is flawed because they were born of a forbidden union or for a different reason. The Ramban himself explains, citing *Tosafot*, that the mishna is referring to a convert, redeemed captive, or liberated slave who was raped by a priest. Since they are forbidden to priests, through intercourse with a priest they are rendered unfit. See the Ritva, who writes contrary to that approach. Several later commentaries question that explanation as well.

A young woman, yes; a minor, no – נַעֲרָה אִין, קְטַנָּה לָא: *Tosafot* ask why the Gemara opted for that inference. The Gemara could have inferred: Young women, yes; adult women, no, and then the mishna would be in accordance with the opinions of all the *tanna'im*. *Tosafot* and other early commentaries explain that the inference is based not on the language of the mishna but on the statement later in the Gemara (40b) that the unattributed mishna is in accordance with the opinion of Rabbi Meir. It is therefore reasonable to posit that this mishna follows the same approach. The Ramban explains that had the *tanna* intended merely to exclude grown women, he could have stated: And these are they for whom there is a fine, as it is clear that grown women receive no fine for rape. By specifying young women, he indicates that the *halakha* applies exclusively to young women and not to minors. In the *Shita Mekubbetzet* it is explained that in cases involving a dispute between *tanna'im*, the *tanna* of the mishna usually enters into greater detail. Therefore, the assumption is that he mentioned young women specifically to take a side in the dispute. The *Yam shel Shlomo* explains that had the *tanna* sought to exclude grown women, he could have written: And these are the virgins, as adult women are not considered full-fledged virgins, since in the course of their physical development their hymens do not remain completely intact.

Who is the *tanna* – מַאן תַּנָּא: *Tosafot* at the beginning of tractate *Moed Katan* state that typically, the Gemara does not ask: Who is the *tanna*, with regard to a mishna that is in accordance with the opinion of Rabbi Meir, as there is a principle that opinions cited in an unattributed mishna are recognized as those of Rabbi Meir. Still, the question is raised here, and the mishna is attributed to Rabbi Meir. In the *Shita Mekubbetzet* it is explained that since the entire mishna is not in accordance with the opinion of Rabbi Meir, as proven later from the *halakha* of one who rapes his daughter, and according to some commentaries from the *halakha* of a Samaritan woman as well, it was therefore necessary to assert that the primary *halakha* in the mishna is in fact in accordance with the opinion of Rabbi Meir. Other commentaries cite this as proof that the *halakha* is not in accordance with the opinion of Rabbi Meir, as the Gemara's question indicates that this is not an unattributed mishna, in accordance with which the *halakha* is ruled, but the opinion of an individual Sage (see *Mishne LaMelekh*).

אמר רב יהודה אמר רב: רבי מאיר היא. דתניא: קטנה, מבת יום אחד ועד שתביא שתי שערות – יש לה מכר ואין לה קנס. ומשתביא שתי שערות ועד שתיבגר – יש לה קנס ואין לה מכר, דברי רבי מאיר. שהיה רבי מאיר אומר: כל מקום שיש מכר – אין קנס, וכל מקום שיש קנס – אין מכר.

Rav Yehuda said that **Rav said:** The *tanna* **is Rabbi Meir, as it is taught** in a *baraita*: **With regard to a minor from** the age of **one day old until she grows two** pubic **hairs, there is** the possibility of **sale for her,**[H] as her father may sell her as a Hebrew maidservant, **but there is no fine** paid **for her** if she is raped. **And once she grows two** pubic **hairs,** from that point **until she matures** into a grown woman **there is a fine for her,** as during that period she is a young woman, with regard to whom the Torah law of a rapist and a seducer applies, **but there is no** possibility of **sale for her.** Once she grows two hairs she is no longer under her father's control and can no longer be sold. This is **the statement of Rabbi Meir, as Rabbi Meir would state** a principle: **Any place where there is a sale, there is no fine; and any place where there is a fine, there is no sale.**

וחכמים אומרים: קטנה, מבת שלש שנים ויום אחד ועד שתיבגר – יש לה קנס. קנס אין, מכר לא?! אימא:

And the Rabbis say: With regard to a minor from the age of **three years and one day old until she matures** into a grown woman, **there is a fine for her.**[H] The Gemara asks: Is that to say that a **fine, yes,** there is, but a **sale, no,** there is not? Do the Rabbis maintain that the father has no right to sell his minor daughter? The Gemara emends the text: **Say:**

HALAKHA

There is the possibility of sale for her – יש לה מכר: The father of a minor girl may sell her as a Hebrew maidservant from the day of her birth until she completes her twelfth year and grows two pubic hairs. However, once she has grown two pubic hairs, he may no longer sell her (Rambam *Sefer Kinyan, Hilkhot Avadim* 4:1).

When is there a fine for her – מתי יש לה קנס: A virgin is entitled to a fine for rape from the age of three years and one day old until puberty, in accordance with the opinion of the Rabbis. Although the unattributed mishna is in accordance with the opinion of Rabbi Meir and as a rule the *halakha* is ruled accordingly, the Gemara indicates that the mishna reflects an individual opinion. That is the ruling of Rif, the Rambam, and the Rosh. Rabbeinu Ḥananel and the Ra'avad rule in accordance with the unattributed mishna (Rambam *Sefer Nashim, Hilkhot Na'ara Betula* 1:8; *Shulḥan Arukh, Even HaEzer* 177:1).

אף קנס במקום מכר.

There is a **fine even in a place** where there is **sale.** That is, not only can a minor girl from the age of three be sold until she matures, but she also receives payment of the fine.

והני בני קנסא נינהו? ואמאי? איקרי כאן "ולו תהיה לאשה" – אשה הראויה לו! אמר ריש לקיש: "נערה", "נערה", "הנערה"; חד – לגופיה, וחד – לאתויי חייבי לאוין, וחד – לאתויי חייבי כריתות.

§ The Gemara questions the basic *halakha* that one who rapes young women of flawed lineage is liable to pay the fine: **And are these** young women **entitled to the fine?**[N] **But why? I read here** with regard to a rapist: **"And to him she shall be as a wife"** (Deuteronomy 22:29),[N] from which the Sages derived that only **a wife who is suitable for him** is eligible to receive payment of a fine from a rapist. **Reish Lakish said** that one verse states: "If a man finds a young woman" (Deuteronomy 22:28), and another states: "And he shall give to the father of the young woman" (Deuteronomy 22:29). This is tantamount to three mentions: **Young woman, young woman, the young woman,** as the superfluous definite article is interpreted as a third mention of the term. **One** mention is required **to teach the matter itself,** that one who rapes a young woman is liable to pay a fine; **and one is to include** payment of a fine to those young women for whose rape one is **liable for** violating **prohibitions; and one is to include** payment of a fine to those young women for whose rape one is **liable to** receive *karet.*

רב פפא אמר: "בתולה", "בתולות", "הבתולות" חד – לגופיה, וחד – לאתויי חייבי לאוין, וחד – לאתויי חייבי כריתות.

Rav Pappa said: This is derived from the *halakha* of the seducer, as the verses state: "And if a man seduce a virgin… he shall weigh money like the dowry of the virgins" (Exodus 22:15–16). This is tantamount to three mentions: **Virgin, virgins, the virgins. One** mention is required **to teach the matter itself; and one is to include** those young women for whose rape one is **liable for** violating **prohibitions; and one is to include** those young women for whom one who rapes them is **liable to** receive *karet.*

ורב פפא מאי טעמא לא אמר כריש לקיש? ההוא מיבעי ליה לכדאביי. דאמר אביי: בא עליה ומתה – פטור, שנאמר "ונתן לאבי הנערה" – לאבי נערה ולא לאבי מתה.

The Gemara asks: **And Rav Pappa, what is the reason** that **he did not** cite the source **as Reish Lakish** did? The Gemara answers: **That** derivation from the three instances of the term young woman is **required by him to** teach **in accordance with that** which **Abaye** said, as **Abaye said:** If one **engaged in** forced **intercourse with** a young woman **and she died**[H] before he stood trial, he is **exempt** from paying the fine, as **it is stated: "And he shall give to the father of the young woman"** (Deuteronomy 22:29). From the fact that the verse does not simply say: To her father, it is inferred: **To the father of the young woman and not to the father of a dead** woman. He is liable only if the young woman is still alive.

NOTES

And are these entitled to the fine – והני בני קנסא נינהו: Rashi indicates that this marks the beginning of a new discussion in which the Gemara analyzes the mishna itself. In the *Shita Mekubbetzet* there is an attempt to tie this matter to the previous one. Had the Gemara explained that the mishna is dealing only with the practical *halakha*, the mishna could be explained as teaching that the young women of flawed lineage are not entitled to the fine by Torah law. The Rabbis instituted that the fine should be paid, for the following reason: So that a sinner will not profit. After asserting that the mishna is dealing with Torah law, and that the fine is paid to the father of a young woman and not the father of a minor, this must be reconciled with the verses in the Torah.

I read here: "And to him she shall be a wife" – איקרי כאן ולו תהיה לאשה: The Ritva contends that this difficulty does not stem from the verse itself, as the verse can be explained in the opposite manner, i.e., that a rapist must marry the woman he raped even if she is unfit to marry him. The *Tosefot Rid* cites the Gemara later (40a), where the question is raised: Why doesn't the positive mitzva to marry the young woman override the prohibition against marrying her? Rather, the difficulty is based primarily on the interpretation of the Sages that "she shall be a wife" refers to a woman suitable for him.

HALAKHA

If one engaged in forced intercourse with a young woman and she died – בא עליה ומתה: If a young woman raped by a man died before he stood trial, he is exempt from paying the fine, as per the opinion of Abaye (Rambam *Sefer Nashim, Hilkhot Na'ara Betula* 1:15; *Tur, Even HaEzer* 177).

וְרֵישׁ לָקִישׁ מַאי טַעְמָא לָא אָמַר כְּרַב פַּפָּא? הַהוּא מִיבָּעֵי לֵיהּ לִגְזֵירָה שָׁוָה. דְּתַנְיָא: "כֶּסֶף יִשְׁקוֹל כְּמוֹהַר הַבְּתוּלוֹת" – שֶׁיְּהֵא זֶה כְּמוֹהַר הַבְּתוּלוֹת, וּמוֹהַר הַבְּתוּלוֹת כָּזֶה. וְרֵישׁ לָקִישׁ נַמִי, מִיבָּעֵי לֵיהּ לִכְדְאַבַּיֵי, וְרַב פַּפָּא נַמִי מִיבָּעֵי לֵיהּ לִגְזֵירָה שָׁוָה!

The Gemara asks: **And Reish Lakish, what is the reason** that he **did not** cite the source **as Rav Pappa** did? The Gemara answers: **That** derivation from the three instances of the term virgin is **required by him to** derive **a verbal analogy,**[B] **as it is taught** in a *baraita* that it is written with regard to a seducer: **"He shall weigh [*yishkol*] money like the dowry of the virgins"** (Exodus 22:16), from which it is derived **that this** fine of a seducer **should be** a sum of fifty *sela* **like the dowry of the virgins**[H] specified in the case of a rapist; **and the dowry of the virgins** must be paid in *sela* **like this** fine of the seducer. Therefore, Reish Lakish holds that no additional matters may be derived from the term virgins. The Gemara asks: **And** for **Reish Lakish too,** isn't it **required by him** to teach **in accordance with that** which **Abaye** said? **And** similarly, for **Rav Pappa,** isn't it **required by him to** derive **a verbal analogy?**

אֶלָּא שִׁיתָּא קְרָאֵי כְּתִיבִי: "נַעֲרָה" "נַעֲרָה" "הַנַּעֲרָה" "בְּתוּלָה" "בְּתוּלוֹת" "הַבְּתוּלוֹת", תְּרֵי – לְגוּפַיְיהוּ, חַד – לִכְדְאַבַּיֵי, וְחַד – לִגְזֵירָה שָׁוָה. אִיַּיתְרוּ לֵיהּ תְּרֵי, חַד – לְאַתּוּיֵי חַיָּיבֵי לָאוִין, וְחַד – לְאַתּוּיֵי חַיָּיבֵי כָּרֵיתוֹת.

Rather, there are **six verses written,**[N] and both Reish Lakish and Rav Pappa derive matters from all of them. In the two passages discussing the rapist and the seducer, it is written: **Young woman, young woman, the young woman; virgin, virgins, the virgins. Two** mentions are required **to** teach the matters **themselves,** the basic *halakhot* of a rapist and a seducer; **one** mention is needed **to** teach **in accordance with that** which **Abaye** said; **and one** mention is necessary **to** derive **a verbal analogy** with regard to the dowry of virgins. **Two** mentions of the term **remain for him; one** is **to include** those young women for whose rape one is **liable for** violating **prohibitions, and one** is **to include** those young women for whom one who rapes them is **liable to** receive ***karet***. Reish Lakish and Rav Pappa do not disagree; the derivation of each complements that of the other.

וּלְאַפּוּקֵי מֵהַאי תַּנָּא; דְּתַנְיָא: "וְלוֹ תִהְיֶה לְאִשָּׁה", שִׁמְעוֹן הַתִּימְנִי אוֹמֵר: אִשָּׁה שֶׁיֵּשׁ בָּהּ הֲוָיָה. רַבִּי שִׁמְעוֹן בֶּן מְנַסְיָא אוֹמֵר: אִשָּׁה הָרְאוּיָה לְקַיְּימָהּ.

§ The Gemara comments: **And** the mishna comes **to exclude** the opinion **of this *tanna*,**[N] **as it is taught** in a *baraita* that it is written: **"And to him she shall be [*tihye*] as a wife"** (Deuteronomy 22:29). **Shimon HaTimni says:** This is referring to **a woman for whom there is betrothal [*havaya*].**[N] If one betroths a woman with whom relations are punishable by *karet*, the betrothal does not take effect. **Rabbi Shimon ben Menasya says:** This is referring to **a woman who is suitable for** him **to sustain,**[H] whom he need not divorce due to her flawed lineage.

מַאי בֵּינַיְיהוּ? אָמַר רַבִּי זֵירָא: מַמְזֶרֶת וּנְתִינָה אִיכָּא בֵּינַיְיהוּ. לְמַאן דְּאָמַר יֵשׁ בָּהּ הֲוָיָה – הָא נַמִי יֵשׁ בָּהּ הֲוָיָה, לְמַאן דְּאָמַר רְאוּיָה לְקַיְּימָהּ – הָא אֵינָהּ רְאוּיָה לְקַיְּימָהּ.

The Gemara begins its analysis of the *baraita* with the question: **What is** the practical difference **between** the statements of Shimon HaTimni and Rabbi Shimon ben Menasya? The Gemara explains that **Rabbi Zeira said:** The difference **between their** opinions is with regard to **a *mamzeret* or a Gibeonite woman,** or any other woman who is forbidden but for whom betrothal takes effect. **According to the one who said** that the criterion is whether **there is betrothal,** for **this** woman **there is also betrothal.** If a Jewish man betroths a *mamzeret* or a Gibeonite woman, although it is prohibited to do so, the betrothal takes effect. However, **according to the one who said** that the criterion is whether the woman is **suitable for** him to **sustain, this** woman **is not suitable for** him to **sustain,** since due to the prohibition he is obligated to divorce her.

BACKGROUND

Verbal analogy – **גְּזֵירָה שָׁוָה**: This is a fundamental talmudic principle of biblical interpretation, appearing in all standard lists of exegetical principles: If the same word or phrase appears in two places in the Torah, and a certain *halakha* is stated explicitly in one of these places, one may infer, on the basis of a verbal analogy, that the same applies in the other case as well. Consequently, inferences drawn on the basis of verbal analogy rely on verbal identity rather than on conceptual similarity. For example, the Torah states concerning those convicted of certain types of sorcery: "Shall be put to death; they shall stone them with stones; their blood shall be upon them" (Leviticus 20:27). Since this verse employs the expression "their blood shall be upon them" when speaking of death by stoning, the Talmud infers by verbal analogy that in all cases where this expression is used, the punishment is capital punishment by stoning.

Generally, inferences are drawn through verbal analogy only if the same word or phrase appears in both of the verses being compared, although verbal analogies are occasionally drawn even if the terms are not identical, if their meanings are similar.

HALAKHA

That this should be like the dowry of the virgins – **שֶׁיְּהֵא זֶה כְּמוֹהַר הַבְּתוּלוֹת**: One who seduces or rapes a virgin young woman must pay a fine of fifty silver *sela* (Rambam *Sefer Nashim, Hilkhot Na'ara Betula* 1:1).

A woman who is suitable for him to sustain – **אִשָּׁה הָרְאוּיָה לְקַיְּימָהּ**: Although the Torah states that a rapist is obligated to marry his victim, if she is forbidden to him, even if the prohibition is due to a positive mitzva or by rabbinic law, he may not marry her, in accordance with the opinion of Rabbi Shimon ben Menasya (see *Kesef Mishne* and *Leḥem Mishne*). The *Halakhot Gedolot* states that this *halakha* is based on the later mishna (40a) (Rambam *Sefer Nashim, Hilkhot Na'ara Betula* 1:5; *Shulḥan Arukh, Even HaEzer* 177:4).

NOTES

There are six verses written – **שִׁיתָּא קְרָאֵי כְּתִיבִי**: In other words, there is no dispute between Reish Lakish and Rav Pappa. Each cited different aspects of the same exposition. One of them specified the terms that include those liable for violating prohibitions, while the other explained the terms that include those liable to receive *karet* (Ritva).

And to exclude the opinion of this *tanna* – **וּלְאַפּוּקֵי מֵהַאי תַּנָּא**: The *Tosafot Yeshanim* and the Rosh maintain that the mishna is actually excluding the opinions of two *tanna'im*, Shimon HaTimni and Rabbi Shimon ben Menasya, and the phrase: This *tanna*, is referring to the *tanna* who taught that *baraita* in which their opinions were cited. However, see the alternative versions of the text for readings that do not require this somewhat implausible interpretation.

For whom there is betrothal [*havaya*] – **שֶׁיֵּשׁ בָּהּ הֲוָיָה**: The term *havaya* is taken from the term used in the Torah: "And if a priest's daughter be married [*tihye*] to a common man" (Leviticus 22:12); "And to him she shall be [*tihye*] as a wife" (Deuteronomy 22:29). *Havaya*, which literally means being, means that the betrothal is effective. Although there is a fundamental dispute between *amora'im* in tractate *Temura* with regard to whether performance of a prohibited action can lead to a halakhically valid result, it is clear from the verses that in certain cases betrothal is effective even though it contravenes Torah law. This is true even according to the extreme opinion of Rabbi Akiva, who says that as a rule, even in cases where one merely violated a prohibition, a child born of that union is a *mamzer*. In this regard, there are many different levels of prohibition and circumstances that affect betrothal differently. Clearly, betrothal of an object or an animal does not take effect. Similarly, since betrothal and marriage are relevant only within the Jewish people, betrothal of a gentile or a slave does not take effect. With regard to other prohibitions there are differences of opinion as to whether the prohibition prevents the betrothal from taking effect, or whether it takes effect only in the sense that it is prohibited for the woman to marry another without first receiving a bill of divorce.

וּלְרַבִּי עֲקִיבָא, דַּאֲמַר: אֵין קִידּוּשִׁין תּוֹפְסִין בְּחַיָּיבֵי לָאוִין, מַאי בֵּינַיְיהוּ? אִיכָּא בֵּינַיְיהוּ אַלְמָנָה לְכֹהֵן גָּדוֹל, כְּרַבִּי סִימַאי. דְּתַנְיָא, רַבִּי סִימַאי אוֹמֵר: מִן הַכֹּל עוֹשֶׂה רַבִּי עֲקִיבָא מַמְזֵרִין, חוּץ מֵאַלְמָנָה לְכֹהֵן גָּדוֹל, שֶׁהֲרֵי אָמְרָה תּוֹרָה "לֹא יִקָּח...וְלֹא יְחַלֵּל" – חִילּוּלִין הוּא עוֹשֶׂה, וְאֵין עוֹשֶׂה מַמְזֵרִין.

The Gemara asks: **And according to Rabbi Akiva,**[N] **who said: Betrothal does not take effect for** women for whose rape one is **liable for** violating **prohibitions, what is** the difference **between them?** According to his opinion, betrothal of a *mamzeret* does not take effect either. The Gemara answers: The difference **between their** statements is the case of **a widow** raped **by a High Priest, in accordance with** the opinion of **Rabbi Simai, as it is taught** in a *baraita* that **Rabbi Simai says: Rabbi Akiva deems** children **from all** illicit relations *mamzerim*, **except for** a child born **from a widow to a High Priest, as the Torah said:** "A widow and a divorcée **he shall not take ... and he shall not profane** [*yeḥallel*] his seed among his people" (Leviticus 21:14–15), from which it is derived: If he has a child with a widow **he creates** *ḥillulin*,[N] i.e., the male offspring of those relations is a *ḥalal*, disqualified from the priesthood, and the female offspring is a *ḥalala*, unfit to marry a priest, **but he does not create** *mamzerim*. Apparently, in that case, the betrothal does take effect.

וּלְרַבִּי יְשֵׁבָב, דְּאָמַר: בּוֹאוּ וְנִצְוַח עַל עֲקִיבָא בֶּן יוֹסֵף, שֶׁהָיָה אוֹמֵר: כָּל שֶׁאֵין לוֹ בִּיאָה בְּיִשְׂרָאֵל הַוָּלָד מַמְזֵר. מַאי בֵּינַיְיהוּ? אִיכָּא בֵּינַיְיהוּ

The Gemara asks: **And according to Rabbi Yeshevav, who said: Come, let us scream at Akiva ben Yosef,** who is proliferating *mamzerim*, **as he would say:** With regard to **anyone who does not have** the possibility of permitted **relations in the Jewish people,** including a widow with a High Priest, **the offspring is a** ***mamzer*****, what is** the difference **between their** opinions, between the one who said that a fine is paid to women with whom the betrothal takes effect and the one who said that a fine is paid to women suitable for one to sustain? Rabbi Yeshevav maintains that betrothal does not take effect even in the case of a widow to a High Priest. The Gemara answers: **There is** a difference **between them** with regard to

NOTES

And according to Rabbi Akiva – וּלְרַבִּי עֲקִיבָא: *Tosafot* note that this question is irrelevant according to the opinion of Rabbi Shimon HaTimni, as the Gemara in *Yevamot* states explicitly that he disagrees with Rabbi Akiva in this regard and maintains that betrothal takes effect in cases of women for whom one who rapes them is liable for violating a prohibition. Instead, the difficulty is in accordance with the opinion of Rabbi Shimon ben Menasya, whose opinion the Gemara seeks to reconcile with that of Rabbi Akiva. The Ramban cites a similar answer in the name of Rabbi Avraham *Av Bet Din*, and other early commentaries explain likewise. The Ra'ah, however, maintains that the question here is not how to reconcile the opinions of these *tanna'im* with that of Rabbi Akiva. Rather, the Gemara is asking: According to Rabbi Akiva, is there a difference between the two interpretations: A woman for whom there is betrothal, and: A woman who is suitable for him to sustain?

He creates *ḥillulin* – חִילּוּלִין הוּא עוֹשֶׂה: *Tosafot* discuss a different aspect of this dilemma at length: Is *mamzer* status of offspring tied to the question of whether or not there is *havaya*, i.e., whether or not betrothal takes effect, between the man and the woman? They maintain that according to most opinions, *mamzer* status is causally related to the betrothal taking effect. In other words, in any case where betrothal does not take effect, the offspring is a *mamzer*. Admittedly, there are exceptions to this principle, as the child of a Jewish man and a gentile woman or a maidservant is not a *mamzer*. However, that is because no relationship outside the congregation of Israel leads to *mamzer* status, which exists only with regard to Jews. See *Tosafot* for their proof that not everyone agrees that there is necessarily a link between the betrothal not taking effect and *mamzer* status.

Perek III
Daf **30** Amud **a**

חַיָּיבֵי עֲשֵׂה – מִצְרִי וַאֲדוֹמִי.

intercourse with women for which one is **liable for** violating a **positive** mitzva,[N] e.g., **an Egyptian** convert **and an Edomite** convert (see Deuteronomy 23:8–9). If he raped a first- or second-generation Egyptian or Edomite convert, even Rabbi Yeshevav agrees that the child is not a *mamzer*, as the betrothal takes effect. On the other hand, it is prohibited for him to sustain her as a wife.

הָנִיחָא לְרַבִּי יְשֵׁבָב, אִי לְאַפּוּקֵי מִטַּעֲמָא דְּרַבִּי סִימַאי קָאָתֵי – שַׁפִּיר. אֶלָּא אִי טַעֲמָא דְּנַפְשֵׁיהּ קָאָמַר, כָּל שֶׁאֵין לוֹ בִּיאָה בְּיִשְׂרָאֵל הַוָּלָד מַמְזֵר – וַאֲפִילּוּ חַיָּיבֵי עֲשֵׂה, מַאי בֵּינַיְיהוּ?

The Gemara asks: **This** works out **well according to Rabbi Yeshevav if he is coming to reject the opinion of Rabbi Simai.** If Rabbi Yeshevav merely takes issue with Rabbi Simai, who said that all offspring of forbidden relations are *mamzerim* according to Rabbi Akiva except for those resulting from relations between a widow and a High Priest, then it may **well** be explained that Rabbi Yeshevav holds that Rabbi Akiva rules that betrothal does not take effect and that there is *mamzerut* when one violates the prohibitions of the priesthood. **However, if he is stating his own opinion,** independent of Rabbi Simai's statement, his ruling is more comprehensive and leads to the conclusion that in the case of relations with **anyone who does not have** the possibility of permitted **relations among the Jewish people, the child is a** ***mamzer*****,** and this is true **even** of women for relations with whom one is **liable for** violating **positive** mitzvot, e.g., Egyptian or Edomite converts. In that case, **what is** the difference **between** the opinions of Shimon HaTimni and Rabbi Shimon ben Menasya?

NOTES

Intercourse with women for which one is liable for violating a positive mitzva – חַיָּיבֵי עֲשֵׂה: The category of positive mitzvot includes all prohibitions that are formulated as a positive mitzva rather than using a negative phrase, e.g.: You may not, lest, do not, take care. One who transgresses and fails to fulfill the command has violated a positive mitzva. In the beginning of tractate *Yevamot* and elsewhere, the Gemara discusses the relative significance of positive mitzvot and prohibitions. There is a fundamental difference between them with regard to punishment: Prohibitions are generally punishable by lashes, whereas positive mitzvot are not. Sexual relations with an Egyptian or Edomite convert are forbidden by a positive mitzva, as explained by Rashi, but there are also other examples of relations forbidden by a positive mitzva. As the Gemara will immediately explain, relations between a non-virgin and a High Priest are also forbidden by a positive mitzva.

אִיכָּא בֵּינַיְיהוּ בְּעוּלָה לְכֹהֵן גָּדוֹל. וּמַאי שְׁנָא? דַּהֲוָה לֵיהּ עֲשֵׂה שֶׁאֵינוֹ שָׁוֶה בַּכֹּל.

The Gemara answers: **There is** a difference **between them** in the case of a **non-virgin** raped **by a High Priest.**[N] **And** the Gemara asks: Here, too, she is a woman for relations with whom one is liable for violating a positive mitzva, as the High Priest fails to fulfill the mitzva "But a virgin of his own people shall he take to wife" (Leviticus 21:14). If Rabbi Akiva rules that betrothal does not take effect when a positive mitzva is violated, **what is different** about this case? The Gemara answers: It is different **because it is a positive** mitzva **whose** application **is not equal for all.**[N] There are two lenient aspects to this mitzva: It is a positive mitzva and not a prohibition, and it applies only to the High Priest and not to all Jews. Even Rabbi Yeshevav would agree that according to Rabbi Akiva, a child born from relations between a High Priest and a non-virgin is not a *mamzer*. However, the High Priest may not sustain the woman as his wife. Therefore, this case is the practical difference between the statements of Shimon HaTimni and Rabbi Shimon ben Menasya.

אָמַר רַב חִסְדָּא: הַכֹּל מוֹדִים בְּבָא עַל הַנִּדָּה שֶׁמְּשַׁלֵּם קְנָס. לְמַאן דְּאָמַר יֵשׁ בָּהּ הֲוָיָה – הָא נַמִי יֵשׁ בָּהּ הֲוָיָה, לְמַאן דְּאָמַר רְאוּיָה לְקַיְּימָהּ – הָא נַמִי רְאוּיָה לְקַיְּימָהּ.

§ **Rav Ḥisda said: Everyone agrees with regard to one who engaged in** forced **intercourse with a menstruating woman**[N] **that he pays the fine.** He elaborates: **According to the one who says** that the criterion is whether **there is betrothal,** for **this** woman **too there is betrothal.**[N] **According to the one who says** that the criterion is whether the woman is **suitable for** him to **sustain, this** woman **is suitable for** him **to sustain.**

NOTES

A non-virgin raped by a High Priest – בְּעוּלָה לְכֹהֵן גָּדוֹל: All commentaries grapple with the following fundamental question, which requires explanation of the case of a non-virgin and a High Priest: If the case is that a High Priest raped a non-virgin, he cannot possibly be liable to pay the fine, as the Torah imposes the fine only for rape of a virgin. The case must perforce involve a more intricate situation. Rashi and the Ra'avad explain that the young woman had engaged in anal intercourse, and therefore she is not considered a non-virgin in terms of the prohibition of a High Priest; however, in terms of the fine, she maintains the status of a virgin, even if she engaged in anal intercourse many times. Most commentaries, though, including *Tosafot*, the Ramban, and the Rashba, accept Rabbeinu Ḥananel's interpretation that it refers to a virgin young woman who was raped by the High Priest himself. He thereby rendered her a non-virgin, whose betrothal takes effect, but it is prohibited for him to remain married to her. In the *Shita Mekubbetzet* Rashi's explanation is questioned: If the anal intercourse rendered her a non-virgin in terms of the High Priest, when he rapes her he renders her a *ḥalala*. Consequently, she is forbidden to him by a Torah prohibition and the betrothal does not take effect. The answer in the *Shita Mekubbetzet* is that although he renders her a *ḥalala* by means of the rape, he incurs the obligation to pay the fine when he initiated intercourse, and she is rendered a *ḥalala* at its conclusion.

A positive mitzva whose application is not equal for all – עֲשֵׂה שֶׁאֵינוֹ שָׁוֶה בַּכֹּל: The Gemara explains in several places that a mitzva that is universally applicable, whether it is a positive mitzva or a prohibition, is more severe than one whose applicability is selective. Rabbi Akiva Eiger notes that the prohibition rendering a widow forbidden to a High Priest is also not universally applicable, just like the mitzva that renders a non-virgin forbidden. The essence of his answer, which is rejected by the Rashash, is that the mitzva that renders a non-virgin forbidden to a High Priest has a twofold leniency: It is a positive mitzva, and it is a mitzva that is not universally applicable. The Meiri explains similarly that the reason for leniency with regard to this mitzva is that it applies exclusively to the High Priest and not even to other priests. Furthermore, there are additional lenient aspects to this prohibition, as the Gemara states in tractate *Yevamot*: Ultimately she will be a non-virgin after her marriage to him, and it stands to reason that the fact that the prohibition will eventually be negated on its own renders it a lenient prohibition. In fact, some assert that if a High Priest married a virgin that he raped, he need not divorce her after the fact (see *Tosafot*).

Everyone agrees with regard to one who engaged in forced intercourse with a menstruating woman – הַכֹּל מוֹדִים בְּבָא עַל הַנִּדָּה: The phrase: Everyone agrees, does not include all of the Sages, as from the statement of Rabbi Neḥunya ben HaKana it appears that one who rapes a menstruating woman does not pay the fine. Admittedly, some take issue with this assertion, but the *Tosafot Yeshanim*, citing the Maharam MiRotenburg, bring conclusive proof from the *Tosefta* in which it is explicitly stated that Rabbi Neḥunya ben HaKana exempts one who rapes a menstruating woman from paying the fine. Rather, the phrase: Everyone agrees, refers to the dispute between Shimon HaTimni and Rabbi Shimon ben Menasya, as according to the criteria established by both of them he is obligated to pay the fine, as there, betrothal with a menstruating woman takes effect and she is suitable for him to sustain as his wife (see *Tosafot* and Ritva). This is the understanding in the Babylonian Talmud; however, in the Jerusalem Talmud the understanding is the opposite, and Rabbi Neḥunya ben HaKana agrees that one who has relations with a menstruating woman or with his wife's sister is liable to pay the fine. The reason is that these relationships can become permitted over the course of time, when the menstruating woman immerses in a ritual bath and when one's wife dies, respectively. However, one who rapes a woman that is forbidden to him by a prohibition punishable by *karet* and whom will remain permanently forbidden to him is exempt from payment of the fine. Rabbi Shimon ben Menasya, in contrast, contends that wherever there is liability to receive *karet* he is exempt from payment of the fine.

A menstruating woman has betrothal – נִדָּה יֵשׁ בָּהּ הֲוָיָה: This is derived from the verse "And her menstruation is [*tehi*] upon him" (Leviticus 15:24), which indicates that the *havaya* of betrothal is effective even when she is menstruating. Although the early commentaries disagree as to whether or not marriage to a menstruating woman takes effect, everyone agrees that her betrothal takes effect (see Ritva).

ולאפוקי מדרבי נחוניא בן הקנה. דתניא: רבי נחוניא בן הקנה היה עושה את יום הכפורים כשבת לתשלומין; מה שבת מתחייב בנפשו ופטור מן התשלומין – אף יום הכפורים מתחייב בנפשו ופטור מן התשלומין.

§ The Gemara comments: **And** the mishna's ruling that one who has relations with his sister is liable to pay the fine comes **to exclude** the opinion **of Rabbi Neḥunya ben HaKana,**[PN] **as it is taught** in a *baraita*: **Rabbi Neḥunya ben HaKana would render Yom Kippur like Shabbat with regard to payment** for damages.[N] **Just as** one who intentionally desecrates **Shabbat is liable to** receive the **death** penalty **and is** therefore **exempt from** the obligation of **payment** for damages caused while desecrating Shabbat, **so too,** one who intentionally desecrates **Yom Kippur is liable to** receive the **death** penalty **and is** therefore **exempt from** the obligation of **payment** for damages caused while desecrating Yom Kippur.

מאי טעמא דרבי נחוניא בן הקנה? אמר אביי: נאמר "אסון" בידי אדם ונאמר "אסון" בידי שמים, מה "אסון" האמור בידי אדם פטור מן התשלומין, אף "אסון" האמור בידי שמים פטור מן התשלומין.

The Gemara asks: **What is the rationale** for the opinion **of Rabbi Neḥunya ben HaKana? Abaye said: It states** the word **harm at the hands of man,** in the verse "But if any harm follow, then you shall give a soul for a soul" (Exodus 21:23) **and it states** the word **harm at the hand of Heaven,** in the verse in which Jacob states: "My son shall not descend with you…and harm befalls him on the way" (Genesis 42:38). **Just as** with regard to **harm that is stated at the hands of man,** e.g., one who kills and is liable to be executed, one is **exempt from the** associated **payment,**[H] **so too,** with regard to **harm that is stated at the hand of Heaven,** one is **exempt from the** associated **payment.**

מתקיף לה רב אדא בר אהבה: ממאי דכי קא מזהר להו יעקב לבניה על צינים ופחים, דבידי שמים נינהו? דלמא על אריא וגנבי, דבידי אדם נינהו! אטו יעקב אהא אזהר, אהא לא אזהר? יעקב על כל מילי אזהר.

Rav Adda bar Ahava strongly **objects to this: From where** is it derived **that when Jacob is warning his sons** he is warning them **about cold and heat [*tzinim paḥim*],**[LN] **which are at the hand of Heaven? Perhaps** he was warning them **about a lion and thieves, which are** harm **at the hands of man,** meaning that unlike heat and cold, these dangers are not calibrated by God. The Gemara refutes this: **Is that to say** that **Jacob warned** them **about this** harm at the hand of man, but **about that** harm at the hand of Heaven **he did not warn** them? **Jacob warned** them **about all** potentially harmful **matters** that might befall Benjamin, not merely one particular form of catastrophe.

וצינים פחים בידי שמים נינהו? והתניא: הכל בידי שמים חוץ מצינים פחים, שנאמר "צינים פחים בדרך עקש שומר נפשו ירחק מהם"! ותו: אריא וגנבי בידי אדם נינהו? והאמר רב יוסף, וכן תני רבי חייא: מיום שחרב בית המקדש, אף על פי שבטלו סנהדרין – ארבע מיתות לא בטלו? לא בטלו?! הא בטלו להו! אלא:

The Gemara asks: **And are cold** and **heat at the hand of Heaven? Isn't it taught** in a *baraita*: **All** matters are **at the hand of Heaven except for cold** and **heat, as it is stated: "Cold and heat are on the path of the crooked, he who guards his soul shall keep far from them"** (Proverbs 22:5)? This indicates that cold and heat are forms of harm caused by man, from which one can protect himself. **And furthermore, are a lion and thieves** forms of harm **at the hands of man? But didn't Rav Yosef say, and similarly, didn't Rabbi Ḥiyya teach** a *baraita*: **From the day that the Temple was destroyed,**[N] **although the Sanhedrin was abolished** the **four death** penalties[B] **were not abolished?** The Gemara asks: Were they **not abolished?** It is clear **that they were abolished,** as today there is neither Sanhedrin nor capital punishment. **Rather,** it means that although there are no court-imposed executions,

PERSONALITIES

Rabbi Neḥunya ben HaKana – רבי נחוניא בן הקנה: Rabbi Neḥunya ben HaKana was a *tanna* during the generation when the Second Temple was destroyed. It is possible that he is the same *tanna* occasionally referred to as Rabbi Neḥunya the Great.

Apparently, he had a close relationship with the students of Rabban Yoḥanan ben Zakkai.

Few of Rabbi Neḥunya ben HaKana's halakhic statements were preserved; however, several aggadic statements are cited in his name. The prayer that he recited upon entering the study hall (*Berakhot* 28b) is widely known. Later in this tractate (28a) his positive attributes and his modesty are recounted. Rabbi Neḥunya is credited with development of the hermeneutical method of generalization and detail, and it is generally attributed to Rabbi Yishmael, his most prominent student. Authorship of *Sefer HaBahir*, a kabbalistic midrash, is also attributed to him, as is the prayer: Please, with the might [*ana bekho'aḥ*].

Kana is the name of a city in the tribal territory of Asher (Joshua 19:28). Perhaps his title is attributable to the place where he lived.

HALAKHA

Death at the hands of man, he is exempt from payment – מיתה בידי אדם פטור מן התשלומין: If one committed a transgression for which he was liable to be executed, even if he was not forewarned and therefore not actually punished, he is nevertheless exempt from any payment for which he may be liable due to this transgression (Rambam *Sefer Nashim, Hilkhot Na'ara Betula* 1:14 and *Sefer Nezikim, Hilkhot Geneiva* 3:2; *Shulḥan Arukh, Ḥoshen Mishpat* 351).

LANGUAGE

Cold and heat [*tzinim paḥim*] – צינים פחים: Most commentaries on the book of Proverbs agree that *tzinim paḥim* means thorns and traps. However, opinions are divided with regard to its use in the Talmud. *Tosafot* cite several different explanations for these words. Some interpret *tzinim paḥim* as gale-force cold winds (Rabbeinu Gershom on *Bava Batra* 144b). Those commentaries who translate *paḥim* as heat apparently connect it to the term for coals, *peḥamim*, as in the verse "Upon the wicked He shall rain coals [*paḥim*], fire, and brimstone" (Psalms 11:6).

BACKGROUND

The four death penalties – ארבע מיתות: There are four forms of court-administered capital punishment in the Torah. They are, in diminishing order of severity: Stoning, burning, decapitation, and strangulation. Capital cases are adjudicated by a court consisting of twenty-three judges.

NOTES

To exclude the opinion of Rabbi Neḥunya ben HaKana – לאפוקי מדרבי נחוניא בן הקנה: Some commentaries maintain that this statement relates to that which Rav Ḥisda said: Everyone agrees with regard to one who engaged in forced intercourse with a menstruating woman that he pays the fine. In that statement, Rav Ḥisda rejects the opinion of Rabbi Neḥunya (*Tosafot*; *Shita Yeshana*, cited in *Shita Mekubbetzet*). However, Rashi and others claim that the Gemara relates to the *halakha* in the mishna with regard to one who rapes his sister. Proof is cited in the *Shita Mekubbetzet* for Rashi's explanation from the fact that the mishna adds the phrase: Although there is *karet* for them, which underscores the fact that despite the prohibition involving *karet* Rabbi Neḥunya's opinion is not taken into account.

The opinion of Rabbi Neḥunya ben HaKana – שיטת רבי נחוניא בן הקנה: Rabbi Neḥunya's opinion is based on two fundamental reasons that are basically accepted by most *tanna'im*. First, one is not punished twice for the same transgression, as the Gemara later explains at length. Second, there is a principle that one receives the greater of two punishments. Rabbi Neḥunya reasons: Since this transgression entails *karet*, it is sufficient that one receive that severe punishment and not be liable to pay. Another factor taken into consideration by Rabbi Neḥunya, as mentioned in the Gemara briefly, is that wherever the Torah imposes the death penalty it does not render one liable to receive any other punishment, and *karet* is essentially death at the hand of Heaven. The Rabbis respond that these principles apply only to punishments administered by man, but not to penalties administered by Heaven. Furthermore, when one's punishment is at the hand of Heaven he can repent, gain atonement for his sin, and avert his punishment. That is not the case with regard to punishments administered by man (Meiri).

Cold and heat [*tzinim paḥim*] – צינים פחים: Rashi and most commentaries explain these words as meaning cold and heat. The Rashbam maintains that *tzinim* is a form of the word *tzina*, meaning cold, while *paḥim* means trap (see *Tosafot*). Rashi and other commentaries explain the verse in Proverbs in an entirely different manner, unrelated to cold and heat. In any case, the idea is that most suffering cannot be prevented no matter what precautions a person takes, except for those matters caused by negligence (see *Tosafot*; Ramban).

From the day that the Temple was destroyed – מיום שחרב בית המקדש: *Tosafot* question this statement, as it is well known that the courts ceased adjudicating capital cases before the destruction of the Temple. They answer that even so, these judgments were not entirely abrogated at the time. Furthermore, as long as the Temple was standing it afforded atonement for certain types of sins through the priestly vestments and the scapegoat. The *Shita Yeshana*, cited in the *Shita Mekubbetzet*, explains that Rabbi Ḥiyya spoke in general terms and did not insist on precision with regard to the date, as it roughly coincided with the destruction. Likewise, it can be explained that even while the Temple was standing, if the Sanhedrin did not have the authority to impose judgment, violators would be punished at the hand of Heaven.

LANGUAGE

Diphtheria [*serunki*] – סְרוּנְכִּי: An extension of the Hebrew/Aramaic roots *samekh, nun, kaf* or *shin, nun, kuf*, and the verb, *lesarnek*, meaning strangulation. The reference here is most likely to diphtheria, which causes the blockage of the trachea and death by strangulation.

HALAKHA

A non-priest who ate *teruma* – זָר שֶׁאָכַל תְּרוּמָה: A non-priest who intentionally ate *teruma* is liable to receive death at the hand of Heaven. If he was forewarned, he is flogged and need not pay for the *teruma* he ate, as one does not both receive lashes and pay. The *halakha* is not decided based on the Gemara here, which is in accordance with the opinion of Rabbi Neḥunya. Rather, it is in accordance with the conclusion in tractate *Terumot* of the Jerusalem Talmud (Rambam *Sefer Zera'im, Hilkhot Terumot* 6:6 and *Kesef Mishne* there).

דִּין אַרְבַּע מִיתוֹת לֹא בָּטְלוּ: מִי שֶׁנִּתְחַיֵּיב סְקִילָה – אוֹ נוֹפֵל מִן הַגַּג, אוֹ חַיָּה דּוֹרַסְתּוֹ. וּמִי שֶׁנִּתְחַיֵּיב שְׂרֵיפָה – אוֹ נוֹפֵל בִּדְלֵיקָה, אוֹ נָחָשׁ מַכִּישׁוֹ. וּמִי שֶׁנִּתְחַיֵּיב הֲרִיגָה – אוֹ נִמְסָר לַמַּלְכוּת, אוֹ לִיסְטִים בָּאִין עָלָיו. וּמִי שֶׁנִּתְחַיֵּיב חֶנֶק – אוֹ טוֹבֵעַ בַּנָּהָר, אוֹ מֵת בִּסְרוּנְכִּי? אֶלָּא אֵיפוֹךְ: אַרְיָא וְגַנָּבֵי – בִּידֵי שָׁמַיִם, צִינִּים וּפַחִים – בִּידֵי אָדָם.

the **punishment** of the **four death** penalties **was not abolished.**[N] How so? **One who was liable** to be executed by **stoning either falls from the roof or a beast tramples him.** That is similar to stoning, which involves being pushed off an elevated place and then stoned. **And one who was liable** to be executed by **burning either falls into a conflagration or a snake bites him,** which creates a burning sensation. **And one who was liable** to be executed by **decapitation is either handed over to the** ruling **monarchy** for execution by sword, **or bandits attack** and kill **him. And one who was liable** to be executed by **strangulation either drowns in a river, or dies of diphtheria [*serunki*].**[L] **Rather, reverse** the order of the previous statement: **A lion and thieves** are cases of harm **at the hand of Heaven,**[N] while **cold and heat** are cases of harm **at the hands of man.**[N]

רָבָא אֲמַר: טַעֲמָא דְּרַבִּי נְחוּנְיָא בֶּן הַקָּנָה מֵהָכָא: ״וְאִם הַעְלֵם יַעְלִימוּ עַם הָאָרֶץ אֶת עֵינֵיהֶם מִן הָאִישׁ הַהוּא בְּתִתּוֹ מִזַּרְעוֹ לַמֹּלֶךְ וְשַׂמְתִּי אֲנִי אֶת פָּנַי בָּאִישׁ הַהוּא וּבְמִשְׁפַּחְתּוֹ וְהִכְרַתִּי אוֹתוֹ״ אָמְרָה תּוֹרָה: כָּרֵת שֶׁלִּי כְּמִיתָה שֶׁלָּכֶם, מַה מִּיתָה שֶׁלָּכֶם – פָּטוּר מִן הַתַּשְׁלוּמִין, אַף כָּרֵת שֶׁלִּי – פָּטוּר מִן הַתַּשְׁלוּמִין.

Rava said an additional explanation: **The rationale** for the opinion **of Rabbi Neḥunya ben HaKana is from here.** It is written that one who gives his children to Molech is liable to be executed by stoning: **"And if the people of the land do at all hide their eyes**[N] **from that man, when he gives of his seed to Molech,** and do not put him to death; **then I will set My face against that man and against his family, and will cut him off [*vehikhrati*]"** (Leviticus 20:4–5). Through the juxtaposition in this verse **the Torah said:** My ***karet*** is **like your death** penalty; **just as** one who is liable to receive **your death** penalty **is exempt from the** associated **payments, so too,** one who is liable to receive **My *karet*** is **exempt from the** associated **payments.**

מַאי אִיכָּא בֵּין רָבָא לְאַבַּיֵּי? אִיכָּא בֵּינַיְיהוּ זָר שֶׁאָכַל תְּרוּמָה. לְאַבַּיֵּי פָּטוּר, וּלְרָבָא חַיָּיב.

The Gemara asks: **What** practical difference **is there between** the opinions of **Rava and Abaye** with regard to the rationale for the opinion of Rabbi Neḥunya ben HaKana? The Gemara answers: **There is** a difference **between them** with regard to **a non-priest who** intentionally **ate *teruma*.**[HN] According **to Abaye** he is **exempt** from paying the priest the value of the *teruma*, as a non-priest who ate *teruma* is liable to receive death at the hand of Heaven. Abaye maintains that the legal status of all forms of death at the hand of Heaven is equivalent to that of death at the hands of man, and therefore, one is exempt from payment. **And** according **to Rava,** who derives the rationale from the juxtaposition between *karet* and death at the hands of man, since a non-priest who ate *teruma* is not liable to receive *karet*, he is **liable** to pay the priest for the *teruma* that he ate.

NOTES

The punishment of the four death penalties was not abolished – דִּין אַרְבַּע מִיתוֹת לֹא בָּטְלוּ: *Tosafot* ask: Aren't there many wicked people who die peacefully and are not punished in these manners? They answer that sometimes the punishment is waived if they repented. Similarly, the Rambam writes that their other merits can protect them, as one is not in a position to assess the actions of others and determine the precise punishment that they deserve. In the *Shita Mekubbetzet* and in the commentary of the Ritva, the explanation is that punishment meted out in this world corresponds to the four death penalties. Not all wicked people are punished in this manner, however, as some enjoy peace in this world to facilitate their more severe punishment in the next world. In the *Shita Mekubbetzet* it is explained that only those who were forewarned and sinned in the presence of witnesses are subject to these punishments, and if the courts had the authority they would have administered the four death penalties.

A lion and thieves are at the hand of Heaven – אַרְיָא וְגַנָּבֵי בִּידֵי שָׁמַיִם: The early commentaries ask: How can any harm be deemed at the hands of man, if even these are considered to be caused by Heaven? They answer, based on Rashi, that when the verse states: "And yet no harm follow, he shall be punished" (Exodus 21:22), harm refers to court-administered death penalties (Ramban). The Ra'ah likewise explains that since the death penalty is imposed due to the misguided choices of the sinner, it is parallel to cold or heat, as there too one's failure to take precautions leads to harm.

Cold and heat are at the hands of man – צִינִּים וּפַחִים בִּידֵי אָדָם: Rabbeinu Ḥananel explains that suffering from cold and heat is sometimes at the hands of man, such as when one carelessly exposes himself to extreme temperatures, and sometimes at the hand of God. Some commentaries maintain that the version of the Gemara before Rabbeinu Ḥananel reflects this explanation.

And if the people of the land do at all hide their eyes – וְאִם הַעְלֵם יַעְלִימוּ עַם הָאָרֶץ: In the *Shita Mekubbetzet*, the question is raised: Why does the Gemara cite this verse rather than the preceding one: "And I will set My face against that man, and will cut him off from among his people, because he has given of his seed unto Molech" (Leviticus 20:3)? The answer is that the preceding verse first refers to one who sinned intentionally but without forewarning or without witnesses, and therefore there is no parallel to one who is liable to receive the death penalty. The Gemara therefore cites a verse that deals with one who was liable to receive court-administered execution, in which case the parallel between the death penalties administered by Heaven and by the court is clear.

A non-priest who ate *teruma* – זָר שֶׁאָכַל תְּרוּמָה: The punishment for a non-priest who intentionally ate *teruma* is death at the hand of Heaven, as it is written: "And they shall die therein if they profane it" (Leviticus 22:9). In several places the Gemara explains that although *karet* is also a death penalty at the hand of Heaven, there is a difference between the two. *Karet* is a more severe punishment, as one dies younger and sometimes one's family is also eliminated. This is especially true according to the explanation of the Rambam, who maintains that *karet* entails the soul ceasing to exist. Since death at the hand of Heaven is less severe, it is possible that even according to Rabbi Neḥunya the sinner would not be exempt from payment.

וּלְאַבָּיֵי פָּטוּר?! וְהָאָמַר רַב חִסְדָּא: מוֹדֶה רַבִּי נְחוּנְיָא בֶּן הַקָּנָה בְּגוֹנֵב חֶלְבּוֹ שֶׁל חֲבֵירוֹ וַאֲכָלוֹ – שֶׁהוּא חַיָּיב, שֶׁכְּבָר נִתְחַיֵּיב בִּגְנֵיבָה קוֹדֶם שֶׁבָּא לִידֵי אִיסּוּר חֵלֶב. אַלְמָא, דְּמֵעִידָּנָא דְּאַגְבְּהֵיהּ קַנְיֵיהּ, מִתְחַיֵּיב בְּנַפְשׁוֹ לָא הָוֵה עַד דְּאָכֵיל לֵיהּ. הָכָא נָמֵי, בְּעִידָּנָא דְּאַגְבְּהֵיהּ קַנְיֵיהּ, מִתְחַיֵּיב בְּנַפְשׁוֹ לָא הָוֵי עַד דְּאָכֵיל לֵיהּ! הָכָא בְּמַאי עָסְקִינַן – כְּגוֹן שֶׁתָּחַב לוֹ חֲבֵירוֹ לְתוֹךְ פִּיו.

The Gemara asks: **And according to Abaye,** is a non-priest actually **exempt** from payment for the *teruma*? **But didn't Rav Ḥisda say that Rabbi Neḥunya ben HaKana concedes**[N] **with regard to** one who **steals another's** forbidden **fat**[B] **and eats it**[H] **that he is obligated** to pay for the fat, even though he is liable to receive *karet*, **as he was already liable for theft before he came to** violate **the prohibition** against eating forbidden **fat? Apparently, from the moment he lifts** the fat to steal **it he acquired it,**[N] and he bears responsibility to repay it, but **he is liable to** receive the **death** penalty **only when he eats it. Here, too,** with regard to a non-priest who ate *teruma*, **at the moment he lifts** the *teruma* **he acquired it** and is responsible to repay it, and **he is liable to** receive the **death** penalty **only when he eats it.** The Gemara answers: **With what are we dealing here?** It is a case **where another inserted** the *teruma* **into his mouth.** In that case, acquisition and liability to receive the death penalty are simultaneous.

סוֹף סוֹף, כֵּיוָן דִּלְעָסֵיהּ – קַנְיֵיהּ, מִתְחַיֵּיב בְּנַפְשׁוֹ לָא הָוֵי עַד דְּבַלְעָהּ! כְּגוֹן שֶׁתָּחַב לוֹ לְתוֹךְ בֵּית הַבְּלִיעָה. הֵיכִי דָּמֵי? אִי דְּמָצֵי לְאַהֲדוּרָהּ – נִיהֲדַר, אִי לָא מָצֵי לְאַהֲדוּרָהּ – אַמַּאי חַיָּיב? לָא צְרִיכָא, דְּמָצֵי לְאַהֲדוּרָהּ עַל יְדֵי הַדְּחֵק.

The Gemara asks: **Ultimately, once he chewed** the *teruma* **he acquired it**[N] and is liable to pay, and **he is liable to** receive the **death** penalty **only when he swallows it.**[N] Since the two are not simultaneous, he should be liable to pay. The Gemara answers: It is a case **where** another **inserted it into the pharynx,**[B] so the liability for payment and liability for the death penalty were both achieved through swallowing. The Gemara asks: **What are the circumstances? If** it is **possible to retrieve** the *teruma* by removing it without ruining it, **let him retrieve** it. If one does so, he would not be liable to pay. If he fails to do so, liability or payment precedes liability for the death penalty. **If** it is **not possible to retrieve**[N] the *teruma*, **why is he liable?** He did nothing; another person inserted the food in his throat. The Gemara answers: It is **necessary only** in a situation **where** it is **possible to retrieve** the *teruma* **under duress,** with great effort.

רַב פָּפָּא אָמַר: כְּגוֹן שֶׁתָּחַב לוֹ חֲבֵירוֹ מַשְׁקִין שֶׁל תְּרוּמָה לְתוֹךְ פִּיו. רַב אָשֵׁי אָמַר: בְּזָר שֶׁאָכַל תְּרוּמָה מִשֶּׁלּוֹ,

Rav Pappa said: It is referring to a case **where another inserted liquids of** *teruma* **into his mouth.** As soon as the liquid enters his mouth, it is ruined. Therefore, the acquisition and his enjoyment are simultaneous. **Rav Ashi said:** It is referring **to a non-priest who partook of his own** *teruma*,[N] e.g., if the non-priest inherited *teruma* from a priest, or acquired ownership from a priest. In that case, he did not steal the *teruma* and there is no payment for it, but he is liable to receive the death penalty for eating *teruma*,

BACKGROUND

Fat – חֵלֶב: The reference is to forbidden animal fats prohibited by Torah law, in contrast to animal fats that are permitted. One who partakes of forbidden fats of a kosher domesticated animal is liable to receive *karet* (Leviticus 7:22–25). One who partakes of those fats unwittingly is liable to bring a sin-offering. It is permitted to eat the fats of non-domesticated kosher animals and of kosher birds. Among the indicators distinguishing forbidden and permitted fats is that the forbidden fats are concentrated in certain areas in the animal's body, form an independent unit, and are not attached to the muscle. They are surrounded by a thin membrane and can easily be peeled away from the meat. Most forbidden fats of a consecrated animal were offered on the altar.

Pharynx – בֵּית הַבְּלִיעָה: This is located in the back of the mouth. Food reaching the pharynx activates a swallowing reflex. At that point, it is only with great effort that one could prevent the food from being swallowed.

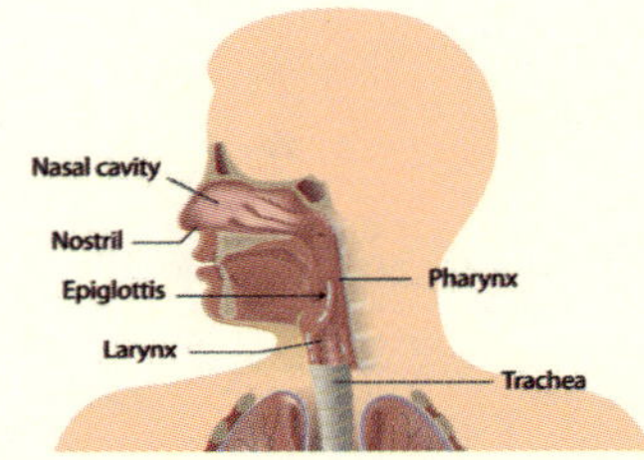

Location of the pharynx

HALAKHA

With regard to one who steals another's forbidden fat and eats it – בְּגוֹנֵב חֶלְבּוֹ שֶׁל חֲבֵירוֹ וַאֲכָלוֹ: One who steals forbidden fat from another and eats it must pay him the value of the fat. The *Sma* and others maintain that this is the *halakha* when one lifted the forbidden fat before consuming it. The *Shakh* notes that this is unnecessary, as the *halakha* is in accordance with the opinion of the Sages that even one who is liable to receive *karet* is obligated to pay for damage that he caused (Rambam *Sefer Nezikim*, *Hilkhot Geneiva* 2:4; *Shulḥan Arukh*, *Ḥoshen Mishpat* 350).

NOTES

Rabbi Neḥunya…concedes, etc. – מוֹדֶה רַבִּי נְחוּנְיָא וכו׳: The Ramban asks: What is novel in Rav Ḥisda's statement, as clearly, with regard to a violation punishable by a court-administered death penalty, Rabbi Neḥunya does not rule more stringently than do the Rabbis, who hold that if one does not incur the liability to be executed and the liability to pay simultaneously he is executed and also pays the damages? The Ramban answers: It is possible that Rav Ḥisda is teaching that the act of lifting the forbidden fat is not considered part of eating but is instead a separate act of acquisition. Furthermore, since Rabbi Neḥunya is lenient with regard to payment, it was necessary to emphasize that even he deems the offender liable in this case.

From from the moment he lifts it he acquired it – מֵעִידָּנָא דְּאַגְבְּהֵיהּ קַנְיֵיהּ: As explained below, it is necessary to precisely define the moment when a particular act is considered theft. Although in the case of misappropriation of a deposit one is liable for merely planning to do so, that is not the case with regard to theft. Instead, the Sages established lifting as the determining factor in theft. One of the ramifications of this determination is with regard to the liability of the thief for damage to the object from the moment he acquired it through the act of theft, even if he derived no benefit from it. Removing an item from its owner's domain also constitutes an act of theft, even if one did not lift it, as explained later in the Gemara.

Once he chewed it he acquired it – כֵּיוָן דִּלְעָסֵיהּ קַנְיֵיהּ: The Meiri maintains that this phrase is superfluous, as merely holding food in one's mouth acquires the food. He suggests that perhaps the thief must perform an action that demonstrates his consent to the proceedings (see Maharam Schiff).

He is liable to receive the death penalty only when he swallows it – מִתְחַיֵּיב בְּנַפְשׁוֹ לָא הָוֵי עַד דְּבַלְעָהּ: The Rosh asks why he is liable only when he swallows the *teruma* if the *teruma* is already profaned when he chews it. He answers that when the Sages said that one who uses *teruma* profanes it, that is only the case when one uses *teruma* and thereby completes his enjoyment of the food. Here, however, the chewing was not the final stage, as he swallowed it thereafter, and only at that point is the *teruma* profaned (see *Tosafot Yeshanim*).

If it is not possible to retrieve – אִי לָא מָצֵי לְאַהֲדוּרָהּ: The Ritva explains that this can also be referring to a case when another inserted the *teruma* with one's knowledge and consent. *Tosafot* approach this possibility from a different perspective. Some write that although he agreed to have the *teruma* placed in his mouth, he did not intend for it to be shoved in so far that he could not change his mind (see Meiri).

Who partook of his own *teruma* – שֶׁאָכַל תְּרוּמָה מִשֶּׁלּוֹ: The Rashba and others state that this does not mean that it is only in a case where the *teruma* is his; rather, Abaye maintains that he is exempt from punishment for tearing his friend's silk even if the *teruma* was his. An issue addressed by the later commentaries is that if the *teruma* belonged to him he could request that a Sage dissolve the consecration of the *teruma*, as that consecration is like any other vow that can be dissolved in that manner (see *Taz*, *Nekuddot HaKesef*, and *Sefer Hafla'a*).

וְקָרַע שִׁירָאִין שֶׁל חֲבֵירוֹ.

and at the same time **he tore another's silk** [*shira'in*].[LN] The question is whether the liability to receive the death penalty exempts him from the liability for payment incurred at precisely the same moment.

גּוּפָא, אָמַר רַב חִסְדָּא: מוֹדֶה רַבִּי נְחוּנְיָא בֶּן הַקָּנָה בְּגוֹנֵב חֶלְבּוֹ שֶׁל חֲבֵירוֹ וַאֲכָלוֹ – שֶׁהוּא חַיָּיב שֶׁכְּבָר נִתְחַיֵּיב בִּגְנֵבָה קוֹדֶם שֶׁיָּבֹא לִידֵי אִיסּוּר חֵלֶב. לֵימָא פְּלִיגָא דְּרַבִּי אָבִין, דְּאָמַר רַבִּי אָבִין: הַזּוֹרֵק חֵץ מִתְּחִילַּת אַרְבַּע לְסוֹף אַרְבַּע וְקָרַע שִׁירָאִין בַּהֲלִיכָתוֹ – פָּטוּר, שֶׁעֲקִירָה צוֹרֶךְ הַנָּחָה הִיא. הָכָא נַמִי – הַגְבָּהָה צוֹרֶךְ אֲכִילָה הִיא.

§ The Gemara analyzes **the matter itself. Rav Ḥisda said: Rabbi Neḥunya ben HaKana concedes in** the case of one who **steals another's** forbidden **fat and eats it that he is obligated to** pay for the fat, **as he is already liable for theft before he comes to** violate **the prohibition** against eating forbidden **fat.** The Gemara comments: **Let us say** that Rav Ḥisda **disagrees with Rabbi Avin, as Rabbi Avin said: One who shoots an arrow**[H] **from the beginning of four** cubits **to the end of four** cubits in the public domain on Shabbat, thereby performing a prohibited labor for which he is liable to receive a court-imposed death penalty, **and the** arrow **ripped silk as it proceeds, is exempt** from the obligation to pay for the silk because he is liable for the more severe punishment for desecrating Shabbat. Although the silk was ripped prior to completion of the prohibited labor, as the arrow had not yet come to rest, he is nevertheless exempt, **as lifting is a prerequisite for placement.** The prohibited labor of carrying on Shabbat[N] is comprised of lifting of the object and placement. Once he shot the arrow, its movement through the air is a continuation of his act of Shabbat desecration, for which he is liable to be executed. **Here, too,** say that **lifting** the fat **is a prerequisite for eating,** and therefore he should be exempt from payment.

הָכִי הָשְׁתָּא? הָתָם – אִי אֶפְשָׁר לְהַנָּחָה בְּלֹא עֲקִירָה, הָכָא אֶפְשָׁר לַאֲכִילָה בְּלֹא הַגְבָּהָה, דְּאִי בָּעֵי – גָּחֵין וְאָכֵיל. אִי נַמִי: הָתָם, אִי בָּעֵי לְאַהֲדוּרָהּ לָא מָצֵי מַהֲדַר לַהּ, הָכָא – מָצֵי מַהֲדַר לַהּ.

The Gemara refutes this argument: **How can** these cases **be compared? There,** in the case of the arrow, **placement is impossible without lifting,** as placement without lifting is not a labor prohibited on Shabbat. Therefore, lifting and placement are a single unit. In contrast, **here, eating is possible without lifting as, if one wishes,** he could **bend down and eat**[N] without lifting the food to his mouth. **Alternatively,** there is another difference between the cases: **There,** in the case of the arrow, even **if he seeks to take back**[N] the arrow after shooting it, **he cannot take** it **back;** therefore, lifting and placement constitute one action. **Here, he could replace** the fat after lifting it.

LANGUAGE

Silk [*shira'in*] – שִׁירָאִין: From the Greek σηρικόν, *sērikon*, a particular variety of silk.

HALAKHA

One who shoots an arrow, etc. – הַזּוֹרֵק חֵץ וכו׳: If one shoots an arrow four cubits in the public domain on Shabbat and it tears silk along its path, he is exempt from payment for the damage as the Shabbat desecration and the damage occur simultaneously. This is in accordance with the statement of Rabbi Avin (Rambam *Sefer Nezikim*, *Hilkhot Geneiva* 3:2).

NOTES

And he tore another's silk – וְקָרַע שִׁירָאִין שֶׁל חֲבֵירוֹ: Rashi, the Ra'avad, and the Meiri maintain that Rav Ashi's statement is in accordance with the opinion that the principle that a guilty person receives the greater punishment applies in a case where his liability to be executed is due to the effect of his actions on one person and his liability to pay is due to the effect of his actions on another. This applies not only if the two liabilities were incurred by a single act, e.g., killing a slave, which renders him liable to be executed for killing the slave and liable to pay the value of the slave to his master. It applies even if he performed two separate actions, as in this case, when he ate *teruma* and tore silk. Some commentaries explain that this refers to silk wrapped around his neck that he tore in the course of eating the *teruma* (*Shita Mekubbetzet*). However, *Tosafot* and most early commentaries contend that this is not actually a case of death to one person and payment to another, as death at the hand of Heaven is not the result of a sin committed against a particular person. Rather, the novel element is that he is exempt from payment even though he performed two separate actions.

The prohibited labor of carrying out on Shabbat – מְלֶאכֶת הוֹצָאָה בְּשַׁבָּת: One of the thirty-nine categories of labor that are prohibited on Shabbat by Torah law is the labor of carrying out, which is treated in detail in a significant portion of tractate *Shabbat*. The labor of carrying out includes two different situations: First, transfer of an object from the private to the public domain or vice versa, regardless of the distance the item was moved; second, carrying an object four cubits in the public domain. Despite the differences between these scenarios, they share several common elements. In both cases, the object in question is lifted from a significant surface with a minimum requisite area and is then placed on another similar surface. If only one of the stages, lifting or placing, was performed by an individual or if each was performed by a different person, it does not constitute labor prohibited on Shabbat by Torah law.

If one wishes, he could bend down and eat – דְּאִי בָּעֵי גָּחֵין וְאָכֵיל: Consistent with his explanation in parallel discussions, Rashi explains here that one who lifts an object acquires it only if he lifted it more than three handbreadths off the ground. Therefore, if he crouched and stood less than three handbreadths off the ground and ate, he did not acquire the food through lifting. Some early commentaries (*Tosafot*) question Rashi's explanation, as it appears from several sources that one acquires the object even by lifting it by less than three handbreadths off the ground. In fact, the Ran states that according to this opinion one must crouch below one handbreadth, as he maintains that by lifting less than one handbreadth off the ground one does not acquire an object. The Meiri, who agrees with Rashi, resolves the difficulty and explains that those sources according to which an acquisition is accomplished by lifting less than three handbreadths are referring to acquisition by rabbinic law. The early commentaries raise an additional difficulty: Independent of lifting, one should acquire the food when it enters his mouth. Therefore, *Tosafot* and other early commentaries explain that the forbidden fat was on a skewer, and he placed it directly at his pharynx when he crouched. Others explain that this matter of crouching and eating is not the primary answer, which is that lifting and placing are integral to the labor of carrying out, whereas lifting fat is not integral to its consumption (Rashba; Ra'ah).

If he seeks to take back – אִי בָּעֵי לְאַהֲדוּרָהּ: This appears to mean that the prohibited labor of carrying out begins with the shooting of the arrow, an act that cannot be reversed. The Ramban, however, explains that the shooting of the arrow necessarily entails the tearing of the silk as it moves, which is not the case with the moving knife. Rashi indicates likewise (see Ramban and *Shita Mekubbetzet*).

מאי איכא בין האי לישנא להא לישנא? איכא בינייהו המעביר סכין ברשות הרבים, וקרע שיראין בהליכתו. להך לישנא דאמרת אי אפשר להנחה בלא עקירה – הכא נמי אי אפשר להנחה בלא עקירה. לדך לישנא דאמרת לא מצי מהדר לה – הכא מצי מהדר לה.

The Gemara asks: **What** practical difference **is there between this formulation,** where the criterion is whether the second stage could be performed independent of the first stage, **and that formulation,** where the criterion is whether the second stage is inevitable after performing the first stage? The Gemara responds: **There is a** practical difference **between them** with regard to **one who carries**[N] **a knife in the public domain and tears silk as he proceeds. According to that formulation, where you said: Lifting is a prerequisite for placement, here too, lifting is a prerequisite for placement.** As these two stages are inexorably connected, they constitute one action, and the one carrying the knife is exempt from paying the damages. Conversely, **according to that formulation where you said: He cannot take back** the arrow and that is why they are considered one action, **here, he can take back** the knife; therefore, lifting and placement are separate actions and he is not exempt from punishment for the damages that he caused.

גופא, אמר רבי אבין: הזורק חץ מתחלת ארבע לסוף ארבע, וקרע שיראין בהליכתו – פטור, שעקירה צורך הנחה היא. מתיב רב ביבי בר אביי: הגונב כיס בשבת – חייב, שכבר נתחייב בגניבה קודם שיבא לידי איסור סקילה. היה מגרר ויוצא, מגרר ויוצא – פטור, שהרי איסור שבת וגניבה באין כאחד.

§ The Gemara analyzes **the** matter **itself. Rabbi Avin said:** With regard to **one who shoots an arrow from the beginning of four** cubits **to the end of four** cubits and the arrow **rips silk as it proceeds, he is exempt, as lifting is a prerequisite for placement. Rav Beivai bar Abaye raised an objection** from that which is taught in a *baraita*: **One who steals a purse on Shabbat**[H] **is liable** for the theft **because he was already liable for theft** as soon as he lifted the purse. This took place **before he came to** violate **the prohibition** against performing prohibited labor on Shabbat by carrying it into the public domain, a violation punishable by **stoning.** However, if he did not lift the purse but **was dragging** it on the ground **and exiting**[NH] the private domain, **dragging and exiting, he is exempt, as the prohibition** against **theft and the prohibition of Shabbat** are violated **simultaneously** when he drags the purse out of the owner's property and into the public domain.

ואמאי? הכא נמי לימא הגבהה צורך הוצאה היא! הכא במאי עסקינן – כגון שהגביהו על מנת להצניעו ונמלך עליו והוציאו.

Rav Beivai concludes: **But why** is he liable if he carried the purse? **Here, too, let us say** that **lifting is a prerequisite for carrying out,**[N] and therefore the theft was performed in the course of performance of the prohibited labor and he is exempt. The Gemara answers: **With what are we dealing here?** We are dealing with a case **where he lifted** the pouch **in order to conceal it** in the same domain, not to carry it out into the public domain, **and he reconsidered** his plan with regard to the purse **and carried it out.** In that case the act of lifting was not performed for the purpose of carrying out. Therefore, he is not exempt from the obligation to pay for the theft.

וכי האי גוונא מי חייב? והאמר רב סימון אמר רבי אמי אמר רבי יוחנן: המפנה חפצים מזוית לזוית, ונמלך עליהם והוציאן – פטור, שלא היתה עקירה משעה ראשונה לכך!

The Gemara asks: **And in a case like that,** where he reconsidered, **is** one **liable** for carrying out an object on Shabbat? **But didn't Rav Simon say** that **Rabbi Ami said** that **Rabbi Yoḥanan said: One who moves objects from** one **corner** of his house to another **corner** on Shabbat, **and he reconsidered** his plan in **their** regard after lifting them **and carried them out** into the public domain, he is **exempt, as the** act of **lifting was not initially** performed **for that** purpose of carrying from one domain to another. Here, too, since the thief did not lift the pouch with the intention of carrying it out, he is not liable to be stoned.

NOTES

There is a difference between them with regard to one who carries – איכא בינייהו המעביר: The early commentaries point out that the Gemara could also have said that there is a difference between the two opinions with regard to one who ate forbidden fat that was inserted into his throat by another. According to the approach that lifting is a prerequisite for placing, here too, placing food in one's mouth is a prerequisite for eating and the two actions can be regarded as simultaneous. According to the opinion that the decisive factor is one's ability to take back the object, in this case one can extract the food after it was placed in one's mouth and therefore the actions are not regarded as simultaneous. (Ritva).

If he was dragging and exiting – היה מגרר ויוצא: The Ramban asks: If he was dragging the object and never lifted it at all, the prohibited labor of carrying out was never completely performed even when the item reached the public domain. The Ra'avad resolves this difficulty and explains that lifting is required only for carrying four cubits in the public domain. However, for transfer of an object from one domain to another one need not lift it completely off the ground, as the very transfer to a different domain is tantamount to lifting. The Ramban explains that in talmudic times the entrance to the private domain was three handbreadths higher than the private domain, and therefore taking an object out of the private domain would necessarily include lifting. Yet others contend that this is not difficult to explain at all, as lifting is required for the object to be considered to have been moved only with regard to an object that remains in place. However, with regard to an object that one is dragging, where he moves the entire object, that itself is considered full-fledged lifting (*Tosafot* on *Shabbat* 8b; Rashba; Ra'ah).

Lifting is a prerequisite for carrying out – הגבהה צורך הוצאה היא: Here too, it could nevertheless be asserted that lifting is not integral to carrying out, as one could drag the object without lifting it, or, according to the other opinion, one could reverse the process. Some commentaries do state that the Gemara could have raised these questions but opted not to raise all possible difficulties. The Ramban claims that this is not difficult to explain, as the Gemara is saying merely that one cannot be liable for placement without lifting; therefore, from the moment one lifts the object he begins assuming liability (see *Tosafot*).

HALAKHA

One who steals a purse on Shabbat – הגונב כיס בשבת: One who steals a purse on Shabbat by lifting it in the owner's domain, is obligated to pay damages even if he later carried it out to the public domain, because the theft preceded the desecration of Shabbat. The *Kesef Mishne* notes that the Rambam omits the Gemara's explanation in this regard because he rules in accordance with the formulation that the decisive factor is whether or not one can take back the object. As the discussion in the Gemara is focused on Rabbi Avin's formulation, it is not relevant to the *halakha*. Therefore, the Rambam omits it (Rambam *Sefer Nezikim*, *Hilkhot Geneiva* 3:2; *Shulḥan Arukh*, *Ḥoshen Mishpat* 351).

If he was dragging and exiting – היה מגרר ויוצא: If one stole a purse on Shabbat without lifting it, but instead dragged it through the owner's property until he reached the public domain, he is exempt from payment, as the desecration of Shabbat and the theft occur simultaneously (Rambam *Sefer Nezikim*, *Hilkhot Geneiva* 3:2; *Shulḥan Arukh*, *Ḥoshen Mishpat* 351).

NOTES

Do not say in order to conceal it, etc. – לָא תֵּימָא עַל מְנָת לְהַצְנִיעוֹ וכו׳: In the *Shita Mekubbetzet* it is explained that many variant versions of the text omit this answer, which may have been inserted under the influence of Rashi's explanation. One can then move to the next explanation in the Gemara with regard to one who stopped, thereby interrupting the transfer of the object.

HALAKHA

Where he stopped – כְּשֶׁעָמַד: One who was carrying an object in the public domain and stopped after walking less than four cubits is exempt. This applies only if he stopped in order to rest; however, if he paused to adjust his burden he is considered to still be in the process of walking, and therefore when he traverses four cubits and stops, he is liable (Rambam *Sefer Zemanim*, *Hilkhot Shabbat* 13:10).

לָא תֵּימָא עַל מְנָת לְהַצְנִיעוֹ, אֶלָּא אֵימָא עַל מְנָת לְהוֹצִיאוֹ, הָכָא בְּמַאי עָסְקִינַן – כְּשֶׁעָמַד.

The Gemara emends the previous answer: **Do not say** that he lifted it **in order to conceal it;**[N] **rather, say** that he lifted it **in order to carry it out.** Nevertheless, the case of shooting the arrow and the case of stealing the purse are different, as **with what** case **are we dealing here?** It is a case **where he stopped**[H] in the courtyard before taking the pouch out to the public domain. Therefore, the initial lifting is exclusively theft and not the start of a prohibited labor, as by stopping, he separated the lifting from the carrying out.

עָמַד לְמַאי? אִי לְכַתֵּף – אוֹרְחֵיהּ הוּא! אֶלָּא בְּעוֹמֵד לָפוּשׁ, אֲבָל לְכַתֵּף מַאי?

The Gemara asks: This is a case where he **stopped. For what** purpose did he stop? **If** he stopped in order **to** adjust the burden on his **shoulder, that is** the typical **manner** of proceeding and would not be considered an interruption in the process of carrying out the object. **Rather,** it must be **in** a case of one who **stopped to rest,** and when he resumes moving he initiates a separate action. The Gemara infers: **But** if he stopped in order **to** adjust the burden on his **shoulder, what** is the *halakha*?

Perek **III**
Daf **31** Amud **b**

NOTES

The legal status of one who walks is like that of one who stops – מְהַלֵּךְ כְּעוֹמֵד דָּמֵי: Ben Azzai's reasoning is clear: Since the act of walking involves the placement of one foot and the lifting of the other foot, one who walks essentially stops between each step. The problem is that according to that understanding, it is difficult to envision how one could perform the prohibited labor of carrying four cubits on Shabbat at all. *Tosafot* briefly cite three answers to this question, which are discussed in greater detail in other early commentaries. The first explanation is that according to ben Azzai carrying four cubits on Shabbat is a special *halakha*, and although one stops between each step it is considered one continuous action. A second resolution maintains that ben Azzai stated his *halakha* only with regard to one who is walking from a private domain to a public domain or vice versa through an exempt domain, and not with regard to walking in one domain. In the Jerusalem Talmud the explanation is that according to ben Azzai one would be liable for carrying out if he jumped four cubits, and the same would be true for one who threw an object that distance. Yet others suggest that the legal status of carrying four cubits is similar to that of carrying out from domain to domain, as the four cubits are considered one's domain. Ben Azzai's *halakha* is irrelevant in that case.

Dragging and exiting was necessary for the ***tanna*** – מְגָרֵר וְיוֹצֵא אִיצְטְרִיכָא לֵיהּ: The Ritva had a variant reading of the text: Rather, dragging and exiting was necessary for the *tanna*, etc. The term rather typically signifies a rejection of the previous explanation, and the Ritva explains that the Gemara here is explaining the matter in accordance with the opinion of the Rabbis, and not merely according to ben Azzai. This also resolves the difficulty raised in *Tosafot*. However, the Rashba rejects the variant reading. He claims that the explanation of the Gemara is in accordance with the opinions of both the Rabbis and ben Azzai, although some commentaries maintain that it is only in accordance with the opinion of ben Azzai.

Rather, it must be referring to intermediate-sized purses – אֶלָּא בְּמִיצְעֵי: Some commentaries maintain that the Gemara here disagrees with the Gemara in *Bava Batra* (86a), which states that objects that are typically lifted cannot be acquired with the acquisition of pulling (see Ramban and Rashba).

פָּטוּר, אַדְּתָנֵי הָיָה מְגָרֵר וְיוֹצֵא מְגָרֵר וְיוֹצֵא פָּטוּר, נִפְלוֹג וְנִיתְנֵי בְּדִידָהּ: בַּמֶּה דְּבָרִים אֲמוּרִים בְּעוֹמֵד לָפוּשׁ, אֲבָל לְכַתֵּף – פָּטוּר!

He would be **exempt.** If that is the case, **rather than teaching:** If **he was dragging and exiting, dragging and exiting, he is exempt, let** the *tanna* **distinguish and teach** the distinction **within** the case of carrying **itself,** as follows: **In what** case **are these matters stated?** It is **in** a case where **he stopped to rest; however,** if **he stopped to** adjust the burden on his **shoulder,** he is **exempt.**

אֶלָּא הָא מַנִּי – בֶּן עַזַּאי הִיא, דְּאָמַר: מְהַלֵּךְ כְּעוֹמֵד דָּמֵי. אֲבָל זוֹרֵק מַאי – פָּטוּר, נִיפְלוֹג [וְנִיתְנֵי] בְּדִידָהּ: בַּמֶּה דְּבָרִים אֲמוּרִים – בִּמְהַלֵּךְ, אֲבָל זוֹרֵק – פָּטוּר!

Rather, the Gemara explains why one is liable in the case where he carries the purse. In accordance with **whose** opinion was **this** *halakha* taught? **It is** in accordance with the opinion of **ben Azzai,** who **said:** The legal status of **one who walks is like** that of **one who stops,**[N] as each step constitutes a pause between the actions of lifting and placement. Therefore, the initial lifting is not part of the prohibited labor of carrying out. The Gemara infers: **But** if **one throws** the object into another domain, **what** is the *halakha*? He would be **exempt** from payment, as the lifting is the start of the prohibited labor of carrying out. If so, **let** the *tanna* **distinguish and teach** the distinction **within** the case **itself,** without resorting to the case of dragging and exiting, as follows: **In what** case **are these matters stated?** It is in the case of **one who walks,** so that there is separation between lifting and carrying out, and therefore the theft and the desecration of Shabbat are not simultaneous. **However, one who throws** is **exempt** from payment, as liability for carrying out and for theft are incurred simultaneously.

מְגָרֵר וְיוֹצֵא אִיצְטְרִיכָא לֵיהּ, סָלְקָא דַּעְתָּךְ אָמִינָא: אֵין דֶּרֶךְ הוֹצָאָה בְּכָךְ, קָא מַשְׁמַע לַן.

The Gemara answers: According to the opinion of ben Azzai, that would in fact be a more appropriate distinction; however, the case of one who was **dragging and exiting was necessary for the** *tanna*[N] to teach because it includes a novel element, as **it might enter your mind to say** that **this is not** a typical **manner of carrying out,** and one is not liable to be executed for performing a prohibited labor in an atypical manner. Therefore, **it teaches us** that this too is a manner of carrying out.

וּבְמַאי? אִי בְּרַבְרְבֵי – אוֹרְחֵיהּ הוּא, אִי בְּזוּטְרֵי – לָאו אוֹרְחֵיהּ הוּא! אֶלָּא, בְּמִיצְעֵי.

And the Gemara asks: **In what** case is this so? **If** it is **in** the case of **large** purses, obviously dragging **is its** typical **manner,** and there is nothing novel in this. **If** it is **in** the case of **small** purses, dragging **is** certainly **not its** typical **manner,** and one would certainly not be liable. **Rather,** it must be referring **to intermediate-sized purses.**[N] Although they are not always carried out in this manner, since they are sometimes dragged, the novelty is that he is liable for desecrating Shabbat and exempt from the payment.

וּדְאַפְּקֵיהּ לְהֵיכָא? אִי דְּאַפְּקֵיהּ לִרְשׁוּת הָרַבִּים אִיסּוּר שַׁבָּת – אִיכָּא, אִיסּוּר גְּנֵיבָה – לֵיכָּא, אִי דְּאַפְּקֵיהּ לִרְשׁוּת הַיָּחִיד – אִיסּוּר גְּנֵיבָה אִיכָּא, אִיסּוּר שַׁבָּת – לֵיכָּא! לָא צְרִיכָא, דְּאַפְּקֵיהּ לְצִידֵּי רְשׁוּת הָרַבִּים.

The Gemara continues: **And** in this case, **to where** did **he** carry out the pouch? **If he carried it out** from the owner's private domain **to the public domain,**[N] **there is** violation of the **prohibition of** Shabbat; however, **there is no** violation of the **prohibition** against **theft,** as one does not acquire an item by pulling it into the public domain. **If he carried it out** from the owner's private domain **to** his own **private domain, there is** violation of the **prohibition** against **theft;** however, **there is no** violation of the **prohibition of Shabbat.** The Gemara answers: This ruling **is necessary only** in a case **where he carried it out to the sides of the public domain.**[N] This is referring to the area in the public domain adjacent to the houses located on its sides, demarcated from the thoroughfare by small pegs and not by a full-fledged partition.

וּכְמַאן? אִי כְּרַבִּי אֱלִיעֶזֶר, דְּאָמַר: צִידֵּי רְשׁוּת הָרַבִּים כִּרְשׁוּת הָרַבִּים דָּמוּ אִיסּוּר שַׁבָּת אִיכָּא אִיסּוּר גְּנֵיבָה לֵיכָּא. אִי כְּרַבָּנַן, דְּאָמְרִי צִידֵּי רְשׁוּת הָרַבִּים לָאו כִּרְשׁוּת הָרַבִּים דָּמוּ – אִיסּוּר גְּנֵיבָה אִיכָּא, אִיסּוּר שַׁבָּת לֵיכָּא.

The Gemara asks: **And in accordance with whose** opinion is this taught? **If** it is **in accordance with** the opinion of **Rabbi Eliezer, who said:** The legal status of **the sides of the public domain is like** that of **the public domain, there is** violation of the **prohibition of** Shabbat; however, **there is no** violation of the **prohibition** against **theft. If** it is **in accordance with** the opinion of **the Rabbis, who said:** The legal status of **the sides of the public domain is not like** that of **the public domain, there is** violation of the **prohibition** against **theft;** however, **there is no** violation of the **prohibition of Shabbat.**

לְעוֹלָם כְּרַבִּי אֱלִיעֶזֶר, וְכִי אֲמַר רַבִּי אֱלִיעֶזֶר צִידֵּי רְשׁוּת הָרַבִּים כִּרְשׁוּת הָרַבִּים דָּמוּ – הָנֵי מִילֵּי לְעִנְיַן חִיּוּבָא דְּשַׁבָּת, דְּזִימְנִין דְּדָחֲקִי רַבִּים וְעָיְילִי לְהָתָם, אֲבָל לְעִנְיַן מִיקְנָא – קָנֵי, מַאי טַעֲמָא – דְּהָא לָא שְׁכִיחִי רַבִּים.

The Gemara answers: **Actually,** it is **in accordance with** the opinion of **Rabbi Eliezer, and when Rabbi Eliezer said:** The legal status of **the sides of the public domain is like** that of **the public domain, that applies only with regard to the liability for** performing prohibited labor on **Shabbat, as occasionally the multitudes crowd and enter there. However,** with regard **to the matter of acquiring**[H] an object, one **acquires** it by dragging it there. **What is the reason** for this *halakha*? It is due to the fact **that the public is not** typically **found** there, and acquisition can be effected in a place where the multitudes are not typically found.

רַב אַשִׁי אָמַר: כְּגוֹן שֶׁצֵּירַף יָדוֹ לְמַטָּה מִשְּׁלֹשָׁה וְקִיבְּלוֹ, כִּדְרָבָא. דְּאָמַר רָבָא: יָדוֹ שֶׁל אָדָם חֲשׁוּבָה לוֹ כְּאַרְבָּעָה עַל אַרְבָּעָה. רַב אַחָא מַתְנֵי הָכִי.

Rav Ashi said: Actually, one is exempt when one dragged the object into the public domain in a case **where he joined his hand** to his other hand at a height **below three handbreadths** off the ground **and received** the purse by passing it from one hand into the other as soon as he brought it into the public domain. This is **in accordance with** the opinion of **Rava,**[N] **as Rava said: A person's hand is considered like four by four** handbreadths **for him.**[H] Therefore, an object placed in one's hand is considered placed with regard to Shabbat, and since his hand is his personal domain he has also acquired the stolen item. **Rav Aḥa taught** the entire discussion **this way,** as above.

HALAKHA

Acquisition in the sides of the public domain – קִנְיָן בְּצִידֵּי רְשׁוּת הָרַבִּים: With regard to an object acquired by pulling in a place that belongs neither to the owner nor to the one acquiring the object, or in the public domain, if the one acquiring the object pulled it into his own domain or into an alleyway, i.e., the sides of the public domain, he acquires it. This is in accordance with the conclusion in the Gemara here that in terms of acquisition, the legal status of the sides of the public domain are not like that of the public domain (Rambam *Sefer Kinyan*, *Hilkhot Mekhira* 4:4; *Shulḥan Arukh*, *Ḥoshen Mishpat* 198:14).

A person's hand is considered like four by four handbreadths for him – יָדוֹ שֶׁל אָדָם חֲשׁוּבָה לוֹ כְּאַרְבָּעָה עַל אַרְבָּעָה: A person's hand is considered for him like a surface with an area of four by four cubits. Consequently, if on Shabbat one carried an object out of one domain and held it in his hand in a different domain, although he did not place it in that domain he is liable for carrying it out, as stated by Rava (Rambam *Sefer Zemanim*, *Hilkhot Shabbat* 13:2).

NOTES

If he carried it out to the public domain, etc. – אִי דְּאַפְּקֵיהּ לִרְשׁוּת הָרַבִּים וכו׳: Some ask: Why not explain that he carried it into another private domain, his own property, via a public domain? The answer is that in that case the prohibition of Shabbat would be violated when the object enters the public domain, and he completes the theft later (*Shita Yeshana*, cited in *Shita Mekubbetzet*).

To the sides of the public domain, etc. – לְצִידֵּי רְשׁוּת הָרַבִּים וכו׳: The definition of public and private domains varies in its application to three different areas of *halakha*: Shabbat, monetary law, and impurity. With regard to monetary law, a private domain is determined by ownership; for Shabbat, a domain is deemed public or private by its area and partitions. With regard to impurity, the decisive factor is the number of people found there. Therefore, it is possible for a place, e.g., the sides of the public domain, to be a private domain with regard to one area of *halakha* and a public domain with regard to another area.

Where he joined his hand below three handbreadths off the ground and received the purse, in accordance with the opinion of Rava – כְּגוֹן שֶׁצֵּירַף יָדוֹ לְמַטָּה מִשְּׁלֹשָׁה וְקִיבְּלוֹ, כִּדְרָבָא: There is a fundamental difficulty with this matter, mentioned in brief by *Tosafot* and discussed at length by the Ramban: Since Rava said in tractate *Shabbat* that the legal status of one's hand is like that of an area of four by four cubits, and therefore an object placed in one's hand is considered as though it were placed in the domain in which he is located, why is it necessary for one to place his hand below three handbreadths? Even if his hand were higher up, the object would still be considered placed in that domain. Apparently, Rashi was aware of this difficulty, as he explains that Rav Ashi's statement that this *halakha* is in accordance with the opinion of Rava is with regard to the *halakhot* of acquisitions, not those of Shabbat. Due to the significance of one's hand, it acquires the object even below three handbreadths. *Tosafot* and others question Rashi's approach, and the early and later commentaries seek to explain Rashi both in terms of different modes of acquisition and in terms of the definition of a person's hand. The *Ḥatam Sofer* writes that according to Rashi, Rava is saying that the legal status of one's hand is that of a larger surface in terms of placement, which explains his opinion with regard to acquisitions. According to *Tosafot*, in contrast, the hand is considered significant but not larger.

The Ramban, consistent with his approach, maintains that the private domain was significantly higher than the public domain, and when the Gemara states that he joined his hand below three handbreadths it means three handbreadths below the private domain, thereby lifting the object above the public domain. The Rid's version, also mentioned by *Tosafot*, reads: Alternatively, it is in accordance with the opinion of Rava. According to this version, the difficulty does not arise at all, as there are two separate answers: First, that he lowered his hand below three handbreadths, and second, that a person's hand is significant, as stated by Rava. The Ramban agrees that this is a worthy reading, but he notes that it does not appear in the manuscripts of Spain (see *Tosafot*).

רָבִינָא מַתְנֵי: לְעוֹלָם דְּאַפְּקֵיהּ לִרְשׁוּת הָרַבִּים וּבִרְשׁוּת הָרַבִּים נַמִּי קָנָה. וְתַרְוַיְיהוּ בְּדִיּוּקָא דְּהָא מַתְנִיתִין קָמִיפַּלְגִי, דִּתְנַן: הָיָה מוֹשְׁכוֹ וְיוֹצֵא, וּמֵת בִּרְשׁוּת בְּעָלִים – פָּטוּר, הִגְבִּיהוֹ אוֹ שֶׁהוֹצִיאוֹ מֵרְשׁוּת בְּעָלִים וּמֵת – חַיָּיב.

Ravina taught otherwise: **Actually,** it is a case **where one carried out** the object **to the public domain, and in the public domain he also acquires**[NH] the stolen object by removing it from the owner's domain, even if he does not transfer it to his own domain. The Gemara comments: **And the two of them,** Rav Aḥa and Ravina **disagree with regard to the inference of this mishna, as we learned** in a mishna (*Bava Kamma* 79a) with regard to one who stole an animal: If he **was pulling** the animal **and exiting, and it died in the domain of the owner,** the thief is **exempt** from payment because he did not yet acquire the animal and therefore did not assume liability for its death through circumstances beyond his control. If **he lifted it or took it out of the owner's domain,** thereby acquiring the animal, **and it died,** the thief is **liable** to pay its value because it died in his possession.

רָבִינָא דָּיֵיק מֵרֵישָׁא, רַב אַחָא דָּיֵיק מִסֵּיפָא. רָבִינָא דָּיֵיק מֵרֵישָׁא: הָיָה מוֹשְׁכוֹ וְיוֹצֵא, וּמֵת בִּרְשׁוּת בְּעָלִים – פָּטוּר. טַעֲמָא – דְּמֵת בִּרְשׁוּת בְּעָלִים, הָא הוֹצִיאוֹ מֵרְשׁוּת בְּעָלִים וּמֵת – חַיָּיב. רַב אַחָא דָּיֵיק מִסֵּיפָא: הִגְבִּיהוֹ אוֹ שֶׁהוֹצִיאוֹ, הוֹצָאָה דּוּמְיָא דְּהַגְבָּהָה; מַה הַגְבָּהָה – דְּאָתֵי לִרְשׁוּתֵיהּ, אַף הוֹצָאָה נַמִּי – דְּאָתֵי לִרְשׁוּתֵיהּ.

Ravina inferred his conclusion **from the first clause** of the mishna, **and Rav Aḥa inferred** his conclusion **from the latter clause. Ravina inferred** his conclusion **from the first clause:** If he **was pulling** the animal **and exiting, and it died in the domain of the owner,** the thief is **exempt** from payment. **The reason** that the thief is exempt **is that** the animal **died in the owner's domain; by inference, if he took it out of the owner's domain**[H] **and it died,** he is **liable** because the thief acquires the item by its very removal from the owner's property, even to the public domain. **Rav Aḥa inferred** his conclusion **from the latter clause** of the mishna: If **he lifted it or took it out of the owner's domain,** he is liable. Based on the juxtaposition of the two, **taking** the animal **out is similar to lifting it: Just as lifting** is an act of acquisition through which the animal **comes into his domain, so too, taking it out** is referring to a case **where it comes into his domain.**

לְרַב אַחָא קַשְׁיָא רֵישָׁא, לְרָבִינָא קַשְׁיָא סֵיפָא! רֵישָׁא לְרַב אַחָא לָא קַשְׁיָא: כַּמָּה דְּלָא אָתֵי לִרְשׁוּתֵיהּ – רְשׁוּת בְּעָלִים קָרֵינָא בֵּיהּ. סֵיפָא לְרָבִינָא לָא קַשְׁיָא: הוֹצָאָה דּוּמְיָא דְּהַגְבָּהָה – לָא אָמְרִינַן.

The Gemara observes: **For Rav Aḥa the first clause** of the mishna **is difficult,** while **for Ravina the latter clause is difficult.** The Gemara answers: **The first clause is not difficult for Rav Aḥa,** as he could explain it as follows: **As long as** the animal **has not come into one's domain,**[N] even if it has left the owner's property, **we** continue to **call it the owner's domain.** Similarly, **the latter clause is not difficult for Ravina,** as in his opinion **we do not say: Taking** the animal **out is similar to lifting** it. Therefore, the mishna's ruling is that the thief acquires the animal merely through its removal from the owner's property.

״הַבָּא עַל אֲחוֹתוֹ וְעַל אֲחוֹת אָבִיו״ כו׳. וּרְמִינְהוּ: אֵלּוּ הֵן הַלּוֹקִין: הַבָּא עַל אֲחוֹתוֹ, וְעַל אֲחוֹת אָבִיו, וְעַל אֲחוֹת אִמּוֹ, וְעַל אֲחוֹת אִשְׁתּוֹ, וְעַל אֵשֶׁת אָחִיו, וְעַל אֵשֶׁת אֲחִי אָבִיו, וְעַל הַנִּדָּה.

§ The mishna continues: Similarly, **one who has** forced **relations with his sister,** i.e., he rapes her, **or with his father's sister,** or with his mother's sister, or with his wife's sister, or with his brother's wife, or with his father's brother's wife after they divorced, or with a menstruating woman, there is a fine paid. **And** the Gemara **raised a contradiction** from the following mishna (*Makkot* 13a): **And these** people **are flogged:**[NH] **One who has relations with his sister, or with his father's sister, or with his mother's sister, or with his wife's sister, or with his brother's wife, or with his father's brother's wife, or with a menstruating woman.** Anyone who intentionally has relations with any of these women is punished with lashes.

NOTES

In the public domain he also acquires – בִּרְשׁוּת הָרַבִּים נַמִּי קָנָה: *Tosafot* point out that this appears to contradict the opinion of Abaye and Rava in *Bava Batra* (84b), who state clearly that pulling, as a mode of acquisition, is not effective in the public domain. In fact, the Rid and other early commentaries maintain that there is a contradiction between the sources in the two tractates, and that is why they do not rule in accordance with the opinion of Ravina (see HALAKHA). Conversely, the Rashba and others accept the explanation of Rabbeinu Yitzḥak in *Tosafot*, who explains that this is not dealing with a standard acquisition; rather, the Gemara is saying that when a thief pulls the object into the public domain he acquires the object to the extent that he is liable for unavoidable accidents that befall the object. However, he does not acquire the object completely. The Ra'ah and the Ritva explain that although pulling does not typically effect acquisition in the public domain, in this case the object was pulled in the public domain after its removal from the owner's domain, and in that case the thief acquires ownership.

As long as it has not come into one's domain, etc. – כַּמָּה דְּלָא אָתֵי לִרְשׁוּתֵיהּ וכו׳: When the mishna refers to the owner's domain, the reference is not to the area currently occupied by the owner but to his domain in terms of legal ownership. Consequently, until the thief acquires the object it remains in the owner's domain (Ritva).

And the Gemara raised a contradiction: These are flogged, etc. – וּרְמִינְהוּ: אֵלּוּ הֵן הַלּוֹקִין וכו׳: Why does the Gemara raise this problem here? The same difficulty could be raised at the beginning of the mishna, as one who rapes a *mamzeret* violates a prohibition and is liable to be flogged. *Tosafot* explain that in fact the Gemara could have raised the question there, but it preferred to cite the question from the mishna in *Makkot*. The Ramban maintains that since the mishna was established earlier in accordance with the opinion of Rabbi Meir, who maintains that one is lashed and pays the fine, as explained later, the difficulty can be raised only with regard to prohibitions punishable by *karet*. In the Jerusalem Talmud there is a different resolution to this problem, as the Gemara there proposes that the mishna is referring to a *mamzer* who raped a *mamzeret*, who is not subject to lashes, as she is permitted to him. According to this interpretation, the novel element in the mishna is that a *mamzeret* is entitled to the fine despite her flawed lineage.

HALAKHA

In the public domain he also acquires – בִּרְשׁוּת הָרַבִּים נַמִּי קָנָה: One who stole a purse on Shabbat by dragging it from the owner's domain into the public domain is exempt from payment, as the desecration of Shabbat and the theft occur simultaneously. The *halakha* is in accordance with the opinion of Ravina, as he is a later Sage, and the *halakha* is generally ruled in accordance with his opinion in disputes with Rav Aḥa. The *Tur* rules in accordance with the opinion of Rav Aḥa because according to the Riva in *Tosafot*, this is also the opinion of Abaye and Rava (Vilna Gaon; Rambam *Sefer Nezikim, Hilkhot Geneiva* 3:2; *Shulḥan Arukh, Ḥoshen Mishpat* 351).

If he took it out of the owner's domain, etc. – הוֹצִיאוֹ מֵרְשׁוּת בְּעָלִים וכו׳: A thief is liable to be punished for theft from the moment he removes an object from its owner's domain, even if it was subsequently destroyed by unavoidable accident. If he did not remove it from the owner's domain he is liable only if he lifted the item, as stated by Ravina (Rambam *Sefer Nezikim, Hilkhot Geneiva* 2:16; *Shulḥan Arukh, Ḥoshen Mishpat* 348:4).

These are flogged, etc. – אֵלּוּ הֵן הַלּוֹקִין וכו׳: With regard to any prohibition punishable by *karet* and not by court-administered execution, if one violated the prohibition in the presence of witnesses and after forewarning, he is liable to be flogged, as explained in the mishna cited here (Rambam *Sefer Shofetim, Hilkhot Sanhedrin* 19:1).

וְקַיְימָא לַן דְּאֵינוֹ לוֹקֶה וּמְשַׁלֵּם! אָמַר עוּלָּא: לָא קַשְׁיָא; כָּאן – בַּאֲחוֹתוֹ נַעֲרָה, כָּאן – בַּאֲחוֹתוֹ בּוֹגֶרֶת.

And since **we maintain** in general **that one is not** both **flogged and** liable to pay, if one receives lashes for having relations with his sister, why must he pay the fine as well? **Ulla said:** This is **not difficult; here,** the *halakha* in the mishna is **with regard to his sister** who is a **young woman,**[N] for whom one pays a fine and is not flogged, whereas **there,** the *halakha* in the mishna is **with regard to his sister** who is a **grown woman,** for whom one does not pay a fine.

אֲחוֹתוֹ בּוֹגֶרֶת נַמִי, הָא אִיכָּא בּוֹשֶׁת וּפְגָם! בְּשׁוֹטָה. וְהָא אִיכָּא צַעֲרָא! בִּמְפוּתָּה.

The Gemara asks: In the case of one who has relations with **his sister** who is a **grown woman, too,** although he does not pay a fine, **isn't there** compensation for **humiliation and degradation?**[H] He should be exempt from lashes in that case as well. The Gemara answers: **There,** the *halakha* in the mishna is **with regard to** his sister who is **an imbecile,**[N] with regard to whom there is no humiliation or degradation beyond her status as an imbecile. The Gemara asks: **But isn't** there payment for **pain**[H] even in the rape of an imbecile? The Gemara responds: The *halakha* is **with regard to a seduced woman,**[H] who is not entitled to payment for pain, as she engaged in relations willingly.

הַשְׁתָּא דְּאָתֵית לְהָכִי, אֲפִילּוּ תֵּימָא אֲחוֹתוֹ נַעֲרָה – בִּיתוֹמָה וּמְפוּתָּה.

The Gemara comments: **Now that you have arrived at this** explanation that the mishna is referring to a seduced woman, the mishna can be understood **even if you say** it is referring **to his sister** who is **a young woman.** The reason that the seducer does not pay the fine is that the *halakha* is **with regard to** one who is **an orphan and a seduced woman.**[N] Were her father alive, he would receive the payment. Because he died, the payment goes to her. Since she willingly participated in the relations, she relinquished her right to the payment, and the seducer is therefore liable to receive lashes.

אַלְמָא קָסָבַר עוּלָּא: כָּל הֵיכָא דְּאִיכָּא מָמוֹן וּמַלְקוֹת – מָמוֹנָא מְשַׁלֵּם מִילְקָא לָא לָקֵי. מְנָא לֵיהּ לְעוּלָּא הָא? גָּמַר מֵחוֹבֵל בַּחֲבֵירוֹ: מָה חוֹבֵל בַּחֲבֵירוֹ, דְּאִיכָּא מָמוֹן וּמַלְקוֹת, מָמוֹנָא מְשַׁלֵּם, מִילְקָא לָא לָקֵי, אַף כָּל הֵיכָא דְּאִיכָּא מָמוֹן וּמַלְקוֹת, מָמוֹנָא מְשַׁלֵּם, מִילְקָא לָא לָקֵי.

The Gemara observes: **Apparently, Ulla maintains** that in **any** case **where there is** liability to both pay **money and** receive **lashes,** e.g., one who has forced relations with his sister who is a young woman, one **pays money** but **is not flogged.** The Gemara asks: **From where does Ulla** derive **this** principle? The Gemara answers: He **derives** it **from the** *halakha* **of one who injures another. Just as** with regard to **one who injures another where there is** liability to both pay **money** for the injury **and** receive **lashes** for violating the prohibition "Lest he continues to strike him" (Deuteronomy 25:3), the *halakha* there is that one **pays money** but **is not flogged, so too,** in **any** case **where there is** liability to both pay **money and** receive **lashes,** one **pays money** but **is not flogged.**

HALAKHA

In the case of…a grown woman, too, isn't there compensation for humiliation and degradation – בּוֹגֶרֶת נַמִי הָא אִיכָּא בּוֹשֶׁת וּפְגָם: One who rapes a grown woman is not liable to pay the fine, but he pays for her humiliation, degradation, and pain (Rambam *Sefer Nashim, Hilkhot Na'ara Betula* 2:11).

But isn't there payment for pain – וְהָא אִיכָּא צַעֲרָא: One who rapes an imbecile or a deaf-mute is liable to pay only for her suffering (Rambam *Sefer Nashim, Hilkhot Na'ara Betula* 2:11).

With regard to a seduced woman – בִּמְפוּתָּה: One who seduced a grown woman, a deaf-mute, or an imbecile is exempt from payment (Rambam *Sefer Nashim, Hilkhot Na'ara Betula* 2:11).

NOTES

With regard to his sister who is a young woman, etc. – בַּאֲחוֹתוֹ נַעֲרָה וכו׳: Similar answers are provided in the Jerusalem Talmud, with certain differences. The responses attributed here to Ulla are cited there in the name of Rabbi Natan bar Oshaya, while the Sages of Caesarea claim that it refers to a seduced woman or to one who waives her right to the payments.

With regard to an imbecile – בְּשׁוֹטָה: Rashi explains that an imbecile has no value. The Rashash points out that an imbecile does have value with regard to valuations (see *Arakhin* 2a), and he therefore explains that Rashi is referring to her degradation. As explained elsewhere, a woman's degradation is determined by estimating the difference between the amount one would pay to purchase her as a maidservant to marry his Hebrew slave before her rape and the amount one would pay after her rape. That is not relevant with regard to an imbecile.

With regard to one who is an orphan and a seduced woman – בִּיתוֹמָה וּמְפוּתָּה: There is a variant reading cited by some early commentaries: With regard to an orphan who is an imbecile and a seduced woman. Rashi deletes the word imbecile, as it is unnecessary. Even if she is a seduced orphan, she is not entitled to payment. The Ramban agrees with Rashi, adding that the other version resulted from the fact that a minor and an imbecile are typically listed together. Conversely, Rabbi Shmuel HaNagid accepts the variant reading, explaining that orphan is not meant literally; rather, the reference is to a young woman who was betrothed and divorced, whose legal status according to the opinion of Rabbi Yosei HaGelili, cited later (38a), is that of an orphan in her father's lifetime and she is not entitled to a fine. It is necessary to add that she is an imbecile as well, to exempt him from the payments for degradation and humiliation. A different interpretation is suggested by the Ritva. He contends that although an orphan who is not an imbecile waives the payment for her humiliation, she cannot exempt one from the payment for the humiliation suffered by her family. Therefore, the Gemara added that she was an imbecile.

מַה לְּחוֹבֵל בַּחֲבֵירוֹ – שֶׁכֵּן חַיָּיב בַּחֲמִשָּׁה דְּבָרִים, וְאִי מָמוֹנָא לְקוּלָּא, שֶׁכֵּן הוּתַּר מִכְּלָלוֹ בְּבֵית דִּין!

The Gemara asks: **What** is the basis for the comparison between other cases and the case of **one who injures another?** One who injures another cannot serve as a paradigm for cases of liability for both money and lashes because the case of one who injures another is particularly stringent, **as he is liable** to pay **five types** of indemnity:[N] Injury, pain, medical costs, loss of livelihood, and humiliation. **And if** payment of **money** is a more **lenient**[N] form of punishment than lashes, one could infer *a fortiori*: If in the stringent case of injuring another, one receives the more lenient punishment, all the more so would he receive the more lenient punishment in less stringent cases; nevertheless, one who injures another cannot serve as a paradigm for cases of liability for both money and lashes. The reason is that there is also a lenient aspect with regard to injuring another, **as it is permitted,** in departure **from its norm, in court.**[N] The court administers lashes, injuring those convicted. The leniency is that its application is selective.

אֶלָּא גָּמַר מֵעֵדִים זוֹמְמִין, מָה עֵדִים זוֹמְמִין דְּאִיכָּא מָמוֹן וּמַלְקוֹת – מָמוֹנָא מְשַׁלֵּם, מִילְקָא לָא לָקֵי! אַף כָּל הֵיכָא דְּאִיכָּא מָמוֹן וּמַלְקוֹת – מָמוֹנָא מְשַׁלֵּם, מִילְקָא לָא לָקֵי!

Rather, the Gemara states that Ulla **derives** this principle **from** the *halakha* of false, **conspiring witnesses.**[B] **Just** as with regard to **conspiring witnesses, where there is** liability to both pay **money,** if they falsely testified to render one liable for payment, **and** receive **lashes,** for violating the prohibition "You shall not bear false witness against your neighbor" (Exodus 20:12), and the *halakha* is that one **pays money** but **is not flogged, so too,** in **any** case **where there is** liability to both pay **money and** receive **lashes,** one **pays money** but **is not flogged.**

מַה לְּעֵדִים זוֹמְמִין – שֶׁכֵּן אֵינָן צְרִיכִים הַתְרָאָה, וְאִי מָמוֹנָא לְקוּלָּא הוּא – שֶׁכֵּן לֹא עָשׂוּ מַעֲשֶׂה!

The Gemara asks: **What** is the basis for the comparison of other cases to the case of **conspiring witnesses?** Conspiring witnesses cannot serve as a paradigm for cases of liability for both money and lashes because the case of conspiring witnesses is particularly stringent, **as they do not require forewarning.**[H] As a rule, the courts administer punishment only to one who was forewarned not to perform the transgression. The fact that this is not a requirement in the case of conspiring witnesses indicates that it is a particularly stringent prohibition. Therefore, no proof can be cited from the case of conspiring witnesses to other cases with regard to monetary payment instead of lashes. **And if** payment of **money** is a more **lenient** form of punishment than lashes, the case of conspiring witnesses also has a lenient aspect, **as they did not perform an action**[N] but merely spoke.

BACKGROUND

False conspiring witnesses – עֵדִים זוֹמְמִין: These are witnesses who are proven to have perjured themselves in order to cause another to lose a monetary dispute or cause him to be punished by the court. Testimony of witnesses can be invalidated in two manners: (1) Two other witnesses testify that an incident did not transpire as it was described by the first pair of witnesses. In that case, the testimony of neither pair is accepted, and the matter remains unresolved. (2) Two witnesses testify that the first pair of witnesses, whose testimony condemned the defendant, were elsewhere when the incident transpired and could not have witnessed the incident about which they testified. The second pair of witnesses does not contradict the version of events described by the first pair, which may in fact be true. They are merely testifying that the first pair was not present and therefore is not in a position to know what transpired. In that case, the testimony of the second pair of witnesses is accepted, and the testimony of the first pair of witnesses is rejected. Furthermore, the first pair of witnesses, once rendered false conspiring witnesses, are punished with the punishment that they sought to inflict on the defendant through their testimony (see Deuteronomy 19:16–19). Therefore, if their testimony would have resulted in the defendant's execution, they are both executed. If their testimony would have resulted in his receiving lashes, they are both flogged. If their testimony would have resulted in a penalty that cannot be applied to them, e.g., if their evidence would have disqualified the defendant from the priesthood, they are flogged.

HALAKHA

Conspiring witnesses…do not require forewarning – עֵדִים זוֹמְמִין...אֵינָן צְרִיכִים הַתְרָאָה: It is not necessary for conspiring witnesses to be forewarned prior to their testimony; rather, they are punished as soon as they are convicted for giving false testimony, as per the Gemara here and the Gemara in *Makkot* (4b; Rambam *Sefer Shofetim*, *Hilkhot Edut* 18:4 and *Kesef Mishne* there).

NOTES

What is the comparison to one who injures another, as he is liable to pay five types of indemnity – מַה לְּחוֹבֵל בַּחֲבֵירוֹ שֶׁכֵּן חַיָּיב בַּחֲמִשָּׁה דְּבָרִים: Although not all those who injure others are liable to pay all five indemnities, they all apply potentially: Injury, for permanent damage caused; pain, for the suffering he inflicted; medical costs, for the doctor's treatment and medicine; loss of livelihood, compensation for the period during which the victim was unable to work; and humiliation, for the shame the victim suffered as a result of the attack. Clearly, depending on the circumstances the aggressor might be liable to pay only some of these indemnities, or even only one of them. Apparently, not all of these categories apply to rape, for which one pays the following: The fine; degradation, which is parallel to injury; pain; and humiliation. An earlier version of Rashi's commentary, cited by the *Shita Mekubbetzet*, states that a rapist is not obligated to pay medical expenses. However, the Rid (42a) states that a rapist is sometimes liable to pay medical costs and loss of livelihood as well. However, in that case, the *halakha* of the five types of indemnity is not unique to one who injures another. It is possible that the payments of medical costs and loss of livelihood do not stem from the rape but from injuries one caused. If so, it falls into the category of one who injures another.

And if payment of money is more lenient – וְאִי מָמוֹנָא לְקוּלָּא: The Ritva, elaborating on *Tosafot*, asks: How can it be suggested that payment of money is the more lenient punishment? The Gemara states below that one who inflicts a wound and causes less than a *peruta* worth of damage is liable to be flogged. If he inflicted more serious damage, he pays. If payment of money is a more lenient punishment, he profits from commission of a more egregious transgression. The Ritva suggests that the Torah had compassion on the injured party. Although the aggressor receives a more lenient punishment, the victim receives compensation for his injury. The *Ḥatam Sofer* states that the comparison between the punishments here is not an attempt to determine the overall relationship between payments and lashes. Rather, the Gemara notes that sometimes one is liable to pay a large sum, in which case the payment of money is the more stringent punishment, whereas other times he is liable to pay a small sum, in which case it is a lenient punishment. The punishment of lashes is fixed, while monetary punishment varies.

As this prohibited action is permitted in departure from its norm in court – שֶׁכֵּן הוּתַּר מִכְּלָלוֹ בְּבֵית דִּין: The Ritva asks: How can it be said that the prohibition against injuring another is lenient because injury is permitted in court? Can there be any comparison between one who criminally assaults another to an officer of the court who performs a mitzva by administering lashes to a convicted criminal? He explains that despite this anomaly, the contention of: As this prohibited action is permitted in departure from its norm, is independent of the nature of the leniency. It merely points to the fact that the prohibition is not in effect in all circumstances.

As they did not perform an action – שֶׁכֵּן לֹא עָשׂוּ מַעֲשֶׂה: Although the Gemara in *Bava Metzia* (90b) states: Moving one's lips while speaking is considered an action, there is a difference between a full-fledged action and speech (Rabbeinu Crescas Vidal). The Rashba similarly distinguishes between a significant action and the insignificant action of moving one's lips. The Ritva suggests that the expression: Did not perform an action, is not referring to the fact that they sinned by speaking. Rather, it is a reference to the principle that false conspiring witnesses are executed only if the person they accused was not himself executed. Consequently, they are punished only if their testimony did not cause the performance of an action.

אֶלָּא, גָּמַר מִתַּרְוַיְיהוּ; מָה הַצַּד הַשָּׁוֶה שֶׁבָּהֶן – דְּאִיכָּא מָמוֹן וּמַלְקוּת – מָמוֹנָא מְשַׁלֵּם מִילְקָא לָא לָקֵי, אַף כָּל הֵיכָא דְּאִיכָּא מָמוֹן וּמַלְקוּת – מָמוֹנָא מְשַׁלֵּם, מִילְקָא לָא לָקֵי. מַה לְּהַצַּד הַשָּׁוֶה שֶׁבָּהֶן – שֶׁכֵּן יֵשׁ בָּהֶן צַד חָמוּר, וְאִי מָמוֹנָא לְקוּלָּא הוּא – שֶׁכֵּן יֵשׁ בָּהֶן צַד הַקַּל!

Rather, Ulla **derives** the principle **from both of them,** the cases of one who injures another and of conspiring witnesses. **The common denominator of** both cases **is that there is** liability to both pay **money and** receive **lashes** and the *halakha* is that one **pays money** but **is not flogged; so too,** in **any** case **where there is** liability to both pay **money and** receive **lashes,** one **pays money** but **is not flogged.** The Gemara asks: **What** is the basis for the comparison of other cases to **the common denominator of** both cases, **as they have an element of stringency**[N] that does not exist in other prohibitions in that one who injures another pays five types of indemnity, and conspiring witnesses are flogged without forewarning? **And if** payment of **money** is a more **lenient** form of punishment than lashes, other cases cannot be derived from it, **as they have an element of leniency** that does not exist in other prohibitions. The prohibition in the case of one who injures another is selectively applied, as it is permitted, in departure from its norm, in court, and the case of conspiring witnesses is lenient because they performed no action.

NOTES

As they have an element of stringency – שֶׁכֵּן יֵשׁ בָּהֶן צַד חָמוּר: This attempt to refute an analogy based on the common denominator appearing elsewhere in the Talmud is questioned by the early commentaries. If an analogy can be refuted due to a common element of stringency, all analogies based on a common denominator can be refuted, as the only reason that the common denominator was necessary is because each of the sources has its own particular stringency or leniency. *Tosafot* explain that this objection is not raised in every case of an analogy based on a common denominator. It is raised only in cases where there is a common extreme stringency or leniency (see *Tosafot*). The Ramban states that the question of whether this explanation fits all the instances in which this refutation is raised requires additional analysis. Rabbeinu Tam in *Tosafot* suggests that the reason this refutation is raised here is because the same stringency and leniency apply in both cases. If conspiring witnesses accused one of injuring another they are liable to pay the five indemnities, and there are certain false testimonies that are permitted in court, with regard to which the prohibition "You shall not bear false witness against your neighbor" (Exodus 20:12) does not apply, e.g., testimony that they saw the new moon. The Ritva and others reject this explanation. A different explanation is suggested by the Ra'ah and his students: The objection of an element of stringency is raised only in cases when the stringent element is the very issue under discussion. In this case, since the relative severity of the various punishments is under discussion, the fact that the two sources both involve especially harsh punishments is in fact a relevant cause for refuting the analogy. By the same token, their particular leniencies are relevant when these *halakhot* are the basis of comparison to other punishments.

Perek **III**
Daf **32** ב Amud **b**

אֶלָּא, עוּלָּא "תַּחַת" "תַּחַת" גָּמַר, כְּתִיב הָכָא "תַּחַת אֲשֶׁר עִנָּהּ" וּכְתִיב הָתָם "עַיִן תַּחַת עַיִן", מָה הָתָם, מָמוֹנָא מְשַׁלֵּם מִילְקָא לָא לָקֵי – אַף כָּל הֵיכָא דְּאִיכָּא מָמוֹנָא וּמַלְקוּת – מָמוֹנָא מְשַׁלֵּם, מִילְקָא לָא לָקֵי.

Rather, Ulla derives the fact that one pays and is not flogged by means of a verbal analogy between the terms **for** and **for.** The verse **states** with regard to rape: "And the man who lay with her shall give to the father of the young woman fifty shekels of silver, and to him she shall be as a wife, **because [*taḥat*] he tormented her**" (Deuteronomy 22:29), **and it states there,** with regard to injury: **"An eye for [*taḥat*] an eye"** (Exodus 21:24). **Just as there,** with regard to injury, one **pays money** and **is not flogged,** so too, in **any** case **where there is** liability to both pay **money** and receive **lashes,** one **pays money** but **is not flogged.**

רַבִּי יוֹחָנָן אָמַר: אֲפִילּוּ תֵּימָא אֲחוֹתוֹ נַעֲרָה. כָּאן – שֶׁהִתְרוּ בּוֹ, כָּאן – שֶׁלֹּא הִתְרוּ בּוֹ.

§ In proposing a different resolution to the apparent contradiction between the mishna here that rules that one pays a fine for raping his sister and the mishna in *Makkot* that rules that one is flogged in that case, **Rabbi Yoḥanan said: Even if you say** that both *mishnayot* are referring to **his sister** who is **a young woman, there** it is referring to a case **where** the witnesses **forewarned him,** and therefore the rapist is flogged; **here,** it is referring to a case **where** the witnesses **did not forewarn him.** Since no lashes are administered without forewarning, the rapist pays the fine.

אַלְמָא קָסָבַר רַבִּי יוֹחָנָן: כָּל הֵיכָא דְּאִיכָּא מָמוֹן וּמַלְקוּת, וְאַתְרוּ בֵּיהּ, מִילְקָא לָקֵי, מָמוֹנָא לָא מְשַׁלֵּם. מְנָא לֵיהּ לְרַבִּי יוֹחָנָן הָא? אָמַר קְרָא: "כְּדֵי רִשְׁעָתוֹ" – מִשּׁוּם רִשְׁעָה אַחַת אַתָּה מְחַיְּיבוֹ, וְאִי אַתָּה מְחַיְּיבוֹ מִשּׁוּם שְׁתֵּי רִשְׁעָיוֹת, וּסְמִיךְ לֵיהּ "אַרְבָּעִים יַכֶּנּוּ".

The Gemara observes: **Apparently, Rabbi Yoḥanan maintains** that in **any** case **where there is** liability to both pay **money and** receive **lashes, and** the witnesses **forewarned him, he is flogged** but does not **pay money.** The Gemara asks: **From where does Rabbi Yoḥanan** derive **this** principle?[N] The Gemara explains that he derives it from that which **the verse states** with regard to one sentenced to lashes in the court: "The judge shall cause him to lie down, and to be beaten before him, **according to the measure of his wickedness**" (Deuteronomy 25:2), from which it is inferred: **For one** act of **wickedness,** i.e., punishment, **you can render him liable, but you cannot render him liable for two** acts of **wickedness. And juxtaposed to** this it states: **"Forty he shall strike him"** (Deuteronomy 25:3), indicating that the punishment that is administered when one is liable to receive two punishments is lashes and not payment.

NOTES

From where does Rabbi Yoḥanan derive this principle – מְנָא לֵיהּ לְרַבִּי יוֹחָנָן הָא: The Gemara asked earlier: From where did Ulla derive that one pays and is not flogged? This question indicates that without that source, the assumption would have been that one is flogged and does not pay. Here, the Gemara questions Rabbi Yoḥanan's source, indicating that the assumption would have been the opposite. Although the Gemara at times questions a certain opinion based on two conflicting lines of reasoning because neither is clear or obvious, the Gemara here is difficult. *Tosafot Yeshanim* and the Rosh explain that once Ulla cited support for his approach from a verbal analogy, the burden of proof shifts, and the Gemara then seeks the source for Rabbi Yoḥanan's opinion.

וַהֲרֵי חוֹבֵל בַּחֲבֵירוֹ, דְּאִיכָּא מָמוֹן וּמַלְקוֹת – מָמוֹנָא מְשַׁלֵּם, מִילְקָא לָא לָקֵי! וְכִי תֵּימָא: הָנֵי מִילֵּי הֵיכָא דְּלָא אַתְרוּ בֵּיהּ, אֲבָל אַתְרוּ בֵּיהּ – מִילְקָא לָקֵי, מָמוֹנָא לָא מְשַׁלֵּם, וְהָאָמַר רַבִּי אַמִי אָמַר רַבִּי יוֹחָנָן: הִכָּהוּ הַכָּאָה שֶׁאֵין בָּהּ שָׁוֶה פְּרוּטָה – לוֹקֶה. הֵיכִי דָּמֵי? אִי דְּלָא אַתְרוּ בֵּיהּ – אַמַּאי לוֹקֶה? אֶלָּא פְּשִׁיטָא. דְּאַתְרוּ בֵּיהּ, וְטַעְמָא – דְּלֵית בָּהּ שָׁוֶה פְּרוּטָה, הָא אִית בָּהּ שָׁוֶה פְּרוּטָה – מָמוֹנָא מְשַׁלֵּם, מִילְקָא לָא לָקֵי!

The Gemara asks: **And** what of the case of **one who injures another where there is** liability to both pay **money and** receive **lashes,** in which case one **pays money** but **is not flogged? And lest you say** that **this applies only when** the witnesses **did not forewarn him, but if they forewarned him** before he struck his friend he **is flogged** but **does not pay money, didn't Rabbi Ami say** that **Rabbi Yoḥanan said:** If one **struck** another with **a blow that** does **not** cause damage that amounts to **the value of a** ***peruta*****,**[H] he is **flogged?** The Gemara asks: **What are the circumstances** of that case? **If** it is a case **where** the witnesses **did not forewarn him, why is he flogged?** No lashes are administered without forewarning. **Rather, obviously** it is a case **where they forewarned him, and the reason** he is flogged is that **there is not** damage that amounts to **the value of a** ***peruta*****.** The damages are not quantifiable. The Gemara infers: However, if **there is** damage that amounts to **the value of a** ***peruta*****,** he **pays money** and **is not flogged,** even though he was forewarned.

כִּדְאָמַר רַבִּי אֶילְעָא: בְּפֵירוּשׁ רִיבְּתָה תּוֹרָה עֵדִים זוֹמְמִין לְתַשְׁלוּמִין, הָכָא נַמִי, בְּפֵירוּשׁ רִיבְּתָה תּוֹרָה חוֹבֵל בַּחֲבֵירוֹ לְתַשְׁלוּמִין. וְהֵיכָא אִיתְּמַר דְּרַבִּי אֶילְעָא – אַהָא: מְעִידִין אָנוּ אֶת אִישׁ פְּלוֹנִי שֶׁחַיָּיב לַחֲבֵירוֹ מָאתַיִם זוּז, וְנִמְצְאוּ זוֹמְמִין – לוֹקִין וּמְשַׁלְּמִין, שֶׁלֹּא הַשֵּׁם הַמְבִיאָן לִידֵי מַכּוֹת מְבִיאָן לִידֵי תַּשְׁלוּמִין, דִּבְרֵי רַבִּי מֵאִיר, וַחֲכָמִים אוֹמְרִים: כָּל הַמְשַׁלֵּם אֵינוֹ לוֹקֶה.

The Gemara answers that the fact that conspiring witnesses pay money can be explained **in accordance with that which Rabbi Ile'a said** in a different context: **The Torah explicitly amplified** the case of **conspiring witnesses** to include liability **for payment.** The Torah employed language indicating that conspiring witnesses who testified falsely in order to render one liable for payment must pay the sum and are not flogged. **Here, too,** with regard to injury, **the Torah explicitly amplified** the case **of one who injures another** to include liability **for payment.**[H] The Gemara asks: **And where is this statement of Rabbi Ile'a stated?** The Gemara answers that it is stated **concerning this** mishna (*Makkot* 4a). If witnesses said: **We testify that so-and-so owes another two hundred dinar, and** these witnesses **were discovered** to be **conspiring** witnesses; **they are flogged and pay,** as **the source** [*shem*] **that brings them to** liability to receive **lashes does not brings them to** liability for **payment.**[N] Each liability has an independent source; the source for lashes is: "You shall not bear false witness against your neighbor," while the source for payment is: "You shall do unto him as he conspired" (Deuteronomy 19:19). This is **the statement of Rabbi Meir. And the Rabbis say: Anyone who pays is not flogged.**[NH]

וְנֵימָא: כָּל הַלּוֹקֶה אֵינוֹ מְשַׁלֵּם! אָמַר רַבִּי אֶילְעָא: בְּפֵירוּשׁ רִיבְּתָה תּוֹרָה עֵדִים זוֹמְמִין לְתַשְׁלוּמִין. – הֵיכָן רִיבְּתָה תּוֹרָה? מִכְּדִי כְּתִיב ״וַעֲשִׂיתֶם לוֹ כַּאֲשֶׁר זָמַם לַעֲשׂוֹת לְאָחִיו״. ״יָד בְּיָד״ לָמָּה לִי – דָּבָר הַנִּיתָּן מִיָּד לְיָד. וּמַאי נִיהוּ – מָמוֹן.

And with regard to that mishna, the Gemara asks: **Let us say,** on the contrary, that **anyone who is flogged does not pay. Rabbi Ile'a said: The Torah explicitly amplified** the case of **conspiring witnesses for payment,** not lashes. The Gemara asks: **Where did the Torah amplify** the case of conspiring witnesses? The Gemara explains: **Now, since it states** with regard to conspiring witnesses: **"And you shall do unto him as he conspired to do unto his brother"** (Deuteronomy 19:19); **why do I require** the Torah to state in his punishment: **"A hand for a hand"** (Deuteronomy 19:21)?[N] This indicates that the punishment that takes precedence is one in which there is **an item that is given from hand to hand, and what is that** item? It is **money.**

NOTES

As the source [*shem*] that brings them to liability to receive lashes does not bring them to liability for payment – שֶׁלֹּא הַשֵּׁם הַמְבִיאָן לִידֵי מַכּוֹת מְבִיאָן לִידֵי תַּשְׁלוּמִין: According to Rashi, the term: The source [*shem*], is referring to the biblical source for his punishment. Rabbi Meir maintains that conspiring witnesses are liable to payment due to the verse "You shall do unto him as he conspired," and the liability to receive lashes is for their transgression of "You shall not bear false witness." *Tosafot* question this understanding, as they cite proof that Rabbi Meir does not distinguish in that manner, and if the liability for lashes and payment are derived from the same verse, he holds that the sinner is lashed and pays. Some early commentaries claim that Rabbi Meir said his statement only in accordance with the opinion of the Rabbis (see *Tosafot*). Many early commentaries follow the approach of the Ramban in tractate *Makkot* (4b), who asserts that were the liability of conspiring witnesses to receive lashes, in fact, derived from the verse "You shall do unto him as he conspired," the witnesses would not be flogged, as the Torah says that they receive the punishment they plotted to inflict on others, but no more. Since they conspired to obligate the defendant to pay and not to be flogged, they too are liable only to pay and not to be flogged. According to Rabbi Meir, in contrast, it is only the obligation to pay that is derived from the verse "You shall do unto him as he conspired," while their liability to be flogged is derived from a different verse. Since Rabbi Meir maintains in general that one can be flogged and pay for a single transgression, these conspiring witnesses are flogged. According to this approach, the decisive point is not that there are two different verses, but that the source for the witnesses' liability to receive lashes is not their conspiracy but the fact that they gave false testimony. Rabbi Meir contends that their liability in this regard is a general one, unrelated to the particular individual who was the object of their testimony.

Anyone who pays is not flogged – כָּל הַמְשַׁלֵּם אֵינוֹ לוֹקֶה: Some early commentaries explain that this is as an elaboration on the opinion of the Rabbis: Not only do they reject Rabbi Meir's ruling that conspiring witnesses are flogged due to the verse "You shall not bear false witness," as this is a prohibition that does not entail an action, but in general they maintain that one does not receive two punishments for a single transgression. Others claim that Rabbi Meir made his statement in accordance with the opinion of the Rabbis. He himself is of the opinion that one can both be flogged and pay; however, he contends that in this case even the Rabbis should concede that the witnesses are liable to receive lashes, as their liability stems from a different source. The Rabbis respond that there is no difference whether their liability results from one verse or two (see Ritva).

Why do I require a hand for a hand – יָד בְּיָד לָמָּה לִי: *Tosafot* ask why this exposition is necessary, as the Torah already stated: "As he conspired," indicating that witnesses who sought to render one falsely liable to pay are themselves liable to pay that sum. Why, then, is another exposition necessary to obligate the witnesses to pay for an item that is given from hand to hand? They answer that otherwise the thought would have been that they are liable for payment only if they conspired to obligate him to pay money. In contrast, in a case where they plotted to obligate him to pay and to be flogged, perhaps they receive both punishments. Therefore, the verse teaches that whenever they are obligated to pay, they are not flogged (see Ritva). *Tosafot* suggest that this exposition is in fact unnecessary for conspiring witnesses, but it serves to emphasize the principle that one who injures another is not literally punished with an eye for an eye but with payment. The Ritva asks: Once this derivation is learned, why not say that conspiring witnesses liable to be executed and liable to pay should pay and should not be executed? He answers that with regard to lashes and payment, it is unclear which punishment is more severe, and therefore, the Sages derived that they pay and are not flogged, whether that constitutes a leniency or a stringency. However, the death penalty is clearly a more severe punishment than payment, and the Torah certainly did not intend to be lenient with one liable to be executed.

HALAKHA

If one struck another with a blow that does not cause damage that amounts to the value of a *peruta* – הִכָּהוּ הַכָּאָה שֶׁאֵין בָּהּ שָׁוֶה פְּרוּטָה: If one injured another and the damage amounts to less than the value of a *peruta*, he is flogged and does not pay. The *halakha* is in accordance with the opinion of Rabbi Ami in the name of Rabbi Yoḥanan (Rambam *Sefer Nezikim, Hilkhot Ḥovel UMazik* 5:3; *Shulḥan Arukh, Ḥoshen Mishpat* 420:2).

The Torah explicitly amplified the case of one who injures another to include liability for payment – רִיבְּתָה תּוֹרָה חוֹבֵל בַּחֲבֵירוֹ לְתַשְׁלוּמִין: One who injures another on the Day of Atonement is obligated to pay damages, even though he is liable to receive lashes or *karet* for his action. Although the principle is that one who is liable both to receive lashes and to pay is flogged and does not pay, the Torah explicitly states that one who injures another pays for the injury. The *halakha* is in accordance with the opinion of Rabbi Yoḥanan in his dispute with Ulla (Rambam *Sefer Nezikim, Hilkhot Ḥovel UMazik* 4:9; *Shulḥan Arukh, Ḥoshen Mishpat* 424:2).

Conspiring witnesses for payment – עֵדִים זוֹמְמִין לְתַשְׁלוּמִין: If witnesses who testified that a person owes money were discovered to be false conspiring witnesses, they pay that sum and are not flogged. The *halakha* is in accordance with the opinion of the Rabbis in their dispute with the individual opinion of Rabbi Meir (Rambam *Sefer Shofetim, Hilkhot Edut* 18:1 and *Kesef Mishne* there; *Tur, Ḥoshen Mishpat* 38).

חובל בחבירו נמי, מכדי כתיב "כאשר עשה כן יעשה לו", "כן ינתן בו" למה לי – דבר שיש בו נתינה, ומאי ניהו – ממון.

The same can be said with regard to **one who injures another. Now, since it states:** "And a man who places a blemish upon his counterpart, **as he has done so shall be done to him**" (Leviticus 24:19), **why do I** require the Torah to state: "As one who places a blemish upon a man, **so shall be placed** [*yinnaten*] **upon him**" (Leviticus 24:20)? This teaches that this is referring to **an item that involves giving** [*netina*], **and what is that** item? It is **money.**

ורבי יוחנן, מאי טעמא לא אמר כעולא? אם כן "בטלת ערות אחותך לא תגלה"

The Gemara asks: **And Rabbi Yoḥanan, what is the reason** that **he did not say** the same *halakha* **as Ulla,**[N] that where there is liability to both pay money and receive lashes, one pays money but is not flogged? The Gemara answers: **If so,** if that were the case, **you have rendered moot** the prohibition **"The nakedness of your sister…you shall not uncover"** (Leviticus 18:9) in that contrary to the standard prohibitions, no lashes would be administered for its violation.

NOTES

What is the reason that he did not say the same *halakha* as Ulla – מאי טעמא לא אמר כעולא: The Ramban notes that it is obvious why the Gemara did not ask why Ulla did not say the same *halakha* as Rabbi Yoḥanan, as Ulla derives his *halakha* from a verbal analogy. However, the question of the Gemara is difficult, as it is clear why Rabbi Yoḥanan rejected Ulla's conclusion; it is because he did not accept his verbal analogy. *Tosafot* explain that Ulla's derivation is universally accepted, and therefore it cannot be said that Rabbi Yoḥanan rejects it. Furthermore, as the Ramban himself explains, Ulla's derivation by means of verbal analogy is more authoritative than Rabbi Yoḥanan's derivation by means of juxtaposed verses. According to the Rashba and other early commentaries, that is the basis for the Gemara's question with regard to Rabbi Yoḥanan's approach. The Ramban maintains that the Gemara is not raising a difficulty with regard to the opinion of Rabbi Yoḥanan but merely seeking to clarify the basis for his opinion.

Perek **III**
Daf **33** Amud **a**

חובל בחבירו נמי, אם כן, בטלת "לא יוסיף פן יוסיף"! עדים זוממין נמי, אם כן, בטלת "והיה אם בן הכות הרשע"! אלא עדים זוממין אפשר לקיומה בבן גרושה ובן חלוצה. חובל בחבירו נמי, איכא לקיומה כגון שהכהו הכאה שאין בה שוה פרוטה.

The Gemara asks: Based on that reasoning, the same would hold true for **one who injures another as well;**[N] **if so,** if he pays and is not lashed, **you have rendered moot** the prohibition "Forty he shall strike him; **he shall not exceed, lest if he should exceed**" (Deuteronomy 25:3). The same would hold true for **conspiring witnesses as well; if so, you have rendered moot** the verse interpreted as addressing the matter of conspiring witnesses: **"And it shall be if the wicked man deserves to be flogged"** (Deuteronomy 25:2).[N] **Rather,** with regard to **conspiring witnesses,** that verse **can be fulfilled** in the case **of the son of a divorcée or the son of a *ḥalutza*.** If witnesses testified that a priest is the son of a divorcée or a *ḥalutza* and were discovered to be conspiring witnesses, there is no payment and they are flogged. With regard to **one who injures another as well,** the verse **can be fulfilled** in a case **where he struck him** with **a blow that** does **not** cause damage amounting to **the value of a *peruta*.**

אחותו נמי, איכא לקיומה באחותו בוגרת! אמר לך רבי יוחנן: האי "תחת אשר עינה" מיבעי ליה לכדאביי, דאמר אביי: אמר קרא "תחת אשר עינה", האי – "תחת אשר עינה", מכלל דאיכא בושת ופגם.

The Gemara raises a difficulty: If so, with regard to **one's sister as well,**[N] the lashes **can be fulfilled** in the case of one who had forced relations **with his sister** who is **a grown woman.** Since there is no fine in that case, he is flogged and the verse is not moot. The Gemara answers: **Rabbi Yoḥanan** could have **said to you** that he does not agree with Ulla because **this** verse: **"Because he tormented her"** (Deuteronomy 22:29), is not available for a verbal analogy, as **he requires it to** derive **in accordance with that** which **Abaye** said, **as Abaye said** that **the verse states:** The fine of fifty dinar is payment **"because he tormented her"; by inference** one may conclude **that** beyond the fine, **there is** compensation for **humiliation and degradation.**

ועולא נפקא ליה מדרבא. דאמר רבא: אמר קרא: "ונתן האיש השכב עמה לאבי הנערה חמשים כסף", הנאת שכיבה – חמשים, מכלל דאיכא בושת ופגם.

The Gemara asks: **And Ulla,** who uses this verse to derive a verbal analogy, from where does he derive the *halakha* stated by Abaye? The Gemara answers: **He derives it from** the statement of **Rava,** who derives that *halakha* from the same verse, **as Rava said** that **the verse states: "And the man who lay with her shall give to the father of the young woman fifty shekels of silver"** (Deuteronomy 22:29). The superfluous phrase "who lay with her" teaches that it is for **the pleasure of lying** with her that he pays **fifty** shekels, i.e., fifty *sela*; **by inference** one may conclude **that** beyond the fine, **there is** compensation for **humiliation and degradation.**

NOTES

One who injures another as well, etc. – חובל בחבירו נמי וכו׳: Why was Rabbi Yoḥanan more concerned about rendering the prohibition with regard to one's sister moot than he was with regard to one who injures another or conspiring witnesses? The Ritva explains that there is no independent prohibition with regard to one who injures another. It is derived from the verse written with regard to the officer of the court: "Lest he exceed" (Deuteronomy 25:3). Likewise, the prohibition against conspiring to bear false witness is also derived from a verse written in another context. In contrast, with regard to a sister, the prohibition is explicit: "The nakedness of your sister…you shall not uncover" (Leviticus 18:9).

You have rendered moot: And it shall be if the wicked man deserves to be flogged – בטלת והיה אם בן הכות הרשע: Why doesn't the Gemara cite the relevant prohibition and say that you have rendered moot the verse "You shall not bear false witness"? One answer is that the prohibition "You shall not bear false witness" is a prohibition that serves as a warning of death at the hands of the court, for which one is not liable to receive lashes (*Shita Yeshana*, cited in *Shita Mekubbetzet*). Alternatively, some Sages maintain that because it is a prohibition that does not involve an action, there are no lashes. Therefore, the Gemara cited the verse from which the punishment of lashes in this case is derived.

One's sister as well, etc. – אחותו נמי וכו׳: Why didn't the Gemara raise the difficulty that according to Rabbi Yoḥanan this negates the obligation "He shall give to the father of the young woman" in the case of one who rapes his sister? The Rashba explains that this mitzva can be fulfilled in the case of a sister if he received no forewarning, whereas according to Ulla's opinion, there would be no possibility of lashes at all in the case of a virgin sister.

HALAKHA

Conspiring witnesses…are not subject to forewarning – עֵדִים זוֹמְמִין...לָאו בְּנֵי הַתְרָאָה נִינְהוּ: Conspiring witnesses do not require forewarning. Although corporal punishment is generally not administered unless the guilty party was forewarned, this does not apply to conspiring witnesses (Rambam *Sefer Shofetim, Hilkhot Edut* 18:4).

They could say: We forgot – אָמְרִי אִישְׁתְּלַין: One is liable to receive corporal punishment only if he committed the transgression after being forewarned within an interval equivalent to the time of speaking. As explained here, the reason is that otherwise he could claim that he forgot the forewarning (Rambam *Sefer Shofetim, Hilkhot Sanhedrin* 12:2).

BACKGROUND

Forewarning – הַתְרָאָה: This is a formal warning to one who is about to violate a prohibition. The forewarning must include the fact that the action that he is about to perform is prohibited, and must also include the punishment that he will receive. Capital and corporal punishment can be administered only with forewarning that is acknowledged by the transgressor. In rare instances, e.g., the cases of false conspiring witnesses or one who incites to idol worship, punishment is administered without forewarning.

רַבִּי אֱלִיעֶזֶר אוֹמֵר: עֵדִים זוֹמְמִין מָמוֹנָא מְשַׁלְּמִי וּמִילְקָא לָא לָקֵי, מִשּׁוּם דְּלָאו בְּנֵי הַתְרָאָה נִינְהוּ. אֲמַר רָבָא: תֵּדַע, נִיתְרֵי בְּהוּ אֵימַת? נִיתְרֵי בְּהוּ מֵעִיקָּרָא – אָמְרִי אִישְׁתְּלַין. נִיתְרֵי בְּהוּ בִּשְׁעַת מַעֲשֶׂה – פָּרְשִׁי וְלָא מַסְהֲדִי. נִיתְרֵי בְּהוּ לְבַסּוֹף – מַאי דַּהֲוָה הֲוָה.

§ **Rabbi Eliezer says:** The reason that **conspiring witnesses pay money**[N] **but are not flogged** is due to the fact **that they are not subject to forewarning,**[HB] and without forewarning there are no lashes. **Rava said: Know** that this is true, since there is no practical manner to forewarn them, as **when would we forewarn them?** Perhaps **let us forewarn them initially,** before they come to testify; in that case, the forewarning would be ineffective because they could **say: We forgot**[H] the forewarning. Then **let us forewarn them at the moment of the action,** just before they testify; in that case they will **leave and not testify**[N] at all, as concern for potential repercussions will intimidate them into silence. Or, **let us forewarn them at the end** after their testimony; in that case **that which was, was,**[N] and forewarning at that point is pointless.

מַתְקִיף לַהּ אַבָּיֵי: וְנִיתְרֵי בְּהוּ בְּתוֹךְ כְּדֵי דִּבּוּר! מַתְקִיף לַהּ רַב אַחָא בְּרֵיהּ דְּרַב אִיקָא: וְנִיתְרֵי בְּהוּ מֵעִיקָּרָא, וְנִרְמַז בְּהוּ רְמוּזֵי!

Abaye strongly **objects to this: And let us warn them within** an interval **equivalent** to the time **of speaking,**[N] during the brief period after they completed their statements, at which time the testimony is not yet considered to have concluded. Since they can still retract or amend their testimony during that period, a warning delivered at that point would be timely and effective. **Rav Aḥa, son of Rav Ika,** also strongly **objects to this: And let us forewarn them initially,** before they testify, **and gesture to them**[N] during the actual testimony, reminding them of the forewarning so they will be unable to claim that they forgot it.

הֲדַר אֲמַר אַבָּיֵי: לָאו מִילְּתָא הִיא דַּאֲמַרִי: אִי סָלְקָא דַּעְתָּךְ עֵדִים זוֹמְמִין צְרִיכִין הַתְרָאָה, כִּי לָא מַתְרֵינַן בְּהוּ לָא קָטְלִינַן לְהוּ – מִי אִיכָּא מִידֵּי דְּאִינְהוּ בָּעוּ קְטֵיל בְּלָא הַתְרָאָה, וְאִינְהוּ בָּעוּ הַתְרָאָה? הָא בָּעֵינַן "וַעֲשִׂיתֶם לוֹ כַּאֲשֶׁר זָמַם לַעֲשׂוֹת לְאָחִיו" וְלֵיכָּא.

Abaye then said: That which I stated is not a significant **matter.** Instead, **if it enters your mind that conspiring witnesses require forewarning, when we do not forewarn them we do not kill them.** However, **is there a matter in which they sought to kill** the defendant **without forewarning** him, as their testimony was false, **and** in order to punish them **they require forewarning?**[N] **Don't we require** that their punishment reflect the verse **"And you shall do unto him as he conspired to do unto his brother"** (Deuteronomy 19:19)? **And** if they require forewarning that **is not** the case.

NOTES

Rabbi Eliezer says: Conspiring witnesses pay money – רַבִּי אֱלִיעֶזֶר אוֹמֵר: עֵדִים זוֹמְמִין מָמוֹנָא מְשַׁלְּמִי: Most early commentaries continue along lines suggested by Rashi and explain that Rabbi Eliezer contends that since there are two possible punishments, money and lashes, it stands to reason that they would pay and not be flogged because, as a rule, corporal punishment is administered only if there was forewarning, a condition that does not affect payment (Ra'ah; Rashba; Rabbeinu Crescas Vidal). This leads to a question raised by Rashi: If so, why are those who testified that a priest is the son of a divorcée liable to receive lashes? He explains that since fulfillment of the verse "And you shall do unto him as he conspired" is impossible, as explained at length in *Makkot*, the sole option remaining is to administer lashes. Rabbi Eliezer, however, was referring to a situation where the choice is between two available punishments for a single transgression. The Maharsha asks: Why not say that one who is liable to be executed and pay should pay, for the same reason that there is no execution without forewarning? He answers that conspiring witnesses are not liable to be executed because they violated the prohibition "You shall not bear false witness"; rather, they are executed due to the verse "And you shall do unto him as he conspired to do unto his brother."

They will leave and not testify – פָּרְשִׁי וְלָא מַסְהֲדִי: Based on Rashi's commentary, apparently they will leave and not testify because they are humiliated by the suspicion that they will testify falsely. The Ritva explains that if they are warned just before they testify they will be concerned that false witnesses might come and render them conspiring witnesses, and they will prefer not to testify at all. The early commentaries inquire into the difference between this *halakha*, where there is concern that they might refrain from testifying, and the *halakha* that in capital cases witnesses are threatened in order to discourage false testimony, where the possibility that they might leave and not testify is not a concern. Several answers were suggested. The most common approach is that in capital cases the witnesses are not actually threatened, as explained in tractate *Sanhedrin*; they are merely informed of the severity of capital cases in general terms, and there is no suspicion voiced that they will testify falsely.

That which was, was – מַאי דַּהֲוָה הֲוָה: Rashi states that they cannot change their testimony once they have delivered it. The *Shita Yeshana*, cited in the *Shita Mekubbetzet*, explains that since they already violated the prohibition with their testimony, warning them is pointless.

Within an interval equivalent to the time of speaking – בְּתוֹךְ כְּדֵי דִּבּוּר: *Tosafot* ask: Doesn't it take longer than that to state the forewarning, and therefore the witnesses would be unable to resume their testimony within that interval? They explain that as long as they remain engaged in the same matter it is considered within an interval equivalent to the time of speaking. A slightly different interpretation is offered by the Ra'avad. He claims that if witnesses require a warning, their testimony would not be complete until after that warning was given. Therefore, the interval is measured only from the conclusion of the warning.

And gesture to them – וְנִרְמַז בְּהוּ רְמוּזֵי: Rashi explains that it is possible to gesture subtly, consistent with his approach that the concern is the embarrassment of the witnesses. The Rashba explains, in keeping with the plain understanding of the Gemara, that the gestures remind them of the earlier warning.

And they require forewarning – וְאִינְהוּ בָּעוּ הַתְרָאָה: Even so, one is not punished for transgressions committed when he was unwitting or unaware. How, then, can it be ascertained that they acted intentionally? One answer is that in general, the assumption is that one is aware that he is violating a prohibition, and therefore the assumption is that a transgressor acted intentionally (*Ketzot HaḤoshen* 28:8). However, there is a Torah decree that no punishment may be administered without forewarning adjacent to the act. Here, there is no need for forewarning, as it is clear that they know it is wrong to testify falsely (*Birkat Avraham*).

מַתְקִיף לָהּ רַב סַמָּא בְּרֵיהּ דְּרַב יִרְמְיָה: אֶלָּא מֵעַתָּה, בֶּן גְּרוּשָׁה וּבֶן חֲלוּצָה, דְּלָא מִכִּ״אֲשֶׁר זָמַם״ קָא מִתְרַבֵּי, לִיבָּעֵי הַתְרָאָה! אָמַר קְרָא: ״מִשְׁפַּט אֶחָד יִהְיֶה לָכֶם״, מִשְׁפָּט הַשָּׁוֶה לְכוּלְּכֶם.

Rav Samma, son of Rav Yirmeya, strongly **objects to this: However, if** what you say is **so,** when witnesses falsely accuse a priest of being **the son of a divorcée or the son of a *ḥalutza*,** as their punishment **is not amplified from** the verse **"As he conspired"** but rather they are punished for violating the prohibition "You shall not bear false witness against your neighbor," **let them require forewarning.** The Gemara answers that **the verse states: "You shall have one manner of law"** (Leviticus 24:22), meaning that there must be **a law equal for all of you.**[N] Since in standard cases of conspiring witnesses no forewarning is required, even in exceptional cases like testimony that a priest is the son of a divorcée or a *ḥalutza*, forewarning is not required.

רַב שִׁישָׁא בְּרֵיהּ דְּרַב אִידִי אָמַר: חוֹבֵל בַּחֲבֵירוֹ נַמִי, מָמוֹנָא מְשַׁלֵּם וּמִילְקָא לָא לָקֵי – מֵהָכָא: ״וְכִי יִנָּצוּ אֲנָשִׁים וְנָגְפוּ אִשָּׁה הָרָה וְיָצְאוּ יְלָדֶיהָ״, וְאָמַר רַבִּי אֶלְעָזָר: בְּמַצּוּת שֶׁבְּמִיתָה הַכָּתוּב מְדַבֵּר, דִּכְתִיב ״וְאִם אָסוֹן יִהְיֶה וְנָתַתָּה נֶפֶשׁ תַּחַת נָפֶשׁ״.

§ **Rav Sheisha, son of Rav Idi, said:** The fact that in the case of **one who injures another as well**[N] **he pays money and is not flogged** is derived not by means of a verbal analogy but **from here: "If men quarrel and hurt a pregnant woman so that her child departs from her,** and yet no harm follow, he shall be punished as imposed upon him by the woman's husband" (Exodus 21:22). **And Rabbi Elazar said: The verse is speaking of a quarrel that involves death,**[N] i.e., they sought to kill each other, **as it is written: "And if any harm follow, then you shall give a soul for a soul"** (Exodus 21:23).

הֵיכִי דָּמֵי? אִי דְּלָא אַתְרוּ בֵּיהּ – אַמַּאי מִיקְּטִיל, אֶלָּא פְּשִׁיטָא דְּאַתְרוּ בֵּיהּ, וּמוּתְרֶה לְדָבָר חָמוּר הָוֵי מוּתְרֶה לְדָבָר הַקַּל, וְאָמַר רַחֲמָנָא ״וְלֹא יִהְיֶה אָסוֹן עָנוֹשׁ יֵעָנֵשׁ״.

The Gemara asks: **What are the circumstances** of this case? **If they did not forewarn one** not to kill the other, **why is he killed** if the death of his opponent ensues? **Rather, obviously** it is a case **where they forewarned him, and** the principle is that **one who is forewarned with regard to a severe matter,** murdering his counterpart, **is forewarned with regard to a lesser matter,**[H] injuring his counterpart. **And** although he is forewarned against injuring another, which violates a prohibition and is punishable by lashes, **the Merciful One states: "And yet no harm follow, he shall be punished"** (Exodus 21:22), indicating that one pays and is not flogged.

מַתְקִיף לָהּ רַב אַשִׁי: מִמַּאי דְּמוּתְרֶה לְדָבָר חָמוּר הָוֵי מוּתְרֶה לְדָבָר הַקַּל, דִּלְמָא לָא הָוֵי? אִם תִּמְצָא לוֹמַר הָוֵי – מִמַּאי דְּמִיתָה חֲמוּרָה,

Rav Ashi strongly **objects to this** proof. First of all, with regard to your initial assumption, **from where** do you ascertain **that one who is forewarned with regard to a severe matter**[N] **is forewarned with regard to a lesser matter? Perhaps he is not** considered forewarned with regard to the lesser matter. Furthermore, even **if you say** that one **is** in fact forewarned with regard to a lesser matter, **from where** do you ascertain **that** the **death** penalty is a more **severe** punishment than lashes?

HALAKHA

Forewarned with regard to a severe matter – מוּתְרֶה לְדָבָר חָמוּר: The question of whether one forewarned with regard to a severe matter is forewarned with regard to a lesser matter remains unresolved. The *Ein Mishpat* claims that the Rambam indicates that one who was forewarned that his action is punishable by death in general is considered forewarned with regard to all forms of executions, regardless of their degree of severity. However, this does not resolve the question with regard to one who was forewarned specifically with regard to a severe death penalty. *Tosafot* suggest that there might be a Torah decree that one must be forewarned specifically with regard to the exact punishment for which he is liable (see Rambam *Sefer Shofetim*, *Hilkhot Sanhedrin* 12:2).

NOTES

A law equal for all of you – מִשְׁפָּט הַשָּׁוֶה לְכוּלְּכֶם: This does not mean that the details of all *halakhot* are the same, as clearly there is a difference between one who injures another, one who pays and is not flogged, and other cases. Rather, the meaning is that when punishment is administered for a particular prohibition, e.g., "You shall not bear false witness," there is no distinction between different cases where the prohibition applies (*Shita Yeshana*, cited in *Shita Mekubbetzet*).

One who injures another as well – חוֹבֵל בַּחֲבֵירוֹ נַמִי: In this context, some commentaries cite the earlier statement of *Tosafot* (32b) that the fact that one who injures another pays and is not flogged is derived from the verse "A hand for a hand" (Deuteronomy 19:21), written with regard to conspiring witnesses. Rabbi Eliezer, at least according to Rava, maintains that this verse is unnecessary in the context of conspiring witnesses, as it can be learned by logical reasoning; therefore, with regard to one who injures another it should be learned by logical reasoning as well (*Shita Mekubbetzet*).

The verse is speaking of a quarrel that involves death – בְּמַצּוּת שֶׁבְּמִיתָה הַכָּתוּב מְדַבֵּר: The verse speaks of two men who were fighting with each other, and in the course of their struggle they hurt a woman. Since "a soul for a soul" is understood literally in this case, although some Sages maintain that here too it is referring to payment of money, the men must have been forewarned not to kill each other. This is according to the opinion that one who intended to kill one person and killed another is liable.

From where do you ascertain that one who is forewarned with regard to a severe matter, etc. – מִמַּאי דְּמוּתְרֶה לְדָבָר חָמוּר וכו׳: The principle that one forewarned with regard to a severe matter is forewarned with regard to a lesser matter seems obvious, since if one is aware that his action is punishable by a severe punishment and decides to perform the action anyway, he certainly accepts a lesser punishment as well. The opposite contention, as explained by *Tosafot*, is that there is a Torah decree that one is punished only if he received forewarning that reflects his precise punishment, whether it is a severe or lesser punishment. Others explain that since it is derived that if a murderer cannot be executed with the death penalty designated for his crime he is executed with another form of death, it can be inferred that those liable to receive other punishments cannot be punished with any other punishment than the one to which they are liable, even if it is a lesser punishment than the designated one (Rabbi David Bonfils on *Sanhedrin* 80b).

דִּלְמָא מַלְקוֹת חָמוּר? דַּאֲמַר רַב: אִילְמָלֵי נַגְדּוּהָ לַחֲנַנְיָה מִישָׁאֵל וַעֲזַרְיָה – פָּלְחוּ לְצַלְמָא! אֲמַר לֵיהּ רַב סַמָּא בְּרֵיהּ דְּרַב אַסִּי לְרַב אַשִׁי, וְאָמְרִי לָהּ רַב סַמָּא בְּרֵיהּ דְּרַב אַשִׁי לְרַב אַשִׁי: וְלָא שָׁנֵי לָךְ בֵּין הַכָּאָה שֶׁיֵּשׁ לָהּ קִצְבָּה לְהַכָּאָה שֶׁאֵין לָהּ קִצְבָּה?!

Perhaps the punishment of **lashes is** more **severe,**[N] **as Rav said: Had they flogged**[N] **Hananiah, Mishael, and Azariah** (see Daniel, chapter 3) instead of casting them into the fiery furnace, these three **would have** been induced to **worship the** graven **image.** Apparently, the punishment of lashes is more severe than death. **Rav Samma, son of Rav Asi, said to Rav Ashi, and some say Rav Samma, son of Rav Ashi, said to Rav Ashi: And is there no difference to you between flogging that has a limit,** e.g., forty lashes by Torah law, which is a less severe punishment, **and flogging that does not have a limit,**[N] i.e., flogging administered to induce compliance, which is more severe?

מַתְקִיף לָהּ רַב יַעֲקֹב מִנְּהַר פְּקוֹד: הָנִיחָא לְרַבָּנַן דְּאָמְרִי נֶפֶשׁ מַמָּשׁ, אֶלָּא לְרַבִּי דַּאֲמַר – מָמוֹן מַאי אִיכָּא לְמֵימַר?

With regard to the basic proof from the case of the two men quarreling, **Rav Ya'akov from Nehar Pekod** strongly **objects to this. This** works out **well according to** the opinion of **the Rabbis, who said** that the verse "And you shall give a soul for a soul" (Exodus 21:23) is referring to **an actual life,** and that if he caused the woman's death he is executed. **However, according to Rabbi** Yehuda HaNasi, **who said** that if he did not intend to injure the woman he is not liable to be executed and instead pays **money** as indemnity for causing her death, **what can be said?** According to that opinion, there was no forewarning for lashes at all, and the only liability is payment for injuring another.

אֶלָּא אֲמַר רַב יַעֲקֹב מִנְּהַר פְּקוֹד מִשְּׁמֵיהּ דְּרָבָא: מֵהָכָא, "אִם יָקוּם וְהִתְהַלֵּךְ בַּחוּץ עַל מִשְׁעַנְתּוֹ וְנִקָּה הַמַּכֶּה". וְכִי תַּעֲלֶה עַל דַּעְתְּךָ שֶׁזֶּה מְהַלֵּךְ בַּשּׁוּק וְזֶה נֶהֱרָג? אֶלָּא מְלַמֵּד שֶׁחוֹבְשִׁין אוֹתוֹ, וְאִי מִית – קָטְלִינַן לֵיהּ, וְאִי לָא מִית – "שִׁבְתּוֹ יִתֵּן וְרַפֹּא יְרַפֵּא".

Rather, Rav Ya'akov from Nehar Pekod said in the name of Rava that the *halakha* that one pays and is not flogged is derived **from here.** With regard to one who struck another with a stone or his fist and did not kill him but caused him to be bedridden, it is written: **"If he rises and walks outside with his staff, he who struck him is absolved"** (Exodus 21:19). **And could it enter your mind that this** victim **is walking in the marketplace and that** aggressor **is executed** as a murderer? **Rather,** the verse **teaches that one imprisons** the aggressor[H] while the injured party recuperates, **and if he dies** due to the blow he received, **we kill him. And if he does not die** and recovers, the aggressor's punishment is based on the verse **"His loss of livelihood he shall give, and he shall cause him to be thoroughly healed"** (Exodus 21:19).

הֵיכִי דָּמֵי? אִי דְּלָא אַתְרוּ בֵּיהּ – אַמַּאי מִיקְּטִיל? אֶלָּא פְּשִׁיטָא – דְּאַתְרוּ בֵּיהּ, וּמוּתְרֶה לְדָבָר חָמוּר מוּתְרֶה לְדָבָר הַקַּל, וְאָמַר רַחֲמָנָא "שִׁבְתּוֹ יִתֵּן וְרַפֹּא יְרַפֵּא.

The Gemara elaborates: **What are the circumstances? If** the witnesses **did not forewarn him, why is** the offender **killed** if the victim dies? **Rather, obviously** it is a case **where** the witnesses **forewarned him, and one who is forewarned for a severe matter,** such as the potential death penalty, is also **forewarned for** the **lesser matter** of injuring another, for which he is liable to be flogged, **and** nevertheless **the Merciful One states: "His loss of livelihood he shall give, and he shall cause him to be thoroughly healed."** Apparently, despite his liability to be flogged, he pays and is not flogged.

מַתְקִיף לָהּ רַב אַשִׁי: מִמַּאי דְּמוּתְרֶה לְדָבָר חָמוּר הָוֵי מוּתְרֶה לְדָבָר הַקַּל? דִּלְמָא לָא הָוֵי, וְאִם תִּמְצָא לוֹמַר הָוֵי – מִמַּאי דְּמִיתָה חֲמוּרָה, דִּלְמָא מַלְקוֹת חָמוּר? דַּאֲמַר רַב: אִילְמָלֵי נַגְדּוּהָ לַחֲנַנְיָה מִישָׁאֵל וַעֲזַרְיָה פָּלְחוּ לְצַלְמָא!

Rav Ashi strongly **objects to this** proof:[N] First of all, with regard to your initial assumption, **from where** do you ascertain **that one who is forewarned with regard to a severe matter is forewarned with regard to a lesser matter? Perhaps he is not** considered forewarned with regard to the lesser matter. Furthermore, even **if you say** that one **is** in fact forewarned with regard to a lesser matter, **from where** do you ascertain **that** the **death** penalty is a more **severe** punishment than lashes? **Perhaps** the punishment of **lashes is** more **severe, as Rav said: Had they flogged Hananiah, Mishael, and Azariah,** instead of casting them into the fiery furnace, **they would have** been induced **to worship the** graven **image.** Apparently, the punishment of lashes is more severe than death.

NOTES

Perhaps the punishment of lashes is more severe – דִּלְמָא מַלְקוֹת חָמוּר: *Tosafot* ask: Why doesn't the Gemara prove that death is the more severe punishment from the fact that it is the punishment administered for the most serious transgressions? The early commentaries suggest various answers, primarily that the issue is not the severity of the punishment itself but its relative harshness from the perspective of the punished. The Ritva states that one sentenced to death might say, as Samson did: "Let me die with the Philistines" (Judges 16:30), and would be prepared to die after murdering his hated enemy. With regard to lashes, in contrast, it is unlikely that one would agree to suffer merely for injuring another. The *Shita Yeshana*, cited in the *Shita Mekubbetzet*, explains that lashes carries with it great suffering and is also very demeaning. Therefore, people consider it a more severe punishment than death.

Had they flogged, etc. – אִילְמָלֵי נַגְדּוּהָ וכו׳: This statement of Rav has raised questions among many early commentaries, as the verse "And you shall love the Lord your God…with all your soul" (Deuteronomy 6:5) indicates that one must be willing to undergo great suffering to sanctify the name of God, as Rabbi Akiva and others did. The Rashba states, citing Rashi, although it does not appear in the standard version of Rashi, that Rav was asking a rhetorical question: Had they been flogged, would they have worshipped the graven image? In any case, Rav's comment proves that lashes are more severe than death. Most early commentaries, however, accept the opinion of *Tosafot* that Nebuchadnezzar's image was not an actual idol, and therefore, by the letter of the law, Hananiah, Mishael, and Azariah were not obligated to give their lives rather than bow to the image. The Ramban agrees with this approach and cites additional proofs that the image was merely an item that could have been mistaken for idolatry and that the three righteous men sought to sanctify the name of God by demonstrating their refusal to accept any authority other than God. He cites a midrash that states that they could have avoided being thrown into the furnace. Others state, citing Rabbi Eliezer, that the *halakha* does not require one to subject himself to suffering greater than death (see *Shita Yeshana*, cited in *Shita Mekubbetzet*).

Flogging that does not have a limit – הַכָּאָה שֶׁאֵין לָהּ קִצְבָּה: In the *Shita Mekubbetzet* it is explained that it is not the number of lashes that determines the sense of the severity of the punishment; rather, it is the very knowledge that the lashes of the court are limited and will eventually end. In contrast, with regard to lashes administered by the monarchy, even if in practice fewer lashes are administered, there is no limit to the lashes that they could inflict.

Rav Ashi strongly objects to this proof – מַתְקִיף לָהּ רַב אַשִׁי: This is difficult, as this statement of Rav Ashi was cited and rejected above. Why is it cited again? In the *Shita Mekubbetzet* it is explained that Rav Ya'akov spoke in accordance with the opinion of Rabbi Yehuda HaNasi that one who sought to kill one person and killed another is exempt. According to that opinion, the questions that Rav Ashi raised are more difficult, as forewarning with regard to one person is ineffective with regard to the other, so forewarning for a severe transgression is ineffective for a lesser transgression.

HALAKHA

The verse teaches that one imprisons the aggressor, etc. – מְלַמֵּד שֶׁחוֹבְשִׁין אוֹתוֹ וכו׳: If one struck another with a stone or his fist, and the court estimated that the blow was capable of killing him, then the aggressor is imprisoned until the fate of the victim is determined. If he dies, the aggressor is executed; if he makes a full recovery, the aggressor pays the five indemnities and is exempt from any other punishment (Rambam *Sefer Nezikim*, *Hilkhot Rotze'aḥ* 4:3).

אמר ליה רב סמא בריה דרב אסי לרב אשי, ואמרי לה רב סמא בריה דרב אשי לרב אשי: ולא שני לך בין הכאה שיש לה קצבה להכאה שאין לה קצבה?	Rav Samma, son of Rav Asi, said to Rav Ashi, and some say Rav Samma, son of Rav Ashi, said to Rav Ashi: And is there no difference to you between flogging that has a limit, e.g., forty lashes by Torah law, which is a less severe punishment, and flogging that does not have a limit, administered to induce compliance, which is more severe?
מתקיף לה רב מרי: ממאי דבמזיד "ונקה" מקטלא, דלמא בשוגג "ונקה" מגלות? קשיא.	Rav Mari strongly objects to this proof that one pays and is not flogged: From where do you ascertain that this is referring to one who struck another intentionally, and that the verse "He who struck him shall be absolved" means that he shall be absolved of the death penalty? Perhaps the verse is referring to one who struck another unwittingly, and the verse means that he shall be absolved of exile?[N] In that case, there would be no forewarning. Therefore, no proof may be cited from here that one who injures another pays and is not flogged. The Gemara concludes: This is difficult, and no proof may be cited from here.
ריש לקיש אמר: הא מני - רבי מאיר היא, דאמר: לוקה ומשלם. אי רבי מאיר - אפילו בתו נמי!	§ The Gemara cites another resolution of the apparent contradiction between the mishna here, which obligates one who rapes his sister to pay a fine, and the mishna in *Makkot*, which rules him liable to be flogged. Reish Lakish said: In accordance with whose opinion is this mishna taught? It is in accordance with the opinion of Rabbi Meir, who said: One is flogged and pays. The Gemara asks: If the mishna is in accordance with the opinion of Rabbi Meir, even if one raped his daughter he should also be obligated to pay the fine. However, the mishna lists only those who raped women for whom one is liable to be punished for violating a prohibition or liable to receive *karet*, not those for whom one is liable to receive court-imposed execution.
וכי תימא רבי מאיר לוקה ומשלם אית ליה, מת ומשלם - לית ליה, ולא? והתניא: גנב וטבח בשבת, גנב וטבח לעבודה זרה, גנב שור הנסקל וטבחו - משלם תשלומי ארבעה וחמשה, דברי רבי מאיר, וחכמים פוטרין.	And lest you say that Rabbi Meir is of the opinion that one is flogged and pays, but is not of the opinion that one dies by execution and pays; and isn't he of the opinion that one who is executed pays? But isn't it taught in a *baraita*: If one stole an animal and slaughtered it on Shabbat,[H] or stole it and slaughtered it for idolatry, or stole an ox that was sentenced to be stoned,[B] from which one may derive no benefit and is therefore worthless, and slaughtered it, he pays the owner a payment of four or five times the principal, as he would in any case of stealing and slaughtering an animal? This is the statement of Rabbi Meir. And the Rabbis exempt him from payment because he is liable to receive the death penalty for slaughtering on Shabbat or for idolatry. Apparently, Rabbi Meir maintains that one is obligated to pay even when he is liable to receive the death penalty.
הא איתמר עלה, אמר רבי יעקב אמר רבי יוחנן, ואמרי לה אמר רבי ירמיה אמר רבי שמעון בן לקיש: רבי אבין ורבי אילעא וכל חבורתא משמיה דרבי יוחנן אמרי: בטובח על ידי אחר.	The Gemara refutes this: Wasn't it stated concerning this *baraita* that Rabbi Ya'akov said that Rabbi Yoḥanan said, and some say that Rabbi Yirmeya said that Rabbi Shimon ben Lakish said, that Rabbi Avin and Rabbi Ile'a and the entire group said in the name of Rabbi Yoḥanan: That case is referring to one who slaughters by means of another?[H] The thief himself did not slaughter the animal; rather, it was his agent. Consequently, the thief pays because the capital crime was committed by his agent. Therefore, this source is unrelated to Rabbi Meir's opinion with regard to the question of whether one is executed and pays.
וכי זה חוטא וזה מתחייב? אמר רבא: אמר רחמנא "וטבחו או מכרו" מה מכירה על ידי אחר - אף טביחה על ידי אחר.	The Gemara analyzes Rabbi Yoḥanan's explanation: And does this agent sin and that thief is liable[N] to pay four and five times the principal? This violates the principle: There is no agent for matters of transgression. The Gemara explains that this is a *halakha* unique to this case. Rava said that the Merciful One states: "If a man steal an ox or a sheep and slaughter it[N] or sell it" (Exodus 21:37). Based on the juxtaposition of slaughter and sale, Rava continues: Just as sale is performed by means of another, as there is no sale without a buyer, so too, one is liable to be punished for slaughter by means of another. Although there is no agent for transgression, here there is a Torah decree that one is liable by means of another.

NOTES

Perhaps the verse is referring to one who struck another unwittingly, and the verse means that he shall be absolved of exile – דלמא בשוגג ונקה מגלות: *Tosafot* ask: In light of the principle that one is not exiled if there is the slightest concern that there was an additional complication that contributed to the death of the victim, the fact that the victim did not die immediately should exempt one from exile (see *Tosafot*). The Ritva maintains that the verse is referring to a situation involving exile and not the death penalty. A different objection is raised in the *Shita Mekubbetzet*: As the verse is clearly speaking of one who struck another, how could it be dealing with exile, which only applies to an unintentional murderer? The answer is that exile is conceivable in a case where one intended to strike one person and struck another.

And does this agent sin and that thief is liable – וכי זה חוטא וזה מתחייב: Rashi says that this question is based on the principle: There is no agent for transgression. In *Derush VeḤiddush*, Rabbi Akiva Eiger explains that this is not a case of an agent for transgression, as were he an agent his legal status would be like that of the sender himself, who would not be liable to pay because he would have desecrated Shabbat. Rather, this is a special *halakha* with regard to an action performed by means of another, unrelated to the laws of agency.

Rava said that the Merciful One states: If a man steals an ox or a sheep and slaughter it, etc. – אמר רבא: אמר רחמנא וטבחו וכו׳: In the *Sefer Hafla'a* the question is raised: Since there are two expositions cited by earlier Sages for this *halakha*, what did Rava add by citing another source? Furthermore, why does the Gemara cite Rava's proof first? Various answers were suggested. Primary among them is that from Rava's statement it can be derived that this *halakha* applies not only to an agent but to anyone who performs an action of this sort on another's behalf, even if he is ineligible for agency, e.g., a deaf-mute or an imbecile (*Beit Ya'akov*). Alternatively, Rava's statement here is consistent with his opinion elsewhere that the thief is liable even if he slaughtered the animal unwittingly (*Beit Aharon*).

HALAKHA

If one stole and slaughtered on Shabbat, etc. – גנב וטבח בשבת וכו׳: If one stole an animal and slaughtered it on Shabbat, or stole it and slaughtered it for idolatry, even if he did so unwittingly he is exempt from payment of four or five times the principal, in accordance with the opinion of the Rabbis (Rambam *Sefer Nezikim*, *Hilkhot Geneiva* 3:3).

One who slaughters by means of another – טובח על ידי אחר: If a thief appointed an agent to slaughter the stolen animal on his behalf, and the agent did so on Shabbat, the thief is liable for the payment of four or five times the principal. The Rosh rules that he is exempt, based on the Gemara's statement below that according to the Rabbis, slaughter on Shabbat is considered an unfit act of slaughter (Rambam *Sefer Nezikim*, *Hilkhot Geneiva* 3:6; *Tur*, *Ḥoshen Mishpat* 350).

BACKGROUND

An ox that was sentenced to be stoned – שור הנסקל: An ox that killed a person is stoned to death, whether or not the ox had previously displayed violent tendencies and whether the victim was an adult, a child, or a Canaanite slave. It is prohibited to derive any benefit from an ox that is stoned, not only after its execution but from the moment the court of twenty-three judges delivered its verdict. The term: Ox that is stoned, is employed to describe any domesticated or non-domesticated animal that killed a person, whether it is a large or small animal, or even a bird.

דְּבֵי רַבִּי יִשְׁמָעֵאל תָּנָא: ״אוֹ״ – לְרַבּוֹת אֶת הַשָּׁלִיחַ. דְּבֵי חִזְקִיָּה תָּנָא: ״תַּחַת״ – לְרַבּוֹת אֶת הַשָּׁלִיחַ.

The Sages **of the school of Rabbi Yishmael taught** a different source for the *halakha* that one is liable for slaughter by means of an agent. It is written: "And slaughter it or sell it"; the term **"or"** comes **to include an agent.**[N] The Sages **of the school of Rabbi Ḥizkiyya taught** a different proof from the same verse: "He shall pay…for an ox…for a sheep"; the term **"for"** comes **to include an agent.**[H]

מַתְקִיף לַהּ מָר זוּטְרָא: מִי אִיכָּא מִידֵּי דְּאִילּוּ עֲבַד אִיהוּ לָא מִיחַיַּיב, וְעָבֵיד שָׁלִיחַ וּמִחַיַּיב? אִיהוּ לָאו מִשּׁוּם דְּלָא מִיחַיַּיב, אֶלָּא מִשּׁוּם דְּקָם לֵיהּ בִּדְרַבָּה מִינֵּיהּ.

Mar Zutra strongly **objects to this** *halakha*. **Is there** any **matter** with regard to **which if one performs** it himself, he is **not liable, and** yet if his **agent performs** it he is **liable?** Had he slaughtered the animal himself on Shabbat he would have been exempt from payment. How, then, is he liable if he does so by means of an agent? The Gemara answers: **He** is exempt **not due to** the fact **that he is not liable** for the slaughter; **rather,** he is exempt **due to** the fact **that he receives the greater of** the two punishments, the death penalty, for his desecration of Shabbat. He is liable for both the slaughter and the desecration of Shabbat. In practice, he receives the more severe punishment. However, when he appoints an agent, there is no liability for the desecration of Shabbat, and therefore he must pay for the slaughter.

אִי בְּטוֹבֵחַ עַל יְדֵי אַחֵר, מַאי טַעֲמַיְיהוּ דְּרַבָּנַן דְּפָטְרִי? מַאן חֲכָמִים?

The Gemara returns to Rabbi Yoḥanan's explanation of the *baraita*. **If** the *baraita* is referring to the case **of one who slaughtered by means of another, what is the** rationale for the opinion **of the Rabbis,**[N] **who exempt** him from payment? As the thief did not perform a transgression for which he is liable to receive the death penalty, why is he exempt from payment for slaughtering the animal? The Gemara answers: **Who are the Rabbis** who disagree with Rabbi Meir in this case?

NOTES

"Or" comes to include an agent – אוֹ לְרַבּוֹת אֶת הַשָּׁלִיחַ: Ostensibly the term "or" is necessary to rule out the possibility that one would be liable to pay four or five times the principal only if he both slaughtered and stole the animal and did not include an agent. Why, then, is it understood in this manner? One answer is that this derivation is in accordance with the *tanna* who maintains that even when the conjunction "and" [*vav*] is written, it would be understood that either slaughter or sale is sufficient to generate liability. Alternatively, it would have been possible to indicate that one is liable for either one of the actions by reversing the order and writing: And he sold it and slaughtered it, as clearly one could not slaughter the animal after selling it. Therefore, this *halakha* of agency can be derived from the fact that the term "or" is used here (*Shita Mekubbetzet*).

What is the rationale for the opinion of the Rabbis – מַאי טַעֲמַיְיהוּ דְּרַבָּנַן: The question is raised: Couldn't the exemption of the Rabbis be attributed to the fact that they maintain that slaughtering by means of an agent does not render the sender liable? The answer is that the derivation from use of the word "or" is the accepted *halakha*, and the Gemara sought to avoid a difficult response. Furthermore, if there is a dispute with regard to the *halakha* of one who slaughters by means of another, there would have been no point in citing the special cases of one who slaughtered on Shabbat or for idolatry (Ra'ah; Rabbeinu Crescas Vidal).

HALAKHA

Slaughter by means of another – טְבִיחָה עַל יְדֵי אַחֵר: If one stole an ox or sheep and gave it as a gift, or gave it to another to slaughter and the recipient did so, or gave it to another to sell and the recipient sold it, the thief is liable for payment of four or five times the principal, in accordance with the exposition of the Sages here that there is a special *halakha* in the case of one who slaughters a stolen animal (Rambam *Sefer Nezikim*, *Hilkhot Geneiva* 2:10).

Perek **III**
Daf **34** Amud **a**

רַבִּי שִׁמְעוֹן הִיא, דְּאָמַר: שְׁחִיטָה שֶׁאֵינָהּ רְאוּיָה – לֹא שְׁמָהּ שְׁחִיטָה. הָתֵינַח עֲבוֹדָה זָרָה וְשׁוֹר הַנִּסְקָל, אֶלָּא שְׁחִיטַת שַׁבָּת – שְׁחִיטָה רְאוּיָה הִיא, דִּתְנַן: הַשּׁוֹחֵט בְּשַׁבָּת וּבְיוֹם הַכִּפּוּרִים, אַף עַל פִּי שֶׁמִּתְחַיֵּיב בְּנַפְשׁוֹ – שְׁחִיטָתוֹ כְּשֵׁרָה!

It is Rabbi Shimon, who said: The legal status of **slaughter that is improper,**[HN] in that it does not render the meat fit to be eaten, **is not that of slaughter.** Therefore, one is not liable for slaughter of the animal. The Gemara asks: **This** works out **well** with regard to **idolatry and the ox that is stoned,** as their slaughter is ineffective in rendering the meat fit to be eaten; **however, the slaughter on Shabbat is a proper** act of **slaughter, as we learned** in a mishna (*Ḥullin* 14a): In the case of **one who slaughters** an animal **on Shabbat**[N] **or on Yom Kippur,**[H] **although he is liable to** receive the **death** penalty for desecrating Shabbat, **his slaughter is valid** and the meat may be eaten.

HALAKHA

Slaughter that is improper – שְׁחִיטָה שֶׁאֵינָהּ רְאוּיָה: In general the ruling is contrary to the opinion of Rabbi Shimon, and improper slaughter is considered an act of slaughter. Consequently, if a thief slaughtered an ox or lamb that was discovered to be a *tereifa*, he is liable to pay four or five times the principal. Similarly, if an animal was slaughtered in a manner that does not permit its consumption, e.g., it was a *tereifa*, one who slaughters its offspring on the same day is liable for transgressing the prohibition against slaughter of an animal itself and its young on a single day. Nevertheless, one who performs an improper act of slaughter on a bird or undomesticated animal is exempt from covering the blood (see *Ḥullin* 85a), as in that regard it is not considered a bona fide act of slaughter, based on the unattributed mishna in accordance with the opinion of Rabbi Shimon (Rambam *Sefer Kedusha*, *Hilkhot Sheḥita* 12:6, 14:10 and *Sefer Nezikim*, *Hilkhot Geneiva* 2:8; *Shulḥan Arukh*, *Yoreh De'a* 16:9, 28:17; *Tur*, *Ḥoshen Mishpat* 350).

One who slaughters on Shabbat or on Yom Kippur – הַשּׁוֹחֵט בְּשַׁבָּת וּבְיוֹם הַכִּפּוּרִים: Although one who slaughters an animal on Shabbat is liable to be executed and one who does so on Yom Kippur is liable to receive *karet* or lashes, the slaughter is valid, in accordance with the mishna in *Ḥullin* (Rambam *Sefer Kedusha*, *Hilkhot Sheḥita* 1:29; *Shulḥan Arukh*, *Yoreh De'a* 11:2).

NOTES

Slaughter that is improper – שְׁחִיטָה שֶׁאֵינָהּ רְאוּיָה: Rabbi Shimon defines slaughter as an action that renders the animal fit to be eaten. If the slaughter is ineffective it is not considered slaughter at all; rather, it is as though one killed the animal by some other means. Consequently, wherever a particular *halakha* depends on performance of an act of slaughter, ineffective slaughter does not meet that requirement. Even the Rabbis concede that one who kills an animal in a manner other than slaughter, e.g., by stabbing it, does not meet the requirement of slaughter. *Tosafot* prove that although the term in the Torah in this context is *teviḥa* and not *sheḥita*, which is the standard term for slaughter, the reference is to slaughter.

One who slaughters on Shabbat, etc. – הַשּׁוֹחֵט בְּשַׁבָּת וכו׳: The early commentaries ask: Isn't one who desecrates Shabbat an apostate, in which case everyone agrees that his slaughter is invalid? How, then, can one say that slaughter on Shabbat is valid? There are several answers offered. *Tosafot* on *Ḥullin* 14a claim that only one who desecrates Shabbat in public is an apostate. The case here is referring to one who slaughtered the animal in private. Rabbeinu Crescas Vidal agrees. In addition, *Tosafot* explain that the act of slaughter that renders one an apostate is not invalid; rather, all subsequent acts of slaughter are invalid. The Ran in tractate *Ḥullin* explains that it is only the conclusion of the act of slaughter that renders one an apostate, but the slaughter that rendered the animal permitted was already complete. In the Rambam's Commentary on the Mishna, it is explained in *Ḥullin* that this is referring only to one who slaughters unwittingly, and therefore the slaughter is not invalidated as that of an apostate.

סָבַר לָהּ כְּרַבִּי יוֹחָנָן הַסַּנְדְּלָר. דְּתַנְיָא: הַמְבַשֵּׁל בְּשַׁבָּת, בְּשׁוֹגֵג – יֹאכַל, בְּמֵזִיד – לֹא יֹאכַל, דִּבְרֵי רַבִּי מֵאִיר. רַבִּי יְהוּדָה אוֹמֵר: בְּשׁוֹגֵג – יֹאכַל לְמוֹצָאֵי שַׁבָּת, בְּמֵזִיד – לֹא יֹאכַל עוֹלָמִית. רַבִּי יוֹחָנָן הַסַּנְדְּלָר אוֹמֵר: בְּשׁוֹגֵג – יֵאָכֵל לְמוֹצָאֵי שַׁבָּת לַאֲחֵרִים, וְלֹא לוֹ. בְּמֵזִיד – לֹא יֵאָכֵל עוֹלָמִית, לֹא לוֹ וְלֹא לַאֲחֵרִים.

The Gemara answers: The *tanna* of the *baraita* under discussion **holds in accordance with** the opinion of **Rabbi Yoḥanan HaSandlar, as it is taught** in a *baraita*:

With regard to **one who cooks on Shabbat,**[HN] if he did so **unwittingly, he may eat** the food he cooked; if he did so **intentionally, he may not eat** it at all. This is **the statement of Rabbi Meir.**[N]

Rabbi Yehuda says: If he cooked **unwittingly he may eat at the conclusion of Shabbat,**[N] as the Sages penalized even one who sinned unwittingly in that they prohibited him from deriving immediate benefit from the dish that he cooked; if he sinned **intentionally, he may not eat** from it **ever.**

Rabbi Yoḥanan HaSandlar says: If he did so **unwittingly,** the food **may be eaten at the conclusion of Shabbat by others but not by him;** if he did so **intentionally, it may not be eaten ever, neither by him nor by other** Jews. According to Rabbi Yoḥanan HaSandlar, food prepared by means of intentional desecration of Shabbat is unfit to be eaten. That is true with regard to cooking food on Shabbat and with regard to slaughtering an animal on Shabbat.

מַאי טַעְמָא דְּרַבִּי יוֹחָנָן הַסַּנְדְּלָר? כִּדְדָרֵישׁ רַבִּי חִיָּיא אַפִּיתְחָא דְּבֵי נְשִׂיאָה: ״וּשְׁמַרְתֶּם אֶת הַשַּׁבָּת כִּי קֹדֶשׁ הִיא לָכֶם״. מַה קוֹדֶשׁ אָסוּר בַּאֲכִילָה אַף מַעֲשֵׂה שַׁבָּת אֲסוּרִין בַּאֲכִילָה. אִי מַה קוֹדֶשׁ אָסוּר בַּהֲנָאָה אַף מַעֲשֵׂה שַׁבָּת אָסוּר בַּהֲנָאָה – תַּלְמוּד לוֹמַר ״לָכֶם״, שֶׁלָּכֶם יְהֵא.

The Gemara asks: **What is the rationale** for the opinion **of Rabbi Yoḥanan HaSandlar?** The Gemara explains: It is **as Rabbi Ḥiyya taught at the entrance to the house of the *Nasi*.** It is written: **"And you shall observe Shabbat, for it is sacred to you;** he who profanes it shall be put to death" (Exodus 31:14); **just as** with regard to a **sacred** item consecrated to the Temple, **eating** it **is prohibited, so too,** with regard to food produced through **action** that desecrates **Shabbat, eating** it **is prohibited.** The Gemara asks: **If** so, perhaps the analogy should be extended to include the following: **Just as** with regard to **a sacred item,** deriving **benefit** from it **is prohibited, so too,** with regard to the product of **an action** that desecrates **Shabbat,** deriving **benefit** from it should be **prohibited.** The Gemara answers: **The verse states:** "It is sacred **to you**" (Exodus 31:14), indicating that **it shall be yours** in the sense that one may derive benefit from it.

יָכוֹל אֲפִילּוּ בְּשׁוֹגֵג. תַּלְמוּד לוֹמַר ״מְחַלְלֶיהָ מוֹת יוּמָת״, בְּמֵזִיד אָמַרְתִּי לְךָ, וְלֹא בְּשׁוֹגֵג.

The Gemara asks: Based on the analogy between actions that desecrate Shabbat and sacred items, one **might** have thought that **even** if the action was performed **unwittingly** it should be prohibited to eat its product, as is the case with regard to sacred items. Therefore, **the verse states: "He who profanes it shall be put to death"** (Exodus 31:14), indicating that it is **with regard to** one who desecrates Shabbat **intentionally** that **I stated to you** this analogy to sacred items,[N] as the verse is clearly referring to one who is liable to receive the death penalty, **and not with regard to** one who desecrates Shabbat **unwittingly,** who is not executed.

HALAKHA

One who cooks on Shabbat – הַמְבַשֵּׁל בְּשַׁבָּת: With regard to a Jew who performed prohibited labor on Shabbat, e.g., cooking, if he did so intentionally, it is permanently prohibited for him to derive benefit from that labor, while others may eat the food immediately at the conclusion of Shabbat. If he did so unwittingly, it is permitted both for him and for others to eat the dish at the conclusion of Shabbat. The *halakha* is ruled in accordance with the opinion of Rabbi Yehuda in his dispute with Rabbi Meir. The Ran adds that the ruling is based on the statement of Rav in *Ḥullin*, where he ruled in accordance with the opinion of Rabbi Meir for Torah scholars but in accordance with the opinion of Rabbi Yehuda for ignorant people, so that they will not come to treat Shabbat prohibitions with contempt (Rambam *Sefer Zemanim*, *Hilkhot Shabbat* 6:23; *Shulḥan Arukh*, *Oraḥ Ḥayyim* 318:1).

NOTES

Benefit from prohibited labor on Shabbat – הֲנָאָה מִמְּלֶאכֶת שַׁבָּת: In the *Shita Mekubbetzet* it is explained that there are three different rationales mentioned here. First, the Sages penalized the sinner so that he would not profit from his transgression. Others explain that the Sages issued a decree penalizing one who acted unwittingly due to an intentional sinner. Second, they did not want people to benefit from prohibited labor performed on Shabbat. Third, due to the verse "It is sacred to you" (Exodus 31:14), the product of labor performed on Shabbat is forbidden.

Intentionally, he may not eat it; this is the statement of Rabbi Meir – בְּמֵזִיד לֹא יֹאכַל דִּבְרֵי רַבִּי מֵאִיר: According to most early commentaries, Rabbi Meir's statement: If he did so intentionally he may not eat it, refers not just to the sinner himself; rather, this dish may not be consumed on Shabbat at all. Rabbi Meir did not formulate his opinion as: It may not be eaten, for stylistic reasons, to use parallel phrasing in both parts of his statement. Similarly, Rabbi Yehuda's statement below must be explained by suggesting that he too employed a uniform mode of expression. The commentaries further state that Rabbi Meir permits even an intentional sinner to partake of the dish after the conclusion of Shabbat. Based on the Gemara in tractate *Ḥullin*, the legal status of an intentional sinner according to Rabbi Meir parallels that of an unwitting transgressor according to Rabbi Yehuda. The legal status of an intentional sinner according to Rabbi Yehuda parallels that of an unwitting sinner according to Rabbi Yoḥanan HaSandlar. However, Rashi here states that according to Rabbi Meir, one who cooks intentionally may never partake of that dish (see *Shita Mekubbetzet*).

He may eat at the conclusion of Shabbat – יֹאכַל לְמוֹצָאֵי שַׁבָּת: Rashi in *Ḥullin* states that this does not mean that the food may be eaten immediately after Shabbat. After the conclusion of Shabbat one must wait until the period of time that would be sufficient for the food to have been prepared from the beginning has elapsed. This is based on the concept that the Sages did not want the sinner to benefit from labor performed on Shabbat.

It is with regard to one who desecrates Shabbat intentionally that I stated to you – בְּמֵזִיד אָמַרְתִּי לְךָ: The Rashash asks why Rabbi Yoḥanan HaSandlar did not explain that the food is prohibited only if one was forewarned, since if he is not forewarned he is not liable to be executed. In fact, in *Gilyon HaShas*, *Sefer HaPardes* is cited, which explains, according to Rashi, that Rabbi Yoḥanan HaSandlar holds that only the product of labor performed on Shabbat by one who was forewarned is permanently forbidden.

פליגי בה רב אחא ורבינא: חד אמר: מעשה שבת דאורייתא, וחד אמר: דרבנן, מאן דאמר דאורייתא – כדאמרן. מאן דאמר דרבנן – אמר קרא: "קדש היא" – היא קודש, ואין מעשיה קודש.

The Gemara comments: **Rav Aḥa and Ravina disagree with regard to this matter.**[N] **One said:** The product of **an action** that desecrates **Shabbat** is prohibited **by Torah** law, **and one said** that it is prohibited **by rabbinic** law. With regard to the **one who said** that it is prohibited **by Torah** law, it is **as we said,** that it is based on the verse interpreted by Rabbi Ḥiyya. **And** the **one who said** that it is prohibited **by rabbinic** law holds that **the verse states: "It is sacred,"** from which he infers: **It is sacred, but** the product of **its actions is not sacred,** and therefore, by Torah law it may be eaten.

ולמאן דאמר דרבנן, מאי טעמייהו דרבנן דפטרי? כי קא פטרי רבנן – אשארא.

The Gemara asks: **And** according to the **one who said** it is prohibited **by rabbinic** law, **what is the rationale**[N] for the opinion **of the Rabbis who exempt** the thief from payment for the slaughter performed by his agent on Shabbat? By Torah law, the slaughter is valid. The Gemara answers: **When the Rabbis exempt** the thief from payment, it is with regard **to the rest** of the cases, i.e., one who slaughters for idolatry or an ox sentenced to stoning, not with regard to Shabbat.

טובח לעבודה זרה, כיון דשחט ביה פורתא איתסר ליה, אידך כי קא טבח – לאו דמריה קא טבח! אמר רבא: באומר "בגמר זביחה הוא עובדה".

The Gemara asks the following question with regard to Rabbi Meir's opinion that **one who slaughters for idolatry** is liable to pay the owner for the animal. **Once he slaughtered** the animal **a bit,**[N] at the very start of the act of slaughter, **it is prohibited for him** to derive benefit from the animal because it is an animal sacrificed to idolatry; **and when he slaughters the rest,** it is **not** the animal that belongs **to its owner** that he **is slaughtering.** Since it is prohibited to derive benefit from the animal, it has no value and there is no ownership. **Rava said:** It is referring **to one who says,** prior to the slaughter, that **he is worshipping** the idol only **at the completion of the slaughter,** and therefore the prohibition takes effect only then.

שור הנסקל – לאו דידיה הוא דקטבח! אמר רבה: הכא במאי עסקינן – כגון שמסרו לשומר, והזיק בבית שומר, ונגמר דיניה בבית שומר, וגנבו גנב מבית שומר.

The Gemara asks the following question with regard to Rabbi Meir's opinion that one who slaughters **the ox that is stoned** is liable to pay for the slaughter. Why is he liable? It is **not** the owner's ox that **he is slaughtering,** since once the ox is sentenced to be stoned it is prohibited to derive benefit from it. **Rabba said: With what are we dealing here?** We are dealing with a case **where** the owners **entrusted** the ox **to a bailee** and the ox **injured** another person while **in the bailee's house, and it was sentenced** to be stoned while **in the bailee's house, and** the **thief** then **stole it from the bailee's house** and slaughtered it.

ורבי מאיר סבר לה כרבי יעקב, וסבר לה כרבי שמעון; סבר לה כרבי יעקב – דאמר: אף משנגמר דינו, החזירו שומר לבעליו – מוחזר. וסבר לה כרבי שמעון, דאמר: דבר הגורם לממון כממון דמי.

And this solution is based on the fact that **Rabbi Meir holds in accordance with** the opinion of **Rabbi Ya'akov and holds in accordance with** the opinion of **Rabbi Shimon. He holds in accordance with** the opinion of **Rabbi Ya'akov, who said: Even after** the ox **was sentenced** to be stoned, if the **bailee returned it to its owners, it is returned.** Despite the fact that the ox is now worthless, as no benefit may be derived from it, since the bailee returned an ox that is physically intact the owner has no claim against him. **And** Rabbi Meir **holds in accordance with** the opinion of **Rabbi Shimon, who said** that the legal status of **an object that effects monetary** loss[NH] **is like** that of **money.** Even in the case of an object that is worthless, if its elimination causes monetary loss because it must be replaced, it is considered to have value. In this case, although the ox has no value in and of itself, slaughtering the animal prevents the bailee from returning it intact to the owner, requiring him to pay the owner the value of the ox before it was sentenced to be stoned. Consequently, the thief must reimburse the bailee, as the ox has value for the bailee.

רבה אמר: לעולם בטובח על ידי עצמו,

Rabba said: Actually, contrary to Rabbi Yoḥanan's explanation of the *baraita*, it is referring **to one who slaughters** the animal **himself,**

NOTES

Rav Aḥa and Ravina disagree with regard to this matter – פליגי בה רב אחא ורבינא: Most early commentaries, beginning with Rabbeinu Ḥananel, maintain that this is a dispute based only on the opinion of Rabbi Yoḥanan HaSandlar. Even so, most halakhic authorities do not consider this as proof that the *halakha* is in accordance with his opinion, although some *ge'onim* rule based on this Gemara that the *halakha* is in accordance with his opinion. The Ramban cites a different interpretation. He suggests that the *tanna'im* disagree with regard to the correct exposition of the verse "It is sacred to you." Rabbi Meir maintains that the product of prohibited labor is sacred only on the sacred day itself, Rabbi Yehuda claims that it is sacred and prohibited only to one who desecrated Shabbat intentionally, while Rabbi Yoḥanan HaSandlar contends that if Shabbat was willfully desecrated, the resulting product is sacred and prohibited to all.

And according to the one who said it is prohibited by rabbinic law what is the rationale, etc. – ולמאן דאמר דרבנן מאי טעמייהו וכו׳: The Maharshal asks: Even if the prohibition is by rabbinic law, the meat may not be eaten, and one should therefore be exempt from punishment for the slaughter of the stolen animal. He cites proof from the fact that if one betroths a woman with an object from which it is prohibited to derive benefit by rabbinic law, the betrothal does not take effect even by Torah law. In the *Shita Mekubbetzet* it is explained that the Sages issued the decree that the meat may not be eaten as a stringency, and not as a leniency. The Rashash maintains that there is a difference between the authority of the court to declare one's property ownerless, which influences the legal status of an item even by Torah law, and issuing a decree that slaughter is unfit, which does not influence the legal status by Torah law.

Once he slaughtered the animal a bit – כיון דשחט ביה פורתא: Even according to the opinion that one cannot render forbidden an object that is not his, that is only with regard to rendering the object forbidden without performing an action. However, if one performs an action that directly affects the object, he renders it forbidden even if it does not belong to him (Ritva; see Rashba).

And Rabbi Meir holds in accordance with the opinion of Rabbi Shimon, who said that the legal status of an object that effects monetary loss – וסבר לה כרבי שמעון דאמר דבר הגורם לממון: *Tosafot* ask why this is necessary, as it is well known that Rabbi Meir adjudicates cases of indirect damage. In other words, if one harms another in a manner that is not discernible, or damages an item that is worthless in and of itself, if he causes financial loss he must reimburse his victim. Several answers are offered. Many early commentaries accept the claim of *Tosafot*, who claim that there is a difference between the two cases. Although Rabbi Meir adjudicates cases of indirect damage, that does not mean that he deems the object itself to be worth money. It is merely an obligation by rabbinic law to compensate the victim. Rabbi Shimon, in contrast, maintains that legal status of an object that effects monetary loss is like that of actual money (see Ramban).

HALAKHA

An object that effects monetary loss – דבר הגורם לממון: If one stole consecrated items from the house of the one who consecrated them, then although the owner is responsible to replace the items the thief is not liable to pay double the principal because, contrary to the ruling of Rabbi Shimon, the legal status of an object that effects monetary loss is not that of money. This is a case of an object that effects monetary loss, as the owner is obligated to bring replacement offerings. The *Shakh* adds that although the *halakha* is that one adjudicates cases of indirect damage and deems one who inflicts that damage liable to pay compensation, most authorities maintain that that is a different issue (Rambam *Sefer Nezikim, Hilkhot Geneiva* 2:1; *Shulḥan Arukh, Ḥoshen Mishpat* 386:2).

וְרַבִּי מֵאִיר, לוֹקֶה וּמְשַׁלֵּם אִית לֵיהּ, מֵת וּמְשַׁלֵּם לֵית לֵיהּ. וְשָׁאנֵי הָנֵי, דְּחִידּוּשׁ הוּא שֶׁחִידְּשָׁה תּוֹרָה בִּקְנָס, אַף עַל גַּב דְּמִיקְטִיל – מְשַׁלֵּם. וְאָזְדָא רַבָּה לְטַעְמֵיהּ, דְּאָמַר רַבָּה: הָיָה גְּדִי גָּנוּב לוֹ וּטְבָחוֹ בְּשַׁבָּת – חַיָּיב, שֶׁכְּבָר נִתְחַיֵּיב בִּגְנֵיבָה קוֹדֶם שֶׁיָּבֹא לִידֵי אִיסּוּר שַׁבָּת. גָּנַב וְטָבַח בְּשַׁבָּת – פָּטוּר, שֶׁאִם אֵין גְּנֵיבָה – אֵין טְבִיחָה וְאֵין מְכִירָה.

and **Rabbi Meir is of** the opinion that one **is flogged and pays,** but **is not of** the opinion that one **dies** by execution **and pays. And these** *halakhot* **are different, as it is a novel element that the Torah innovated with regard to** the halakhic category of **fines;**[N] **although he is killed, he pays. And Rabba followed his** line of **reasoning**[N] stated elsewhere, **as Rabba said:** If one **had a stolen kid in his** possession that he had stolen previously, **and he slaughtered it on Shabbat, he is liable** to pay five times the principal for slaughtering the kid, **as he was already liable for stealing before he came to** violate **the prohibition** against performing labor on **Shabbat.** Although he slaughtered the goat on Shabbat, a capital crime, he is liable for the payment because it is a fine. However, if **he stole** the goat **and slaughtered** it **on Shabbat,**[N] he is **exempt** from the payment of five times the principal **as, if** there is **no** payment for **theft,**[N] due to his liability to receive the death penalty for desecrating Shabbat, and his obligation to repay the theft is not a fine, there is **no** liability for **slaughter and** there is **no** liability for **sale.**

וְאָמַר רַבָּה: הָיָה גְּדִי גָּנוּב לוֹ וּטְבָחוֹ בְּמַחְתֶּרֶת – חַיָּיב, שֶׁכְּבָר נִתְחַיֵּיב בִּגְנֵיבָה קוֹדֶם שֶׁיָּבֹא לִידֵי אִיסּוּר מַחְתֶּרֶת. גָּנַב וְטָבַח בְּמַחְתֶּרֶת – פָּטוּר, שֶׁאִם אֵין גְּנֵיבָה – אֵין טְבִיחָה וְאֵין מְכִירָה.

And Rabba said: If one **had a stolen kid in his** possession that he had stolen previously, **and he slaughtered it in** the course of an act of **burglary,**[N] he is **liable** to pay four or five times the principal, **as he was already liable for theft before he came to** violate **the prohibition** against **burglary.** However, if **he stole and slaughtered** an animal **in** the course of an act of **burglary,**[H] he is **exempt.** Because the owner of the house is permitted to kill the burglar, the status of the burglar is tantamount to one liable to receive the death penalty. **As,** if there is **no** payment **for theft,** there is **no** liability for **slaughter and** there is **no** liability for **sale.** Rabba's statements indicate that one pays the fines for slaughter or sale even if he is liable to receive the death penalty.

HALAKHA

If he stole and slaughtered in the course of an act of burglary – גָּנַב וְטָבַח בְּמַחְתֶּרֶת: If a burglar broke into a house and stole an animal and slaughtered it there, he is exempt, as it is permitted to take his life at the time, as per the statement of Rabba (Rambam *Sefer Nezikim, Hilkhot Geneiva* 9:13; *Tur, Ḥoshen Mishpat* 351).

NOTES

As it is a novel element that the Torah innovated with regard to the halakhic category of fines – דְּחִידּוּשׁ הוּא שֶׁחִידְּשָׁה תּוֹרָה בִּקְנָס: In the *Shita Mekubbetzet* it is explained that Rashi is not saying that the novel element in the Torah is that one who is liable to pay a fine is executed and pays. Rather, the novel element is the very imposition of a fine. Therefore, one cannot derive the legal status of fines from other similar payments, and as a result, one is liable to be executed and to pay. Whenever a *halakha* in the Torah is characterized as novel, that means that it is exceptional in certain respects, as the principles in effect in similar cases do not apply. Its *halakhot* are therefore unique; elements of other *halakhot* cannot be derived from it, nor can its elements be derived from other *halakhot*. As for the novel element of fines, the *Ḥatam Sofer* writes that it is not that one pays more than the damage he caused, as that is true about other Torah punishments, e.g., corporal punishment, where there is no necessary connection between the damage caused and the penalty imposed. Instead, the novel element is that the fine is paid to the victim rather than to the public treasury or to the Sanctuary, which is generally the case with regard to sinners.

And Rabba followed his line of reasoning – וְאָזְדָא רַבָּה לְטַעְמֵיהּ: A general question is raised here: When an *amora* repeats a *halakha*, why does the Gemara sometimes react by asking: Didn't he already state that once, while on other occasions the Gemara simply notes: And the Sage followed his line of reasoning stated elsewhere. In *Sefer HaḤokhma*, Rabbeinu Barukh explains that when the statement of the Sage is stated as an elucidation of a mishna or the like, the Gemara says that he followed his standard line of reasoning, as his explanation is consistent with his practical halakhic ruling. However, if both statements are halakhic rulings, the Gemara will question the repetition.

If he stole and slaughtered on Shabbat – גָּנַב וְטָבַח בְּשַׁבָּת: The early and later commentaries discuss the case of one who stole on Shabbat and proceeded to slaughter or sell the animal during the week. The Ritva and others infer from Rashi that in that case he is liable to pay four or five times the principal. The reason is that the theft committed on Shabbat is no longer relevant, and when he takes the animal to slaughter or sells it is as though the theft began at that moment. The Rashba disagrees and maintains that in that case he is exempt, in accordance with the principle that if there is no theft there is no slaughter or sale either. Since one is not liable to pay for theft on Shabbat, there is no liability for slaughter or sale. The *Shita Yeshana*, cited in the *Shita Mekubbetzet* explains likewise. Several later commentaries address the fundamental aspects of this dilemma. It appears that the dispute among the early commentaries is dependent on the precise definition of theft performed in the course of desecrating Shabbat. Is it considered a full-fledged acquisition in every sense but the thief is exempt from payment, or is it viewed as an incomplete acquisition and considered as though there were no theft at all (Rabbi Akiva Eiger; *Or Same'aḥ*; *Kovetz Shiurim*)?

As, if there is no payment for theft, etc. – שֶׁאִם אֵין גְּנֵיבָה וכו׳: Although the fine for slaughter or sale is an independent fine, independent of the mitzva to restore the stolen item to its owner, it is a biblical decree that one is liable to pay four or five times the principal, not merely three or four times. Based on that biblical decree, if one is exempt from the obligation to return the principal, he is exempt from paying the fine as well (Ritva).

The prohibition against burglary – אִיסּוּר מַחְתֶּרֶת: The *halakha* of a burglar who breaks into a private home is stated in the Torah: "If the thief is found breaking in, and is struck and dies, there is no blood for him" (Exodus 22:1). The basic concept, which is elucidated in tractate *Sanhedrin*, is that a thief breaking into a house is considered, with certain exceptions, as one with the intention to commit murder if necessary. Therefore, if the homeowner kills him, he is exempt. Since taking the life of the burglar is permitted, his legal status is like that of one sentenced to death, and therefore he is exempt from payment for any damage that he may have caused at that moment. That status is temporary, as once the burglar leaves the premises it is no longer permitted to kill him and he is liable to pay for any monetary liability that he may incur.

וצריכא, דאי אשמעינן שבת – משום דאיסורה איסור עולם, אבל מחתרת דאיסור שעה הוא – אימא לא; ואי אשמעינן מחתרת – משום דמחתרתו זו היא התראתו, אבל שבת דבעיא התראה – אימא לא, צריכא.

The Gemara comments: **And** it was **necessary** for Rabba to state this *halakha* with regard to both Shabbat and burglary; as, **if he** had **taught us**[N] that one is exempt from payment only with regard to **Shabbat,** it is **because** Shabbat is severe since punishment for violation of **its prohibition is an eternal prohibition,** as whenever witnesses testify that one desecrated Shabbat, he can be executed. **However,** in the case of **burglary,** as punishment for violating its **prohibition is transitory,** e.g., it is permitted for the homeowner to kill the burglar only as long as the burglar remains on his property, **say** that he is **not** exempt from payment. **And if he taught us** the exemption only with regard to **burglary,** that would be **because his burglary is his forewarning.** Because he certainly intends to kill the homeowner, it is permitted for the homeowner to kill him without forewarning. In that respect, burglary is a severe prohibition and exempts one from payment. **However, Shabbat, which requires forewarning,** is a less severe prohibition, and in that case, say that one **is not** exempt from payment. Therefore, it was **necessary** for Rabba to state the exemption in both cases.

אמר רב פפא: היתה פרה גנובה לו וטבחה בשבת – חייב, שכבר נתחייב בגניבה קודם שיבא לידי איסור שבת. היתה פרה שאולה לו, וטבחה בשבת – פטור. אמר ליה רב אחא בריה דרבא לרב אשי: רב פפא פרה אתא לאשמועינן?!

Rav Pappa said: If one **had a stolen cow** in **his** possession that he had stolen previously **and he slaughtered it on Shabbat,** he is **liable** to pay four or five times the principal **as he was already liable for theft before he came to** violate **the prohibition of Shabbat.** If **a cow was lent to him and he slaughtered it on Shabbat,**[H] he is **exempt** from paying the fine. **Rav Aha, son of Rava, said to Rav Ashi: Is Rav Pappa coming to teach us** the case **of a cow?** In other words, what did Rav Pappa add that was not already clear from Rabba's statement? The same principle applies with regard to both a kid and a cow. If one was liable to pay for the theft when he stole the animal, he is liable to pay the fine for slaughter as well, even if he is liable to receive the death penalty.

אמר ליה: רב פפא שאולה אתא לאשמועינן; סלקא דעתך אמינא, הואיל ואמר רב פפא: משעת משיכה הוא דאתחייב ליה במזונותיה, הכא נמי משעת שאלה אתחייב באונסיה. – קא משמע לן.

Rav Ashi **said to him: Rav Pappa is coming to teach us** the *halakha* with regard to a **borrowed** cow, as **it could enter your mind to say** that **since Rav Pappa said:** It is **from the moment of pulling** the animal into his domain **that** the borrower **is obligated**[H] **to** provide the animal's **sustenance,** then **here too, from the moment of borrowing**[N] **he is liable** to pay **for its unavoidable accidents.** From that point, the animal is legally in his possession and therefore, even if he slaughtered the animal on Shabbat he should be liable. Therefore, **he teaches us** that one assumes liability for unavoidable accidents only when they actually occur, and if that is on Shabbat, he is exempt.

NOTES

And it was necessary; as, if he had taught us, etc. – וצריכא דאי אשמעינן וכו׳: Rashi and several other commentaries explain that the Gemara here emphasizes that although one might have thought otherwise, in each of these cases one is exempt from punishment. Conversely, *Tosafot* and other early commentaries (Ramban; Rashba) contend that the opposite is true: The point is that one is obligated to pay the fine even though he violated a prohibition that is punishable by death.

Here too, from the moment of borrowing, etc. – הכא נמי משעת שאלה וכו׳: The reason for the difference between these two *halakhot* is that since one who borrows an animal is obligated to guard it from that moment, he is also obligated to see to the animal's sustenance. In contrast, liability to pay for accidental damage does not stem from his obligation to care for the animal; rather, there is an independent obligation to compensate the owner if there is an accident. Therefore, his liability begins only from the moment that the accident transpires.

HALAKHA

If a cow was lent to him and he slaughtered it on Shabbat – היתה פרה שאולה לו וטבחה בשבת: One who borrowed a cow from another before Shabbat and stole and slaughtered it on Shabbat is exempt from payment, as the liability to be punished for theft and Shabbat desecration coincide. The *halakha* is in accordance with the opinion of Rav Pappa, as his opinion does not contradict the latter version of Rava's statement. The early commentaries disagree, both in terms of the understanding of the Gemara and in terms of the Rambam's ruling. Some (Meiri; *Netivot HaMishpat, Hoshen Mishpat* 341:9) state that he is exempt only from paying four or five times the principal but is liable to pay the principal, while others (Rabbi Meir HaLevi; *Nimmukei Yosef*) state that he is exempt from the principal as well (Rambam *Sefer Nezikim, Hilkhot Geneiva* 3:4; *Tur, Hoshen Mishpat* 350).

From the moment of pulling that he is obligated – משעת משיכה הוא דאתחייב ליה: One who borrows an animal is obligated to see to its sustenance and is liable for accidents (*Shakh*) from the moment he pulls the animal, as per the opinion of Rav Pappa. The Rema cites the opinion of Rabbeinu Yitzhak and the Rosh that even without pulling the animal, he is liable from the moment its owners leave (Rambam *Sefer Mishpatim, Hilkhot She'ela* 1:4; *Shulhan Arukh, Hoshen Mishpat* 340:4).

אמר רבא: הניח להן אביהן פרה שאולה – משתמשין בה כל ימי שאלתה, מתה – אין חייבין באונסה. כסבורין של אביהם היא וטבחוה ואכלוה – משלמין דמי בשר בזול. הניח להן אביהן אחריות נכסים – חייבין לשלם.

Rava said: If **their father** died and **left them a borrowed cow,**[H] **they may use it** for **the entire** duration of the **period** for which **it was borrowed.** The right to use a borrowed article continues even after the borrower himself dies. However, if the cow **died, they are not liable** to pay **for its unavoidable accident,**[N] as they did not borrow the animal themselves. Similarly, if **they thought** the cow **was their father's**[H] **and they slaughtered it and ate it, they pay only a reduced** assessment **of the price of the meat.**[N] They are required to pay only for the benefit they received, not the damage they caused the owner. However, if **their father left them**[N] **property** as a **guarantee**[N] for return of the borrowed item, i.e., there was a lien on the father's property during his lifetime, **they are obligated to pay** the entire sum of the damage.

איכא דמתני לה ארישא, ואיכא דמתני לה אסיפא. מאן דמתני לה ארישא – כל שכן אסיפא, ופליגא דרב פפא, ומאן דמתני לה אסיפא – אבל ארישא לא, והיינו דרב פפא.

The Gemara comments: **Some teach this** statement, that if the father left property as a guarantee his heirs are liable to pay the entire damage, **with regard to the first clause** of this *halakha*, **and some teach it with regard to the latter clause.** The Gemara elaborates: According to the **one who teaches it with regard to the first clause,**[N] when the animal died, **all the more so** would he teach this *halakha* **with regard to the latter clause,** as since they slaughtered the animal they must pay full damages. **And** this approach **differs** with the opinion **of Rav Pappa,** who said that a borrower is liable for accidents only when the incident occurs. **And** according to the **one who teaches it with regard to the latter clause,** this *halakha* applies only when they slaughtered and ate it; **however, with regard to the first clause,** when it died, they would **not** be liable, as the *tanna* too maintains that liability for unavoidable accidents begins only when the incident occurs, not from when the cow was borrowed. **And this is** consistent with the ruling **of Rav Pappa.**

HALAKHA

If their father left them a borrowed cow – הניח להן אביהן פרה שאולה: If one borrowed an animal and died, his heirs may use the animal until the end of the period for which it was borrowed. If the animal dies, they are not liable to pay for the accident, as per the opinion of Rava. However, their liability is like that of paid bailees, as the Gemara states that they are exempt only from accidents, from which it may be inferred that they are liable for theft and loss (*Baḥ*). The Rosh writes that if the lender says to the heirs: Return the article I lent or assume responsibility to pay for accidents, it is binding upon the heirs (Rambam *Sefer Mishpatim, Hilkhot She'ela* 1:5; *Shulḥan Arukh, Ḥoshen Mishpat* 341:3).

If they thought the cow was their father's, etc. – כסבורין של אביהם וכו׳: If the heirs inherited no property from their father and slaughtered and ate the borrowed cow under the mistaken impression that it belonged to their father, they are required to pay only for the benefit they received, not the damage they caused the owner. If their father bequeathed property to them and the borrowed cow died or they slaughtered it, they reimburse the owner the full value of his cow from the inherited property. This is the opinion of the Rambam. His view is disputed by the Ramban and the Rashba, who contend that the Rambam's approach corresponds with neither the first version nor the latter version in the Gemara. They rule in accordance with the latter version, and Rava's ruling is parallel to that of Rav Pappa. Therefore, if the cow dies the heirs are exempt from payment even if their father left them property as a guarantee. The Rosh agrees. The *Kesef Mishne* and other commentaries explain that the Rambam had a variant version of the Gemara. The *Shulḥan Arukh*, like most authorities, rules in accordance with the latter version of Rava's statement to exempt the heirs (Rambam *Sefer Mishpatim, Hilkhot She'ela* 1:5; *Shulḥan Arukh, Ḥoshen Mishpat* 341:4).

NOTES

If it died they are not liable for its unavoidable accident – מתה אין חייבין באונסה: The Ra'avad states that the heirs are exempt from payments for accidents even if they actually use the animal. He explains that the heirs inherit the rights to use the animal, whereas the obligation to pay for accidents is a personal obligation assumed by the borrower, which lapses upon his death. The heirs never accepted responsibility to pay for accidents. The Rashba questions this approach, in light of the *halakha* that one who borrowed from a hirer is considered to have borrowed from the owner himself. Accordingly, heirs should also be viewed as having borrowed from their father and therefore should be obligated to pay the owner of the animal for accidents. The Ritva answers that even in a case of a second borrower, his liability does not stem from his use of the object but from the fact that he actually borrowed it and thereby incurred the responsibility, as opposed to heirs, who never assumed that. A different explanation is suggested by Rabbi Avraham *Av Beit Din*. He contends that heirs are exempt from financial responsibility for accidents only if they had not made use of the animal, but if they had used it they are considered to have borrowed it themselves. See HALAKHA for further elaboration. The Ra'avad adds that even if they did not use the animal, their responsibility is no less than the responsibility of paid bailees, stemming from their right to use the animal.

Reduced assessment of the price of the meat – דמי בשר בזול: Based on *Bava Kamma* 146b, Rashi explains that this means that they return the hide to the owner and pay two-thirds of the standard market price of the meat. The Rid agrees. The Ramban maintains that even in *Bava Kamma* that ruling is a later addition by the early *ge'onim*. Therefore, he asserts that there is no connection between the two passages, and the Gemara here simply means the value of meat sold at a reduced price.

If their father left them, etc. – הניח להן אביהן וכו׳: The rationale for the opinion that this statement relates to the latter clause is subject to dispute among the early commentaries. According to most versions of Rashi's commentary, the heirs are liable due to the fact that they neglected to assess the situation properly, although some (*Shita Mekubbetzet*; Rashash) cite a variant reading that aligns Rashi's opinion with that of most of the other commentaries. The Ramban questions Rashi's interpretation: If that is the reason for their liability, what is the difference whether or not their father left them property? He therefore agrees with *Tosafot* that the heirs' father should have informed them that this cow did not belong to him. Since he neglected to do so, payment is collected from his property, if any of his property remains. Most early commentaries explain in this way, despite the difficulty raised by the Rashba, that it is conceivable that he neglected to inform them due to circumstances beyond his control, e.g., if he died suddenly, a difficulty that does not exist according to Rashi's explanation. Rabbi Meir HaLevi explains that had their father not left them property, there would be no need to consider the possibility that there is some obligation incurred by their father when they come to slaughter the animal, as he left them no property from which it could be collected. Since they did not know the cow was borrowed, they are not liable. If, however, they inherited property from their father, they know that if he was liable, e.g., because he stole the animal, they are obligated to pay due to their own assumption of responsibility for the animal and due to their father's obligation as well.

Property as a guarantee – אחריות נכסים: According to Rashi this refers specifically to property that can be mortgaged to guarantee a loan, i.e., land. Although there are different versions of the Rambam's ruling, apparently he maintains that after the ordinance instituted by the *ge'onim* that when one takes a loan there is a lien on all of one's property, there is no difference between land and other types of property. The commentaries state that this dispute is related to the issue of whether the ordinance that the debts of the father are bequeathed to an heir is limited to a debt due to a loan or whether it applies to all debts.

The one who teaches it with regard to the first clause, etc. – מאן דמתני לה ארישא וכו׳: The Rambam rules that if the heirs thought the cow was their father's and their father left them property, they are obligated to pay even if the cow died. Other early commentaries question this ruling, as it appears to correspond neither with the first nor with the second version of the Gemara. See HALAKHA for further elaboration. The Meiri claims that the duty of the heirs to pay for the dead cow does not result from their liability to pay for accidents, but from their father's obligation to return the article he borrowed. According to his opinion, this *halakha* is unrelated to the Gemara's discussion with regard to the relationship between the statement of Rava and Rav Pappa.

NOTES

What is the reason that he didn't state his opinion in accordance with the opinion of Rabbi Yoḥanan – מַאי טַעְמָא לָא אָמַר כְּרַבִּי יוֹחָנָן: Although ostensibly the Gemara could have said that Reish Lakish bases his opinion on the fact that a careful reading of the mishna leads to the conclusion that it is in accordance with the opinion of Rabbi Meir, it was already proven above that it cannot be said that the entire mishna is in accordance with the opinion of Rabbi Meir. Therefore, that is not sufficient to clarify why he explained it according to Rabbi Meir's opinion (Ritva). In the *Shita Mekubbetzet* it is explained at length that all of the problems of the mishna are resolved by Rabbi Yoḥanan's explanation, including contradictions with other *mishnayot*. That is not the case with the explanation of Reish Lakish.

Those unwittingly liable – חַיָּיבֵי...שׁוֹגְגִין: The word unwittingly is inaccurate here because the same *halakha* applies even if they sinned intentionally, as according to Rabbi Yoḥanan the decisive factor is not their state of mind but whether or not they received a warning and consequently whether or not they are punished. However, it could be explained that Rabbi Yoḥanan deems anyone who acted without forewarning as one who acted unwittingly (Ritva).

בִּשְׁלָמָא רַבִּי יוֹחָנָן לָא אָמַר כְּרֵישׁ לָקִישׁ – דְּקָא מוֹקִים לַהּ כְּרַבָּנַן. אֶלָּא רֵישׁ לָקִישׁ מַאי טַעְמָא לָא אָמַר כְּרַבִּי יוֹחָנָן? אָמַר לָךְ: כֵּיוָן דְּאִילּוּ אַתְרוּ בֵּיהּ – פָּטוּר, כִּי לָא אַתְרוּ בֵּיהּ – נַמִי פָּטוּר.

Several possible solutions were proposed to resolve the apparent contradiction between the mishna here that says that one who rapes his sister pays a fine and the mishna in *Makkot* that says that he is flogged. The Gemara comments: **Granted, Rabbi Yoḥanan,** who explains the mishna as referring to a case where he was not forewarned, **did not state** his opinion **in accordance with** the opinion of **Reish Lakish,** who explains that the mishna is in accordance with the opinion of Rabbi Meir, **as he establishes** the mishna **in accordance with** the opinion of **the Rabbis,** a preferable option, as that aligns the unattributed mishna with the *halakha*. **However, what is the reason** that **Reish Lakish didn't state** his opinion **in accordance with** the opinion of **Rabbi Yoḥanan?**[N] The Gemara answers: Reish Lakish could have **said to you: Since if they forewarned him** he is **exempt** from payment, **when they did not forewarn him,** he is **exempt as well.**

וְאָזְדוּ לְטַעֲמַיְיהוּ: דְּכִי אֲתָא רַב דִּימִי אָמַר: חַיָּיבֵי מִיתוֹת שׁוֹגְגִין וְחַיָּיבֵי מַלְקִיּוֹת שׁוֹגְגִין וְדָבָר אַחֵר, רַבִּי יוֹחָנָן אָמַר: חַיָּיב, וְרֵישׁ לָקִישׁ אָמַר: פָּטוּר. רַבִּי יוֹחָנָן אָמַר: חַיָּיב, דְּהָא לָא אַתְרוּ בֵּיהּ. רֵישׁ לָקִישׁ אָמַר: פָּטוּר, כֵּיוָן דְּאִילּוּ אַתְרוּ בֵּיהּ – פָּטוּר, כִּי לָא אַתְרוּ בֵּיהּ נַמִי פָּטוּר.

And Rabbi Yoḥanan and Reish Lakish each **follow their** standard lines of **reasoning** in this regard, **as when Rav Dimi came** from Eretz Yisrael to Babylonia, **he said:** With regard to **those** who **unwittingly** performed a transgression for which one is **liable**[N] **to** receive the **death** penalty, or **those** who **unwittingly** performed a transgression for which one is **liable** to receive **lashes, and** that transgression also involved **another matter,** monetary payment, **Rabbi Yoḥanan said:** He is **liable** to pay; since he sinned unwittingly he did not receive the severe punishment. **And Reish Lakish said** he is **exempt.** The Gemara clarifies the rationales for their statements. **Rabbi Yoḥanan said** he is **liable; since they did not forewarn him,** he sinned unwittingly. **Reish Lakish said** he is **exempt; since if they forewarned him** he is **exempt** from payment, **when they did not forewarn him,** he is **exempt as well.**

אֵיתִיבֵיהּ רֵישׁ לָקִישׁ לְרַבִּי יוֹחָנָן: ״וְלֹא יִהְיֶה אָסוֹן עָנוֹשׁ יֵעָנֵשׁ״

Reish Lakish raised an objection to the opinion of **Rabbi Yoḥanan** from the following verse, which describes a case where two people fought and during their struggle they hurt a pregnant woman, causing her to miscarry: **"And yet no harm follow, he shall be punished** as imposed upon him by the woman's husband" (Exodus 21:22).

Perek **III**
Daf **35** Amud **a**

מַאי לָאו אָסוֹן מַמָּשׁ? לָא, דִּין אָסוֹן. אִיכָּא דְּאָמְרִי, אֵיתִיבֵיהּ רַבִּי יוֹחָנָן לְרֵישׁ לָקִישׁ: ״וְלֹא יִהְיֶה אָסוֹן עָנוֹשׁ יֵעָנֵשׁ״ מַאי לָאו – דִּין אָסוֹן? לָא, אָסוֹן מַמָּשׁ.

Is this not referring to **actual harm,** i.e., the woman's death? And the verse states that he pays only if she did not die, but if she died is he exempt, even if he was not forewarned? The Gemara answers: **No,** the verse can be explained to mean: If there is no **sentence of harm.**[N] If the court does not actually sentence him to death, he pays the damages for the miscarried fetus. He is exempt from payment only if he is actually executed. **Some say** a different version of this exchange: **Rabbi Yoḥanan raised an objection to** the opinion of **Reish Lakish: "And yet no harm follow, he shall be punished"** (Exodus 21:22); **is this not** referring to **a sentence of harm?** The Gemara answers: **No,** the verse can be explained to mean: If there is no **actual harm.**

NOTES

Harm and sentence of harm – אָסוֹן וְדִין אָסוֹן: Rashi explains that the harm referred to in the verse is that of the woman dying. He therefore explains that according to the opinion that the verse refers to actual harm, when it says: "And yet no harm follow, he shall be punished" (Exodus 21:22), it means that whenever the woman dies, the one who caused the miscarriage is not liable. According to the opinion that the verse refers to a sentence of harm, it means that the fact that the woman dies is not sufficient to exempt the aggressor from payment, as there must be a sentence of death for her killer, which can be administered only if there was forewarning.

Rabbeinu Ḥananel's version of the text has the names in the text reversed. Rabbi Yoḥanan asks the first version of the question: Is this not referring to actual harm? Reish Lakish asks the second version: Is this not referring to sentence of harm? Accordingly, he understands the harm mentioned in the verse to be the fate of the killer; Rabbi Yoḥanan asks: Is it not only when the killer experiences actual harm, when he is executed by the court, as there were witnesses and forewarning, that he is exempt from payment? The Gemara's response in defense of Reish Lakish's opinion is that no, the verse is referring to the sentence of harm, i.e. to an action for which one is potentially liable to be executed.

אמר רבא: ומי איכא למאן דאמר חייבי מיתות שוגגין חייבים? והא תנא דבי חזקיה: מכה אדם ומכה בהמה,

Rava said: Is there anyone who said that **those** who **unwittingly** performed a transgression for which one is **liable to** receive the **death** penalty **are obligated** to pay? **But didn't** the Sage **of the school of Ḥizkiyya teach:**[N] The verse speaks of **one who smites a person,** and the verse speaks of **one who smites an animal.**[N] The two cases are juxtaposed in the verse "And one who smites an animal shall pay for it, and one who smites a person shall die" (Leviticus 24:21).

מה מכה בהמה – לא חילקת בו בין בשוגג בין במזיד, בין מתכוין לשאין מתכוין, בין דרך ירידה לדרך עלייה, לפוטרו ממון אלא לחייבו ממון – אף מכה אדם לא תחלוק בו בין בשוגג בין במזיד, בין מתכוין לשאין מתכוין, בין דרך ירידה לדרך עלייה – לחייבו ממון, אלא לפוטרו ממון.

Just as in the case of one **who smites an animal, you did not distinguish between** one who did so **unwittingly and** one who did so **intentionally,**[N] **between** one who acted **with intent and one who** acted **with no intent, between** one who smites **in** the course of a **downward motion and** one who smites **in** the course of **an upward motion,** and in all those cases it is not **to exempt** him from paying **money but rather to obligate him to** pay **money; so too, in** the case of one **who smites a person, do not distinguish between** one who did so **unwittingly and** one who did so **intentionally,**[H] **between** one who acted **with intent and one who** acted **with no intent, between** one who smites **in** the course of **a downward motion and** one who smites **in** the course of **an upward motion.** In all those cases as well it is not **to obligate him** to pay **money but rather to exempt him** from paying **money.** The *halakha* in both cases is unconditional; when he smites an animal he is always liable to pay and when he smites a person he is always exempt from payment, regardless of whether or not he is actually executed.

אלא, כי אתא רבין אמר: חייבי מיתות שוגגין כולי עלמא לא פליגי דפטורין. כי פליגי בחייבי מלקות שוגגין ודבר אחר. רבי יוחנן אמר: חייב, חייבי מיתות איתקוש, חייבי מלקיות – לא איתקוש. ריש לקיש אמר: פטור, בפירוש ריבה תורה חייבי מלקיות כחייבי מיתות.

Rather, when Ravin came from Eretz Yisrael to Babylonia, **he said:** With regard to **those** who **unwittingly** performed a transgression for which one is **liable to** receive the **death penalty, everyone agrees that** they **are exempt,** as per the derivation of the Sages of the school of Ḥizkiyya. **When they disagree** it is **with regard to those** who **unwittingly** performed a transgression for which one is **liable to** receive **lashes, and another matter,**[H] for which he is liable to pay money. **Rabbi Yoḥanan said** that he is **obligated** to pay, as **those liable to** receive the **death penalty are juxtaposed** to cases of monetary payment and are unconditionally exempt from payment. However, **those liable** to receive **lashes are not juxtaposed.** Therefore, in the case of one who is liable to receive lashes, unless one is actually flogged, he is obligated to pay for the damage he inflicted. **Reish Lakish said:** He is **exempt, as the Torah explicitly included those liable to** receive **lashes, like those liable to** receive the **death** penalty, and unconditionally exempted them from payment.

HALAKHA

So too, in the case of one who smites a person, do not distinguish between one who did so unwittingly and one who did so intentionally – **אף מכה אדם לא תחלוק בו בין בשוגג בין במזיד**: If one performed a transgression punishable by death and simultaneously performed an action for which he is liable to pay, he is exempt from that payment even if he sinned unwittingly or with no intent, as per the statement of the Sage of the school of Ḥizkiyya (Rambam *Sefer Nashim, Hilkhot Na'ara Betula* 1:13; *Sefer Nezikim, Hilkhot Ḥovel* 4:7; *Shulḥan Arukh, Ḥoshen Mishpat* 423:4).

When they disagree it is with regard to those who unwittingly performed a transgression for which one is liable to receive lashes, and another matter – **כי פליגי בחייבי מלקות שוגגין ודבר אחר**: One who commits a transgression for which he is liable both to be flogged and to pay is flogged and is exempt from payment. However, if he is not flogged for his transgression, e.g., if he performed it unwittingly or without forewarning, he is obligated to pay. The *halakha* is in accordance with the opinion of Rabbi Yoḥanan in his dispute with Reish Lakish (Rambam *Sefer Nashim, Hilkhot Na'ara Betula* 1:11 and *Sefer Nezikim, Hilkhot Geneiva* 3:1).

NOTES

But didn't the Sage of the school of Ḥizkiyya teach – **והא תנא דבי חזקיה**: *Tosafot* and other early commentaries discuss whether this statement of the school of Ḥizkiyya is undisputed. In the Jerusalem Talmud there is no dispute in this regard, and both Rabbi Yoḥanan and Reish Lakish accept this exposition completely. The commentaries ask: Couldn't Rabbi Yoḥanan prove from the mishna that one who is liable to receive the death penalty is exempt from paying the fine, as he maintains that the mishna is referring to a sinner who received no forewarning? Why, then, is it necessary for him to cite proof from a different source? The answer is that the difficulty raised from the statement of the school of Ḥizkiyya is also based on this inference from the mishna. The Rashba claims that the Gemara could have cited proof from the mishna, but it preferred to cite an explicit teaching rather than rely on an inference. Furthermore, unlike the statement of the school of Ḥizkiyya, the mishna does not provide the biblical source for the *halakha*.

One who smites a person and one who smites an animal – **מכה אדם ומכה בהמה**: This exposition is based on the fact that both parts of the verse "And one who smites an animal shall pay for it, and one who smites a person shall die" are superfluous, as the *halakhot* of causing injury to an animal and killing another person are both stated elsewhere. The purpose of this verse, therefore must be to equate the two *halakhot* (Ramah). It cannot be that the Torah is teaching that one who smites a person is also liable to pay in all cases, as clearly one who commits intentional murder receives the greater of the two punishments and is exempt from payment. He therefore derived that just as one who strikes an animal is liable to pay in every case, so too, one who kills a person is exempt from payment in every case (Ritva).

Between one who did so unwittingly and one who did so intentionally – **בין בשוגג בין במזיד**: *Tosafot* explain that these three categories: Unwitting versus intentional, with intent versus with no intent, and one who smites in the course of a downward motion versus one who smites in the course of an upward motion, refer to three different types of monetary liability. Other early commentaries, and *Tosafot* elsewhere, elaborate on this point. Specifically, they explain that unwitting versus intentional relates to intention to kill, generally determined by forewarning; with intent versus with no intent refers to one who intended to kill one person but killed another; in the course of a downward motion versus in the course of an upward motion is relevant to exile. It is a Torah decree that one is liable to be exiled to a city of refuge only if he killed another in a downward movement, e.g., if one fell on the victim or dropped an object upon him. If one killed another in an upward motion, e.g., one who struck another with an ax while lifting it upward, he is exempt, as explained at length in tractate *Makkot*.

NOTES

It is derived by means of a verbal analogy between the term wicked and the term wicked – אָתְיָא רָשָׁע רָשָׁע: The Gemara does not specify the verses upon which this verbal analogy is based, as it appears in several places. Although the meaning is not the same in all of those places, the basic comparison between those liable to be executed and those liable to be flogged is an accepted principle, and the Gemara did not find it necessary to elaborate (see *Shita Mekubbetzet*).

It is derived by means of a verbal analogy between the term smites and the term smites – אָתְיָא מַכֵּה מַכֵּה: The early commentaries discuss the precise nature of this derivation. At first glance, it appears that it is based on juxtaposition of the verses. However, if that is the case, how does the Gemara proceed to reject it based on the term smites when the derivation is not based on a verbal analogy? The Ritva explains that the Gemara was merely questioning the fact that Rava stated that the term smites appears in both verses. *Tosafot* conclude that Rava's derivation is in fact a verbal analogy, which accounts for the question of the Gemara. Accordingly, the phrase: And juxtaposed to it, does not mean that it is a derivation based on juxtaposed verses but is merely noting that the other verse appears adjacent to the first. The notion that a verbal analogy can be based on similar concepts rather than identical terms is well established, as the school of Rabbi Yishmael derives verbal analogies from different words with the same meaning.

HALAKHA

Smiting that causes damage that is not equivalent to the value of a *peruta* – הַכָּאָה שֶׁאֵין בָּהּ שָׁוֶה פְּרוּטָה: One who struck another with a blow that causes damage that is not the equivalent of a *peruta* is liable to be flogged, as he is exempt from payment. The *halakha* is in accordance with the opinion of Rabbi Yoḥanan (Rambam *Sefer Nezikim, Hilkhot Ḥovel* 4:9, 5:3; *Shulḥan Arukh, Ḥoshen Mishpat* 420:2).

הֵיכָן רִיבְּתָה תּוֹרָה? אֲמַר אַבַּיֵי: אָתְיָא "רָשָׁע" "רָשָׁע". רָבָא אֲמַר: אָתְיָא "מַכֵּה" "מַכֵּה". אֲמַר לֵיהּ רַב פַּפָּא לְרָבָא: הֵי מַכֵּה? אִילֵימָא "וּמַכֵּה בְהֵמָה יְשַׁלְּמֶנָּה וּמַכֵּה אָדָם יוּמָת" – הַאי בְּקַטְלָא כְּתִיב! אֶלָּא הַאי "מַכֵּה": "מַכֵּה נֶפֶשׁ בְּהֵמָה יְשַׁלְּמֶנָּה נֶפֶשׁ תַּחַת נָפֶשׁ" וּסְמִיךְ לֵיהּ "וְאִישׁ כִּי יִתֵּן מוּם בַּעֲמִיתוֹ [כַּאֲשֶׁר עָשָׂה כֵּן יֵעָשֶׂה לּוֹ]".

The Gemara asks: **Where did** the **Torah include** those liable to be flogged? **Abaye said:** It is **derived** by means of a verbal analogy between the term **wicked** in the verse "That he is wicked and liable to die" (Numbers 35:31), and the term **wicked**[N] in the verse "That he is wicked and liable to be flogged" (Deuteronomy 25:2). **Rava said:** It is **derived** by means of a verbal analogy between the term **smites** in one verse and the term **smites**[N] in another verse. **Rava Pappa said to Rava:** To **which** term **smites** are you referring? **If we say** that it is the verse **"And one who smites an animal shall pay for it, and one who smites a person shall die"** (Leviticus 24:21), clearly that is not so, as **that is written with regard to death.** Smiting a person in that verse is referring to murder. **Rather,** it is to **this** term **smites** that Rava is referring: **"And he who smites an animal shall pay for it, a life for a life"** (Leviticus 24:18), **and juxtaposed to it,** it is written: **"And a man who places a blemish upon his counterpart, as he has done so shall be done to him"** (Leviticus 24:19). The verses liken those liable to receive lashes to those obligated to pay money, from which it is derived that those liable to receive lashes are exempt from payment.

וְהַאי לָאו "מַכֵּה" הִיא! אֲנַן הַכָּאָה הַכָּאָה קָאָמְרִינַן. וְהָא כִּי כְּתִיב – בְּחוֹבֵל בַּחֲבֵירוֹ הוּא דִּכְתִיב, וְחוֹבֵל בַּחֲבֵירוֹ בַּר תַּשְׁלוּמִין הוּא! אִם אֵינוֹ עִנְיָן לְהַכָּאָה שֶׁיֵּשׁ בָּהּ שָׁוֶה פְּרוּטָה – תְּנֵהוּ עִנְיָן לְהַכָּאָה שֶׁאֵין בָּהּ שָׁוֶה פְּרוּטָה.

The Gemara raises a difficulty: **But this** term that appears in the latter verse **is** "places a blemish," **not smites.** How, then, can one derive a verbal analogy? The Gemara answers: This is not a verbal analogy based on identical terms; rather, it is based on identical concepts. **We are saying** that it is a verbal analogy between **smiting** an animal in the first verse and **smiting** a person in the latter verse. The Gemara asks: **However, when** the second verse **is written, it is written with regard to one who injures another, and one who injures another is subject to payment** and not to lashes. This undermines the proof, as lashes are not mentioned in either verse. The Gemara answers: **If it is not a matter of smiting that** causes damage equivalent to the **value of a *peruta*,** in which case he would pay and would not be flogged, **apply it** to the **matter of smiting that** causes damage that is not equivalent to the **value of a *peruta*.**[H] Since in that case there is no payment for the injury, one is flogged for striking that blow.

Perek **III**
Daf **35** Amud **b**

סוֹף סוֹף לָאו בַּר תַּשְׁלוּמִין הוּא! לָא צְרִיכָא, דִּבַהֲדֵי דְּמַחְיֵיהּ קָרַע שִׁירָאִין דִּילֵיהּ.

The Gemara raises a difficulty: **Ultimately,** one who injured another and is flogged **is not subject to payment,** as he inflicted damage worth less than a *peruta*. How then can a principle be derived that one who is liable to receive lashes does not pay even when he is not actually flogged? The Gemara answers: The juxtaposition of the verses is **necessary only** with regard to a situation **where at the same time that he struck**[N] him **he tore his silk.** In that case, where he performed a transgression for which he is liable to be flogged and is also liable to pay damages, it is derived that he would be exempt from paying damages even if he is not actually flogged.

NOTES

Necessary only with regard to a situation where at the same time that he struck, etc. – לָא צְרִיכָא, דִּבַהֲדֵי דְּמַחְיֵיהּ וכו׳: Based on the formulation of the Gemara, this appears to be a continuation of the previous statement, i.e., it is dealing with a blow that caused damage that is not the equivalent of a *peruta*. This is the implied meaning, as the Gemara did not introduce this section with the term: Rather. The Maharshal, however, claims that this solution renders it unnecessary to explain the verse as referring to a blow that caused damage that is not the equivalent of a *peruta* (see *Penei Yehoshua*). The rationale is that the Torah exempted one who injured another from being punished with lashes only if the obligation to pay stems from that very same transgression. If the obligation for payment results from violation of a different prohibition, the injurer is not exempt from being punished with lashes.

אמר ליה רב חייא לרבא: ולתנא דבי חזקיה, דאמר: "מכה אדם ומכה בהמה" ממאי דבחול כתיב, וליכא לאיפלוגי, דלמא בשבת כתיב, דבבהמה גופה איכא לאיפלוגי?

§ **Rav Ḥiyya said to Rava: And according to the** derivation **of the** *tanna* **of the school of Ḥizkiyya, who said:** The verse speaks of **one who smites a person,** and the verse speaks of **one who smites an animal. From where** does that *tanna* know **that it is written with regard to a weekday and** therefore **there is no** reason **to distinguish** between an unwitting and a purposeful sinner; **perhaps** this case **is stated with regard to** one who injured an animal on **Shabbat,**[N] **when concerning the animal itself there is** reason **to distinguish** between one who did so unwittingly and one who did so intentionally. In the case of one who acted unwittingly, he is not liable to receive the death penalty and should therefore be obligated to pay, whereas one who acted intentionally is exempt from payment because he receives the death penalty for desecrating Shabbat. If so, there is no source to exempt from payment one who is not actually executed.

לא סלקא דעתך, דכתיב "ומכה בהמה ישלמנה ומכה אדם יומת". היכי דמי? אי דלא אתרו ביה – מכה אדם אמאי יומת? אלא פשיטא – דאתרו ביה, ואי בשבת – מכה בהמה ישלמנה?! אלא לאו – בחול.

The Gemara answers: That notion **should not enter your mind, as it is written: "And one who smites an animal shall pay for it, and one who smites a person shall die"** (Leviticus 24:21). **What are the circumstances** discussed in this verse? **If** it is a case **where** the witnesses **did not forewarn him,** i.e., when **one who smites a person** is not forewarned, **why should he be executed?** There is no corporal punishment, neither lashes nor execution, without forewarning. **Rather,** it is **obvious that they forewarned him. And if** the verse is referring to one who sinned **on Shabbat** after forewarning, would **one who smites an animal** be obligated to **pay for it?** He is executed and certainly exempt from payment. **Rather, isn't** the verse clearly referring to a case **during the week?**

אמר ליה רב פפא לאביי: לרבה, דאמר: חידוש הוא שחידשה תורה בקנס, ואף על גב דמיקטיל משלם, מתניתין כמאן מוקים לה? אי כרבי מאיר – קשיא בתו, אי כרבי נחוניא בן הקנה – קשיא אחותו, אי כרבי יצחק – קשיא ממזרת!

§ **Rav Pappa said to Abaye: According to Rabba,** who **said: It is a novel element that the Torah innovated with regard to** the halakhic category **of fine, and even though he is executed he pays** the fine; **in accordance with whose** opinion **does** Rabba **establish the mishna? If** it is **in accordance with** the opinion **of Rabbi Meir,**[N] it is **difficult;** why is he exempt if he raped **his daughter?** According to Rabba, Rabbi Meir is of the opinion that even one liable to receive the death penalty pays the fine. **If** it is **in accordance with** the opinion of **Rabbi Neḥunya ben HaKana,** it is **difficult,** as why does the mishna rule that he pays the fine for raping **his sister?** Rabbi Neḥunya holds that one liable to receive *karet* is exempt from the fine, like those liable to receive the death penalty. **If** the mishna is **in accordance with** the opinion of **Rabbi Yitzḥak,**[N] who rules that lashes are not administered to those liable to receive *karet* and therefore they are obligated to pay the fine; however, one who is flogged is exempt from payment, it is **difficult,** as why did the mishna rule that he is obligated to pay the fine for raping a ***mamzeret,***[N] for which he is liable to receive lashes?

NOTES

Perhaps this case is stated with regard to Shabbat – דלמא בשבת כתיב: Some commentaries explain that the Gemara is not suggesting that the verse refers only to Shabbat, but rather states a principle that applies equally to blows struck on weekdays and those struck on Shabbat. Once it is established that the verse refers to Shabbat as well, an additional distinction can be made between unwitting and intentional actions. If that is the case, this superfluous verse could teach that there is indeed a distinction between unwitting and intentional acts both in the case of one who kills an animal and one who kills a person (Ritva; *Shita Mekubbetzet*).

In accordance with whose opinion…if it is in accordance with Rabbi Meir – מתניתין כמאן...אי כרבי מאיר: *Tosafot* note that the Gemara did not list all the Sages whose opinions did not correspond with the mishna. Rather, it mentions those opinions cited earlier, and which were suggested as the opinion of the *tanna* of the mishna. Only after listing those *tanna'im* does the Gemara mention Rabbi Yitzḥak, whose opinion was not cited earlier, even though the *mamzeret* appears first in the mishna, (*Shita Mekubbetzet*).

The opinion of Rabbi Yitzḥak – שיטת רבי יצחק: His opinion, which is merely alluded to here, is that even though most of those liable to receive *karet* violate a prohibition, they do not receive lashes. The reason is that just as prohibitions punishable by death at the hands of the court do not render the offender liable to be flogged, the same applies to prohibitions punishable by death at the hand of Heaven, e.g., *karet*.

If the mishna is in accordance with the opinion of Rabbi Yitzḥak, it is difficult…a *mamzeret* – אי כרבי יצחק קשיא ממזרת: Ostensibly, it could be explained that Rabbi Yitzḥak agrees with Rabbi Meir that one receives lashes and pays, in which case there would be no difficulty from the case of a *mamzeret*. Why then does the Gemara say that it is difficult? Various answers were suggested. The Rashba explains that the Gemara did not want to establish Rabbi Yitzḥak's opinion in accordance with the individual opinion of Rabbi Meir. In the *Shita Mekubbetzet* there is an inference from *Tosafot* that even though the opinion of Rabbi Neḥunya was established in accordance with that of Rabbi Meir, as is indicated in the language of his statement, there is no indication from the statement of Rabbi Yitzḥak that he agrees with Rabbi Meir. Rabbeinu Ḥananel contends that according to Rabbi Yitzḥak lashes are a more severe punishment than *karet*, and those liable to receive *karet* are exempt from lashes only because it is derived from the verses to be lenient in their regard. He therefore maintains that just as those liable to be executed are exempt from payment, the same applies to those who receive lashes. All this is in accordance with the approach of the Gemara.

In the Jerusalem Talmud, it is explained that there is no difficulty, as the mishna can be understood as referring to a *mamzer* who raped a *mamzeret*, in which case there is no liability to receive lashes at all. The Ramban and other commentaries explain that the Gemara does not understand the mishna in this manner because in the case of a *mamzer* who raped a *mamzeret* there is nothing novel, as she is permitted to him, and therefore it is no different from a case of a Jew who rapes a Jewish woman.

הָנִיחָא אִי סָבַר לַהּ כְּרַבִּי יוֹחָנָן – הוּא נָמֵי מְתָרֵץ לַהּ כְּרַבִּי יוֹחָנָן, אֶלָּא אִי סָבַר כְּרֵישׁ לָקִישׁ – הֵיכִי מְתָרֵץ לַהּ? עַל כָּרְחָךְ כְּרַבִּי יוֹחָנָן סְבִירָא לֵיהּ.

This works out **well if** Rabba **holds in accordance with** the opinion of **Rabbi Yoḥanan,** who says that one who did not receive forewarning is obligated to pay even if he performed a transgression for which he is liable to be flogged, as **he can explain** the mishna **as well, in accordance with** the opinion of **Rabbi Yoḥanan,** that he is obligated to pay in cases where there was no forewarning. **However, if he holds in accordance with** the opinion of **Reish Lakish,** that one who violated a prohibition for which one is liable to be flogged is exempt from payment even if he was not forewarned, **how does** he **explain** the mishna? The mishna does not correspond to any of the aforementioned opinions. The Gemara answers: **You** must **say perforce** that **he holds in accordance with** the opinion of **Rabbi Yoḥanan**[N] in this regard.

אָמַר לֵיהּ רַב מַתָּנָא לְאַבָּיֵי: לְרֵישׁ לָקִישׁ, דְּאָמַר: בְּפֵירוּשׁ רִיבְּתָה תּוֹרָה חַיָּיבֵי מַלְקִיּוֹת כְּחַיָּיבֵי מִיתוֹת, מַאן תַּנָּא דִּפְלִיג עֲלֵיהּ דְּרַבִּי נְחוּנְיָא בֶּן הַקָּנָה – אִי רַבִּי מֵאִיר, אִי רַבִּי יִצְחָק.

Rav Mattana said to Abaye: According to Reish Lakish, who said that **the Torah explicitly included those** who are **liable to receive lashes** and accorded them legal status **like those** who are **liable to receive the death** penalty, unconditionally exempting them from payment; **who is the *tanna* who disagrees**[N] **with Rabbi Neḥunya ben HaKana** and obligates one who is liable both to receive *karet* and to be flogged to pay, and the lashes do not exempt him from payment? The Gemara answers: He holds in accordance with **either Rabbi Meir,** who says that one who is liable to receive lashes is liable to pay a fine, **or Rabbi Yitzḥak,** who rules that those liable to receive *karet* are not flogged.

תָּנוּ רַבָּנַן: עֲרָיוֹת וּשְׁנִיּוֹת לָעֲרָיוֹת אֵין לָהֶן לֹא קְנָס וְלֹא פִּיתּוּי. הַמְּמָאֶנֶת אֵין לָהּ לֹא קְנָס וְלֹא פִּיתּוּי. אַיְילוֹנִית אֵין לָהּ לֹא קְנָס וְלֹא פִּיתּוּי, וְהַיּוֹצֵאת מִשּׁוּם שֵׁם רָע אֵין לָהּ לֹא קְנָס וְלֹא פִּיתּוּי.

§ The Gemara turns its attention to a related issue. **The Sages taught:** Women who are **forbidden relatives and secondary forbidden relatives**[B] receive **neither** payment of **a fine**[H] for rape **nor** payment of a fine for **seduction.**[N] Similarly, a girl **who refuses**[N] to remain married to her husband receives **neither** payment of **a fine** for rape **nor** payment of a fine for **seduction.**[N] Because she was married, she no longer has the presumptive status of a virgin. **A sexually underdeveloped woman** [*ailonit*] who will never reach puberty and therefore her legal status is not that of a young woman, receives **neither** payment of **a fine** for rape **nor** payment of a fine for **seduction. And one who leaves** her **husband due to a bad reputation** receives **neither** payment of **a fine** for rape **nor** payment of a fine for **seduction.**

BACKGROUND

Secondary forbidden relatives – שְׁנִיּוֹת לָעֲרָיוֹת: These are relatives with whom relations are prohibited as incestuous by rabbinic decree. The Torah (Leviticus, chapters 18 and 20) lists many forbidden incestuous relationships. The Sages expanded this list to include relations with one's maternal and paternal grandmother; the mother of one's maternal and paternal grandfather; the wife of one's maternal and paternal grandfather, even though she is not one's grandmother; the wives of one's father's maternal brothers, while his paternal brother's wives are prohibited by Torah law; the wives of one's maternal uncles; one's son's or daughter's daughter-in-law; one's great-granddaughters; one's wife's great-granddaughters from previous marriages; and one's wife's maternal and paternal great-grandmothers. Relations with these forbidden relatives are also referred to as prohibitions resulting from a mitzva. Violation of these prohibitions is punishable by lashes for rebelliousness administered for transgression of a rabbinic decree.

HALAKHA

These do not have a fine – אֵלּוּ שֶׁאֵין לָהֶן קְנָס: The Rambam writes that one who refuses her husband, a sexually underdeveloped woman [*ailonit*], and a woman with a bad reputation as a minor are not entitled to payment of the fine. The Ra'avad states that the ruling that an *ailonit* does not receive the fine is not the *halakha*, as it is the opinion of Rabbi Meir; while the Rabbis maintain that she is considered a minor until the age of twenty, and she is therefore entitled to the fine. The *Tur* agrees (Rambam *Sefer Nashim*, *Hilkhot Na'ara Betula* 1:9; *Tur*, *Even HaEzer* 177).

NOTES

You must say perforce that he holds in accordance with the opinion of Rabbi Yoḥanan – עַל כָּרְחָךְ כְּרַבִּי יוֹחָנָן: The early commentaries ask: Why not say that Rabba explains the mishna in accordance with the opinion of Ulla that one always pays and is not flogged? Rashi resolves this difficulty and explains that one who does not accept Rabbi Yoḥanan's opinion certainly would not accept Ulla's opinion. Rabbi Aharon HaLevi proves that Ulla's opinion cannot be reconciled with that of Reish Lakish, and the two Sages certainly disagree. The Ramban maintains that it is theoretically possible for Rabba to interpret the mishna in accordance with the opinion of Ulla, but the Gemara does not seek to completely clarify the matter at this juncture. Instead, it merely notes that with regard to the dispute between Reish Lakish and Rabbi Yoḥanan, Rabba's statement is in accordance with the opinion of the latter.

Who is the *tanna* who disagrees, etc. – מַאן תַּנָּא דִּפְלִיג וכו׳: Rashi infers that although Reish Lakish maintains that the mishna disagrees with Rabbi Neḥunya, he cannot establish it in accordance with the opinion of Rabbi Yitzḥak, as explained above with regard to Rabba's statement, but only in accordance with the opinion of Rabbi Meir. Rashi's explanation here is consistent with his opinion that this question does not relate specifically to this mishna in particular, but rather relates to several *mishnayot* that clearly indicate that those liable to receive *karet* must pay as well. Those *mishnayot* correspond to the opinion of Rabbi Yitzḥak. The Ritva agrees. Rabbeinu Ḥananel explains that Reish Lakish maintains that since Rabbi Yitzḥak is of the opinion that no lashes are administered to those liable to receive *karet*, a person can be liable both to receive *karet* and to pay, but not to receive lashes and pay. In the Jerusalem Talmud, it is similarly explained that a person does not receive two punishments for a single transgression if he was convicted by a court, but a liability to be punished at the hand of Heaven does not exempt him from a debt to others.

Neither a fine for rape nor a fine for seduction – לֹא קְנָס וְלֹא פִּיתּוּי: *Tosafot* explain that the term fine is more suitable for a rape, as the perpetrator is also penalized with the obligation to marry his victim. In the *Shita Mekubbetzet* it is explained according to Rashi that the payment is not called a fine in the case of a seduction, as he acted with her consent. Furthermore, a seducer is liable for speaking, whereas a rapist is punished for acting.

A girl who refuses – הַמְּמָאֶנֶת: A girl who refuses her husband is a fatherless girl who was married off by her mother or brothers when she was a minor. That marriage is not valid by Torah law, and the Sages ruled that if the minor expresses that she does not wish to remain with her husband, not only does she leave the marriage but the marriage is retroactively negated, and it is as though she was never married. Rashi claims that the reason there is no fine with regard to a girl who refused is that she is no longer considered a virgin because she was married. According to his opinion, this *halakha* contains no novel element, and it is only stated to enable the Gemara to infer that other minors are entitled to the fine.

The Ramban asks: If there are witnesses that she never entered into seclusion with her husband, why shouldn't she be entitled to the fine? And if there are no witnesses to that effect, this *halakha* is obvious. He answers that even if there were witnesses that there was seclusion, one might have thought that since she claims she is a virgin, the rapist should not receive the benefit of the doubt and should be required to pay the fine. The Rashba contends that even if witnesses testified that she was never in seclusion with her husband, she still does not receive the fine, as the witnesses are unable to achieve a degree of certainty that would remove all doubt; the rapist is not required to pay in a case of uncertainty.

Tosafot question Rashi's interpretation, as they point out that according to his approach there is no difference whether he raped or seduced her when she was a minor or whether he did so when she was a young woman, and therefore perhaps the inference should have been that all other young women receive the fine. In the *Shita Mekubbetzet* that assertion is rejected: One who refuses, in present tense, indicates a minor, as she cannot refuse her husband once she reaches puberty. Were the *baraita* referring to a young woman, it should have said: One who refused, in past tense. In any case, *Tosafot* explain otherwise: The Gemara is referring to one who was raped or seduced by her husband while she was still married to him. The novel element is that one does not say that if she refuses him his act is retroactively rendered rape or seduction. Later commentaries explain that the reason that this is not considered rape is that it is deemed rape or seduction only if it is outside the framework of marriage. Otherwise, the categories of rape and seduction are inapplicable.

Nor seduction – וְלֹא פִּיתּוּי: *Tosafot* explain that these words are merely added because the terms are usually listed together, as this *halakha* applies to a young woman as well, and one who seduces a fatherless young woman certainly is not liable to pay the fine, as she consented. The Rashba and the Rosh maintain that even a fatherless minor is not entitled to receive the fine for seduction, as a competent minor can also relinquish her right to the fine, and she does so by agreeing to be seduced. The Ritva disagrees and contends that it can be learned from here that the legal status of the seduction of any minor is like that of rape, as even though she has a certain measure of competency in terms of forgiving a debt, she is not considered to be fully competent in terms of complicity with seduction.

מַאי עֲרָיוֹת וּמַאי שְׁנִיּוֹת לַעֲרָיוֹת? אִילֵימָא עֲרָיוֹת

The Gemara elaborates. **What is** the meaning of **forbidden relatives, and what is** the meaning of **secondary forbidden relatives** in the context of this *baraita*? **If we say that forbidden relatives** means

Perek **III**
Daf **36** Amud **a**

עֲרָיוֹת מַמָּשׁ, שְׁנִיּוֹת – מִדִּבְרֵי סוֹפְרִים, כֵּיוָן דְּמִדְּאוֹרַיְיתָא חַזְיָא לֵיהּ – אַמַּאי אֵין לָהֶן קְנָס? אֶלָּא: עֲרָיוֹת – חַיָּיבֵי מִיתוֹת בֵּית דִּין, שְׁנִיּוֹת – חַיָּיבֵי כָרֵיתוֹת, אֲבָל חַיָּיבֵי לָאוִין – יֵשׁ לָהֶן קְנָס, וּמַנִּי – שִׁמְעוֹן הַתִּימְנִי הִיא.

actual forbidden relatives[N] prohibited by Torah law, and **secondary relatives** means, as it does in most cases, relatives prohibited **by rabbinic law,**[N] that cannot be, for **since** those secondary relatives **are suitable for him** to marry and are not prohibited **by Torah** law,[N] **why do they not** receive **a fine** if they are raped or seduced? **Rather,** the meaning of these terms in this context is different: **Forbidden relatives** are **those** for which one is **liable** to receive a **court-imposed death** penalty; **secondary relatives** are **those** for which one is **liable** to receive ***karet,*** which are relatively less severe than those for which one is executed. **However, those liable for** violating regular **prohibitions** receive payment of a **fine** if they are raped or seduced. **And** according to **whose** opinion is the *baraita* taught? **It is** the opinion of **Shimon HaTimni,** who exempts from paying a fine only one who rapes a woman with whom betrothal is ineffective.

אִיכָּא דְּאָמְרִי: עֲרָיוֹת – חַיָּיבֵי מִיתוֹת ב״ד וְחַיָּיבֵי כָרֵיתוֹת, שְׁנִיּוֹת – חַיָּיבֵי לָאוִין, מַנִּי – רַבִּי שִׁמְעוֹן בֶּן מְנַסְיָא הִיא.

Some say that we can explain **that forbidden relatives** refers to all relatives with whom relations are forbidden by severe prohibitions, both **those** for which one is **liable to death** by the **court and those** for which he is **liable to *karet,*** and **secondary** relatives refers to **those** relatives with whom one who engages in relations is **liable for** violating regular **prohibitions.** According to this approach, **whose** opinion does this follow? **It is** that of **Rabbi Shimon ben Menasya,** who maintains that even a woman raped by a man forbidden to her by a regular prohibition is not entitled to the fine, despite the fact that betrothal is effective in that case.

״הַמְמָאֶנֶת אֵין לָהּ לֹא קְנָס וְלֹא פִּיתּוּי״. הָא קְטַנָּה בְּעָלְמָא – אִית לַהּ, מַנִּי – רַבָּנַן הִיא, דְּאָמְרִי: קְטַנָּה יֵשׁ לָהּ קְנָס. אֵימָא סֵיפָא: אַיְילוֹנִית אֵין לָהּ לֹא קְנָס וְלֹא פִּיתּוּי. אֲתָא לְרַבִּי מֵאִיר, דַּאֲמַר: קְטַנָּה אֵין לָהּ קְנָס, וְהָא – מִקַּטְנוּתָהּ יָצְתָה לְבֶגֶר. רֵישָׁא רַבָּנַן וְסֵיפָא רַבִּי מֵאִיר!

§ The *baraita* stated: A girl **who refuses** to remain married to her husband receives **neither** payment of **a fine** for rape **nor** payment of a fine for **seduction,** because she was married and therefore lost her presumptive status as a virgin. The Gemara infers: But **an ordinary minor** girl **has** a fine for rape. If so, in accordance with **whose** opinion is the *baraita* taught? **It is** the opinion of **the Rabbis, who say: A minor** girl **has** a fine for rape. The Gemara asks: **Say the latter clause** of the *baraita*: **A sexually underdeveloped woman** [*ailonit*] **has neither a fine** for rape **nor** a fine for **seduction,** as she will not develop the signs of puberty and her legal status is that of a minor until she is twenty, at which point she assumes the status of a grown woman. In that *halakha*, the *baraita* **comes to** the opinion of **Rabbi Meir, who said: A minor** girl **does not have** a **fine** for rape, **and** the same is true for **this** *ailonit*, who **emerged from her** status as a **minor** at the age of twenty **to** the status of **a grown woman,** skipping the stage of a young woman. **The first clause** of the *baraita* **is** in accordance with the opinion of **the Rabbis, and the latter clause is** in accordance with the opinion of **Rabbi Meir.**

NOTES

Actual forbidden relatives – עֲרָיוֹת מַמָּשׁ: The phrase: Actual forbidden relatives, refers to those relatives with whom relations are prohibited by Torah law (see Leviticus, chapter 18). An intermediate category of people with whom relations are prohibited by Torah law, even though they do not fall into the category of actual forbidden relatives, is omitted from the *baraita*, which is an additional reason the term: Secondary relatives, should not be interpreted in the standard manner.

Secondary relatives by rabbinic law – שְׁנִיּוֹת מִדִּבְרֵי סוֹפְרִים: As explained by Rashi, there is a list of secondary forbidden relatives, women who are not close relatives by Torah law but are prohibited by rabbinic decree as a safeguard to Torah law. In the second chapter of *Yevamot*, sixteen women are listed as secondary relatives, with whom marriage takes effect but the man is required to divorce her; the Sages penalized these women by stripping them of the right to a marriage contract and other rights to which a married woman is entitled. However, a child born of such a relationship is not rendered unfit, and the woman herself is not disqualified from marrying a priest due to this marriage.

Since they are suitable for him by Torah law – כֵּיוָן דְּמִדְּאוֹרַיְיתָא חַזְיָא לֵיהּ: The question is raised: With regard to a woman in the category of a secondary forbidden relative, the assertion that since she is suitable for him by Torah law, she is entitled to the fine, is by no means obvious. It could be asserted that since he is required to divorce her and is not allowed to sustain her as his wife, even though it is by rabbinic decree, he does not fulfill the requirement "And to him she shall be as a wife" (Deuteronomy 22:19). The fact is that a Gibeonite woman, who is prohibited by rabbinic law, is listed in the mishna together with a *mamzeret*.

The answer given is that there is a distinction between the *halakha* of a Gibeonite, with regard to whom there is a general rabbinic decree prohibiting her from entering the congregation of Israel, and secondary prohibitions, prohibited as a safeguard, with regard to which the Sages certainly did not deny them their right to the fine (*Shita Mekubbetzet*; *Beit Aharon*).

HALAKHA

Until when can a girl refuse to remain married – עַד מָתַי הַבַּת מְמָאֶנֶת: A girl can refuse to remain married to her husband until two pubic hairs emerge after she reaches the age of twelve years and one day. The *halakha* is in accordance with the opinion of Rabbi Meir in this regard, as the discussion in several places in the Gemara is according to his opinion. If two hairs did not grow and she did not give birth, as that is also a sign of puberty, she remains a minor even after the age of twelve. This applies only if it was definitely determined that the hairs did not grow, as the assumption is that two hairs are present in a girl that age. Even if she was examined and no hairs were discovered, if she engaged in sexual intercourse the assumption is that the hairs were severed as a result. Some authorities maintain that today one should rule stringently and not allow refusal after she reaches the age of twelve under any circumstances (Rambam *Sefer Nashim, Hilkhot Geirushin* 11:4; *Shulḥan Arukh, Even HaEzer* 155:12, and see 19–22).

NOTES

Until the black is greater than the white – עַד שֶׁיִּרְבֶּה שָׁחוֹר עַל הַלָּבָן: Although everyone agrees that the girl becomes a young woman as soon as two pubic hairs emerge, there is a distinction between a young woman and a grown woman, one of whose characteristic signs is the area covered by the black pubic hairs is greater than the white skin of the genital area. A young woman is in certain respects an intermediate stage between a minor and a grown woman, as her father retains certain rights over his daughter while she is still a young woman. Therefore, one might have thought that until she becomes a grown woman, she can refuse to remain married to her husband and dissolve a marriage into which she entered as a minor. According to one opinion in tractate *Yevamot*, even a woman with children can refuse and thereby dissolve a marriage that she entered as a minor.

Rav should have said: This is the statement of Rabbi Meir and Rabbi Yehuda – זוֹ דִּבְרֵי רַבִּי מֵאִיר וְרַבִּי יְהוּדָה מִיבְּעֵי לֵיהּ: This question is unusual, as there is no expectation that all the Sages who share a particular opinion would be listed. Indeed, *Tosafot* prove that other *tanna'im* also agree with Rabbi Meir's opinion. Here, however, the Gemara should have mentioned that this is the opinion of Rabbi Yehuda as well, both because he disagrees with Rabbi Meir with regard to several *halakhot* related to this topic, and because there is an attempt to prove that the *mishnayot* in this chapter are not necessarily all in accordance with the opinion of Rabbi Meir (see *Shita Mekubbetzet*).

They have a claim concerning virginity – יֵשׁ לָהֶן טַעֲנַת בְּתוּלִים: There are two distinct, albeit similar, interpretations of this expression. According to Rashi, it means these women can claim they are virgins, whereas the Rid and Ramban maintain that others can register a claim that contrary to pre-marriage expectations, she was not a virgin. The novel element here is that the Sages did not enact a marriage contract for a deaf-mute, so if there is a claim concerning virginity, the husband must have written a marriage contract for her as a virgin, and he now claims that his was an erroneous transaction.

וְכִי תֵּימָא: כּוּלָּהּ רַבִּי מֵאִיר הִיא, וּבִמְמָאֶנֶת סָבַר לָהּ כְּרַבִּי יְהוּדָה; וּמִי סָבַר לָהּ?! וְהָתַנְיָא: עַד מָתַי הַבַּת מְמָאֶנֶת? עַד שֶׁתָּבִיא שְׁתֵּי שְׂעָרוֹת, דִּבְרֵי רַבִּי מֵאִיר. רַבִּי יְהוּדָה אוֹמֵר: עַד שֶׁיִּרְבֶּה שָׁחוֹר עַל הַלָּבָן!

And if you say that **the entire** *baraita* **is** in accordance with the opinion of **Rabbi Meir, and with regard to** a girl **who refuses** to remain married Rabbi Meir **holds in accordance with** the opinion of **Rabbi Yehuda,** that not only a minor girl but a young woman may also end her marriage through refusal, and the *baraita* is referring to a young woman and not to a minor; **but does he maintain that** opinion? **But isn't it taught** in a *baraita* that he disagrees with Rabbi Yehuda in this matter? It was taught: **Until when can a girl refuse** to remain married?[H] **Until she develops two** pubic **hairs,** signs of puberty rendering her a young woman; this is **the statement of Rabbi Meir. Rabbi Yehuda says:** She can refuse **until** the area covered by the **black** pubic hairs **is greater than the white**[NB] skin of the genital area. That occurs approximately six months later, at which point she becomes a grown woman.

אֶלָּא רַבִּי יְהוּדָה הִיא, וּבִקְטַנָּה סָבַר לָהּ כְּרַבִּי מֵאִיר. וּמִי סָבַר לָהּ? וְהָאָמַר רַב יְהוּדָה אָמַר רַב: זוֹ דִּבְרֵי רַבִּי מֵאִיר. וְאִם אִיתָא, זוֹ דִּבְרֵי רַבִּי מֵאִיר וְרַבִּי יְהוּדָה מִיבְּעֵי לֵיהּ! הַאי תַּנָּא סָבַר לָהּ כְּרַבִּי מֵאִיר בַּחֲדָא, וּפָלֵיג עֲלֵיהּ בַּחֲדָא.

Rather, the Gemara suggests: The *baraita* **is** in accordance with the opinion of **Rabbi Yehuda, and with** regard to **a minor** girl, **he holds in accordance with** the opinion of **Rabbi Meir, who says** that a minor girl does not receive payment of a fine for rape, and therefore, an *ailonit* is not entitled to payment. The Gemara asks: **But does he maintain that** opinion? **But didn't Rav Yehuda say** that **Rav said** with regard to the mishna below (40b), which states: Any case where there is the right of a father to effect the sale of his daughter as a Hebrew maidservant, i.e., when she is a minor, there is no fine if she is raped, **this is the statement of Rabbi Meir? And if it is so** that Rabbi Yehuda maintains that opinion, Rav **should have** said: **This is the statement of Rabbi Meir and Rabbi Yehuda.**[N] Rather, **this** *tanna* of the *baraita* **holds in accordance with** the opinion of **Rabbi Meir with regard to one** *halakha*, that there is no fine for the rape of a minor, **and disagrees with him with regard to one** *halakha*, that a young woman may conclude her marriage through refusal.

רַפְרָם אָמַר: מַאי מְמָאֶנֶת – הָרְאוּיָה לְמָאֵן. וְלִיתְנֵי קְטַנָּה! קַשְׁיָא.

Rafram said: This entire *baraita* is in accordance with the opinion of Rabbi Meir, and **what is** the meaning of the statement: With regard to a girl **who refuses,** there is neither a fine for rape nor a fine for seduction? It is referring to **one who is fit to refuse,** i.e., as long as she is a minor she is not entitled to the fine. The Gemara asks: **And** if that is the case, **let** the *tanna* simply **teach** the *halakha* with regard to **a minor.** Why teach a simple *halakha* in so convoluted a manner? The Gemara concludes: Indeed, this is **difficult.**

״אַיְילוֹנִית אֵין לָהּ לֹא קְנָס וְלֹא פִּיתּוּי״. וּרְמִינְהִי: הַחֵרֶשֶׁת וְהַשּׁוֹטָה וְהָאַיְילוֹנִית יֵשׁ לָהֶן קְנָס וְיֵשׁ לָהֶן טַעֲנַת בְּתוּלִים! וְהָא מַאי רוּמְיָא? הָא – רַבִּי מֵאִיר, הָא – רַבָּנַן. וּדְקָאָרֵי לָהּ מַאי קָאָרֵי לָהּ?

§ The *baraita* stated: **An** *ailonit* **has neither a fine** for rape **nor** a fine for **seduction. And** the Gemara **raises a contradiction** from a *baraita*: **A deaf-mute, an imbecile, and an** *ailonit* **have a fine** for rape **and they have a claim concerning virginity.**[N] If one of these women married with the presumptive status of a virgin and received a corresponding marriage contract, her husband can cause her to lose her marriage contract by claiming that she was not a virgin. The Gemara rejects this argument: **And what is the contradiction in this?** It can be explained simply: **This** *baraita*, in which it was taught that the *ailonit* receives no fine, is in accordance with the opinion of **Rabbi Meir; that** *baraita*, in which it was taught that the *ailonit* receives a fine, is in accordance with the opinion of **the Rabbis.** The Gemara is puzzled: **And** as the resolution is so obvious, **he who raised** the contradiction, **why did he raise it?** The dispute between Rabbi Meir and the Rabbis in this matter is known.

BACKGROUND

Until the black is greater than the white – עַד שֶׁיִּרְבֶּה שָׁחוֹר עַל הַלָּבָן: One of the first stages is the appearance of pubic hair, which indicates the passage from minority to majority. Only after the passage of time do hairs cover most of the pubic region. The *halakha* does not require that the entire area be covered with hair, but once the area covered by the black pubic hairs is greater than the white skin of the genital area is she considered a grown woman.

מִשּׁוּם דְּאִית לֵיהּ לְמִירְמָא אַחֲרִיתִי עִילָּוֵיהּ: הַחֵרֶשֶׁת וְהַשּׁוֹטָה וְהַבּוֹגֶרֶת וּמוּכַּת עֵץ – אֵין לָהֶן טַעֲנַת בְּתוּלִים, הַסּוּמָא וְאַיְילוֹנִית – יֵשׁ לָהֶן טַעֲנַת בְּתוּלִים. סוּמְכוֹס אוֹמֵר מִשּׁוּם רַבִּי מֵאִיר: סוּמָא אֵין לָהּ טַעֲנַת בְּתוּלִים!

The Gemara answers: He cited this *baraita* **due to the fact that he has another** *baraita* from which **to raise as a contradiction to it: A deaf-mute, and an imbecile, and a grown woman,**[H] **and a woman whose hymen was torn** not in the course of sexual relations,[H] **do not have a claim concerning virginity,** as they do not have the presumptive status of a virgin. However, **a blind** woman **and an** *ailonit*[H] **have a claim concerning virginity. Sumakhos says in the name of Rabbi Meir: A blind** woman **does not have a claim concerning virginity.** The *baraitot* contradict each other with regard to the claim concerning virginity of a deaf-mute and an imbecile.

אָמַר רַב שֵׁשֶׁת: לָא קַשְׁיָא; הָא – רַבָּן גַּמְלִיאֵל, וְהָא – רַבִּי יְהוֹשֻׁעַ. אֵימַר דִּשְׁמַעַתְּ לֵיהּ לְרַבָּן גַּמְלִיאֵל הֵיכָא דְּקָא טָעֲנָה אִיהִי, הֵיכָא דְּלָא קָא טָעֲנָה אִיהִי מִי שְׁמַעַתְּ לֵיהּ? אִין, כֵּיוָן דְּאָמַר רַבָּן גַּמְלִיאֵל מְהֵימְנָא, כְּגוֹן זוֹ "פְּתַח פִּיךָ לְאִלֵּם" הוּא.

Rav Sheshet said: This is **not difficult,** as **this** *baraita* is in accordance with the opinion of **Rabban Gamliel,**[N] who holds that a woman who, in response to a claim concerning her virginity, is believed if she says that she was raped after her betrothal and therefore does not lose her marriage contract. **And that** *baraita* is in accordance with the opinion of **Rabbi Yehoshua,** who says that a woman is not believed if she makes that claim, and therefore she loses her marriage contract. The Gemara asks: **Say that you heard** that **Rabban Gamliel** accepts her contention in a case **where she claims** that she was raped after the betrothal; however, in a case **where she did not claim** that that was the case, **did you hear** that **he** accepts her contention? The Gemara answers: **Yes, since Rabban Gamliel said** she is **believed** when she states that she was raped after betrothal, the deaf-mute and the imbecile are also believed even though they are unable to make the claim, as in a cases **like that,** it **is** a case of: **"Open your mouth for the mute"** (Proverbs 31:8). When a person lacks the capacity to proffer the claim on his own, the court makes the claim on her behalf.

"וְהַבּוֹגֶרֶת אֵין לָהּ טַעֲנַת בְּתוּלִים". וְהָאָמַר רַב: בּוֹגֶרֶת נוֹתְנִין לָהּ לַיְלָה הָרִאשׁוֹן!

§ The *baraita* stated: **A grown woman does not have a claim concerning virginity**[B] because of changes as her body matures, her hymen is no longer completely intact. The Gemara asks: **But didn't Rav say:** The Sages **give a grown** woman who had relations on her wedding night, **the entire first night,**[H] during which she may have relations with her husband several times? Any blood seen during that night is attributed to the blood of her hymen, which is ritually pure, and not menstrual blood. Apparently, even a grown woman has her hymen intact.

NOTES

This *baraita* is in accordance with the opinion of Rabban Gamliel – הָא רַבָּן גַּמְלִיאֵל: Rashi explains that this refers to the claim: I was raped after you betrothed me. In the first chapter of this tractate, Rabban Gamliel maintains that a woman is believed when she makes that claim. According to his opinion, although a deaf-mute lacks the halakhic intelligence to make that claim, the court makes the claim on her behalf. The Ramban asks: Isn't a case conceivable where he betrothed her and then consummated the marriage immediately, in which case that claim would not be accepted even from a woman with halakhic intelligence; so how can the court make that claim on behalf of a deaf-mute? Therefore, he explains that the claim made on her behalf is that her hymen was accidentally torn, which is effective even if they had relations immediately after betrothal. Rabbi Meir maintains that a woman in that condition is entitled to a marriage contract of two hundred dinars. This interpretation is especially apt according to Rabbi Shmuel HaNagid's variant reading: This is the opinion of Rabbi Meir in the name of Rabban Gamliel; this is the opinion of Rabbi Meir in the name of Rabbi Yehoshua. Rabbi Zeraḥya HaLevi contends that the reference is to Rabban Gamliel and Rabbi Yehoshua's opinion with regard to the presumptive status of her body. He explains that Rabban Gamliel considers her presumptive status of virginity to be the determining factor, whereas Rabbi Yehoshua rules that the burden of proof is incumbent upon the claimant and the husband's possession of the money is the determining factor (see Ramban and *Tosafot*; Rashba; Rabbi Aharon HaLevi).

BACKGROUND

A grown woman does not have a claim concerning virginity – הַבּוֹגֶרֶת אֵין לָהּ טַעֲנַת בְּתוּלִים: Most women have a natural opening in the hymen, although the ratio between open and blocked areas varies in each woman, just as there are significant differences in the size of the vagina. In any event, while the girl matures and her body develops, the opening in the hymen also grows. In certain cases, the opening can become large enough that a grown woman who is a virgin could have sexual relations with no tearing of the hymen whatsoever. Even in a case where the hymen is torn and bleeds, the hymen might be so small that the husband would not feel its presence at all, and be under the impression that he encountered an open entrance.

HALAKHA

A grown woman – הַבּוֹגֶרֶת: The marriage contract of a grown woman is two hundred dinars, and there is a claim concerning her virginity (Rambam *Sefer Nashim, Hilkhot Ishut* 11:4; *Shulḥan Arukh, Even HaEzer* 68:1).

The claim concerning virginity with regard to a deaf-mute, an imbecile, and a woman whose hymen was torn not in the course of sexual relations – טַעֲנַת בְּתוּלִים בְּחֵרֶשֶׁת וּבְשׁוֹטָה וּבְמוּכַּת עֵץ: Any woman whose marriage contract is one hundred dinars, or for whom the Sages did not institute a marriage contract, is not vulnerable to a claim concerning her virginity. The marriage contract of a woman whose hymen was accidentally torn is one hundred dinars, there is no marriage contract for a deaf-mute, and the marriage of an imbecile does not take effect (Rambam *Sefer Nashim, Hilkhot Ishut* 11:4–5; *Shulḥan Arukh, Even HaEzer* 66:1, and see 67:5 and 67:7–8).

A blind woman and an *ailonit* – הַסּוּמָא וְאַיְילוֹנִית: For a virgin who is blind or an *ailonit* whose status was known at the time of her betrothal, there is a marriage contract of two hundred dinars, and they are vulnerable to a claim concerning their virginity (Rambam *Sefer Nashim, Hilkhot Ishut* 11:4; *Shulḥan Arukh, Even HaEzer* 67:6; 68:1).

Give a grown woman the entire first night – בּוֹגֶרֶת נוֹתְנִין לָהּ לַיְלָה הָרִאשׁוֹן: Fundamentally, as long as a grown woman has not seen the blood of virginity, any blood that she sees after intercourse is attributed to losing her virginity and she is not rendered impure. However, the daughters of Israel imposed a stringency upon themselves, and therefore, even a man who marries a minor virgin must refrain from contact with her after fulfilling the mitzva of consummating the marriage (Rambam *Sefer Kedusha, Hilkhot Issurei Bia* 4:9, 11:8; *Shulḥan Arukh, Yoreh De'a* 193:1).

אִי דְּקָא טָעֵין טַעֲנַת דָּמִים – הָכִי נַמִי, הָכָא בְּמַאי עָסְקִינַן – דְּקָטָעֵין טַעֲנַת פֶּתַח פָּתוּחַ.

The Gemara answers: **If he proffers a claim** that there was no **blood** after consummating the marriage, **indeed** he can cause her to lose her marriage contract with that claim. However, **with what are we dealing here** in the *baraita*? We are dealing **with** one who **proffers a claim** that he encountered **an open entrance,** i.e., there was no hymen. As the hymen of an adult woman is no longer completely intact, the claim is of no consequence.

״סוּמָכוֹס אוֹמֵר מִשּׁוּם רַבִּי מֵאִיר: סוּמָא אֵין לָהּ טַעֲנַת בְּתוּלִים״. מַאי טַעֲמָא דְּסוּמָכוֹס? אָמַר רַבִּי זֵירָא: מִפְּנֵי שֶׁנֶּחְבֶּטֶת עַל גַּבֵּי קַרְקַע. כּוּלְּהוּ נַמִי חֲבוּטֵי מִיחַבְּטִי! כּוּלְּהוּ רוֹאוֹת וּמַרְאוֹת לְאִמָּן, זוֹ אֵינָהּ רוֹאָה, וְאֵינָהּ מַרְאָה לְאִמָּהּ.

The *baraita* continues: **Sumakhos says in the name of Rabbi Meir: A blind** woman **does not have a claim concerning virginity.** The Gemara asks: **What is the rationale** for the statement **of Sumakhos? Rabbi Zeira said: Due to** the fact **that** a blind woman **is struck** by falling **onto the ground,** causing her hymen to break. The Gemara asks: **All** girls tend **to be struck** by falling onto the ground **as well;**[N] what is unique about blind girls? The Gemara answers: When **all of** the other girls fall, they **see** the blood flow **and show** it to **their mother.** The mother would then examine them and discover that her hymen was broken. **This** blind girl **does not see** the flow of blood **and** therefore **does not show** it to **her mother.** Due to that possibility, the man who married the blind woman must have considered the likelihood that her hymen is not intact, and therefore he cannot make a claim concerning virginity.

״וְהַיּוֹצֵאת מִשּׁוּם שֵׁם רַע אֵין לָהּ לֹא קְנָס וְלֹא פִּיתּוּי״. הַיּוֹצֵאת מִשּׁוּם שֵׁם רַע בַּת סְקִילָה הִיא! אָמַר רַב שֵׁשֶׁת: הָכִי קָאָמַר: מִי שֶׁיָּצָא עָלֶיהָ שֵׁם רַע בְּיַלְדוּתָהּ – אֵין לָהּ לֹא קְנָס וְלֹא פִּיתּוּי.

§ The previous *baraita* concluded: **And one who leaves** her husband **due to a bad reputation**[N] **has neither a fine** for rape **nor a** fine for **seduction.** The initial understanding is that the *baraita* is referring to a young betrothed woman who leaves her husband because she committed adultery. The Gemara asks: **One who leaves** her husband **due to a bad reputation is subject to stoning** as an adulteress; clearly she is not entitled to the fine. **Rav Sheshet said: This is what** the *baraita* **is saying: One about whom a bad reputation emerged in her youth** that she engaged in sexual relations **has neither a fine** for rape **nor a** fine for **seduction,** as the assumption is that she is no longer a virgin.

אֲמַר רַב פַּפָּא: שְׁמַע מִינָּהּ, הַאי שְׁטָרָא רִיעָא לָא מַגְבִּינַן בֵּיהּ. הֵיכִי דָּמֵי? אִילֵימָא דְּנָפַק קָלָא עֲלֵיהּ דִּשְׁטָרָא דְּזַיְיפָא הוּא, דִּכְוָותָהּ הָכָא – דְּנָפַק עֲלָהּ קָלָא דִּזְנַאי, וְהָא אֲמַר רָבָא: יָצָא לָהּ שֵׁם מְזַנָּה בָּעִיר – אֵין חוֹשְׁשִׁין לָהּ!

Rav Pappa said: Conclude from it with regard to **this tainted document** whose authenticity was compromised that **we do not collect** a debt **with it.** The Gemara asks: **What are the circumstances? If you say that a rumor emerged about it that it is a forged document,** and in **the corresponding** case **here,** the case of a bad reputation, **that a rumor emerged about her that she engaged in** promiscuous **sexual relations; but didn't Rava say: If a rumor emerged about** a woman **in a town** as one **who engaged in** promiscuous **sexual relations,**[H] **one need not be concerned about it?** The assumption is that it is insubstantial, as a reputation based on rumor is disregarded.

אֶלָּא, דְּאָתוּ בֵּי תְּרֵי וְאָמְרִי: לְדִידְהוּ תַּבְעַתַנְהִי בְּאִיסּוּרָא. דִּכְוָותָהּ הָכָא – דְּאָתוּ בֵּי תְּרֵי וְאָמְרִי: לְדִידְהוּ אֲמַר לְהוּ ״זַיְּיפוּ לִי״. בִּשְׁלָמָא הָתָם – שְׁכִיחִי פְּרוּצִין, אֶלָּא הָכָא – אִם הוּא הוּחְזַק – כׇּל יִשְׂרָאֵל מִי הוּחְזְקוּ?! הָכָא נַמִי, כֵּיוָן דְּקָא מְהַדַּר אַזִּיוּפָא – אֵימַר זִיּוּפֵי זַיֵּיף וְכָתַב.

Rather, it is **that two** witnesses **came and said: She propositioned us** to engage **in forbidden** relations,[H] and in **the corresponding** case **here** with regard to a document, it is a case where **two** people **came and said** that **he said to us: Forge** a document **for me.**[NH] The Gemara asks: **Granted, there,** in the case of the rumor of promiscuity, **immoral men are common,** and even if they refused her, presumably she found someone willing to engage in relations with her. **However, here,** with regard to forgery, even **if he assumed presumptive status** as one seeking a forgery, **do all the Jewish people assume presumptive status** as forgers? Why is the assumption that the document was forged? The Gemara answers: **Here too, since he is** actively **seeking a forgery, say that** he **forged** the document **and wrote** it. Even if others are not suspected of cooperating with him, there is suspicion with regard to the document. Therefore, the case of the tainted document and the woman with a bad reputation are comparable.

NOTES

All girls tend to be struck as well – כּוּלְּהוּ נַמִי חֲבוּטֵי מִיחַבְּטִי: Although the Sages stated that the case of a woman's hymen accidentally tearing is rare, there is a difference between one whose genitals tear from direct contact and one whose genitals tear from a fall. Furthermore, only if she was struck with a heavy blow could her hymen be broken (see Rashba). Rabbi Pinehas HaLevi, cited by the Ritva, explains that the statement: When all of the other girls fall they see and show, is for two reasons. First, they can see their surroundings and avoid a heavy blow; and second, if they fall they would show the blood to their mothers.

One who leaves due to a bad reputation – הַיּוֹצֵאת מִשּׁוּם שֵׁם רַע: The Gemara's initial assumption is based on the idea that the expression: One who leaves due to a bad reputation, refers to a married woman who was divorced due to rumors of adultery. It cannot be explained that she was divorced due to the rape itself, e.g., if he raped a betrothed maiden, as that is addressed in the next mishna, which enumerates those to whom the fine is not paid based on the principle: One receives the greater of the punishments, in this case, stoning. According to Rashi and most early commentaries, witnesses came and testified that she solicited them to engage in relations with her, and the assumption is that someone accepted her offer and she is no longer a virgin. The Rambam, however, explains that once witnesses testified that she solicited them to engage in relations with her, the claim that she was raped or seduced is rejected, as based on her conduct chances are that she initiated the relations, which exempts him from the fine. The Ran notes that the discussion in the Gemara does not support that interpretation, but several later commentaries explain the Rambam's approach at length, and reconcile it with the Gemara.

He said to us forge a document for me – לְדִידְהוּ אֲמַר לְהוּ זַיְּיפוּ לִי: The Ritva cites the opinion of certain Sages that if one issued a general request: Forge a document for me, all documents that he produces are suspect. He likewise states in the name of Rabbi Aharon HaLevi that once a person solicits a forgery, any document that he produces is suspected of being forged. The Meiri cites similar opinions (see HALAKHA).

HALAKHA

If a rumor emerged about a woman in a town as one who engaged in promiscuous sexual relations – יָצָא לָהּ שֵׁם מְזַנָּה בָּעִיר: If a woman had a reputation of having engaged in promiscuous sexual relations, those rumors are ignored, as per the statement of Rava (Rambam *Sefer Kedusha, Hilkhot Issurei Bia* 17:21; *Shulḥan Arukh, Even HaEzer* 6:16).

She propositioned us to engage in forbidden relations – לְדִידְהוּ תַּבְעַתַנְהִי בְּאִיסּוּרָא: If a young woman had a bad reputation, as two men testified that she solicited them to engage in sexual relations, she is not entitled to the fine (Rambam *Sefer Nashim, Hilkhot Na'ara Betula* 1:9; *Shulḥan Arukh, Even HaEzer* 177:4).

He said to us forge a document for me – לְדִידְהוּ אֲמַר לְהוּ זַיְּיפוּ לִי: If a person produced a promissory note and two witnesses claimed that he had asked them to forge that document, even if the document was ratified by its signatories, it cannot be used to collect the debt. The only way to collect the debt is by producing the witnesses who signed the document to testify that they witnessed the loan, or for others to testify that they saw the pair signing the document and the signatories testify that it is their signature. The Rema states that some authorities disagree and maintain that the testimony validating their signatures is ineffective (*Tur*, citing Rabbi Meir HaLevi). However, with regard to other documents that this man produces that affect other people, the debts may be collected, and there is no suspicion that they too were forged (*Shakh*, citing Ran and Rosh; Rambam *Sefer Shofetim, Hilkhot Edut* 11:4; *Shulḥan Arukh, Ḥoshen Mishpat* 63:2).

מתני׳ ואלו שאין להן קנס: הבא על הגיורת, ועל השבויה, ועל השפחה, שנפדו ושנתגיירו ושנשתחררו יתירות על בנות שלש שנים ויום אחד. רבי יהודה אומר שבויה שנפדית הרי היא בקדושתה, אף על פי שגדולה.

MISHNA **And these** are the cases of young women **who do not** have **a fine** paid to their fathers when they are raped or seduced: **One who has intercourse with a convert**[H] **or with a captive**[N] woman **or with a gentile maidservant, who were redeemed, converted, or emancipated** when they were **more than three years and one day** old, as presumably they are no longer virgins. **Rabbi Yehuda says: A captive** woman **who was redeemed** remains **in her** state of **sanctity even though** she is **an adult**, as it cannot be stated that she certainly engaged in intercourse.

הבא על בתו, על בת בתו, על בת בנו, על בת אשתו, על בת בנה, על בת בתה – אין להן קנס, מפני שמתחייב בנפשו, שמיתתן בידי בית דין, וכל המתחייב בנפשו אין משלם ממון, שנאמר ״ואם לא יהיה אסון ענוש יענש״.

The mishna resumes its list of the cases of young women who are not entitled to a fine when raped or seduced by the following men: In the case of **one who engages in intercourse with his daughter,**[NH] **with his daughter's daughter,**[N] **with his son's daughter, with his wife's daughter, with her son's daughter, or with her daughter's daughter; they do not** receive payment of **a fine.** That is **due to** the fact **that he is liable** to receive the **death** penalty, and **that their death** penalty is administered by **the court, and anyone who is liable** to receive the **death** penalty **does not pay money, as it is stated: "And yet no harm follow, he shall be punished"** (Exodus 21:22). This verse indicates that if a woman dies and the one who struck her is liable to receive the death penalty, he is exempt from payment.

גמ׳ אמר רבי יוחנן: רבי יהודה ורבי דוסא אמרו דבר אחד; רבי יהודה – הא דאמרן, רבי דוסא – דתניא: שבויה אוכלת בתרומה, דברי רבי דוסא. אמר רבי דוסא: וכי מה עשה לה ערבי הלז? וכי מפני שמיעך לה בין דדיה פסלה מן הכהונה?

GEMARA **Rabbi Yoḥanan said: Rabbi Yehuda and Rabbi Dosa**[N] **said one** and the same **thing** with regard to a captive woman. The statement of **Rabbi Yehuda is that** which **we said** in the mishna. The statement of **Rabbi Dosa is as it is taught** in a *baraita*: **A captive** daughter or wife of a priest, who was redeemed, **partakes of *teruma*;**[NH] this is **the statement of Rabbi Dosa.** In explanation, **Rabbi Dosa said: And what did this Arab** who took her captive **do to her? And due to** the fact **that he** lasciviously **squeezed between her breasts,** did he **render her unfit** to marry into **the priesthood?** Although he may have taken liberties with her, there is no concern that he had relations with her.

אמר רבה: דלמא לא היא; עד כאן לא קאמר רבי יהודה הכא אלא שלא יהא חוטא נשכר, אבל התם – כרבנן סבירא ליה. אי נמי: עד כאן לא קאמר רבי דוסא התם – אלא בתרומה דרבנן, אבל קנס דאורייתא – כרבנן סבירא ליה.

Rabba said: Perhaps that is not so, and their opinions differ. Perhaps **Rabbi Yehuda states** his opinion **only here** with regard to payment of a fine, **so that the sinner will not profit** through exemption from the fine because this girl was taken captive in her youth. **However, there,** with regard to *teruma*, **he holds in accordance with** the opinion of **the Rabbis,** and she is unfit to marry a priest. **Alternatively,** there is another distinction between their opinions. Perhaps **Rabbi Dosa stated** his opinion **only there, with regard to *teruma*** whose legal status today is **by rabbinic** law, and therefore he rules leniently. **However,** with regard to payment of **a fine,** which is mandated **by Torah law, he holds in accordance with** the opinion of **the Rabbis,** and the rapist is exempt from payment based on the principle: The burden of proof is incumbent upon the claimant, and she cannot prove that her captors did not engage in intercourse with her and that she is a virgin.

NOTES

A captive woman with regard to the matter of a fine – שבויה לענין קנס: The early commentaries ask: Doesn't everyone agree that there is merely a suspicion that a captive woman was violated, and it is a rabbinic decree that she does not have the presumptive status of a virgin, so how does the mishna rule unequivocally that she is not entitled to a fine? *Tosafot* explain that if a captive woman was entitled to a fine there is concern lest she marry a priest. In the *Shita Mekubbetzet* it is explained that even though it is based merely on suspicion, her presumptive status as a virgin was undermined, and one does not collect money based on weakened presumptive status.

One who engages in intercourse with his daughter – הבא על בתו: In the Jerusalem Talmud the question is raised: If she had relations with another, her father would be entitled to the fine, and therefore it is obvious in this case that she does not receive payment of the fine, as it is her father who would be entitled to the payment. One answer is that this refers to a case where the father died in the meantime, and the fine would therefore have been collected from his estate; his heirs would then have no right to it. The Rashba adds that it could also be referring to a girl who was betrothed and divorced, in accordance with the opinion that in that case the fine is paid to her, as her father is not entitled to the payment after her divorce.

With his daughter's daughter, etc. – על בת בתו וכו׳: As the mishna includes forbidden relatives by marriage, e.g., relations with his wife's daughter, why doesn't it list his daughter-in-law and other relatives? *Tosafot* maintain that the *tanna* could indeed have enumerated those cases as well, but he taught some cases and omitted others. In the *Shita Mekubbetzet* the suggestion is made that the mishna lists only those cases with regard to which all the Sages agree, even those Sages who maintain that one who was betrothed and divorced is not entitled to the fine.

Rabbi Yehuda and Rabbi Dosa – רבי יהודה ורבי דוסא: In the Jerusalem Talmud, these opinions are also cited, with certain differences. There Rabbi Yoḥanan said that Rabbi Yehuda referred only to the fine, while the Sage of the school of Rabbi Ḥiyya said that Rabbi Yehuda was also referring to the marriage contract, as in the *baraita* quoted below. Reish Lakish alone maintains that the two opinions are equal in all regards, including with regard to the *halakha* of *teruma*.

As it is taught in a *baraita*: A captive partakes of *teruma* – דתניא שבויה אוכלת בתרומה: Although fundamentally, this *halakha* appears in a mishna in tractate *Eduyyot*, since the Gemara adds Rabbi Dosa's rationale for his ruling, which does not appear in the mishna, it introduces the entire passage: As it is taught in a *baraita*.

HALAKHA

A convert, etc. – הגיורת וכו׳: A gentile woman older than the age of three who converted, and likewise a captive older than the age of three who was redeemed, and similarly a maidservant older than the age of three who was freed are not entitled to the fine. The *halakha* is in accordance with the mishna, contrary to the individual opinion of Rabbi Yehuda (Rambam *Sefer Nashim, Hilkhot Na'ara Betula* 1:10).

One who engages in intercourse with his daughter, etc. – הבא על בתו וכו׳: One who rapes a woman for whom he is liable to receive a court-administered death penalty, e.g., his daughter or his wife's daughter, whether or not he was forewarned, is exempt from paying the fine (Rambam *Sefer Nashim, Hilkhot Na'ara Betula* 1:13–14).

A captive woman with regard to partaking of *teruma* – שבויה באכילת תרומה: The wife of a priest who was taken captive may not eat *teruma*, due to the concern that she was violated by her gentile captor. However, if she claims that she is pure, or if there were witnesses to that effect, she is permitted to her husband the priest, and she is permitted to eat *teruma*. The *halakha* is in accordance with the opinion of the Rabbis in their dispute with Rabbi Dosa (Rambam *Sefer Zera'im, Hilkhot Terumot* 6:11).

אֲמַר לֵיהּ אַבַּיֵי: וְטַעֲמֵיהּ דְּרַבִּי יְהוּדָה הָכָא שֶׁלֹּא יְהֵא חוֹטֵא נִשְׂכָּר הוּא? וְהָא תַּנְיָא, רַבִּי יְהוּדָה אוֹמֵר: שְׁבוּיָה שֶׁנִּשְׁבֵּית הֲרֵי הִיא בִּקְדוּשָּׁתָהּ, אֲפִי׳ בַּת עֶשֶׂר שָׁנִים כְּתוּבָּתָהּ מָאתַיִם, וְהָתָם – מַאי שֶׁלֹּא יְהֵא חוֹטֵא נִשְׂכָּר אִיכָּא? הָתָם נַמִי, דִּלְמָא מִימְנְעִי וְלָא נָסְבִי לָהּ.

Abaye said to Rabba: **And is the rationale** for the opinion of **Rabbi Yehuda here**, in the case of a fine, to ensure **that the sinner will not profit? But isn't it taught** in a *baraita* that **Rabbi Yehuda says: A captive** woman **who was taken captive** remains **in her** state of **sanctity** with the presumptive status of a virgin? **Even** if she was in captivity when she was **ten years old, her marriage contract is two hundred** dinars. **And there,** in that case, **what** relevance **is there** for the rationale: To ensure **that the sinner will not profit?** That *baraita* refers to a marriage contract and no transgression is involved. The Gemara answers: **There too,** Rabbi Yehuda issues the same ruling for a different reason. She receives the marriage contract of a virgin because if she didn't, **perhaps men would refrain and not marry her,** due to their suspicion that her captors violated her.

וְסָבַר רַבִּי יְהוּדָה בִּקְדוּשָּׁתָהּ קַיְימָה? וְהָתַנְיָא: הַפּוֹדֶה אֶת הַשְּׁבוּיָה יִשָּׂאֶנָּה; מֵעִיד בָּהּ – לֹא יִשָּׂאֶנָּה. רַבִּי יְהוּדָה אוֹמֵר: בֵּין כָּךְ וּבֵין כָּךְ – לֹא יִשָּׂאֶנָּה! הָא גּוּפָהּ קַשְׁיָא; אָמְרַתְּ: הַפּוֹדֶה אֶת הַשְּׁבוּיָה יִשָּׂאֶנָּה, וַהֲדַר תָּנָא: מֵעִיד בָּהּ – לֹא יִשָּׂאֶנָּה, מִשּׁוּם דְּמֵעִיד בָּהּ לֹא יִשָּׂאֶנָּה?!

The Gemara asks: **And does Rabbi Yehuda maintain** that a captive woman remains **in her** state of **sanctity? But isn't it taught** in a *baraita*: **One who redeems a captive may marry her,** even if he is a priest, but if he **testifies**[H] that **she** did not engage in sexual relations while in captivity, **he may not marry her? Rabbi Yehuda says: Both** in **this** case, where he redeemed her, **and** in **that** case, where he testified, **he may not marry her,** lest she was violated and rendered unfit to marry a priest. The Gemara comments: **This** *baraita* **itself is difficult.** On the one hand **you said: One who redeems a captive may marry her, and then it was taught:** If he **testifies** that **she** did not engage in sexual relations while in captivity, **he may not marry her.** Is that to say that **due to** the fact **that he** also **testifies** that **she** was not violated **he may not marry her?**

הָא לָא קַשְׁיָא; הָכִי קָאָמַר: הַפּוֹדֶה אֶת הַשְּׁבוּיָה וּמֵעִיד בָּהּ – יִשָּׂאֶנָּה, מֵעִיד בָּהּ כְּדִי – לֹא יִשָּׂאֶנָּה.

The Gemara answers: This is **not difficult,** as **this is what** the *baraita* **is saying: One who redeems a captive** woman **and testifies** that **she** was not violated **may marry her.** However, if he **only testifies** that **she** was not violated **he may not marry her.**

מִכָּל מָקוֹם קַשְׁיָא לְרַבִּי יְהוּדָה! אֲמַר רַב פָּפָּא: אֵימָא; רַבִּי יְהוּדָה אוֹמֵר בֵּין כָּךְ וּבֵין כָּךְ – יִשָּׂאֶנָּה. רַב הוּנָא בְּרֵיהּ דְּרַב יְהוֹשֻׁעַ אוֹמֵר: לְעוֹלָם כִּדְקָתָנֵי, רַבִּי יְהוּדָה לְדִבְרֵיהֶם דְּרַבָּנַן קָאָמַר לְהוּ: לְדִידִי – בֵּין כָּךְ וּבֵין כָּךְ יִשָּׂאֶנָּה, אֶלָּא לְדִידְכוּ – בֵּין כָּךְ וּבֵין כָּךְ לֹא יִשָּׂאֶנָּה מִבָּעֵי לֵיהּ!

With regard to the apparent contradiction between the two statements of Rabbi Yehuda, the Gemara says: **In any case,** this *baraita* is **difficult** according **to Rabbi Yehuda,** as contrary to his earlier statement, he states that a captive woman does not retain the presumptive status of a virgin. **Rav Pappa said:** Emend the text and **say** that **Rabbi Yehuda says:**[N] **Both** in **this** case and in **that** case **he may marry her. Rav Huna, son of Rav Yehoshua, says: Actually,** do not emend the *baraita* and learn it **as it was taught.** In the *baraita*, **Rabbi Yehuda spoke to them** according **to the statement of the Rabbis.** According **to my** opinion, that the presumptive status of a redeemed captive woman is that of a virgin, **both** in **this** case **and** in **that** case **he may marry her. However,** according **to your** opinion that there is concern lest she was violated, the *halakha* **should be** that **both** in **this** case **and** in **that** case **he may not marry her.**

וְרַבָּנַן? הַפּוֹדֶה אֶת הַשְּׁבוּיָה וּמֵעִיד בָּהּ יִשָּׂאֶנָּה – לָא שָׁדֵי אִינִישׁ זוּזֵי בְּכְדִי, מֵעִיד בָּהּ כְּדִי לֹא יִשָּׂאֶנָּה – שֶׁמָּא עֵינָיו נָתַן בָּהּ.

The Gemara asks: **And** how do **the Rabbis** explain their ruling? They explain: **One who redeems a captive** woman and **testifies** that **she** was not violated **may marry her,** as **a person does not throw** away **money for nothing.** If he paid the ransom to redeem her, he must be certain that she is a virgin. One who **only testifies** that **she** was not violated **may not marry her, lest he had his eye on her** to marry her and is prepared to lie to facilitate that marriage.

רָמֵי לֵיהּ רַב פָּפָּא בַּר שְׁמוּאֵל לְרַב יוֹסֵף:

Rav Pappa bar Shmuel raised a contradiction before Rav Yosef:

HALAKHA

One who testifies with regard to a captive – הַמֵּעִיד עַל הַשְּׁבוּיָה: If a priest testifies that a captive woman is pure, he is not permitted to marry her based on his testimony, due to the concern that he lied because he had his eye on marrying her. However, his testimony is accepted to permit her to others (*Beit Shmuel*). If he was not certain that she was not violated, he would not have redeemed her, as he would not have spent his money. If he redeemed her and testified in her regard, he may marry her (Rambam *Sefer Kedusha, Hilkhot Issurei Bia* 18:20; *Shulḥan Arukh, Even HaEzer* 7:3).

NOTES

Say that Rabbi Yehuda says – אֵימָא רַבִּי יְהוּדָה אוֹמֵר וכו׳: The Ritva questions the suggestion that the attribution of the opinion in the *baraita* can be reversed in this manner. He therefore claims that perhaps Rav Pappa is suggesting that Rabbi Yehuda's statement can be read as a question: And may he not marry her? He cites similar instances from elsewhere in the Talmud.

וסבר רבי יהודה בקדושתה קיימא? והתניא: הגיורת שנתגיירה וראתה דם, רבי יהודה אומר דיה שעתה, רבי יוסי אומר: הרי היא ככל הנשים, ומטמאה מעת לעת ומפקידה לפקידה

And does **Rabbi Yehuda maintain** that a captive woman **remains in her** state of **sanctity? But isn't it taught** in a *baraita*: With regard to a female **convert who converted and saw** the flow of menstrual **blood**[N] on that same day, **Rabbi Yehuda says:** Deeming **her** impure from the **hour** that she saw the menstrual flow **is sufficient for her.** There is no decree of retroactive impurity on objects that she touched earlier, due to the concern that the blood flow might have started earlier. **Rabbi Yosei says: Her** legal status **is like** that of **all of the** Jewish **women, and she** therefore **transmits impurity** retroactively **for a twenty-four hour period** following her conversion, or **from examination to examination,** i.e., from the last time she examined herself.

וצריכה להמתין שלשה חדשים, דברי רבי יהודה. רבי יוסי מתיר ליארס ולינשא מיד! אמר ליה: גיורת אשבויה קא רמית?! גיורת – לא מנטרא נפשה, שבויה – מנטרא נפשה.

And a convert **is required to wait**[N] **three months** after her conversion before marrying a Jew, due to the concern that she is pregnant, leading to confusion whether the child was conceived before or after her conversion; this is **the statement of Rabbi Yehuda. Rabbi Yosei permits her to be betrothed and to be married immediately.** Clearly, Rabbi Yehuda is concerned that she engaged in sexual relations prior to her conversion. Rav Yosef **said to** Rav Pappa bar Shmuel: **Are you raising a contradiction** from the *halakha* of **a convert to** that of **a captive** woman? **A convert does not protect herself** from engaging in sexual relations before conversion, whereas **a captive protects herself,** as she is conscious of the sanctity of the Jewish people and does not want to be violated.

ורמי שבויה אשבויה; דתניא: הגיורת והשבויה והשפחה שנפדו ושנתגיירו, ושנשתחררו יתרות על בנות שלש שנים ויום אחד – צריכות להמתין שלשה חדשים, דברי רבי יהודה. רבי יוסי מתיר ליארס ולינשא מיד! אשתיק.

And Rav Pappa bar Shmuel **raised a contradiction from** one *halakha* with regard to **a captive to** another *halakha* with regard to **a captive, as it is taught** in a *baraita*: **The convert, or the captive** woman **or the** gentile **maidservant, who were redeemed, converted, or emancipated** when they were **more than three years and one day** old,[N] **are required to wait three months** before marrying; this is **the statement of Rabbi Yehuda. Rabbi Yosei permits** these women **to be betrothed and to be married immediately.** Apparently, Rabbi Yehuda is concerned that she engaged in sexual relations prior to her redemption, contradicting his opinion here. Rav Yosef **was silent,** unable to respond.[H]

HALAKHA

Waiting with regard to a convert and a maidservant – המתנה בגיורת ובשפחה: An emancipated maidservant and a convert must wait ninety days before they can marry. The *Mishne LaMelekh* claims that this applies only to women who were previously married and therefore took no steps to prevent conception. The same *halakha* applies to a male convert and his wife who converted together; they too must wait so that it can be determined whether conception predated or postdated conversion. That is the ruling in the *Shulḥan Arukh* as well. Although the *Beit Yosef* questions this approach, apparently he reconsidered his ruling (Rambam *Sefer Nashim*, *Hilkhot Geirushin* 11:21; *Shulḥan Arukh*, *Even HaEzer* 13:5 and *Beit Shmuel* there).

NOTES

Who converted and saw the flow of menstrual blood – שנתגיירה וראתה דם: When a woman sees menstrual blood the concern is whether the blood flowed earlier but was not immediately obvious. Therefore, all pure items with which she came into contact during a previous period of time are rendered ritually impure. The precise length of this period of time is subject to a dispute between Hillel and Shammai at the beginning of tractate *Nidda*. The *halakha* is that this concern extends either for the twenty-four-hour period before she noticed the blood or from her most recent examination, whichever of the two periods is shorter. Consequently, if her last examination was more than twenty-four hours earlier, she renders the items impure retroactively for twenty-four hours, and if she examined herself more recently than that, any pure item with which she came into contact after that examination is impure.

Rashi and most commentaries explain that the convert referred to here saw blood on the day of her conversion. Rabbi Yosei maintains that she is like all Jewish women, and therefore renders items impure retroactively from the time of her conversion, whereas Rabbi Yehuda claims that since it cannot be for the entire twenty-four hour period, as she was a gentile for part of that time, she does not render the items impure retroactively at all, but merely from the moment of her sighting: Deeming her impure from the hour that she saw the menstrual flow is sufficient.

The *Shita Yeshana*, cited in the *Shita Mekubbetzet*, suggests a slightly different interpretation. There it is claimed that the reference is to a convert who saw blood for the first time after her conversion. Accordingly, the dispute is whether a decree is issued in her regard like the decree that applies to all Jewish women, or whether they did not decree impurity in her case, due to her former gentile state.

And a convert is required to wait – וצריכה להמתין: The Sages decreed that a woman who was married may not wed another man immediately after the end of her marriage, as she might be unknowingly pregnant from her first husband. In that case, if she gives birth seven months into her second marriage it will be unclear whether the child was born to the first husband after a pregnancy of nine months or to the second husband after a pregnancy of seven months. That would lead to complications with regard to prohibitions, lineage, and inheritance. The Sages therefore required her to wait three months, at which point a pregnancy would be noticeable and it would be clear that the first husband is the father. The *tanna'im* disagreed whether this decree is applied to cases where there is no concern that there might be a previous pregnancy. A similar concern exists in the case of a woman who engaged in forbidden relations, or a convert, where it is necessary to determine whether or not the lineage of the child is flawed. In the case of a convert, there are halakhic ramifications dependent on whether or not the child was conceived and born in sanctity as a member of the Jewish people.

More than three years and one day old – יתירות על בנות שלש שנים ויום אחד: *Tosafot* question whether this phrase belongs here. First of all, it does not appear in other places in the Talmud where an identical discussion appears. In addition, it presents a difficulty for the opinion of Rabbi Yehuda, as he does not require a waiting period for a minor who was married. Although some commentaries (Ramban; Rashba) contend that there is no need to be particular in this regard, as adult women are included in this phrase, and the mention of three years and one day is merely the usual expression in this regard, most early commentaries agree that this version is inaccurate.

אֲמַר לֵיהּ: מִידִי שְׁמִיעַ לָךְ בְּהָא? אֲמַר לֵיהּ, הָכִי אֲמַר רַב שֵׁשֶׁת: שֶׁרָאוּהָ שֶׁנִּבְעֲלָה. אִי הָכִי מַאי טַעֲמָא דְּרַבִּי יוֹסֵי? אֲמַר רַבָּה: קָסָבַר רַבִּי יוֹסֵי אִשָּׁה מְזַנָּה מְשַׁמֶּשֶׁת בְּמוֹךְ שֶׁלֹּא תִּתְעַבֵּר.

Later, Rav Yosef **said to him: Have you heard anything with regard to this** matter? Rav Pappa bar Shmuel **said to him: This** is what **Rav Sheshet said:** Rabbi Yehuda is referring to a captive **whom** witnesses **saw engage in intercourse.** The Gemara asks: **If so, what is the rationale** for the ruling of **Rabbi Yosei** that she may marry immediately? Shouldn't he be concerned lest she is pregnant? **Rabba said: Rabbi Yosei holds** that **a woman who engages in** promiscuous **sexual relations has relations with** a contraceptive **resorbent** at the entrance of her womb, so **that she will not become pregnant.**

בִּשְׁלָמָא גִּיּוֹרֶת, כֵּיוָן דְּדַעְתָּהּ לְאִיגַּיּוֹרֵי – מְנַטְּרָא נַפְשָׁהּ; שְׁבוּיָה נַמִי, דְּלָא יָדְעָה הֵיכָא מַמְטוּ לָהּ; שִׁפְחָה נַמִי, דְּשָׁמְעָה מִפִּי מָרָהּ; אֶלָּא יוֹצְאָה בְּשֵׁן וָעַיִן – מַאי אִיכָּא לְמֵימַר?

The Gemara asks: **Granted, a convert** uses the resorbent; **since it is her intention to convert, she protects herself** from pregnancy. **A captive too** uses the resorbent because **she does not know where they are taking her,** and she does not want to become pregnant. **A maidservant** uses the resorbent **too, as she heard from her master** that he intends to free her, and she seeks to avoid confusion with regard to the lineage of her offspring. **However,** with regard a maidservant who **emerges** from slavery **with** the extraction by her master of her **tooth or** her **eye, what is there to say?** She has no advance knowledge that she will be freed and therefore would not take precautions to avoid becoming pregnant, and Rav Sheshet explained that this is a case where she was seen engaging in sexual relations.

וְכִי תֵּימָא כָּל מִמֵּילָא לָא אָמַר רַבִּי יוֹסֵי – הֲרֵי אֲנוּסָה וּמְפוּתָּה, דְּמִמֵּילָא, וְתַנְיָא: אֲנוּסָה וּמְפוּתָּה צְרִיכוֹת לְהַמְתִּין שְׁלֹשָׁה חֳדָשִׁים, דִּבְרֵי רַבִּי יְהוּדָה, רַבִּי יוֹסֵי מַתִּיר לֵיאָרֵס וְלִינָּשֵׂא מִיָּד!

And if you say that with regard to **any** situation that occurs **on its own,** without advance knowledge, **Rabbi Yosei** concedes to Rabbi Yehuda and **did not say** that it is permitted for her to marry immediately, that cannot be so. There is the case of **a raped or seduced** woman, which happens **on its own** without advance knowledge, **and it is taught** in a *baraita*: **A raped woman and a seduced woman must wait three months** before marrying; this is **the statement of Rabbi Yehuda; Rabbi Yosei permits** these women **to be betrothed and to be married immediately.**

אֶלָּא אֲמַר רַבָּה: קָסָבַר רַבִּי יוֹסֵי: אִשָּׁה מְזַנָּה מִתְהַפֶּכֶת כְּדֵי שֶׁלֹּא תִּתְעַבֵּר. וְאִידָּךְ: חָיְישִׁינַן שֶׁמָּא לֹא נֶהֶפְכָה יָפֶה יָפֶה.

Rather, Rabba said: The rationale for the ruling of Rabbi Yosei is not because the woman uses a contraceptive resorbent that she inserts before engaging in relations. Rather, **Rabbi Yosei holds: A woman** who **engages in** promiscuous **sexual relations**[H] **turns over**[NB] at the conclusion of the sexual act so **that she will not become pregnant.** Therefore, even if she engaged in unplanned sexual relations, she can take steps afterward to prevent unwanted pregnancy. The Gemara asks: **And** how does **the other** *tanna*, Rabbi Yehuda respond to this contention? The Gemara answers: **We are concerned lest** the semen remain in her womb because **she did not turn over properly,** and she will become pregnant.

שֶׁנֶּאֱמַר "וְלֹא יִהְיֶה אָסוֹן עָנוֹשׁ יֵעָנֵשׁ" וכו׳. וְהָא מֵהָכָא נָפְקָא? מֵהָתָם נָפְקָא: "כְּדֵי רִשְׁעָתוֹ" – מִשּׁוּם רִשְׁעָה אַחַת אַתָּה מְחַיְּיבוֹ, וְאִי אַתָּה מְחַיְּיבוֹ מִשּׁוּם שְׁתֵּי רְשָׁעִיּוֹת!

§ The mishna states that one liable to receive the death penalty is exempt from payment, **as it is stated: "And yet no harm follow, he shall be punished, etc."** (Exodus 21:22). The Gemara asks: **And is this** principle **derived from here?** Actually, **it is derived from there:** "And to be beaten before his face **according to the measure of his iniquity**" (Deuteronomy 25:2).[N] From the term: His iniquity, it is inferred: **You can hold** one who performs one action **liable for one iniquity,** i.e., punishment for violating one prohibition, **but you do not hold him liable for two iniquities,** i.e., punishments for violating two prohibitions.

חֲדָא בְּמִיתָה וּמָמוֹן, וַחֲדָא בְּמַלְקוֹת וּמָמוֹן. וּצְרִיכָא: דְּאִי אַשְׁמְעִינַן מִיתָה וּמָמוֹן – מִשּׁוּם דְּאִיכָּא אִיבּוּד נְשָׁמָה, אֲבָל מַלְקוֹת וּמָמוֹן דְּלֵיכָּא אִיבּוּד נְשָׁמָה, אֵימָא לָא.

The Gemara answers: **One** of these derivations, from the verse "And yet no harm follow" is stated **with regard to** one who performed an action for which he is liable to receive the **death** penalty **and** to pay **money,** and the liability to be executed exempts him from payment. **And one** of these derivations, from the verse "According to the measure of his iniquity," is stated **with regard to** one who performed an action for which he is liable to receive **lashes and** to pay **money,** and he receives only one punishment. The Gemara elaborates: **And** both derivations **are necessary,** as **if** the Torah **taught us** this *halakha* only with regard to **death and money,** one would assert that the exemption from payment is **due to** the fact **that there is loss of life,**[N] the ultimate punishment, leaving no room for additional punishment; **however,** in the case of **lashes and money, where there is no loss of life, say no,** there is no exemption and he is flogged and pays.

HALAKHA

Waiting with regard to a captive, a raped or seduced woman, and one who engaged in promiscuous relations – הַמְתָּנָה בִּשְׁבוּיָה, בַּאֲנוּסָה וּמְפוּתָּה, וּבִמְזַנָּה: A redeemed captive woman need not wait before marrying, even if she was an adult, since she turns over to prevent conception, as stated by Rabbi Yosei. For the same reason a rape victim and seduced woman need not wait three months either, and the same applies to any woman who engaged in promiscuous relations. The Rema states that some authorities, e.g., Rabbi Zeraḥya HaLevi, the Rosh, and the *Tur*, claim that in all cases, if a woman was capable of conception, she must wait, as Shmuel in the latter version of his statement in *Yevamot* (32b) rules in accordance with the opinion of Rabbi Yehuda that there is concern lest she did not turn over properly (Rambam *Sefer Nashim, Hilkhot Geirushin* 11:22; *Shulḥan Arukh, Even HaEzer* 13:6).

NOTES

A woman who engages in promiscuous sexual relations turns over, etc. – אִשָּׁה מְזַנָּה מִתְהַפֶּכֶת וכו׳: Rashi maintains that this reason is accepted; a woman who is freed from enslavement by the loss of a tooth or eye would not have to wait either, as she too would turn over. In his opinion, no woman who engages in acts of promiscuous relations wants to conceive, and therefore she will turn over even if she has no particular reason to protect herself. However, many early commentaries, including *Tosafot* and the Ramban, contend that even Rabbi Yosei agrees that a maidservant is required to wait in that case, as she has no particular reason to prevent conception and therefore would not have turned over. They add that it is possible that she was married to a slave, and as such would certainly have had no reason to avoid conception, as she was engaging in legitimate conjugal relations.

It is derived from there: According to the measure of his iniquity – מֵהָתָם נָפְקָא כְּדֵי רִשְׁעָתוֹ: The Ritva raises the question that although from the verse "According to the measure of his iniquity" it can be derived that one is not punished twice for a single transgression, which of the two punishments he receives cannot be derived. It is only from the verse "And yet no harm follow" that it is derived that he is executed and does not pay. He answers that it is logical that one would not be exempted from the severe punishment of execution, because there is additional liability to pay. The *Beit Aharon* suggests that the question is not why the verse "And yet no harm follow" is necessary; on the contrary, why not suffice with that verse alone, from which both principles can be derived? Although that interpretation resolves the Ritva's question, it does not fit well with the language of the Gemara.

There is loss of life – דְּאִיכָּא אִיבּוּד נְשָׁמָה: Although the *halakha* concludes that he is exempt from any other punishment even if he is not actually executed, the exemption is due to the fact that a transgression that entails the loss of life is so serious that no other punishment would be appropriate. A careful reading of Rashi leads to a similar understanding (*Shita Mekubbetzet*).

BACKGROUND

Turns over – מִתְהַפֶּכֶת: According to modern medicine, turning over after intercourse would be ineffective in preventing conception. Therefore, it stands to reason that the Gemara is not referring merely to turning over; rather, it is referring to additional steps taken to prevent pregnancy. In terms of the language of the Gemara, perhaps it is referring to turning over during the sexual act, leading to an uncommon position that might significantly reduce the odds of conception.

ואי אשמעינן מלקות וממון – משום דלא חמיר איסוריה, אבל מיתה וממון דחמיר איסוריה אימא לא, צריכא.	**And if** the Torah **taught us** this *halakha* only with regard to **lashes and money,** one would assert that the exemption from payment is **due to** the fact **that** the **prohibition** that he violated **is not severe,** as it is punishable by lashes, and for violating a prohibition that is not severe one does not receive two punishments. **However,** with regard to **death and money, where** the **prohibition** that he violated **is severe, say no,** he is not exempt from receiving two punishments. Therefore, it was **necessary** for the Torah to teach both derivations.
ולרבי מאיר, דאמר לוקה ומשלם, תרתי למה לי? חדא במיתה וממון	The Gemara asks: **And according to Rabbi Meir, who said** that one **is flogged and pays** in cases where he violated a prohibition punishable by both, **why do I** require **two** derivations teaching that one does not receive the death penalty and pay? The Gemara answers: **One** derivation is **with regard to death and money,** exempting one liable to be executed from payment,

Perek **III**
Daf **37** Amud **b**

וחדא במיתה ומלקות. וצריכא; דאי אשמעינן מיתה וממון – משום דחדא בגופיה וחדא בממוניה לא עבדינן, אבל במיתה ומלקות דאידי ואידי בגופיה – אימא מיתה אריכתא היא, ונעביד ביה.	**and one** derivation is **with regard to death and lashes,**[N] exempting one liable to be executed from lashes. The Gemara comments: **And** both verses **are necessary, as if** the Torah **taught us** this *halakha* only with regard to **death and monetary** payment, one would assert that the exemption from payment is **due to** the fact **that we do not administer one** punishment **to his body and one to his money. However, with regard to death and lashes, that both this,** death, **and that,** lashes, are administered **to his body, say it is an extended death** penalty **and let us administer** lashes and then the death penalty **to him** so that his death will ensue from affliction.
ואי אשמעינן מיתה ומלקות – דתרתי בגופיה לא עבדינן, אבל מיתה וממון דחדא בגופיה וחדא בממוניה – אימא נעביד ביה, צריכא.	**And if** the Torah **taught us** this *halakha* only with regard to **death and lashes,** one would assert that the exemption from lashes is **due to** the fact **that we do not administer two** punishments **to his body. However,** with regard to **death and money, where one** is administered **to his body and one** is administered **to his money, say: Let us administer** both **to him.** Therefore, both verses are **necessary,** to teach that one receives only one punishment in both cases.
"ולא תקחו כופר לנפש רוצח" למה לי? דאמר רחמנא: לא תשקול ממונא מיניה ותפטריה מקטלא – "לא תקחו כופר לנוס אל עיר מקלטו" למה לי? דאמר רחמנא: לא תשקול ממונא מיניה ותפטריה מן גלות.	The Gemara asks with regard to the verse **"And you shall take no ransom for the life of a murderer,** who is guilty of death" (Numbers 35:31), which means that one does not take payment from a person sentenced to death, **why do I** require this verse, if that principle was already derived from another verse? The Gemara explains **that the Merciful One says: Do not take money from him and exempt him from** the **death** penalty.[H] Similarly, the following verse: "**And you shall take no ransom for him that is fled to his city of refuge"** (Numbers 35:32), **why do I** require this verse? The Gemara explains **that the Merciful One says: Do not take money from him and exempt him from exile.**[H]
ותרי קראי למה לי? חד בשוגג וחד במזיד, וצריכי; דאי אשמעינן מזיד – משום דחמיר איסוריה, אבל שוגג דלא חמיר איסוריה – אימא לא. ואי אשמעינן שוגג – משום דליכא איבוד נשמה, אבל מזיד דאיכא איבוד נשמה – אימא לא, צריכא.	The Gemara asks: **And why do I** require **two verses** to teach the same principle? The Gemara explains: **One** verse refers **to** one who killed **unwittingly, and one** verse refers **to** one who killed **intentionally.** The Gemara comments: **And** both verses **are necessary, as if** the Torah **taught us** this *halakha* only with regard to **an intentional** murderer, one would assert that payment is not accepted **due to** the fact **that** the **prohibition** that **he** violated **is severe. However,** with regard to **an unwitting** killer, **where** the **prohibition is not severe, say no,** he may pay in lieu of exile. **And if** the Torah **taught us** this *halakha* only with regard to **an unwitting** killer, one would assert that payment is not accepted **due to** the fact **that there is no loss of life,** as the killer is not executed, and therefore, there is no reason to allow payment in lieu of exile. **However,** with regard to **an intentional** killer, **where there is loss of life,** as he will be executed, **say no,** he may pay in lieu of execution. Therefore, both verses are **necessary.**

NOTES

And one is with regard to death and lashes – וחדא במיתה ומלקות: The Rabbis maintain that no special verse is required for this principle, as it stands to reason that if one is not punished with both lashes and payment, all the more so is he not punished with lashes and execution, as the death penalty is a far more severe punishment than lashes (Rashba; Ritva).

HALAKHA

There is no ransom for a murderer – אין כופר לרוצח: The court may not accept a ransom payment from a murderer in order to exempt him from the death penalty. They may not do so even if he offers all the money in the world, and even if the avenging relative of the victim agrees, as the soul of the murderer does not belong to the avenger but to God (Rambam *Sefer Nezikim, Hilkhot Rotze'aḥ* 1:4).

There is no ransom for exile – אין כופר לגלות: The court may not accept a ransom payment from an unintentional murderer in order to exempt him from exile (Rambam *Sefer Nezikim, Hilkhot Rotze'aḥ* 5:1).

"וְלָאָרֶץ לֹא יְכוּפַּר לַדָּם אֲשֶׁר שׁוּפַּךְ בָּהּ כִּי אִם בְּדַם שׁוֹפְכוֹ" לָמָּה לִי?

The Gemara asks with regard to the following verse: **"And no expiation can be made for the land for the blood that is shed therein, but by the blood of him that shed it"** (Numbers 35:33), which also indicates that he cannot be exempted by money, **why do I** require another verse to teach that one cannot absolve himself from the death penalty by means of payment?

מִבָּעֵי לֵיהּ לְכִדְתַנְיָא: מִנַּיִן שֶׁאִם נִתְעָרְפָה עֶגְלָה וְאַחַר כָּךְ נִמְצָא הַהוֹרֵג, מִנַּיִן שֶׁאֵין פּוֹטְרִין אוֹתוֹ – שֶׁנֶּאֱמַר "וְלָאָרֶץ לֹא יְכוּפַּר לַדָּם אֲשֶׁר שׁוּפַּךְ בָּהּ" וגו׳,

The Gemara explains: **It is necessary to** teach **that which is taught** in a *baraita* with regard to the matter of the calf that is beheaded. If a corpse whose murderer is unknown is found between two towns, the elders of the town nearest to the corpse bring a heifer and behead it in a riverbed, after which they pray for atonement for this murder. The *baraita* states: **From where** is it derived **that if the calf was beheaded and the murderer was found thereafter,**[H] it is derived **that one does not exempt him**[N] from punishment? It **is as it is stated: "And no expiation can be made for the land for the blood that is shed therein,** but by the blood of him that shed it" (Numbers 35:32), from which it is inferred: And not by the blood of the calf.

"וְאַתָּה תְּבַעֵר הַדָּם הַנָּקִי מִקִּרְבֶּךָ" לָמָּה לִי? מִיבָּעֵי לֵיהּ לְכִדְתַנְיָא: מִנַּיִן לַמּוּמָתִים בְּסַיִיף שֶׁהוּא מִן הַצַּוָּאר – תַּלְמוּד לוֹמַר "וְאַתָּה תְּבַעֵר הַדָּם הַנָּקִי מִקִּרְבֶּךָ", הוּקְשׁוּ כָּל שׁוֹפְכֵי דָמִים לְעֶגְלָה עֲרוּפָה, מַה לְּהַלָּן מִן הַצַּוָּאר – אַף שׁוֹפְכֵי דָמִים מִן הַצַּוָּאר.

The Gemara asks: What about the following verse, from the conclusion of the chapter of the heifer: The verse **"And so shall you put away the innocent blood from your midst"** (Deuteronomy 21:9) appears to be teaching the very same *halakha*, that a murderer must be executed. **Why do I** need it? The Gemara answers that **it is necessary to** teach **that which is taught** in a *baraita*: **From where** is it derived **that** with regard to **those executed by sword,** e.g., murderers, their execution **is** administered **from the neck,** and nowhere else? **The verse states: "And so shall you put away the innocent blood from your midst"** (Deuteronomy 21:9), **likening all spillers of blood to the beheaded calf**[B] brought for an unresolved murder. **Just as there,** the calf is beheaded **from the neck, so too, murderers** are beheaded **from the neck.**

אִי מַה לְּהַלָּן בְּקוֹפִיץ, וּמִמּוּל עוֹרֶף, אַף כָּאן בְּקוֹפִיץ וּמִמּוּל עוֹרֶף? אָמַר רַב נַחְמָן אָמַר רַבָּה בַּר אֲבוּהּ: אָמַר קְרָא "וְאָהַבְתָּ לְרֵעֲךָ כָּמוֹךָ" – בְּרוֹר לוֹ מִיתָה יָפָה.

The Gemara asks: **If so, just as there,** in the case of the beheaded calf, it is beheaded **with a cleaver** [*kofitz*][BL] **and at the nape of the neck,**[H] **here too** the court executes murderers **with a cleaver and at the nape of the neck. Rav Naḥman said** that **Rabba bar Avuh said** that **the verse says: "And you shall love your neighbor as yourself"** (Leviticus 19:18),[N] from which it is derived: **Choose for him an agreeable death.**[N] It is prohibited to abuse a guilty person while executing him, and chopping off his head with a cleaver is an unseemly death. The murderer is beheaded from the neck, not with a cleaver, and not by the other methods employed in beheading the calf.

"כָּל חֵרֶם אֲשֶׁר יָחֳרַם מִן הָאָדָם לֹא יִפָּדֶה" לָמָּה לִי? מִיבָּעֵי לֵיהּ לְכִדְתַנְיָא. מִנַּיִן לַיּוֹצֵא לֵיהָרֵג וְאָמַר אֶחָד "עֶרְכּוֹ עָלַי", מִנַּיִן שֶׁלֹּא אָמַר כְּלוּם,

The Gemara asks with regard to the following verse: **"Anything dedicated** [*ḥerem*], **that may be dedicated of men, shall not be redeemed;** he shall surely be put to death" (Leviticus 27:29), which is interpreted here as: Anyone sentenced to be executed shall not be redeemed; this appears to teach the same *halakha* as above, so **why do I need** it? The Gemara explains: **It is necessary** to teach **that which is taught** in a *baraita*: **From where** is it derived **with regard to one taken to be executed, and one** person **said: His valuation**[H] **is upon me** to donate to the Temple, **that he did not say anything** and his vow is not binding?

NOTES

From where is it derived that one does not exempt him – מִנַּיִן שֶׁאֵין פּוֹטְרִין אוֹתוֹ: *Tosafot* note that Rashi on the Torah cites a verse as the source of this *halakha* other than the one cited by the Gemara. They explain that this is related to the dispute concerning whether decapitation or strangulation is the more severe death penalty; *Tosafot* add that the Gemara here does not correspond to the ultimate halakhic ruling. The Ritva and Meiri indicate that the early commentaries had a different version of this passage in *Sanhedrin*, and perhaps Rashi relied on that text. The Rambam, like Rashi on the Torah, cites the verse "And you shall clear away the innocent blood" (Deuteronomy 19:13) as the proof text.

And you shall love your neighbor as yourself – וְאָהַבְתָּ לְרֵעֲךָ כָּמוֹךָ: At first glance, this derivation is difficult, as it applies this significant Torah principle of loving one's neighbor to the choice of an agreeable means of execution. However, the concept is that the mitzva: And you shall love your neighbor, applies to all Jews, even to a wicked person facing execution. Therefore every effort must be expended to provide him with an agreeable death. In a homiletic vein, Rabbeinu Meir HaLevi in *Sanhedrin* (52b) reads the term: Your neighbor [*re'akha*], as your wicked [*ra'akha*], meaning that one must love even the wicked members of the Jewish people.

An agreeable death – מִיתָה יָפָה: The use of a cleaver is a less agreeable death as it does not immediately sever all the blood vessels. Furthermore, a cleaver is duller than a sword, and therefore inflicts greater pain (Rabbi Meir HaLevi in *Sanhedrin* 52b).

BACKGROUND

The beheaded calf – עֶגְלָה עֲרוּפָה: When a murder victim's corpse is found outside a town and the identity of the person who caused his death in unknown, the Torah mandates a course of action (Deuteronomy 21:1–9): First, members of the Great Sanhedrin measure the distance between the corpse and the nearest town, to determine which town must perform the rite of the beheaded calf. This measurement is carried out even if it is obvious which town is closest. Afterward, the elders of that town bring a calf that has never been used for any labor, and they behead it in a riverbed that is not tilled. The elders wash their hands and make a statement absolving themselves of guilt. If the murderer is discovered before the calf was killed, the rite is not performed.

Cleaver – קוֹפִיץ:

Ancient Roman cleaver

LANGUAGE

Cleaver [*kofitz*] – קוֹפִיץ: From the Greek κοπίς, *kopis*, meaning a thick, large knife.

HALAKHA

The calf was beheaded and the murderer was found thereafter – נִתְעָרְפָה עֶגְלָה וְאַחַר כָּךְ נִמְצָא הַהוֹרֵג: Even if the murderer was discovered only after the calf was beheaded, he is executed (Rambam *Sefer Nezikim*, *Hilkhot Rotze'aḥ* 10:8).

The manner of beheading the calf – דֶּרֶךְ עֲרִיפַת הָעֶגְלָה: The calf is beheaded by cutting it with a large knife on the back of its neck (Rambam *Sefer Nezikim*, *Hilkhot Rotze'aḥ* 9:3).

Valuation of one taken to be executed – עֶרְכּוֹ שֶׁל הַיּוֹצֵא לֵיהָרֵג: One condemned to death by a Jewish court has no valuation. In other words, if he or anyone else takes a vow to donate his valuation, the vow does not take effect, in accordance with the opinion of the first *tanna* (Rambam *Sefer Hafla'a*, *Hilkhot Arakhin* 3:11).

שֶׁנֶּאֱמַר ״כָּל חֵרֶם אֲשֶׁר יָחֳרַם מִן הָאָדָם לֹא יִפָּדֶה״. יָכוֹל אַף קוֹדֶם שֶׁנִּגְמַר דִּינוֹ כֵּן – תַּלְמוּד לוֹמַר. ״מִן הָאָדָם״ – וְלֹא כָּל הָאָדָם.

It is derived **as it is stated: "Anything dedicated** [*ḥerem*], **that may be dedicated of men** [*yoḥoram*], **shall not be redeemed"** (Leviticus 27:29). This verse is taken to mean that anything dedicated, through which a man who is condemned [*yoḥoram*] is valuated, shall not be redeemed, as the person in question is already considered dead. One **might** think that **even before his verdict** is issued this should be **so**, and that one who said: The valuation of so-and-so on trial for murder is upon me, said nothing of consequence. Therefore, **the verse states:** "That may be dedicated **of men,"** implying "of men," **but not entire men.** If it is valuation of an entire man, one not yet sentenced to death, it is binding. If it is valuation of a partial man, one sentenced to death, it is not binding.

וּלְרַבִּי חֲנַנְיָא בֶּן עֲקַבְיָא, דְּאָמַר: נֶעֱרָךְ, מִפְּנֵי שֶׁדָּמָיו קְצוּבִין, הַאי ״כָּל חֵרֶם״ מַאי עָבֵיד לֵיהּ?

The Gemara asks: **And according to Rabbi Ḥananya ben Akavya,** who **said** that even a person taken to his execution **is valuated,**[N] and the vow is binding, **because** the **money** of **his** valuation **is fixed.** The sum of the valuation established in the Torah is not based on the worth of the individual; rather, there is a fixed sum determined by age and gender. Therefore, one may be valuated as long as he is alive. According to that opinion, the question remains with regard to **this** verse: **"Anything dedicated," what does** he derive from **it?**

מִיבְּעֵי לֵיהּ לְכִדְתַנְיָא, רַבִּי יִשְׁמָעֵאל בְּנוֹ שֶׁל רַבִּי יוֹחָנָן בֶּן בְּרוֹקָה אוֹמֵר: לְפִי שֶׁמָּצִינוּ לַמּוּמָתִים בִּידֵי שָׁמַיִם שֶׁנּוֹתְנִין מָמוֹן וּמִתְכַּפֵּר לָהֶן, שֶׁנֶּאֱמַר ״אִם כּוֹפֶר יוּשַׁת עָלָיו״, יָכוֹל אַף בִּידֵי אָדָם כֵּן – תַּלְמוּד לוֹמַר ״חֵרֶם מִן הָאָדָם לֹא יִפָּדֶה״.

The Gemara answers: **He requires it** to teach **that which is taught** in a *baraita*: **Rabbi Yishmael, son of Rabbi Yoḥanan ben Beroka, says: Because we found with regard to those executed at the hand of Heaven,** and not through court-administered execution, **that they give money and their** sins **are atoned, as it is stated:** "The ox shall be stoned, and its owner shall also be put to death. **If there be laid upon him a ransom** then he shall give for the redemption of his life whatsoever is laid upon him" (Exodus 21:29–30). One whose ox kills a person is essentially liable to receive the death penalty at the hand of Heaven, and pays money instead.[H] You **might** think that **even** with regard to those liable to receive the death penalty **at the hands of man** it is **so,** and one can pay in lieu of execution. Therefore, **the verse states: "Dedicated of men shall not be redeemed"** (Leviticus 27:29). One who is executed by man cannot be redeemed with money.

וְאֵין לִי אֶלָּא מִיתוֹת חֲמוּרוֹת, שֶׁלֹּא נִיתְּנָה שִׁגְגָתָן לְכַפָּרָה, מִיתוֹת קַלּוֹת, שֶׁנִּיתְּנָה שִׁגְגָתָן לְכַפָּרָה מִנַּיִן – תַּלְמוּד לוֹמַר ״כָּל חֵרֶם״.

And I have derived this restriction **only** with regard to prohibitions punishable by **severe** penalties of **death,**[N] e.g., striking one's father, **for which no atonement is designated** in the Torah **for their unwitting** violation. However, with regard to prohibitions punishable by **less severe** penalties of **death,** e.g., performing labor on Shabbat, **for which atonement,** a sin-offering, **is designated** in the Torah **for their unwitting** violation, **from where** is it derived that there is no payment in lieu of execution? **The verse states: "Anything dedicated,"** to include all prohibitions punishable by court-administered execution.

וְלָא מִמֵּילָא, מִ״לֹּא תִקְחוּ כוֹפֶר״ שָׁמְעַתְּ מִינָּהּ: לָא תִּשְׁקוֹל מָמוֹנָא מִינֵּיהּ וְתִפְטְרֵיהּ, ״כָּל חֵרֶם״ לָמָּה לִי? אָמַר רָמִי בַּר חָמָא: אִיצְטְרִיךְ; סָלְקָא דַּעְתָּךְ אָמִינָא:

The Gemara asks: **And didn't you incidentally learn** the following conclusion **from** the verse **"And you shall take no ransom** for the life of a murderer, who is guilty of death" (Numbers 35:31): **Do not take money from him and exempt him** from death? **Why,** then, **do I** require the phrase: **Any *ḥerem*? Rami bar Ḥama said:** It is **necessary,** as **it might enter your mind to say**

HALAKHA

Payment of ransom for death at the hand of Heaven – כּוֹפֶר לַמּוּמָתִים בִּידֵי שָׁמַיִם: The owner of a forewarned ox that killed a person is liable to receive death at the hand of Heaven, in accordance with the verse "And its owner shall also be put to death" (Exodus 21:29). If he pays ransom equivalent to the value of the victim, he thereby gains atonement (Rambam *Sefer Nezikim, Hilkhot Nizkei Mamon* 10:4).

NOTES

Is valuated – נֶעֱרָךְ: The *halakhot* of valuations are detailed in the Torah (Leviticus 27), and an entire tractate, *Arakhin*, is devoted to it. There is a fundamental difference between one who vows to give the monetary worth of a particular person and one who vows to donate his valuation. The former is a vow to donate the monetary value of that person, which is typically determined by his worth in the slave market. In that regard, everyone agrees that one taken to be executed has no monetary value. Valuations, in contrast, are unrelated to one's worth on the slave market, but are fixed sums determined by the age and gender of the subject. The dispute, then, is whether the legal status of one taken to be executed is that of a dead person, who has no valuation, or whether as long as he remains alive he can still be valuated.

Severe penalties of death – מִיתוֹת חֲמוּרוֹת: Rashi and *Tosafot* disagree over whether a murderer is considered one whose punishment is lenient or one whose punishment is severe. They both agree, though, that the determining factor of severity or leniency is whether there is atonement for unwitting transgressors. If that is the case, why doesn't the Gemara explicitly distinguish between capital crimes for unwitting sinners, for which there is atonement, and capital crimes for which there is no atonement; why refer to them cryptically as severe and lenient? Moreover, those transgressions characterized in the Gemara as lenient, e.g., performing prohibited labor on Shabbat, are typically punishable by the more severe penalties of death, stoning, and burning. The *Shita Mekubbetzet* suggests that a prohibition with regard to which the Torah did not specify that it is punishable by *karet* receives a punishment from Heaven as well, rendering his punishment more severe than the punishment of one liable to receive *karet*.

הָנֵי מִילֵּי הֵיכָא דַּהֲרָגוֹ דֶּרֶךְ עֲלִיָּיה, שֶׁלֹּא נִיתְּנָה שִׁגְגָתוֹ לְכַפָּרָה. אֲבָל הֲרָגוֹ דֶּרֶךְ יְרִידָה, דְּנִיתְּנָה שִׁגְגָתוֹ לְכַפָּרָה, אֵימָא נִישְׁקוֹל מָמוֹנָא מִינֵּיהּ וְנִיפַטְרֵיהּ, קָא מַשְׁמַע לַן.

this principle, that one cannot pay in lieu of execution, **applies only when one** intentionally **killed him in an upward motion,**[NH] **for which no atonement is designated** in the Torah **for its unwitting** performance. **However,** with regard to one who intentionally **killed him in a downward motion, for which atonement,** i.e., exile, **is designated** in the Torah **for its unwitting** performance, **say: Let us take money from him and exempt him.** Therefore, the phrase "any *ḥerem*" **teaches us** that even in that case there is no payment in lieu of execution.

אֲמַר לֵיהּ רָבָא: הָא – מִדְּתָנָא דְּבֵי חִזְקִיָּה נָפְקָא, דְּתָנָא דְּבֵי חִזְקִיָּה: מַכֵּה אָדָם וּמַכֵּה בְהֵמָה,

Rava said to him: That principle **is derived** from that which the Sage **of the school of Ḥizkiyya taught,**[N] as the Sage **of the school of Ḥizkiyya taught:** The verse juxtaposes the cases of **one who smites a person, and one who smites an animal** (Leviticus 24:21).

מַה מַּכֵּה בְהֵמָה לֹא חִלַּקְתָּ בּוֹ בֵּין שׁוֹגֵג לְמֵזִיד, בֵּין מִתְכַּוֵּין לְשֶׁאֵין מִתְכַּוֵּין, בֵּין דֶּרֶךְ יְרִידָה לְדֶרֶךְ עֲלִיָּיה, לְפוֹטְרוֹ מָמוֹן אֶלָּא לְחַיְּיבוֹ מָמוֹן, אַף מַכֵּה אָדָם לֹא תַּחֲלוֹק בּוֹ בֵּין שׁוֹגֵג לְמֵזִיד, בֵּין מִתְכַּוֵּין לְשֶׁאֵין מִתְכַּוֵּין, בֵּין דֶּרֶךְ יְרִידָה לְדֶרֶךְ עֲלִיָּיה, לְחַיְּיבוֹ מָמוֹן אֶלָּא לְפוֹטְרוֹ מָמוֹן!

Just as in the case of one **who smites an animal, you did not distinguish between** one who did so **unwittingly and** one who did so **intentionally; between** one who acted **with intent and** one who acted **with no intent; between** one who smites **in the** course of a **downward motion and** one who smites **in the** course of **an upward motion;** and in all those cases it is not **to exempt** him from paying **money but rather to obligate him** to pay **money; so too** in the case of one **who smites a person: Do not distinguish between** one who did so **unwittingly and** one who did so **intentionally; between** one who acted **with intent and** one who acted **with no intent; between** one who smites **in the** course of **a downward motion and** one who smites **in the** course of **an upward motion;** and in all those cases it is not **to obligate him** to pay **money but rather to exempt him** from paying **money.** Apparently, one who kills another in any manner is exempt from payment, and therefore no additional verse is required to derive that principle.

אֶלָּא אֲמַר רָמִי בַּר חָמָא: אִיצְטְרִיךְ; סָלְקָא דַּעְתָּךְ אָמִינָא: הָנֵי מִילֵּי – הֵיכָא דְּסִימֵּא אֶת עֵינוֹ וַהֲרָגוֹ בָּהּ, אֲבָל הֵיכָא דְּסִימֵּא אֶת עֵינוֹ וַהֲרָגוֹ בְּדָבָר אַחֵר – אֵימָא נִישְׁקוֹל מָמוֹנָא מִינֵּיהּ. אֲמַר לֵיהּ רָבָא: הָא נַמִי מֵאִידָּךְ תַּנָּא דְּבֵי חִזְקִיָּה נָפְקָא. דְּתָנָא דְּבֵי חִזְקִיָּה: ״עַיִן תַּחַת עַיִן״ וְלֹא עַיִן וְנֶפֶשׁ תַּחַת עַיִן!

Rather, Rami bar Ḥama said that the phrase "any *ḥerem*" (Leviticus 27:29) **is necessary, as it might enter your mind to say** that **this** *halakha*, that one who is liable to be executed is exempt from payment, **applies only** in a case **where one blinded** another's **eye and killed him with** that same blow. **However,** in a case **where one blinded** another's **eye and killed him by** means of a **different** blow, **say: Let us take money from him** to pay the damage inflicted to the eye. Therefore, the verse teaches that this is not the case. **Rava said to him: This** case of one who blinded another's eye and killed him **is also derived from** that which **another *tanna*** of the school of **Ḥizkiyya** taught, as the Sage **of the school of Ḥizkiyya taught** that the verse states: **"An eye for an eye"** (Exodus 21:24), from which it may be inferred, **but not an eye and a life**[NH] **for an eye.** When he gives his life for killing another while blinding him, he need not pay the worth of the eye as well.

NOTES

When one intentionally killed him in an upward motion – הֵיכָא דַּהֲרָגוֹ דֶּרֶךְ עֲלִיָּיה: *Tosafot* note that killing in an upward motion is considered a less severe crime than killing in a downward motion. The Rambam maintains that this is because an accident of this kind is unusual and it cannot be attributed to negligence. However, *Tosafot* continue, here only one particular aspect of the comparison is under consideration, whether or not atonement is available to one who commits this transgression. Other stringent or lenient elements are not taken into account. The reasoning is that if the Torah provided a remedy for the sin other than the prescribed punishment, it stands to reason that atonement for his transgression could be achieved through monetary payment.

It is derived from that which the Sage of the school of Ḥizkiyya taught – מִדְּתָנָא דְּבֵי חִזְקִיָּה נָפְקָא: Rashi follows his earlier explanation: The main point of the derivation of the Sage of the school of Ḥizkiyya is that there is no monetary payment for violating any prohibition whose violation is punishable by death when it is performed intentionally. According to this, clearly no special derivation is required with regard to one who kills in a downward motion. However, according to the Ramban and others, who maintain that the Sage of the school of Ḥizkiyya is teaching that one does not receive two punishments, the Gemara's statement is difficult, as theoretically, one could be obligated to pay money and at the same time be exempt from any other punishment. The commentaries answer that according to all opinions, the *halakha* is derived from both the statement of the school of Ḥizkiyya and the derivation from the verse "And yet no harm follow" (Exodus 21:22).

An eye for an eye, but not an eye and a life, etc. – עַיִן תַּחַת עַיִן וְלֹא עַיִן וְנֶפֶשׁ וכו׳: This statement of the school of Ḥizkiyya is unrelated to liability for two punishments; rather, as explained by Rashi, it is one of the proofs that the verse "An eye for an eye" is not to be interpreted literally. Were the punishment of one who injured another's eye to have his own eye injured, there is the risk that he might die as a result, meaning that it was an eye and a life for an eye. The early commentaries therefore questioned the relevance of this source to the matter under discussion.

Various explanations of that relevance were proposed. *Tosafot* maintain that the point is from the continuation of the statement of the school of Ḥizkiyya. Just as one does not punished with an eye and a life for an eye, so too, one is not punished with a life and an eye for a life. Others explain that the principle underlying this statement of the school of Ḥizkiyya is that one does not receive two punishments for transgressions committed simultaneously (Rosh; Rabbi Aharon HaLevi; Ritva). An additional interpretation, attributed to one of the Tosafists, is that this is a form of juxtaposition: Just as with regard to the eye of the attacker, he is punished only with payment for one eye, so too, with regard to the eye of the victim, only one punishment is meted out. The Ritva cites Rabbeinu Menaḥem's version of the text: And not an eye for an eye and a life, which is explained like the explanations of the early commentaries.

HALAKHA

Killed him in an upward motion – הֲרָגוֹ דֶּרֶךְ עֲלִיָּיה: One who unintentionally kills another in an upward motion is not liable to be exiled, as detailed in the second chapter of tractate *Makkot* (Rambam *Sefer Nezikim, Hilkhot Rotze'aḥ* 6:13).

Not an eye and a life – לֹא עַיִן וְנֶפֶשׁ: One who injures another is not punished by having the same injury inflicted upon him; rather, he pays for the damage he caused. The reason is that inflicting an injury could cause the attacker's death. See *Bava Kama* 84a, where the Gemara derives this principle from this verse (Rambam *Sefer Nezikim, Hilkhot Ḥovel* 1:3).

אלא אמר רב אשי: איצטריך; סלקא דעתך אמינא: הואיל וחידוש הוא שחידשה תורה בקנס, אף על גב דמיקטיל משלם – קא משמע לן. ולרבה דאמר: חידוש הוא שחידשה תורה בקנס, אף על גב דמיקטיל משלם, האי "כל חרם" מאי עביד ליה? סבר לה כתנא קמא דרבי חנניא בן עקביא.

Rather, after the Gemara rejected the above explanations, **Rav Ashi said:**[N] The phrase "any *ḥerem*" is nonetheless **necessary,** as **it might enter your mind to say: Since it is a novel element that the Torah introduced with regard to** the payment of a **fine,** which is not payment for any damage caused but is a Torah decree, in that case, **even though he is killed he pays** the fine. Therefore, the verse **teaches us** that one who is executed is exempt from payment of the fine. The Gemara asks: **And according to Rabba, who said** that this is indeed the *halakha*: Since **it is a novel element that the Torah introduced with regard to** the payment of a **fine, even though he is killed he pays** the fine, **what does** he **do with this** phrase: **"Any *ḥerem*"?** The Gemara answers: Rabba **holds** with regard **to this** matter **in accordance with** the opinion of **the first *tanna*,** who disagrees with **Rabbi Ḥananya ben Akavya** and explains that the phrase "Any *ḥerem*" teaches that the vow one takes to donate the valuation of one being taken to his execution is not binding.

מתני׳ נערה שנתארסה ונתגרשה, רבי יוסי הגלילי אומר: אין לה קנס, רבי עקיבא אומר: יש לה קנס, וקנסה לעצמה.

MISHNA With regard to **a young woman who was betrothed and divorced,**[NH] and then raped, **Rabbi Yosei HaGelili says: She does not** receive payment of a **fine** for her rape. **Rabbi Akiva says: She** receives payment of a **fine** for her rape **and her fine** is paid **to herself,** not her father, as since she was betrothed and divorced she is no longer subject to her father's authority.

גמ׳ מאי טעמא דרבי יוסי הגלילי? אמר קרא "אשר לא אורשה", הא אורסה – אין לה קנס. ורבי עקיבא: "אשר לא אורשה" – לאביה, הא אורסה – לעצמה,

GEMARA **What is the rationale** for the opinion of **Rabbi Yosei HaGelili?** It is as **the verse states:** "If a man finds a young woman who is a virgin **who was not betrothed"** (Deuteronomy 22:28), from which it may be inferred: If **she was betrothed she does not have a fine** for rape. The Gemara asks: **And** how does **Rabbi Akiva** explain this verse? The Gemara answers that the verse states: If it is a young woman **who was not betrothed,** the fine is paid **to her father,** from which it may be inferred: If **she was betrothed,** the fine is paid **to** the betrothed woman **herself.**

אלא מעתה "נערה" ולא בוגרת, דכי נמי דלעצמה? "בתולה" ולא בעולה, דכי נמי דלעצמה? אלא, לגמרי – הכא נמי לגמרי!

The Gemara asks: **But if** that is **so,** that the inference from the verse is that the fine is levied on one who rapes **a young woman and not** on one who rapes **a grown woman,**[N] **so too,** there is the *halakha* in the latter case that the fine is paid **to** the grown woman **herself.** Similarly, with regard to the inference that the fine is levied on one who rapes **a virgin and not** on one who rapes **a non-virgin, so too,** there is the *halakha* that in the latter case the fine is paid **to** the non-virgin **herself.** A distinction of that kind has never been encountered. **Rather,** with regard to a grown woman and a non-virgin, the rapist is **completely** exempt from paying the fine; **here too,** with regard to a betrothed woman, the rapist is **completely** exempt from paying the fine.

אמר לך רבי עקיבא: האי "לא אורשה" מיבעי ליה לכדתניא: "אשר לא אורשה" – פרט לנערה שנתארסה ונתגרשה, שאין לה קנס, דברי רבי יוסי הגלילי. רבי עקיבא אומר: יש לה קנס, וקנסה לאביה. והדין נותן: הואיל ואביה זכאי בכסף קידושיה, ואביה זכאי בכסף קנסה, מה כסף קידושיה, אף על פי שנתארסה ונתגרשה – לאביה, אף כסף קנסה, אף על פי שנתארסה ונתגרשה – לאביה.

The Gemara answers: **Rabbi Akiva** could have **said to you** that **this verse: "Who was not betrothed," is required by him** to teach another *halakha* **that is taught** in a different *baraita*. **"Who was not betrothed"** (Deuteronomy 22:28) comes to **exclude a young woman who was betrothed and divorced** and establish **that she does not** receive payment of a **fine** for her rape; this is **the statement of Rabbi Yosei HaGelili. Rabbi Akiva says: She** receives payment of a **fine** for her rape, **and her fine goes to her father,** contrary to the ruling attributed to Rabbi Akiva in the mishna. **And** ostensibly, no verse is required to derive this *halakha*, as **logic dictates** that it is so: **Since her father is entitled to the money of her betrothal**[N] if she is betrothed before she becomes a grown woman, **and** likewise **her father is entitled to the money of her fine; just as the money of her** subsequent **betrothal** as a young woman, **even though she was betrothed and divorced,** is paid **to her father,**[H] **so too, the money of her fine, although she was betrothed and divorced,** is paid **to her father.**

NOTES

Rather, Rav Ashi said, etc. – אלא אמר רב אשי וכו׳: If, as Rav Ashi claims, the phrase "Any *ḥerem*" refers to the case of one who is liable to be executed and to pay a fine, it should have been cited as proof in the mishna, which deals with the fine of a rapist. Why did the mishna cite proof from the verse "And yet no harm follow"? One answer is that the mishna established a principle that one is exempt from payment, even payment of a fine, for a transgression punishable by death, and the *tanna* did not cite all relevant verses. Alternatively, since there is proof for the basic *halakha* from the verse that he cited, the *tanna* did not cite the verse that refers to that particular detail (Rabbi Aharon HaLevi; Ritva).

Who was betrothed and divorced – שנתארסה ונתגרשה: The same *halakha* applies if she was betrothed and widowed. Rabbi Yosei HaGelili does not agree with Rabbi Akiva even in that case, but consistently maintains that a young woman who was once betrothed is not entitled to the fine (*Shita Mekubbetzet*).

A young woman and not a grown woman, etc. – נערה ולא בוגרת וכו׳: Rashi notes that since there is no source that requires payment of a fine to a grown woman or a non-virgin, even Rabbi Akiva agrees with this *halakha*. He does not, however, explain why Rabbi Akiva agrees with this *halakha*. One approach is that since ultimately there is a verbal analogy between the seduced and raped woman, the words "young woman" and "virgin" that appear in both passages come to emphasize that only a young woman who is a virgin is entitled to the fine (see *Or Same'aḥ*).

Since her father is entitled to the money of her betrothal – הואיל ואביה זכאי בכסף קידושיה: This is problematic, as there is a distinction between a father's right to the money received for his daughter's betrothal and his right to her fine if she is raped. In the case of betrothal, he has the right to betroth her to the man of his choice, but he does not have the right to give her to a man for intercourse outside the context of marriage. Why, then, does he receive the money paid as a fine for her rape? One answer is that Rabbi Akiva maintains that the father's right to the money received for his daughter's betrothal is based on a source other than his discretionary rights with regard to her betrothal, and therefore just as the money of her betrothal goes to her father, so does her fine. As the Meiri stated, betrothal does not release a daughter from her father's authority (see *Shita Mekubbetzet*).

HALAKHA

A young woman who was betrothed and divorced – נערה שנתארסה ונתגרשה: The fine of one who raped or seduced a girl who was betrothed and divorced is paid to her, as the *halakha* is in accordance with the opinion of Rabbi Akiva in disputes with an individual *tanna* (Rif; Rambam *Sefer Nashim, Hilkhot Na'ara Betula* 2:16).

The money of her betrothal is paid to her father – כסף קידושיה לאביה: With regard to a daughter who was betrothed and divorced or widowed, as long as she remains a young woman, the money of any subsequent betrothal belongs to her father (Rambam *Sefer Nashim, Hilkhot Ishut* 3:11; *Shulḥan Arukh, Even HaEzer* 37:1).

אם כן, מה תלמוד לומר "אשר לא אורשה" – מופנה להקיש לו, ולדון הימנו גזירה שוה: נאמר כאן "אשר לא אורשה" ונאמר להלן "אשר לא אורשה" מה כאן חמשים – אף להלן חמשים; ומה להלן שקלים – אף כאן שקלים.

If so, and the *halakha* can be logically inferred, **why does the verse state: "Who was not betrothed"?** This verse is **free,** as it is superfluous in its own context, **and** it is written **to liken** another case to it, **and to derive from it a verbal analogy: It is stated here** with regard to a woman who was raped: **"Who was not betrothed," and it is stated below:** "And if a man seduce a virgin **who was not betrothed"** (Exodus 22:15). **Just as here,** with regard to rape, the Torah specifies that the payment is **fifty** silver pieces (Deuteronomy 22:29), **so too below,** with regard to seduction, the payment is **fifty. And just as below,** with regard to seduction, the payment is in **shekels,** as it is written: "He shall weigh [*yishkol*] money" (Exodus 22:16), **so too here,** the payment is in **shekels.**

ורבי עקיבא, מאי חזית ד"אשר לא אורשה" לגזירה שוה, ו"בתולה" למעוטי בעולה,

The Gemara asks: **And Rabbi Akiva, what did you see** that led you to utilize the phrase: **"Who was not betrothed" for a verbal analogy,** and the term **"virgin" to exclude a non-virgin** from the fine?

Perek **III**
Daf **38** Amud **b**

אימא "בתולה" – לגזירה שוה ו"אשר לא אורסה" – פרט לנערה שנתארסה ונתגרשה!

Say to the contrary; the term **"virgin,"** written with regard to both rape and seduction, is **to** derive **a verbal analogy,**[N] and not to exclude a non-virgin, **and** the phrase **"Who was not betrothed"** will be interpreted as Rabbi Yosei HaGelili interpreted it, to **exclude a young woman who was betrothed and divorced.**

מסתברא "אשר לא אורסה" לגזירה שוה, שהרי אני קורא בה "נערה בתולה". אדרבה, "בתולה" לגזירה שוה, שהרי אני קורא בה "אשר לא אורסה"! מסתברא, הא – אישתני גופה, והא – לא אישתני גופה.

The Gemara answers: **It stands to reason** that the phrase **"Who was not betrothed"** is utilized **to** derive **a verbal analogy,** and not to exclude one who was betrothed and divorced, **as** even after the divorce **I can still read** the phrase **"A young woman who is a virgin"** as applying **to her.** The Gemara asks: **On the contrary,** utilize the term **virgin to** derive **a verbal analogy, as** even if she is not a virgin, **I can still read** the phrase **"Who was not betrothed"** as applying **to her.** The Gemara answers: **It stands to reason** that the term "virgin" excludes a non-virgin, and the phrase "Who was not betrothed" is utilized to derive a verbal analogy, as **this** woman who engaged in relations, **her body changed,**[N] **and that** woman who was betrothed and divorced, **her body did not change,** and therefore her status with regard to the fine should similarly not change.

ורבי יוסי הגלילי האי סברא מנא ליה? נפקא ליה מדתניא: "כסף ישקול כמוהר הבתולות" – שיהא זה כמוהר הבתולות, ומוהר הבתולות כזה.

The Gemara asks: **And from where** does **Rabbi Yosei HaGelili** derive **this conclusion** with regard to the amount of the payment for seduction and the type of money used in the payment for rape? The Gemara responds: **He derives it from that which was taught** in a *baraita* that it is written with regard to seduction: **"He shall weigh money like the dowry of the virgins"** (Exodus 22:16), from which it is derived **that this** fine for seduction **will be like the dowry** paid **to the virgins** elsewhere for rape, fifty silver coins, **and the dowry** paid **to the virgins** for rape **will be like this** fine for seduction in shekels.

NOTES

Say virgin is to derive a verbal analogy – אימא בתולה לגזירה שוה: There is a fundamental difficulty, as this question runs counter to one of the basic principles of verbal analogy, i.e., one may not derive a verbal analogy on his own; only those he has received as a tradition from his teachers are valid. All verbal analogies are based on ancient tradition, like a *halakha* transmitted to Moses from Sinai. Yet here, and in several other places, there appears to be no established tradition. The early commentaries suggest several answers. One approach (Ritva) is that there was a tradition linking two verses by verbal analogy, but it was not clear which particular words served as the basis of the analogy (see *Tosafot*). Others maintain that the terms in the analogy were also part of the tradition, but the meaning of the analogy was not always clear (see *Shita Mekubbetzet*).

This woman, her body changed – הא אישתני גופה: This change is obvious in the case of a non-virgin. With regard to a grown woman, some commentaries explain that her body is also considered to have undergone changes over time affecting her status as a virgin (see *Shita Mekubbetzet*).

קשיא דרבי עקיבא אדרבי עקיבא! תרי תנאי ואליבא דרבי עקיבא.

§ The Gemara comments: It is **difficult** as there is a contradiction between one statement **of Rabbi Akiva** and another statement **of Rabbi Akiva.**[N] In the mishna he ruled that the fine for the rape of a young woman who was betrothed and divorced is paid to the woman, and in the *baraita* he ruled that it is paid to her father. The Gemara answers: These are conflicting traditions of **two *tanna'im* in accordance with** the opinion of **Rabbi Akiva.**

בשלמא רבי עקיבא דמתניתין – לא אתיא גזירה שוה ומפקא ליה לקרא מפשטיה לגמרי, אלא לרבי עקיבא דברייתא – אתיא גזירה שוה ומפקא מפשטיה לגמרי!

The Gemara observes: **Granted,** the statement of **Rabbi Akiva of the mishna** is reasonable, as **a verbal analogy does not come and divert the verse from its plain meaning entirely.** The plain meaning of the phrase: "Who was not betrothed" is that there is a difference between a young woman who was betrothed, who receives payment of the fine, and one who was not, whose father receives payment of the fine. **However,** according **to Rabbi Akiva of the *baraita*,** does **a verbal analogy come and divert the verse from its plain meaning entirely,**[N] and teach that there is no difference at all between a young woman who was betrothed and one who was not?

אמר רב נחמן בר יצחק: קרי ביה "אשר לא ארוסה". ארוסה בת סקילה היא! סלקא דעתך אמינא: הואיל וחידוש הוא שחידשה תורה בקנס, אף על גב דמיקטיל – משלם.

Rav Naḥman bar Yitzḥak said: Interpret the verse as: **Who is not betrothed.**[N] It does not mean that the young woman was not betrothed in the past, rather, that she is not currently betrothed. The Gemara asks: There is no need for a verse to derive that the rapist is exempt from paying a fine if the young woman is betrothed, as the rape of **a betrothed** young woman **is** punishable **by stoning,** and the rapist is certainly exempt from paying the fine. The Gemara answers: As **it might enter your mind to say: Since it is a novel element that the Torah introduced with regard to** the payment of **a fine, even though he is killed he pays** the fine. Therefore, the verse **teaches us** that one who is executed is exempt from payment of the fine.

ולרבה, דאמר: חידוש הוא שחידשה תורה בקנס, אף על גב דמיקטיל משלם – מאי איכא למימר? סבר לה כרבי עקיבא דמתניתין.

The Gemara asks: **And according to Rabba, who said** that this is indeed the *halakha*: Since **it is a novel element that the Torah introduced with regard to** the payment of **a fine, even though he is killed he pays** the fine, **what is there to say?** What is derived from the verse that says that there is no fine if the young woman is betrothed? The Gemara answers: Rabba **holds in accordance with** the opinion of **Rabbi Akiva of the mishna,** who interpreted the verse as it is written, meaning that it is referring to one who was betrothed and divorced.

תנו רבנן: קנסה למי – לאביה, ויש אומרים: לעצמה. לעצמה אמאי? אמר רב חסדא: הכא בנערה שנתארסה ונתגרשה עסקינן, וקמיפלגי בפלוגתא דרבי עקיבא דמתניתין ורבי עקיבא דברייתא.

The Sages taught: With regard to a young woman who was raped, **to whom is her fine** paid? It is paid **to her father; and some say:** It is paid **to her.** The Gemara asks: **To her? Why?** The verse explicitly states that the fine is paid to her father. **Rav Ḥisda said: Here we are dealing with a young woman who was betrothed and divorced, and these *tanna'im*** in the ***baraita*** **disagree in the dispute between Rabbi Akiva of the mishna and Rabbi Akiva of the *baraita*,** with regard to whom the rapist pays the fine in that case.

NOTES

It is difficult as there is a contradiction between one statement of Rabbi Akiva and another statement of Rabbi Akiva – קשיא דרבי עקיבא אדרבי עקיבא: Why did the Gemara postpone raising this contradiction instead of raising it immediately, especially as it provides no novel resolution but merely affirms that these are two opinions? In the *Shita Mekubbetzet* it is explained that since the Gemara elaborates on and provides a source for Rabbi Akiva's opinion, it was necessary to cite the *baraita* in order to explain his reasoning, which appears contrary to the verses. As the *baraita* includes a detailed explanation, the Gemara cannot be dismissed as corrupted and thereby rejected in favor of the mishna (*Shita Mekubbetzet*).

Divert the verse from its plain meaning entirely – מפקא מפשטיה לגמרי: Even though the ideal verbal analogy is free, i.e., the words that serve as the basis of the analogy are superfluous in their context, the meaning of these words cannot be entirely disregarded just because they were written primarily for the verbal analogy. *Tosafot* note that there are other cases where this is more problematic, as here it is merely the inference of the verse, that a young woman who was betrothed and divorced does not receive the fine, that runs counter to the halakhic conclusion. In other places, the verbal analogy appears to subvert the meaning of the verse entirely (see *Shita Mekubbetzet*).

Interpret the verse as: Who is not betrothed – קרי ביה אשר לא ארוסה: This does not require adapting the letters or vowels of this word. Rather, the expression "not betrothed" should not be understood in the past tense: Who was not betrothed; rather it is a kind of present participle: One who is not betrothed. This is a common usage in the Bible, particularly in the language of the prophets (Ritva; Rabbeinu Crescas Vidal).

HALAKHA

If one had intercourse with a young woman, and she died – בָּא עָלֶיהָ וּמֵתָה: If the young woman died before the rapist or seducer stood trial, he is exempt from the fine. The *halakha* is in accordance with the opinion of Abaye, as his conclusion is not rejected due to Rava's dilemma (Rambam *Sefer Nashim, Hilkhot Na'ara Betula* 1:15 and the *Kesef Mishna* there; *Tur, Even HaEzer* 177).

אָמַר אַבַּיֵי: בָּא עָלֶיהָ וּמֵתָה – פָּטוּר, שֶׁנֶּאֱמַר ״וְנָתַן לַאֲבִי הַנַּעֲרָה״ – וְלֹא לַאֲבִי מֵתָה. מִלְּתָא דִּפְשִׁיטָא לֵיהּ לְאַבַּיֵי, מִיבַּעְיָא לֵיהּ לְרָבָא.

§ **Abaye said:** If **one had intercourse with a** young woman, **and she died**[H] before he was sentenced, he is **exempt** from paying the fine, **as it is stated: "And the man who lay with her shall give to the father of the young woman"** (Deuteronomy 22:29), from which it is inferred, **and not to the father of a dead girl.**[N] The Gemara comments: This **matter that was obvious to Abaye** was **raised as a dilemma to Rava.**[N]

דְּבָעֵי רָבָא: יֵשׁ בֶּגֶר בַּקֶּבֶר אוֹ אֵין בֶּגֶר בַּקֶּבֶר? יֵשׁ בֶּגֶר בַּקֶּבֶר – וְדִבְנָהּ הָוֵי, אוֹ דִּלְמָא אֵין בֶּגֶר בַּקֶּבֶר – וּדְאָבִיהָ הָוֵי?

As Rava raised a dilemma: Is there achievement of **grown-woman status in the grave or is there** not achievement of **grown-woman status in the grave?**[N] The *halakha* is that if a young woman is raped and the rapist did not pay the fine until she became a grown woman, the rapist pays the fine to her and not to her father. Rava's dilemma is in a case where a young woman dies and her rapist was convicted only after the time elapsed that were she alive she would have reached grown-woman status. **Is there** achievement of **grown-woman status in the grave, and** therefore she is entitled to the fine and **it is the** property **of her son**[N] as his mother's heir? **Or perhaps there is no** achievement of **grown-woman status in the grave, and the fine is** the property **of her father,** as she was a young woman when she died.

NOTES

And not to the father of a dead girl – וְלֹא לַאֲבִי מֵתָה: The early commentaries point out that the Gemara does not interpret the term young woman consistently. Sometimes it interprets a young woman as referring to one who was a young woman, even though she is already a grown woman. *Tosafot*, the Rosh, and others explain that it would have been sufficient for it to have been written in the verse: And he gives to her father. The use of the phrase "To the father of the young woman" indicates that she remains a young woman at the time of the rapist's conviction. The *Penei Yehoshua* asks: Wasn't it necessary to write: "To the father of the young woman" to exclude the father of a grown woman? Conceivably, both conclusions may be derived as they emanate from the same principle: The time that determines the father's right to the payment is when the rapist is convicted. If his daughter's status then is no longer what it was at the time of the rape, he forfeits that right.

Raised as a dilemma to Rava – מִיבַּעְיָא לֵיהּ לְרָבָא: Rashi explains later that Rava's dilemma exists neither according to the first version nor according to the second version of Rava's teaching, as in both versions he clearly maintains that death does not release the rapist from the obligation to pay the fine. Rather, the dilemma raised is according to Mar bar Rav Ashi's explanation of Rava's statement.

Is there achievement of grown-woman status in the grave – יֵשׁ בֶּגֶר בַּקֶּבֶר: There are different aspects to the definition of the daughter as a grown woman, both in terms of the changes to her body and in terms of her legal status. The dilemma of whether there is achievement of grown-woman status in the grave is not in terms of her physical state but in terms of her legal status. More specifically, it is with regard to the fact that a grown woman is entirely removed from her father's authority. The problem stems from the fact that a young woman is transformed into a grown woman six months after puberty, which is the time at which she becomes a young woman. The dilemma is as follows: Is the daughter's exit from her father's authority dependent on her development during those six months, which would lead to the conclusion that there is no achievement of grown-woman status in the grave; or is it merely dependent on the passage of time, and once the six months pass she is no longer subject to her father's authority, leading to the conclusion that there is achievement of grown-woman status in the grave (*Birkat Avraham*)?

It is the property of her son – דִּבְנָהּ הָוֵי: The Meiri notes that this son must have been born out of wedlock, as had the daughter been married, her marriage itself would have fully removed her from her father's authority, leaving him with no rights over her.

Many early commentaries question the matter of the son inheriting his mother's fine, as it appears to contradict the principle that one does not bequeath a fine to his heirs, as stated at the start of the next chapter. *Tosafot* discuss this issue at length and provide various resolutions. One approach, attributed to Rabbeinu Yitzḥak, and cited by the Ritva and other early commentaries, is that the principle that one does not bequeath a fine to his heirs refers only to a fine that is not his by right, but which he receives due to actions done to others. Consequently, a father's right to the fine paid by the man who raped his daughter is not inherited by his sons. However, since the rape victim is herself entitled to the fine, she does bequeath it to her heirs. *Tosafot* explain that the discussion here is with regard to payments accompanying the fine, e.g., compensation for humiliation and degradation, and not the fine itself. These are standard monetary payments and therefore are bequeathed to others.

Rabbi Aharon HaLevi states, in the name of Rabbi Zeraḥya HaLevi, that this statement in the Gemara is according to Rabbi Shimon's opinion that if she became a grown woman after the trial she receives the fine herself. Here too, she died after the trial but before she became a grown-woman. The dilemma then is whether she is considered to have achieved grown woman status in the grave, and therefore the money is transferred to her heirs, or perhaps she did not achieve that status, and the money remains her father's. The Rashba rejects this approach. A different interpretation is suggested by the Ramban. He contends that the statement: It is her son's, does not mean literally that it belongs to her son, as a fine cannot be bequeathed. Instead, it means that if there is achievement of grown-woman status in the grave the father no longer has rights to it, as she would have received it, which would have afforded her the theoretical right to give it away or bequeath it. The Ra'avad suggests simply that initially, Rava maintained that a person can bequeath his rights to a fine, and the Gemara could have responded by challenging that assumption. However, the Gemara cited better reasons for rejecting the dilemma. Many early commentaries, including the Ramban and the Rashba, believe that the Ra'avad's answer is the most suitable in the context of the discussion in the Gemara.

וּמִי מִעַבְּרָא? וְהָתָנֵי רַב בֵּיבָי קַמֵּיהּ דְּרַב נַחְמָן: שָׁלֹשׁ נָשִׁים מְשַׁמְּשׁוֹת בְּמוֹךְ, אֵלּוּ הֵן: קְטַנָּה, וּמְעוּבֶּרֶת, וּמֵינִיקָה; קְטַנָּה – שֶׁמָּא תִּתְעַבֵּר וְתָמוּת, מְעוּבֶּרֶת – שֶׁמָּא תַּעֲשֶׂה עוּבָּרָהּ סַנְדָּל, מֵינִיקָה – שֶׁמָּא תִּגְמוֹל אֶת בְּנָהּ.

Rava's dilemma is based on the assumption that a rape victim is able to conceive before she is a grown woman. The Gemara asks: **And can a minor conceive? But didn't Rav Beivai teach** a *baraita* **before Rav Naḥman:** It is permitted for **three women to engage in relations with a** contraceptive **resorbent.**[N] **These are they: A minor, and a pregnant woman, and a nursing woman.** The *baraita* elaborates: **A minor** may do so **lest she conceive and die;**[NB] **a pregnant** woman, **lest her** existing **fetus** be crushed[B] by another fetus and **assume** the shape of **a sandal** fish[B] if she conceives a second time; and **a nursing** woman, **lest** she conceive, causing her milk to spoil, which will lead **her** to **wean her son** prematurely, endangering his health.

וְאֵיזוֹהִי קְטַנָּה – מִבַּת אַחַת עֶשְׂרֵה שָׁנָה וְיוֹם אֶחָד עַד שְׁתֵּים עֶשְׂרֵה שָׁנָה וְיוֹם אֶחָד. פָּחוֹת מִיכֵּן וְיָתֵר עַל כֵּן – מְשַׁמֶּשֶׁת כְּדַרְכָּהּ וְהוֹלֶכֶת, דִּבְרֵי רַבִּי מֵאִיר. וַחֲכָמִים אוֹמְרִים: אַחַת זוֹ וְאַחַת זוֹ מְשַׁמֶּשֶׁת כְּדַרְכָּהּ וְהוֹלֶכֶת, וּמִן הַשָּׁמַיִם יְרַחֲמוּ, מִשּׁוּם שֶׁנֶּאֱמַר "שׁוֹמֵר פְּתָאִים ה'"!

And the *baraita* further states: **What is a minor girl?**[N] A minor girl is a girl **from eleven years and one day old until twelve years and one day old.** If she was **less than that** age or **more than that** age, **she proceeds and engages in relations in her usual manner;** this is **the statement of Rabbi Meir. And the Rabbis say: Both this** woman **and that** woman, i.e., in the cases of all these women, **she proceeds and engages in relations in her usual manner, and from Heaven they will have mercy** and prevent any mishap, **due to the fact that it is stated: "The Lord preserves the simple"** (Psalms 116:6).[N] Apparently, a minor is unable to conceive.

וְכִי תֵּימָא דְּאִיעַבְּרָא כְּשֶׁהִיא נַעֲרָה וְאוֹלִידָה כְּשֶׁהִיא נַעֲרָה, וּבְשִׁיתָּא יַרְחֵי מִי קָא יָלְדָה? וְהָאָמַר שְׁמוּאֵל: אֵין בֵּין נְעָרוֹת לְבַגְרוּת אֶלָּא שִׁשָּׁה חֳדָשִׁים! וְכִי תֵּימָא: בְּצִיר הוּא דְּלֵיכָּא, הָא טְפֵי אִיכָּא – הָא "אֶלָּא" קָאָמַר!

And if you say that she conceived when she was a young woman, twelve years old, **and gave birth when she was a young woman,** and died before she reached the status of a grown woman, can a woman **give birth in six months** after conception? **But didn't Shmuel say: There are only six months between** becoming **a young woman and** becoming **a grown woman?**[H] **And if you say** that Shmuel is saying that it is **less** than six months **that there is not** transition from young woman to grown woman status; however, **more** than six months **there is** transition, as different women develop differently, and therefore she could conceive and give birth while she is a young woman, that is not so, as Shmuel **said: Only,** indicating that the period is neither less nor more than six months.

BACKGROUND

Lest she conceive and die – שֶׁמָּא תִּתְעַבֵּר וְתָמוּת: A minor girl, who has not yet reached puberty, cannot conceive. However, the age of puberty is not uniform but is heavily influenced by genetics and nutrition. There are documented cases of young girls who have indeed conceived and given birth. Regardless, the younger the girl is when she conceives, the greater the danger posed by the pregnancy. Presumably, due to the narrowness of the pelvis of a young girl, she would not survive delivery of her child.

Lest her existing fetus be crushed, etc. – שֶׁמָּא...עוּבָּרָהּ: In the case of twins or simultaneous pregnancies, which are possible albeit infrequent, one of the fetuses occasionally develops more quickly and thereby severely reduces the blood supply to the other fetus. In these situations the undernourished fetus does not develop properly but remains a fleshy mass adjoined to the placenta, similar in shape to the sandal fish.

Sandal fish – סַנְדָּל: This fish is referred to today as the species sole, a group of flatfish, a name derived from the Latin solea, referring to both the fish and the sole of a shoe. The common sole, *Solea solea*, possesses an interesting feature: Both of its eyes are on the right side of its body.

Sandal fish

HALAKHA

There are only six months between becoming a young woman and becoming a grown woman – אֵין בֵּין נְעָרוֹת לְבַגְרוּת אֶלָּא שִׁשָּׁה חֳדָשִׁים: A minor who develops the signs of puberty, two pubic hairs, becomes a young woman. Precisely six months later she becomes a grown woman, as per the statement of Shmuel (Rambam *Sefer Nashim, Hilkhot Ishut* 2:2; *Shulḥan Arukh, Even HaEzer* 234:1, and in the comment of Rema).

NOTES

It is permitted for three women to engage in relations with a contraceptive resorbent, etc. – שָׁלֹשׁ נָשִׁים מְשַׁמְּשׁוֹת בְּמוֹךְ וכו': The early commentaries disagree over the meaning of this statement. Some explain that she inserts the material to cover the entrance of her uterus before engaging in relations, while others maintain that she uses it after intercourse to absorb the semen (see *Tosafot*). The precise nature of this *halakha* is also a matter of dispute among the early commentaries. Rashi maintains that only these three types of women may engage in relations with this resorbent, and it is prohibited for others to do so. However, many other early commentaries, among them Rabbeinu Tam, contend that the Sages were advising or even requiring these three women to use the resorbent due to the danger involved.

Lest she conceive and die – שֶׁמָּא תִּתְעַבֵּר וְתָמוּת: The Gemara's question is clear according to this version of the text, as the indication is that a minor who conceived cannot survive the ordeal of childbirth, and certainly her child will not live. However, according to the variant reading in *Yevamot* (12b): Lest she conceive and lest she die, apparently it is possible for her to conceive and give birth. The Ramban and his students maintain that this version is according to the opinion that children are an indication of grown-woman status, suggesting that she was a grown woman when she conceived, even though both in terms of age and in terms of physical development there was no indication of puberty.

What is a minor girl – אֵיזוֹהִי קְטַנָּה: The meaning is: Whose legal status is that of a minor in terms of this *halakha*? In principle, as long as she has yet to develop the requisite physical indicators, she is still classified as a minor. Here, however, a special definition is necessary, as even Rabbi Meir concedes that under a certain age, there is no concern that a minor might conceive.

The Lord preserves the simple – שׁוֹמֵר פְּתָאִים ה': Many commentaries question this attitude: In a life-threatening situation, how can one say that from Heaven they will have mercy, and rely on the notion that the Lord preserves the simple, when the Torah commands that one must avoid all dangers and violate virtually all prohibitions in order to avoid endangering one's life (see *Avoda Zara* 18a)? One opinion is that the Gemara employs this approach only with regard to people conducting themselves in a conventional manner and according to the standard mode of conduct. The assumption is that God protects them, as the fact is that most people are not harmed (*Kovetz Shiurim*). Alternatively, the Gemara employs this approach only in a case where this potential danger affects only a minority of cases, and people need not take special precautions to avoid unlikely occurrences.

אֶלָּא הָכִי קָמִיבַּעְיָא לֵיהּ: יֵשׁ בֶּגֶר בַּקֶּבֶר וּפָקַע אָב, אוֹ דִּלְמָא: אֵין בֶּגֶר בַּקֶּבֶר וְלָא פָּקַע אָב? מָר בַּר רַב אַשִׁי בָּעֵי לַהּ הָכִי: מִיתָה עוֹשָׂה בַּגְרוּת, אוֹ אֵין עוֹשָׂה בַּגְרוּת? תֵּיקוּ.

Rather, Rava's dilemma is unrelated to whether or not her son inherits the fine payment. **This is his dilemma: Is there** achievement of **grown-woman status in the grave and** therefore the right of the **father** to receive payment of the fine **lapsed;** and since there is no one claiming the payment, the rapist need not pay? **Or perhaps there is no** achievement of **grown-woman status in the grave, and** the right of the **father did not lapse. Mar bar Rav Ashi raised the dilemma** in **this** manner: Does **death effect grown-woman status**[N] **or does it not effect grown-woman status?** No resolution was found for this dilemma, and the Gemara concludes that the dilemma **stands** unresolved.

בָּעֵי מִינֵּיהּ רָבָא מֵאַבָּיֵי: בָּא עָלֶיהָ וְנִתְאָרְסָה מַהוּ אֲמַר לֵיהּ: מִי כְּתִיב ״וְנָתַן לַאֲבִי הַנַּעֲרָה אֲשֶׁר לֹא אֹרָשָׂה״? וּלְטַעְמִיךְ, הָא דְּתַנְיָא: בָּא עָלֶיהָ וְנִשֵּׂאת – לְעַצְמָהּ, מִי כְּתִיב ״וְנָתַן לַאֲבִי הַנַּעֲרָה אֲשֶׁר לֹא נְשׂוּאָה״?

On a similar note, **Rava inquired of Abaye:** If he forcibly **had intercourse with** a young woman **and she was** later **betrothed,**[HN] **what is the** *halakha*? Abaye **said to him: Is it written: And he shall give to the father of the young woman who is not betrothed?** Actually it is written: "If a man finds a young woman…who was not betrothed" (Deuteronomy 22:28), which indicates that the determining factor is whether she was betrothed before the rape and not whether she is engaged at the moment of payment. Rava asked him: **And according to your reasoning, that which was taught** in a *baraita*: If he forcibly **had intercourse** with a young woman **and she** later **married,**[N] the fine is paid **to her,** not to her father. There too, ask: **Is it written: And he shall give to the father of the young woman who is not married?** Even though the verse does not address the moment of payment, if she married the fine is paid to her.

הָכִי הָשְׁתָּא?! הָתָם, הוֹאִיל וּבַגְרוּת מוֹצִיאָה מֵרְשׁוּת אָב, וְנִישּׂוּאִין מוֹצִיאִין מֵרְשׁוּת אָב, מָה בַּגְרוּת, בָּא עָלֶיהָ וּבָגְרָה – לְעַצְמָהּ, אַף נִישּׂוּאִין, בָּא עָלֶיהָ וְנִשֵּׂאת – לְעַצְמָהּ, אֶלָּא אֵירוּסִין – מִי קָא מַפְּקִי מֵרְשׁוּתָא דְּאָב לְגַמְרֵי? הָא תְּנַן: נַעֲרָה הַמְאוֹרָסָה אָבִיהָ וּבַעְלָהּ מְפִירִין לָהּ נְדָרֶיהָ.

Abaye retorted: **How can** these cases be **compared? There,** in the case of marriage, there is reason to diverge from the plain meaning of the verse, **as grown-woman status removes her from the authority of the father and marriage removes her from the authority of the father. Just as** with regard to **grown-woman status,** if he forcibly **had intercourse with her and she became a grown woman,** the fine is paid **to her,** as it is written: "And he shall give to the father of the young woman" (Deuteronomy 22:29); **so too,** with regard to **marriage,** if he forcibly **had intercourse with her and she** later **married,**[H] the fine is paid **to her. However,** with regard to **betrothal, does it remove**[N] her **from the authority of the father entirely? Didn't we learn** in a mishna (*Nedarim* 66b): With regard to **a betrothed young woman, her father and her husband** together **nullify her vows?**[H] Apparently, betrothal does not remove her entirely from her father's authority, and therefore, the *halakha* with regard to betrothal cannot be derived from the *halakha* with regard to grown-woman status. Therefore, Rava's question is not difficult.

HALAKHA

If he forcibly had intercourse with a young woman and she was later betrothed – בָּא עָלֶיהָ וְנִתְאָרְסָה: If a girl who was raped or seduced was later betrothed to another, her fine and the other payments belong to her father, as betrothal does not release her from her father's authority (Rambam *Sefer Nashim, Hilkhot Na'ara Betula* 2:16; *Tur, Even HaEzer* 177).

If he forcibly had intercourse with her and she later married – בָּא עָלֶיהָ וְנִשֵּׂאת: If one who seduced or raped a young woman did not pay the fine and the accompanying payments until she became a grown woman or married, the fine and the other payments are paid to her (Rambam *Sefer Nashim, Hilkhot Na'ara Betula* 2:15).

A betrothed young woman with regard to the nullification of vows – נַעֲרָה הַמְאוֹרָסָה לְהָתָרַת נְדָרִים: The vows of a betrothed young woman may be nullified only if they are annulled by both the father and the husband. If only one of them annulled her vow, it remains intact, as stated in the mishna in *Nedarim* cited in the Gemara (Rambam *Sefer Hafla'a, Hilkhot Nedarim* 11:9; *Shulḥan Arukh, Yoreh De'a* 374:5).

NOTES

Does death effect grown-woman status – מִיתָה עוֹשָׂה בַּגְרוּת: It is clear from Rashi and other commentaries that the question is not whether death always effects grown-woman status, or even whether she is considered a grown woman in the grave. Rather, this statement should be read in the negative: Does the father forfeit his right to the fine when she dies just as he would if she became a grown woman? The later commentaries add that the difference between these two interpretations is that if she actually were to achieve grown-woman status in the grave, her creditors could collect the debt from the fine.

If he forcibly had intercourse with a young woman and she was later betrothed – בָּא עָלֶיהָ וְנִתְאָרְסָה: The commentaries explain that this is not a question according to the opinions of Rabbi Yosei HaGelili or Rabbi Akiva cited in the *baraita*, but only according to the opinion of Rabbi Akiva of the mishna, who maintains that a betrothed woman is entitled to payment of a fine that is paid directly to her. Others maintain that Rava posed this question according to Abaye's opinion that the decisive time for determining payment of a fine is when the rapist stands trial: Does her change in status mean that she herself receives the payment?

If he forcibly had intercourse with a young woman and she later married – בָּא עָלֶיהָ וְנִשֵּׂאת: In the Jerusalem Talmud, the ruling is that even if she later married, the fine belongs to her father. According to the discussion in the Talmud there, since she was raped while still under her father's authority, the payment is to the father, even if she left his authority entirely in the interim.

Betrothal, does it remove, etc. – אֵירוּסִין מִי קָא מַפְּקִי וכו׳: The Ritva writes that the Gemara sought to cite a proof for this claim from the *halakhot* of vows, as it is clear that with regard to monetary matters, betrothal does not release her from her father's authority. The suggestion is that since payment of the fine is a Torah decree, it should be viewed as a unique *halakha* rather than a standard monetary obligation, and therefore the father could lose the right to this money upon her betrothal.

מתני׳ הַמְפַתֶּה נוֹתֵן שְׁלֹשָׁה דְּבָרִים, וְהָאוֹנֵס אַרְבָּעָה. הַמְפַתֶּה נוֹתֵן בּוֹשֶׁת וּפְגָם וּקְנָס, מוֹסִיף עָלָיו אוֹנֵס שֶׁנּוֹתֵן אֶת הַצַּעַר. מַה בֵּין אוֹנֵס לִמְפַתֶּה? הָאוֹנֵס – נוֹתֵן אֶת הַצַּעַר, וְהַמְפַתֶּה – אֵינוֹ נוֹתֵן אֶת הַצַּעַר. הָאוֹנֵס – נוֹתֵן מִיָּד, וְהַמְפַתֶּה – לִכְשֶׁיּוֹצִיא. הָאוֹנֵס – שׁוֹתֶה בַּעֲצִיצוֹ, וְהַמְפַתֶּה – אִם רָצָה לְהוֹצִיא, מוֹצִיא.

MISHNA

The seducer gives the father of his victim **three things, and the rapist** gives the father **four.**[H] The mishna specifies: **The seducer gives** the father payments for **humiliation, degradation, and the fine. A rapist adds** an addition to **his** payments, **as he** also **gives** payment for **the pain. What** are the differences **between** the *halakha* of **a rapist** and that of **a seducer? The rapist gives** payment for **the pain, and the seducer does not give** payment for **the pain. The rapist gives** payment **immediately,**[H] **and the seducer** does not pay those payments immediately but only **when he releases** her. **The rapist drinks from his vessel [*atzitzo*],**[BLHN] i.e., marries the woman he raped, perforce, **and the seducer, if he wishes to release** her, **he releases** her.

כֵּיצַד שׁוֹתֶה בַּעֲצִיצוֹ – אֲפִילּוּ הִיא חִיגֶּרֶת, אֲפִילּוּ הִיא סוּמָא, וַאֲפִילּוּ הִיא מוּכַּת שְׁחִין. נִמְצָא בָּהּ דְּבַר עֶרְוָה, אוֹ שֶׁאֵינָהּ רְאוּיָה לָבֹא בְּיִשְׂרָאֵל – אֵינוֹ רַשַּׁאי לְקַיְּימָהּ, שֶׁנֶּאֱמַר ״וְלוֹ תִהְיֶה לְאִשָּׁה״ – אִשָּׁה הָרְאוּיָה לוֹ.

The mishna clarifies: **How does** the rapist **drink from his vessel? Even if** the woman he raped **is lame, even if she is blind, and even if she is afflicted with boils,** he is obligated to marry her and may not divorce her. However, if **a matter of licentiousness is found in her,**[H] e.g., if she committed adultery, **or if she is unfit to enter the Jewish people,** e.g., if she is a *mamzeret*, **he is not permitted to sustain her**[N] as his wife, **as it is stated: "And to him she shall be as a wife"** (Deuteronomy 22:29), from which it is inferred that she must be **a woman who is** legally **suitable for him.**

גמ׳ צַעַר דְּמַאי? אָמַר אֲבוּהּ דִּשְׁמוּאֵל: צַעַר שֶׁחֲבָטָהּ עַל גַּבֵּי קַרְקַע. מַתְקִיף לָהּ רַבִּי זֵירָא: אֶלָּא מֵעַתָּה, חֲבָטָהּ עַל גַּבֵּי שִׁירָאִין הָכִי נַמִי דְּפָטוּר? וְכִי תֵּימָא הָכִי נַמִי – וְהָתַנְיָא, רַבִּי שִׁמְעוֹן בֶּן יְהוּדָה אוֹמֵר מִשּׁוּם רַבִּי שִׁמְעוֹן: אוֹנֵס אֵינוֹ מְשַׁלֵּם אֶת הַצַּעַר מִפְּנֵי

GEMARA

The mishna taught that a rapist pays for the pain that he caused. The Gemara asks: **For what pain**[N] is he obligated to pay? **Shmuel's father said:** It is for **the pain that** he caused when **he slammed her onto the ground** while raping her. **Rabbi Zeira** strongly **objects to this: But if** what you say is so, **if he slammed her onto silk, so too is the** *halakha* **that** he is **exempt** from payment for pain? **And if you say** indeed that it is **so, but isn't it taught** in a *baraita* that **Rabbi Shimon ben Yehuda says in the name of Rabbi Shimon: A rapist does not pay** for **the pain due to** the fact

BACKGROUND

Vessel [*atzitz*] – עָצִיץ: The descriptions of the sources indicate that the reference is to a ceramic or wooden vessel, usually unfinished or not completely fired in the kiln. This type of vessel was used for tasks that required a simple receptacle, but not one with exacting craftsmanship. An *atzitz* was often used for potted plants or as a chamber pot. Sometimes it was crafted from the bottom of a broken jug.

LANGUAGE

Vessel [*atzitz*] – עָצִיץ: Similar to the Arabic اصيص, *'aṣīṣ*, which has the same meaning.

HALAKHA

The seducer gives three things and the rapist four – הַמְפַתֶּה נוֹתֵן שְׁלֹשָׁה דְּבָרִים וְהָאוֹנֵס אַרְבָּעָה: One who seduces a virgin must pay the fine, and the payments for humiliation and degradation. The rapist pays these and must compensate her for her pain as well (Rambam *Sefer Nashim, Hilkhot Na'ara Betula* 2:7; *Shulḥan Arukh, Even HaEzer* 177:1).

The rapist gives payment immediately – הָאוֹנֵס נוֹתֵן מִיָּד: The rapist must pay the four indemnities for which he is liable immediately, and then marry the young woman. In contrast, the seducer pays the fine only if he opts not to take her as a wife (Rambam *Sefer Nashim, Hilkhot Na'ara Betula* 2:7).

Drinks from his vessel – שׁוֹתֶה בַּעֲצִיצוֹ: A man who rapes a virgin is obligated to marry her if she and her father consent. He must do so even if she is lame or blind, and he may never divorce her against her wishes (Rambam *Sefer Nashim, Hilkhot Na'ara Betula* 1:3; *Shulḥan Arukh, Even HaEzer* 177:3).

If a matter of licentiousness is found in her – נִמְצָא בָּהּ דְּבַר עֶרְוָה: If his rape victim was forbidden to him, even if the prohibition is by rabbinic law, he is not permitted to marry. Similarly, if he married her and she acted in a licentious manner, he is required to divorce her (Rambam *Sefer Nashim, Hilkhot Na'ara Betula* 1:5; *Shulḥan Arukh, Even HaEzer* 177:4).

NOTES

Drinks from his vessel – שׁוֹתֶה בַּעֲצִיצוֹ: This refers to a rudimentary earthenware vessel, fit only for potted plants (Rambam's Commentary on the Mishna) or other base uses, such as sewage and the like (*Talmidei Rabbeinu Yona*; see *Shita Mekubbetzet*). In short, this is not a vessel used for drinking and was chosen by the *tanna* for that very reason. Since this man chose to drink from a lowly vessel, he must continue to do so.

The Maharik writes that the *halakha* that a rapist must marry his victim serves to protect the daughters of Israel, so that powerful men will not abuse them. The Radbaz therefore states that this should not be viewed as a penalty but as a positive mitzva. Consequently, even if there were no witnesses and he admits to the rape and is thereby exempted from paying the fine, he is obligated to marry her. As explained above, the reason is that he drinks from his vessel. Once he raped her, he can no longer claim that he does not desire her.

He is not permitted to sustain her – אֵינוֹ רַשַּׁאי לְקַיְּימָהּ: The *tanna* uses this expression in order to include both cases: That of a rapist who married her and later found her behaving in a licentious manner, necessitating their divorce; and one who cannot marry her in the first place because she is prohibited to him. Instead of saying that he divorces her or he may not marry her, the *tanna* states: He may not sustain her (Rashba).

For what pain – צַעַר דְּמַאי: *Tosafot* ask a simple question: Were the Sages unaware that the first time a virgin engages in intercourse it is painful? That seems to be indicated by their question. *Tosafot* and other early commentaries answer that it is clear that this *tanna* does not consider the pain of the tearing of the hymen sufficient to render one liable for payment, as otherwise a seducer would also be deemed liable.

BACKGROUND

Pain – צַעַר: Pain experienced during sexual intercourse might be the result of a lack of lubrication or due to vaginal muscle contractions. Typically, if a woman willingly engages in intercourse, those two problems do not exist, or at least are greatly mitigated. However, a woman who is raped does not want intercourse and does not cooperate in performance of the act, and therefore she could very well experience intense pain that could lead to actual injury. The same applies to a minor girl, as described in *Tosafot*. In contrast, the pain experienced by the breaking of the hymen is not as intense and, as the Gemara describes, is nothing more than a light wound in a sensitive area.

שֶׁסּוֹפָהּ לְהִצְטַעֵר תַּחַת בַּעְלָהּ, אָמְרוּ לוֹ: אֵינוֹ דּוֹמֶה נִבְעֶלֶת בְּאוֹנֶס לְנִבְעֶלֶת בְּרָצוֹן! אֶלָּא אָמַר רַב נַחְמָן אָמַר רַבָּה בַּר אֲבוּהּ: צַעַר שֶׁל פִּיסּוּק הָרַגְלַיִם. וְכֵן הוּא אוֹמֵר: ״וַתְּפַשְּׂקִי אֶת רַגְלַיִךְ לְכָל עוֹבֵר״.

that she will ultimately suffer[N] the same pain during intercourse when **under** the authority of **her husband? They said to him: One who has intercourse against** her **will is not comparable to one who has intercourse willingly.** Apparently, the pain associated with rape is a direct result of the forced intercourse and not of some associated cause.[B] **Rather, Rav Naḥman said** that **Rabba bar Avuh said:** It refers to the **pain of spreading** her **legs** during intercourse. **And likewise,** the verse **says:**[N] **"And you opened your legs to every passerby"** (Ezekiel 16:25).

אִי הָכִי מְפוּתָּה נָמֵי! אָמַר רַב נַחְמָן אָמַר רַבָּה בַּר אֲבוּהּ: מָשָׁל דִּמְפוּתָּה לְמָה הַדָּבָר דּוֹמֶה – לְאָדָם שֶׁאָמַר לַחֲבֵירוֹ: קְרַע שִׁירָאִין שֶׁלִּי וְהִפָּטֵר. שֶׁלִּי?! דַּאֲבוּהָ נִינְהוּ! אֶלָּא אָמַר רַב נַחְמָן אָמַר רַבָּה בַּר אֲבוּהּ: פִּקְחוֹת שֶׁבָּהֶן אוֹמְרוֹת: מְפוּתָּה אֵין לָהּ צַעַר.

The Gemara asks: **If so, a seduced woman** should **also**[N] be obligated to make that payment as well. **Rav Naḥman said** that **Rabba bar Avuh stated a parable: To what can** this **matter** of a seducer **be compared?** It can be compared **to a person who said to another: Tear my silk**[N] **and be exempt** from payment. Since she engaged in relations of her own volition, she certainly absolved him of payment for the pain. The Gemara asks: Tear **my silk**? It is not her silk, and therefore she may not waive payment for damage to it; **it is** the silk **of her father,** as the fine and the other payments are paid to him. **Rather, Rav Naḥman said**[N] that **Rabba bar Avuh said** that **the clever** women **among them say**[N] that **a seduced woman** has **no pain** during intercourse, as she is a willing participant.

NOTES

That she will ultimately suffer, etc. – שֶׁסּוֹפָהּ לְהִצְטַעֵר וכו׳: In the Jerusalem Talmud this is deemed comparable to removing the wart from someone who was planning on doing so anyway. She cannot demand compensation as she would have experienced the pain of her loss of virginity at some point. The Rabbis respond that although the act itself would have been performed eventually, her suffering is greater if it is performed against her will. In the Jerusalem Talmud, it is explained that Rabbi Shimon agrees that the rapist must pay for any pain other than the pain of the intercourse itself, e.g., if he pushed her onto thorns, as he disputes the need to pay for pain only with regard to the pain of the sexual act itself. The Ḥatam Sofer asks: Can't the woman claim that she would have never been subject to the pain of intercourse, as since a woman is not obligated to take a husband, she might never have married? He answers that since the fine is compensation for diminishing her prospects of marriage, if she claims she does not want to marry at all, she would no longer be entitled to the fine.

And likewise, the verse says, etc. – וְכֵן הוּא אוֹמֵר וכו׳: Some commentaries explain that this verse is cited in order to explain the spreading of legs to which it refers. The Ritva contends that the meaning of this expression is clear from the context; rather, the verse indicates that this act involves pain, as the prophet is castigating the Jewish people for the fact that it was willing to suffer the pain in order to engage in licentious behavior with others.

If so, a seduced woman should also – אִי הָכִי מְפוּתָּה נָמֵי: The Ramban views the Gemara here as one component of a complex question: If this pain is significant, then a seducer should also have to pay for it, and if it is not significant, the Rabbis should agree that even a rapist should be exempt. The *Shita Mekubbetzet* summarizes the question: The pain of losing her virginity is a one-time occurrence, and therefore she will not experience this pain again. The argument that she will eventually suffer pain during intercourse when under the authority of her husband does not apply to the pain of spreading her legs, as the pain she suffers now will not reduce that of any later cohabitation (see *Tosafot*).

Tear my silk – קְרַע שִׁירָאִין שֶׁלִּי: The logic is that since she suffers the pain to her own body, it is hers and she can waive her right to it (Rabbeinu Crescas Vidal; see Ritva). The *Kovetz Shiurim* explains that her forgiving the debt is insufficient to exempt the rapist for payments of humiliation and degradation, as even though the action that rendered him liable was performed on her body, her father is also affected by the humiliation and degradation. With regard to her pain, in contrast, even when the father is entitled to the payment, the pain affects her exclusively. The Ra'avad rules that the payment for the pain of rape is paid to the victim herself, not to her father.

The *Ḥakham Tzvi* explains that that although a father has the right to give his daughter away in marriage, he cannot give her away to undergo suffering. Apparently, the Torah did not entitle him to the payment for her pain. The Ran, in the next chapter, contends that since he has the right to marry her to a repulsive person, e.g., one who is afflicted with boils, with whom she would only agree to engage in intercourse unwillingly, apparently, he has the right to give her away to undergo suffering, and therefore the payment for her pain also belongs to the father.

Rather, Rav Naḥman said, etc. – אֶלָּא אָמַר רַב נַחְמָן וכו׳: The word rather indicates that Rav Naḥman's statement is not necessarily based on the previous answer with regard to the spreading of legs. Instead, it could be explained that he reverts back to the first opinion, that the pain is the pain of intercourse, and the difference between the two cases is that a seduced woman does not suffer pain. Some commentaries have a variant reading excluding the word rather (see Ritva and *Shita Mekubbetzet*). The later commentaries continue to discuss whether a seduced woman experiences no pain, as any suffering is obscured by the pleasure of the act, or whether she does experience pain but it is not taken into consideration due to her desire.

The clever women among them say, etc. – פִּקְחוֹת שֶׁבָּהֶן אוֹמְרוֹת וכו׳: The significance of clever women is not immediately apparent in this context. The *Shita Mekubbetzet* explains that a significant factor in the pain of intercourse for a woman, even the first time, is the failure to prepare her body properly. Clever women know how to prepare their bodies so that the tearing of their hymen causes merely slight discomfort, as indicated by the various metaphors cited in the Gemara.

וְהָא קָא חָזֵינַן דְּאִית לָהּ! אֲמַר אַבַּיֵי, אָמְרָה לִי אֵם: כְּמַיָּא חַמִּימֵי עַל רֵישֵׁיהּ דְּקָרְחָא. רָבָא אֲמַר: אָמְרָה לִי בַּת רַב חִסְדָּא: כִּי רִיבְדָּא דְּכוּסִילְתָּא. רַב פַּפָּא אֲמַר: אָמְרָה לִי בַּת אַבָּא סוּרָאָה: כִּי נַהֲמָא אַקּוּשָׁא בְּחִינְכֵי.

The Gemara asks: **But don't we see that** even a married woman **has** pain when she engages in sexual relations for the first time? **Abaye said:** My foster **mother told me** that the pain is **like hot water on the head of a bald** man. **Rava said:** My wife, **Rav Ḥisda's daughter, told me** that it is **like the stab of a bloodletting knife. Rav Pappa said:** My wife, **Abba Sura's daughter, told me** that it is like the feeling of **hard bread on the gums.** When a woman engages in intercourse willingly, the pain is negligible. Therefore, the seducer is not obligated to pay for pain.

״הָאוֹנֵס נוֹתֵן מִיָּד, הַמְפַתֶּה לִכְשֶׁיּוֹצִיא״ וכו׳. לִכְשֶׁיּוֹצִיא, אִשְׁתּוֹ הִיא?! אֲמַר אַבַּיֵי: אֵימָא לִכְשֶׁלֹּא יִכְנוֹס. תַּנְיָא נַמִי הָכִי: אַף עַל פִּי שֶׁאָמְרוּ הַמְפַתֶּה נוֹתֵן לִכְשֶׁלֹּא יִכְנוֹס, בּוֹשֶׁת וּפְגָם – נוֹתֵן מִיָּד. וְאֶחָד הָאוֹנֵס וְאֶחָד הַמְפַתֶּה, בֵּין הִיא וּבֵין אָבִיהָ יְכוֹלִין לְעַכֵּב.

§ The mishna continues: **The rapist gives** payment **immediately, and the seducer when he releases her, etc.** The Gemara asks: **When he releases** her?[N] **Is she his wife?**[N] He did not yet marry her, so how can the mishna use the language of divorce? **Abaye said: Say** that he gives payment **when** he opts **not** to **marry** her.[H] If he marries her he need not pay. **That** opinion **was also taught** in a *baraita*: **Although they said** that **the seducer gives** the fine **when** he opts **not** to **marry** her, the compensation for her **humiliation and degradation he gives immediately.** The *baraita* continues: Although **both the rapist and the seducer** are obligated to marry their victim, **both she and her father**[NH] **are able to prevent** the marriage.

בִּשְׁלָמָא מְפוּתָּה – כְּתִיב ״אִם מָאֵן יְמָאֵן אָבִיהָ״, אֵין לִי אֶלָּא אָבִיהָ, הִיא עַצְמָהּ מִנַּיִן – תַּלְמוּד לוֹמַר ״יְמָאֵן״, מִכׇּל מָקוֹם.

The Gemara asks: **Granted,** with regard to **a woman who was seduced, it is written: "If her father refuses** [*maen yemaen*] to give her to him" (Exodus 22:16), and the Sages interpreted: **I have only** derived that **her father** can prevent the marriage; **from where do we** derive that **she herself** can do so? **The verse states:** ***Maen yemaen***, a double verb indicating that the marriage can be prevented **in any case**, i.e., she too may do so.

אֶלָּא אוֹנֵס, בִּשְׁלָמָא אִיהִי – כְּתִיב ״וְלוֹ תִהְיֶה״ – מִדַּעְתָּהּ. אֶלָּא אָבִיהָ מְנָלַן?

However, from where is it derived that they can prevent the marriage in the case of **a rapist? Granted, she** herself can prevent the marriage, as **it is written: "And to him she shall be** as a wife" (Deuteronomy 22:29), and the term "shall be" indicates **with her consent. However, from where do we** derive that **her father** can prevent the marriage?

אָמַר אַבַּיֵי: שֶׁלֹּא יְהֵא חוֹטֵא נִשְׂכָּר. רָבָא אָמַר: קַל וָחוֹמֶר: וּמָה מְפַתֶּה שֶׁלֹּא עָבַר אֶלָּא עַל דַּעַת אָבִיהָ בִּלְבַד, בֵּין הִיא וּבֵין אָבִיהָ יְכוֹלִין לְעַכֵּב, אוֹנֵס שֶׁעָבַר עַל דַּעַת אָבִיהָ וְעַל דַּעַת עַצְמָהּ – לֹא כׇּל שֶׁכֵּן.

Abaye said: No verse is necessary as it stands to reason that the father too can prevent the marriage **so that a sinner will not profit.** If her father could not prevent the marriage, the rapist would acquire the right to marry the young woman despite the father's refusal, a right not accorded to one who seeks to betroth a young woman in a conventional manner. **Rava said** it is derived through **an *a fortiori* inference: Just as** in the case of **a seducer, who contravened only her father's will,** as she acquiesced to his proposition, nevertheless **both she and her father can prevent** the marriage; in the case of **a rapist, who contravened** both **her father's will and her own will, all the more so** is it **not** so that both she and her father can prevent the marriage?

HALAKHA

When does the seducer pay – **מָתַי מְשַׁלֵּם הַמְפַתֶּה:** A seducer pays compensation for humiliation and degradation immediately, but he pays the fine only if he does not marry his victim (Rambam *Sefer Nashim, Hilkhot Na'ara Betula* 2:7).

Both she and her father, etc. – **בֵּין הִיא וּבֵין אָבִיהָ וכו׳:** In the cases of both a raped and a seduced young woman, if either she or her father refuses the marriage, the rapist or seducer pays the fine and is not obligated to marry her (Rambam *Sefer Nashim, Hilkhot Na'ara Betula* 1:3).

NOTES

When he releases her – **לִכְשֶׁיּוֹצִיא:** The Ritva's explanation clarifies the phrase: When he releases her, in this context. He explains that it means that the man releases her in court when he declares that he does not wish to marry her.

Is she his wife – **אִשְׁתּוֹ הִיא:** Almost all commentaries read this expression in the form of a question: Is she his wife? If he didn't marry her yet, how can he release her? The Ra'avad, however, understands it as a statement: If he married her and she is his wife, upon their divorce he must pay her marriage contract of one hundred dinars, consistent with the Ra'avad's approach with regard to a seduced woman. The Rashba questions this interpretation, for it would mean that the sinner profited, as he paid only one hundred dinars instead of the fifty *sela* fine, which is two hundred dinars, like the dowry of virgins. Furthermore, a seducer can subvert the *halakha* by marrying and immediately divorcing her, thereby saving one hundred dinars.

Both she and her father – **בֵּין הִיא וּבֵין אָבִיהָ:** *Tosafot* ask: How can the young woman object? After all, her father has the right to marry her to the man of his choice. Some commentaries (Ritva; Rabbeinu Crescas Vidal) maintain that this is referring specifically to an orphan or a grown woman. They explain that the phrase: Both she and her father, refers to different cases. Sometimes she can object, if she is no longer subject to her father's authority, and in other cases, her father has the right of refusal. Others accept Rashi's explanation in tractate *Kiddushin*: Even though her refusal cannot prevent him from marrying her if her father agrees, it obligates the seducer to pay the fine immediately.

Several other interpretations are proposed by the Ran. One suggestion is that if she does not want to be his wife, although her father still retains the power to marry her to him, there is no longer a mitzva for the rapist or seducer to wed her. Alternatively, he suggests that this is a unique *halakha* in that the Torah granted her the right of refusal due to the ordeal she went through, despite the fact that in standard circumstances she cannot refuse her father's choice of a husband for her. The *Yam shel Shlomo* writes that the purpose of the statement that both she and her father can refuse is to emphasize that the mitzva to marry the victim of one's rape and seduction victim applies only to the man, but there is no mitzva incumbent on the woman or her father.

רָבָא לָא אֲמַר כְּאַבַּיֵי, כֵּיוָן דְּקָא מְשַׁלֵּם קְנָס – לָאו חוֹטֵא נִשְׂכָּר הוּא. אַבַּיֵי לָא אֲמַר כְּרָבָא, מְפַתֶּה דְּאִיהוּ מָצֵי מְעַכֵּב – אָבִיהָ נַמִי מָצֵי מְעַכֵּב, אוֹנֵס דְּאִיהוּ לָא מָצֵי מְעַכֵּב – אָבִיהָ נַמִי לָא מָצֵי מְעַכֵּב.

The Gemara elaborates: **Rava did not say in accordance with** the explanation of **Abaye,** as **since** the rapist **pays the fine he is not a sinner** who **profits,** as he too must pay the dowry of a virgin even if he marries her. Likewise, **Abaye did not say in accordance with** the explanation of **Rava** because in the case of **a seducer, where** the seducer himself **can prevent** the marriage, **her father can also prevent** the marriage. In the case of **a rapist, where** the rapist himself **cannot prevent** the marriage, **her father also cannot prevent** the marriage.

תַּנְיָא אִידָךְ: אַף עַל פִּי שֶׁאָמְרוּ אוֹנֵס נוֹתֵן מִיָּד, כְּשֶׁיּוֹצִיא הוּא – אֵין לָהּ עָלָיו כְּלוּם. כְּשֶׁיּוֹצִיא? מִי מָצֵי מַפֵּיק לָהּ?! אֵימָא: כְּשֶׁתֵּצֵא הִיא – אֵין לָהּ עָלָיו כְּלוּם. מֵת – יָצָא כֶּסֶף קְנָסָהּ בִּכְתוּבָּתָהּ. רַבִּי יוֹסֵי בְּרַבִּי יְהוּדָה אוֹמֵר: יֵשׁ לָהּ כְּתוּבָּה מָנֶה.

It was taught in **another** *baraita*: **Although** the Sages **said** that **the rapist gives** payment **immediately, when he releases** her **she has no claim upon him.**[N] The Gemara asks: **When he releases** her? **Can he release her?** It is prohibited by Torah law for him to do so. Rather, emend the *baraita* and **say: When she leaves,** if she seeks to divorce him and demands a bill of divorce, **she has no** monetary **claim upon him.** Similarly, if **he died,** the **money of her fine offsets her marriage contract.**[H] The fine, which was the equivalent of the dowry of virgins, replaces her marriage contract. **Rabbi Yosei, son of Rabbi Yehuda, says:** Even a rape victim **has a marriage contract of one hundred dinars,**[N] like the marriage contract of all non-virgin wives.

בְּמַאי קָמִיפַּלְגִי? רַבָּנַן סָבְרִי: טַעֲמָא מַאי תַּקִּינוּ רַבָּנַן כְּתוּבָּה – כְּדֵי שֶׁלֹּא תְּהֵא קַלָּה בְּעֵינָיו לְהוֹצִיאָהּ, וְהָא לָא מָצֵי מַפֵּיק לָהּ. וְרַבִּי יוֹסֵי בְּרַבִּי יְהוּדָה סָבַר: הָא נַמִי מְצַעֵר לָהּ עַד דְּאָמְרָה הִיא ״לָא בָּעֵינָא לָךְ״.

The Gemara asks: **With regard to what** principle **do they disagree?** The Gemara explains: **The Rabbis maintain: What is the reason** that **the Sages instituted a marriage contract** for the woman? They instituted it **so that she will not be inconsequential in his eyes,** enabling him **to** easily **divorce her.** Because divorcing her will cost money, he will not do so rashly. **And this** woman whom he raped, **he cannot release her** by Torah law, obviating the need for a marriage contract. **And Rabbi Yosei, son of Rabbi Yehuda, maintains:** With regard to **this** woman **too,** although he cannot divorce her, he can **torment her until she says: I do not want you.** When she initiates the divorce, he can divorce her. Therefore, the Sages instituted that she receives the marriage contract of a non-virgin to prevent him from doing so.

״אוֹנֵס שׁוֹתֶה בַּעֲצִיצוֹ״. אֲמַר לֵיהּ רָבָא מִפַּרְזְקָיָא לְרַב אַשִׁי: מִכְּדִי, מִיגְמַר גָּמְרֵי מֵהֲדָדֵי

The mishna continues: **A rapist drinks from his vessel,** and the seducer is not obligated to marry the woman he seduced. **Rava from Parzakya said to Rav Ashi: Since** the *halakhot* of a rapist and a seducer **are derived from each other** with regard to the sum of the fine,

לְהָא מִילְּתָא נַמִי לִיגְמְרוּ מֵהֲדָדֵי! אָמַר קְרָא: ״מָהֹר יִמְהָרֶנָּה לּוֹ לְאִשָּׁה״ לוֹ – מִדַּעְתּוֹ.

for this matter too, marrying the woman against his will, **let them be derived from each other.** Rav Ashi replied that **the verse says** with regard to a seducer: **"He shall pay a dowry for her to be a wife to him"** (Exodus 22:15);[N] **"to him"** means **in accordance with his will.**

NOTES

She has no claim upon him – אֵין לָהּ עָלָיו כְּלוּם: The Gemara provides different explanations for a divorcée and a widow because the reason for the marriage contract varies in each case. With regard to a divorcée the Sages instituted a marriage contract so that her husband would not divorce her lightly, and the Gemara therefore states that there is no need for that ordinance for a rape victim, as he cannot divorce her at all; therefore, she has no claim upon him. In the case of a widow the purpose of her marriage contract is to make her a more attractive marriage prospect, and therefore the Gemara states that she has already received the money in payment of the fine (*Tosafot*; Rosh; Ritva). The Rosh adds that even according to those who maintain that the obligation of the marriage contract of a virgin is by Torah law, since the verse states: "Like the dowry of the virgins" (Exodus 22:16), it is clear that the fine replaces the marriage contract.

The marriage contract of a raped woman – כְּתוּבַּת אֲנוּסָה: The ruling authorities disagree with regard to the basic question of whether or not a rape victim receives a marriage contract. The Rambam maintains that she is not entitled to a marriage contract, whereas the Ra'avad states that she receives a marriage contract of one hundred dinars, like any other non-virgin. The conclusion in the Jerusalem Talmud seems to support the opinion of the Ra'avad. The Gemara there discusses whether a seduced woman or a raped woman is entitled to the other conditions of a marriage contract, such as provision for her male children that predated her marriage, and sustenance for her daughters, among other stipulations.

HALAKHA

The money of her fine offsets her marriage contract – יָצָא כֶּסֶף קְנָסָהּ בִּכְתוּבָּתָהּ: The Sages did not institute a marriage contract for a raped young woman, as it is prohibited for her husband to divorce her. She does not even receive payment of the marriage contract in the event of his death, in accordance with the opinion of the first *tanna* (Rambam *Sefer Nashim, Hilkhot Na'ara Betula* 1:4; *Shulḥan Arukh, Even HaEzer* 177:3).

NOTES

He shall pay a dowry for her to be a wife to him – מָהֹר יִמְהָרֶנָּה לוֹ לְאִשָּׁה: *Tosafot* ask: If the term "to him" indicates that his consent is required, why not derive a similar *halakha* with regard to a rapist, where it is written: "And to him she shall be as a wife"? The Ritva explains that the derivation is not from the term "to him" but from the phrase "He shall pay a dowry for her," indicating that the seducer's agreement is required. *Talmidei Rabbeinu Yona* maintain that the difference is whether the term "to him" appears at the beginning of a sentence, in which case there is no indication that his agreement is necessary, or whether it appears at the end of the verse, which indicates that his consent is required.

"כֵּיצַד שׁוֹתֶה בַּעֲצִיצוֹ" כו׳. אֲמַר רַב כָּהֲנָא, אֲמַרִיתָא לִשְׁמַעְתָּא קַמֵּיהּ דְּרַב זְבִיד מִנְּהַרְדְּעָא: נֵיתֵי עֲשֵׂה וְנִדְחֶה לֹא תַעֲשֶׂה!

§ The mishna continues: **How does** the rapist **drink from his vessel?** The mishna proceeds to explain that he is obligated to marry her despite the physical flaws she might have. However, if the marriage is prohibited, either due to the fact that she committed adultery or due to her flawed lineage, he is not obligated to marry her, and therefore he may not marry her. **Rav Kahana said: I stated this *halakha* before Rav Zevid of Neharde'a,** and I asked him: Let the **positive** mitzva: "And to him she shall be as a wife" (Deuteronomy 22:29), **come and override** the **prohibition**[N] of marriage to a woman who is forbidden to him, according to the principle that positive mitzvot override prohibitions.

אֲמַר לִי: הֵיכָא אָמְרִינַן נֵיתֵי עֲשֵׂה וְנִידְחֵי לֹא תַעֲשֶׂה – כְּגוֹן מִילָה בְּצָרַעַת, דְּלָא אֶפְשָׁר לְקַיּוֹמֵיהּ לַעֲשֵׂה. אֲבָל הָכָא, אִי אָמְרָה דְּלָא בָּעֵינָא מִי אִיתֵיהּ לַעֲשֵׂה כְּלָל?

He said to me: Where do we say the principle that **a positive** mitzva **comes and overrides a prohibition?** It is in a case **where** one performs **circumcision** of a foreskin afflicted **with leprosy.**[H] Although there is a prohibition against removing leprous skin, the positive mitzva of circumcision overrides that prohibition, **as it is not possible to fulfill the positive** mitzva without violating the prohibition. **However, here,** in the case of the rapist, **if she says: I do not want him** as a husband, **is there a positive** mitzva **at all?**[N] Since in that case the mitzva need not be performed, as it is negated when the woman refuses to marry him, it does not override the prohibition.

מתני׳ יְתוֹמָה שֶׁנִּתְאָרְסָה וְנִתְגָּרְשָׁה, רַבִּי אֱלְעָזָר אוֹמֵר: הָאוֹנֵס חַיָּיב, וְהַמְפַתֶּה פָּטוּר.

MISHNA With regard to **an orphan who was betrothed**[N] **and divorced, Rabbi Elazar says: One who rapes** her **is obligated** to pay the fine, as she is a virgin young woman, **and one who seduces her is exempt**[H] from payment. Because she is an orphan, or because she was betrothed and divorced, she is independent, and by consenting to the seduction she forgoes her right to the fine.

HALAKHA

Circumcision of a foreskin afflicted with leprosy – מִילָה בְּצָרַעַת: The mitzva of circumcision overrides the prohibition against severing leprosy, whether or not the circumcision is performed at its proper time. Therefore, if there was a leprous spot on the foreskin, one may perform the circumcision and sever it, despite the fact that severing leprosy is prohibited by Torah law (Rambam *Sefer Ahava, Hilkhot Mila Betula* 1:9; *Shulḥan Arukh, Yoreh De'a* 266:1).

One who rapes her is obligated to pay the fine and one who seduces her is exempt – הָאוֹנֵס חַיָּיב וְהַמְפַתֶּה פָּטוּר: If a young woman who was betrothed and divorced was raped, the fine is paid to her. If she was seduced she is not entitled to the fine, as she consented to the act. The *halakha* is in accordance with the opinion of Rabbi Elazar and the ruling of Rav (Rambam *Sefer Nashim, Hilkhot Na'ara Betula* 2:14, 16; *Tur, Even HaEzer* 177).

NOTES

A positive mitzva and a prohibition – עֲשֵׂה וְלֹא תַעֲשֶׂה: The Gemara at the beginning of *Yevamot* explains at length that when there is a conflict between a positive mitzva and a prohibition, and it is impossible to fulfill both, the positive mitzva overrides the prohibition. That is the ruling despite the fact that the punishment for violating a prohibition is generally more severe than the punishment for failure to fulfill a mitzva.

Several questions arise in this regard. One basic issue is the identity of the prohibition in question. Rashi, and most commentaries, explains that it refers to the prohibition of the woman, e.g., a *mamzeret*. *Tosafot* question this approach, as it is derived from the verse "And to him she shall be as a wife" that a rapist is under no obligation to marry a woman prohibited to him. They suggest various answers. Other early commentaries elaborate on *Tosafot*'s answers, and suggest additional answers. The Ramban prefers *Tosafot*'s final answer and explains the Gemara's difficulty as follows: As the Torah establishes here that this positive mitzva does not override a prohibition, why not derive a principle from here that a positive mitzva does not in fact override a prohibition?

Rabbi Aharon HaLevi and his disciples explain that the verse "And to him she shall be as a wife" comes primarily to teach that her consent is required for marriage to the rapist, and it is cited as a mere support for the *halakha*, as the source of that *halakha* is in fact the reason articulated here (see *Tosafot*). The Ritva attributes this approach to the Ramban. The Ramban also maintains that this can be explained in a fundamentally different manner, that the Gemara is not referring to a prohibition of lineage, but to a woman forbidden due to adultery. We can therefore say that even if he found her acting immorally after marriage he is obligated to retain her as a wife, because she was suitable for him when they married. The Ramban is not bothered by *Tosafot*'s rejection of that approach.

Is there a positive mitzva at all – מִי אִיתֵיהּ לַעֲשֵׂה כְּלָל: Rashi explains that because she can neutralize the positive mitzva for the rapist, she is instructed to refuse him. The problem with this interpretation is what happens if the woman does not comply and insists on marrying him? The Ramban answers that according to Rashi it is self-evident that a woman would not want to wed a man with whom marriage is prohibited, and therefore she is induced to refuse him. Most commentaries, however, maintain that the Gemara does not mean that the victim must refuse to marry him. Rather, the very fact that she has the right to do so indicates that it is an insubstantial mitzva and therefore does not override a prohibition (see *Tosafot*, Rid, Ran, and Ramban). The Rid adds that her right of refusal indicates that it is not a full-fledged positive mitzva; rather it is one designed to appease her.

Rabbeinu Crescas Vidal adopts the reading: A positive mitzva overrides a prohibition only when there is no alternative to fulfilling the mitzva and he is completely obligated to perform it. Here, however, the positive mitzva can be bypassed, and therefore it does not negate the prohibition. *Tosafot Yeshanim* suggest that even though the prohibition is overridden by the positive mitzva from the man's perspective, it is also prohibited for her to violate the negative command, and it is certainly not permitted for her to violate a prohibition due to a mitzva incumbent upon him.

An orphan who was betrothed, etc. – יְתוֹמָה שֶׁנִּתְאָרְסָה וכו׳: In the *Shita Mekubbetzet* there are four different interpretations of the term orphan. One possibility is that the mishna is speaking of a single case, an orphan who was betrothed and divorced. Another possibility is that it is referring to a daughter who was betrothed and divorced, and she is called an orphan because her legal status is that of an orphan. A third option is that there are two entirely separate cases; one, an orphan, the other, one who was betrothed and divorced. Finally, the mishna can be explained as dealing with two cases in which the *halakha* is different; an orphan receives no payment, and although a girl who was betrothed and divorced is not entitled to the fine, she receives the payment for degradation. Indeed, the commentaries adopt various interpretations of the mishna. The Ritva explains at length that according to Rashi the word orphan refers literally to a girl without a father and also indicates that the legal status of a girl who was betrothed and divorced is that of an orphan.

גמ׳ אָמַר רַבָּה בַּר בַּר חָנָה אָמַר רַבִּי יוֹחָנָן: רַבִּי אֱלִיעֶזֶר בְּשִׁיטַת רַבִּי עֲקִיבָא רַבּוֹ אֲמָרָהּ, דְּאָמַר: יֵשׁ לָהּ קְנָס, וּקְנָסָהּ לְעַצְמָהּ. מִמַּאי – מִדְּקָתָנֵי: יְתוֹמָה, רַבִּי אֱלְעָזָר אוֹמֵר: הָאוֹנֵס חַיָּיב וְהַמְפַתֶּה פָּטוּר.

GEMARA **Rabba bar bar Ḥana said** that **Rabbi Yoḥanan said: Rabbi Elazar stated** his opinion **in accordance** with the opinion of **Rabbi Akiva, his teacher,**[N] **as** with regard to a young woman who was betrothed and divorced and then raped, Rabbi Akiva **said** in an earlier mishna: **She is entitled to a fine** for rape **and her fine** is paid **to her.** Rabbi Yosei HaGelili says: She is not entitled to a fine for rape. **And from where** do we know that Rabbi Elazar's opinion corresponds to the opinion of his teacher? **From the fact that** the mishna **teaches** with regard to **an orphan** that **Rabbi Elazar says: One who rapes** her **is obligated** to pay the fine **and one who seduces** her **is exempt** from payment.

יְתוֹמָה פְּשִׁיטָא! אֶלָּא הָא קָא מַשְׁמַע לָן: דְּנַעֲרָה שֶׁנִּתְאָרְסָה וְנִתְגָּרְשָׁה כִּיתוֹמָה, מַה יְתוֹמָה לְעַצְמָהּ – אַף נַעֲרָה שֶׁנִּתְאָרְסָה וְנִתְגָּרְשָׁה לְעַצְמָהּ.

The Gemara asks: **An orphan?** That is **obvious,** as she has no father and is not subject to the authority of anyone else. Clearly the seducer is exempt from payment because she was complicit. **Rather, this is** what the mishna is **teaching us: That** the legal status of **a young woman who was betrothed and divorced,** even if her father is alive, is **like** that of **an orphan: Just as** with regard to **an orphan,** payment of the fine is **to her, so too,** with regard to **a young woman who was betrothed and divorced,**[H] payment of the fine is **to her.**

אָמַר רַבִּי זֵירָא אָמַר רַבָּה בַּר שֵׁילָא אָמַר רַב הַמְנוּנָא סָבָא אָמַר רַב אַדָּא בַּר אַהֲבָה אָמַר רַב: הֲלָכָה כְּרַבִּי אֱלְעָזָר. קָרֵי רַב עֲלֵיהּ דְּרַבִּי אֱלְעָזָר: טוּבִינָא דְּחַכִּימֵי.

Rabbi Zeira said that **Rabba bar Sheila said** that **Rav Hamnuna the Elder said** that **Rav Adda bar Ahava said** that **Rav said: The** ***halakha*** **is in accordance** with the opinion of **Rabbi Elazar.**[PN] **Rav** would **exclaim about Rabbi Elazar:** He is the **happiest of the Sages,** as he held that the *halakha* was ruled in accordance with his opinion in many instances.

מתני׳ אֵיזֶהוּ בּוֹשֶׁת? הַכֹּל לְפִי הַמְבַיֵּישׁ וְהַמִּתְבַּיֵּישׁ. פְּגָם – רוֹאִין אוֹתָהּ כְּאִילּוּ הִיא שִׁפְחָה נִמְכֶּרֶת בַּשּׁוּק, כַּמָּה הָיְתָה יָפָה וְכַמָּה הִיא יָפָה. קְנָס שָׁוֶה בְּכָל אָדָם. וְכָל שֶׁיֵּשׁ לוֹ קִצְבָּה מִן הַתּוֹרָה – שָׁוֶה בְּכָל אָדָם.

MISHNA **What is humiliation?**[N] How is the payment for humiliation during rape or seduction assessed? It is **all based on the one who humiliated and the one who was humiliated.**[HN] The price will vary depending on the lineage of the family of the rape victim and the nature of the attacker. How is her **degradation** assessed? **One considers her as though she were a maidservant sold in the marketplace,** and assesses **how much she was worth** beforehand **and how much she is** currently **worth,** after the rape or seduction. The sum of the **fine is equal for all people,**[H] and the principle is: **Any** payment **that has a fixed** sum **by Torah law is equal for all people,** regardless of the lineage and the physical state of the attacker or the victim.

HALAKHA

An orphan…one who was betrothed and divorced – יְתוֹמָה...מִי שֶׁנִּתְאָרְסָה וְנִתְגָּרְשָׁה: The fine for the rape of a girl without a father is paid to her; the same is true for a young woman who was betrothed and divorced (Rambam *Sefer Nashim, Hilkhot Na'ara Betula* 2:14, 16; *Tur, Even HaEzer* 177).

It is all based on the one who humiliated and the one who was humiliated – הַכֹּל לְפִי הַמְבַיֵּישׁ וְהַמִּתְבַּיֵּישׁ: How is the humiliation of a raped woman assessed? It is all based on the one who humiliated and the one who was humiliated. The humiliation of a young woman of significance from a distinguished family is not comparable to the humiliation of a poor girl of lowly lineage. Likewise, the payment to a woman humiliated by a man of significance is lower than the payment to one humiliated by a lowly person (Rambam *Sefer Nashim, Hilkhot Na'ara Betula* 2:4; *Shulḥan Arukh, Even HaEzer* 407:24).

The sum of the fine is equal for all people – קְנָס שָׁוֶה בְּכָל אָדָם: Whether one had relations with the daughter of a High Priest or a *mamzer*, the fine is fifty silver coins (Rambam *Sefer Nashim, Hilkhot Na'ara Betula* 2:3; *Tur, Even HaEzer* 177).

PERSONALITIES

Rabbi Elazar – רַבִּי אֶלְעָזָר: This is Rabbi Elazar ben Shammua, a *tanna* in the generation prior to the redaction of the Mishna and among the greatest of Rabbi Akiva's students. Rabbi Elazar was a leader of the Jewish people in the years following the persecution in the wake of the failure of the bar Kokheva rebellion. Despite the dire situation, many students studied with him. One of his primary students was Rabbi Yehuda HaNasi, the redactor of the Mishna. Not many of Rabbi Elazar's *halakhot* are cited in the Mishna; however, he was held in high esteem by the Sages of the following generations. Rav, an *amora*, referred to him as the happiest of the Sages, and Rabbi Yoḥanan said of him: The hearts of the early Sages were like the Entrance Hall to the Sanctuary. In the Mishna and in *baraitot*, he is called simply Rabbi Elazar.

Rabbi Elazar ben Shammua lived a long life. According to one tradition he was 105 years old when he was killed. He is listed among the ten martyrs executed by the Romans.

NOTES

Stated it in accordance with the opinion of Rabbi Akiva, his teacher – בְּשִׁיטַת רַבִּי עֲקִיבָא רַבּוֹ אֲמָרָהּ: The Ramban explains that the Gemara is not saying that Rabbi Elazar agrees with Rabbi Akiva as opposed to Rabbi Yosei HaGelili, as that is self-evident. Rather, it is emphasizing that he accepts Rabbi Akiva's opinion cited in the mishna, not the opinion attributed to him in the *baraita*. The Gemara therefore asks: From where is that known; perhaps he agrees with Rabbi Akiva of the *baraita* and that is why he referred specifically to an orphan, as the fine for one who is not an orphan is paid to her father? The Gemara answers that since the mishna mentions an orphan, and there is nothing novel in that *halakha*, as she certainly does not receive payment for willingly performing an act, it is clear that the reference is to a girl who is not an orphan but rather one who was betrothed and divorced. The Ritva adds that by specifying that one who seduces her is exempt, Rabbi Elazar is demonstrating that he is not referring to a literal orphan, as there is no need to state that she receives no payment when she is seduced. Rather, he mentions an orphan in order to explain why she does not receive the fine; a young woman who was betrothed and divorced is considered an orphan in her father's lifetime.

The *halakha* is in accordance with the opinion of Rabbi Elazar – הֲלָכָה כְּרַבִּי אֶלְעָזָר: The question is raised: Since Rabbi Elazar's opinion is in accordance with the opinion of Rabbi Akiva, why did the Gemara not issue the ruling in accordance with the source of his opinion, Rabbi Akiva? The Ritva explains that had the Gemara issued a ruling in accordance with Rabbi Akiva, there would have been uncertainty whether the reference was to his opinion as cited in the mishna or to the opinion cited in the *baraita*. The Gemara therefore preferred to state that the *halakha* is in accordance with the opinion of Rabbi Elazar, who adopts the opinion of Rabbi Akiva in the mishna, as stated above. The Ritva adds that this is why Rabbi Elazar is called the happiest of the Sages, as he was able to accurately approximate the opinion of his teacher. According to the *Yam shel Shlomo*, Rabbi Elazar indeed adds to Rabbi Akiva's opinion; he teaches that this *halakha* applies to the payments of humiliation and degradation as well as to the fine. This also accounts for the fact that this mishna is placed here, rather than adjacent to Rabbi Akiva's opinion.

What is humiliation – אֵיזֶהוּ בּוֹשֶׁת: The appropriate question would appear to be: How much is the payment of humiliation? After all, that is the topic of the mishna. The *Melekhet Shlomo* explains that since one might have thought that the humiliation and degradation of a rape victim are identical, the mishna underscores that these are two separate *halakhot*.

It is all based on the one who humiliated and the one who was humiliated – הַכֹּל לְפִי הַמְבַיֵּישׁ וְהַמִּתְבַּיֵּישׁ: Rashi here explains that humiliation is greatest when the humiliator is neither particularly prominent nor particularly inconsequential. If he is a person of importance her humiliation is less, and similarly the action of a man of lowly standing is considered insignificant and the humiliation in that case is less. The Rid agrees.

The Ran maintains that this is the case in standard instances of humiliation, but a rape victim is humiliated more when she is violated by a man of lowly standing. He agrees though that a woman raped by a great man suffers less humiliation. See, however, the *Yam shel Shlomo*, who argues to the contrary, and concludes that each case must be considered on its own merits, dependent on time and place. The Meiri agrees with Ran, and cites proof from the Jerusalem Talmud, where it states that the humiliation suffered by a great man is extensive and his humiliation of others is minor, while the humiliation suffered by a lowly man is insignificant while his humiliation of others is major. He explains that the humiliation suffered by a great person corresponds to his significance, and therefore the humiliation payment for a woman of significance will be greater, whereas his humiliation of others is relatively insignificant.

גמ׳ וְאֵימָא חֲמִשִּׁים סְלָעִים אָמַר רַחֲמָנָא, מִכֹּל מִילֵּי! אָמַר רַבִּי זֵירָא: יֹאמְרוּ בָּעַל בַּת מְלָכִים – חֲמִשִּׁים, בָּעַל בַּת הֶדְיוֹטוֹת – חֲמִשִּׁים?! אֲמַר לֵיהּ אַבָּיֵי: אִי הָכִי, גַּבֵּי עֶבֶד נַמִּי יֹאמְרוּ: עֶבֶד נוֹקֵב מַרְגָּלִיּוֹת – שְׁלֹשִׁים, עֶבֶד עוֹשֶׂה

GEMARA The Gemara asks: **And say** that **the Merciful One said** that the payment is **fifty** ***sela*** **from all** these **matters,** i.e., the fine, degradation, humiliation, and pain. **Rabbi Zeira said:** That cannot be, as **they will say:** If **one who engaged in forced intercourse with a daughter of kings** pays a sum of **fifty** *sela,* does **one who engaged in forced intercourse with the daughter of commoners** [*hedyotot*][L] also pay **fifty** *sela?* **Abaye said to him:** This is not a decisive argument, as **if so, with regard to a** Canaanite **slave** killed by an ox, the Torah says that the owner of the ox pays the master of the slave thirty *sela.* There too, **they will say:** For **a slave who pierces** precious **pearls** [*margaliyyot*],[LB] a valuable skill, the fine is **thirty** *sela,* and for **a slave who performs**

LANGUAGE

Commoners [*hedyotot*] – הֶדְיוֹטוֹת: From the Greek ἰδιώτης, *idiotēs,* meaning a common man with no official office. The Sages use it to distinguish between a common person, e.g., a common priest, and one with a special position.

Pearls [*margaliyyot*] – מַרְגָּלִיּוֹת: From the Greek μαργαρίτης, *margarites,* meaning pearl. Sometimes it is used as a general term for a precious stone, both in Greek and in the language of the Sages.

BACKGROUND

A slave who pierces precious pearls – עֶבֶד נוֹקֵב מַרְגָּלִיּוֹת: Since pearls, especially valuable ones, were usually made into necklaces, they had to be pierced. This was a specialized form of craftsmanship that required expertise. The artisan would choose the ideal place to pierce the jewel, and the resultant hole had to be completely straight so as not to mar the beauty of the pearl. That craftsman was well paid, and a slave who could perform this task would be considered highly valuable.

מַעֲשֵׂה מַחַט שְׁלֹשִׁים?!

the **needlecraft** of a tailor, a common, less valuable skill, is the fine also **thirty** *sela?* Rather, just as with regard to the slaves, the sum is not dependent on the standing of the victim, so too with regard to a woman who was raped.

אֶלָּא אָמַר רַבִּי זֵירָא: אִילּוּ בָּאוּ עָלֶיהָ שְׁנַיִם, אֶחָד כְּדַרְכָּהּ וְאֶחָד שֶׁלֹּא כְּדַרְכָּהּ, יֹאמְרוּ: בָּעַל שְׁלֵימָה חֲמִשִּׁים, בָּעַל פְּגוּמָה – חֲמִשִּׁים?! אֲמַר לֵיהּ אַבָּיֵי: אִי הָכִי, גַּבֵּי עֶבֶד נַמִּי יֹאמְרוּ, עֶבֶד בָּרִיא – שְׁלֹשִׁים, עֶבֶד מוּכֵּה שְׁחִין – שְׁלֹשִׁים?!

Rather, Rabbi Zeira said a different proof: **Had two** men **engaged in forced intercourse with her, one vaginal intercourse, and one anal intercourse,**[N] **they will say:** If one who **engaged in forced intercourse** with **an untainted** virgin pays **fifty** *sela,* does one who **engaged in forced intercourse** with her when she is **tainted,** i.e., after she has engaged in anal intercourse, also pay **fifty** *sela?* Apparently, the fifty *sela* is the fixed sum of the fine, while the rest of the payment varies on a case-by-case basis. **Abaye said to him:** This too is no proof, as **if so, with regard to a slave as well, they will say** if one whose ox gored **a healthy slave** pays **thirty** *sela,* does one whose ox gored **a slave afflicted with boils** also pay **thirty** *sela?*

אֶלָּא אֲמַר אַבָּיֵי: אָמַר קְרָא ״תַּחַת אֲשֶׁר עִנָּהּ״, הָנֵי – תַּחַת אֲשֶׁר עִינָּהּ, מִכְּלָל דְּאִיכָּא בּוֹשֶׁת וּפְגָם. רָבָא אָמַר: אָמַר קְרָא ״וְנָתַן הָאִישׁ הַשּׁוֹכֵב עִמָּהּ לַאֲבִי הַנַּעֲרָה חֲמִשִּׁים כָּסֶף״ הֲנָאַת שְׁכִיבָה – חֲמִשִּׁים, מִכְּלָל דְּאִיכָּא בּוֹשֶׁת וּפְגָם.

Rather, Abaye said a different proof. **The verse says:** "Fifty shekels of silver… **because he tormented her**" (Deuteronomy 22:29); **these** fifty *sela* are the fine paid **because he tormented her.** From which it **may be inferred that there are** the additional payments of **humiliation and degradation** beyond that sum mentioned in the verse. **Rava said** an alternative proof. **The verse says: "And the man who lay with her shall give to the father of the young woman fifty shekels of silver"** (Deuteronomy 22:29). For **the pleasure of lying** with her he pays **fifty** *sela;*[H] from which it **may be inferred that there are** the additional payments of **humiliation and degradation,** beyond payment of the fine.

וְאֵימָא לְדִידַהּ? אָמַר קְרָא: ״בִּנְעֻרֶיהָ בֵּית אָבִיהָ״ – כׇּל שֶׁבַח נְעוּרֶיהָ לְאָבִיהָ.

The Gemara asks: **And say** that these additional payments are paid **to her?**[N] The Gemara answers that **the verse says:** "Between a father and his daughter, **being in her young womanhood, in her father's house**" (Numbers 30:17), from which it is derived that **all profits of her young womanhood go to her father.**[H]

NOTES

And one anal intercourse – וְאֶחָד שֶׁלֹּא כְּדַרְכָּהּ: The authorities disagree as to whether a rapist or seducer by means of anal intercourse is liable to pay the fine. According to the Rambam there is no fine for anal intercourse, whereas the Ra'avad deems the rapist liable, as do *Tosafot.* These opinions both depend upon and influence the interpretation of the Gemara. According to those who maintain that there is no fine for anal intercourse, the Gemara is referring to two women, one of whom engaged in anal intercourse before engaging in vaginal intercourse. The Gemara is stating that there is no difference with regard to the sum of the fine for the vaginal intercourse. The other opinion maintains that the Gemara is referring to one woman who receives payment of the fine both from the one who engaged in anal intercourse with her as well as from the one who engaged in vaginal intercourse with her, despite her impaired status. The early commentaries add that it appears that Rashi, at least according to his interpretation here, agrees with the Rambam that the reference is to two women. The Ritva and others note that in the Jerusalem Talmud it is clear that one who performs anal intercourse is also liable to pay the fine.

And say that these additional payments are paid to her – וְאֵימָא לְדִידַהּ: This difficulty hearkens back to the earlier statements of Abaye and Rava. According to Rabbi Zeira's reasoning this is not a question, as he holds that the need to emphasize that fifty *sela* is the sum of the fine is to prevent mistaken impressions and to indicate that the humiliation and degradation are paid to the same person to whom the fine is paid. However, according to Abaye and Rava, who derive this from a verse that indicates that the fine is paid as compensation only for the torment of the intercourse, the question can be raised: Who is entitled to the other payments? (*Shita Mekubbetzet*).

HALAKHA

The pleasure of lying is fifty *sela* – הֲנָאַת שְׁכִיבָה חֲמִשִּׁים: The fine of fifty *sela* paid by a rapist or a seducer is for the pleasure of the act itself. It does not include other forms of indemnity that he owes her (Rambam *Sefer Nashim, Hilkhot Na'ara Betula* 2:1; *Shulḥan Arukh, Even HaEzer* 177:1).

All profits of her young womanhood go to her father – כׇּל שֶׁבַח נְעוּרֶיהָ לְאָבִיהָ: The four categories of indemnity owed by a rapist and the three owed by a seducer are paid to the girl's father, as all profits of her young womanhood go to her father (Rambam *Sefer Nashim, Hilkhot Na'ara Betula* 2:15).

HALAKHA

The handiwork of the daughter goes to her father – מַעֲשֵׂה הַבַּת לְאָבִיהָ: The handiwork of a minor girl, until she becomes a young woman, goes to her father (Rambam *Sefer Nashim, Hilkhot Ishut* 3:11; *Shulḥan Arukh, Even HaEzer* 37:1).

Assessment of degradation – אוֹמְדִין הַפְּגַם: How is the degradation of a rape victim assessed? She is considered as though she was a maidservant for sale in the slave market and the difference between her value as a virgin and her value as a non-virgin is assessed, as a person would pay more for a virgin maidservant in order to marry her to a slave whom he wishes to please (Rambam *Sefer Nashim, Hilkhot Na'ara Betula* 2:6).

וְאֶלָּא הָא דְּאָמַר רַב הוּנָא אָמַר רַב: מִנַּיִן שֶׁמַּעֲשֵׂה הַבַּת לְאָבִיהָ? שֶׁנֶּאֱמַר ״וְכִי יִמְכּוֹר אִישׁ אֶת בִּתּוֹ לְאָמָה״ מָה אָמָה מַעֲשֵׂה יָדֶיהָ לְרַבָּהּ, אַף בַּת מַעֲשֵׂה יָדֶיהָ לְאָבִיהָ – לָמָּה לִי? תֵּיפּוֹק לֵיהּ מִ״בִּנְעוּרֶיהָ בֵּית אָבִיהָ״! אֶלָּא, הַהִיא בַּהֲפָרַת נְדָרִים הוּא דִּכְתִיב.

The Gemara asks: **However,** with regard to **that which Rav Huna said** that **Rav said: From where** is it derived **that the handiwork of the daughter** goes **to her father?**[H] It is **as it is stated: "And if a man sells his daughter as a maidservant"** (Exodus 21:7), juxtaposing his daughter to a maidservant: **Just as a maidservant, her handiwork** belongs **to her master,** as she was sold for that purpose; **so too a daughter, her handiwork** goes **to her father. Why do I** need this complicated proof? **Let him derive it** directly from the verse **"Being in her young womanhood, in her father's house." Rather,** this cannot be derived from that verse because **that** verse **is written with regard to the nullification of vows.** A young woman is subject to her father's authority with regard to her vows, which he has the right to nullify. The matter of monetary rights is not addressed in that verse.

וְכִי תֵּימָא: נֵילַף מִינֵּיהּ – מָמוֹנָא מֵאִיסּוּרָא לָא יָלְפִינַן. וְכִי תֵּימָא: נֵילַף מִקְּנָסָא – מָמוֹנָא מִקְּנָסָא לָא יָלְפִינַן. אֶלָּא מִסְתַּבְּרָא דְּאָבִיהָ הָוֵי, דְּאִי בָּעֵי – מָסַר לָהּ לִמְנוּוָּל וּמוּכֵּה שְׁחִין.

And if you say: Let us derive monetary matters **from** vows, i.e., just as she is subject to her father's authority with regard to vows the same is true with regard to monetary matters, **we do not derive monetary** matters **from ritual** matters. **And if you say: Let us derive** that her father receives payment **from the** *halakha* **of a fine,** i.e., just as the fine is paid to her father, as explicitly stated in the Torah, so too, other payments are also paid to her father, **we do not derive monetary** matters **from fines.**[N] The payment of a fine is a novel element decreed by the Torah and cannot serve as a paradigm for standard monetary matters. **Rather,** the Gemara explains that **it is reasonable that** the payments of humiliation and degradation are paid **to her father, as if he wished** to do so he could **give her** hand in marriage **to a repulsive man**[N] **or one afflicted with boils,** thereby humiliating her. Since her humiliation is under his control, payment for her humiliation is similarly his.

״פְּגָם – רוֹאִין אוֹתָהּ כְּאִילּוּ הִיא שִׁפְחָה נִמְכֶּרֶת״. הֵיכִי שָׁיְימִינַן לַהּ? אָמַר אֲבוּהּ דִּשְׁמוּאֵל: אוֹמְדִין כַּמָּה אָדָם רוֹצֶה לִיתֵּן בֵּין שִׁפְחָה בְּתוּלָה לְשִׁפְחָה בְּעוּלָה לְשַׁמְּשׁוֹ,

The mishna continues: How is her **degradation** assessed? **One considers her as though she was a maidservant sold** in the marketplace, and assesses how much she would have been worth beforehand and how much she would be worth currently. The Gemara asks: **How do we assess her** value? **Shmuel's father said: One estimates** the difference **between how much a person is willing to give** to purchase **a virgin maidservant and** how much he is willing to give **to** purchase **a non-virgin maidservant**[N] **to serve him.**

מַאי נָפְקָא לֵיהּ מִינַּהּ? אֶלָּא: בֵּין שִׁפְחָה בְּעוּלָה לְשִׁפְחָה שֶׁאֵינָהּ בְּעוּלָה לְהַשִּׂיאָהּ לְעַבְדּוֹ. וּלְעַבְדּוֹ מַאי נָפְקָא לֵיהּ מִינַּהּ? בְּעֶבֶד שֶׁיֵּשׁ לוֹ לְרַבּוֹ קוֹרַת רוּחַ הֵימֶנּוּ.

The Gemara asks: With regard to **a non-virgin maidservant to serve him;** if he purchases her for service, **what difference is there to him** whether or not she is a virgin? **Rather,** the difference **between a maidservant who engaged in intercourse and a maidservant who did not engage in intercourse** is with regard to how much one is willing **to marry her to his slave.** The Gemara further asks: **And** with regard to marrying her **to his slave, what difference is there to him** whether or not she is a virgin? The Gemara answers: It is **with regard to a slave from whom his master has** a sense of **satisfaction,** and he seeks a virgin for the slave in order to reciprocate. The difference between the price that the master is willing to pay for each of the maidservants is the degradation that the offender pays the victim.[H]

NOTES

We do not derive monetary matters from fines – מָמוֹנָא מִקְּנָסָא לָא יָלְפִינַן: The students of the Rashba cite in his name that the reason for this principle is not due to any fundamental difference between payments of money and fines, like the difference between ritual matters and monetary payment. Rather, fines are a novel *halakha* from which a general principle cannot be derived. Consequently, everyone agrees that the *halakhot* of fines can be derived from the *halakhot* of payments of money.

As if he wished to do so he could give her hand in marriage to a repulsive man, etc. – דְּאִי בָּעֵי מָסַר לָהּ לִמְנוּוָּל וכו׳: Rav Hai Gaon explains that he can betroth her to any man he chooses while she is a minor, and the humiliation, degradation, and even the pain resulting from that betrothal would continue into her young womanhood. Therefore, her humiliation and degradation belong to her father. The problem with this explanation is that the same reasoning leads to the conclusion that the humiliation and degradation of a grown woman should also be paid to her father. Rabbi Aharon HaLevi answers that since a grown woman has completely left her father's control, he retains no rights to anything of hers (see Ramban and Rashba).

One estimates…between purchasing a virgin maidservant and purchasing a non-virgin maidservant, etc. – אוֹמְדִין...בֵּין שִׁפְחָה בְּתוּלָה לְשִׁפְחָה בְּעוּלָה וכו׳: *Tosafot* explain that this does not mean every woman is evaluated as though she were a maidservant, as there is certainly no comparison between the degradation of a maidservant to that of an woman of significance from a distinguished family. Rather, the Gemara cited a common case, as only a maidservant can be married to a slave. However, with regard to every woman, the assessment involves that particular woman and how much more a man would be willing to give for her as a virgin. *Tosafot Yeshanim* maintain that degradation is always assessed in terms of a maidservant, as the difference between injury of a woman of significance and injury of a maidservant is covered by the payment for humiliation.

מתני׳ כׇּל מָקוֹם שֶׁיֵּשׁ מֶכֶר – אֵין קְנָס, וְכׇל מָקוֹם שֶׁיֵּשׁ קְנָס – אֵין מֶכֶר. קְטַנָּה – יֵשׁ לָהּ מֶכֶר וְאֵין לָהּ קְנָס, נַעֲרָה – יֵשׁ לָהּ קְנָס וְאֵין לָהּ מֶכֶר. הַבּוֹגֶרֶת – אֵין לָהּ לֹא מֶכֶר וְלֹא קְנָס.

MISHNA **Any place where there is sale**[N] by a father of his minor daughter as a Hebrew maidservant, **there is no fine** if she is raped. **And any place where there is a fine,** when a young woman is raped; **there is no sale** by the father. The Gemara specifies: **A minor is subject to sale** by her father, **and she is not entitled to a fine** if she is raped. **A young woman is entitled to a fine** if she is raped **and is not subject to sale. A grown woman is neither subject to sale nor entitled to a fine.**

גמ׳ אָמַר רַב יְהוּדָה אָמַר רַב: זוֹ דִּבְרֵי רַבִּי מֵאִיר, אֲבָל חֲכָמִים אוֹמְרִים: יֵשׁ לָהּ קְנָס בִּמְקוֹם מֶכֶר. דְּתַנְיָא: קְטַנָּה מִבַּת יוֹם אֶחָד וְעַד שֶׁתָּבִיא שְׁתֵּי שְׂעָרוֹת – יֵשׁ לָהּ מֶכֶר וְאֵין לָהּ קְנָס, מִשֶּׁתָּבִיא שְׁתֵּי שְׂעָרוֹת עַד שֶׁתִּיבָּגֵר יֵשׁ לָהּ קְנָס וְאֵין לָהּ מֶכֶר, דִּבְרֵי רַבִּי מֵאִיר, שֶׁהָיָה רַבִּי מֵאִיר אוֹמֵר: כׇּל מָקוֹם שֶׁיֵּשׁ מֶכֶר – אֵין קְנָס, וְכׇל מָקוֹם שֶׁיֵּשׁ קְנָס – אֵין מֶכֶר. וַחֲכָמִים אוֹמְרִים: קְטַנָּה מִבַּת שָׁלֹשׁ שָׁנִים וְיוֹם אֶחָד וְעַד שֶׁתִּיבָּגֵר – יֵשׁ לָהּ קְנָס.

GEMARA **Rav Yehuda said that Rav said: This** *halakha* in the mishna **is the statement of Rabbi Meir, but the Rabbis say: She is entitled to a fine** even **where there is a sale, as it is taught** in a *baraita*: **A minor** girl, **from one day old until she grows two** pubic **hairs, is subject to sale and is not entitled to a fine. From when she grows two** pubic **hairs** and becomes a young woman **until she matures** into a grown woman, **she is entitled to a fine and she is not subject to sale;** this **is the statement of Rabbi Meir, as Rabbi Meir would state** the principle: **Any place where there is a sale there is no fine, and any place where there is a fine there is no sale. And the Rabbis say: A minor girl from the age of three years and one day until she matures** into a grown woman **is entitled to a fine.**

קְנָס אִין, מֶכֶר לָא?! אֵימָא: אַף קְנָס בִּמְקוֹם מֶכֶר. אָמַר רַב חִסְדָּא: מַאי טַעְמָא דְּרַבִּי מֵאִיר – אָמַר קְרָא ״וְלוֹ תִהְיֶה לְאִשָּׁה״ – בִּמְהַוָּה עַצְמָהּ הַכָּתוּב מְדַבֵּר. וְרַבָּנַן? אָמַר רֵישׁ לָקִישׁ: אָמַר קְרָא ״נַעַר״ – אֲפִילּוּ קְטַנָּה בְּמַשְׁמָע.

The Gemara questions the statement of the Rabbis in the *baraita* with regard to a girl more than three years of age: **A fine, yes, but sale, no?** Do the Rabbis maintain that a father cannot sell his minor daughter as a Hebrew maidservant? Rather, emend the text and **say:** She **is even** entitled to **a fine**[H] **where** she is subject to **sale. Rav Ḥisda said: What is the rationale** for the opinion **of Rabbi Meir?** It is as **the verse says** with regard to a rapist: "And the man who lay with her shall give to the father of the young woman fifty *sela*, **and to him she shall be as a wife**" (Deuteronomy 22:29). **The verse is speaking with regard to one** halakhically competent to **marry** by **herself,** which means she must be a young woman. The Gemara asks: **And** what is the rationale for the opinion of **the Rabbis? Reish Lakish said** that **the verse says "young woman [*na'ara*]";** however, although the term is pronounced *na'ara*, it is written as *na'ar*,[N] without the letter *heh*, and **even a minor girl is indicated** by that term.

שְׁמָעָהּ רַב פַּפָּא בְּרֵיהּ דְּרַב חָנָן מִבֵּי כְלוֹחִית, אֲזַל אֲמָרָהּ קַמֵּיהּ דְּרַב שִׁימִי בַּר אַשִׁי. אֲמַר לֵיהּ: אַתּוּן אַהָא מַתְנִיתוּ לַהּ, אֲנַן אַהָא מַתְנֵינַן לַהּ: אָמַר רֵישׁ לָקִישׁ: הַמּוֹצִיא שֵׁם רַע עַל הַקְּטַנָּה – פָּטוּר, שֶׁנֶּאֱמַר ״וְנָתְנוּ לַאֲבִי הַנַּעֲרָה״ – נַעֲרָה מָלֵא דִּיבֵּר הַכָּתוּב.

The Gemara relates: **Rav Pappa, son of Rav Ḥanan, from** a place called **Bei Kelohit, heard** this *halakha* **and went and said it before Rav Shimi bar Ashi.** Rav Shimi **said to him: You teach this** statement **concerning that** matter. **We,** based on our traditions, **teach it concerning this** matter, **as Reish Lakish said: One who slanders a minor girl,** falsely claiming that she was not a virgin on the wedding night, **is exempt** from paying the fine, **as it is stated: "And they shall give them to the father of the young woman [*na'ara*]"** (Deuteronomy 22:19). **The verse spoke of *na'ara*,** not only pronounced but written **in full,**[N] indicating that this payment is in effect only with regard to a young woman, not a minor girl.[H] However, in places where the term is written *na'ar*, even a minor girl would be included.

מַתְקִיף לַהּ רַב אַדָּא בַּר אַהֲבָה: טַעְמָא דִּכְתַב רַחֲמָנָא ״נַעֲרָה״, הָא לָאו הָכִי – הֲוָה אָמִינָא אֲפִילּוּ קְטַנָּה? וְהָא כְּתִיב ״וְאִם אֱמֶת הָיָה הַדָּבָר הַזֶּה לֹא נִמְצְאוּ בְתוּלִים לַנַּעֲרָה וְהוֹצִיאוּ אֶת הַנַּעֲרָה אֶל פֶּתַח בֵּית אָבִיהָ וּסְקָלוּהָ״ – וּקְטַנָּה לָאו בַּת עוֹנָשִׁין הִיא! אֶלָּא: כָּאן – נַעֲרָה, הָא כׇּל מָקוֹם שֶׁנֶּאֱמַר ״נַעַר״ – אֲפִילּוּ קְטַנָּה בְּמַשְׁמָע.

Rav Adda bar Ahava strongly **objects to this: The reason is that the Merciful One writes "*na'ara*"** with a *heh*. Is that to say that **if that were not the case I would have said that** this *halakha* applies **even to a minor girl?** How is that possible? **But isn't it written: "And if this matter was true, that the hymen of this young woman was not found intact; then they shall remove the young woman to the entrance of her father's house and stone her"** (Deuteronomy 22:20–21). And this verse clearly refers to a young woman old enough to be punished, as **a minor is not subject to punishment.**[N] **Rather, here,** with regard to the payment of a slanderer, the verse speaks of **a *na'ara*,** written with a *heh*, and a minor is excluded. This is a paradigm from which **it may be inferred** that in any place **that it is stated "*na'ara*"** without a *heh*, **even a minor girl is indicated.**

NOTES

Any place where there is a sale, etc. – כׇּל מָקוֹם שֶׁיֵּשׁ מֶכֶר וכו׳: The *Tosefot Yom Tov* explains that this principle does not teach anything new; it merely serves as a mnemonic for the fact that a minor can be sold but is not entitled to a fine. The *Melekhet Shlomo* contends that there is a new *halakha* that emerges from this principle: Since even a young woman for whom there is no payment of humiliation or degradation, e.g., a deaf-mute or an imbecile, can be sold as a minor, she is entitled to the fine as a young woman.

Na'ara*, with and without the letter *heh – נַעֲרָה מָלֵא וְחָסֵר: Throughout the Torah the word *na'ara* is written without a *heh*, with the lone exception in the case of a slanderer. Admittedly, in certain very ancient Torah scrolls predating Ezra, *na'ara* is consistently written with a *heh*; however, the Masoretic tradition is without the *heh*. As for the derivation itself, one explanation is that when the word is written without a *heh*, it refers to both males and females, and it is only the vocalization that distinguishes between them. Therefore, when it is written without a *heh* it refers even to a minor girl, whose development into a young woman is not yet discernible and is therefore not clearly distinguishable from a male.

The verse spoke of *na'ara* written in full – נַעֲרָה מָלֵא דִּיבֵּר הַכָּתוּב: In the Jerusalem Talmud the question is raised: In the verses concerning the slanderer, other than the single instance where it is written with a *heh*, *na'ara* is written without a *heh* as well. The Gemara there answers that in that context, the fact that it is written without a *heh* indicates that it does not include a minor, but comes to include anal intercourse, which is common to both males and females.

And a minor is not subject to punishment – וּקְטַנָּה לָאו בַּת עוֹנָשִׁין הִיא: *Tosafot* ask: Perhaps the *halakha* of a slanderer applies even if she was a minor, and it is merely the punishment for adultery that is not administered to a minor. They answer that the case of a slanderer is one where a husband is trying to frame his wife and have her executed. As he cannot cause a minor to be executed, he cannot be punished as a slanderer.

HALAKHA

A minor is entitled to a fine – קְטַנָּה יֵשׁ לָהּ קְנָס: With regard to a minor three years and one day old and older, although she can be sold she is nonetheless entitled to the fine if she was raped or seduced, in accordance with the opinion of the Rabbis (Rambam *Sefer Nashim, Hilkhot Na'ara Betula* 1:8; *Shulḥan Arukh, Even HaEzer* 177:1).

One who slanders a minor girl – הַמּוֹצִיא שֵׁם רַע עַל הַקְּטַנָּה: One who slanders a minor girl is exempt from both the fine and lashes, as the term *na'ara* is written with a *heh* in the verse where the punishment is mentioned (Rambam *Sefer Nashim, Hilkhot Na'ara Betula* 3:2).

MISHNA מתני׳ הָאוֹמֵר: ״פִּתִּיתִי אֶת בִּתּוֹ שֶׁל פְּלוֹנִי״ – מְשַׁלֵּם בּוֹשֶׁת וּפְגָם עַל פִּי עַצְמוֹ, וְאֵין מְשַׁלֵּם קְנָס. הָאוֹמֵר ״גָּנַבְתִּי״ – מְשַׁלֵּם אֶת הַקֶּרֶן עַל פִּי עַצְמוֹ, וְאֵין מְשַׁלֵּם תַּשְׁלוּמֵי כֶּפֶל וְתַשְׁלוּמֵי אַרְבָּעָה וַחֲמִשָּׁה. ״הֵמִית שׁוֹרִי אֶת פְּלוֹנִי״ אוֹ ״שׁוֹרוֹ שֶׁל פְּלוֹנִי״ – הֲרֵי זֶה מְשַׁלֵּם עַל פִּי עַצְמוֹ. ״הֵמִית שׁוֹרִי עַבְדּוֹ שֶׁל פְּלוֹנִי״ – אֵין מְשַׁלֵּם עַל פִּי עַצְמוֹ. זֶה הַכְּלָל: כָּל הַמְשַׁלֵּם יָתֵר עַל מַה שֶּׁהִזִּיק – אֵינוֹ מְשַׁלֵּם עַל פִּי עַצְמוֹ.

One who says:[N] I seduced[H] **the daughter of so-and-so, pays** compensation for **humiliation and degradation** based **on his own** admission, **but does not pay the fine.** Similarly, **one who says: I stole,**[H] **pays the principal,** the value of the stolen goods, **based on his own** admission, **but does not pay the double payment and the payment four and five** times the principal for the slaughter or sale of the sheep or ox that he stole. Likewise if he confessed: **My ox killed so-and-so,**[H] **or:** My ox killed **an ox** belonging **to so-and-so, this** owner **pays** based **on his own** admission. However, if he said: **My ox killed a slave** belonging **to so-and-so,**[HN] **he does not pay** based **on his own** admission as that payment is a fine. **This is the principle:**[N] **Anyone who pays more than what he damaged,**[N] the payments are fines and therefore **he does not pay** based **on his own** admission. He pays only based on the testimony of others.

GEMARA גמ׳ וְלִיתְנֵי ״אָנַסְתִּי״! לָא מִבָּעְיָא קָאָמַר; לָא מִבָּעְיָא ״אָנַסְתִּי״ דְּלָא קָא פָּגֵים לַהּ, דִּמְשַׁלֵּם בּוֹשֶׁת וּפְגָם עַל פִּי עַצְמוֹ, אֲבָל ״פִּתִּיתִי״ דְּקָא פָּגֵים לַהּ – אֵימָא לָא מְשַׁלֵּם עַל פִּי עַצְמוֹ – קָא מַשְׁמַע לַן.

The Gemara asks: **And let the** *tanna* **teach** this *halakha* with regard to one who said: **I raped**[N] the daughter of so-and-so. Why did the mishna cite the case of seduction? The Gemara answers: The *tanna* **is speaking** employing the style: **It is not necessary. It is not necessary** for the mishna to cite the case of one who says: **I raped** her,[N] **where he does not tarnish her** reputation and merely incriminates himself, as it is obvious that **he pays** compensation for **humiliation and degradation** based **on his own** admission. **However,** in the case of one who says: **I seduced** her, **where he tarnishes her** reputation as he testifies that she willingly engaged in relations with him, and he is not deemed credible to do so, **say** that **he does not pay** based **on his own** admission. Therefore, the mishna **teaches us** that even in the case of seduction he pays compensation for humiliation and degradation based on his own admission.

מַתְנִיתִין דְּלָא כִּי הַאי תַּנָּא; דְּתַנְיָא, רַבִּי שִׁמְעוֹן בֶּן יְהוּדָה אוֹמֵר מִשּׁוּם רַבִּי שִׁמְעוֹן: אַף בּוֹשֶׁת וּפְגָם אֵינוֹ מְשַׁלֵּם עַל פִּי עַצְמוֹ, לֹא כׇּל הֵימֶנּוּ שֶׁיִּפְגּוֹם בִּתּוֹ שֶׁל פְּלוֹנִי.

The Gemara comments: **The mishna is not in accordance with** the opinion of **this** *tanna***, as it is taught** in a *baraita*: **Rabbi Shimon ben Yehuda says in the name of Rabbi Shimon: Even** the payments of **humiliation and degradation, he does not pay** them based **on his own** admission as **it is not within his power to tarnish** the reputation of **the daughter of** so-and-so based merely on his confession. Consequently, unless his account is corroborated by the testimony of others, his admission that she was complicit in her seduction is rejected.

HALAKHA

One who says: I seduced, etc. – הָאוֹמֵר פִּתִּיתִי וכו׳: One who confesses: I seduced or raped so-and-so's daughter, is exempt from payment of the fine, but is obligated to pay compensation for humiliation and degradation (Rambam *Sefer Nashim, Hilkhot Na'ara Betula* 2:12).

One who says, I stole, etc. – הָאוֹמֵר גָּנַבְתִּי וכו׳: One who confesses to stealing and slaughtering or selling is liable to pay only the principal, but is exempt from payment of double or four or five times the principal (Rambam *Sefer Nezikim, Hilkhot Geneiva* 3:9; *Tur, Ḥoshen Mishpat* 348).

My ox killed so-and-so, etc. – הֵמִית שׁוֹרִי אֶת פְּלוֹנִי וכו׳: One who confesses that his ox killed so-and-so, or in the case of a forewarned ox, that it killed so-and-so's ox, pays based on his confession (Rambam *Sefer Hafla'a, Hilkhot Shevuot* 8:4; *Sefer Shofetim, Hilkhot Sanhedrin* 4:14).

My ox killed a slave belonging to so-and-so, etc. – הֵמִית שׁוֹרִי עַבְדּוֹ שֶׁל פְּלוֹנִי וכו׳: One who confesses that his ox killed another person's slave is exempt from paying the thirty *sela*, as it is a fine (Rambam *Sefer Hafla'a, Hilkhot Shevuot* 8:2).

NOTES

The order of the mishna – סִדְרָהּ שֶׁל הַמִּשְׁנָה: The commentaries explain that the mishna employs the style: Not only this but also that. In other words, there is a novel element in each succeeding case. The principle here is that one who admits that he is liable to pay a fine is exempt. The mishna teaches that not only is one exempt in a case where he confesses that he raped or seduced a girl, where the exemption could be attributed to the fact that his admission casts aspersions on the girl, but one who confesses that he stole is also exempt from the double payment, although his testimony casts no aspersions. Furthermore, this *halakha* applies not only to a thief, who although he is exempt from the fine, is obligated to pay the principal; it applies even to a case where one confesses that his ox killed a slave, in which case his confession exempts him from any payment. There is a Torah decree that one whose incrimination is based exclusively on his own confession is exempt from the fine (*Melekhet Shlomo*; see *Tosefot Yom Tov*).

My ox killed a slave belonging to so-and-so – הֵמִית שׁוֹרִי עַבְדּוֹ שֶׁל פְּלוֹנִי: In the Jerusalem Talmud, the question is raised with regard to a slave worth less than thirty *sela*: Is part of the sum considered a monetary payment and the rest a fine, or is the entire amount deemed a fine? The *Yam shel Shlomo* explains that the phrase: Anyone who pays more than what he damaged, should not be taken literally, as it is possible that the slave is worth exactly thirty *sela*, in which case he would pay precisely the sum of the damage he caused. Rather, since the sum is fixed and is not always equal to the value of the slave, it is a fine.

This is the principle – זֶה הַכְּלָל: Based on *Tosafot* the commentaries on the mishna explain that the phrase: This is the principle: Anyone who pays more than what he damaged does not pay based on his own admission, comes to include other fines omitted here: The one hundred silver coins that a slanderer pays the father of his wife, and the obligation to free one's slave if he severed one of his extremities, i.e., he is freed with extraction of a tooth or an eye.

Anyone who pays more than what he damaged – כָּל הַמְשַׁלֵּם יָתֵר עַל מַה שֶּׁהִזִּיק: This principle, which establishes the difference between fines and payments of money, is problematic in the case of the ransom paid by one whose forewarned ox kills a person, as the *tanna'im* disagree about the meaning of the verse "If a ransom is placed upon him, then he shall give the redemption of his soul" (Exodus 21:30). Is this assessment of ransom based on the value of the victim or the value of the owner of the ox? According to the opinion that he pays his own value, in certain cases he pays more than the damage he caused, and therefore the payment should be considered a fine. *Tosafot*, and in greater detail *Tosefot HaRosh* and other commentaries, explain that since he pays the assessment of his own value, it is considered a monetary payment, as he is essentially redeeming himself from death at the hand of Heaven.

And let the *tanna* teach with regard to one who said: I raped – וְלִיתְנֵי אָנַסְתִּי וכו׳: According to *Tosafot* the question is: Why didn't the *tanna* cite a case of rape rather than one of seduction? The later commentaries add that had the mishna cited the case of rape, there would have been an additional novel element according to the Rambam's opinion that one pays for her pain based on his own admission. However, the Ritva and others claim that the Gemara is merely asking why the *tanna* did not teach both rape and seduction as he did in the other *mishnayot*. See *Tosafot* for a discussion of the novel element in the case of rape.

It is not necessary for the mishna to cite the case of one who says: I raped her, etc. – לָא מִבָּעְיָא אָנַסְתִּי וכו׳: The *ge'onim* had a variant reading of the Gemara, according to which the case of a rapist is unnecessary, as he did not significantly tarnish her reputation, whereas a seducer severely tarnishes her reputation, and therefore one might think that he pays based on his own confession (see also *Shita Mekubbetzet*).

אֲמַר לֵיהּ רַב פַּפָּא לְאַבַּיֵי: נִיחָא לָהּ לְדִידָהּ מַאי? דִּלְמָא לָא נִיחָא לֵיהּ לְאָבִיהָ. נִיחָא לֵיהּ לְאָבִיהָ מַאי? דִּלְמָא לָא נִיחָא לְהוּ לִבְנֵי מִשְׁפָּחָה. נִיחָא לְהוּ לִבְנֵי מִשְׁפָּחָה מַאי? אִי אֶפְשָׁר דְּלֵיכָּא חַד בִּמְדִינַת הַיָּם דְּלָא נִיחָא לֵיהּ.

Rav Pappa said to Abaye: According to Rabbi Shimon, if **she herself is amenable** to his claim, and admits that his version of the events is accurate, **what** is the *halakha*? Is he exempt from payments of humiliation and degradation in that case as well? Abaye responded: **Perhaps her father is not amenable** to his daughter's reputation being tarnished. We therefore do not rely on his statement even in this case. Rav Pappa continued: If **her father is** also **amenable** to his claim, **what** is the *halakha*? Abaye responded: **Perhaps her** other **family members are not amenable,** as the reputation of the entire family would be tarnished. Rav Pappa asked: If the **family members** too are **amenable, what** is the *halakha*? Abaye answered: Even if all the local relatives are amenable, **it is impossible that there** will not be at least **one** relative **in a country overseas**[N] **who is not amenable** to his claim.

״הָאוֹמֵר גָּנַבְתִּי מְשַׁלֵּם אֶת הַקֶּרֶן״ וכו׳. אִיתְּמַר, פַּלְגָא נִיזְקָא; רַב פַּפָּא אֲמַר: פַּלְגָא נִיזְקָא מָמוֹנָא, רַב הוּנָא בְּרֵיהּ דְּרַב יְהוֹשֻׁעַ אֲמַר: פַּלְגָא נִיזְקָא קְנָסָא.

The mishna continues. **One who says: I stole, pays the principal,** but does not pay the double payment and the payment four and five times the principal. **It is stated** that *amora'im* disagreed with regard to the payment of **half the damage** that the owner of an innocuous ox, which was not yet witnessed goring a person or an ox three times, must pay to the owner of the ox that he gored. **Rav Pappa said: Half the damage** is considered a payment of **money,** compensation for the damage caused. **Rav Huna, son of Rav Yehoshua, said** that **half the damage** is considered payment of a **fine.**

רַב פַּפָּא אֲמַר: פַּלְגָא נִיזְקָא מָמוֹנָא, קָסָבַר: סְתָם שְׁוָורִים לָאו בְּחֶזְקַת שִׁימּוּר קַיְימִי, וּבְדִין הוּא דִּמְשַׁלֵּם כּוּלֵּיהּ, וְרַחֲמָנָא הוּא דְּחָיֵיס עֲלָוֵיהּ, דְּאַכַּתִּי לָא אִיַּעַד תּוֹרָא. רַב הוּנָא בְּרֵיהּ דְּרַב יְהוֹשֻׁעַ אֲמַר: פַּלְגָא נִיזְקָא קְנָסָא. קָסָבַר: סְתָם שְׁוָורִים בְּחֶזְקַת שִׁימּוּר קַיְימִי, וּבְדִין הוּא דְּלָא לִישַׁלֵּם כְּלָל, וְרַחֲמָנָא הוּא דִּקְנָסֵיהּ, כִּי הֵיכִי דְּנִינְטְרֵיהּ לְתוֹרֵיהּ.

The Gemara elaborates. **Rav Pappa said: Half the damage** is considered a payment of **money,** as **he maintains: Standard oxen do not exist in the presumptive status of safety,**[N] and therefore are likely to cause damage. **And by right,** the owner **should pay the entire** damage caused by his animal, **and it is the Merciful One that has compassion on him, as his ox is not yet forewarned** until it has gored a person or an animal three times. Fundamentally, the payment is for damage that the animal caused. **Rav Huna, son of Rav Yehoshua, said** that **half the damage** is payment of a **fine,** as **he maintains: Standard oxen exist in the presumptive status of safety,** and are not dangerous. **And by right,** the owner **should not pay at all,** as the ox goring could not have been anticipated, and therefore the owner bears no responsibility. **And it is the Merciful One that penalized him so that he would guard his ox.** The sum that he pays is a fine.

סִימָן: היזיק מה והמית כלל. תְּנַן: הַנִּיזָּק וְהַמַּזִּיק בְּתַשְׁלוּמִין. בִּשְׁלָמָא לְמַאן דַּאֲמַר פַּלְגָא נִיזְקָא מָמוֹנָא – הַיְינוּ דְּשַׁיָּיךְ נִיזָּק בְּתַשְׁלוּמִין. אֶלָּא לְמַאן דְּאָמַר פַּלְגָא נִיזְקָא קְנָסָא – הַשְׁתָּא, דְּלָאו דִּידֵיהּ קָא שָׁקֵיל, בְּתַשְׁלוּמִין אִיתֵיהּ?!

The Gemara provides **a mnemonic**[B] for the proofs cited with regard to this dispute: **Damaged; what; and killed; principle. We learned** in a mishna that if an innocuous ox gored and killed another's ox, both **the damaged and the damager** share **in the payments. Granted, according to the one who said** that **half the damage** is a payment of **money; that** is how the **damaged party shares in the payments.** By right, the owner of the dead ox should be compensated for his entire loss. However, since the ox that gored his ox was innocuous, the owner of the gored ox bears half the costs. The mishna characterizes him as sharing in the payments. **However, according to he who said** that **half the damage** is payment of **a fine,** by right, the injured party himself is entitled to nothing. **Now,** the owner **takes** half the damage **that** by right **is not his; can he** be characterized as sharing **in the payments?**

לָא נִצְרְכָא אֶלָּא לְפְחַת נְבֵילָה. פְּחַת נְבֵילָה תְּנֵינָא: תַּשְׁלוּמֵי נֶזֶק מְלַמֵּד שֶׁהַבְּעָלִים מְטַפְּלִין בַּנְּבֵילָה.

The Gemara answers: This *halakha* is **necessary only for the degradation of the carcass.** Initially, half the damage is assessed by calculating the difference between the value of a living ox and the value of its carcass when the owner of the ox that gored the other ox stands trial. The degradation in the value of the carcass from when it was gored until the owner is able to sell it is borne by the owner of the carcass. The owner thereby shares in the payment, as he loses that sum. The Gemara asks: **We** already **learned** the *halakha* with regard to **the degradation of the carcass** in a *baraita* in *Bava Kamma* (10b) in which it is taught that the passage in the mishna: I have become liable to pay **payments of damage,**[N] **teaches that the owners tend to the carcass**[H] and bear the costs of its degradation.

NOTES

Family members in a country overseas – **בְּנֵי מִשְׁפָּחָה בִּמְדִינַת הַיָּם:** Although her family, certainly those living overseas, have no monetary claim, the issue here is not their monetary or legal rights. Rather, the question is whether the statement that he seduced the daughter constitutes degradation. In this regard, the fact that she has relatives who would be displeased is enough to establish the claim. Consequently, that confession would not be accepted, as it tarnishes the reputation of the family (Rabbi Aharon HaLevi).

Do not exist in the presumptive status of safety – **לָאו בְּחֶזְקַת שִׁימּוּר קַיְימִי:** The Ritva and others explain that this does not mean that the assumption is that every ox will gore a person. It means that even those oxen that do not typically gore people must be guarded. Consequently, one who fails to guard them is liable to pay; he cannot be seen as the victim of unavoidable circumstances.

Payments of damage etc. – **תַּשְׁלוּמֵי נֶזֶק וכו׳:** The inference is as follows: Had it stated simply damage, the understanding would have been that the owner of the ox that gored another ox must pay the victim the entire damage or half the damage in the case of an innocuous ox. In contrast, the phrase: Payments of damage, indicates that he is liable to payment determined when he stands trial, deducting degradation from the sum that he is liable to pay, but not payment to cover all the damage he caused (Rabbeinu Crescas Vidal).

BACKGROUND

A mnemonic – **סִימָן:** Because the Talmud was studied orally for many generations, mnemonic devices were necessary to facilitate memorizing a series of *halakhot* and the order in which they were taught.

HALAKHA

That the owners tend to the carcass – **שֶׁהַבְּעָלִים מְטַפְּלִין בַּנְּבֵילָה:** The owner of the ox that was gored bears the cost of the degradation of the carcass. How so? Consider the case of an ox worth two hundred dinars that was gored and killed, and its carcass, which was worth one hundred dinars at the time of its death, was worth only eighty dinars at trial. If the ox that gored a person or animal was forewarned, its owner pays one hundred dinars; if it was innocuous, the owner pays fifty dinars. The owner of the dead ox is not compensated for the twenty dinars of degradation of the carcass. The Rema writes that this *halakha* applies only if the owner of the ox that was gored is immediately apprised of his loss. However, if he was not apprised, and therefore could not have tended to the carcass and sold it immediately, the owner of the ox that gored a person or animal must pay for the degradation in its value. The *Tur* claims that this *halakha* applies also if the market price of the carcass decreased, whereas others contend that the owner of the ox that was gored bears the cost of the decrease in the market price of the carcass (Rambam *Sefer Nezikim*, *Hilkhot Nizkei Mamon* 7:8; *Shulḥan Arukh*, *Ḥoshen Mishpat* 403:20).

חֲדָא בְּתָם וַחֲדָא בְּמוּעָד. וּצְרִיכָא, דְּאִי אַשְׁמְעִינַן תָּם – מִשּׁוּם דְּאַכַּתִּי לָא אִיַּעַד, אֲבָל מוּעָד דְּאִיַּעַד – אֵימָא לָא. וְאִי אַשְׁמְעִינַן מוּעָד – מִשּׁוּם דְּקָא מְשַׁלֵּם כּוּלֵּיהּ, אֲבָל תָּם – אֵימָא לָא, צְרִיכָא.

The Gemara answers: **One** of these *halakhot* is **with regard to an innocuous** ox **and one** is **with regard to a forewarned** ox. The Gemara adds: **And** it is **necessary** to teach both *halakhot*, **as if** the mishna **had taught us** only with regard to **an innocuous** ox, one would understand that its owner is treated with leniency and the owner of the carcass bears the cost of degradation **due to** the fact **that** the ox **has not yet been forewarned; however,** with regard to **a forewarned** ox, **that was forewarned, say no,** the owner of the carcass does not bear the cost of degradation. **And if** the mishna **had taught us** only with regard to **a forewarned** ox, one would understand that its owner is treated with leniency and the owner of the carcass bears the cost of degradation **due to** the fact **that he pays** for the **entire damage,** and therefore, the relatively insignificant cost of degradation is overlooked. **However,** with regard to **an innocuous** ox, **say no,** since the owner pays only half the damage, he must bear the cost of degradation. Therefore, it was **necessary** to state the *halakha* in both cases. Therefore, there is no proof from this mishna whether half the damage is payment of a money or payment of a fine.

תָּא שְׁמַע: מַה בֵּין תָּם לְמוּעָד? שֶׁהַתָּם מְשַׁלֵּם חֲצִי נֶזֶק מִגּוּפוֹ, וּמוּעָד מְשַׁלֵּם נֶזֶק שָׁלֵם מִן הָעֲלִיָּיה. וְלָא קָתָנֵי שֶׁהַתָּם אֵינוֹ מְשַׁלֵּם עַל פִּי עַצְמוֹ וּמוּעָד מְשַׁלֵּם עַל פִּי עַצְמוֹ!

The Gemara continues. **Come** and **hear** an additional proof from a *baraita*: **What is** the difference **between an innocuous and a forewarned** ox? The difference is **that** the owner of **an innocuous** ox **pays half** of the **damage from its body.** Compensation for the damage may be collected only from the body of the ox that gored another ox. If the ox that gored another ox is worth less than half the damage, e.g., if an inexpensive ox killed an expensive one, the injured party receives less than half the damage. **And** the owner of **a forewarned** ox **pays the entire damage from the** owner's **property,** and the value of the ox that gored another ox has no effect on the payment. The *tanna* **did not teach** an additional difference that the owner of **an innocuous** ox **does not pay** based **on his own** admission **and** the owner of **a forewarned** ox **pays** based **on his own** admission.[H] Apparently, the half damage is a payment of money and not a fine.

תָּנָא וְשַׁיֵּיר. מַאי שַׁיֵּיר דְּהַאי שַׁיֵּיר? שַׁיֵּיר חֲצִי כּוֹפֶר. אִי מִשּׁוּם חֲצִי כּוֹפֶר – לָאו שִׁיּוּרָא הוּא.

The Gemara refutes this claim: This *baraita* is no proof, as the *tanna* **taught** some cases **and omitted** others[N] and did not list all the differences between innocuous and forewarned oxen. The Gemara asks: **What else did he omit that he omitted this?** The failure to include an item in a list can be deemed insignificant only if it is one of at least two omissions. If there is only one omission, apparently it was omitted advisedly. The Gemara replies: **He omitted** the *halakha* of the **half ransom**[H] as well. If a forewarned ox killed a person, its owner pays a ransom, and if an innocuous ox killed a person, the owner does not pay even half the ransom. The Gemara rejects this claim: **If** it is **due to** the **half ransom** that the failure to list the difference with regard to payment based on one's own admission is insignificant, it **is not an omission.**

HALAKHA

Innocuous and forewarned – תָּם וּמוּעָד: The owner of a forewarned ox pays full damages from his highest quality property. The same applies to any damage caused by an animal in the course of its typical conduct and which therefore is considered forewarned. If an innocuous ox caused damage its owner pays half of the damage, paid from the body of the ox itself (Rambam *Sefer Nezikim, Hilkhot Nizkei Mamon* 1:2–3; *Shulḥan Arukh, Ḥoshen Mishpat* 389:2, 9).

Half ransom – חֲצִי כּוֹפֶר: The owner of an innocuous ox that killed a person pays nothing, not even half the ransom, as explicitly stated in *Bava Kamma* (Rambam *Sefer Nezikim, Hilkhot Nizkei Mamon* 10:2).

NOTES

The *tanna* taught some cases and omitted others – תָּנָא וְשַׁיֵּיר: This is a standard response to an attempted inference from an omission in a mishna. The idea is that an omission of a case from a mishna is not significant if the *tanna* did not list all of the possible cases. An alternative manner of expressing the same concept is the phrase: Is that to say that the *tanna* should have continued reckoning cases like a peddler? The immediate rejoinder to this answer, as here, is for the Gemara to inquire: What else did he omit that he omitted this? In other words, in order to assert that the *tanna* did not list all possible cases, it must be proven that the *tanna* omitted additional examples.

הָא מַנִּי – רַבִּי יוֹסֵי הַגְּלִילִי הִיא, דְּאָמַר: תָּם מְשַׁלֵּם חֲצִי כּוֹפֶר.

As it can be explained: According to **whose** opinion **is this** *baraita* taught? **It is** according to the opinion of **Rabbi Yosei**[N] **HaGelili,**[N] **who said:** The owner of **an innocuous** ox **pays half** the **ransom.** According to his opinion, the only differences between innocuous and forewarned oxen are those specified in the mishna.

תָּא שְׁמַע: ״הֵמִית שׁוֹרִי אֶת פְּלוֹנִי״, אוֹ ״שׁוֹרוֹ שֶׁל פְּלוֹנִי״ – הֲרֵי זֶה מְשַׁלֵּם עַל פִּי עַצְמוֹ. מַאי לָאו בְּתָם? לָא, בְּמוּעָד.

The Gemara suggests: **Come** and **hear** an additional proof from the mishna. One who said: **My ox killed so-and-so, or:** My ox killed **an ox** belonging **to so-and-so, this** owner **pays** based **on his own** admission. **What, is** this **not** referring **to an innocuous** ox, for which he pays half the damage, proving that it is a payment of money and not a fine? The Gemara rejects the proof: **No,** the *tanna* is referring **to a forewarned** animal.

אֲבָל בְּתָם מַאי – אֵינוֹ מְשַׁלֵּם עַל פִּי עַצְמוֹ. אַדְּתָנֵי סֵיפָא: ״עַבְדּוֹ שֶׁל פְּלוֹנִי״ אֵינוֹ מְשַׁלֵּם עַל פִּי עַצְמוֹ – נִיפְלוֹג וְנִיתְנֵי בְּדִידָהּ: בַּמֶּה דְּבָרִים אֲמוּרִים – בְּמוּעָד, אֲבָל תָּם אֵינוֹ מְשַׁלֵּם עַל פִּי עַצְמוֹ! כּוּלָּהּ בְּמוּעָד קָמַיְירֵי.

The Gemara asks: **However,** in the case **of an innocuous** ox, **what** is the *halakha*? If it is that **he does not pay** based **on his own** admission, then, **rather than teaching the latter clause** of the mishna: One whose ox **killed a slave** belonging to **so-and-so does not pay** based **on his own** admission, **let him distinguish and teach** the distinction **within the case itself: In what** case **is this statement said?** It is **with regard to a forewarned** ox; **however,** the owner of **an innocuous** ox **does not pay** based **on his own** admission. The Gemara rejects this proof: The **entire** mishna **is speaking of a forewarned** ox, and does not address the *halakha* of an innocuous ox at all. Therefore, no proof can be cited with regard to the nature of half the payment.

תָּא שְׁמַע, זֶה הַכְּלָל: כָּל הַמְשַׁלֵּם יָתֵר עַל מַה שֶּׁהִזִּיק אֵינוֹ מְשַׁלֵּם עַל פִּי עַצְמוֹ. הָא פָּחוֹת מִמַּה שֶּׁהִזִּיק – מְשַׁלֵּם עַל פִּי עַצְמוֹ! לָא תֵּימָא: הָא פָּחוֹת מִמַּה שֶּׁהִזִּיק, אֶלָּא אֵימָא: הָא כְּמַה שֶּׁהִזִּיק – מְשַׁלֵּם עַל פִּי עַצְמוֹ.

The Gemara suggests: **Come** and **hear** an additional proof from the mishna: **This is the principle: Anyone who pays more than what he damaged,** the payments are fines, and therefore **he does not pay** based **on his own** admission. The Gemara infers: If he pays **less than what he damaged, he pays** based **on his own** admission. Apparently, payment of half the damage is a payment of money, not a fine. The Gemara rejects this proof: **Do not** infer and **say:** If he pays **less than what he damaged,** he pays based on his own admission. Infer and **say:** If he pays precisely **what he damaged, he pays** based **on his own** admission.

אֲבָל פָּחוֹת מַאי – אֵינוֹ מְשַׁלֵּם עַל פִּי עַצְמוֹ. לִיתְנֵי: זֶה הַכְּלָל: כָּל שֶׁאֵינוֹ מְשַׁלֵּם כְּמַה שֶּׁהִזִּיק – אֵינוֹ מְשַׁלֵּם עַל פִּי עַצְמוֹ, דְּמַשְׁמַע פָּחוֹת וּמַשְׁמַע יָתֵר! תְּיוּבְתָּא.

The Gemara asks: **But** according to that explanation, if he pays **less** than the damage he caused, **what** is the *halakha*? If it is that **he does not pay** based **on his own** admission, **let** the *tanna* **teach** a more general principle: **This is the principle: Anyone who does not pay** the amount **that he damaged does not pay** based **on his own** admission, **as** that formulation both **indicates** one who pays **less and indicates** one who pays **more** than the damage he inflicted. The Gemara concludes: This is **a conclusive refutation** of the opinion of Rav Huna, son of Rav Yehoshua, that payment of half the damage is a fine.

NOTES

According to whose opinion is this *baraita* taught? It is according to Rabbi Yosei, etc. – **הָא מַנִּי רַבִּי יוֹסֵי וכו׳**: The structure of the Gemara appears to indicate the following: The Gemara attempts to prove that apparently the payment of half the damage is a monetary payment and not a fine, from the fact that the distinction between a forewarned ox, whose owner pays based on his confession, and an innocuous ox, whose owner does not pay based on his confession, was omitted from the mishna. The Gemara answers: The *tanna* taught some cases and omitted others. The Gemara asks: What else did he omit that he omitted this? The Gemara answers: He omitted payment of half the ransom, as there is no payment of ransom at all for an innocuous ox. The Gemara notes: That is not an omission, as the mishna is in accordance with the opinion of Rabbi Yosei HaGelili who holds that there is a payment of half the ransom in the case of an innocuous ox. Indeed, Rabbeinu Simḥa, cited in *Tosefot HaRosh*, explains the Gemara in this manner. However, that explanation is difficult. The entire difficulty raised by the Gemara is based on establishing that the mishna is according to the individual opinion of Rabbi Yosei HaGelili, which is by no means the most obvious possibility.

The Ra'avad explains in the name of one of his teachers that the contention that the *tanna* included some cases and omitted others is far-fetched, and therefore, the Gemara prefers an explanation of the mishna that does not rely on that contention, even if it requires adoption of a minority opinion. However, some difficulty remains, and therefore, most early commentaries explain the exchange in the Gemara differently. The Gemara is saying that once it was established that the *tanna* omitted the difference between the forewarned and innocuous oxen with regard to ransom, apparently there is another difference that he omitted. It must be that he omitted the difference with regard to liability to pay half the damage based on one's own confession. This proves that the payment of half the damage is a fine and poses a difficulty to the one who holds that it is a monetary payment. The Gemara responds that it is not an absolute proof as it could be established that the mishna is according to the opinion of Rabbi Yosei HaGelili, in which case there is no difference between them with regard to ransom, and therefore there is no need to search for an additional difference with regard to payment based on confession (Ra'avad; Rosh; Ritva).

Rabbi Yosei HaGelili – **רַבִּי יוֹסֵי הַגְּלִילִי**: *Tosafot* discuss at length why the Gemara attributes this opinion to Rabbi Yosei HaGelili, as there is no source where he is cited expressing this opinion, and it is merely inferred from his statements. Furthermore, if we are willing to ascribe this opinion based on inference, it could be attributed to Rabbi Akiva and to other Sages as well. The Ritva claims that in cases of this kind, the Gemara is not particular about the precise identity of the *tanna*, but is satisfied with the fact that there is a tannaitic opinion to this effect, even if there are other Sages who might also concur with this opinion.

וְהִלְכְתָא: פַּלְגָא נִיזְקָא קְנָסָא. תְּיוּבְתָּא וְהִלְכְתָא?! אִין, טַעֲמָא מַאי אִיתּוֹתַב – מִשּׁוּם דְּלָא קָתָנֵי כְּמַה שֶׁהִזִּיק. לָא פְּסִיקָא לֵיהּ, כֵּיוָן דְּאִיכָּא חֲצִי נֶזֶק צְרוֹרוֹת דְּהִלְכְתָא גְּמִירִי לַהּ דְּמָמוֹנָא הוּא – מִשּׁוּם הָכִי לָא קָתָנֵי.

The Gemara further concludes: **And the *halakha* is that** payment of **half the damage**[H] **is a fine.** The Gemara asks: Is there **a conclusive refutation** of the opinion of Rav Huna, son of Rav Yehoshua, **and** the *halakha*[N] is in accordance with that opinion? The Gemara responds: **Yes,** the *halakha* is in accordance with his opinion, as, **what is the reason** that his opinion **was conclusively refuted?** It is **because** the *tanna* **does not teach:** This is the principle: Anyone who does not pay the amount **that he damaged.** However, the reason the *tanna* did not employ that formulation **is not clear-cut for him, since there is** the payment of **half** the **damage** caused by **pebbles**[H] dispersed by an animal proceeding in its usual manner. **As it is a *halakha* transmitted** to Moses from Sinai **that** the payment for pebbles **is a monetary** payment, not a fine; it is **due to that** fact that the *tanna* **did not teach** the principle: Anyone who does not pay the amount that he damaged does not pay based on his own admission. In the case of pebbles, although he does not pay the amount that he damaged, he pays based on his own admission.

וְהָשְׁתָּא דְּאָמְרַתְּ פַּלְגָא נִיזְקָא קְנָסָא, הַאי כַּלְבָּא דַּאֲכַל אִימְּרֵי, וְשׁוּנְרָא דְּאָכֵיל תַּרְנְגוֹלֵי רַבְרְבֵי – מְשׁוּנֶּה הוּא, וְלָא מַגְבִּינַן בְּבָבֶל. אֲבָל זוּטְרֵי – אוֹרְחֵיהּ הוּא, וּמַגְבִּינַן.

Based on that ruling, the Gemara concludes: **And now that you said** that payment of **half the damage is a fine,**[N] **this dog that ate lambs,**[H] **and a cat that ate large roosters,**[N] **is unusual**[N] damage, for which the owner is liable to pay only half the damage if the animal was innocuous, **and** therefore, **we do not collect** it **in Babylonia.** The payment for unusual damage is a fine, and fines cannot be collected in Babylonia, as there are no ordained judges authorized to adjudicate cases involving fines. **However,** if the cat ate **small** roosters, that **is its usual manner, and we collect** the damages in Babylonia, as it is a payment of money.

HALAKHA

Half the damage – פַּלְגָא נִיזְקָא: The payment of anyone obligated to pay a sum equivalent to the amount of damage caused is considered a monetary payment, whereas the payment of anyone obligated to pay either more or less than the amount of damage caused is a fine. A person is liable to pay a fine based only on the testimony of witnesses (Rambam *Sefer Nezikim, Hilkhot Nizkei Mamon* 2:8).

Half the damage caused by pebbles – חֲצִי נֶזֶק צְרוֹרוֹת: If an animal dispersed pebbles from under its feet in the course of walking, and those pebbles caused damage, it is a sub-category of the primary category of damage of foot, which includes any damage caused by the animal in the course of its standard conduct, and the animal's owner is obligated to remit a monetary payment to the person whose property was damaged, from his highest quality property. However, there is a *halakha* transmitted to Moses from Sinai that he pays only half of the damages (Rambam *Sefer Nezikim, Hilkhot Nizkei Mamon* 2:2; *Shulḥan Arukh, Ḥoshen Mishpat* 390:3).

A dog that ate lambs, etc. – כַּלְבָּא דַּאֲכַל אִימְּרֵי וכו׳: If an undomesticated animal killed and ate an animal or ate raw meat, this is typical conduct, and its owner must pay the complete amount of the damage caused. However, in the case of a dog that killed a lamb or in the case of a cat that killed a large rooster and ate it, that is atypical conduct and therefore the owner of the cat or dog is liable to pay only half the damage. A person liable to pay half the damage pays only based on the ruling of judges ordained in Eretz Yisrael (Rambam *Sefer Nezikim, Hilkhot Nizkei Mamon* 3:7; *Sefer Shofetim, Hilkhot Sanhedrin* 5:9; *Shulḥan Arukh, Ḥoshen Mishpat* 391:6; 1:5).

NOTES

A conclusive refutation and *halakha* – תְּיוּבְתָּא וְהִלְכְתָא: There is a difference between the Gemara's use of the expressions conclusive refutation and difficulty. If the opinion of a Sage is characterized as difficult, his opinion was not completely rejected. The Gemara is merely noting that there is a difficulty with that opinion. There is a tradition among the early commentaries that there is an answer to each of those difficulties. Indeed, several books, e.g., Rabbi Yeshaya Berlin's *Kashot Meyushav*, are devoted to providing answers in all of the places where the Gemara concludes that it is difficult. In contrast, when the Gemara concludes that there is a conclusive refutation of an opinion, the difficulty is significant to the extent that the opinion of that Sage is rejected. That explains the astonishment expressed by the Gemara: A conclusive refutation and *halakha*?

And now that you said that payment of half the damage is a fine – וְהָשְׁתָּא דְּאָמְרַתְּ פַּלְגָא נִיזְקָא קְנָסָא: Even though fundamentally, ordained judges are required to adjudicate monetary cases as well as cases of fines, the Sages instituted that in this regard the Sages in each place are the agents of the original ordained Sages. Although they said that this principle is implemented only in common cases, damage caused by animals is deemed a frequent occurrence and is therefore within the jurisdiction of Babylonian judges when the payment for damages is a monetary payment and not a fine (Ritva).

Large roosters – תַּרְנְגוֹלֵי רַבְרְבֵי: The early commentaries state that this distinction between large and small animals applies only to a cat that killed roosters. However, with regard to the case of a dog that ate lambs, it is unusual for a dog to eat even undersized lambs, and therefore those cases may not be adjudicated in Babylonia (Rashi and Meiri on *Bava Kamma*).

It is unusual – מְשׁוּנֶּה הוּא: As explained by Rashi, any damage caused to an object by a domesticated or undomesticated animal eating it falls into the primary category of damage of tooth, which includes any damage caused by the animal by eating an item that it typically eats. However, if the animal ate an item that it does not typically eat, it no longer falls into the category of tooth. Instead, the animal is considered to have acted with the intention to cause damage, which places it in the category of horn, which includes any damage that the animal causes intentionally. Consequently, as long as it was not forewarned, that act has the legal status of goring by an innocuous ox, and the owner only pays half the damage from the animal itself.

וְאִי תָּפַס – לָא מַפְּקִינַן מִינֵּיהּ. וְאִי אָמַר: אַקְבְּעוּ לִי זִימְנָא לְאֶרֶץ יִשְׂרָאֵל, מַקְבְּעִינַן לֵיהּ, וְאִי לָא אָזֵיל, מְשַׁמְּתִינַן לֵיהּ.

The Gemara comments: **And** in cases of fines, **if** the injured party **seized**[NH] property from the offender in the amount of the fine, even in Babylonia **we do not repossess it from him,** as according to the letter of the law he is entitled to that payment, and the party from whom he seized the property cannot claim that he does not owe that payment. **And if** the injured party **said: Set me a time** to go to a court **in Eretz Yisrael,** where cases of fines are adjudicated, **we set** a time **for him, and if** the other disputant **does not go** to Israel as demanded, **we excommunicate him.**

בֵּין כָּךְ וּבֵין כָּךְ מְשַׁמְּתִינַן לֵיהּ. דְּאָמְרִינַן לֵיהּ: סַלֵּיק הֶיזֵּיקָךְ, מִדְּרַבִּי נָתָן. דְּתַנְיָא, רַבִּי נָתָן אוֹמֵר: מִנַּיִן שֶׁלֹּא יְגַדֵּל אָדָם כֶּלֶב רַע בְּתוֹךְ בֵּיתוֹ וְלֹא יַעֲמִיד סוּלָּם רָעוּעַ בְּתוֹךְ בֵּיתוֹ – שֶׁנֶּאֱמַר ״וְלֹא תָשִׂים דָּמִים בְּבֵיתֶךָ״.

The Gemara adds: **Either way,** whether or not he agrees to go to Eretz Yisrael, if he keeps the cause of the damage, **we** in Babylonia **excommunicate him, as we say to him: Remove your** cause of **damage,**[N] in accordance with the opinion of **Rabbi Natan. As it is taught** in a *baraita* that **Rabbi Natan says: From where** is it derived **that a person may not raise a vicious dog**[HB] **in his house, and may not place an unsteady ladder**[H] **in his house?** It is as it is stated: "And you shall make a parapet for your roof **that you shall not place blood in your house"** (Deuteronomy 22:8). It is prohibited to leave a potentially dangerous object in one's house, and one who refuses to remove it is excommunicated.

הדרן עלך אלו נערות

NOTES

And if he seized – **וְאִי תָּפַס**: Rabbeinu Tam maintains that seized in this context means that he seized the animal that caused the damage, as, if the legal status of this situation is like that of the damage caused by the horn of an innocuous ox, payment may be collected only from the animal itself, not from the rest of the owner's property. The Meiri agrees. Many early commentaries, however, maintain that since he is not collecting the damages through the legal system but is seizing compensation for the damage he suffered, the above distinction does not apply. As a result, even if the owner of the rooster or the lamb seized other assets of the owner of the dog and the cat, the courts do not repossess them. The Rivan attributes this explanation to Rashi in *Bava Kamma*. This explanation also stands to reason, as it is unlikely that the value of a cat would be sufficient to offset half the damage to a large rooster.

Remove your cause of damage – **סַלֵּיק הֶיזֵּיקָךְ**: The Ritva writes, and the *Nimmukei Yosef* cites in his name, that this principle applies only to a nuisance like a dog, when the owner can be ostracized until he kills it or removes it by some other means. If, however, it was an ox that he utilizes for his work, the court does not compel the owner to remove it from his possession. He is forced to upgrade his supervision over it. In the Jerusalem Talmud, there is an opinion cited by the authorities that even though the party that suffered the damage has the right to seize the possessions of the one whose animal caused the damage, and despite the fact that the latter is required to remove the source of damage from his possession, the owner of the animal that caused the damage is under no obligation, not even by the laws of Heaven, to pay a fine if the court lacks the authority to force him to do so (see *Nimmukei Yosef*).

HALAKHA

And if he seized – **וְאִי תָּפַס**: Even though courts do not collect fines outside Eretz Yisrael, where the judges are not ordained, the person liable to pay the fine is ostracized until he attempts to appease the person who incurred the damage and pays him an appropriate sum. If he does so, the ostracism is repealed, even if the one who incurred the damage refuses to be placated. Similarly, if the victim seizes the property of the person liable to pay the fine equal to the value of the fine, the court does not repossess it from him. The Rema states in the name of the Rosh that although the court does not assess the damage *ab initio* so that if he chooses to do so the victim will know how much to seize, if the victim seized the other's property, the court assesses the damage and informs him whether he is allowed to keep the entire sum that he seized. All these limitations apply to fines fixed by Torah or rabbinic law. However, Sages located in each place have the authority to institute ordinances and collect fines from those who violate their ordinances (Rambam *Sefer Shofetim, Hilkhot Sanhedrin* 5:17; *Shulḥan Arukh, Ḥoshen Mishpat* 1:5).

A vicious dog – **כֶּלֶב רַע**: It is prohibited to raise a vicious dog unless it is tied with iron chains. In a border town one may raise a vicious dog, but he must tie it by day and release it at night. The Rema cites an opinion that if Jews are living among gentiles and require protection they may raise dogs for that purpose; however, if the dog is so vicious that it poses a real danger to people beyond the need for protection, the owner must tie it with chains, as stated here and in *Bava Kamma* 83b (Rambam *Sefer Nezikim, Hilkhot Nizkei Mamon* 5:9; *Shulḥan Arukh, Ḥoshen Mishpat* 409:3).

An unsteady ladder – **סוּלָּם רָעוּעַ**: It is a mitzva to remove any potential danger from one's property. One who keeps a dangerous item in his house has failed to fulfill the positive mitzva of making a parapet and has violated the prohibition: You shall not place blood in your house (Rambam *Sefer Nezikim, Hilkhot Rotze'aḥ UShmirat HaNefesh* 11:4; *Shulḥan Arukh, Ḥoshen Mishpat* 427:8).

BACKGROUND

Damages of cats and dogs – **נִזְקֵי כֶּלֶב וְחָתוּל**: Apparently, based on the Gemara, cats were not completely domesticated and trained in those times. However, some people kept cats in their houses in order to battle snakes, mice, and other small vermin. However, in many cases, the cat would pounce on birds or even on the children of the house.

Most of the dogs in that period were either shepherd dogs or guard dogs. Later in this tractate (61b), it is clear that raising a dog in one's home as a pet was uncommon. Moreover, there were those who kept a vicious dog, a savage guard dog trained to attack and even kill people. It was no wonder that a dog of that kind could pounce on domesticated animals and kill them.

Summary of **Perek III**

In this chapter, the Gemara concluded that one who rapes or seduces a young woman who is forbidden to him, regardless of whether the prohibition is by Torah law or by rabbinic law, need not and may not marry her. However, he is required to pay her father the fine mentioned in the Torah. However, if she was forbidden to him by a prohibition punishable by death, then even if in this particular case the death penalty is not administered, the perpetrator is exempt from paying the fine.

These *halakhot* are based on several principles analyzed in this chapter. One is that a person is not punished with two punishments for one prohibited action; rather he receives the more severe punishment. Another is that in the case of any prohibition whose violation incurs both lashes and monetary payment, one pays and is not flogged. One is obligated to make that payment even if the prohibition was punishable by *karet*.

With regard to the details mentioned in the verse, the Gemara concluded that the rapist is obligated to pay the fine only if the victim is a virgin and not one who lost her presumptive virgin status, e.g., an emancipated maidservant or a woman who participated in a marriage ceremony; however, the rapist is obligated to pay even if he raped a minor girl and not only if the victim is a young woman. Furthermore, even if the victim was a young woman who was betrothed and widowed from betrothal, he is obligated to pay. In addition, although the verse refers to a young woman with a father, even if the victim was an orphan the rapist pays a fine. However, with regard to this detail, there is a difference between the victim of rape and the victim of seduction, as one who seduces an orphaned young woman is exempt, because she was complicit in performing the action. With regard to refusal to marry the perpetrator, the Sages derived that this applies to both the victim of rape and the victim of seduction, and both the father and the daughter have the right of refusal.

The Gemara concluded that the sum written in the Torah is a fine and the perpetrator pays it to every young woman that he victimizes. However, in addition, like any person who injures another, he pays for pain, humiliation, loss of livelihood, medical costs, and degradation. The fine is payment for the act of intercourse alone. Since that sum is a fine and not a monetary obligation, like all fines it is collected only through the testimony of witnesses and not by his own admission and it may be levied and collected only by ordained judges.

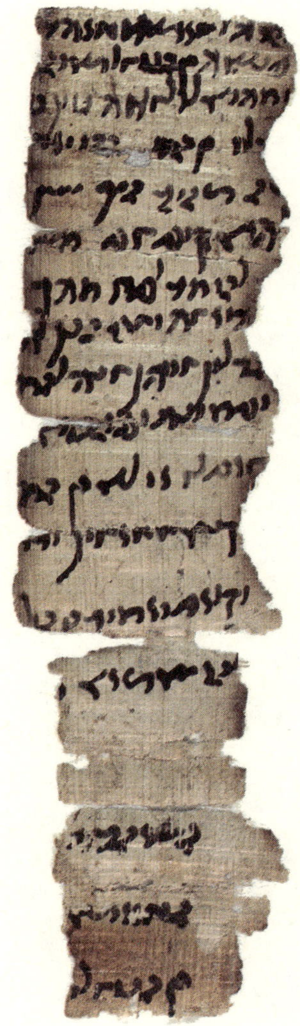

Remnant of an ancient *ketuba*, marriage document, found in a cave in the Judean Desert. Dating back to the second century, it is the oldest *ketuba* ever discovered. It was hidden, along with other objects, by refugees at the end of the bar Kokheva revolt. Although most of the text of the *ketuba* is missing, many significant details can be derived from what remains.

Image **Credits**

All images are copyright © Koren Publishers Jerusalem Ltd., except:

p208 © Wolfgang Sauber; **p215** © Hans Hillewaert; **p262** © Jastrow; **p278** © Biehler Michael, www.shutterstock.com; **p336** © Matthias Kabel; **p363** © Giovanni Dall'Orto; **p364** © Guy de la Bedoyere; **p233** © Shai Halevi, Clara Amit, Yoram Lehman, Yael Yolovitch, Miki Koren, and Mariana Salzberger, courtesy of the Israel Antiquities Authority.

My Notes

My Notes

My Notes

My Notes

אֵלּוּ *א נְעָרוֹת שֶׁיֵּשׁ לָהֶן קְנָס: הַבָּא עַל הַמַּמְזֶרֶת, וְעַל הַנְּתִינָה, וְעַל הַכּוּתִית. הַבָּא עַל הַגִּיּוֹרֶת, וְעַל הַשְּׁבוּיָה. וְעַל הַשִּׁפְחָה שֶׁנִּפְדּוּ וְשֶׁנִּתְגַּיְּירוּ וְשֶׁנִּשְׁתַּחְרְרוּ פְּחוּתוֹת מִבְּנוֹת שָׁלֹשׁ שָׁנִים וְיוֹם אֶחָד. *הַבָּא עַל אֲחוֹתוֹ וְעַל אֲחוֹת אָבִיו וְעַל אֲחוֹת אִמּוֹ וְעַל אֲחוֹת אִשְׁתּוֹ וְעַל אֵשֶׁת אָחִיו וְעַל אֵשֶׁת אֲחִי אָבִיו וְעַל הַנִּדָּה – יֵשׁ לָהֶם קְנָס, אע"פ שֶׁהֵן בְּהִכָּרֵת – אֵין בָּהֶן מִיתַת בֵּית דִּין.§ **גמ'** הָנֵי נְעָרוֹת פְּסוּלוֹת – אִית לְהוּ קְנָס, כְּשֵׁירוֹת – לָא?! הָכִי קָאָמַר: אֵלּוּ נְעָרוֹת פְּסוּלוֹת שֶׁיֵּשׁ לָהֶם קְנָס: הַבָּא עַל הַמַּמְזֶרֶת וְעַל הַנְּתִינָה וְעַל הַכּוּתִית.§ נַעֲרָה – אִין, קְטַנָּה – לָא, מַאן תַּנָּא? אָמַר רַב יְהוּדָה אָמַר רַב: רַבִּי מֵאִיר הִיא. דְּתַנְיָא*: בקְטַנָּה, מִבַּת יוֹם אֶחָד וְעַד שֶׁתָּבִיא שְׁתֵּי שְׂעָרוֹת – יֵשׁ לָהּ מֶכֶר *וְאֵין לָהּ קְנָס. וּמִשֶּׁתָּבִיא שְׁתֵּי שְׂעָרוֹת וְעַד שֶׁתִּיבָּגֵר – יֵשׁ לָהּ קְנָס וְאֵין לָהּ מֶכֶר, דִּבְרֵי רַבִּי מֵאִיר. שֶׁהָיָה רַבִּי מֵאִיר אוֹמֵר: כָּל מָקוֹם שֶׁיֵּשׁ מֶכֶר – אֵין קְנָס, וְכָל מָקוֹם שֶׁיֵּשׁ קְנָס – אֵין מֶכֶר. גוַחֲכָמִים אוֹמְרִים: קְטַנָּה, מִבַּת שָׁלֹשׁ שָׁנִים וְיוֹם אֶחָד וְעַד שֶׁתִּיבָּגֵר – *יֵשׁ לָהּ קְנָס. קְנָס אִין, מֶכֶר לָא?! אֵימָא: אַף

רש"י

אֵלּוּ נְעָרוֹת. דַּוְקָא נַעֲרָה, מִשֶּׁהֵבִיאָה שְׁתֵּי שְׂעָרוֹת עַד שֶׁתִּתְבַּגֵּר, וְהֵם שִׁשָּׁה חֳדָשִׁים שֶׁבֵּין נַעֲרוּת לְבַגְרוּת. אֲבָל קְטַנָּה וּבוֹגֶרֶת – אֵין לָהֶם קְנָס. שֶׁיֵּשׁ לָהֶן קְנָס. אִם אֲנָסָהּ אָדָם – נוֹתֵן לְאָבִיהָ חֲמִשִּׁים כֶּסֶף, כְּדִכְתִיב "וְנָתַן הָאִישׁ הַשּׁוֹכֵב" וגו' (דברים כב). הַבָּא עַל הַמַּמְזֶרֶת. בַּגְּמָרָא פָּרֵיךְ: אֲבָל כְּשֵׁירוֹת לָא? וּמְשַׁנֵּי: פְּסוּלוֹת אִיצְטְרִיכָא לֵיהּ לְאַשְׁמוּעִינַן. נְתִינָה. מִן הַגִּבְעוֹנִים, וְהִיא אֲסוּרָה לַקָּהָל, דְּדָוִד גָּזַר עֲלֵיהֶם, כִּדְאָמְרִינַן בִּיבָמוֹת (ד' עח:). וְעַל שֵׁם "וַיִּתְּנֵם יְהוֹשֻׁעַ חוֹטְבֵי עֵצִים וְשׁוֹאֲבֵי מַיִם" וגו' (יהושע ט) קָרֵי לְהוּ נְתִינִים. כּוּתִית. קָסָבַר: גֵּירֵי אֲרָיוֹת הֵן, וְיֶשְׁנָן בִּכְלָאו "לֹא תִתְחַתֵּן בָּם" (דברים ז). וְעַל הַשְּׁבוּיָה. יִשְׂרְאֵלִית שֶׁנִּפְדֵּית פְּחוּתָה מִבַּת שָׁלֹשׁ שָׁנִים, דְּמֻחְזֶקֶת בְּתוּלָה הִיא. שֶׁאֲפִי' נִבְעֲלָה בַּשִּׁבְיָה – בְּתוּלֶיהָ חוֹזְרִים. וְעַל אֵשֶׁת אָחִיו. שֶׁנִּתְקַדְּשָׁה לוֹ לְאָחִיו, וְגֵירְשָׁהּ, שֶׁאֵין בָּהּ מִיתָה אֶלָּא כָּרֵת. וְעַל אֵשֶׁת אֲחִי אָבִיו. שֶׁנִּתְקַדְּשָׁה לוֹ וְגֵירְשָׁהּ. אע"פ שֶׁהֵן בְּהִכָּרֵת הֲרֵי אֵין בָּהֶם מִיתַת ב"ד. וְכָרֵת לָא פָּטַר לֵיהּ מִן הַתַּשְׁלוּמִין. **גמ'** ר"מ הִיא. כִּדְמַיְיתֵי בָּרַיְיתָא לְקַמֵּיהּ. יֵשׁ לָהּ מֶכֶר. יֵשׁ לְאָבִיהָ בָּהּ זְכִיָּיה לְמָכְרָהּ לְשִׁפְחוּת. וְאֵין לָהּ קְנָס. שֶׁהַבָּא עָלֶיהָ אֵינוֹ חַיָּיב קְנָס. וְאֵין לָהּ מֶכֶר. כִּדְתַנְיָא (ערכין דף כט:): יָכוֹל יִמְכּוֹר אָדָם אֶת בִּתּוֹ כְּשֶׁהִיא נַעֲרָה? אָמַרְתָּ ק"ו: מְכוּרָה – כְּבָר יוֹצְאָה עַכְשָׁיו; שֶׁאֵינָהּ מְכוּרָה – אֵינוֹ דִּין שֶׁלֹּא תִּמָּכֵר? מִבַּת ג' שָׁנִים וְיוֹם אֶחָד. שֶׁהִיא רְאוּיָה לְבִיאָה. מֶכֶר לָא. בִּתְמִיָּה. אַף

תוספות

אלו נערות. הבא על הנתינה. פי' בקונטרס: דדוד גזר עליהם שלא לבא בקהל, והיינו משום עבדות, כדאמרינן ב"הערל" (יבמות עח: ושם). ואין נראה לר"ת, דהא משמע בגמרא (ע"ב) דנתינה הויא דאורייתא, דקאמר: ממזרת ונתינה איכא בינייהו, למ"ד ראויה לקיימה כו' – משמע דהויא דאורייתא, דהא בקראי פליגי. וברים "יש מותרות" (שם דף פה: ושם) אמרינן: ממזרת ונתינה איכא בינייהו, מ"ד דאורייתא – הא נמי דאורייתא! ועוד: דתנן (מכות דף יג.): אלו הן הלוקין, ממזרת ונתינה לישראל. משמע דלקי עלה מדאורייתא, דומיא דכל הנך דחשיב התם! ומיהו, איכא למימר דבכל הנהו נקט נתינה אגב ממזרת. וכן צריך לומר ע"כ לרבא, למאי דס"ד ב"הערל" (יבמות דף עו. ושם) דבגירותן לית להו איסור חתנות. ומ"מ אין נראה לר"ת פירושו, דהא מסיק רבא ב"הערל" (ג"ז שם) דבגירותן אית להו איסור חתנות, וכל היכא דחשיב נתינה בהדי ממזרת – איירי בגירות, כמו הכא. דבגויותה לית לה קנס, כדאמרינן לעיל בפ"ק (דף יא. ושם): יהבינן לה קנס ואזלה ואכלה בגויותה?! וכן בקדושין, בפרק "האומר" (דף סו:): תנן: כל מקום שיש קדושין ויש עבירה – כגון ממזרת ונתינה כו'. ועוד: לפירוש הקונטרס, כיון דעבדות ממש גזר עלייהו, שמתוך כך נאסרו לבוא בקהל משום "לא יהיה קדש" – א"כ אמאי יש לה קנס? הא תנן בהדיא במתניתין דשפחה אין לה קנס! ואי משום דנתינה מנטרא – נפשה הא אמרינן בירושלמי דשפחה אפילו משומרת אין לה קנס. ועוד: דתנן בפרק "עשרה יוחסין" (שם דף סט.) דחרורי ונתיני מותרים לבא זה בזה, ואמאי, והא חרורי אסירי בשפחה, כדתנן (גיטין דף מג.): לישא שפחה אינו יכול! ומיהו, הא י"ל: דלאו ממש גזר עלייהו עבדות לאסור ב"לא יהיה קדש". ונראה לר"ת: דנתינה אסורה דאורייתא משום "לא תתחתן", כדמסיק רבא ב"הערל" (יבמות דף עו. ושם). ודוד לא גזר עלייהו אלא שיעבוד, ולאו לאוסרן בבנות ישראל – דהא אסירי וקיימי מלאו ד"לא תתחתן", אלא כדי שלא יטמעו ישראל. והא דגזר בהו טפי מבשאר פסולי קהל – משום דהוו אומה שלימה. והא דקאמר התם*: כל מי שיש בו שלשה סימנים הללו – ראוי לידבק בהן, לא לישא מהן, אלא להיות בן חורין כמותן. וכן הא דקאמר התם*: בימי רבי בקשו להתיר נתינים, א"ר: אם חלקנו נתיר – חלק מזבח מי יתיר? לא שהיו רוצים להתירם לבא בקהל – דהא מדאורייתא אסירי, אלא בקשו לפטרן מעבדות, להיות בני חורין. ואמר להו רבי דאין יכולין להפקיע חלק מזבח. ואע"ג דקיימא לן* דהפקר ב"ד היה הפקר – היינו לצורך, אבל זה אינו צורך כל כך. ומיהו, בירושלמי משמע כפי' הקונט', בפ' "עשרה יוחסין" דקאמר התם: נתינים יהושע ריחקם. כלום ריחקם אלא משום פסול משפחה, דא"ת משום פסול עבדות – אלא מעתה הבא על הנתינה לא יהיה לה קנס? משמע משום דיהושע גזר עליהם נפסלו מלבא בקהל, וגזרת יהושע ודוד הכל גזירה אחת היא, כדמוכח ב"הערל" (שם דף עט.). ומיהו, בירושלמי איכא למימר דסבר כמו שהיה ס"ד דרבא מעיקרא ב"הערל", דבגירותן לית להו איסור חתנות. ועוד י"ל: דריחקן היינו שלא יטמעו בהן. והא דאמרינן ב"האומר" בקדושין (דף סח: ושם): גויה מנא לן דלא תפסי בה קדושין – דכתיב "לא תתחתן בם", אומר ר"ת: דאסיפיה דקרא סמיך "ובתו לא תקח לבנך". אבל רישיה דקרא – מיירי בגירות. וכענין זה מצינו ב"הערל" (יבמות דף עט.) דפריך גבי בני שאול: והכתיב "לא יומתו אבות על בנים", וע"כ לא פריך אלא מסיפא דקרא "איש בחטאו יומתו", דרישא דקרא מוקמינן ליה לפסול קרובים לעדות בפרק "החובל" (ב"ק דף פח.) ובפרק "זה בורר" (סנהדרין דף כז:)*. **ועל** הכותית. פירש בקונטרס: דקסבר כותים גירי אריות הן, וישנן בלאו ד"לא תתחתן" – וזהו לפי שיטתו, כדסלקא דעתין מעיקרא ב"הערל" (יבמות דף עו. ושם) דבגויותן אית להו איסור חתנות. ומה שפי' דקסבר כותים גירי אריות הן – ל"נ לרבינו יצחק בן רבינו מאיר, דא"כ גויה היא, וגויה אין לה קנס, כדפריך בפ"ק (לעיל יא.): יהבינן לה קנס ואזלה ואכלה בגויותה? ועוד: דבגמרא מוקי מתני' כר"מ, ור"מ אית ליה דגירי אמת הן, ואע"ג דכולה מתניתין לא אתיא כר"מ, דהא בתו אמר בגמרא דלא אתיא כוותיה – מ"מ בהא דסבר דגירי אמת הן אתיא כוותיה, דהא ב"שור שנגח ד' וה'" (ב"ק דף לח: ושם) מסקינן דשור ישראל שנגח שור של כותי פטור, משום דקנס הוא דקניס רבי מאיר בממונם, אע"ג דמן הדין חייב, דגירי אמת הם, ופריך ממתני' דהכא, דכותית יש לה קנס. ואי ס"ד דקנס הוא שקנס ר"מ בממונם – ה"נ לקנוס כו', אלמא דמתניתין דהכא סברה דגירי אמת הן! וא"ת: אם כן מאי קמ"ל? פשיטא דיש לה קנס, דישראלית גמורה היא! וי"ל: דס"ד דלא יהבינן לה קנס, שלא יטמעו בהן. *וא"ת: למ"ד בפרק "עשרה יוחסין" (קדושין דף עו.) דפסול כותים משום דעבד ושפחה נטמעו – בהן אמאי יש לה קנס? נימא לה: אייתי ראיה דלאו שפחה את, וסקילי. לשמואל דאמר (ב"ק דף מו:) אין הולכין בממון אחר הרוב, ואפילו לרב, אי דאזיל איהו גבה ה"ל קבוע, וכל קבוע כמחצה על מחצה דמי! ויש לומר: דכל אחת מוקמינן לה אחזקת אבהתא שהיו כותים. אע"ג דלענין פסול לא מוקמינן לה אחזקתה, לענין קנס – מוקמינן להו, שלא יהא חוטא נשכר. *ואם תאמר: *ואמאי לא חשיב נמי אלמנה לכ"ג, גרושה וחלוצה לכהן הדיוט? וי"ל: דבפסול כהונה לא קמיירי. והא דלא תני מצרי ואדומי – משום שיש להם היתר [א"נ לא חשיב אלא חייבי לאוין]. אבל קשה: דליתני מחזיר גרושתו משניסת ונבעלה שלא כדרכה, ואע"ג דאמרי' בפ' "עשרה יוחסין" (קדושין עח.) הכל מודים שאם בעל ולא קידש שאינו לוקה – מ"מ לר"ע, דאמר אין קדושין תופסין במחזיר גרושתו – ליתני! ועוד הוה מצי למיתני יבמה לשוק! [ועבד הבא על הכותית הולד ממזר ויש לה קנס. ת"י]! וי"ל: דתנא ושייר. ואע"ג דבפ"ק דקדושין (דף טז:) דייק: תנא תני "אלו", ואת אמרת תנא ושייר?! הכא דתני בסיפא ואלו שאין להם קנס – לא שייך למידק הכי, כדאשכחן בפרק "המזבח מקדש" (זבחים דף פד.), דקתני: ואלו פסולן בקדש ואלו שאין פסולן בקדש, ומשייר ברישא ובסיפא. *ועי"ל: דהכא לא חשיב אלא פסולי קהל. **והבא** על הגיורת. חילקן, לשנות חייבי לאוין לחודייהו, וגיורת ומשוחררת דכשירות הן לחודייהו, וחייבי כריתות לחודייהו, משום דבעי למיתני סיפא: "אע"פ שהם בהכרת כו'". אבל ב"אלו הן הלוקין" (מכות יג.) לא תני אלא הבא אחד על כולם. **ועל** אשת אחיו. פר"ת: דפריך בירושלמי: אשת אחיו! ולא יבמה היא לו, וזקוקה לו, ומה קנס וכרת שייך בה? ומשני: בשיש לו בנים מאשה אחרת, ואיירי במת מן האירוסין. והוא הדין דהוה מצי לאוקמה כשגירשה. וקשה לר"י ב"ר אברהם: לרב פפא דמוקי הך מתניתין במפותה, בפרק "בן סורר" (סנהדרין דף עג. ושם) תקשי: דהיכי מצי לאוקומי הכי? הא נתארסה ונתגרשה קנסה לעצמה (לקמן דף לח.), וכיון דלעצמה – מפותה אין לה קנס, כדאמרינן בגמרא (לקמן מ.) וברים "נערה" משום דמדעתה עבדה! וכ"ת: דקסבר תנא דמתניתין כר"ע דברייתא, דקנסה לאביה הוי – אם כן אכתי *תיקשי ליה סיפא, דקתני (שם לו:): הבא על בתו – פטור. משום דקס ליה בדרבה מיניה, תיפוק ליה דקנסה לאביה הוי, דאי לעצמה – תיקשי ליה דמחלה, וממה נפשך תקשי סיפא! ומיהו, בירושלמי מוקי לה כשבא עליה עד שלא מת, ומת, והוא הדין עד שלא בגרה, ובגרה. ולמאי דאמר בירושלמי דמפותה אינו פטור אלא מבושת ופגם, אבל קנס אינה יכולה למחול – אתי שפיר. ומיהו, בתלמוד דידן משמע דאין לה אפי' קנס, דמוקי הא ד"אלו הן הלוקין" לקמן בגמ' (דף לג.) ביתומה ומפותה שאין לה קנס. **נערה** אין קטנה לא. תימה: מנא ליה! דלמא לא אתי למעוטי אלא בוגרת, דהא משמע* בס"פ "ארבע מיתות" (סנהדרין דף סו:) גבי הא דתנן אינו חייב אלא עד שתהא נערה בתולה מאורסה, דאי הוה תני אלא על נערה בתולה כו' הוה מוקמינן לה אפילו כרבנן ולא הוה אתי למעוטי קטנה אלא בוגרת! ותירץ ריצב"א: °דאסיפא דמתניתין סמיך, דתנן (לקמן דף מ:): כל מקום שיש מכר אין קנס. נערה

עין משפט נר מצוה

א א מיי' פ"א מהל' נערה הלכה י סמג עשין נד טור אה"ע סי' קעז:

ב ב מיי' פ"ד מהל' עבדים הלכה א סמג עשין פה:

ג ג מיי' פ"א מהלכות נערה הלכה ח סמג עשין נד טוש"ע אה"ע סי' קעז סעיף א בהג"ה:

תוספות רי"ד

אלו נערות שיש להן קנס. פי' אנסה אדם נותן לאביה נ' כסף כדכתיב ונתן האיש וגו'. הבא על הממזרת ועל הנתינה ועל הכותית על הגיורת ועל השבויה. פי' ישראלית שנשבית. ועל השפחה. שנפדו ושנתגיירו ושנשתחררו פחותות מבנות ג"ש ויום אחד. הבא על אחותו ועל אחות אביו ועל אחות אמו ועל אחות אשתו ועל אשת אחיו ועל אשת אחי אביו ועל הנדה יש להן קנס. אע"פ שהן בכרת אין בהן מיתת ב"ד. פי' דוקא נערה ולא בוגרת וקטנה. שהבוגרת כלו בתוליה ואין להם קנס. וקטנה הויא כעין א) שמדמעת וחוזרת ומדמעת. ונערה היא מבת י"ב שנים ויום אחד אם הביאה ב' שערות וממתנת ששה חדשים אחר שהביאה ב' שערות והיא בוגרת שאין בין נערות לבוגרת אלא ו' חדשים בלבד. נתינה היא מן הגבעונים ע"ש ויתנם יהושע חוטבי עצים ושואבי מים. ומשום צד עבדות הן אסורות. והכותיות קסבר גירי אמת הן ומ"ה יש להן קנס. שאילו היו גירי אריות הויא לה גויה. ואין קנס לגויה אלא שהכותים פסולים כדתנן בעשרה יוחסין אלו הן הספיקות שתוקי ואסופי וכותי. והתם מפרש טעמא למה הן הכותים פסולין: ועל אשת אחיו. כגון שקידש את הבתולה וגירשה. א"נ שמת ויש לו בן מאשה אחרת דקיימי עליה בכרת אע"פ שהן בהכרת אין הכרת פוטרו מן התשלומין אלא מיתת ב"ד: נערה אין קטנה לא. דהיינו קודם שתביא ב' שערות. מאן תנא אר"י א"ר ר"מ הוא דתניא קטנה ב) מבת ג' שנים ויום אחד. פירוש שמזמן זה היא ראויה לביאה ועד שתביא ב' שערות יש לה מכר ואין לה קנס. ומשתביא ב' שערות ועד שתבגר יש לה קנס ואין לה מכר דברי ר"מ שהיה ר"מ אומר כ"מ שיש מכר אין קנס וכל מקום שיש קנס אין מכר. וחכ"א קטנה מבת ג' שנים ויום אחד עד שתבגר יש לה מכר ויש

א) דברי רבינו אינו מובן דהך סברא אמרינן בנדה (מ"ה) לענין קטנה פחותה מבת שלש דבתוליה חוזרין אבל מתני' הא ס"ל דאין קנס בקטנה כלל רק בנערה ונ"ע. ב) לפנינו בגמ' הגירסא בדברי ר"מ מבת יום אחד וגירסת רבינו צ"ע.

דפריך עד שתהא נערה איננו חייב אלא על נערה מבעי ליה. ת"י

מסורת הש"ס

לעיל יח. ב"ק לח:

סנהדרין עג:

[תוספתא פ"ג ע"ש] לקמן מ: חולין כו.

[לקמן לו.]

[לקמן לו.]

[דף עט.]

שם:

[שם פט:]

גליון הש"ס

תוס' ד"ה נערה וכו' דאסיפא דמתני' סמיך. עי' נדה מד ע"ב תוס' ד"ה שלשים יום:

[ועי' תוס' יבמות עט. ד"ה ונתינים ותוס' ע"ז לו: ד"ה דכתיב]

א"נ היא גופא קמ"ל דגירי אמת הן. ת"י

[ועי' תוס' ב"ק לח: ד"ה ועל הכותית]

ועבד הבא על הכותית הולד ממזר ויש לה קנס. ת"י

[עי' תוס' יבמות פד: ד"ה אלא ותוס' זבחים פד. ד"ה הלן ותוס' שבועות לט. ד"ה ואלו נאמרין ותוס' שם מז: ד"ה כל הנשבעין ותוס' שבת עה: ד"ה חסר אחת]

אבל ליכא לאוקמי הבא על בתו אחר שנכנסה לחופה ולא נבעלה וגירשה דא"כ בלאו הכי אין לה קנס כיון דמוקי לה במפותה דמחלה וא"ל דסיפא בא על בתו לא איירי במפותה אלא באנוסה א"כ כתנס נקט בא על בתו דחייבי כריתות נמי אין לה קנס כיון דניתנה להצילה בנפשו דמשום הכי מוקי לה התם במפותה:

ד א מיי' פ"א מהלכות נערה הל' טו סמג עשין נל טור אה"ע סי' קעז:
ה ב מיי' שם הל' א:
ו ג מיי' שם הל' ה:

אַף קְנָס בִּמְקוֹם מֶכֶר. וְהָנֵי בְּנֵי קְנָסָא נִינְהוּ? וְאַמַּאי? אִיקְּרֵי כָּאן: °"וְלוֹ *תִהְיֶה לְאִשָּׁה" — אִשָּׁה הָרְאוּיָה לוֹ! אָמַר רֵישׁ לָקִישׁ: °"נַעֲרָה", "נַעֲרָה", "הַנַּעֲרָה"; חַד — לְגוּפֵיהּ, וְחַד — לְאַתּוֹיֵי חַיָּיבֵי לָאוִין, וְחַד — לְאַתּוֹיֵי חַיָּיבֵי כָרֵיתוֹת. רַב פַּפָּא אָמַר: °"בְּתוּלָה", "בְּתוּלוֹת", "הַבְּתוּלוֹת" חַד — לְגוּפֵיהּ, וְחַד — לְאַתּוֹיֵי חַיָּיבֵי לָאוִין, וְחַד — לְאַתּוֹיֵי חַיָּיבֵי כָרֵיתוֹת. וְרַב פַּפָּא מ"ט לֹא אָמַר כְּר"ל? הַהוּא מִיבָּעֵי לֵיהּ לְכִדְאַבַּיֵי. *דְּאָמַר אַבַּיֵי: [א]בָּא עָלֶיהָ וּמֵתָה — פָּטוּר, שֶׁנֶּאֱמַר: °"וְנָתַן לַאֲבִי הַנַּעֲרָה" — לַאֲבִי נַעֲרָה וְלֹא לַאֲבִי מֵתָה. וְרֵישׁ לָקִישׁ מ"ט לֹא אָמַר כְּרַב פַּפָּא? הַהוּא מִיבָּעֵי לֵיהּ לִגְזֵירָה שָׁוָה. דְּתַנְיָא: *°"כֶּסֶף יִשְׁקוֹל כְּמוֹהַר הַבְּתוּלוֹת" — [ב]שֶׁיְּהֵא זֶה כְּמוֹהַר הַבְּתוּלוֹת, וּמוֹהַר הַבְּתוּלוֹת כָּזֶה. וְרֵישׁ לָקִישׁ נַמִי, מִיבָּעֵי לֵיהּ לְכִדְאַבַּיֵי, וְרַב פַּפָּא נַמִי מִיבָּעֵי לֵיהּ לִגְזֵירָה שָׁוָה! אֶלָּא שִׁיתָּא קְרָאֵי כְּתִיבִי: "נַעֲרָה" "נַעֲרָה" "הַנַּעֲרָה" "בְּתוּלָה" "בְּתוּלוֹת" "הַבְּתוּלוֹת", תְּרֵי — לְגוּפַיְיהוּ, חַד — לְכִדְאַבַּיֵי, וְחַד — לִגְזֵירָה שָׁוָה. אַיְיתְרוּ לֵיהּ תְּרֵי, חַד — לְאַתּוֹיֵי חַיָּיבֵי לָאוִין, וְחַד — לְאַתּוֹיֵי חַיָּיבֵי כָרֵיתוֹת. וּלְאַפּוֹקֵי מֵהַאי תַּנָּא; דְּתַנְיָא: "וְלוֹ תִהְיֶה לְאִשָּׁה", *שִׁמְעוֹן הַתִּימְנִי אוֹמֵר: אִשָּׁה שֶׁיֵּשׁ בָּהּ הֲוָיָה. רַבִּי שִׁמְעוֹן בֶּן מְנַסְיָא אוֹמֵר: [ג]אִשָּׁה הָרְאוּיָה לְקַיְּימָהּ. מַאי בֵּינַיְיהוּ? אָמַר ר' זֵירָא: מַמְזֶרֶת וּנְתִינָה אִיכָּא בֵּינַיְיהוּ. לְמַאן דְּאָמַר יֵשׁ בָּהּ הֲוָיָה — הָא נַמִי יֵשׁ בָּהּ הֲוָיָה, לְמַאן דְּאָמַר רְאוּיָה לְקַיְּימָהּ — הָא אֵינָהּ רְאוּיָה לְקַיְּימָהּ. וּלְרַבִּי עֲקִיבָא, דְּאָמַר: *אֵין קִידּוּשִׁין תּוֹפְסִין בְּחַיָּיבֵי לָאוִין, מַאי בֵּינַיְיהוּ? אִיכָּא בֵּינַיְיהוּ אַלְמָנָה לְכֹהֵן גָּדוֹל, כְּרַבִּי סִימַאי. דְּתַנְיָא, רַבִּי סִימַאי אוֹמֵר:* מִן הַכֹּל עוֹשֶׂה רַבִּי עֲקִיבָא מַמְזֵרִין, חוּץ מֵאַלְמָנָה לְכֹהֵן גָּדוֹל, שֶׁהֲרֵי אָמְרָה תּוֹרָה: °"לֹא יִקָּח" "וְלֹא יְחַלֵּל" — חִילּוּלִין הוּא עוֹשֶׂה, וְאֵין עוֹשֶׂה מַמְזֵרִין — וּלְרַבִּי יְשֵׁבָב, דְּאָמַר: בּוֹאוּ וְנִצְוַח עַל עֲקִיבָא בֶּן יוֹסֵף, שֶׁהָיָה אוֹמֵר: כָּל שֶׁאֵין לוֹ בִּיאָה בְּיִשְׂרָאֵל הַוָּלָד מַמְזֵר. מַאי בֵּינַיְיהוּ? אִיכָּא בֵּינַיְיהוּ חַיָּיבֵי

(דברים כב; שם; שמות כב; דברים כב; שמות כב; ויקרא כא)

רש"י

אַף קְנָס בִּמְקוֹם מֶכֶר. וּמִשּׁוּם קְנָס נָקַט בַּת שָׁלֹשׁ. אֲבָל לְמֶכֶר – מִבַּת יוֹם אֶחָד וְעַד שֶׁתָּבִיא שְׁתֵּי שְׂעָרוֹת. וְאַמַּאי. יֵשׁ לָהֶן קְנָס לִנְעָרוֹת פְּסוּלוֹת? אִיקְּרֵי כָּאן כו'. אַמַּתְנִי' מַקְשֵׁי: ה"ג. נַעֲרָה נַעֲרָה הַנַּעֲרָה. בְּאוֹנֵס כְּתִיב "כִּי יִמְצָא אִישׁ נַעֲרָה בְתוּלָה" וגו', וּכְתִיב בַּתְרֵיהּ "וְנָתַן הָאִישׁ הַשּׁוֹכֵב עִמָּהּ לַאֲבִי הַנַּעֲרָה", וְדָרְשִׁינַן "נַעֲרָה" יְתֵירָה, וְהֵ"א יְתֵירָה דְּ"הַנַּעֲרָה", דְּמָצֵי לְמִיכְתַּב "וְנָתַן לְאָבִיהָ". חַד לְגוּפֵיהּ. לִכְשֵׁרָה. בְּתוּלָה בְּתוּלוֹת הַבְּתוּלוֹת. בִּמְפַתֶּה כְּתִיב "וְכִי יְפַתֶּה אִישׁ בְּתוּלָה", וּקְרָא אַחֲרִינָא בַּתְרֵיהּ "כֶּסֶף יִשְׁקוֹל כְּמוֹהַר הַבְּתוּלוֹת". וּמָצֵי לְמִיכְתַּב "כְּמוֹהַר בְּתוּלוֹת", הָא תְּלָת, דְּדָרְשִׁינַן ה' יְתֵירָה וּ"בְתוּלוֹת", דְּמָצֵי לְמִיכְתַּב "כְּמוֹהַר" וְלִשְׁתּוֹק. הַהוּא מִיבָּעֵי לֵיהּ. הַהוּא "הַנַּעֲרָה", הָא דְּלָא כְּתִיב "וְנָתַן לְאָבִיהָ", מִיבָּעֵי לֵיהּ לְכִדְאַבַּיֵי, שֶׁאִם לֹא הִסְפִּיק הָאָב לְהַעֲמִידוֹ בַּדִּין עַד שֶׁמֵּתָה – פָּטוּר. לַאֲבִי הַנַּעֲרָה. מַשְׁמַע שֶׁהִיא קַיֶּימֶת. מִיבָּעֵי לֵיהּ לג"ש. "בְּתוּלָה" דִּכְתִיב גַּבֵּי מְפַתֶּה – מִיבָּעֵי לֵיהּ לג"ש, "בְּתוּלָה" "בְּתוּלָה" לג"ש: מַה כֶּסֶף הָאָמוּר בְּאוֹנֵס חֲמִשִּׁים – אַף מְפַתֶּה חֲמִשִּׁים. וּמַה מְּפַתֶּה שְׁקָלִים, דִּכְתִיב בֵּיהּ "יִשְׁקוֹל" – אַף חֲמִשִּׁים שֶׁל אוֹנֵס – שְׁקָלִים קָאָמַר. כְּמוֹהַר הַבְּתוּלוֹת. חֲמִשִּׁים כֶּסֶף הַמְפוֹרָשִׁים בִּמְאַנֵּס אֶת הַבְּתוּלָה. שֶׁיְּהֵא זֶה. חֲמִשִּׁים כְּמוֹהַר הַבְּתוּלוֹת. וּמוֹהַר הַבְּתוּלוֹת. יִהְיוּ שְׁקָלִים כָּזֶה. וְחַד לג"ש. וּתְהִי מוּפְנָה מִצַּד אֶחָד, וּלְמֵידִים הֵימֶנָּה. וּלְאַפּוֹקֵי מֵהַאי תַּנָּא. מַתְנִי' דְּקָתָנֵי יֵשׁ קְנָס לְמַמְזֶרֶת וְלַאֲחוֹתוֹ – לְאַפּוֹקֵי מֵהַאי תַּנָּא. שֶׁיֵּשׁ בָּהּ הֲוָיָה. שֶׁקִּדּוּשִׁין תּוֹפְסִין לוֹ בָּהּ, פְּרָט לַאֲחוֹתוֹ וּלְכָל חַיָּיבֵי כָרֵיתוֹת, דִּילְפִינַן בְּקִדּוּשִׁין שֶׁאֵין קִדּוּשִׁין תּוֹפְסִין בָּהֶן, בְּפֶרֶק שְׁלִישִׁי (דף סז:). וּמַשְׁמַע לֵיהּ "תִּהְיֶה" לְשׁוֹן הֲוָיַת קִדּוּשִׁין. וְר"ש בֶּן מְנַסְיָא מַשְׁמַע לֵיהּ "תִּהְיֶה" – לְשׁוֹן קִיּוּם. הָא נַמִי אִית בָּהּ הֲוָיָה. דְּקִדּוּשִׁין תּוֹפְסִין בְּחַיָּיבֵי לָאוִין, וְהָתָם יָלֵיף לָהּ. וּלְר"ע דְּאָמַר אֵין קִדּוּשִׁין תּוֹפְסִין בְּחַיָּיבֵי לָאוִין. בִּיבָמוֹת בְּ"הַחוֹלֵץ" (דף מד:) בְּבָרַיְיתָא: הַמַּחֲזִיר גְּרוּשָׁתוֹ, ר"ע אוֹמֵר: אֵין לוֹ בָּהּ קִדּוּשִׁין. מַאי בֵּינַיְיהוּ. מִשּׁוּם ר"ש בֶּן מְנַסְיָא קָא פָּרֵיךְ לָהּ. דְּאִילּוּ שִׁמְעוֹן הַתֵּימְנִי שָׁמְעִינַן לֵיהּ בִּיבָמוֹת (דף מט.) דְּפָלֵיג עֲלֵיהּ דְּר"ע בְּהָא, דִּתְנַן: אֵיזֶהוּ מַמְזֵר – כָּל שְׁאֵר בָּשָׂר שֶׁהוּא בְּ"לֹא יָבֹא", דִּבְרֵי ר"ע. שִׁמְעוֹן הַתֵּימְנִי אוֹמֵר: כָּל שֶׁחַיָּיבִין עָלָיו כָּרֵת בִּידֵי שָׁמַיִם. אֶלָּא לְר"ש בֶּן מְנַסְיָא קָא בָּעֵינַן לָהּ, אִי ס"ל כְּר"ע – מַאי אִיכָּא בֵּין מַשְׁמָעוּתָא דְּ"תִהְיֶה" לְשׁוֹן קִיּוּם, לְמַשְׁמָעוּת דְּשִׁמְעוֹן הַתֵּימְנִי? אִי נַמִי, מַשְׁמַע לֵיהּ לְר"ש בֶּן מְנַסְיָא לְשׁוֹן הֲוָיָה אִימְעִיטָא לָהּ מַמְזֵר, וּמַה בֵּין רְאוּיָה לְקַיְּימָהּ לְיֵשׁ בָּהּ הֲוָיָה? אַלְמָנָה לְכֹהֵן גָּדוֹל. דְּמוֹדֶה בָּהּ ר"ע שֶׁקִּדּוּשִׁין תּוֹפְסִין לוֹ בָּהּ, וְאע"פ שֶׁהִיא בְּלָאו, וּכְרַבִּי סִימַאי. וְהוּא הַדִּין גְּרוּשָׁה לְהֶדְיוֹט. מִן הַכֹּל. כָּל הַנּוֹלָדִים מֵחַיָּיבֵי לָאוִין. לֹא יִקָּח. וּסְמִיךְ לֵיהּ "וְלֹא יְחַלֵּל זַרְעוֹ" – מִדִּין כְּהוּנָּה הוּא מְחַלְּלוֹ, וְלֹא שֵׁם מַמְזֵרִים עֲלֵיהֶם. בּוֹאוּ וְנִצְוַח עַל עֲקִיבָא בֶּן יוֹסֵף. שֶׁמַּרְבֶּה מַמְזֵרִים בְּיִשְׂרָאֵל חִנָּם. שֶׁהוּא אוֹמֵר כָּל שֶׁאֵין לוֹ בִּיאָה בְּיִשְׂרָאֵל. הַבָּא עַל אִשָּׁה שֶׁאֵין לוֹ בָּהּ הֶיתֵּר בִּיאָה – הַוָּלָד מַמְזֵר, וַאֲפִי' אַלְמָנָה לְכ"ג נַמִי.

[לקמן לה.] [לקמן לח:] [לעיל י. לקמן לח:] [לקמן לו.] [יבמות י: ושם נסמן] [יבמות סט. קידושין סד. סח.]

תוספות

נערה נערה הנערה. פי' רבינו חננאל: דמחד "נערה" דריש כולה מלתא, "נער" "נערה" "הנערה". ואין נראה לר"ת, דלא כתיב "נערה" מלא בה"א אלא ההוא דמוציא שם רע לחודיה, כדמוכח בסוף פרקין. ועוד הקשה רבינו יצחק: מה צריך חד לגופה? הא איכא "נערה" אחרינא בפרשה! אלא פי' הקונטרס עיקר.

בתולה בתולות הבתולות. כאן נמי פר"ח דמחד קרא נפקי כולהו. ואין נראה, דלא צריך חד לגופיה, דבתולה אחרינא כתיב.

וחד לאיתויי חייבי לאוין. הקשה ר"י בן רבינו מאיר, אכתי נימא: חד – לאתויי חייבי עשה, וחד – לאתויי חייבי לאוין, ואכתי חייבי כריתות מנא לן? ותירץ: דלחייבי לאוין ועשה לא צריך אלא חד קרא, דהא אי לאו דכתיב "ולו תהיה לאשה", דמשמע שיש בה הויה וראויה לקיימה, לא הוה צריך קרא לרבויינהו, הלכך מחד ריבויא מרבינן אין ראויה לקיימה, דהיינו חייבי עשה וחייבי לאוין, כיון דאית בהו הויה, ואידך ריבויא לחייבי כריתות. ולמאן דאמר אין קדושין תופסין בחייבי לאוין – הוי חד ריבויא לחייבי עשה, ואידך לחייבי לאוין וחייבי כריתות. וא"ת: ולשתוק מ"ולו תהיה לאשה" ולא יצטרך להנך ריבויי? וי"ל: דאיצטריך למידרש "ולו תהיה לאשה" – מדעתה*. [לקמן לט:]

אייתרו להו תרי כו'. וחד ריבויא כתב באונס וחד במפתה. וא"ת: ומנא לן דחד לאתויי חייבי כריתות? אימא דתרוייהו אתו לרבויי חייבי לאוין, וחד לאונס וחד למפתה? וי"ל: דלהא לא צריך, דמגזרה שוה ילפינן אונס ומפתה מהדדי.

ת"י [**ולאפוקי** מהאי תנא. פי': תנא דברייתא, אבל מפיק מתרוייהו תנאי שמוזכרים בברייתא].

ולרבי עקיבא דאמר כו'. ואף ע"ג דר"ש התימני פליג בהדיא אר' עקיבא ב"החולץ" (יבמות דף מד. ודף מט.) – הכא לר"ש בן מנסיא פריך, דאי סבר כר"ע – מאי בינייהו, פי': בינו לר"ש התימני? דמדנקט ראויה לקיימה ולא נקט שיש בה הויה – משמע דיש שאין ראויה לקיימה ויש בה הויה.

חילולין הוא עושה ואינו עושה ממזרים. משמע דהא בהא תליא, דכיון דלא הוי ממזר – קדושין תופסין. וכן משמע בפרק "החולץ" (שם דף מה:): מה אשת אב דלא תפסי בה קדושין והוולד ממזר כו', [ור"ע נמי, משום דיליף ב"החולץ" דיש ממזר מחייבי לאוין קאמר דאין קדושין תופסין בחייבי לאוין]. ותימה: דלרבי יהושע, אע"ג דאין ממזר מחייבי כריתות, כדיליף בשילהי "החולץ" (שם דף מט.) מודה דאין קדושין תופסין בחייבי כריתות, כדפריך ס"פ "ר"ג", ביבמות (דף נג. ושם): איצטריך לאשמעינן דאין קדושין תופסין בחייבי כריתות? ובפ' "החולץ" (שם דף מד: ושם) קאמר דלרבי יהושע פגום מיהא הוי מחייבי כריתות, משום דעשאה זונה, וזונה לא הויא אלא מהנהו דלא תפסי בה קדושין, כדמוכח בתמורה (דף כט: ושם). וקאמרינן נמי ב"החולץ" (יבמות דף מד: ושם): הכל מודים בכותי ועבד הבא על בת ישראל הוולד ממזר. מאן הכל מודים – שמעון התימני, דאע"ג דאמר אין ממזר מחייבי לאוין – ה"מ חייבי לאוין דתפסי בהו קדושין, אבל כותי ועבד כו'. ולא קאמר מאן הכל מודים ר' יהושע, דאע"ג דאמר אין ממזר מחייבי כריתות ה"מ חייבי כריתות דתפסי בהו קדושין כו'. אלמא דלר' יהושע אין קדושין תופסין בחייבי כריתות, ואפ"ה לא הוי ממזר, ולהכי לא מצי למימר דמודה בכותי ועבד! ויש לומר: דלר"ש התימני ולר"ע ודאי הא בהא תליא, דליכא מידי דלא תפסי בה קדושין והוולד כשר, רק שהוא דומה לאשת אב. אבל לר' יהושע, אע"ג דאין קדושין תופסין בחייבי כריתות, כדילפי' בסוף "האומר" (קדושין סח. ושם) לא הוי ממזר אלא מחייבי מיתות ב"ד, כדיליף ר' יהושע בסוף "החולץ" (יבמות מט. ושם). אבל קשה: דא"כ לר' יהושע אין קדושין תופסין באלמנה לכ"ג לרבא, דאמר בפ"ק דתמורה (דף ד: ושם): כל דאמר רחמנא לא תעביד, אי עביד – לא מהני. דהתם* פריך ליה: והרי אלמנה לכ"ג דקאמר רחמנא "לא יקח" ותנן: כל מקום שיש קדושין ויש עבירה כגון אלמנה לכ"ג כו'? ומשני: אמר לך רבא: שאני התם, דא"ק "לא יחלל" – חלולין הוא עושה, ואינו עושה ממזרים. ולר' יהושע ליכא לשנויי הכי. וא"ת: בקדושין בסוף "האומר" (דף סז: ושם) כי מסכח דלא תפסי קדושין באשת אב, מאי פריך התם ואימא תרוייהו באשת אב הא לכתחלה הא דיעבד? אמאי לא יליף מינה דכל היכא דהוי ממזר לא תפסי בה קדושין, כיון דהא בהא תליא, כדפירשנו! וי"ל: דאכתי לא שמעינן ממזרות בשאר חייבי כריתות כל כמה דלא מייתי התם היקישא דר' יונה, דמ"לא יקח" ו"לא יגלה" דאיירי באשת אב ובשומרת יבם של אביו לא שמעינן מינה ממזרות באשת איש ובאחות אשה דיש היתר לאיסורן, וכל דכוותייהו. אבל לבסוף דמייתי היקישא דרבי יונה התם – איכא למילף בעלמא כדפירשנו. [דף ה:]

ת"י כ"י [וכן משמע בפרק "ד' מיתות" דליכא מאן דפליג דבחייבי כריתות לא תפסי קידושין. וט"ו נשים דפוטרות צרותיהן מן החליצה, ואי קידושין תופסין בחייבי כריתות א"כ היו עולין לחליצה כמו חייבי לאוין, כדאמר התם בפ"ב: מסתברא חייבי לאוין תפסי בהו קידושין, ולכך עולין לחליצה. והאיא מתני' אתיא כר"ע, דהא קאמר עלה דפלוגתא לא קא מיירי. **מאי** בינייהו. תימה: אמאי לא קאמר איכא בינייהו סוטה שאירסה וזינתה תחתיו שלא כדרכה, וגירשה, דאית בה הויה לכ"ע, כדאמרינן בסוף "החולץ": הכל מודים בבא על הסוטה שאין הוולד ממזר].

תוספות רי"ד

לה קנס: ומקשינן אמתני' קרי כאן ולו תהיה לאשה אשה הראוי' לו. פי' באשה הראויה לו יתן קנס דמקיים בה ולו תהיה לאשה. אבל באשה שאינה ראויה לו דלא מקיים בה ולו תהיה לאשה גם מן הקנס יהא פטור. אר"ל נער נערה הנערה. חד לגופיה. פי' לכשירה. וחד לאתויי חייבי לאוין. וחד לאתויי חייבי כריתות. פי' גבי אונס כתיב וכי ימצא איש נערה בתולה. וכתיב בתרי' ונתן האיש השוכב עמה לאבי הנערה דהו"ל למיכתב לאביה וקרא יתירה הוא. ודרשי' נערה וה' דהנערה תרי קראי יתירי חד לרבויי חייבי לאוין וחד לאתויי חייבי כריתות. ואי קשיא והא בפ"ב דיבמות תנן כלל אמרו ביבמה כל שאיסורה איסור ערוה (קדושה) לא חולצת ולא מתיבמת עד אסור קדושה אלמנה לכ"ג גרושה וחלוצה לכהן הדיוט [חולצת ולא מתייבמת]. ומקשה בגמ' ואמאי אין מתייבמת ליתי עשה ולידחה את ל"ת. ותירץ רבא גזירה ביאה ראשונה אטו ביאה שניה. ותנ"ה אם בעלו קנו בביאה ראשונה ואסור לקיימם בביאה שניה. ופי' אלא מוציא בגט שכבר פרחה מצות יבמה בביאה ראשונה. ואע"ג דמצי למיחלץ. אמרי' התם חליצה במקום ייבום אינה מצוה. והתם נמי כתיב ולקחה לו לאשה ויבמה. דאיכא למימר באשה הראויה לו. ואפ"ה אתי עשה ודחי את ל"ת וה"נ ליתי עשה דולו תהיה לאשה ולידחי את ל"ת ואע"פ שהיא ממזרת יקחנה לו לאשה דהאי ולו תהיה לאשה עשה הוא כדאמרי' בפ' אלו הן הלוקין בהלכה זר טמא שאכל את הקודש אונס שגירש. אם ישראל הוא מחזיר ואינו לוקה. והוי לאו שניתק לעשה דהאי ולו תהיה לאשה קאי אכל ימיו דכל ימיו בעמוד והחזר קאי. וכיון דעשה הוא ליתי ולדחי את ל"ת ואמאי דרשי' אשה הראויה לו. ולקמן בפירקין [דף מ ע"א] מקשה לה ר"כ ומתרץ לה:

חייבי עשה – מצרי ואדומי. הניחא לר' ישבב, אי לאפוקי מטעמא דר' סימאי קאתי – שפיר. אלא אי טעמא דנפשיה קאמר, כל שאין לו ביאה בישראל הולד ממזר – ואפי' חייבי עשה, מאי בינייהו? *איכא בינייהו בעולה לכ"ג. ומ"ש? דהוה ליה עשה שאינו שוה בכל. אמר רב חסדא: הכל מודים בבא על הנדה שמשלם קנס. למ"ד יש בה הויה – הא נמי יש בה הויה, למ"ד ראויה לקיימה – הא נמי ראויה לקיימה. ולאפוקי מדרבי נחוניא בן הקנה. דתניא: *רבי נחוניא בן הקנה היה עושה את יום הכפורים כשבת לתשלומין; מה שבת מתחייב בנפשו ופטור מן התשלומין – אף יום הכפורים מתחייב בנפשו ופטור מן התשלומין. מ"ט דר' נחוניא בן הקנה? אמר אביי: נאמר °"אסון" בידי אדם (שמות כא) ונאמר °"אסון" בידי שמים (בראשית מב), אמה "אסון" האמור בידי אדם פטור מן התשלומין, אף "אסון" האמור בידי שמים פטור מן התשלומין. מתקיף לה רב אדא בר אהבה: ממאי דכי קא מזהר להו יעקב לבניה על צינים ופחים, דבידי שמים נינהו? דלמא על אריא וגנבי, דבידי אדם נינהו! אטו יעקב אהא אזהר, אהא לא אזהר? יעקב על כל מילי אזהר. וצינים פחים בידי שמים נינהו? והתניא: *הכל בידי שמים חוץ מצינים פחים, שנאמר: °"צינים פחים בדרך עיקש שומר נפשו ירחק מהם"! (משלי כב) ותו: אריא וגנבי בידי אדם נינהו? *והאמר רב יוסף, וכן תני רבי חייא: מיום שחרב בית המקדש, אף על פי שבטלו סנהדרין – ארבע מיתות לא בטלו? לא בטלו?! הא בטלו להו! אלא:

דין

[יבמות נב:]

חייבי עשה מצרי ואדומי. בתוך שלשה דורות, דכתיב (דברים כג) "דור שלישי יבא להם", דור שני – לא, ולאו הבא מכלל עשה – עשה. הניחא. אי רבי ישבב האי כל שאין לו היתר ביאה דקאמר אליבא דר"ע לאו כללא הוא, אלא לאפוקי מדרבי סימאי לחודיה אתא, ואחייבי לאוין הוא דפליג, לאוסופי חייבי לאוין *בכהונה, אבל שום חייבי עשה לא הוסיף. שפיר. מצינו למימר איכא בינייהו דשמעון התימני ור"ש בן מנסיא חייבי עשה. אלא. אי לאו אדרבי סימאי קאי, וטעמא דנפשיה קאמר כשם ר"ע, שכל שאין לו היתר ביאה באשה זו הולד ממזר – מאי איכא למימר? בעולה לכ"ג. שאין בה לאו דאלמנות וגירושין אלא עשה ד"בתולה יקח" (ויקרא כא), ולא בעולה. וא"ת: יש כאן לאו דזונה! לא אשכחן תנא דאמר פנוי הבא על הפנויה עשאה זונה אלא ר' אלעזר*, (א) ולית הלכתא כוותיה, ואין זונה אלא הנבעלת לפסול לה. ובבעולה שלא כדרכה איירי, דאי כדרכה – תו ליכא קנס. ומאי שנא. האי עשה משאר עשה דמודה ביה ר"ע. דהוה ליה עשה שאינו שוה בכל. שאינו נוהג אלא בכ"ג, אבל עשה דמצרי ואדומי נוהג בכל הקהל. הא נמי יש בה הויה. המקדש אשה בימי נדותה מקודשת. ולאפוקי מדר' נחוניא. מתני' דמחייב תשלומין לבא על אחותו, ואע"פ שמתחייב כרת בביאתו – מפקא מדר' נחוניא. את יום הכפורים כשבת. לפטור המדליק את הגדיש ביום הכפורים כאילו הדליקו בשבת. מה שבת. שהוא מיתת ב"ד. פטור מן התשלומין. כדתנן במתני' גבי בא על בתו, ויליף לה מ"ולא יהיה אסון ענוש יענש". אף יום הכפורים. שהוא בכרת, חיוב נפש הוא זה – ופטור מן התשלומין. אסון בידי אדם. "ולא יהיה אסון" דמשתעי במיתת ב"ד, למימר דהיכא דליכא מיתת ב"ד – משלם דמי ולדות. אסון בידי שמים. "וקראהו אסון". צינים פחים. קור וחום. בידי שמים. אם באים פורעניות על האדם – גזירת המלך הוא. חוץ מצינים ופחים. שפעמים שבאין בפשיעה. בידי אדם נינהו. שלא מגזירת מלך.

דין

תורה אור

נ"ל דכהונה

[תוספתא ב"ק פ"ז] שבועות לג. מגילה ז: פסחים כט. לב. [תוספתא פ"ג תוספתא דמגילה פ"א]

ב"מ קז: ב"ב קמד: ע"ש ע"ז ג: ע"ש

סוטה ח: סנהדרין לז: ע"ש

הגהות הב"ח

(א) רש"י ד"ה בעולה וכו' אלא ר' אלעזר ולית. נ"ב וביבמות נ"ט ע"ב מסיק דאף אליבא דר"א משכחת לה בממאנת ע"ש:

גליון הש"ס

גמ' איכא בינייהו בעולה לכ"ג. עי' פסחים מא ע"ב תוד"ה אכל:

אי לאפוקי מדרבי סימאי קאתי. תימה, תיפשוט דרבי ישבב טעמא דנפשיה קאמר, אליבא דמ"ד בפ"ק דיבמות (דף יא. ושם): הבא על יבמתו וחזר ובא אחד מן האחים על צרתה – בעשה. דהא תנן בפרק "ר"ג" (יבמות דף נ.): ר"ג אומר דאין בעילה אחר בעילה, ע"כ רבי ישבב טעמא דנפשיה קאמר, והוי התם כר' ישבב דאין קידושין תופסין בחייבי עשה, ולהכי אין אחר בעילה כלום, כדאמר התם בגמרא*, אמתני' דאין אחר חליצה כלום, אמר רב הונא אמר רב: זו דברי ר"ע, דאמר דאין קידושין תופסין בחייבי לאוין. ומסתמא הכא אליבא דר"ע מספקא ליה אי טעמא דנפשיה קאמר אי לאו! לכן נראה לר"ת דגרסי' בפ"ק דיבמות (דף יא.) חד אמר בלאו. ובלא זה מוכיח ר"ת בההיא שמעתא דל"ג "בעשה". וכן פר"ת דהיינו לאו שהלך לאחת, דאמר קרא "אשר לא יבנה" כיון שלא בנה שוב לא יבנה אחרת, ה"נ כיון שבנה שוב יבמה – לא יבנה אחרת.

איכא בינייהו בעולה לכ"ג. פי' בקונט': בעולה שלא כדרכה. וקשה: דפלוגתא דר"מ ורבי אלעזר היא בפרק "הבא על יבמתו" (יבמות דף נט. ושם) אי כשירה לכ"ג, וה"ל למימר: ולר"מ דאמר כשירה לכ"ג מאי איכא למימר? כדקאמר ולר"ע דאמר כו'! ואור"י: דמר"ע פריך שפיר כדי לאוקומי ר"ש בן מנסיא שהוא בתרא כר"ע שהיה רבו, אבל בהא לא חייש אי פליג ר"מ אר"ש בן מנסיא. ור"ת פי': דהכא לא איירי בבעולה מאחר, אלא בכ"ג שאנס בתולה גמורה, ולא חשיבה ראויה לקיימה, אע"ג דאמר ב"הבא על יבמתו"*: אנוסת עצמו ומפותת עצמו לא ישא, ואם נשא – נשוי, מ"מ כיון דלכתחלה לא ישא – לא חשיבה ראויה לקיימה, דהאי "לא ישא" – הוי מן התורה, אף ע"ג דאם נשא נשוי. ה"נ אמר בוגרת ומוכת עץ לא ישא, ואם נשא – נשוי, אע"ג דהוי מן התורה, כדמוכח התם. ועוד דקאמר התם*: מתיב רבא "ולו תהיה לאשה" – באשה הראויה לו, פרט אלמנה לכ"ג. היכי דמי: אילימא בכדרכה – מאי איריא משום אלמנה, תיפוק ליה דהויא לה בעולה! משמע דבעולת עצמו אסורה לו מן התורה. ור"ת לא פירש כן.

הכל מודים בבא על הנדה שמשלם קנס. תימה לר"י: מנלן דר"ש בן מנסיא מודה בה? דלמא כר' נחוניא בן הקנה ס"ל דחייבי כריתות פטורים מן התשלומין? ומיהו, ר"ש התימני ע"כ לית ליה דר' נחוניא, מדאיצטריך למעוטי חייבי כריתות מ"ולו תהיה לאשה" אשה שיש בה הויה. דע"כ לא איצטריך למעוטי אלא חייבי כריתות, דחייבי לאוין ס"ל בסוף "החולץ" (יבמות דף מט. ושם) דאית בהו הויה. אבל מר"ש בן מנסיא קשה: מנלן דלית ליה דר' נחוניא? ועוד, אפי' ר"ש התימני דלמא אית ליה דר' נחוניא, ואיצטריך למעוטי מ"ולו תהיה לאשה" יבמה לשוק, דאין קידושין תופסין בה לר"ע, כדאמר ב"האשה רבה" (שם דף צב: ושם)! וי"ל: דרב חסדא ס"ל דאין שום תנא סובר כרבי נחוניא, ולה"ק ולאפוקי כו'. ובקונטר' פירש דאמתני' קאי דמפקא מדר' נחוניא. ותימה: מנ"ל דמפקא מיניה? דלמא מודה ר' נחוניא דחייבי כריתות. יש להן קנס דרבינהו קרא חד לחייבי לאוין וחד לחייבי כריתות ולר"ע ניחא דמפקא מתני' מדר' נחוניא דכיון דאין קידושין תופסין בחייבי לאוין – איכא לאוקומי הנך תרי ריבויי חד לחייבי עשה וחד לחייבי לאוין, אבל חייבי כריתות לר' נחוניא – לא. *ונראה לרשב"א לתרץ: *דע"כ מפקא מתני' מר' נחוניא, דלר' נחוניא אין חילוק בין חייבי כריתות לחייבי מיתות ב"ד, או מ"אסון" "אסון", או כדדריש רבא: כרת שלי כמיתה שלכם. ואם יש קנס לר' נחוניא בחייבי כריתות – יש ג"כ בחייבי מיתות ב"ד, ומתני' קתני: בא על בתו פטור. **הכל** בידי שמים חוץ מצינים פחים. והא דאמרי' (שבת דף לב.): לעולם אל יעמוד אדם במקום סכנה, אלמא יכול לשמור עצמו מן הפורענות! וכן קיר נטוי דאסור לעבור תחתיו! התם מן הפשיעה יכול לשמור עצמו, דהא ודאי שבידו להמית עצמו, אבל כשמביאין עליו מן השמים באונס – אי אפשר לו לשמור, אבל צינים פחים לעולם אל יבואו עליו באונס אם רוצה ליזהר. וא"ת: והא דרשינן (ב"מ דף קז:) "והסיר ה' ממך כל חולי" – זה צינה, אלמא דבידי שמים הוא! וי"ל: דהיינו שיתם הקב"ה עולמו, או יתן לו מלבושים, ולא יצטרך ליזהר. וא"ת: והא פחים בידי שמים הוא, כדאמרי' בבראשית רבה בפרשה ט"ו, א"ל אנטונינוס לרבי: צלי עלי. א"ל: רחמנא שיזבך מצינתא. א"ל: דא צלותא היא? יתיר חד כסו וצינתא אזלא. א"ל: תשתזב משרבא. א"ל: הא כדו צלותא, דכתיב "אין נסתר מחמתו"! וי"ל דקרא כתיב בעוברי דרכים, או במלחמה, כדרך שהמלכים עושים, דבדרך אין אדם יכול ליזהר מן החום. אבל אם רוצה לישב בביתו – יכול להזהר שישב בבית של אבנים או יכנס במרתף. ויש מפרשים דצינים פחים חדא מילתא היא, כלומר: צינים שהם פחים לאדם, לשון פח ומוקש. ואינו כן, דבפ"ק דמסכת ע"ז (דף ג: ושם) מייתי לה [אהא דכתיב "ותעשה אדם כדגי הים" מה] דגים שבים, כיון שקדרה עליהן חמה מיד מתים – [אף בני אדם כיון שקדרה עליהם חמה מיד מתים]. והא דאמר (ברכות דף לג:): הכל בידי שמים חוץ מיראת שמים – אין ענינו לכאן, דהתם קאי על הולד במעי אמו (נדה טז:), שגוזרין אם יהא עני או עשיר גבור או חלש טפש או חכם, אבל צדיק ורשע – לא, *והכא איירי במאורעות הבאות על האדם*. **מיום** שחרב בית כו'. וא"ת: אמאי לא נקט מ' שנה קודם שחרב בהמ"ק? דמ' שנה קודם חורבן גלתה סנהדרין כו', שלא דנו דיני נפשות! וי"ל: דלפעמים לצורך שעה היו חוזרין סנהדרין ללשכת הגזית, ולהכי לא פסיקא ליה למיתני מ' שנה קודם חורבן. וא"ת: א"כ מאי פריך בפרק "היו בודקין" (סנהדרין דף מא.) גבי מעשה ובדק ר' יוחנן בן זכאי בעוקצי תאנים, ופריך: מי הוה בסנהדרין? והא תניא כל שנותיו של רבן יוחנן בן זכאי מאה ועשרים שנה, מ' עסק בפרקמטיא, ומ' למד ומ' לימד. ותניא: מ' שנה קודם חורבן גלתה סנהדרין כו'. והשתא מאי קשיא ליה? כיון דלפעמים היו חוזרין ודנין! וי"ל: דרבן יוחנן בן זכאי דבדק בעוקצי תאנה – אמעשה דרציחה היה, ומשום דיני נפשות דרציחה לא היו חוזרין לעולם, דעיקרם לא גלו אלא משום רציחה, דחזו דנפישי רוצחים, כדאמרינן בפ"ק דמסכת ע"ז (דף ח: ושם). וי"מ דלהכי נקט משחרב בהמ"ק, משום דקודם לכן אע"פ שגלו היו בגדי כהונה מכפרים על מזיד דלא אתרו ביה, כדאמרינן בפרק יש בערכין (ערכין דף טז. ושם). ואין נראה, דהא בימי שמעון בן שטח היו בגדי כהונה, והיה דין ארבע מיתות, כדאמרינן בפרק "אחד דיני ממונות" (סנהדרין דף לז: ושם): אר"ש בן שטח: אראה בנחמה אם לא ראיתי אחד שרץ אחר חברו לחורבה וכו' לא זז משם עד שנשכו נחש. ופריך: והאי בר נחש הוא? והא תני ר' חייא: אע"פ שבטלו סנהדרין כו'? ועוד אמר (מכות י:) "מרשעים יצא רשע כו'" *)והתם בזמן שבהמ"ק קיים איירי, מדקאמר: ונמצא זה מת וזה גולה**).

דין

*) [ומיהו אפשר לומר לפי שלפעמים היו מכפרים לא פסיקא ליה. ת"י] **) [וע"ע תוס' סוטה ח: וזבחים פח: ד"ה מכפרים]

ז א (מיי' פ"א מהלכות נערה הלכה יג ופ"ג מהלכות גניבה הלכה ב טוש"ע ח"מ סי' שנא):

תוספות רי"ד

מתני' דלא כר"נ בן הקנה. פירוש מתני' דמחייב קנס לבא על אחותו ואע"פ שמתחייב כרת בביאתו. דתניא ר"נ [בן הקנה] היה עושה יוה"כ כשבת לתשלומין. פי' לפטור המדליק את הגדיש ביוה"כ כאילו הדליקו בשבת מה שבת שהיא מיתת ב"ד פטור מתשלומין כדתנן מתני' לקמן בבא על בתו וילפי' לה מולא יהי' אסון. אף יוה"כ שהוא בכרת מתחייב בנפשו ופטור מן התשלומין. מ"ט דר"נ ב"ה. אמר אביי נאמר אסון בידי שמים. פי' וקראהו אסון ונאמר אסון בידי אדם ואם אסון יהיה מה אסון הנאמר בידי אדם פטור מן התשלומין. פי' דמשתעי במיתת ב"ד למימר היכא דליכא מיתת ב"ד משלם דמי וולדות. אף אסון האמור בידי שמים פטור מן התשלומין:

[יבמות דף נט:]

[דף נט. ושם ד"ה אילימא]

[ומהר"מ אומר כי מצא בתוספתא פרק אלו נערות ר' נחוניא אומר הבא על אחותו ועל אחות אביו כו' אין להם קנס וכן היה עושה רבי נחוניא בן הקנה יוה"כ כשבת]

[ול"נ לתרץ דע"כ מפקא מתני' מר' נחוניא דלר' נחוניא איצטריך לאוקמי חד לחייבי לאוין ועשה וחד ללאו דיבמה לשוק אבל חייבי כריתות קים ליה בדרבה מיניה וכ"מ לקמן בפירקין אי כרבי נחוניא קשיא אחותו משמע דבחייבי כריתות לא מתוקמא כוותיה. ת"י]

[והא דתנן (פ"ד דאבות) על כרחך אתה חי היינו שאין לך אדם שמניח להרוג עצמו ועוד נראה לר"י דע"כ אתה חי לעתיד קאמר וגרסי' ע"כ אתה מת וע"כ אתה חי והוי כמו המתים להחיות והחיים לידון. ת"י]

[וע"ע תוס' מגילה כה. ד"ה הכל ותוס' נדה טז: ד"ה הכל]

ח א מיי' פ"י מהלכות תרומות הל' ו סמג לאוין רכו:
ט ב מיי' פ"ב מהלכות גניבה הלכה ד סמג עשין עא טוש"ע ח"מ סימן שנ:

דין ארבע מיתות לא בטלו: מי שנתחייב סקילה — או נופל מן הגג, או חיה דורסתו. ומי שנתחייב שריפה — או נופל בדליקה, או נחש מכישו. ומי שנתחייב הריגה — או נמסר למלכות, או ליסטים באין עליו. ומי שנתחייב חנק — או טובע בנהר, או מת בסרונכי? אלא איפוך: אריא וגנבי — בידי שמים, צינים ופחים — בידי אדם. רבא אמר: טעמא דרבי נחוניא בן הקנה מהכא: °"ואם העלם יעלימו עם הארץ את עיניהם מן האיש ההוא בתתו מזרעו למולך ושמתי אני את פני באיש ההוא ובמשפחתו והכרתי אותו" אמרה תורה: כרת שלי כמיתה שלכם, מה מיתה שלכם — פטור מן התשלומין, אף כרת שלי — פטור מן התשלומין. מאי איכא בין רבא לאביי? איכא בינייהו זר שאכל תרומה. לאביי [א]פטור, ולרבא חייב. ולאביי פטור?! והאמר רב חסדא: מודה ר' נחוניא בן הקנה [ב]בגונב חלבו של חבירו ואכלו — שהוא חייב, שכבר נתחייב בגניבה קודם שבא לידי איסור חלב. אלמא, דמעידנא דאגביה קנייה, מתחייב בנפשו *לא הוה עד דאכיל ליה. הכא נמי, בעידנא דאגביה קנייה, מתחייב בנפשו לא הוי עד דאכיל ליה! הכא במאי עסקינן — כגון שתחב לו חבירו לתוך פיו. סוף סוף, כיון דלעסיה — קנייה, מתחייב בנפשו לא הוי עד דבלעה! כגון *שתחב לו לתוך בית הבליעה. היכי דמי? אי דמצי לאהדורה — ניהדר, אי לא מצי לאהדורה — אמאי חייב? לא צריכא, דמצי לאהדורה ע"י הדחק. רב פפא אמר: כגון שתחב לו חבירו משקין של תרומה לתוך פיו. רב אשי אמר: בזר שאכל תרומה משלו, וקרע

ויקרא כ

תורה אור

דין ד' מיתות. עונש דוגמתם. נופל מן הגג. דומה לנסקל, שדוחפין אותו מבית הסקילה לארץ. דגבוה ב' קומות היה, כדאמרי' ב"נגמר הדין" (סנהדרין דף מה.). חיה דורסתו. ארי מפילו לארץ והורגו בדריסה. נחש מכישו. והארס שורפו. נמסר למלכות. והן מתיזין ראשו בסייף, כי כן דרך המומתין על ידיהן, וזו היא מיתת סייף. סרונכי. אסכרא, והוא בגרון, מלנ"ט. מן האיש ההוא. שהוא חייב מיתת ב"ד. ושמתי אני את פני והכרתי. למדנו שהכרת במקום מיתה וחילופה. זר שאכל תרומה. במזיד, הוא במיתה בידי שמים ולא בכרת. כרת — הוא וזרעו נענשין, דכתיב (ויקרא כ) "ערירים יהיו". לאביי פטור. מתשלומין, דנפקא ליה מאסון בידי שמים, ולכל אסון במשמע, בין במיתה בין בכרת. ולאביי פטור. בתמיה; נהי נמי דמיתה בידי שמים פוטרת מתשלומין, אבל היכא דאכיל תרומה דגזילה מי מיפטר? הא כיון דאגבהה קנייה, וחייב בתשלומין, ואפילו תישרף, ומתחייב בנפשו לא הוי עד דאכיל לה. שתחב לו חברו. דלא אגבהה ולא קנייה ולא מיחייב בתשלומין, אלא בבליעתו מתחייב דמי הניית מעיו, ולא דמי כולה. ובההיא שעתא חיוב מיתה נמי איכא. איבעי ליה לאהדורה. וכי לא אהדרה — מההיא שעתא איהו מזיק לה. דראשון לאו מידי עבד, ולא נתחייב לכהן כלום. ואי דלא מצי לאהדורה אמאי חייב. מיתה? אנוס הוא! ע"י הדחק. דאי נמי אהדרה — ממאסה, ולא חזיא לבעלים. הלכך, מגזל לא גזלה. אמאי קא מחייבת ליה בתשלומין — אהנאת גרונו ומעיו? ההיא שעתא חיוב מיתה איכא! משקין של תרומה. ולא תדחקה לשנויה בבית הבליעה, אלא מכיון שתחבה לתוך פיו אימאסא לה, ולא מגיע לאיחיובי משום גזילה — דהא לא חזיא למידי, אלא אהניית גרונו ומעיו מיחייב, ומיתה ותשלומין באים כאחד. וקרע

דין ד' מיתות לא בטלו. וא"ת: והא אמר ב"השוכר את הפועלים" (ב"מ פג:) בההוא דזקפוהו, אע"פ שהיה חייב סקילה, שבעלו הוא ובנו נערה המאורסה! וי"ל: כשבעל בנו תחלה ואח"כ הוא, דהוי בעולה, והרי הוא בחנק. אבל קשה: דחזינן כמה עבריינים ועובדי עבודה זרה שמתים על מטותם? ויש לומר דע"י תשובה הקב"ה מיקל, ולפעמים מוחל לגמרי, או זכות תולה לו ואינו נפרע ממנו בחייו. ובפ' "אחד דיני ממונות" (סנהדרין דף לז: ושם) דפריך: והא בר נחש הוא! לפי שהחמיר עליו יותר. זר שאכל תרומה לאביי פטור. ואוכל תרומה בשוגג והזיד במעילה, לרבי דאמר במיתה (פסחים דף לג.) דחייב — גזירת הכתוב הוא. וא"ת: לאביי דפטר חייבי מיתות בידי שמים, אי ר' נחוניא ס"ל כרבי דאמר הזיד במעילה במיתה — אמאי תניא בפרק "כל שעה" (פסחים דף כט. ושם): האוכל חמץ של הקדש במועד — יש אומרים לא מעל. ואמרינן: מאן י"א — רבי נחוניא בן הקנה. והא כיון דגלי רחמנא גבי הקדש, דלא שייך קים ליה (א), דאם לא כן אין לך אדם שמועל בהקדש — א"כ בפסח נמי, דאיכא כרת — ליחייב, ולא הוה לן למימר דקים ליה בדרבה מיניה! וכ"ת: במיתה דהקדש דוקא גלי רחמנא דלא אמרינן דקים ליה בדרבה מיניה, אבל התם דהוי בפסח דאיכא כרת לא גלי קרא — א"כ הא דתנן התם (שם דף לא:): האוכל תרומת חמץ בפסח, בשוגג — משלם קרן וחומש, במזיד — פטור מן התשלומין, ומפרש בגמ': במזיד פטור דקים ליה בדרבה מיניה, כרבי נחוניא. והשתא בשוגג נמי ליפטר משום כרת דפסח, דאפי' בשוגג אמרי' דקים ליה בדרבה מיניה, כדאמרינן לקמן בפירקין (דף לה.)! אלא ע"כ משום דגלי רחמנא במיתה דתרומה בשוגג, דלא אמרינן קים ליה בדרבה מיניה, וה"ה כי איכא כרת. ולא אמרינן דוקא במיתה דגלי גלי, אבל כי איכא כרת לא. וי"ל: דשאני שוגג דתרומה, משום דתשלומין דידיה כפרה ולא ממונא, כדאמרינן במסכת תרומות (פ"ו מ"א) דאם רצה כהן למחול — אינו יכול למחול, משום דלא הוי ממון אלא כפרה. ואפילו אוכל תרומת עצמו, דלא גזל מידי, משלם כפרה לעצמו וחומש לכהן. ולכך לא שייך קים ליה בדרבה מיניה לפוטרו מכפרה. אבל קרן וחומש של הקדש אינו משום כפרה, אלא משלם ממון שגזל הקדש. ותדע, דבתרומה חייב משום דכפרה הוא, ולא משום כיון דגלי גלי, דהא לרבא דלא פטר במיתה מטעם דקים ליה בדרבה מיניה — מאי טעמא לא מיפטר אוכל תרומת חמץ בפסח? אלא ודאי משום כפרה הוא*. וא"ת: והא דתנן בפרק "נושאין" (יבמות דף נט:): כהנת שנתערב ולדה בולד שפחתה, ושחררו זה את זה. וכן ספק בן תשעה לראשון או בן ז' לאחרון, דאמרינן אם אכלו בתרומה — אין משלמין קרן וחומש, ואמאי? כיון דכפרה הוא — ליחייבו מספק! וי"ל: דודאי צריכין להפריש אבל אין נותנין לכהן. ולפי זה צריך לומר שהכפרה תלויה בהפרשה, והא דאין הכהן יכול למחול — היינו לענין שלא יהיה צריך להפריש, אבל לאחר שהפריש — יכול למחול לו שיהא שלו. ולאביי פטור והאמר רב חסדא כו'. הכי נמי הוה מצי לאקשויי אמתניתין ד"כל שעה" (פסחים דף לא:) דקתני: פטור מן התשלומין, לפי מה דמוקמינן לה כרבי נחוניא בן הקנה. אי דמצי לאהדורה ניהדרה. וכי לא מיהדר — חייב, דמיתה לא פטרה ליה, דלא אתיא עד דבלע לגמרי. ואי דלא מצי לאהדורה אמאי חייב. פירש בקונטרס אמאי חייב מיתה. וקשה לר"י: דלוקי כגון שמרצונו מניח לו לתחוב, דהשתא ודאי חייב מיתה, אע"ג דלא מצי לאהדורה, וממון נמי לא מיחייב, כיון דלא מצי לאהדורה, אלא על הנאת גרונו ומעיו, וההיא שעתא קים ליה בדרבה מיניה! ונראה לר"י דה"פ: אמאי חייב ממון? והרי הוא לא גזלו, ואהנאתו לא מיחייב, דאע"ג דאמרי' (ב"ק דף קיא:): גזל ולא נתייאשו הבעלים, ובא אחר ואכלו — רצה מזה גובה כו'. היינו דוקא לפי שהדבר הגזול ישנו בעולם בשעה שזה שני גוזלו, אבל הכא, דבשעה שזה נהנה ממנו כבר הוא אבוד מן העולם, שהוא במקום דלא אפשר לאהדוריה — אין לו על השני כלום. *וריצב"א מפרש כשיטת רש"י. ופשיטא ליה להתלמוד דאיירי כשתוחב לו בע"כ, דכשתוחב לו מרצונו — מיד כשמשים בפיו ולא אהדרה — קנאה מיד להתחייב באונסין, ואין בא כאחד, דמסתמא מניחה בפיו, ואח"כ תוחב לו כשלבעו או בכוס. וא"ת שהוא כראש הכוס מתחלתו ועד גמר בית הבליעה — מ"מ קונה אותו בפיו להתחייב באונסים, אע"ג דיכול לנתקו ולהביאו אצלו. ⊛דדוקא לענין הגט אמרי' היכא דיכול לנתקו דלא הוי גט משום דבעינן כריתות, והא אגידא ביה. אבל לענין זכיה אשכחן בפ"ק דב"מ (דף ט. ושם) טלית, תליה על גבי קרקע ותליה על גבי העמוד, והגביה תליה שעל גבי קרקע — דלא קני, מטעם שיכול לנתקה ולהביאה אצלו. וכיון שאינו זוכה מטעם זה — ה"ה דאינו מגרע זכיית האחר, שהוא מונח בתוך ידו או בתוך פיו, מטעם זה. ועוד: דלכל הפחות קונה מחלה, כמו שנים שהגביהו מציאה. ולכך פשיטא ליה להתלמוד דבאונס מיירי, וה"פ: אנוס הוא ופטור ממיתה וממון, דאנן סהדי דלא ניחא ליה באכילת איסור. לא צריכא דמצי לאהדורה על ידי הדחק. והשתא ליכא למימר דניהדרה, דאין מרויחין בעלים בכך, דכבר נמאסו. הלכך ליכא חיוב ממון אלא ע"י הנאת מעיו ואז באין כאחד. ואע"ג שחבירו גזלה, הואיל ויכול להחזירה הויא כמו שהיא בעין, והרי הוא בולעה ונהנה בה. ואם תאמר: והא אמרינן בפרק "בהמה המקשה" (חולין דף עא.) גבי טומאה בלועה [דלא מטמאה לא משום דלא חזיא, דנהי בפניו לא חזיא] שלא בפניו מיהא חזיא, א"כ אי הוה מהדר לה הויא חזיא! וי"ל: כגון דמעיקרא לא הוי בה כי אם שוה פרוטה, או מעט יותר, ועתה, שנתקלקלה קצת, אינה שוה פרוטה. ואפילו אי זה נהנה וזה לא חסר פטור — ⊛מ"מ כיון דשוין כל שהוא אז מיחייב בכל, כדאמרינן התם (ב"ק דף כ:): משום דא"ל את גרמת לי היקפא יתירתא מיחייב בכל הנאה, או משום שחרוריתא דאשיתא מיחייב לכולי עלמא בכל. וריצב"א פי' דמיירי אפי' באוכלין דלא מאיסי, וכיון דתחב לו בבית הבליעה ובלע ונהנה מיד — חשוב באין כאחת אע"פ שאין כאחד ממש. כדאשכחן בסוף פרק "ד' אחין" (יבמות דף לג. ושם) דמפרש: בעל מום ששמש בטומאה דאתו בהדי הדדי, כגון שחתך אצבעו בסכין טמאה, אע"פ שאי אפשר שלא יגע בסכין קודם שיחתוך*. רב אשי אמר בזר שאכל תרומה משלו וקרע שיראים כו'. פ"ה דסבירא ליה לרב אשי דמיתה לזה ותשלומין לזה פטור, ופליג אדרבא דאמר בפרק קמא דסנהדרין (דף י. ושם): פלוני בא על בת פלוני והוזמו — נהרגין ומשלמין — ממון לזה ונפשות לזה. *פי': ממון לבת שרצו להפסיד לה כתובתה, ונפשות לזה שאומר שבא עליה. ואין נראה, **) דאי חשיב אכילת תרומה וקריעת שיראין ממון לזה ונפשות לזה — א"כ תקשי ליה לרבא הא דתנן ב"המניח את הכד" (ב"ק דף לד: ושם):

והוא

[עי' תוס' בבא קמא כ: ד"ה הא]

גליון הש"ס
תוס' ד"ה ואי וכו' דדוקא לענין הגט. תמוה לי הא להדיא איתא כן בב"מ ז ע"א ודלע"ג: ד"ה לא צריכא וכו' מ"מ כיון דשוין כל שהוא. עי' בב"ק דף כ ע"ב תוד"ה הא איתהנית:

הגהות הב"ח
(א) תוס' ד"ה זר וכו' קים ליה בדרבה מיניה ל"ס:

[וא"ת כיון דלעס ליה נתקלקל והיאך חייב תו עלה כדאמר פ"ק דכריתות [דף ז.] כהן שסך שמן של תרומה בן בתו ישראל מתעגל בו ואינו חושש וי"ל דהתם ודאי נתקלקל שכבר נגמרה כל הנאתו אבל הכא לא נגמרה כל הנאתו בלעיסה לחודיה. ת"י]

[ועוד יש להוכיח דכפרה הוי מדפטרי' לאביי מזיד בתרומה ואע"ג דגלי רחמנא גבי שוגג דלא אמרי' קים ליה בדרבה מיניה במיתה דתרומה אלא ודאי משום כפרה הוא ויש לחות דשאני שוגג דתרומה לפי שמצינו שהוא חמור שמשלם חומש. ת"י]

[פי' ריצב"א לא יתיישב בסמוך דקאמר אי בעי גחין ואכיל. ת"י]

[פי' ממון לאב שרצו להפסידו כתובה כצ"ל מהרש"א]

[ור"ת פירש כיון שהוא במקום דלא מצי לאהדור אלא ע"י הדחק כבר נהנה גרונו ובאין כאחד ואח"כ והיאך יתחייב ממון כיון שתחב לו באונס וי"ל כיון דמצי לאהדורה ע"י הדחק ולא הדרה ניחא ליה בהנאה זו. ת"י]

**) [ועוד דלהכי מאי איכא בין רבא לאביי דלאפי' אי הוי סבר רבא דיליף מאסון אסון הוי מיחייב כיון דהוי ממון לזה ונפשות לזה. ת"י]

וקרע שיראין של חבירו. גופא, אמר רב חסדא: מודה רבי נחוניא בן הקנה בגונב חלבו של חבירו ואכלו — שהוא חייב שכבר נתחייב בגניבה קודם שיבא לידי איסור חלב. לימא פליגא דרבי אבין, דאמר רבי אבין: *[א]הזורק חץ מתחילת ארבע לסוף ארבע וקרע שיראין בהליכתו — פטור, שעקירה צורך הנחה היא. הכא נמי — הגבהה צורך אכילה היא; הכי השתא? התם — אי אפשר להנחה בלא עקירה, הכא אפשר לאכילה בלא הגבהה, דאי בעי — *גחין ואכיל. אי נמי: התם, אי בעי לאהדורה לא מצי מהדר לה, הכא — מצי מהדר לה. מאי איכא בין האי לישנא להאי לישנא? איכא בינייהו המעביר סכין ברה"ר, וקרע שיראין בהליכתו. להך לישנא דאמרת אי אפשר להנחה בלא עקירה — הכא נמי אי אפשר להנחה בלא עקירה. להך לישנא דאמרת לא מצי מהדר לה — הכא מצי מהדר לה. גופא, אמר רבי אבין: הזורק חץ מתחלת ארבע לסוף ארבע, וקרע שיראין בהליכתו — פטור, שעקירה צורך הנחה היא. מתיב רב ביבי בר אביי: *[ב]הגונב כיס בשבת — חייב, שכבר נתחייב בגניבה קודם שיבא לידי איסור סקילה. [ג]היה מגרר ויוצא, מגרר ויוצא — פטור, שהרי איסור שבת וגניבה באין כאחד. ואמאי? הכא נמי לימא הגבהה צורך הוצאה היא! הכא במאי עסקינן — כגון שהגביהו על מנת להצניעו ונמלך עליו והוציאו. וכי האי גוונא מי חייב? והאמר רב סימון אמר רבי אמי אמר רבי יוחנן: *[ד]המפנה חפצים מזוית לזוית, ונמלך עליהם והוציאן — פטור, שלא היתה עקירה משעה ראשונה לכך! לא תימא ע"מ להצניעו, אלא אימא ע"מ להוציאו, הכא במאי עסקינן — [ה]כשעמד. עמד למאי? אי לכתף — אורחיה הוא! אלא בעומד לפוש, אבל לכתף מאי — פטור

רש"י

וקרע שיראים. בשעה שבולעת. ואע"ג דמיתה לאו משום ממונא דניזק אתיא ליה — מיפטר. וסבירא ליה לרב אשי מיתה לזה ותשלומין לזה — פטור. שעקירה צורך הנחה היא. הלכך, אע"ג דחיוב ממון מקמי הנחה אתיא ליה — פטור, הואיל ובין עקירה והנחה אתיא ליה, מיתה ותשלומין באין כאחד, שעקירה צורך הנחה היא, ומההיא שעתא אתחלה לה מלאכה. דאי בעי גחין. למטה מג' טפחים ואכיל. ובציר מג' לאו הגבהה היא. לא מצי לאהדורה. משנזרק את החץ. הלכך משעת עקירה סופו לקרוע לו שיראין. הכא מצי מהדר ליה. הלכך לא אמרי' משעת הגבהה אתחלה לה אכילה. המעביר סכין. בידו בהליכה. הגונב כיס בשבת. הגביהו ברשות הבעלים, והוציאו לרה"ר. חייב. בתשלומין, אף על פי שנהרג. שכבר נתחייב בגניבה. לשלם, דהגבהה קונה בכל מקום וקמה לה ברשותיה אף להתחייב באונסים. היה מגרר ויוצא. שלא הגביהו ברשות הבעלים. ולא קנאו אלא בהוצאה מרשות הבעלים — פטור, שאיסור שבת כו'. ואמאי. כי הגביהו ברשות הבעלים וקנאו אמאי חייב? נימא משעת הגבהה אתחלה לה הוצאה. וכה"ג מי חייב. משום שבת. לכך. להוציאו. לא תימא בהגביהו ע"מ להצניעו אלא הגביהו ע"מ להוציאו. ודקשיא לך נימא הגבהה צורך הוצאה היא. הכא במאי עסקינן בשעמד. ועמידתו היא הנחה לעקירה ראשונה, ואין חיוב שבת בא לו ע"י עקירת חפץ הראשונה, אלא ע"י עקירת גופו שעוקר עצמו אחר העמידה על מנת להוליך, ועקירת גופו כעקירת חפץ. אורחיה הוא. ואין עמידתו הנחה לבטל עקירה ראשונה ממלאכת שבת.

תוספות

והוא שהדליק את הגדיש בשבת פטור מפני שנידון בנפשו, והיינו מיתה לזה משום שבת, ותשלומין לזה משום גדיש. אלא על כרחך חשיב מיתה ותשלומין לאחד, הואיל ולא מתחייב מיתה בשביל אדם אלא לשמים. וה"נ אכילת תרומה וקריעת שיראין — הוי מיתה ותשלומין לאחד. ור"י רצה ליישב פי' הקונט' דחשיב הכא מיתה לזה ותשלומין לזה לפי שהן ב' מעשים, אכילת תרומה וקריעת שיראין. וכן פלוני בא על בתו של פלוני, הם ב' עדיות. שהיו יכולין להעיד עליו בלא הבת, ועל הבת בלא עליו: פלוני בא על נערה המאורסה, פלונית זינתה. אבל מדליק גדיש — הכל בא על מעשה אחד, ולכך חשיב מיתה ותשלומין לאחד. ואין נראה לרשב"א, דהא אמר רב יוסף בפ"ק דסנהדרין (דף ט: ושם): הביא הבעל עדים שזינתה, והביא האב עדים והזימום לעידי הבעל, עידי הבעל נהרגים ואין משלמין ממון. חזר והביא הבעל עדים והזימום לעידי האב, עדי האב נהרגין ומשלמין ממון. ממון לזה, פירוש: לבעל, שרצו להפסידו כתובה. ונפשות, לעדים. והתם על הזמה אחת בא להם הכל! ונראה לר"ת: דרבא דוקא גבי עדים זוממים אית ליה דממון לזה ונפשות לזה חייב, משום דבעינן שתתקיים הזמה כלפי כל אחד. ומיהו, ממון ונפשות בחד גברא — פטור, כיון דמתקיים בו קצת הזמה. אבל בעלמא מודה רבא דממון לזה ונפשות לזה פטור, דהא גבי סמוך לו ועבד כפות לו, דתנן פטור, ומוקמינן בפרק "כיצד הרגל" (ב"ק דף כב: ושם) בגדי דחד ועבדא דחד. ועוד: דרבא גופיה אית ליה בפרק "בן סורר ומורה" (סנהדרין דף עד.) דרודף ששבר כלים, בין של נרדף בין של כל אדם, פטור, אע"ג דהוי מיתה לנרדף ותשלומין לבעל הכלים. ומיהו, התם גבי רודף רבה גרס, כדמוכח ב"הגוזל בתרא" (ב"ק דף קיז:) ובפ"ק דסנהדרין (דף י.) הוי רבא. ועוד אומר ר"ת: דע"כ לכ"ע מיתה לזה ותשלומין לזה פטור, דהא קים ליה בדרבה מיניה דפטור — נפקא לן מ"לא יהיה אסון וגו'" והתם הוי מיתה לאשה ותשלומין לבעל שהולדות שלו. ואומר ר"י דאינה ראיה, דהתם כיון שהולדות הן בגוף האשה — חשיב מיתה ותשלומין לאחד. תדע, דבפרק "בן סורר ומורה" (שם דף עד.) בעי לחייב כשאין אסון באשה אף ע"ג דניתן להצילו בנפשו, דבמלות שבמיתה הכתוב מדבר, משום דהוי מיתה לזה שרצה להורגו, ותשלומין לבעל. ואפי' הכי כשיש אסון — פטור, והיינו משום דחשיב מיתה ותשלומין לאחד, לפי שהן בגוף האשה, כדפרישית. וריב"א אומר: דבכל מקום מיתה לזה ותשלומין לזה חייב, ועבד כפות לו ורודף שאני, דניתן להציל לכל אדם, וחייב מיתה לכל העולם, [אף לבעל העבד ולבעל הכלים], ולהכי חשיב מיתה ותשלומין לאחד. ואע"ג דמעיקרא בפרק "בן סורר" (ג"ז שם) חשיב רודף מיתה לזה ותשלומין לזה, לפי המסקנא דקאמר: אלא לא שנא — חזר בו מאותה סברא. וה"פ: אלא לא שנא משום דהוי מיתה ותשלומין לאחד [והכא חשיב מיתה ותשלומין לאחד. כמו במדליק גדיש]. **שעקירה** צורך הנחה היא. קשה: דאמרינן ב"מרובה" (ב"ק דף ע:) גבי גנב ומכר בשבת דפטור, כגון דאמר ליה זרוק גניבותיך לחצרי ותיקני לי חצירי גניבותיך. ופריך: מכי מטי לאויר חצירו קנה, ומתחייב בנפשו משום שבת לא הוי עד שתנוח! ומאי פריך? והא עקירה צורך הנחה היא, כדאמר הכא! ולפר"ת אתי שפיר. דפירש דאי אפשר לניסוך בלא הגבהה, ואפ"ה קאמר רב מנסך ממש ב"הניזקין" (גיטין דף נב: ושם). ולא קא מפטר משום דקים ליה בדרבה מיניה, כדרבי ירמיה, דמשעת הגבהה קונה, ומתחייב בנפשו לא הוי עד שעת ניסוך. והשתא רבי ירמיה לית ליה דהגבהה צורך ניסוך היא, וה"ה דלית ליה דעקירה צורך הנחה היא, ולא הוה מפליג בין מצי לאהדורי ללא מצי לאהדורי. תדע, ללישנא דאי אפשר להנחה בלא עקירה אמאי נקט רבי אבין זרק חץ? לינקוט מעביר! אלא ודאי כי הדדי נינהו. ומאן דפליג אמעביר — פליג נמי אזורק. ואליבא דרבי ירמיה פריך ב"מרובה" (ב"ק דף ע: ושם). אבל אם אפשר לניסוך בלא הגבהה — לא פליג רבי ירמיה אדרבי אבין, וב"הגוזל בתרא" (שם דף קיז.) משמע קצת דרבי ירמיה פליג אדרבי אבין, גבי חזרו לומר אף המנסך. דקאמר התם: מעיקרא סבור כדרבי אבין, ולבסוף סבור כדרבי ירמיה. [ומיהו יש לדחות: דמעיקרא סבור דדמיא לדרבי אבין, ולבסוף סבור דדמיא לדר' ירמיה]. **דאי** בעי גחין ואכיל. פי' בקונט': למטה מג' דלא הויא הגבהה. וקשה לר"י: דמה שייך הגבהה בדבר שהוא תופס בידו או בפיו? ד"ונתן בידה" אמר רחמנא, ואמרינן בגיטין (דף עח.) זרק לתוך קלתה — מגורשת, קשורה אע"פ שאינה תלויה, אע"ג דמיירי ברשות הבעל. ואפי' מאן דבעי התם תלויה — אינו מצריך שתהא גבוה ג'! אלא נראה לר"י *דה"פ: דאי בעי גחין ואכיל, אם הוא בראש קנה יכול הוא לשחות ולתוחבה עד בית בליעתו, אע"ג דבכך אכילה אינו עושה כן והויא הגבהה זו לצורך אכילה, מ"מ הואיל ויכול להתחייב בלא הגבהה — לאו צורך אכילה היא. וה"ה דה"מ למימר דאפשר לאכילה בלא הגבהה, כגון אם תחבה לו חבירו. **הכא** נמי נימא הגבהה צורך הוצאה היא. ללישנא דאי בעי לאהדורי לא מצי מיהדר א] לא פריך מידי, אבל ללישנא דאי אפשר להנחה בלא עקירה פריך, דהכא נמי אי אפשר להנחה בלא הגבהה. אע"ג דאפשר בגרירה, כך לי עקירה זו כמו עקירה אחרת, דמ"מ האיסור מתחיל משעת הגבהה. דאם היה אחר עושה עקירה — לא היה מתחייב בהנחה, נמצא עקירה גורמת החיוב, ועד שעת הנחה מושך החיוב. **נימא** הגבהה צורך הוצאה היא. תימה: לפר"ת דהגבהה קונה פחות משלשה טפחים — *מאי פריך? והא כיון דקנאה קודם התחלת העקירה, דעקירה לא הויא עד שיגביה שלשה, דלמטה משלשה הוי כלבוד, כדאמרינן ב"המוציא" (שבת דף פ. ושם): העביר חצי גרוגרת דרך עליה — חייב. ואם כן דין הוא שיתחייב, כמו לבן עזאי, דאמר: מהלך כעומד דמי, דחייב לפי שקנאה קודם שהתחיל העקירה! ואומר רשב"א: דמשמע ליה בכל ענין גונב כיס אפילו מונח על גבי מקל שהוא גבוה שלשה טפחים, שבא הקנין והעקירה בבת אחת. **שהגביהו** על מנת להצניעו ונמלך להוציאו. ואם תאמר: וכיון דסלקא דעתיה השתא דמיחייב אהך הוצאה, אם כן הדרא קושיא לדוכתין, דצורך הוצאה היא! ויש לומר: דסלקא דעתין הא דנמלך והוציאו הוי עקירה שניה. **אבל** לכתף מאי פטור כו'. אפילו הוי לכתף חייב, הוי מצי למיפרך דליפלוג בדידיה, בין עמד ללא עמד כלל.

מהלך

עין משפט נר מצוה

י א מיי' פ"ג מהל' גניבה הלכה ב:

יא ב ג מיי' שם טוש"ע ח"מ סימן שנא:

יב ד ה מיי' פי"ג מהל' שבת הלכה יב:

תוספות רי"ד

א"ר אבין הזורק חץ מתחילת ד' לסוף ד' וקרע שיראין בהליכתו פטור שעקירה צורך הנחה היא. פי' ומההיא שעתא אתחלה לה מלאכה והלכך אע"ג דחיוב ממון מקמי הנחה אתיא ליה פטור הואיל א) וכן עקיר להנחה אתיא לה מיתה ותשלומין באין כאחד ולא תימא תשלומין קדמי למיתה: תניא הגונב כיס בשבת חייב. פי' חייב בתשלומין אע"פ שנהרג שכבר נתחייב בגניבה קודם שיבוא לידי איסור שבת פי' דמשעה דאגבהה קניא שהגבהה קונה בכ"מ אפילו ברה"ר. ופי' אף להתחייב באונסים מתחייב בנפשו לא הוי עד דמפיק ליה היה מגרר ויוצא פירוש שלא הגביהו ברשות הבעלים ולא קנאה אלא בהוצאה מרשות בעלים פטור. שהרי איסור שבת ואיסור גניבה באין כא'. בפ' בן סורר ומורה מוקי לה כגון דשדייה בנהרא שאין הכים בעין שאם הוא בעין א"י לזכות בו אלא בעל הכים בא ונוטלו.

א) נראה דל"ל הואיל דהא דקא עקיר להנחה אתיא לה הוי לה מיתה ותשלומין וכו'.

[וע"ע תוס' עירובין עט: ד"ה צריך ותוס' קדושין כו. ד"ה אי נמי ותוס' ב"ק כט: ד"ה אלא]

מסורת הש"ס

ב"ק קיז.

[מנחות ע.]

ב"ב פו. סנהדרין עב. שבת לא: תוספתא דב"ק פט

שבת ה: עירובין כ: ע"ש

גליון הש"ס

גמ' הגונב כיס בשבת. עיין ירושלמי ב"ק פ"ג הלכה ד:

הגהות מהר"ב רנשבורג

א] תוס' ד"ה הכא וכו' לא פריך מידי. עי' פ"י בשם הרא"ה דלהך לישנא נמי פריך ולדבריו צ"ל דרב ביבי בר אביי המותיב לית ליה אוכא בינייהו דעביד הש"ס לעיל בסמוך. ועי' הרא"ה ושיטה מקובצת בשם הרמב"ן והרא"ה וקרובים דבריהם לדברי וזה ברור ודו"ק:

[וכן רוצה לומר הספר התם מתחיל האיסור משעת עקירה הכא אין האיסור מתחיל אלא משעת אכילה דאי בעי גחין ואכיל ליה בלא הגבהה אבל באם לא היה אפשר בלא הגבהה היה מתחיל נמי האיסור משעת הגבהה. ת"י]

פָּטוּר, אַדְּתָנֵי הָיָה מְגָרֵר וְיוֹצֵא מְגָרֵר וְיוֹצֵא פָּטוּר, נִפְלוֹג וְנִיתְנֵי בְּדִידָהּ: בַּמֶּה דְּבָרִי' אֲמוּרִים בְּעוֹמֵד לָפוּשׁ, אֲבָל לְכַתֵּף – פָּטוּר! אֶלָּא הָא מַנִּי – *בֶּן עַזַּאי הִיא, דְּאָמַר: מְהַלֵּךְ כְּעוֹמֵד דָּמֵי. אֲבָל זוֹרֵק מַאי – פָּטוּר, נִיפְלוֹג [וְנִיתְנֵי] בְּדִידָהּ: בַּמֶּה דְּבָרִים אֲמוּרִים – בִּמְהַלֵּךְ, אֲבָל זוֹרֵק – פָּטוּר! מְגָרֵר וְיוֹצֵא אִיצְטְרִיכָא לֵיהּ, ס"ד אָמִינָא: אֵין דֶּרֶךְ הוֹצָאָה בְּכָךְ, קמ"ל. וּבְמַאי? אִי בְּרַבְרְבֵי – אוֹרְחֵיהּ הוּא, אִי בְּזוּטְרֵי – לָאו אוֹרְחֵיהּ הוּא! אֶלָּא, בְּמִיצְעֵי. וּדְאַפְּקֵיהּ לְהֵיכָא? אִי דְּאַפְּקֵיהּ לִרְהַ"ר אִיסּוּר שַׁבָּת – אִיכָּא, אִיסּוּר גְּנֵיבָה – לֵיכָּא, אִי דְּאַפְּקֵיהּ לִרְשׁוּת הַיָּחִיד – אִיסּוּר גְּנֵיבָה אִיכָּא, אִיסּוּר שַׁבָּת – לֵיכָּא! לָא צְרִיכָא, דְּאַפְּקֵיהּ לְצִידֵּי רְשׁוּת הָרַבִּים. וּכְמַאן? אִי כְּר' אֱלִיעֶזֶר, דְּאָמַר: *צִידֵּי רה"ר כִּרה"ר דָּמוּ אִיסּוּר שַׁבָּת אִיכָּא אִיסּוּר גְּנֵיבָה לֵיכָּא, אִי כְּרַבָּנַן דְּאָמְרִי צִידֵּי רה"ר לָאו כִּרה"ר דָּמוּ – אִיסּוּר גְּנֵיבָה אִיכָּא, אִיסּוּר שַׁבָּת לֵיכָּא. לְעוֹלָם כְּר' אֱלִיעֶזֶר, וְכִי אָמַר ר"א צִידֵּי רה"ר כִּרה"ר דָּמוּ – הָנֵי מִילֵּי לְעִנְיַן חִיּוּבָא דְּשַׁבָּת, דְּזִימְנִין דְּדָחֲקֵי רַבִּים וְעָיְילֵי לְהָתָם, [א]אֲבָל לְעִנְיַן מִיקְנָא – קָנֵי, מ"ט – דְּהָא לָא שְׁכִיחִי רַבִּים. רַב אַשִׁי אָמַר: כְּגוֹן שֶׁצֵּירֵף יָדוֹ לְמַטָּה מִשְּׁלֹשָׁה וְקִיבְּלוֹ, כִּדְרָבָא. דְּאָמַר רָבָא: *[ב]יָדוֹ שֶׁל אָדָם חֲשׁוּבָה לוֹ כְּאַרְבָּעָה עַל אַרְבָּעָה. רַב אַחָא מַתְנֵי הָכִי. רָבִינָא מַתְנֵי: לְעוֹלָם דְּאַפְּקֵיהּ לִרה"ר [ג]וּבִרה"ר נַמִּי קָנָה. וְתַרְוַיְיהוּ בְּדִיוּקָא דְּהָא מַתְנִי' קָמִיפַּלְגִי, דִּתְנַן: *[ד]הָיָה מוֹשְׁכוֹ וְיוֹצֵא, וּמֵת בִּרְשׁוּת בְּעָלִים – פָּטוּר, הִגְבִּיהוֹ אוֹ שֶׁהוֹצִיאוֹ מֵרְשׁוּת בְּעָלִים וּמֵת – חַיָּיב. רָבִינָא דָּיֵיק מֵרֵישָׁא, רַב אַחָא דָּיֵיק מִסֵּיפָא. רָבִינָא דָּיֵיק מֵרֵישָׁא: הָיָה מוֹשְׁכוֹ וְיוֹצֵא, וּמֵת בִּרְשׁוּת בְּעָלִים – פָּטוּר. טַעְמָא – דְּמֵת בִּרְשׁוּת בְּעָלִים, [ה]הָא הוֹצִיאוֹ מֵרְשׁוּת בְּעָלִים וּמֵת – חַיָּיב. רַב אַחָא דָּיֵיק מִסֵּיפָא: הִגְבִּיהוֹ אוֹ שֶׁהוֹצִיאוֹ, הוֹצָאָה דּוּמְיָא דְּהַגְבָּהָה; מָה הַגְבָּהָה – דְּאָתֵי לִרְשׁוּתֵיהּ, אַף הוֹצָאָה נַמִּי – דְּאָתֵי לִרְשׁוּתֵיהּ. לְרַב אַחָא קַשְׁיָא רֵישָׁא, לְרָבִינָא קַשְׁיָא סֵיפָא! רֵישָׁא לְרַב אַחָא לָא קַשְׁיָא: כַּמָּה דְּלָא אָתֵי לִרְשׁוּתֵיהּ – רְשׁוּת בְּעָלִים קָרֵינָא בֵּיהּ. סֵיפָא לְרָבִינָא לָא קַשְׁיָא: הוֹצָאָה דּוּמְיָא דְּהַגְבָּהָה – לָא אָמְרִינַן. § הַבָּא עַל אֲחוֹתוֹ וְעַל אֲחוֹת אָבִיו כו'. § וּרְמִינְהוּ: *[ו]אֵלּוּ הֵן הַלּוֹקִין: הַבָּא עַל אֲחוֹתוֹ, וְעַל אֲחוֹת אָבִיו, וְעַל אֲחוֹת אִמּוֹ, וְעַל אֲחוֹת אִשְׁתּוֹ, וְעַל אֵשֶׁת אָחִיו, וְעַל אֵשֶׁת אֲחִי אָבִיו, וְעַל הַנִּדָּה. וְקַיְימָא

פָּטוּר. מִתַּשְׁלוּמִין, דְּאָתֵי עֲלֵיהּ חִיּוּב שַׁבָּת מֵחֲמַת הַגְבָּהָה רִאשׁוֹנָה שֶׁבָּהּ נִקְנָה לוֹ הַכִּיס, וּמִיתָה וְתַשְׁלוּמִין בָּאִין כְּאֶחָד. נִיפְלוֹג בְּדִידָהּ. בְּמַגְבִּיהַּ עַצְמוֹ יָכוֹל לִשְׁנוֹת בּוֹ חִיּוּב וּפְטוּר. אֶלָּא. לָא תּוֹקְמָהּ כְּשֶׁעָמַד, וְאַפ"ה חִיּוּב שַׁבָּת דַּעֲקִירָה לָאו מֵחֲמַת עֲקִירָה רִאשׁוֹנָה דְּהַגְבָּהָה אָתְיָא לֵיהּ, אֶלָּא בַּעֲקִירַת גּוּפוֹ שֶׁל פְּסִיעָה אַחֲרוֹנָה כְּשֶׁיּוֹצֵא מִן הַבַּיִת, וּבֶן עַזַּאי הִיא. דְּאָמַר. בְּפ"ק דְּשַׁבָּת. מְהַלֵּךְ כְּעוֹמֵד דָּמֵי. וַעֲקִירַת כָּל פְּסִיעָה הָוְיָא עֲקִירָה, וְהַנָּחַת הָרֶגֶל הִיא הַנָּחָה, הִלְכָּךְ קָנְיֵיהּ מִשְּׁעַת הַגְבָּהָה, וְחִיּוּב מִיתָה בִּפְסִיעָה בַּתְרַיְיתָא קָא אָתְיָא לֵיהּ. אֲבָל זוֹרֵק מַאי. הִגְבִּיהוֹ וּזְרָקוֹ. פָּטוּר. מִתַּשְׁלוּמִין, דְּאָתְיָא לֵיהּ חִיּוּב שַׁבָּת ע"י חִיּוּב הַגְבָּהָה, דְּתוּ לֵיתָא עֲקִירָה אַחֲרִיתִי. אֵין דֶּרֶךְ הוֹצָאָה בְּכָךְ. וְאֵין כָּאן חִיּוּב שַׁבָּת. וּבְמַאי. אִיצְטְרִיךְ לְאַשְׁמוּעִינַן דְּדֶרֶךְ הוֹצָאָה בְּכָךְ. אִי בְּרַבְרְבֵי. כִּיס גָּדוֹל שֶׁיֵּשׁ בּוֹ מַשּׂוֹי לְהַגְבִּיהוֹ. אוֹרְחֵיהּ הוּא. לְגָרְרוֹ, וּפְשִׁיטָא דְּהוֹצָאָה הִיא. לָאו אוֹרְחֵיהּ הוּא. וְאַמַּאי חַיָּיב מִשּׁוּם שַׁבָּת? אִיסּוּר גְּנֵיבָה לֵיכָּא. דִּמְשִׁיכָה בְּלֹא הַגְבָּהָה, קס"ד דְּלָא קָנְיָא בִּרה"ר. לִרְשׁוּת הַיָּחִיד. לִרְשׁוּתוֹ, שֶׁהָיְתָה חֲצֵירוֹ סְמוּכָה לַחֲצַר הַבְּעָלִים. צִידֵּי רה"ר. סָמוּךְ לַבָּתִּים, שֶׁנּוֹתְנִין לְהַלָּן מִן הַבָּתִּים אֲבָנִים וּמִכְשׁוֹלִין לְהַרְחִיק חִיכּוּךְ הָעֲגָלוֹת. וּמֵאוֹתָן חִיפּוּפֵי וְלִפְנִים קָרֵי צִידֵּי רה"ר. פְּלוּגְתָּא דְּרַבִּי אֱלִיעֶזֶר וְרַבָּנַן בְּעֵירוּבִין בְּפֶרֶק "כָּל גַּגּוֹת". דְּהָא לָא שְׁכִיחִי רַבִּים. וַהֲוֵי לֵיהּ כְּסִימְטָא, דְּתִיקּוּן בָּהּ מְשִׁיכָה. רַב אַשִׁי אָמַר. מְגָרֵר וְיוֹצֵא דְּקָאָמַר פָּטוּר – לְעוֹלָם בִּרְשׁוּת הָרַבִּים, וּדְקַשְׁיָא לָךְ אִיסּוּר גְּנֵיבָה לֵיכָּא. כְּגוֹן שֶׁצֵּירַף יָדוֹ. הַשְּׁנִיָּה לְפָחוֹת מִשְּׁלֹשָׁה סָמוּךְ לַקַּרְקַע, וּבְיָדוֹ אַחַת גֵּירְרָהּ, וְנָפְלָה לְתוֹךְ חֲבֶרְתָּהּ, וְיָדוֹ קָנְיָא לֵיהּ. כִּדְרָבָא דְּאָמַר רָבָא יָדוֹ שֶׁל אָדָם חֲשׁוּבָה. לְעִנְיַן הַנָּחַת שַׁבָּת, כְּמָקוֹם אַרְבָּעָה עַל אַרְבָּעָה. וְכִי הֵיכִי דִּלְעִנְיַן שַׁבָּת חָשׁוּב מָקוֹם – לְעִנְיַן מִיקְנָא נַמִּי חָשׁוּב מָקוֹם לְמִיקְנֵי, כְּאִילּוּ הִגְבִּיהָהּ לְמַעְלָה מִשְּׁלֹשָׁה. וּמִיהוּ, בִּרְשׁוּת הַיָּחִיד לָא אַגְבְּהָהּ דְּתִיקְנֵי לֵיהּ מִקַּמֵּי דְּלֵיתֵי חִיּוּב שַׁבָּת עֲלֵיהּ, וּבִיאָתָהּ לִרה"ר וּקְנִיָּיתָהּ בָּאִין כְּאֶחָד. וּלְהָכִי מְשַׁנֵּי כְּשֶׁצֵּירַף, דְּלָא תֶּיהֱוֵי הַגְבָּהָה בִּרְשׁוּת הַיָּחִיד, כִּדְקָתָנֵי "מְגָרֵר וְיוֹצֵא". רַב אַחָא מַתְנֵי הָכִי. כְּדַאֲמַרַן, דִּמְשִׁיכָה בִּרְשׁוּת הָרַבִּים לָא קָנֵי, וּמוֹקִים לָהּ כְּשֶׁצֵּירַף יָדוֹ וְקִיבְּלָהּ לְתוֹכָהּ. הָיָה מוֹשְׁכוֹ. בְּגוֹנֵב בְּהֵמָה בִּרְשׁוּת בְּעָלִים קָאֵי, בְּפֶרֶק "מְרוּבֶּה". וּמֵת. הַשּׁוֹר. בִּרְשׁוּת הַבְּעָלִים פָּטוּר. הַגַּנָּב מִלְּשַׁלֵּם כְּלוּם, דְּלָא קָנֵי לְהִתְחַיֵּיב בְּאוֹנָסִין. הִגְבִּיהוֹ. אֲפִי' בִּרְשׁוּת הַבְּעָלִים. הָא הוֹצִיאוֹ. כָּל הֵיכָא דְּאַפְּקֵיהּ, וַאֲפִי' לִרה"ר. אֵלּוּ הֵן הַלּוֹקִין. אִם הִתְרוּ בָּהֶן. וְקַיְימָא לָן דְּאֵין לוֹקֶה וּמְשַׁלֵּם. דְּנַפְקָא לָן לְקַמָּן מִ"כְּדֵי רִשְׁעָתוֹ" – מִשּׁוּם רִשְׁעָה אַחַת אַתָּה מְחַיְּיבוֹ, וְאִי אַתָּה מְחַיְּיבוֹ מִשּׁוּם שְׁתֵּי רִשְׁעָיוֹת. מַתְנִי'

מהלך בעומד דמי. ומעביר ארבע אמות דחייב ברה"ר – הלכתא גמירי לה, כדאמרינן ב"הזורק" (שבת דף צו:) ולא ילפינן מינה, דהתם מקום חיובא הוא. אבל בן עזאי מיירי במהלך מחנות לפלטיא דרך סטיו שהוא מקום פטור. ובירושלמי פריך: לבן עזאי היכי משכחת מעביר ד"א ברה"ר דמיחייב? ומשני: בקופץ*.

אבל זורק מאי פטור ליפלוג וליתני בדידה. משום הכי חשיב זורק בדידה טפי ממגרר, משום דבמוציא ובזורק בשניהם בא בהגבהה הקנין, קודם שיבא חיוב הוצאה. אבל במגרר – ההוצאה והקנין באין כאחד.

מגרר ויוצא איצטריך ליה. לעיל דפריך: דליפלוג בין לפוש ובין לכתף, לא בעי לשנויי הכי, משום דלכתף פטור נראה לו חידוש טפי מחידוש דמגרר. [ועוד, דהכא לא הוי לגמרי בדידה, אבל לעיל, דהוי ממש בדידה – לא שייך לשנויי הכי].

אי דאפקיה לרה"ר איסור גניבה ליכא. אף על גב דאיכא למ"ד בפ"ק דב"מ (דף י. ושם) דד' אמות קונות לו לאדם אפילו ברה"ר – ה"מ גבי מציאה, דלא ליתו לאנצויי, ובגט משום עיגונא. אבל לגנב – לא תקינו שיקנו לו ד' אמות. **אלא** במיצעי. תימה לר"י: דבפרק "הספינה" (ב"ב דף פו. ושם) גבי דברים שדרכן להגביהן אין נקנין במשיכה אלא בהגבהה, ופריך מהגונב כיס, דבר הגבהה הוא, ומשני: במידי דבעי מיתנא. משמע דאי הוה אמר דבר הגבהה נמי נקנה במשיכה – הוה אתי ליה שפיר אפילו בזוטרי, ואמאי? הא על כרחך לא מצי איירי בזוטרי, דא"כ היכי מיחייב לענין שבת בגרירה? דאין דרך הוצאה בכך? וי"ל: דאפשר שיהא דרך הוצאה בכך אפילו בזוטרי, כגון שמוציאו דרך מחתרת, דדרכו בגרירה, ואינו נקנה אלא בהגבהה. אי נמי: הוה מצי למימר ולטעמיך, ולא פריך. וכן דרך התלמוד בכמה מקומות.

רב אשי אמר כגון שצירף ידו למטה מג' וקיבלה, וכדרבא. פירש בקונטרס, דקאי אמאי דפריך לעיל איסור גניבה ליכא, והשתא משני דאיכא נמי איסור גניבה, כדרבא. וקשה לר"י: חדא, דמה ענין חשיבות מקום ד' דלענין שבת לקנין? ועוד: דאין צריך שום ראיה להביא דקניא ליה ידו, דפשיטא ד"ונתן בידה" אמר רחמנא, כדפרישית לעיל. ועוד: *) דאמאי לא מוקי אפילו כשצירף ידו למעלה מג', כגון שהאסקופה גבוהה ג' דליכא הגבהה ברה"י, והוה מייתי מדרבא אקנין ואשבת! ונראה כגירסת הספר שמצא ר"י בן רבינו מאיר בספרי אשכנז דגרס: אי נמי כדרבא. וכולה מילתא אשבת קאי, כשצירף ידו למטה מג', דאע"ג דלא חשיבא לענין שבת הנחה אלא על גבי מקום ד', איכא הכא חיוב שבת כשצירף ידו למטה מג', דלמטה מג' לא בעינן מקום ד', דכלבוד דמי, *וכמונחת אארעא דמיא. אי נמי, אפי' צירף ידו למעלה מג', וכדרבא, דידו חשובה כד' על ד'. ור"ת ל"ג דאמר רבא ידו של אדם, אלא וכדרבא, ותו לא. ואתא לשנויי דמגרר ויוצא איצטריך ליה לאשמועינן, דאגד יד לא שמיה אגד, והא מייתי כדרבא דאמר ב"המצניע" (שבת דף צב.) דאגד יד לא שמיה אגד. ומיירי כשהוא נשאר בפנים והוציא ידו אחת, ובאחרת מגרר לתוכה. ודוקא צירף למטה מג', דלמעלה משלשה שמיה אגד, דבתר גופו גרירא. [ולפי' קמא קשה: דלשנויא קמא לית ליה דרבא, וכולהו מתנייתא דשבת וכן ר' יוחנן (שבת ה.) אתו כרבא]. **וברשות** הרבים נמי קנה. והא דאמר ב"המוכר את הספינה" (ב"ב פד:) דאביי ורבא דאמרי תרוייהו דמשיכה לא קניא ברה"ר, אומר ר"י: דלא פליגי אדרבינא דהכא, דהא דקאמר דקני – היינו לענין להתחייב באונסין, אבל אינו קונה שיהא שלו לגמרי. וריצב"א נראה לו דפליג, דהא ב"מרובה" (ב"ק דף עט. ושם) גבי נתנה לבכורות בנו דקתני סיפא, איכא נמי למידק כמו שמדקדק כאן. והתם לענין משיכה דקנין איירי, ללשון ראשון שפי' שם בקונט', ואפילו ללשון שני הא מוכח התם בגמ' (דף סה.) שאין לגנב להתחייב אלא במשיכה הראויה לקנין. **ורמינהי** אלו הן הלוקין הבא על אחותו. ארישא דמתניתין הוה מצי למיפרך, דקתני: הבא על הממזרת יש לה קנס, והתם קתני דלקי עלה, אלא נטר הכא עד "הבא על אחותו" למיפרך מרישא דמתניתין דהתם, דחייבי לאוין שנויין שם בתר חייבי כריתות והיה צריך להביא כל המשנה עד "הבא על הממזרת". וקיימא

*) [ור' אליהו פי' כגון שהאסקופה כרמלית ולהכי צריך כשצירף ידו למטה מג' מגב האסקופה דאי בתוך ג' לראשה הוי כרמלית כמו אסקופה עצמה ולא מחייב. ת"י]

עין משפט נר מצוה

יג א מיי' פ"ד מהל' מכירה הלכה ד טוש"ע ח"מ סימן קלח סעיף יז:

יד ב מיי' פי"ג מהל' שבת הלכה (טו) [ג]:

[ביתר ביאור כתבו תוס' שבת ה: ד"ה בשלמא]

טו ג מיי' פ"ג מהל' גניבה הלכה ב טור ש"ע ח"מ סימן שנח:

טז ד ה מיי' פ"ב מהל' גניבה הל' טז סמג עשין עא טוש"ע ח"מ סי' שמח סעיף ד:

יז ו מיי' פי"ט מהל' סנהדרין הלכה א:

תוספות רי"ד

ע"ש בפסקי: ובמאי. פי' ובמאי איצטריך לאשמועינן דדרך הוצאה בכך אי בגדול שיש בו משוי להגביה אורחיה הוא לגוררו ופשיטא דהוצאה היא ואי בזוטרא לאו אורחי' הוא ואמאי חייב משום שבת (איסור א) גניבה ליכא דמשיכה בלא הגבהה לא קניא ברה"ר) אלא במיצעי. פי' אם היה הכיס קטן שדרכו להוציאו בהגבהה והוציאו בגרירה פטור לענין שבת דהוצאה כלאחר יד הוא. וגם לענין קני' נמי אמרינן בפ' המוכר את הספינה דדברים שדרכן להגביהן אינן נקנים אלא בהגבהה לא במשיכה ומוקמי להא דתני היה מגרר ויוצא במידי דצריך מיתנא. ודאפקוה היכא אי דאפקי' לרה"ר איסור שבת איכא איסור גניבה ליכא פי' (אי) דמשיכה [אינה] קונה ברה"ר ואי דאפקה לרה"י איסור גניבה איכא איסור שבת ליכא ר"א אמר כגון שצירף ידו למטה מג' וקבלה. פי' מכי נפלה לתוך ידו איכא איסור גניבה שידו קונה לו ואיכא איסור שבת שכל פחות מג' כלבוד דמי וכאילו נחה ברשות הרבים דמי פי' המורה: לעולם הא דקתני מגרר ויוצא פטור לעולם דאפקה לרה"ר ודק' לך איסור גניבה ליכא איכא ודאי כגון שצירף ידו השנית לפחות מג' סמוך לקרקע ובידו הא' גירדה והפילה לתוך יד חברתה וידו של אדם קני' ליה כדרבא דאמר ידו של אדם חשובה לו כד' על ד'. פי' לענין הנחת שבת וכי היכי דלענין שבת חשיבא מקום לענין מיקנא נמי חשיב מקום למיקני' כאילו הגביה למעלה מג' מיהו ברה"י לא אגביה דתיקני לי' מקמי דליתי חיוב שבת עלי' ויציאתה וביאתה לרה"ר וקנייתה באין כא' ולהכי משני כשצירף דלא תהוי הגבהה ברשות היחיד כדקתני היה (מכנים) [מגרר] ויוצא. א"נ כדרבא ב) דאמר ידו של אדם חשובה לו כד' על ד'. פי' ואע"פ שהיתה למעלה מג' יש בה איסור שבת דידו של אדם פי' לענין שבת בעינן שיעשה הנחה ע"ג מקום חשוב שיש בו ד' על ד' והיד היא חשובה כד' על ד': רב אחא מתני הכי פי' כדאמרי' דמשיכ' ברה"ר לא קניא ומוקי לה כשצירף ידו וקבלה לתוכה. רבינא מתני לעולם דאפקיה לרה"ר וברה"ר נמי קני. פי' דמשיכה ברה"ר קונה. ואע"ג דקיי"ל דכל היכא דפליגי רב אחא ורבינא הלכתא כרבינא. הכא הלכתא כר"א משום דקיימו כוותיה אביי ורבא בפרק המוכר את הספינה ואמרי שאין משיכה קונה ברה"ר. ותלמודא נמי מקשה ממילתיה וקיי"ל שאין התלמוד מקשה אלא מהלכה פסוקה: הבא על אחותו וכו'. ורמינהו אלו הן הלוקין הבא על אחותו וכו' וקי"ל דאין לוקה המשלם. פי' דנפקא לן מכדי רשעתו משום רשעה א' אתה מחייבו ולא משום ב' רשעיות. פי' המורה והא דאוקי מתני' דמכות בבוגרת ולא אוקי מתני' דהכא בשלא היתרו בו ש"מ אפילו איתרו ביה נמי ממונא משלב וכו':

א) מתניתא איסור גניבה ליכא עד ברה"ר שייך להכן. ב) גירסת רבינו א"נ כדרבא וכ"ה בתוס' בד"ה רב אשי בשם הריב"ס.

מסורת הש"ס

[שבת ה: עירובין לג.]

שבת ו. עירובין לג.

שבת ה.

ב"ק עט.

מכות יג.

גליון הש"ס

תום' ד"ה רב אשי וכו' דקניא ליה ידו. עי' בב"ק כט ע"ב תוד"ה אלא אמר רב אשי:

[ורש"י דפי' לגריר בהגבהה הא דאמרי' בהספינה (דף כט:) כשהגביה בפחות מג' וקאמר דקני הא פי' התם בקונט' משום דהכי הפקר ואיכא למ"ד דאפ' הבטיה בהפקר קני ושיתופי מבואות דאמר שצריך שיגביה טפח התם נמי בעירוב הקילו. ת"י]

וקיימא לן דאינו לוקה ומשלם! אמר עולא: לא קשיא; כאן — באחותו נערה, כאן — באחותו בוגרת. אחותו בוגרת נמי, הא איכא [א]בושת ופגם! [ב]בשוטה. והא איכא [ג]צערא! במפותה. השתא דאתית להכי, אפי' תימא אחותו נערה — ביתומה ומפותה. אלמא קסבר עולא: כל היכא דאיכא ממון ומלקות — ממונא משלם, מילקא לא לקי. מנא ליה לעולא הא? גמר מחובל בחבירו: מה חובל בחבירו, דאיכא ממון ומלקות, ממונא משלם, מילקא לא לקי, אף כל היכא דאיכא ממון ומלקות, ממונא משלם, מילקא לא לקי. מה לחובל בחבירו — שכן חייב בחמשה דברים, ואי ממונא לקולא, שכן הותר מכללו בבית דין! אלא גמר מעדים זוממין, מה עדים זוממין דאיכא ממון ומלקות — ממונא משלם, מילקא לא לקי! אף כל היכא דאיכא ממון ומלקות — ממונא משלם, מילקא לא לקי! [ד]מה לעדים זוממין — שכן אינן צריכים התראה, ואי ממונא לקולא הוא — שכן לא עשו מעשה! אלא, גמר מתרוייהו; מה הצד השוה שבהן — דאיכא ממון ומלקות — ממונא משלם מילקא לא לקי, אף כל היכא דאיכא ממון ומלקות — ממונא משלם, מילקא לא לקי. מה להצד השוה שבהן — *שכן יש בהן צד חמור, ואי ממונא לקולא הוא — שכן יש בהן צד הקל!
אלא

רש"י

מתני' באחותו נערה. דאיכא קנס, וסבירא ליה דממונא משלם ולא לקי. והיא דמכות — בבוגרת, דאין לה קנס. בושת ופגם. דגבי קנס הוא דבעינן נערה, אבל בושת — ממונא הוא. ופגם. כאילו היא שפחה נמכרת בשוק, כמה פיחתה מדמיה להשיאה לעבד שיש לרבו קורת רוח הימנה, כדלקמן (דף מ:). והא בוגרת נמי איתא. בשוטה. שאין לה בושת, ודמים למכור בשוק נמי אין לה. והא איכא צערא. דהכי תנן במתניתין: המפתה נותן בושת ופגם וקנס. מוסיף עליו האונס, שנותן את הצער. במפותה. דאין לה צער, כדאמרי' לקמן בפירקין (ד' לט:): פקחות שבהן אומרות, מפותה אין לה צער. ביתומה. שקנסה ובושתה ופגמה שלה. ומפותה. כיון שהכל שלה — אין כאן חיוב ממון, דהא עבדא מדעתה, ואחולי אחלה גביה. שוטה לא גרסי', דבפקחת נמי אין שום חיוב ממון במפותה יתומה. קסבר עולא. דאוקי מתני' דמכות בבוגרת, ולא אוקמה למתני' דהכא בשלא התרו בו — שמעת מינה: אפי' אתרו ביה, נמי ממונא משלם ולא לקי. חובל בחבירו. איכא מלקות ד"לא יוסיף" (דברים כה), וממונא משלם, כדכתיב (שמות כא) "שבתו יתן". ואפילו אתרו ביה, נמי מרבי ליה לקמן בשמעתין בהדיא לתשלומין. מה לחובל בחבירו. דין הוא לידון בממון שהוא חמור ממלקות, שכן יש בו חומר אחר. שחייב בחמשה דברים. נזק צער ריפוי שבת ובושת. ואי ממונא לקולא הוא. וא"ת: ממון קל מן המלקות, ואין זו תשובה שהשבנו, דכ"ש בעלמא, מה זה שחמור להתחייב בחמשה דברים נדון בקלה שבשני חיובין שבהן — ק"ו לשאר חייבי ממון הקלין, שידונו בממון הקל, איכא למיפרך: מה לחובל בחבירו — שכן הותר מכללו בב"ד, דניתן רשות לב"ד להלקותו. תאמר בשאר חייבי ממון, כגון קנס דאונס ומפתה, שלא הותרו מכללן בב"ד. אלא גמר מעדים זוממים. במה מצינו. דאיכא ממון. ד"כאשר זמם". ומלקות. ד"לא תענה". ממונא משלם. לקמן יליף לה בשמעתין. שכן אין צריכין התראה. ונענשין במיתה או במלקות או בממון, ודין הוא שידונו בחמורה כי איכא תרתי. ואי ממונא קולא הוא. תשכחן בהן צד הקל, ודין הוא שידונו בקלה. שכן לא עשו מעשה. אלא בדיבורא בעלמא מיענשי. מתרווייהו. כי פרכת מה לחובל בחבירו שכן חייב בחמשה דברים — עדים זוממין יוכיחו, מה לעדים זוממין שכן אין צריכין התראה — חובל יוכיח; וחזר הדין.
תחת

תוספות

וקיימא לן דאינו לוקה ומשלם. נראה לר"י דלא פריך *אמתני' דהתם אמאי לוקה, דהא פשיטא דמשכחת לה מלקות בלא קנס, כגון בוגרת ומפותה או בעולה, אלא אמתניתין קשיא ליה: אמאי משלם קנס כיון דאיכא מלקות? ואפילו בלא אתרו ביה, מצינן למימר דס"ד דמקשה דחייבי מלקיות שוגגים פטורים מן התשלומין. ומשני עולא דמתניתין אפילו בהתרו בו, דממונא משלם ולא לקי, ורבי יוחנן משני דמיירי בלא התרו בו. ואזיל לטעמיה דאית ליה דחייבי מלקיות שוגגים חייבין בתשלומין. **דאין** לוקה ומשלם. תימה דבפ"ק דמכות (דף ד: ושם) משמע דבקנס לוקה ומשלם. דקאמר אפלוגתא דר' מאיר ורבנן דמעידין אנו באיש פלוני שחייב לחברו מאתים זוז: בשלמא רבנן — כי טעמייהו, משום רשעה אחת כו'. אלא ר"מ מ"ט? גמר ממוציא שם רע. מה למוציא שם רע — שכן קנס! קסבר ר"מ עדים זוממין נמי קנסא. משמע דלרבנן לא ילפינן ממוציא שם רע, משום דסברי דעדים זוממין ממונא, אבל קנסא ילפינן שפיר ממוציא שם רע דלוקה ומשלם! ועולא גופיה דדחיק הכא לשנויי: כאן באחותו נערה — הוא דמסיק התם הכי. וליכא למימר דמבושת ופגם שהן ממון פריך, דהא מדמשני: כאן באחותו בוגרת, משמע דלאו מבושת ופגם פריך, דא"כ לא הוה משני מידי! וי"ל: כיון דלרבנן דר' מאיר עדים זוממין לאו קנסא הוא, ולכך לא ילפינן ממוציא שם רע, אלא אין לוקין ומשלמין מ"כדי רשעתו", דהשתא אית לן למילף בכל דוכתין מעדים זוממין ולא ממוציא שם רע, דכל מלקיות ילפינן ממלקות דעדים זוממין, דסמיך ליה לאו דחסימה, ד"ארבעים יכנו" בעדים זוממין כתיב, ולפי שמפורש בהן מלקות — ילפינן כולהו לאוי דליהוי דומין ללאו דחסימה דסמיך ליה. וכי היכי דעדים זוממין אין לוקין ומשלמין בכל ענין, בין בממון בין בקנס, דמקרא מלא דבר הכתוב "כדי רשעתו" — משום רשעה אחת אתה מחייבו כו', אפילו נתחייבו קנס כגון בשעה שהעידו טבחו או מכרו שור של גניבה, הם או אחרים בשבילם — הכי נמי בכל מלקיות. ועוד תירץ ריצב"א: דרבנן נמי מצו סברי דעדים זוממין קנסא, ומ"מ לא ילפינן ממוציא שם רע, משום ד"כדי רשעתו" משמע בממון ומלקות. אבל לר"מ, משום בנין אב דמוציא שם רע, מוקי "כדי רשעתו" למיתה ומלקות, ומפיק ליה ממשמעותיה. אי נמי, טעמא דרבנן כדמפרש בירושלמי דמוציא שם רע חידוש הוא, דבדיבור גרידא מיחייב. דאע"ג דעדים זוממין נמי בדיבורייהו מיחייבי — מ"מ לא הוי חידוש כולי האי, דע"י דבורם היה נפסד, אבל במוציא שם רע — לא איתעבד מעשה בדבורו, אלא ע"י עדים. וכן משמע לקמן (דף לה:): דאפילו עדים זוממין קנסא — אין לוקה ומשלם קנס, דאמר: ולרבה דאמר לר"מ חידוש הוא שחידשה תורה בקנס מתני' במאי מוקים להו? ואמאי לא מוקים לה כר' עקיבא, דס"ל בפ' קמא דב"ק (דף ה.): עדים זוממין קנסא הוא, דלדידיה לא שמעינן דאית ליה מת ומשלם! אלא משמע דאין שום תנא דסבר לוקה ומשלם, אלא רבי מאיר לחודיה. **אלמא** קסבר עולא כל היכא דאיכא ממון ומלקות ממונא משלם מילקא לא לקי. וא"ת מנא ליה להש"ס, דלמא בעלמא סבר דמילקא לקי וממונא לא משלם, והכא דוקא הוא דמשלם ממונא דגלי קרא, כדאמרינן לעיל (דף כט:): "נערה" "נערה" "הנערה"? ואין לומר כמו שפירש ר"ת דאי ס"ל דבעלמא מילקא לקי ולא משלם, הוה ליה לאוקומי מתני' דמכות (דף יג.) נמי באחותו נערה והתרו בו, ומתני' בשלא התרו בו, אלא ודאי סבר דבעלמא נמי ממונא משלם ולא לקי, ולהכי לא הוה מצי לאוקומי מתניתין דמכות באחותו נערה. דאין זה דיוק, דאיכא למימר דעולא סבר לה כריש לקיש דלא בעי לשנויי: כאן בהתרו בו, כאן שלא התרו בו, כדאמרינן לקמן, דאין חילוק לדידיה דאית ליה דחייבי מלקיות שוגגין פטורין מן התשלומין בין התרו בו בין לא התרו בו, ואי מרבינן לקנס מקרא בלא התרו ה"ה התרו. ונראה לר"י דע"כ ס"ל ממונא משלם מילקא לא לקי, מדמרבינן מחד קרא חייבי לאוין ומחד חייבי כריתות, דאי בעלמא מילקא לקי, דלמא חד לחייבי עשה וחד לחייבי לאוין אע"ג דבעלמא לוקה ואינו משלם, *אבל חייבי כריתות לא, משום דבעינן אשה שיש בה הויה, וכדרבנן דאמרי קדושין תופסין בחייבי לאוין.

[ועוד פי' ר"ת דדייק דממונא משלם, מדפריך: בוגרת, והא איכא בושת ופגם! ומשני, בשוטה. ולא משני דלוקה ואינו משלם, אלא ודאי סבר דבעלמא נמי ממונא משלם ולא לקי. וקשה, דאין נראה שיהא זה מדברי עולא אלא תלמודא הוא דקאמר ליה! ועוד, מדמסיק: אלא [עולא] "תחת" "תחת" גמר — משמע דבקנס גופיה בעי קרא דממונא משלם, ואמאי לא שמעינן מ"נער" "נערה" "הנערה"?! ועוד, מאי קאמר "מנ"ל"? לעולא נימא דיליף בושת ופגם מקנס דרבי קרא! וכ"ת מקנס לא ילפינן, נילף מקנס וחובל ועדים זוממים! ועוד, היך דאבושת ופגם קאי, מאי קאמר בסמוך: מה לחובל שכן חייב בד' דברים, אטו בושת לאו חובל הוא?! וכמה ענייני חבלות שאין בהן כל ה' דברים כדאמר ב"החובל"! ומיהו ריב"ס פי' דהכי פריך: מה ללאו דחובל שכן פעמים יש בו כל ה' דברים, תאמר בלאו ד"ערות אחותך לא תגלה" שלעולם אין בו כל ה' דברים?! ופי' ר"י נראה עיקר].

ואי ממונא קולא הוא. וא"ת איתגורי איתגור שנידון בקלה? דהכי פריך בפרק "הנשרפין" (סנהדרין דף פא.) גבי מי שנתחייב שתי מיתות! וי"ל: דשאני הכא דחס רחמנא אממונא של נחבל. **שכן** יש בהן צד חמור. קשה דא"כ לא נלמד עוד מהצד השוה בשום מקום, דאכולהו איכא למיפרך או צד חמור או צד קל! ונראה לר"י דהכא פריך הכי: שכן יש בהן צד חמור משונה, כי ההיא דבפרק "ד' מיתות" (שם דף סו.): מה להצד השוה שבהן שכן משונין, גבי דיין נשיא וחרש. דהכא חמשה דברים שאין צריכין התראה הוי צד חמור יותר משאר דברים, וצד הקל נמי הוי קולא יתירא בחובל — שהותר מכללו, שמותר לחבול. בחבירו וכן עדים זוממין לא עשו מעשה הוי קולא יתירא, ואפילו למ"ד עקימת שפתים הוי מעשה, הא אמרי' בסנהדרין (דף סה: ושם): שאני עדים זוממין הואיל וישנן בראיה. *ובפרק "כשם" (סוטה כט:) יש לפרש נמי דפריך גבי טבול יום וכלי חרס: מה להצד השוה שבהן שכן צד חמור! דקרי צד חמור משונה: כלי חרס שמטמא באוירו. וטבול יום נמי יש לפרש בדוחק שקורא צד חמור מה שנעשה אב הטומאה במגע, שלא היה נראה שיהיה שום דבר אב הטומאה אלא אם כן טומאה יוצאה מגופו. ועוד יש לומר דצד חמור דהתם, היינו: דאיכא למפרך שכן במינו אב הטומאה, דנהי דכלי חרס אינו נעשה אב מכל מקום
יש

עין משפט נר מצוה

[נראה איפכא דאמתני' לא קשיא ליה הא דמשלם דהא רבי קרא חייבי לאוין וכריתות דמשלמין אלא אההיא מתני' קשיא ליה אמאי לוקה דמשמע ליה דאיירי התם בנערה דומיא דמתני' ומיהו איכא למימר דפריך אמתני' אמאי משלם בחייבי כריתות כדפי' ר"י בסמוך. ת"י]

יח א מיי' פ"ב מהלכות נערה הלכה יא טור אה"ע סימן קעז:

יט ב מיי' פ"ג מהל' חובל ומזיק הל' ז ופ"ב מהל' נערה הל' יא טור שם טוש"ע ח"מ סי' תכ סעיף לז:

כ ג מיי' פ"א שם הלכה ב סמג עשין ע טור אה"ע שם:

כא ד מיי' פי"ח מהל' עדות הלכה ז סמג עשין קי טור ח"מ סי' לח:

תוספות רי"ד

אמר עולא ל"ק כאן באחותו נערה כאן באחותו בוגרת אחותו נערה דאיכא קנס משלם ולא לקי. בוגרת דליכא קנס לקי פי' המורה מתני' דהכא בנערה. ומתני' דמכות בבוגרת. אלמא קסבר עולא כל היכא דאיכא ממון ומלקות ממונא משלם מילקי לא לקי דגמיר לה מחובל בחבירו ומעדים זוממין דממונא משלם ומילקי לא לקי. פי' חובל בחבירו איכא מלקות בלא יוסיף פן יוסיף. וממונא משלם כדכתיב רק שבתו יתן ואפי' אתרו בי' נמי עדים זוממין נמי (במה) מצינו דאיכא ממון דכאשר זמם ומלקות מלא תענה:

[ורשב"ל נמי לא אוקמי כרבנן משום חייבי כריתות ולר"י דאמר מלקי לקי כר' דסבר ממונא קילא דאי חומרא וכי אתגורי אתגור והשתא א"ש דקאמר מנ"ל הא דע"כ מדמוקי חד לחייבי כריתות נפקא ליה בעלמא דממונא משלם ולא לקי ולפי המסקנא דגמר תחת אילטריך קרא לחייבי עשה דאי לאו ההוא קרא הוי דרשי תחת לדרשא אחריתי ואידך לחייבי כריתות. ת"י]

[פסחים עז. סוטה כט: מכות ד:]

ת"י כ"י

הג"ה עיקר ויובא בא ע"י הראיה שבעדין שראו וראיה לית בה מעשה. לשון רש"י

עין משפט נר מצוה

כב א מיי' פי"ט מהל' סנהדרין הל' ד סי' קלא טוש"ע ח"מ סימן תכ סעיף ב:
כג ב מיי' פ"ד מהל' חובל ומזיק הל' א סמג עשין ע טוש"ע ח"מ סימן תכ סעיף ב:
כד ג מיי' פי"ח מהל' עדות הל' א סמג עשין קי טור ח"מ סי' לח:

גמרא

אֶלָּא, עוּלָּא "תַּחַת" "תַּחַת" גָּמַר, כְּתִיב הָכָא: (דברים כב) "תַּחַת אֲשֶׁר עִנָּהּ", וּכְתִיב הָתָם: (שמות כא) "עַיִן תַּחַת עַיִן", מָה הָתָם, מָמוֹנָא מְשַׁלֵּם מִילְקָא לָא לָקֵי – אַף כָּל הֵיכָא דְּאִיכָּא מָמוֹנָא וּמַלְקוּת – מָמוֹנָא מְשַׁלֵּם, מִילְקָא לָא לָקֵי. רַבִּי יוֹחָנָן אָמַר: אֲפִי' תֵּימָא אֲחוֹתוֹ נַעֲרָה. כָּאן – שֶׁהִתְרוּ בּוֹ, כָּאן – שֶׁלֹּא הִתְרוּ בּוֹ. אַלְמָא קָסָבַר רַבִּי יוֹחָנָן: כָּל הֵיכָא דְּאִיכָּא מָמוֹן וּמַלְקוּת, וְאַתְרוּ בֵּיהּ, מִילְקָא לָקֵי, מָמוֹנָא לָא מְשַׁלֵּם. מְנָא לֵיהּ לְר' יוֹחָנָן הָא? אָמַר קְרָא: (דברים כה) "כְּדֵי רִשְׁעָתוֹ" – *מִשּׁוּם רִשְׁעָה אַחַת אַתָּה מְחַיְּיבוֹ, וְאִי אַתָּה מְחַיְּיבוֹ מִשּׁוּם שְׁתֵּי רִשְׁעָיוֹת, וּסְמִיךְ לֵיהּ "אַרְבָּעִים יַכֶּנּוּ". וַהֲרֵי חוֹבֵל בַּחֲבֵירוֹ, דְּאִיכָּא מָמוֹן וּמַלְקוּת – מָמוֹנָא מְשַׁלֵּם, מִילְקָא לָא לָקֵי! וְכִי תֵּימָא: הָנֵי מִילֵּי הֵיכָא דְּלָא אַתְרוּ בֵּיהּ, אֲבָל אַתְרוּ בֵּיהּ – מִילְקָא לָקֵי, מָמוֹנָא לָא מְשַׁלֵּם, *וְהָאָמַר ר' אַמִּי א"ר יוֹחָנָן: הִכָּהוּ [א]הַכָּאָה שֶׁאֵין בָּהּ שָׁוֶה פְּרוּטָה – לוֹקֶה. הֵיכִי דָּמֵי? אִי דְּלָא אַתְרוּ בֵּיהּ – אַמַּאי לוֹקֶה? אֶלָּא פְּשִׁיטָא. דְּאַתְרוּ בֵּיהּ, וְטַעְמָא – דְּלֵית בָּהּ שָׁוֶה פְּרוּטָה, הָא אִית בָּהּ שָׁוֶה פְּרוּטָה – מָמוֹנָא מְשַׁלֵּם, מִילְקָא לָא לָקֵי! כִּדְאָמַר רַבִּי אֶילְעָא: בְּפֵירוּשׁ רִיבְּתָה תּוֹרָה עֵדִים זוֹמְמִין לְתַשְׁלוּמִין, [ב]הָכָא נַמִי, בְּפֵירוּשׁ רִיבְּתָה תּוֹרָה חוֹבֵל בַּחֲבֵירוֹ לְתַשְׁלוּמִין. וְהֵיכָא אִיתְּמַר דְּר' אֶילְעָא – אַהָא: *מְעִידִין אָנוּ אֶת אִישׁ פְּלוֹנִי שֶׁחַיָּיב לַחֲבֵירוֹ מָאתַיִם זוּז, וְנִמְצְאוּ זוֹמְמִין – לוֹקִין וּמְשַׁלְּמִין, שֶׁלֹּא הַשֵּׁם הַמְבִיאָן לִידֵי מַכּוֹת מְבִיאָן לִידֵי תַּשְׁלוּמִין, דִּבְרֵי ר"מ, וַחֲכָמִים אוֹמְרִים: [ג]כָּל הַמְשַׁלֵּם אֵינוֹ לוֹקֶה. וְנֵימָא: כָּל הַלּוֹקֶה אֵינוֹ מְשַׁלֵּם! א"ר אֶילְעָא: בְּפֵירוּשׁ רִיבְּתָה תּוֹרָה עֵדִים זוֹמְמִין לְתַשְׁלוּמִין. הֵיכָן רִיבְּתָה תּוֹרָה? מִכְּדִי כְּתִיב: (דברים יט) "וַעֲשִׂיתֶם לוֹ כַּאֲשֶׁר זָמַם לַעֲשׂוֹת לְאָחִיו". (שם) "יָד בְּיָד" לָמָּה לִי – דָּבָר הַנִּיתָּן מִיָּד לְיָד. וּמַאי נִיהוּ – מָמוֹן. חוֹבֵל בַּחֲבֵירוֹ נַמִי, מִכְּדִי כְּתִיב: (ויקרא כד) "כַּאֲשֶׁר עָשָׂה כֵּן יֵעָשֶׂה לוֹ", "כֵּן יִנָּתֶן בּוֹ" לָמָּה לִי – דָּבָר שֶׁיֵּשׁ בּוֹ נְתִינָה, וּמַאי נִיהוּ – מָמוֹן. וְרַבִּי יוֹחָנָן, מ"ט לָא אָמַר כְּעוּלָּא? אִם כֵּן בִּטַּלְתָּ (שם יח) "עֶרְוַת אֲחוֹתְךָ לֹא תְגַלֶּה" חוֹבֵל

מסורת הש"ס: לקמן לו. ב"ק פג: מכות ד: יג: | סנהדרין פה. מכות ט. | מכות ד.

רש"י

תַּחַת תַּחַת גָּמַר. וּגְזֵירָה שָׁוָה מוּפְנָה הִיא, וּלְמֵדִין וְאֵין מְשִׁיבִין. אֲפִי' תֵּימָא. הָהִיא דְּמַכּוֹת בַּאֲחוֹתוֹ נַעֲרָה, וּכְשֶׁהִתְרוּ בּוֹ – דְּאִיכָּא מָמוֹן וּמַלְקוֹת, וְאַשְׁמְעִינַן דְּלָקֵי וְלָא מְשַׁלֵּם. וּמַתְנִיתִין דִּכְתוּבּוֹת – בְּשֶׁלֹּא הִתְרוּ בּוֹ, דְּלֵיכָּא מַלְקוֹת. וּסְמִיךְ לֵיהּ אַרְבָּעִים יַכֶּנּוּ. דְּהֵיכָא דְּאִיכָּא שְׁתֵּי רְשָׁעִיּוֹת נֵיעֲבַד בֵּיהּ הַכָּאָה. בְּפֵירוּשׁ רִיבְּתָה. לְקַמֵּיהּ מְפָרֵשׁ הֵיכָא. שֶׁלֹּא הַשֵּׁם הַמְבִיאוֹ לִידֵי מַכּוֹת כו'. הַמִּקְרָא הַמְבִיאוֹ לִידֵי מַלְקוֹת אֵינוֹ מְבִיאוֹ לְתַשְׁלוּמִין. מַלְקוֹת מִ"לֹּא תַעֲנֶה", תַּשְׁלוּמִין מִ"כַּאֲשֶׁר זָמַם", וְכֵיוָן דִּשְׁנֵי שֵׁמוֹת הֵן – חַיָּיב עַל שְׁנֵיהֶם. נֵימָא כָּל הַלּוֹקֶה אֵינוֹ מְשַׁלֵּם. וְנִידַיְינֵיהּ בְּמַלְקוֹת, מַאי שְׁנָא מָמוֹן דִּפְשִׁיטָא לְהוּ? יָד בְּיָד. דִּסְמִיךְ לֵיהּ "לֹא תָחוֹס עֵינֶךָ, נֶפֶשׁ בְּנֶפֶשׁ" וגו'. כֵּן יִנָּתֶן. "כַּאֲשֶׁר יִתֵּן מוּם בָּאָדָם" וגו'. מַאי טַעְמָא לָא אָמַר כְּעוּלָּא. דְּגָמַר גְּזֵירָה שָׁוָה לְעוֹנְשׁוֹ מָמוֹן וְלֹא מַלְקוֹת לְכָל חַיָּיבֵי מָמוֹן וּמַלְקוֹת. אִם כֵּן. דְּפָטַרְתָּ בָּא עַל אֲחוֹתוֹ מִמַּלְקוֹת – בִּטַּלְתָּ לָאו שֶׁבָּהּ, שֶׁעוֹנֶשׁ לָאו בְּמַלְקוֹת. וּפָרְכִינַן

תוספות

יש במינו אב הטומאה יותר מככר שהרי יש בו שום כלי שהוא אב הטומאה, כגון כלי עץ, אבל שום אוכל אינו נעשה אב הטומאה. ועל שני הפירושים קשה לרשב"א: דנימא, התם אוכל ראשון יוכיח שאין במינו אב הטומאה ומטמא תרומה, אף אני אביא שני! וכי תימא: מה לאוכל ראשון שכן עושה שני בחולין? טבול יום יוכיח. וליכא למיפרך נמי השתא שכן משונה, דאין כאן שום שינוי! ונראה לפרש צד חמור דהתם לפי שבאין מכח אב הטומאה, דטבול יום וכלי חרס ואוכל ראשון כולם נגעו באב הטומאה, מה שאין כן בשני דלא נגע אלא בראשון. ור"ת מפרש: דגבי עדים זוממין שייך צד חמור משום דאותו צד חמור של חובל יכול להיות בעדים זוממין, אם העידו על אחד שחבל בחבירו והוזמו, דמשלמין חמשה דברים מה שרצו לחייבו. וצד הקל יש לפרש, שכן לאו דחובל ועדים זוממין אין בהן כרת אלא לאו גרידא, ולא נגמר מינייהו חייבי כריתות. וכן בפ"ק דמכות (דף ד:): דיליף ממוציא שם רע ועדים זוממין דלאו שאין בו מעשה לוקין עליו, ופריך: מה להצד השוה שבהם שכן צד חמור – יש לפרש כי הכא לרבינו תם ולרבינו יצחק. ובפרק "כיצד צולין" (פסחים דף עז.) גבי "במועדו" ואפילו בטומאה, דאמר: אי כתב בתמיד – שכן כליל, ואי כתב בפסח – שכן כרת, בתרוייהו – שכן יש בהן צד חמור! התם יש שום פירכא אחריתי דלא מצינו למילף במה הצד, ולא חש התלמוד לפרשה, ובטעם מועט מסתלק לומר דצריכי. **אלא** עולא תחת תחת גמר. מצינו למימר לפי מסקנא זו דלא קאמר עולא דממונא משלם ולא לקי – אלא בהנהו תלת דגלי בהו קרא. וליכא למימר דילפינן לעולא בכל דוכתא מ"תחת" "נתינה" "ישלם" "כסף", דמהאי גזירה שוה ילפינן* מיטב בכולהו. דדוקא לענין מיטב נתקבל, שהוא גוף התשלומין, דאם לא כן תקשי לר' יוחנן ולאביי דפליגי אעולא – דאטו מי לית להו גזירה שוה לענין מיטב? והכא לעולא אייתר ליה האי "תחת" למיפטר ממלקות מגזירה שוה דחובל בחברו. הלכך צריך לומר לקמן לעולא דנפקא ליה בושת ופגם מדרבא.

[**מנא** ליה לר"י הא. וא"ת: לעיל בעי מנא ליה לעולא דממונא משלם ולא לקי כו' והשתא בעי איפכא! וי"ל: דהכא משום ג"ש ד"תחת" "תחת" קאמר, מנ"ל לר"י דלא דרשינן ג"ש להכי? דג"ש זו נתקבלה לכ"ע בבכורות (דף יב.) לגבי בכור].

שלא השם המביאו לידי מלקות מביאו כו'. פירש בקונטרס: משום דממון ומלקות אתו מתרי קראי, מלקות מ"לא תענה" וממון מ"ועשיתם לו כאשר זמם". וקשה: דכ"ש דאי הוו כתיבי בחד קרא שילקה וישלם – שהיה לוקה ומשלם! ומיהו – שמא יש לפרש לפ"ה משום דממון ומלקות אתו מתרי קראי – אין לנו לבטל פסוק אחד לגמרי ולקיים האחר. אבל אם היו באים שניהם מ"ועשיתם לו כאשר זמם", כגון שהעידו על אחד שהוציא שם רע על אשתו, דבאין לחייבו ממון ומלקות – אין לוקין ומשלמין. ואין נראה לר"י: דלא מסתבר שלא יהו חייבין ממון ומלקות בכה"ג, כיון שרצו לחייבו שניהם! ונראה לר"י לפרש: שלא השם המביאו לידי מכות כו', כלומר שהתשלומין לא נכתבו בסמוך למלקות. דאם היה כתוב באותו פסוק עצמו "לא תענה ואם ענה ועשיתם לו כאשר זמם" – אז ודאי הוה אמינא דה"ל לאו שניתק לעשה, ולא ילקה עליו, אבל עתה שנכתב רחוק זה מזה – לא הוי ניתק לעשה. ולא דמי ללאו דגזילה דחשיב ליה ניתק לעשה בפ' בתרא דמכות (דף טז.) וב"שלוח הקן" (חולין קמא.) אע"ג דעשה ד"והשיב את הגזילה" לא כתיב אצל לאו ד"לא תגזול" – דהתם ודאי ע"כ הוא ניתק לעשה, שהרי עוקר גזילה מתחת ידו, אבל קרא ד"ועשיתם לו כאשר זמם" אינו עוקר הלאו ד"לא תענה", דעל ידי שאנו עושין לו "כאשר זמם" אינו נעקר עדותו, אלא ע"י שהוזם, הלכך לא חשבינן ליה ניתק לעשה, כיון שלא נכתב אחריו סמוך לו. והר"ר שלמה מדרוי"ש מפרש: שלא השם המביאו לידי מכות – דהיינו: "לא תענה", מביאו לידי תשלומין, פי': אינו בא להיות אזהרה לענוש תשלומין, כדאמרינן במכות, דממון לא בעי אזהרה. ועוד: דר' מאיר נפקא ליה אזהרה ל"כאשר זמם" מ"וכל ישראל ישמעו ויראו ולא יוסיפו" כדאמרינן בפ"ק דמכות (דף ד:), שאם היה צריך "לא תענה" לאזהרה ממון – אז לא היה לוקה עליו, דמחד לאו לא הוה ענשינן ליה ממון ומלקות.

[כדמשמע בפ"ק דמכות אההיא דתנן: מעידין אנו באיש פלוני שחייב מלקות מ' – לוקים שמונים, א' מ"ועשיתם כאשר זמם" וא' מ"לא תענה". ותכ"א: אין סופג אלא מ'. ורבנן האי "לא תענה" מאי עבדי ליה? מיבעיא להו לאזהרת עדים זוממים. ור"מ אזהרה נפקא ליה מ"וכל ישראל וגו'". משמע דאי לאו קרא אחרינא לאזהרה, מ"לא תענה" לא הוה ענשינן ליה תרי מלקיות. ולרבנן, אע"ג ד"לא תענה" לא צריך לאזהרת ממון, מ"מ אינו לוקה ומשלם משום "כדי רשעתו", ולא לקי לרבנן אלא כשמעידים שהוא בן גרושה דליכא כאשר זמם. ואע"ג ד"לא תענה" לאו שאין בו מעשה, ועוד דניתן לאזהרת מיתת ב"ד, הכא גלי קרא דלקי מ"והיה אם בן הכות הרשע"].

מכדי כתיב ועשיתם לו כאשר זמם יד ביד למה לי. וליכא למימר דלמה לי "יד ביד" דמ"ועשיתם לו כאשר זמם" משמע בהדיא ממון, דכמו שהיה רוצה לחייבו ממון כן יתחייב לו ממון? דמצינו למימר ד"כאשר זמם" איירי במיתה ומלקות אבל בממון – מילקא לקי ממונא לא משלם. ומיהו, קשה לישנא דמכדי כתיב "ועשיתם לו כו'" "יד ביד" למה לי, דמשמע דמייתורא דלא איצטריך לגופיה הוא דמפיק ליה, והא אפילו לא מייתר "יד ביד" משמע שפיר ממון, דליכא לפרושי יד ביד ממש כדנפקא לן ב"החובל" (ב"ק דף פג: ופד.) מ"עין תחת עין". ועוד, הא דקאמר גבי חובל בחבירו: "כן ינתן בו" למה לי, דבר הניתן מיד ליד, ומאי ניהו ממון. אימא הני מילי היכא דלא אתרו ביה דמ"כן ינתן בו" נפקא ב"החובל" נזק ולא מ"כאשר עשה", אבל היכא דאתרו ביה אימא דמילקא לקי? ונראה לר"י דהך סוגיא אתיא כמאן דמפיק התם "עין תחת עין" – ממון, מקרא ד"יד ביד", והיינו דקאמר: מכדי כתיב "ועשיתם לו כאשר זמם" ואי ס"ד *עין תחת עין ממש, א"כ "יד ביד" בעדים זוממין למה לי – מ"כאשר זמם" נפקא! אלא אייתר "יד ביד" למידרש דבר הניתן מיד ליד דהיינו ממון, אבל אי לא אייתר הוה אמינא יד ביד ממש. (א) **חובל** בחבירו מכדי כתיב כאשר עשה כן יעשה לו. דמשמע ממון, כדאוכחן מייתורא ד"יד ביד" כדפרישית. וא"כ "כן ינתן בו" למה לי? והא ליכא למימר דאתא להיכא דלא אתרו ביה, דמ"יד ביד" נפקא, אלא ע"כ לא איצטריך אלא היכא דאתרו ביה. ומיהו הא לא קשיא ליה אמאי איצטריך "כאשר עשה וגו'", דנשנה כאן לשום נורך, כדאמרינן: כל פרשה שנאמרה ונשנית כו'. אבל "כן ינתן בו" למה חזר ושנה שתי פעמים? אלא לומר לך דבר הניתן מיד ליד להיכא דאתרו ביה. והוא הדין דהוה מצי למימר מכדי כתיב "יד ביד" "כן ינתן בו" למה לי. **ורבי** יוחנן מ"ט **לא אמר** כעולא. והא ליכא למימר דלא שמיע ליה גזירה שוה ד"תחת" "תחת" – דהא ילפינן לה בבכורות* גבי בכור, ובכמה מקומות. **אם** כן בטלת ערות אחותך לא תגלה. וא"ת: כל לאו שאין בו מעשה ולאו הניתק לעשה ביטלנו הלאו כיון שאין לוקין עליו! הא לאו מילתא היא, דההיא לאו בר מלקות הוא, אבל הכא דשייך ביה מלקות, לית לן למידרש גזירה שוה לאפוקי מלקות מיניה, כיון דאיכא לאוקומי גז"ש אמילתא אחריתי.

אלא

מסורת הש"ס: [ב"ק ה.] | ת"י כ"י | ס"א יד תחת יד | [דף יב. נז.]

תוספות רי"ד

ור"י אמר אפילו תימא באחותו נערה. כאן שהתרו בו כאן שלא התרו בו אלמא קסבר ר"י כל היכא דאיכא ממון ומלקות מילקא לקי ממונא לא משלם פי' המורה. אפילו תימא ההיא דמכות באחותו נערה וכשהתרו בו דאיכא ממון ומלקות דלקי ולא משלם. ומתני' דהכא בשלא אתרו בי' דליכא מלקות כ"א ממון.

הגהות הב"ח

(א) תוס' ד"ה מכדי וכו' חובל בחבירו נמי מכדי הד"כ:

חובל בַּחֲבֵירוֹ נַמִי, א"כ, בִּטַּלְתָּ °"לֹא יוֹסִיף פֶּן יוֹסִיף"! עֵדִים זוֹמְמִין נַמִי, א"כ, בִּטַּלְתָּ °"וְהָיָה אִם בִּן הַכּוֹת הָרָשָׁע"! אֶלָּא עֵדִים זוֹמְמִין אֶפְשָׁר לְקַיּוּמָהּ בְּבֶן גְּרוּשָׁה וּבֶן חֲלוּצָה. – חוֹבֵל בַּחֲבֵירוֹ נַמִי, אִיכָּא לְקַיּוּמָהּ כְּגוֹן שֶׁהִכָּהוּ הַכָּאָה שֶׁאֵין בָּהּ שָׁוֶה פְּרוּטָה. אֲחוֹתוֹ נַמִי, אִיכָּא לְקַיּוּמָהּ בַּאֲחוֹתוֹ בּוֹגֶרֶת! (א)אָמַר לָךְ ר' יוֹחָנָן: הַאי "תַּחַת אֲשֶׁר עִנָּהּ" מִיבָּעֵי לֵיהּ לְכִדְאַבַּיֵי, *דְּאָמַר אַבַּיֵי: אָמַר קְרָא °"תַּחַת אֲשֶׁר עִנָּהּ", הַאי – "תַּחַת אֲשֶׁר עִנָּהּ", מִכְּלָל דְּאִיכָּא בּוֹשֶׁת וּפְגָם. וְעוּלָּא נָפְקָא לֵיהּ מִדְּרָבָא. דְּאָמַר רָבָא: אָמַר קְרָא: °"וְנָתַן הָאִישׁ הַשֹּׁכֵב עִמָּהּ לַאֲבִי הַנַּעֲרָה חֲמִשִּׁים כָּסֶף", הֲנָאַת שְׁכִיבָה – חֲמִשִּׁים, מִכְּלָל דְּאִיכָּא בּוֹשֶׁת וּפְגָם. רַבִּי *אֶלְיעֶזֶר אוֹמֵר: עֵדִים זוֹמְמִין מָמוֹנָא מְשַׁלְּמֵי וּמִילְקָא לָא לָקֵי, מִשּׁוּם [א]דְּלָאו בְּנֵי הַתְרָאָה נִינְהוּ. אָמַר רָבָא: תֵּדַע, נִיתְרֵי בְּהוּ אֵימַת? נִיתְרֵי בְּהוּ מֵעִיקָּרָא – [ב]אָמְרִי אִישְׁתַּלִּין. נִיתְרֵי בְּהוּ בִּשְׁעַת מַעֲשֶׂה – פָּרְשֵׁי וְלָא מַסְהֲדֵי. נִיתְרֵי בְּהוּ לְבַסּוֹף – מַאי דַּהֲוָה הֲוָה. מַתְקִיף לָהּ אַבַּיֵי: וְנִיתְרֵי בְּהוּ בְּתוֹךְ כְּדֵי דִּבּוּר! מַתְקִיף לָהּ רַב אַחָא בְּרֵיהּ דְּרַב אִיקָא: וְנִיתְרֵי בְּהוּ מֵעִיקָּרָא, וְנִרְמַז בְּהוּ רְמוּזֵי! הֲדַר אָמַר אַבַּיֵי: לָאו מִילְּתָא הִיא דַּאֲמַרִי: אִי סָלְקָא דַּעְתָּךְ עֵדִים זוֹמְמִין צְרִיכִין הַתְרָאָה, כִּי לָא מַתְרִינַן בְּהוּ לָא קָטְלִינַן לְהוּ – מִי אִיכָּא מִידֵּי דְּאִינְהוּ בָּעוּ קָטֵיל בְּלָא הַתְרָאָה, וְאִינְהוּ בָּעוּ הַתְרָאָה? הָא בָּעֵינַן "וַעֲשִׂיתֶם לוֹ כַּאֲשֶׁר זָמַם לַעֲשׂוֹת לְאָחִיו" וְלֵיכָּא. מַתְקִיף לָהּ רַב סָמָא בְּרֵיהּ דְּרַב יִרְמְיָה: אֶלָּא מֵעַתָּה, בֶּן גְּרוּשָׁה וּבֶן חֲלוּצָה, דְּלָא מִ"כַּאֲשֶׁר זָמַם" קָא מִיתְרַבֵּי, לִיבָּעֵי הַתְרָאָה! •אָמַר קְרָא: °"מִשְׁפַּט אֶחָד יִהְיֶה לָכֶם", *מִשְׁפָּט הַשָּׁוֶה לְכוּלְּכֶם. רַב שִׁישָׁא בְּרֵיהּ דְּרַב אִידִי אָמַר: חוֹבֵל בַּחֲבֵירוֹ נַמִי, מָמוֹנָא מְשַׁלֵּם וּמִילְקָא לָא לָקֵי – מֵהָכָא: °"וְכִי יִנָּצוּ אֲנָשִׁים וְנָגְפוּ אִשָּׁה הָרָה וְיָצְאוּ יְלָדֶיהָ", וְאָמַר רַבִּי אֶלְעָזָר: *בְּמַצּוּת שֶׁבְּמִיתָה הַכָּתוּב מְדַבֵּר, דִּכְתִיב: °"וְאִם אָסוֹן יִהְיֶה וְנָתַתָּה נֶפֶשׁ תַּחַת נָפֶשׁ". הֵיכִי דָּמֵי? אִי דְּלָא אַתְרוּ בֵּיהּ – אַמַּאי מִיקְטִיל, אֶלָּא פְּשִׁיטָא דְּאַתְרוּ בֵּיהּ, *[ג]וּמוּתְרֶה לְדָבָר חָמוּר הָוֵי מוּתְרֶה לְדָבָר הַקַּל, וְאָמַר רַחֲמָנָא: "וְלֹא יִהְיֶה אָסוֹן עָנוֹשׁ יֵעָנֵשׁ". מַתְקִיף לָהּ רַב אַשִׁי: מִמַּאי דְּמוּתְרֶה לְדָבָר חָמוּר הָוֵי מוּתְרֶה לְדָבָר הַקַּל, דִּלְמָא לָא הָוֵי? אִם תִּמְצָא לוֹמַר הָוֵי – מִמַּאי דְּמִיתָה חֲמוּרָה, דִּלְמָא

תורה אור: דברים כה; שם; שם כב; שם; ויקרא כד; שמות כא; שם

ופרכינן. חובל בַּחֲבֵירוֹ. דְּעַל כָּרְחָךְ בְּמָמוֹן נִידּוֹן – תִּקְשֵׁי: בִּטַּלְתָּ לָאו דְּ"לֹא יוֹסִיף פֶּן יוֹסִיף", שֶׁהוּא אַזְהָרָה לְמַכֶּה אֶת חֲבֵירוֹ! וְהָיָה אִם בִּן הַכּוֹת. בְּמַסֶּכֶת מַכּוֹת (דף ב:) מוֹקְמִינַן לָהּ בְּעֵדִים זוֹמְמִין. אֶלָּא. עַל כָּרְחָךְ, כֵּיוָן דְּרַבְּיֵיהּ קְרָא לְתַשְׁלוּמִין, אִיכָּא לְאוֹקְמָא לְעוֹנֶשׁ מַלְקוֹת דְּלָאו דִּידֵיהּ, בִּמְעִידִין אָנוּ אֶת אִישׁ פְּלוֹנִי כֹּהֵן שֶׁהוּא בֶּן גְּרוּשָׁה. דְּלֵיכָּא לְאוֹקְמֵי "כַּאֲשֶׁר זָמַם" וְלוֹמַר יְהֵא הוּא בֶּן גְּרוּשָׁה תַּחְתָּיו, אֶלָּא סוֹפֵג אֶת הָאַרְבָּעִים. וְהָכִי תְּנַן בְּמַסֶּכֶת מַכּוֹת. וְחוֹבֵל בַּחֲבֵירוֹ נַמִי מוֹקְמִינַן לֵיהּ בְּשֶׁאֵין בָּהּ שָׁוֶה פְּרוּטָה בְּכָל חֲמִשָּׁה דְּבָרִים שֶׁבָּהּ, כְּגוֹן שֶׁלֹּא פִּיחֲתוֹ מִכַּסְפּוֹ וּמִמְּלַאכְתּוֹ, וְרִיפּוּי לֹא הוּצְרַךְ, וְלֹא צַעַר הָיָה בָּהּ, וּבְשׁוֹטָה שֶׁאֵין לָהּ בּוֹשֶׁת. וְהָכָא נַמִי בַּאֲחוֹתוֹ מָצֵית לְאוֹקְמֵי מַלְקוֹת דִּידָהּ בְּבוֹגֶרֶת. אֲבָל נַעֲרָה – לִישַׁלֵּם וְלָא לִילְקֵי, הוֹאִיל וְרִיבְּתָה גְּזֵירָה שָׁוָה דְּ"תַחַת" "תַּחַת" לְתַשְׁלוּמִין. לְכִדְאַבַּיֵי. בְּשִׁילְהֵי פִּירְקִין, דְּפָרְכִינַן: וְאֵימָא חֲמִשִּׁים אָמַר רַחֲמָנָא מִכָּל מִילֵּי? וְשַׁנֵּי אַבַּיֵי: חֲמִשִּׁים *כֶּסֶף נִתְקַדְּשׁוּ תַּחַת קְנָס הָעִינּוּי, אֲבָל בּוֹשֶׁת וּפְגָם שֶׁהוּא בִּשְׁאָר חוֹבְלִים – לֹא כָּלַל כָּאן. הַשּׁוֹכֵב עִמָּהּ. קְרָא יְתֵירָא הוּא לִדְרָשָׁה, נֵימָא: וְנָתַן לַאֲבִי הַנַּעֲרָה חֲמִשִּׁים כֶּסֶף. מִכְּלָל דְּבוֹשֶׁת וּפְגָם. דְּלָאו מֵחֲמַת הֲנָאַת שְׁכִיבָה נִינְהוּ, שֶׁהֲרֵי יֶשְׁנָן בִּשְׁאָר חוֹבְלִים – לָא כַּיְילִינְהוּ בְּגַוַּויְיהוּ דְּהָנֵי. רַבִּי אֶלְעָזָר אוֹמֵר עֵדִים זוֹמְמִין דְּמָמוֹנָא מְשַׁלְּמֵי וְלָא לָקוּ. לָא צְרִיכִי קְרָא, דִּסְבָרָא הִיא דְּמַלְקוֹת לָא שַׁיָּיךְ בְּהוּ. דְּלָאו בְּנֵי הַתְרָאָה נִינְהוּ. קוֹדֶם עֵדוּת, כִּדְמְפָ' רָבָא וְאָזֵיל. הִלְכָּךְ, אִי אִיכָּא לְמֶעֱנְשִׁינְהוּ – לָא מַעַנְשִׁינַהוּ אֶלָּא מָמוֹן, דְּאֵין עוֹנֶשׁ הַגּוּף בְּלֹא הַתְרָאָה. וְאע"ג דְּגַבֵּי בֶּן גְּרוּשָׁה וּבֶן חֲלוּצָה עָנְשִׁינַן לְהוּ מַלְקוֹת בְּלֹא הַתְרָאָה – הָתָם גְּזֵירַת הַכָּתוּב, דְּאַשְׁכְּחַן בְּהוּ מַלְקוֹת בְּהֶדְיָא "וְהָיָה אִם בִּן הַכּוֹת", וּמוֹקְמִינַן לִקְרָא בְּמִידֵי דְּלָא מָצֵית לְמֶעֱנְשִׁינְהוּ מִ"כַּאֲשֶׁר זָמַם". אֲבָל הֵיכָא דְּמָצֵית לְמֵיעֲבַד בְּהוּ הֲזָמָה – לָא שַׁיָּיךְ בְּהוּ מַלְקוֹת. תֵּדַע. שֶׁאִי אֶפְשָׁר לְהַתְרוֹת בָּהֶם. מֵעִיקָּרָא. יוֹם אוֹ שָׁעָה קוֹדֶם שֶׁיָּעִידוּ הָעֵדוּת. אָמְרִי אִישְׁתַּלִּין. שָׁכַחְנוּ הַהַתְרָאָה, הֲרֵי שֶׁבָּטְלָה הַהַתְרָאָה. פָּרְשֵׁי וְלָא מַסְהֲדֵי. אֲפִילּוּ אֱמֶת. הוֹאִיל וְאָנוּ חֲשׁוּדִים בְּעֵינֵיכֶם, מַה לָּנוּ וְלַצָּרָה? לְבַסּוֹף. לְאַחַר שֶׁהֵעִידוּ. מַאי דַּהֲוָה הֲוָה. דְּכֵיוָן שֶׁהִגִּיד אֵינוֹ חוֹזֵר וּמַגִּיד, וְאֵינָן יְכוֹלִין לַחֲזוֹר. וְנִיתְרֵי בְּהוּ בְּתוֹךְ כְּדֵי דִּבּוּר. לְאַחַר שֶׁהֵעִידוּ, דְּתוֹךְ כְּדֵי דִּבּוּר כְּדִבּוּר דָּמֵי, וִיכוֹלִים לַחֲזוֹר. תּוֹךְ כְּדֵי דִבּוּר. כְּדֵי שְׁאֵילַת שָׁלוֹם. וְנִרְמַז רְמוּזֵי. בִּשְׁעַת הָעֵדוּת נִרְמוֹז לָהֶם רְמָזִים עַל הַהַתְרָאָה לְהַזְכִּירָם, וּבְלָשׁוֹן רַךְ, שֶׁלֹּא יַקְפִּידוּ. לָאו מִילְּתָא הִיא דַּאֲמַרִי. שֶׁיְּהוּ עֵדִים זוֹמְמִין צְרִיכִין הַתְרָאָה. ה"ג: דְּאִינְהוּ בָּעוּ לְמִיקְטַל בְּלֹא הַתְרָאָה, וְאִינְהוּ בָּעוּ הַתְרָאָה כו'. כַּאֲשֶׁר זָמַם. וְהֵם זָמְמוּ לַהֲרוֹג אֶת זֶה בְּעֵדוּתָן שֶׁלֹּא הָיָה וְלֹא נִבְרָא, וְלֹא הִתְרוּ בּוֹ הַהַתְרָאָה שֶׁהֵעִידוּ עָלֶיהָ. אֶלָּא מֵעַתָּה. דְּהַאי דְּלָא בָּעוּ הַתְרָאָה מִשּׁוּם "כַּאֲשֶׁר זָמַם" הוּא, מַלְקוֹת שֶׁל זוֹמְמֵי עֵדוּת בֶּן גְּרוּשָׁה וּבֶן חֲלוּצָה. דְּלָאו מִכַּאֲשֶׁר זָמַם אָתֵי. עוֹנֶשׁ דִּידְהוּ, שֶׁהֲרֵי לֹא זָמְמוּ לְהַלְקוֹתוֹ אֶלָּא לְחַלְּלוֹ. מִשְׁפַּט הַשָּׁוֶה. וְכֵיוָן דְּרוֹב זוֹמְמִין לָאו בְּנֵי הַתְרָאָה נִינְהוּ, הָנֵי נַמִי לָא בָּעוּ הַתְרָאָה. בְּמַצּוּת שֶׁבְּמִיתָה. שֶׁמִּתְכַּוֵּין הָיָה לְהוֹרְגוֹ. הַכָּתוּב מְדַבֵּר. דִּכְתִיב "אִם אָסוֹן יִהְיֶה", שֶׁמֵּתָה הָאִשָּׁה – "וְנָתַתָּ נֶפֶשׁ", וְאע"פ שֶׁלֹּא נִתְכַּוֵּין אֶלָּא לַחֲבֵירוֹ. וְאַשְׁמְעִינַן: נִתְכַּוֵּין לַהֲרוֹג אֶת זֶה וְהָרַג אֶת זֶה – חַיָּיב. אִי דְּלָא אַתְרוּ בֵּיהּ. אִם תְּמִיתֶנּוּ תֵּהָרֵג. לְדָבָר חָמוּר. מִיתָה. הָוֵי מוּתְרֶה לְדָבָר הַקַּל. שֶׁאִם יַכֶּנּוּ וְלֹא יָמוּת יִלְקֶה, וַאֲפִילּוּ הָכִי אָמַר רַחֲמָנָא דְּכִי אֵין שָׁם חִיּוּב מִיתָה – יֵעָנֵשׁ דְּמֵי וְלָדוֹת, וְאַף עַל גַּב דְּאִיכָּא הַתְרָאָה לְמַלְקוֹת. אַלְמָא: מְשַׁלֵּם וְאֵינוֹ לוֹקֶה. נַגְדּוּהּ

לקמן מ:

ס"א כסף נתחייבו תחת

[ב"ק פג: פד. סנהדרין כח.]

סנהדרין עב. עט. [וע"ש על הגליון מ"ש בשם רש"י]

[סנהדרין פ:]

אלא אפשר לקיומי בבן גרושה או בבן חלוצה. ואם תאמר: אמאי לקו – אעדות דבן גרושה, הא הוי עדות שאין אתה יכול להזימה! ויש לומר: דלא חשיב עדות שאין אתה יכול להזימה אלא במעידין על הטרפה, דאי אפשר לקיומי בשום דבר, לא במיתה ולא במלקות, דגברא קטילא בעו למיקטל. אבל הכא נתקיימה הזמה במלקות*. **מיבעי** ליה לכדאביי. ואם תאמר: כיון דאיצטריך "תחת" להך דרשה, א"כ מנא לן מיטב? וי"ל: דיליף מנתינה או מכסף.

ועולא נפקא ליה מדרבא. משמע דרבא סבר כעולא, דרבי יוחנן גופיה הוה דריש כעולא אי לאו משום דמיבעי ליה לכדאביי. וקשה לרשב"א: דבפרק "השוכר את הפועלים" (ב"מ צא. ושם) משמע בהדיא דסבר כרבי יוחנן גבי חוסם פרה ודש בה – לוקה ומשלם, דמוקי לה אביי כרבי מאיר. ורבא אמר לעולם כרבנן, ואתנן אסרה תורה אפי' בא על אמו. פירוש: ומשלם לצאת ידי שמים. משמע דבדין לוקה ואינו משלם! ולמאי דפרישי' לעיל – דלמסקנא דווקא בהני תלת אית ליה לעולא דממונא משלם ולא לקי – אתי שפיר, דבעלמא סבר כרבי יוחנן דלוקה ואין משלם, כדדריש רבי יוחנן, וסמיך ליה "ארבעים יכנו".

ניתרי בהו מעיקרא וכו'. ואם תאמר: תיפוק ליה דהויא התראת ספק, דאין אנו יודעין אם מעידים שקר? ויש לומר: דהתראת ספק לא הויא אלא כגון אל תותיר, שאף למותרה עצמו הוא ספק, שסבור שעדיין יש שהות ביום, אבל הכא המותרין יודעין שמעידין שקר.

וניתרי בהו בתוך כדי דבור. ואם תאמר: היכי מצי תו הדרי בהו? והא בהתראה איכא טפי מכדי דבור, שהוא כדי שאילת שלום! ויש לומר: דכל זמן שעסוקים באותו דבר חשיב הכל תוך כדי דבור, כדאמרינן במכות (דף ו.) דאפי' מעידין מאה, כל אחד תוך כדי דבור של חבירו – חשובין כולן תוך כדי דבור של ראשון, ואם נמצא אחד מהן קרוב או פסול – עדותן בטילה.

אלא פשיטא דאתרו ביה. וא"ת: היכי משלם ממון אפי' כי אין אסון? הא כיון דמתכוין להרוג – הוי ליה רודף, ומתחייב בנפשו, וקים ליה בדרבה מיניה! וי"ל: בשיכולין להצילו באחד מאבריו. והכי אמרינן ב"בן סורר" (סנהדרין דף עד.).

ממאי דמותרה לדבר חמור הוי מותרה לדבר הקל דלמא לא הוי. אין לומר דטעמא משום דאהריגה הוא דקיבל התראה, דניחא ליה ליהרג על מנת שיהרוג שונאו, ד"תמות נפשי עם פלשתים" הוא דקאמר. אבל לא ניחא ליה להכות את חבירו על מנת שילקוהו. דהא אמתני' דפרק "הנשרפין" (סנהדרין ד' עט:) דקתני דחייבי מיתות שנתערבו ידונו בקלה, וקאמר בגמ' (שם דף פ:): ש"מ מותרה לדבר חמור הוי מותרה לדבר הקל. והתם פשיטא דכיון דהתרו בו לסקילה וקבל – כ"ש שאם התרו בו חנק על אותו דבר עצמו שהיה מקבל. ואפ"ה בעי למימר דמותרה לדבר חמור לא הוי מותרה לדבר הקל. אלא יש לומר דגזירת הכתוב הוא, דבעינן שיתיר עצמו לאותה מיתה, בין קלה בין חמורה. ודלמא

כה א מיי' פי"ח מהל' עדות הל' ז סמג עשין קי טור ח"מ סי' לח:

[ועיין תוס' מכות ב. ד"ה מעידין וכו' ביתר ביאור]

כו ב ג מיי' פי"ב מהל' סנהדרין הלכה ב [דין דמותרה לדבר חמור לא מצאתי במיי' שם מבואר רק כשהתרו בו בשתי מיתה פסק דהוי התראה והיינו דהוי כמקבל עליו בין מיתה חמורה כגון סקילה ובין קלה אבל כשהתרו בו בחמורה לבד לא נתבאר שם ועי' בתוספות דהכא סד"ה אמאי וכו' דגזירת הכתוב הוא וכו']

[נ"ל אלעזר]

הגהות הב"ח

(א) גמ' אמר לך ר"י נ"ב ס"א אלא ר' יוחנן:

גליון הש"ס

גמ' אמר קרא משפט אחד. עיין מכות דף ד ע"ב ברש"י ד"ה עדים זוממין א"צ התראה ונע"ק:

עין משפט
נר מצוה

כז א מיי' פ"ד מהל' רוצח ושמירת נפש הל' ג:
כח (ב) ג מיי' פ"ג מהל' גניבה הל' ו:
כט ד מיי' פ"ב שם הל' י:
ל ה מיי' פ"ג שם ה"ג

תורה אור

דִּלְמָא מַלְקוֹת חָמוּר? דְּאָמַר רַב: אִילְמָלֵי נַגְּדוּהּ לַחֲנַנְיָה מִישָׁאֵל וַעֲזַרְיָה — פָּלְחוּ לְצַלְמָא! א"ל רַב סָמָא בְּרֵיהּ דְּרַב אַסִּי לְרַב אַשִׁי, וְאָמְרִי לָהּ רַב סָמָא בְּרֵיהּ דְּרַב אַשִׁי לְרַב אַשִׁי: וְלָא שָׁנֵי לָךְ בֵּין הַכָּאָה שֶׁיֵּשׁ לָהּ קִצְבָה לְהַכָּאָה שֶׁאֵין לָהּ קִצְבָה?! מַתְקִיף לָהּ רַב יַעֲקֹב מִנְּהַר פְּקוֹד: הָנִיחָא לְרַבָּנַן *דְּאָמְרִי נֶפֶשׁ מַמָּשׁ, אֶלָּא לְרַבִּי דְּאָמַר *מָמוֹן מַאי אִיכָּא לְמֵימַר? אֶלָּא אָמַר רַב יַעֲקֹב מִנְּהַר פְּקוֹד מִשְּׁמֵיהּ דְּרָבָא: מֵהָכָא: °"אִם יָקוּם וְהִתְהַלֵּךְ בַּחוּץ עַל מִשְׁעַנְתּוֹ וְנִקָּה הַמַּכֶּה". *וְכִי תַּעֲלֶה עַל דַּעְתְּךָ שֶׁזֶּה מְהַלֵּךְ בַּשּׁוּק וְזֶה נֶהֱרָג? [א]אֶלָּא מְלַמֵּד שֶׁחוֹבְשִׁין אוֹתוֹ, וְאִי מִית — קָטְלִינַן לֵיהּ, וְאִי לָא מִית — "שִׁבְתּוֹ יִתֵּן וְרַפֹּא יְרַפֵּא". הֵיכִי דָּמֵי? אִי דְּלָא אַתְרוּ בֵּיהּ — אַמַּאי מִיקְטִיל? אֶלָּא פְּשִׁיטָא — דְּאַתְרוּ בֵּיהּ, וּמוּתְרֶה לְדָבָר חָמוּר מוּתְרֶה לְדָבָר הַקַּל, וְאָמַר רַחֲמָנָא "שִׁבְתּוֹ יִתֵּן וְרַפֹּא יְרַפֵּא". מַתְקִיף לָהּ רַב אַשִׁי: מִמַּאי דְּמוּתְרֶה לְדָבָר חָמוּר הָוֵי מוּתְרֶה לְדָבָר הַקַּל? דִּלְמָא לָא הָוֵי, וְאִם תִּמְצָא לוֹמַר הָוֵי — מִמַּאי דְּמִיתָה חֲמוּרָה, דִּלְמָא מַלְקוֹת חָמוּר? דְּאָמַר רַב: אִילְמָלֵי נַגְּדוּהּ לַחֲנַנְיָה מִישָׁאֵל וַעֲזַרְיָה פָּלְחוּ לְצַלְמָא! א"ל רַב סָמָא בְּרֵיהּ דְּרַב אַסִּי לְרַב אַשִׁי, וְאָמְרִי לָהּ רַב סָמָא בְּרֵיהּ דְּרַב אַשִׁי לְרַב אַשִׁי: וְלָא שָׁנֵי לָךְ בֵּין הַכָּאָה שֶׁיֵּשׁ לָהּ קִצְבָה לְהַכָּאָה שֶׁאֵין לָהּ קִצְבָה? מַתְקִיף לָהּ רַב מָרִי: מִמַּאי דִּבְמֵזִיד "וְנִקָּה" מִקְטָלָא, דִּלְמָא בְּשׁוֹגֵג "וְנִקָּה" מִגָּלוּת? קַשְׁיָא.§ רֵישׁ לָקִישׁ אָמַר: הָא מַנִּי — רַבִּי מֵאִיר הִיא, *דְּאָמַר: לוֹקֶה וּמְשַׁלֵּם. אִי רַבִּי מֵאִיר — אֲפִי' בִּתּוֹ נַמִי! וְכִי תֵּימָא ר' מֵאִיר לוֹקֶה וּמְשַׁלֵּם אִית לֵיהּ, מֵת וּמְשַׁלֵּם — לֵית לֵיהּ, וְלָא? וְהָתַנְיָא: גָּנַב וְטָבַח בְּשַׁבָּת, גָּנַב וְטָבַח לַעֲבוֹדָה זָרָה, גָּנַב שׁוֹר הַנִּסְקָל וּטְבָחוֹ — (ב)מְשַׁלֵּם תַּשְׁלוּמֵי אַרְבָּעָה וַחֲמִשָּׁה, דִּבְרֵי רַבִּי מֵאִיר, וַחֲכָמִים פּוֹטְרִין. הָא אִיתְּמַר עֲלָהּ, אָמַר רַבִּי יַעֲקֹב א"ר יוֹחָנָן, וְאָמְרִי לָהּ אָמַר רַבִּי יִרְמְיָה אָמַר ר' שִׁמְעוֹן בֶּן לָקִישׁ: ר' אָבִין וְרַבִּי אֶילְעָא וְכָל חֲבוּרָתָא מִשְּׁמֵיהּ דְּרַבִּי יוֹחָנָן אָמְרִי: [ג]בְּטוֹבֵחַ עַל יְדֵי אַחֵר. וְכִי זֶה חוֹטֵא וְזֶה מִתְחַיֵּיב? אָמַר רָבָא, אָמַר רַחֲמָנָא: °"וּטְבָחוֹ אוֹ מְכָרוֹ" *[ד]מַה מְּכִירָה עַל יְדֵי אַחֵר — אַף טְבִיחָה עַל יְדֵי אַחֵר. דְּבֵי רַבִּי יִשְׁמָעֵאל תָּנָא: "אוֹ" — לְרַבּוֹת אֶת הַשָּׁלִיחַ. דְּבֵי חִזְקִיָּה תָּנָא: "תַּחַת" — לְרַבּוֹת אֶת הַשָּׁלִיחַ. *מַתְקִיף לָהּ מָר זוּטְרָא: מִי אִיכָּא מִידֵּי דְּאִילּוּ עָבֵד אִיהוּ לָא מִיחַיַּיב, וְעָבֵיד שָׁלִיחַ וּמִחַיַּיב? אִיהוּ לָאו מִשּׁוּם דְּלָא מִיחַיַּיב, [ה]אֶלָּא מִשּׁוּם דְּקָם לֵיהּ בִּדְרַבָּה מִינֵּיהּ. אִי בְּטוֹבֵחַ עַל יְדֵי אַחֵר, מַאי טַעֲמַיְיהוּ דְּרַבָּנַן דְּפָטְרִי? *מַאן חֲכָמִים — רַבִּי

(שמות כא) ... (שם)

רש"י

נַגְּדוּהּ. יִסּוּרִין. וְלָא שָׁנֵי לָךְ כו'. יִסּוּרֵי הַמַּלְכוּת — הַכָּאָה שֶׁאֵין לָהּ קִצְבָה הִיא. אֲבָל מַלְקוֹת יֵשׁ לָהּ קִצְבָה — אַרְבָּעִים. הָנִיחָא לְרַבָּנַן דְּאָמְרִי. בְּסַנְהֶדְרִין, בְּ"אֵלּוּ הֵן הַנִּשְׂרָפִים" (עט.): נִתְכַּוֵּון לַהֲרוֹג אֶת זֶה וְהָרַג אֶת זֶה — חַיָּיב, וְהַאי "וְנָתַתָּ נֶפֶשׁ" — מַמָּשׁ קָאָמַר, אִית לָן לְמֵידַק וְאוֹקְמֵי קְרָא בְּשֶׁהִתְרוּ בּוֹ, וּלְמֵילַף דְּאַע"ג דְּאִיכָּא הַתְרָאָה — יַעֲנֹשׁ מָמוֹן כְּשֶׁאֵין שָׁם מִיתָה. אֶלָּא לְרַבִּי דְּאָמַר. הָתָם: נִתְכַּוֵּון לַהֲרוֹג אֶת זֶה וְהָרַג אֶת זֶה — אֵינוֹ נֶהֱרָג, אֶלָּא מְשַׁלֵּם דְּמֵי הָאִשָּׁה לְיוֹרְשֶׁיהָ, אִם כֵּן אֶפְשָׁר לְאוֹקְמֵי קְרָא בְּשֶׁלֹּא הִתְרוּ בּוֹ, וּמִשּׁוּם הָכִי, כִּי אֵין אָסוֹן מְשַׁלֵּם דְּמֵי וְלָדוֹת, וְכִי יֵשׁ אָסוֹן מְשַׁלֵּם דְּמֵי אִשָּׁה. אֲבָל אַתְרוּ בֵּיהּ — אֵימָא לָךְ לוֹקֶה וְאֵינוֹ מְשַׁלֵּם. מַאי אִיכָּא לְמֵימַר. מֵהֵיכָא תֵּיתֵי חוֹבֵל בַּחֲבֵירוֹ לְתַשְׁלוּמִין, וְאַף כְּשֶׁהִתְרוּ בּוֹ? עַל מִשְׁעַנְתּוֹ. כִּדְמִתַּרְגְּמִינַן: "עַל בּוּרְיוֹ", שֶׁשָּׁב לְכֹחוֹ וּלְאֵיתָנוֹ הָרִאשׁוֹן. אֶלָּא מְלַמֵּד שֶׁחוֹבְשִׁין אוֹתוֹ. לֹא נֶאֱמַר מִקְרָא זֶה אֶלָּא לְלַמֶּדְךָ דְּהֵיכָא דְּהִכָּהוּ וְלֹא מֵת וְנָפַל לְמִשְׁכָּב — יַחְבְּשׁוּ אֶת הַמַּכֶּה הַהוּא בְּבֵית הָאֲסוּרִין, עַד שֶׁנִּרְאֶה: "אִם יָקוּם וְהִתְהַלֵּךְ בַּחוּץ", אָז "וְנִקָּה הַמַּכֶּה". מִכְּלָל דְּעַד הַשְׁתָּא לֹא יָצָא מִידֵי בֵּית דִּין, אֶלָּא נֶחְבָּשׁ. וְאִי מָיֵית קָטְלִינַן לֵיהּ. [כֵּיוָן דְּאָמְרַתְּ חוֹבְשִׁין, מִכְּלָל דְּאִי מָיֵית נִיזָּק — קָטְלִינַן לֵיהּ לְהַאי. דְּאִי לָאו לְקַטְלָא, לְמַאי חָבְשִׁינַן לֵיהּ? לְדָבָר חָמוּר. מִיתָה. לְדָבָר הַקַּל. מַלְקוֹת דְּ"לֹא יוֹסִיף" דְּחוֹבֵל וְלֹא מֵת]. וְאָמַר רַחֲמָנָא. לְהֵיכָא דְּלֹא מֵת, דְּאִיכָּא מָמוֹן וּמַלְקוֹת — נִידוֹן בְּמָמוֹן, דִּכְתִיב "שִׁבְתּוֹ יִתֵּן". מִמַּאי. דְּהַאי "וְהִכָּה אִישׁ אֶת רֵעֵהוּ" בְּמֵזִיד קָא מִשְׁתָּעֵי, וְהַאי "וְנִקָּה" דְּיָלְפִינַן מִינֵּיהּ חֲבִישָׁה — וְנִקָּה מִקְטָלָא קָאָמַר, דְּתִשְׁמַע מִינָּהּ דְּאִי מָיֵית קָטְלִינַן לֵיהּ, וְעַל כָּרְחִין בְּהִתְרוּ בּוֹ. דִּלְמָא בְּשׁוֹגֵג. מִשְׁתָּעֵי, וְלֹא הִתְרוּ בּוֹ. וַחֲבִישָׁה לָאו לְקַטְלָא, "וְנִקָּה" נַמִי לָאו לְקַטְלָא, אֶלָּא מִגָּלוּת דְּעָרֵי מִקְלָט. וַחֲבִישָׁה דְּיָלְפִינַן מִינָּהּ לְגָלוּת קָאָמַר, וּמִשּׁוּם הָכִי כִּי נִקָּה מִגָּלוּת — יְשַׁלֵּם מָמוֹן. אֲבָל הֵיכָא דְּאַתְרוּ בֵּיהּ, אֵימָא לָךְ דְּכִי לָא מָיֵית — לוֹקֶה וְאֵינוֹ מְשַׁלֵּם. רֵישׁ לָקִישׁ מְהַדַּר אַשִּׁינּוּיָא דְּרוּמְיָא דְּרָמִינַן בְּרֵישׁ שְׁמַעְתִּין מַתְנִי' דְּמַכּוֹת אַדִּכְתוּבּוֹת. הָא מַנִּי. מַתְנִיתִין דְּקָתָנֵי בָּא עַל אֲחוֹתוֹ נוֹתֵן קְנָס — ר"מ הִיא דַּאֲמַר לְעֵיל לוֹקֶה וּמְשַׁלֵּם, שֶׁלֹּא הַשֵּׁם הַמְבִיאוֹ לִידֵי מַכּוֹת מְבִיאוֹ לִידֵי תַּשְׁלוּמִין. אֲפִי' בִּתּוֹ נַמִי. דְּמִיקְטִיל עֲלָהּ, לִישַׁלֵּם. דְּהָא לָא סְבִירָא לֵיהּ לְר"מ דְּפָטוּר מִשּׁוּם דְּרַבָּה מִינֵּיהּ, וְאַמַּאי תְּנַן מַתְנִי' הַבָּא עַל בִּתּוֹ פָּטוּר מִן הַקְּנָס? וְטָבַח בְּשַׁבָּת. אִיכָּא חִיּוּב מִיתָה, וְכֵן לַעֲבוֹדָה זָרָה. שׁוֹר הַנִּסְקָל. לְקַמָּן פָּרֵיךְ: הָא לֹא שָׁוֶה מִידֵּי. בְּטוֹבֵחַ עַל יְדֵי אַחֵר. הַגַּנָּב צִוָּה לִשְׁלוּחוֹ לִשְׁחוֹט. וְכִי. שָׁלִיחַ חוֹטֵא, וְשׁוֹלֵחַ מִתְחַיֵּיב קְנָס דְּאַרְבָּעָה וַחֲמִשָּׁה? וְהָא קַיְימָא לָן בְּקִדּוּשִׁין (מב:): אֵין שָׁלִיחַ לִדְבַר עֲבֵירָה. מְכִירָה אִי אֶפְשָׁר אֶלָּא ע"י אַחֵר, שֶׁהַלּוֹקֵחַ לוֹקְחוֹ מִמֶּנּוּ. תַּחַת הַשּׁוֹר. מָלֵי לְמִכְתַּב "יְשַׁלֵּם בְּשׁוֹר". עָבֵד אִיהוּ לָא מִיחַיַּיב. דְּהָא מִיקְטִיל. לָאו מִשּׁוּם דְּלָא מִיחַיַּיב הוּא. דְּחִיּוּבָא רַמְיָא עֲלֵיהּ, אֶלָּא מִשּׁוּם דְּקָם לֵיהּ בִּדְרַבָּה מִינֵּיהּ.

רַבִּי

תוספות

ודלמא מלקות חמור. הוה מלי לשנויי: מסתברא מיתה חמורה שכן ניתנה לאנשי עיר הנידחת, כדאמרי' בפ' "ד מיתות" (סנהדרין נ.). **אילמלי** נגדוה לחנניה מישאל ועזריה הוו פלחי לצלמא. תימה מנא לן (א) דהא אמרי' בהרואה (ברכות סא:) כשהוליאו את ר"ע אמר כל ימי הייתי מצטער על פסוק זה אימתי יבא לידי ואקיימנו בכל נפשך אלמא משמע דבכל נפשך איירי אפי' היו מייסרין את האדם ביסורין קשין דומיא דר' עקיבא שהיו מסרקין בשרו במסרקי ברזל וכ"ש לנגודי ואור"ת דאותו צלם לא היה עבודה זרה ממש אלא היה עשוי לכבוד המלך ואעפ"כ היה בו קידוש השם ולכך מסרו עצמן למיתה, והיינו דכתיב (דניאל ג) "לאלהך לית אנן פלחין ולצלם דהבא די אקימת לא נסגוד" משמע שהצלם לא היה תופס באלהות. ומיהו, "פלחו לצלמא" משמע שהצלם היה עבודה זרה, מדקאמר "פלחו"*.

דלמא בשוגג ונקה מגלות. תימה לר"י: היכי שייך גלות אם מת אחר שחבשוהו ב' או שלשה ימים? הא אמרינן ב"מי שאחזו" (גיטין ע: ושם): שחט בו שנים או רוב שנים — הרי זה אינו גולה, דחיישינן שמא הרוח בלבלתו. וטעמא, דגבי גלות אשכחן מילי טובא דפטור, כגון דרך עלייה, דגבי מיתה אין חילוק בין דרך עלייה לדרך ירידה. הכי נמי גבי גלות בעינן שימות מיד, כדכתיב "ויפל עליו וימות" משמע מיד. ואע"ג דגבי מיתה נמי כתיב "מכה איש ומת" — וי"ל: דמשכחת לה בגיטא דשישא, דלא חיישינן שמא הרוח בלבלתו, כדאמרינן התם. אי נמי: דוקא בשחט בו רוב שנים חיישינן שמא הרוח בלבלתו, דבקל הרוח מבלבלו, אבל בשאר חבלות — אין הרוח מזיק כל כך, שיכולין לשמור יפה מבלבול רוח, לכרוך על המכה שום דבר. וא"ת: היכי מיתוקם קרא בשוגג? הא כתיב שבת בקרא "רק שבתו יתן וגו'" ובשוגג לא מיחייב, כדאמרינן בס"פ "כילד הרגל" (ב"ק כו: ושם) דמרבה מ"פצע תחת פצע" לחייב על השוגג כמזיד נזק, אבל לא ד' דברים! וי"ל: דמשכחת לה בהוסיף לו רצועה אחת, דאמר ב"המניח" (שם לג:) דגולה, ואם לא מת — חייב בד' דברים, ולא דמי לשאר שוגג. או כגון שנכנס לחנותו של נגר (שלא) ברשות, דמוכח התם לרב פפא דשייך ביה גלות וד' דברים. או נפל מן הגג ברוח מצויה דחייב בד' דברים כדאמרי' בסוף "כילד הרגל" (שם כז.) ומסתברא דאם מת — דגולה. ועוד, דאפשר דהוי שוגג על המיתה ומזיד על החבלה*. **גנב** שור הנסקל וטבחו משלם תשלומי ד' וה'. תימה: דתיקשי מהכא לריש לקיש, דאמר בפ' "מרובה" (שם עז: ושם): כל היכא דליתיה במכירה ליתיה בטביחה, והכא שור הנסקל ליתיה במכירה! וי"ל: דהתם קדשים תמירי, דליתנהו כלל במכירה! אבל שור הנסקל, אם ימכרנו לגוי אין תופס דמיו. ולר"ת שאומר דאין שור הנסקל °נאסר מחיים ניחא. **לאו** משום דלא מיחייב כו'. אע"ג דהכא אפי' לצאת ידי שמים אינו חייב, דדוקא בממון הוא דאמר רבא ב"השוכר את הפועלים" (ב"מ צא. ושם): אתנן אסרה תורה אפי' בא על אמו, דמיחייב בבא לצאת ידי שמים. אבל קנס לא מיחייב אלא ע"פ ב"ד, כדאמרי': "אשר ירשיעון אלהים" — פרט למרשיע עצמו. מ"מ ניחא, דכיון שהיה ראוי להתחייב אם לא היה מתחייב בנפשו — מתחייב נמי אממון ע"י שליח, כיון שאינו מתחייב בנפשו.

רבי

[וע"ע תוס' פסחים נג: ד"ה מה ראו ותוס' ע"ז ג. ד"ה שלא]

הגהות הב"ח

(א) תוס' ד"ה אלמלי כו' מנא לן ועוד דהא:

רש"א מ"ז

[וע"ע תוס' יבמות קכ: ד"ה אלא ור"ה חיישינן ותוס' גיטין ע: ובשבועות לב. ד"ה ע"פ]

מסורת הש"ס

[סנהדרין עט.] [שם]

[שם עח: תוס' דב"ק פ"ט]

גליון הש"ס

תוס' ד"ה גנב וכו' נאסר מחיים ניחא. עי' זבחים קף ע"א תוס' ד"ה (בכמות הקודם) אפי'

[לקמן לד: לה.] ב"ק עא. ב"מ צא.

קדושי מג. ב"ק עא. [עט.]

ב"ק עא.

[ערובין סג. וש"נ]

ר' שמעון היא, *דאמר: [א]שחיטה שאינה ראויה – לא שמה שחיטה. התינח עבודה זרה ושור הנסקל, אלא שחיטת שבת – שחיטה ראויה היא, דתנן: *[ב,ג]השוחט בשבת וביום הכפורים, אע"פ שמתחייב בנפשו – שחיטתו כשרה! סבר לה כר' יוחנן הסנדלר, *דתניא: *המבשל בשבת, בשוגג – יאכל, במזיד – לא יאכל, דברי ר"מ. ר' יהודה אומר: [ג]בשוגג – יאכל למוצאי שבת, במזיד – לא יאכל עולמית. רבי יוחנן הסנדלר אומר: בשוגג – יאכל למוצאי שבת לאחרים, ולא לו. במזיד – לא יאכל עולמית, לא לו ולא לאחרים. מאי טעמא דרבי יוחנן הסנדלר? כדדריש ר' חייא אפיתחא דבי נשיאה: °"ושמרתם את השבת כי קדש היא לכם". מה קודש אסור באכילה אף מעשה שבת אסורין באכילה. אי מה קודש אסור בהנאה אף מעשה שבת אסור בהנאה – ת"ל: "לכם", שלכם יהא. יכול אפילו בשוגג – ת"ל: "מחלליה מות יומת", במזיד אמרתי לך, ולא בשוגג. פליגי בה רב אחא ורבינא: חד אמר: מעשה שבת דאורייתא, וחד אמר: דרבנן. מאן דאמר דאורייתא – כדאמרן. מאן דאמר דרבנן – אמר קרא: "קדש היא" – *היא קודש, [ד]ואין מעשיה קודש. ולמאן דאמר דרבנן, מאי טעמייהו דרבנן דפטרי? כי קא פטרי רבנן – אשארא. טובח לעבודה זרה, *כיון דשחט ביה פורתא איתסר ליה, אידך כי קא טבח – לאו דמריה קא טבח! אמר רבא: *באומר "בגמר זביחה הוא עובדה". שור הנסקל – לאו דידיה הוא דקטבח! אמר רבה: הכא במאי עסקינן – כגון שמסרו לשומר, והזיק בבית שומר, ונגמר דיניה בבית שומר, וגנבו גנב מבית שומר. ורבי מאיר סבר לה כר' יעקב, וסבר לה כר"ש; סבר לה כר' יעקב – *דאמר: אף משנגמר דינו, החזירו שומר לבעליו – מוחזר. וסבר לה כר"ש, *דאמר: [ה]דבר הגורם לממון כממון דמי. רבה אמר: לעולם בטובח על ידי עצמו, ור'

שמות לא | קדושין נז. [ב"ק עו: חולין פ. פא. פה.] | חולין יד. ב"ק עא. | [משום פלוגתא דר"י ור"י הסנדלר דליתא במשנה שפיר גרסי' "תניא"] | [חולין קטו.] | [ב"ק עא: ע"ז לב: חולין מ:] | ב"ק מה. עא: לח: | ב"ק סב פסחים כט: שבועות לב. לג. [ב"ק קה:]

רש"י

רבי שמעון. בפרק "מרובה" וב"כסוי הדם" וב"אותו ואת בנו". התינח עבודה זרה. דזבחי מתים אסורים, וכן שור הנסקל, דמשנגמר דינו אסור בהנאה, כדאמרינן בב"ק (דף מא.) ובפסחים (דף כב:): ממשמע שנאמר "סקול יסקל" איני יודע שהוא נבילה, ונבילה כו'? בשוגג יאכל. אפי' בו ביום. במזיד לא יאכל. הוא לעולם, אבל אחרים ישראלים – אוכלים. ר' יהודה אומר בשוגג יאכל. הוא למוצאי שבת, ולא בו ביום. דקנסינן שוגג אטו מזיד. במזיד לא יאכל. הוא עולמית, אלא אחרים. כדרבי יוחנן הסנדלר גרסינן יאכל. לאחרים. לישראל. לא לו ולא לאחרים. ישראל, אבל מוכרו ונותנו לגוים. מ"ט דר' יוחנן הסנדלר. דקאמר: מעשה שבת אסורין באכילה. יכול אפילו בשוגג. תאסר באכילה, אם שגג בבישול, שלא ידע שהוא שבת. מחלליה וגו'. היכא דאיכא חיוב מיתה אסירי באכילה כי קודש. במזיד אמרתי. שהוא אסור כקודש, דהא גבי חיוב מיתה כתיב, ולא בשוגג. מעשה שבת. במזיד אסורין מן התורה באכילה, לר' יוחנן הסנדלר. מ"ט דרבנן. דפליגי אדרבי מאיר, ופטרי מקנס ארבעה וחמשה, הואיל ובטובח על ידי אחר אוקימתא – הא שחיטה ראויה היא מדאורייתא. אשארא. אעבודה זרה ואשור הנסקל. כיון דשחט ביה פורתא איתסר ליה. דאמר מר (חולין דף מ.): היתה בהמת חבירו רבוצה לפני עבודה זרה, כיון ששחט בה סימן אחד – אסרה. לאו דמריה קא טבח. דהא איתסרא עליה. וחיובא דתשלומי ארבעה וחמשה "טביחה" כתיב בהו, ועד גמר שחיטה לא מיחייב. ומקמי דמטי גמר שחיטה איתסרא בהנאה על בעליה, ומההיא שעתא אפקדה מיניה, דאי איתא – לא הדרא בעינא, ולאו דמריה היא. באומר בגמר זביחה הוא עובדה. לעבודה זרה, אינו עובד לעבודה זרה עד גמר זביחה. פלוגתא דר' יעקב בבבא קמא. החזירו שומר לבעליו מוחזר. דאמר ליה: תורא אשלמת לי – תורא אשלימית לך. כממון דמי. והאי נמי, אע"ג דלא שוי מידי – גורם לממון הוא, דכי ליתא בעי לשלומי ליה תורא מעליא. דר' שמעון בבבא קמא, בפרק "מרובה": קדשים שחייב באחריותן משלם ארבעה וחמשה, משום דגורם לממון הוא, ואע"ג דהקדש לאו ממון בעלים הוא, ובהקדש לא שייך קנס, ד"רעהו" כתיב. רבה גרסינן בכולהו. ותדע, מדקאמר לקמן: א"ל רב פפא לאביי: לרבה דאמר חידוש הוא כו', ואם איתא דרבא גרסינן – הא רב פפא תלמידו של רבא היה, כדאמר לקמן: אמר ליה רב פפא לרבא: הי מכה? מאי שנא דשבקיה לרבא ולא שייליה [לתרולי שמעתיה], ושייליה לאביי [שמעתא דרבא]? אלא רבה גרסינן. ורב פפא לא היה בימיו, ושייל לאביי שהיה תלמידו של רבה. רבה אמר לעולם בטובח בעצמו ור'

תוספות

רבי שמעון היא דאמר שחיטה שאינה ראויה לא שמה שחיטה. תימה: דעד כאן לא פליגי רבנן התם גבי אותו ואת בנו אלא כדמפרש התם בחולין (דף פה.) טעמא: דנין שחיטה משחיטה, פירוש: משחוטי חוץ, ואין דנין שחיטה מטביחה. אבל הכא, גבי תשלומי ד' וה' דכתיב טביחה – אית לן למילף טביחה מטביחה, ולא שמה שחיטה! ואור"י: דאיכא למימר דנין דבר הנאמר בסיני, מדבר הנאמר בסיני ואין דנין דבר הנאמר בסיני מ"טבוח טבח והכן" שלא נאמר בסיני. והתם נמי, ה"מ למימר הכי, אלא דאית ליה שינויא אחרינא. א"נ י"ל: דצריך שינויא, דהתם דנין שחיטה משחיטה, דאי הוה כתיב טביחה גבי אותו ואת בנו – הוה ילפינן הכא והתם מ"טבוח טבח והכן" טביחה מטביחה, אע"ג דלא נאמרה בסיני, דהוי בדדמי, מדנילף טביחה משחיטה דלא דמי אע"ג דנאמרה בסיני. אבל השתא דכתיב שחיטה גבי אותו ואת בנו – דנין שחיטה משחיטה. וילפינן נמי השתא אטביחה דד' וה'. ואיפכא ליכא למימר דנין טביחה דתשלומי ד' וה' מטביחה, ולמילף מהתם אשחיטה דאותו ואת בנו, דכיון דשקולים הן, ואיכא למילף הכי ואיכא למילף הכי, אית לן למימר: דנין דבר הנאמר בסיני ממה שנאמר בסיני*.

המבשל בשבת בשוגג יאכל. פי': בו ביום, ואפילו הוא, כדמוכח בפ' "כירה" (שבת לח.) דבעו מרבי חייא בר אבא: שכח קדירה על גבי כירה ובשלה בשבת כו', עד המבשל בשבת כו' בשוגג יאכל. ולאותו שבת קא בעי התם, אי אסיר גזרה שלא יאמר "שוכח אני". במזיד לא יאכל – פירוש: בין הוא בין אחרים בו ביום, אבל במוצאי שבת – לדידיה נמי שרי, דהא בפ' קמא דחולין (דף טו. ושם) אההיא מתני' דהשוחט בשבת וביה"כ, אע"פ שמתחייב בנפשו – שחיטתו כשרה, פריך: ונוקמא במזיד ור' מאיר? ומשני: לא סלקא דעתין, דקתני שבת דומיא דיה"כ, מה יה"כ לא שנא שוגג ול"ש מזיד. והשתא, אי לאחרים שרי בו ביום – לפרוך ממזיד גופיה: מה יוה"כ לא שנא לו ולא שנא לאחרים כו', ואי לדידיה אסור אף למוצאי שבת – הוה ליה למימר: שחיטתו כשרה קתני, ל"ש לו לא שנא לאחרים, כדקאמר התם על ר' יוחנן הסנדלר. ועוד: דא"כ היינו מזיד דר' יהודה, כמו שאפרש. ומדאצטריך לרבי יהודה לאפוקי מזיד במילתיה – משמע דפליג נמי אמזיד. **בשוגג** יאכל במוצאי שבת. שוגג דר' יהודה הוי כמו שפירשתי מזיד דר"מ. דהא מוקי התם מתני' דהשוחט בשבת כוותיה. **במזיד** לא יאכל עולמית. הוא, אבל אחרים אוכלים. דאי אחרים נמי לא יאכלו עולמית – היינו מזיד דרבי יוחנן הסנדלר. כללא דמילתא: מזיד דרבי מאיר – שוגג דרבי יהודה, מזיד דרבי יהודה – שוגג דרבי יוחנן הסנדלר. **אמר** קרא לכם. וא"ת ולא לכתוב לא קדש ולא לכם ואנא ידענא דאסירי באכילה מלא תאכל כל תועבה דכל שתעבתי לך הרי הוא בבל תאכל וי"ל דאי מהתם ה"א בין שוגג בין מזיד להכי איצטריך למכתב הכא לאסמכיה למחלליה לומר במזיד אמרתי לך ולא בשוגג. **היא** קדש ואין מעשיה קודש. ואין להקשות דלא לכתוב לא היא ולא קדש דהוה אסורה באכילה מכל אשר תיעבתי לך והכי אמרי' בהדיא בפ' כל הבשר (חולין קטו. ושם). **מאי** טעמא דרבנן דפטרי. לא בעי למימר דלא דרשי "או" ו"תחת" לרבות את השליח – דלא ניחא ליה למימר דפליגי בשליח. **כי** קא פטרי רבנן אשארא. וא"ת: אמאי אצטריך למתני כלל טבח בשבת? דאפי' בשחיטה שאינה ראויה מחייב ר"מ, כ"ש הא דשחיטה ראויה היא! וי"ל: דזו אף זו קתני. וא"ת: כל טובח נמי, לאו דמריה קא טבח, דמכי שחט פורתא – קניא בשינוי? אלא ע"כ בהכי חייב רחמנא, והכא נמי לא שנא! ואור"י: דלא חשיב שינוי לקנותה בכך. **כיון** דשחט בה פורתא אסרה ואידך כו'. **סבר** לה כר"ש דאמר דבר הגורם לממון כו'. וא"ת: ואמאי לא קאמר דר"מ לטעמיה דדאין דינא דגרמי (ב"ק ק.) גבי מקדש תבואת חבירו או שורף שטרות חבירו (שם צח:), וכ"ש דמחייב בדבר הגורם לממון, כדאמר התם ב"הגוזל" (שם צח:): דלמא עד כאן לא קאמר ר"ש אלא בדבר שעיקרו ממון, אבל שטר דאין גופו ממון – לא! וי"ל: דאיכא למימר נמי איפכא, דעד כאן לא קאמר ר"מ אלא בשורף שטרות של חבירו, או מקדש תבואת חבירו, שהוא ממון הראוי לכל העולם. אבל שור הנסקל – אין ראוי אלא לזה השומר, שיפטור עצמו. וי"מ: דמשום הכי קאמר ס"ל כר"ש משום דר"ש קאמר דבר הגורם לממון הוי ממון לענין תשלומי ד' וה', דהכי תני ליה ב"מרובה" (שם עא:), ואילו ר' מאיר לא חזינא דמחייב בדינא דגרמי אלא קרן, אבל לחייב לשלם על ידו תשלומי ד' וה' – לא חזינא. ועוד אומר ריצב"א: דמשום דינא דגרמי לא מחייב אלא מדרבנן, כדמוכח בסוף "הכונס" (שם סב.)*.

ורבי

עין משפט נר מצוה

לא א מיי' (פ' יב הל' ה) ופי"ד מהל' שחיטה הל' י ופ"ב מהל' גניבה הל' ח סמג עשין סד ועא ולאוין קמט טוש"ע י"ד סימן עז סעיף ט וסי' כח סעיף יז וטור ח"מ סימן שז:

לב ב מיי' פ"א מהל' שחיטה הל' כט סמג עשין סג טוש"ע י"ד סי' יא סעיף ב:

ב"ק עא. חולין טו. גיטין נג: ביצה יז: תרומות פ"ב מ"ג שבת לח. [תוספתא דשבת פ"ג]

לג ג ד מיי' פ"ו מהל' שבת הל' כג סמג לאוין סה טוש"ע א"ח סימן שיח סעיף א:

לד ה מיי' פ"ז מהל' חובל הל' ז טוש"ע ח"מ סי' שפו סעי' ב:

[וע"ע תוס' ב"ק עא: ד"ה איסורא ותוס' חולין פה. ד"ה דנין]

[ופריך אפי' למ"ד יבנה לשחיטה מתחלה ועד סוף כדאמרי' במרובה וטבחו כולו בעינן ה"נ וטבחו כולו בעינן. ת"י עה:ג]

[וע' תוס' ב"ק נג. ד"ה חמור עוד שם עא: ד"ה וסבר]

תורה אור

ור' מאיר, *לוקה ומשלם אית ליה, מת ומשלם לית ליה. ושאני הני, דחידוש הוא שחידשה תורה בקנס, אע"ג דמיקטיל – משלם. ואזדא רבה לטעמיה, דאמר רבה: היה גדי גנוב לו וטבחו בשבת – חייב, שכבר נתחייב בגניבה קודם שיבא לידי איסור שבת. גנב וטבח בשבת – פטור, שאם אין גניבה – אין טביחה ואין מכירה. ואמר רבה: היה גדי גנוב לו וטבחו במחתרת – חייב, שכבר נתחייב בגניבה קודם שיבא לידי איסור מחתרת. [א]גנב וטבח במחתרת – פטור, שאם אין גניבה – אין טביחה ואין מכירה. וצריכא, דאי אשמעינן שבת – משום דאיסורה איסור עולם, אבל מחתרת דאיסור שעה הוא – אימא לא; ואי אשמעינן מחתרת – משום *דמחתרתו זו היא התראתו, אבל שבת דבעיא התראה – אימא לא, צריכא. אמר רב פפא: *היתה פרה גנובה לו וטבחה בשבת – חייב, שכבר נתחייב בגניבה קודם שיבא לידי איסור שבת. [ב]היתה פרה שאולה לו, וטבחה בשבת – פטור. אמר ליה רב אחא בריה דרבא לרב אשי: רב פפא פרה אתא לאשמועינן?! אמר ליה: רב פפא שאולה אתא לאשמועינן; סלקא דעתך אמינא. הואיל ואמר רב פפא: *[ג]משעת משיכה הוא דאתחייב ליה במזונותיה, הכא נמי [ד]משעת שאלה אתחייב באונסיה, קא משמע לן. *אמר רבא: [ה]הניח להן אביהן פרה שאולה – משתמשין בה כל ימי שאלתה, מתה – אין חייבין באונסה. [ו]כסבורין של אביהם היא וטבחוה ואכלוה – [א] משלמין *דמי בשר בזול. הניח להן אביהן אחריות נכסים – חייבין לשלם. איכא דמתני לה ארישא, ואיכא דמתני לה אסיפא. מאן דמתני לה ארישא – כל שכן אסיפא, ופליגא דרב פפא, ומאן [ז]דמתני לה אסיפא – אבל ארישא לא, והיינו דרב פפא. בשלמא ר' יוחנן לא אמר כריש לקיש – דקא מוקים לה כרבנן. אלא ריש לקיש מ"ט לא אמר כר' יוחנן? אמר לך: כיון דאילו אתרו ביה – פטור, כי לא אתרו ביה – נמי פטור. *ואזדו לטעמייהו: דכי אתא רב דימי אמר: חייבי מיתות שוגגין וחייבי מלקיות שוגגין ודבר אחר, ר' יוחנן אמר: חייב, וריש לקיש אמר: פטור. ר' יוחנן אמר: חייב, דהא לא אתרו ביה. ר"ל אמר: פטור, כיון דאילו אתרו ביה – פטור, כי לא אתרו ביה נמי פטור. איתיביה ר"ל לרבי יוחנן: °"ולא יהיה אסון ענוש יענש" (שמות כא) מאי

רש"י

ור' מאיר. בעלמא בתשלומי ממון לית ליה מת ומשלם, והכא תשלומי ארבעה וחמשה קנס הם, וכל משפט קנס חידוש הוא. הלכך, אע"ג דמיקטיל נמי לא מיפטר מיניה. ולקמן פריך: לרבה אליבא דרבי מאיר קשיא בתו, דמתניתין נמי קנס הוא, וקא פטר ליה אבתו. היה גדי גנוב לו. גנב גדי בחול ונתחייב הקרן וטבחו בשבת, דלא אתי עליה חיובא דממון באיסור שבת, אלא חיוב קנס. [לעיל לג: וש"נ] חייב. ד' וה'. דקנס חידוש הוא, ורבה סבירא ליה כרבי מאיר. גנב וטבח בשבת. דחיוב ממון דקרן אתא עליה באיסור שבת. פטור. דקיימא לן: אין מת ומשלם. וכיון דאקרן לא מיחייב – קנס נמי לא משלם, דתשלומי ד' וה' אמר רחמנא, ולא תשלומי שלשה וארבעה. ולא סבירא לן כרבי נתן דאמר (שבת דף לד.): חי נושא את עצמו. אי נמי: בכפות. שאם אין גניבה. כלומר, שמאחר שפטור על הקרן משום מיתה. אין טביחה ואין מכירה. אינו מחויב קנס, כדפירשתי, דתשלומי ארבעה וחמשה כתיב ולא תשלומי שלשה וארבעה. מחתרת. שחתר בית והוליאו. [סנהדרין עב:] וטבחו במחתרת. עצמה, דההיא שעתא בר קטלא הוא אי הוה אשכחיה בעל הבית, כדכתיב (שמות כב) "אין לו דמים". משום דאיסוריה איסור עולם. כל זמן שיעידו עליו שחילל שבת ימיתוהו בית דין. הלכך חמירא מיתה דילה לפוטרו מממון. [ב"ק קיב.] דאיסור שעה. אי לא משכח ליה ההיא שעתא – תו לא מיקטיל. היתה פרה שאולה לו וטבחה בשבת פטור. [ב"מ לא.] דההיא שעתא דקא טבח לה גזיל לה ממרה, ומיתה וממון באין כאחד. ולא גרסינן שאם אין גניבה אין טביחה ואין מכירה, דגבי שואל לא שייך לא כפל ולא ארבעה וחמשה, שהרי חייב בקרן לעולם, אפילו טוען טענת גנב. [ב"ק קיב.] ואין קנס אלא או בגנב או בשומר חנם הפוטר עצמו בטוען טענת גנב, שאומר "נגנבה". [ב"ק שם קו. ב"מ מב: ב"ב קמו:] פרה אתא לאשמועינן. בתמיה: מה למדנו ממנה שלא למדנו מגדי דקאמר רבה? שאולה אתא לאשמועינן. דטובחה בשבת פטור. ס"ד אמינא הואיל ואמר רב פפא. ב"השוכר את הפועלים". הכא נמי. נימא משעת שאלה רמיא עליה חיוב קרן, וכי טבחה בשבת ליחייב. קמ"ל. כיון דכל כמה דאיתא הדרא בעינא, ההיא שעתא דקא טבח לה – קא גזיל לה. [חולין פא:] כל ימי שאלתה. כל ימי משך הזמן ששאלה אביהן מן הבעלים. אין חייבין באונסה. דאינהו לאו שואלין נינהו עלה. דמי בשר בזול. כל זוזא שמינן בארבעה דנקי. הכי אמרינן בפרק "מי שמת" (ב"ב קמו:) והעור יחזירו לבעלים. אחריות נכסים. קרקעות. איכא דמתני ארישא. להאי הניח להן אביהן אחריות נכסים חייבין לשלם, ואמרינן דחייבין באונסין, דאישתעבוד נכסים דאבוהון מחיים, משעת שאלה. כ"ש אסיפא. כשטבחוה ואכלוה. ופליגא דרב פפא. דאמר לעיל ההיא שעתא דמטו לה אונסין הוא דאתי חיובא עליה, ולא משעת שאלה. ואיכא דמתני לה אסיפא. היכא דטבחוה, אם הניח להן אביהן אחריות נכסים – משלמין תשלומי מעליא ולא בזול, דאיבעי להו למידק. אבל ארישא. אם מתה לא מיחייבי לשלומי, ולא אמרינן אישתעבוד נכסי דאבוהון משעת שאלה. והיינו דרב פפא. דאמר לעיל: לא אמרינן משעת שאלה רמו עליה תשלומין, אלא משעת אונסין ואילך, וההיא שעתא ליתיה לשואל דליחייב. בשלמא רבי יוחנן. דמוקי מתניתין בשלא התרו בו. לא אמר כריש לקיש. דאוקמיה כר' מאיר. כי לא אתרו ביה נמי פטור. הואיל ואיכא לד מלקות. שוגגין. שלא התרו בהן. ודבר אחר. ממון. ואכולה מילתא קאי, כלומר: חייבי מיתות שוגגין וממון, או חייבי מלקיות שוגגין וממון. ר' יוחנן אומר חייב. בתשלומין. דהא לא אתרו ביה. ואין מיתה מחייבו אלא משום רשעה אחת דממון. כי לא אתרו ביה נמי פטור. ולקמן יליף טעמא. מאי

תוספות

ורבי מאיר לוקה ומשלם אית ליה מת ומשלם לית ליה ושאני הני. משמע דרבי מאיר אית ליה לוקה ומשלם אף בממון שאינו קנס, וכן משמע ב"השוכר את הפועלים" (ב"מ צא.) שהבאתי לעיל* ותימה: דבפ"ק דמכות (ד' ד:) קאמר עולא: טעמא דרבי מאיר דאמר עדים זוממין לוקין ומשלמין – משום דגמר ממוציא שם רע. ופריך: מה למוציא שם רע – שכן קנס. סבר לה כר' עקיבא, דאמר: עדים זוממין קנס הוא. משמע דבממון אינו לוקה ומשלם! ויש לומר: דודאי, אי עדים זוממין הוי ממונא – לא הוה גמר ממוציא ש"ר, שכן הוא קנס, אלא הוה דרשינן מ"כדי רשעתו" שאינו לוקה ומשלם, אבל השתא, דסבר עדים זוממין קנסא, וגמר ממוציא שם רע דלוקין ומשלמין – ע"כ מוקי "כדי רשעתו" במיתה ומלקות, כיון ד"כדי רשעתו" לא הוי במלקות וממון, מהשתא בכל דוכתא לוקה ומשלם, דמהיכא נמעיט שלא ילקה וישלם? דאמר רבה היה גדי גנוב לו. אליבא דרבי מאיר קאמר ולא משום דסבר הכי. משום דאיסורו איסור עולם כו'. שאם חלל שבת, לאחר השבת יעידו עליו ויהרגוהו. אבל מחתרת, אע"פ שמתחייב בנפשו בעודו במחתרת, מ"מ אחר שילא – תו לא הוי בר קטלא, ולא הוי דומיא ד"אם יהיה אסון". אבל שבת דבעי התראה אימא לא. תימה: דעיקר קים ליה בדרבה מיניה ברליחה כתיב, דבעינן התראה? ועוד, דשבת ומחתרת תרווייהו תננהי, דבפרק "המניח" (ב"ק דף לד:) תנן: והוא שהדליק את הגדיש בשבת – פטור, מפני שנידון בנפשו. ומחתרת נמי תנינא בפרק "בן סורר" (סנהדרין עב.): היה בא במחתרת ושיבר את החבית, אם אין לו דמים פטור! ונראה דהכא עביד צריכותא אמאי דבקנס מיקטיל ומשלם. וה"ק: משום דחמיר איסוריה, והוה אמינא דהתם דווקא הוא דליחייב קנס עם המיתה, וכה"ג עביד צריכותא לקמן (דף לז.) גבי "לא יהיה אסון" ו"כדי רשעתו", דמשום דחמור הוי אמרינן דלעביד ביה תרתי. אבל קשה: למאי דפרישית דרבה אליבא דרבי מאיר קאמר, אם כן – היכי קאמר: אבל שבת דבעיא התראה – אימא לא מיקטיל ומשלם. והא עיקר מילתיה דרבי מאיר גבי שבת תניא לעיל! ואיכא למימר: דרבה אשמועינן דשייך קים ליה בדרבה מיניה, אע"ג דבשעה דמתחייב עדיין הממון בעין – לא הוה לן למימר קים לי' בדרבה מיניה. כדאמר רבה גופיה בפרק "בן סורר" (סנהדרין עב. ושם) אמר *רבה: מסתברא מילתיה דרב כשיבר – דליתנהו, אבל נטל – דאיתנהו – לא, אפ"ה, כיון דטבח אחרי כן – מיפטר על הגנבה. והא דפטור אגנבה אף על גב דבאותה שעה הוי בעין עביד צריכותא. מתה אין חייבין באונסין. אבל בגנבה ואבדה נראה לר"י שהן חייבין, דהואיל ונהנין, דמשתמשין בה, והכי (א) אמר ב"השואל" (ב"מ לו. ושם). אבל ארישא לא והיינו דרב פפא. דלא אמרינן משעת שאלה חייב באונסין. וא"ת: אם כן, בסיפא נמי בשטבחוה, אמאי משלמין כשהניח להן אביהן אחריות נכסים? הא לא נתחייב בהן האב! וי"ל: דהתם פשע בה האב, שהיה לו לומר לבניו שאינה שלו, הלכך מחיים פשע בה, ונתחייב בה באותה שעה, ונשתעבדו נכסיו. מאי

עין משפט נר מצוה

לה א מיי' פ"ז מהל' גנבה הל' יג סג לאוין קס:
[דף לג. ד"ה ושולא]
לו ב מיי' פ"ג שם הל' ד סמג שם:
לז ג ד מיי' פ"א מהל' שאלה הל' ד סמג עשין נב טוש"ע ח"מ סימן שמ סעיף ז:
לח ה מיי' שם הל' ה וסמג שם טוש"ע שם סי' שמא סעיף ג:
לט ו ז מיי' שם טוש"ע שם סעי' ד:

תוספות רי"ד

אמר רבא הניח להן אביהם פרה שאולה משתמשין בה כל ימי שאלה. מתה אין חייבים באונסיה פי' שלא שאלו הן ולא קבלו עליהן אונסים. כסבורין של אביהן היא טבחוה ואכלוה משלמין דמי בשר בזול. פי' כל זוזי בארבע דנקא והעור יחזירו לבעלים. ואם הניח להן אביהן אחריות נכסים. פי' קרקעות חייבים לשלם משום דאישתעביד נכסיה. פי' נכסי דאבוהון מחיים משעת שאלה:
כי אתא רב דימי אמר חייבי מיתות שוגגין וד"א. פי' ממון או חייבי מלקות שוגגין וד"א ר"י אמר חייב בתשלומין ור"ל אמר פטור ר"י אמר חייב דהא לא התרו ביה פי' ואי אתה מחייבו אלא משום רשעה א' בממון ור"ל אמר פטור א) כי אתרו בי' נמי פטור פי' הואיל ואיכא צד מלקות:
א) נ"ל כיון דאילו אתרו ביה פטור כי לא אתרו ביה נמי פטור פי' וכו'.

הגהות הב"ח

(א) תוס' ד"ה מתה וכו' והכי אמרי' בהאומנין דף פא ע"א:

הגהות מהר"ב רנשבורג

א] גמ' משלמין דמי בשר בזול. עי' רש"י ד"ה דמי בשר וכו' ורשב"ם בב"ב דף קמו ע"ב בד"ה ושמין להם וכו':

[בסנהדרין שם איתא רבא]

מאי לָאו אָסוֹן מַמָּשׁ? לֹא, דִּין אָסוֹן. אִיכָּא דְּאָמְרִי, אֵיתִיבֵיהּ רַבִּי יוֹחָנָן לְר"ל: "וְלֹא יִהְיֶה אָסוֹן עָנוֹשׁ יֵעָנֵשׁ" מַאי לָאו – דִּין אָסוֹן? לֹא, אָסוֹן מַמָּשׁ. אָמַר רָבָא: וּמִי אִיכָּא לְמ"ד חַיָּיבֵי מִיתוֹת שׁוֹגְגִין חַיָּיבִים? וְהָא תָּנָא *) דְּבֵי חִזְקִיָּה: [א]מַכֵּה אָדָם וּמַכֵּה בְהֵמָה, מַה מַּכֵּה בְהֵמָה – לֹא חִילַּקְתָּ בּוֹ בֵּין בְּשׁוֹגֵג בֵּין בְּמֵזִיד, בֵּין מִתְכַּוֵּין לְשֶׁאֵין מִתְכַּוֵּין, בֵּין דֶּרֶךְ יְרִידָה לְדֶרֶךְ עֲלִיָּיה, לְפוֹטְרוֹ מָמוֹן אֶלָּא לְחַיְּיבוֹ מָמוֹן – אַף מַכֵּה אָדָם לֹא תַחֲלוֹק בּוֹ בֵּין בְּשׁוֹגֵג בֵּין בְּמֵזִיד, בֵּין מִתְכַּוֵּין לְשֶׁאֵין מִתְכַּוֵּין, בֵּין דֶּרֶךְ יְרִידָה לְדֶרֶךְ עֲלִיָּיה – לְחַיְּיבוֹ מָמוֹן, אֶלָּא לְפוֹטְרוֹ מָמוֹן. אֶלָּא, כִּי אֲתָא רָבִין אָמַר: [ב]חַיָּיבֵי מִיתוֹת שׁוֹגְגִין כּוּלֵּי עָלְמָא לָא פְּלִיגִי דִּפְטוּרִין. כִּי פְּלִיגִי בְּחַיָּיבֵי מַלְקוֹת שׁוֹגְגִין וְדָבָר אַחֵר. [ג]רַבִּי יוֹחָנָן אָמַר: חַיָּיב, חַיָּיבֵי מִיתוֹת אִיתְקוּשׁ, חַיָּיבֵי מַלְקִיּוֹת – לָא אִיתְקוּשׁ. רֵישׁ לָקִישׁ אָמַר: פָּטוּר, בְּפֵירוּשׁ רִיבְּתָה תּוֹרָה חַיָּיבֵי מַלְקִיּוֹת כְּחַיָּיבֵי מִיתוֹת. הֵיכָן רִיבְּתָה תּוֹרָה? *אָמַר אַבַּיֵי? אָתְיָא "רָשָׁע" "רָשָׁע". רָבָא אָמַר: אָתְיָא "מַכֵּה" "מַכֵּה". אֲמַר לֵיהּ רַב פַּפָּא לְרָבָא: *הֵי מַכֵּה? אִילֵימָא "וּמַכֵּה בְהֵמָה יְשַׁלְּמֶנָּה וּמַכֵּה אָדָם יוּמָת" – הַאי בִּקְטָלָא כְּתִיב! אֶלָּא הַאי "מַכֵּה": "מַכֵּה נֶפֶשׁ בְּהֵמָה יְשַׁלְּמֶנָּה נֶפֶשׁ תַּחַת נָפֶשׁ" וּסְמִיךְ לֵיהּ "וְאִישׁ כִּי יִתֵּן מוּם בַּעֲמִיתוֹ [כַּאֲשֶׁר עָשָׂה כֵּן יֵעָשֶׂה לּוֹ]". – וְהַאי לָאו "מַכֵּה" הִיא! אֲנַן הַכָּאָה הַכָּאָה קָאָמְרִינַן. וְהָא כִּי כְּתִיב – בְּחוֹבֵל בַּחֲבֵירוֹ הוּא דִּכְתִיב, וְחוֹבֵל בַּחֲבֵירוֹ בַּר תַּשְׁלוּמִין הוּא! אִם אֵינוֹ עִנְיָן לְהַכָּאָה שֶׁיֵּשׁ בָּהּ שָׁוֶה פְּרוּטָה – [ד]תְּנֵהוּ עִנְיָן לְהַכָּאָה שֶׁאֵין בָּהּ שָׁוֶה פְּרוּטָה.

(שמות כא | במדבר לה | דברים כה | ויקרא כד | שם)

*) לקמן לח. ב"ק לה. סנהדרין עט: פד:

סוף

רש"י

מאי לאו אסון ממש. אם לא מתה האשה – יענש הנוגף בדמי ולדות. הא אם מתה – לא יענש, ואפי' לא התרו בו, וקשיא לר' יוחנן. לא דין אסון. הכי קאמר קרא: אם אין משפט מות לנוגף, כגון שלא מתה האשה, או מתה ולא התרו בו – ענוש יענש. מכה אדם ומכה בהמה. מכה בהמה ישלמנה, ומכה אדם לא ישלם, אלא יומת. הקיש פטור ממון דמכה אדם לחיוב ממון דמכה בהמה: מה מכה בהמה אין לך בו חילוק *לחיוב, אף מכה אדם אין לך בו חילוק *לפטור. מכה בהמה לעולם חייב, דאמרי' בב"ק (דף כו:): "פצע תחת פצע" – לחייב על השוגג כמזיד, ואונס כרצון. שאין מתכוין. אין בו חיוב מיתה באדם. דרך עלייה. שהכהו בהגבהת ידו, או שחתכו בחרבו מלמטה למעלה. בין דרך ירידה לדרך עלייה. משום דגבי גלות דהורג בשוגג איכא חילוק בין דרך ירידה לדרך עלייה, כדאמרי' במכות (דף ז:): כל שבדרך ירידתו גולה, דכתיב "ויפל עליו", עד שיפול כדרך נפילה. כולי עלמא לא פליגי דפטור. מדתנא דבי חזקיה. חייבי מיתות איתקוש. למכה בהמה. אתיא רשע רשע. נאמר בחייבי מיתות "אשר הוא רשע למות", ונאמר בחייבי מלקות "והיה אם בן הכות הרשע". רבא אמר אתיא מכה מכה. דמלקות נמי איתקוש למכה בהמה, ולאו מגזרה שוה דחייבי מיתות ילפינן. ואיש כי יתן מום בעמיתו כאשר עשה כן יעשה לו. והאי "יעשה לו" – מלקות קאמר. ולקמן פריך: והא חובל בחבירו בתשלומין, ולא מלקות! והאי. מלקות לאו מכה כתיב, אלא "כי יתן מום", ומאי אתיא "מכה" "מכה" דקאמר רבא? הכאה הכאה קאמרינן. ומום ע"י הכאה הוא ניתן. וחובל בחבירו בר תשלומין הוא. והיכי מוקמת ליה את במלקות ופטור ממון? אם אינו ענין. האי קרא. להכאה שיש בה שוה פרוטה. ולתשלומין, דהא מקרא דבתריה ילפינן, דכתיב ביה "כן ינתן בו" – דבר הניתן מיד ליד. תנהו ענין. לאי "כן יעשה לו". להכאה שאין בה שוה פרוטה. ולמלקות, ואיתקיש למכה בהמה שלא תחלוק בו.

סוף

תוספות

מאי לאו אסון ממש. אע"ג דסיפיה דקרא ד"אם אסון יהיה" ע"כ היינו דין אסון, כדכתיב "ונתת נפש" וגו' – מ"מ "לא יהיה אסון" הוה משמע ליה אסון ממש. אי נמי: "אם אסון יהיה" נמי בעי למימר דהוי אסון ממש, ודריש "ונתת נפש" וגו' – היינו ממון. **ומי** איכא למאן דאמר חייבי מיתות שוגגין חייבין והא תנא דבי חזקיה וכו'. וא"ת: והא אמרינן בפ' "הנשרפין" (סנהדרין עט: ושם): תנא דבי חזקיה מפקא מדרבי, ומפקא מדרבנן. אלמא פליגי תנאי אתנא דבי חזקיה! וי"ל: דלענין ממון אחר אית להו לכולהו היקישא דתנא דבי חזקיה, ולא פליגי עליה *אלא במאי דקתני בין מתכוין לשאינו מתכוין, דמשמע בין מתכוין להרוג האשה בין אין מתכוין להורגה, אלא להרוג את חברו והרגה, דבכל ענין פטור מדמי האשה. דלענין ממון אחר כבר תנא דלא תחלוק בין שוגג בין מזיד, והיינו דמפקא מדרבי ומדרבנן, דלר' נתכוין להרוג את זה והרג את זה חייב ממון, ולרבנן חייב מיתה, ולתנא דבי חזקיה פטור ממיתה וממון. אבל קשה לרבינו יצחק: דבריש "הנחנקין" (שם פד:) אמרינן: הניחא למאן דאית ליה דתנא דבי חזקיה, אבל למאן דלית ליה כו'. משמע דאיכא תנא דפליג! ואומר רבינו יצחק: דהיינו רבי חגא מדרומא, דאייתי מתניתא בידיה. כדאמרינן בפרק "שור שנגח ארבעה וחמשה" (ב"ק מב. ושם) דשני אנשים כי נתכוונו זה לזה, אע"פ שיש אסון באשה – יענשו בדמי ולדות. אלמא לית ליה היקישא דבין שוגג למזיד. והא דקאמר מי איכא למאן דאמר כו' – היינו משום דתנא דבי חזקיה עיקר, שהיה שונה ברייתות של רבי חייא שהיה אביו, כדמוכח בסוף פרק "הבא על יבמתו" (יבמות סה:), והן עיקר, ומותבינן תיובתא מינייהו. ולרשב"א נראה: דמשום הכי קא פריך ליה מתנא דבי חזקיה – משום דרבי יוחנן מוקי מתניתין (לעיל לג:) בשלא התרו בו, וקתני סיפא דחייבי מיתות פטורין – א"כ מתני' סברה דחייבי מיתות שוגגין פטורין. דאי סיפא מיירי בשהתרו בו – ליפלוג בחייבי מלקיות גופייהו. והוה מצי למיפרך ממתני', אלא דלא מצי למיפרך אלא מדיוקא, ולהכי פריך ליה מתנא דבי חזקיה, ומתניתין סמיך. ולפי זה מצינן למימר דמפקא מדרבי ורבנן בכולה מילתא. ועוד אומר רשב"א: דר' ישמעאל בנו של רבי יוחנן בן ברוקה לקמן בפירקין (דף לז:) *הוא תנא דלית ליה דתנא דבי חזקיה. וצריך לומר דלתנא דבי חזקיה "לא יהיה אסון" – היינו אסון ממש, וקרא ד"אם אסון יהיה" – היינו דין אסון, כגון שנתכוין לאשה. דאם לא נתכוין לה – פטור ממיתה וממון לתנא דבי חזקיה. א"נ: לא קאי קרא דאסון אאשה, אלא אחברו שנתכוין לו, ולא איירי קרא שנתכוין להרוג את זה והרג את זה. ובפ' "הנשרפין" דדייק לר"ש דפטר נתכוין להרוג את זה והרג את זה היכי מפרש קראי – הוה מצי למימר כדפרישית, אלא אליבא דר"א, דאמר: קראי בנתכוין להרוג את זה והרג את זה דייק.

אף מכה אדם לא תחלוק בו כו'. וקרא ד"לא יהיה אסון" דאשמעינן דלא ישלם דמי ולדות בהדי מיתה, והא נמי דדרשינן בשילהי פרק "כיצד הרגל" (ב"ק כו.) עליו – ולא על האדם, דלא תשקול מיניה ממונא וקטליה על הרציחה לחוד, וקרא ד"לא תקחו" דדרשינן מיניה דלא תשקול ממונא מיניה ונפטריה – אצטריכו כולהו, דלא מצי למילף מהיקישא דתנא דבי חזקיה, כדפירש בקונטרס לקמן (דף לח.) דמ"מכה בהמה" לא מצי למילף פטור ממון, דאדרבה חיוב היה לו למילף, דמכה בהמה חייב, להכי איצטריך למכתב כולהו. והכי ילפינן: מה מכה בהמה לא חלקת במה שכתוב בו, דהיינו חיוב, דבכל ענין חייב – אף מכה אדם כל עניני פטור ממון שכתוב בו – לא תחלוק בין שוגג בין מזיד, ובין דרך עלייה לדרך ירידה. ושוגג למזיד היינו ממון אחר בהדי מיתה, ודרך עלייה וירידה בכל ענין לא תשקול ממונא מיניה ונפטריה, כדאמרינן לקמן. ומתכוין לשאין מתכוין – לענין דמי האשה.

רבא אמר אתיא מכה מכה. תימה: לרבא לית ליה הכא גזרה שוה ד"רשע" "רשע", וכן ר' יוחנן. ולקמן (דף לז.) נמי מצרכינן חד קרא למיתה וממון; וחד למלקות וממון, ולא ילפינן מלקות וממון ממיתה וממון בגזרה שוה ד"רשע" "רשע", וסתמא דהתלמוד דריש ליה בפ"ק דמכות (דף ה:) גבי אין עדים זוממין נהרגין עד שיגמר הדין על פיהן, דאמרינן: חייבי מלקיות מנין? אתיא "רשע" "רשע". וברייתא נמי איכא בר"פ "אחד דיני ממונות" (סנהדרין לג: ושם) גבי דיני נפשות מחזירין לזכות אבל לא לחובה, דאמרינן: חייבי מלקיות מנין – אתיא "רשע" "רשע", תניא נמי הכי כו'. ור' יהודה נמי דריש ליה ב"החובל" (ב"ק פו: ושם) גבי וכן היה ר"י פוטרו, פירוש: את הסומא, מחייבי גליות ומחייבי מלקיות ומחייבי מיתות ב"ד. וגמר התם חייבי מיתות ב"ד מ"רוצח" "רוצח", וחייבי מלקיות אתיא "רשע" "רשע". ורבנן דפליגי עליה התם – לאו משום דלית להו "רשע" "רשע" אלא משום דמחייבי ליה כחייבי מיתות ב"ד! וי"ל: דרבא ור' יוחנן אית להו *בכ"מ גז"ש ד"רשע" "רשע" בדבר שהוא בגוף המלקות, אבל הכא לענין פטור ממון שהוא עם המלקות, וכן לקמן – לא ילפינן "רשע" "רשע". וטעמא – משום דקרא מוכח דרשע כתיב לענין מלקות "והיה אם בן הכות הרשע". והא דדריש "מכה" "מכה" – משום דמכה גבי תשלומין כתיב, שנאמר "מכה בהמה ישלמנה". ואביי אית ליה גזרה שוה ד"רשע" "רשע" בכ"מ. וסוגיא דלקמן כרבא ודלא כאביי. ואביי מוקי קרא במיתה ומלקות כר"מ, דלמלקות וממון לא צריך קרא, דאתיא "רשע" "רשע". ואם תאמר: ר' יוחנן אמאי לא דריש "מכה" "מכה", הא ברייתא היא בריש "החובל" (שם פג: ושם)! וי"ל: דסבר כאידך תנאי דהתם, דלא דרשי "מכה" "מכה" אלא ילפי מאידך קראי דלאו עין תחת עין ממש.

וכתיב ואיש כי יתן מום וגו'. אית דגרסי: וסמיך ליה, ולא מגזרה שוה יליף אלא מסמוכין. וכן משמע קצת, מדשביק קרא ד"מכה בהמה ישלמנה" ונקיט קרא אחרינא. ומיהו, מדפריך בריש "החובל" (שם פג:): מאי חזית דילפת ממכה בהמה, נילף ממכה אדם! משמע דגזרה שוה הוא, והא דהדר ביה מקרא קמא – משום דאיצטריך למהדר ממכה אדם ולאתויי "כי יתן מום בעמיתו", הדר ביה נמי מ"מכה בהמה ישלמנה" ומייתי "מכה נפש בהמה" דסמיך ליה. אי נמי משום דאיצטריך קרא קמא לכדתנא דבי חזקיה. ולמאן דלית ליה נמי איצטריך, מה מכה בהמה לרפואה פטור אף מכה אדם כו', כדאמרינן בריש "הנחנקין" (סנהדרין פד: ושם).

אם

עין משפט נר מצוה

מ א ב מיי' פ"א מהל' נערה בתולה הל' יג ופ"ד מהל' חובל הל' ז סמג עשין ע טוש"ע ח"מ סי' תכג סעיף ד:

מא ג מיי' פ"א מהל' נערה בתולה הל' יא ופ"ג מהל' גניבה הל' א סמג עשין נד:

מב ד מיי' פ"ד מהל' חובל הל' ט ופ"ה הל' ג סמג עשין ע טוש"ע ח"מ סי' תכ סעי' ב:

[וטעמא דרבי דדריש ונתת וגו' ממון ורבנן דרשי נפש ממש ולהכי לא מצי לאוקמי הקישא לאין מתכוין אבל לענין שוגג ומזיד כולהו אית להו הקישא. ת"י]

תוספות רי"ד

א"ר ומי איכא למ"ד חייבי מיתות שוגגין חייבין והתנא דבי חזקי' מכה אדם ומכה בהמה ישלמנה מה מכה בהמה לא חלקת בה בין בשוגג בין במזיד בין מתכוין לאינו מתכוין בין דרך ירידה לדרך עלייה לפוטרו ממון אלא לחייבו ממון אף מכה אדם לא חלקת בו בין שוגג למזיד בין מתכוין לא"מ בין דרך ירידה לד"ע לחייבו ממון אלא לפוטרו ממון. פי' המורה (מכה אדם) מכה בהמה ישלמנה ומכה אדם לא ישלם אלא יומת הקיש פטור ממון דמכה אדם לחיוב ממון דמכה בהמה. מה מכה בהמה אין לך בו חילוק לפטור מלשלם דאדם מועד לעולם בין ער ובין ישן בין שוגג בין מזיד אף מכה אדם אין לך בו חילוק לחיובא ומכה בהמה לעולם חייב דאמרי' בב"ק פצע תחת פצע לחייב השוגג כמזיד ואונס כרצון פי' שאין מתכוין אין בו חיוב מיתה באדם פי' דרך עלי' שהכהו בהגבהת ידו או בחרבו ממטה למעלה פי' בין דרך עליה וכו' משום דגבי גלות דהורג בשוגג איכא חילוק בין דרך ירידה לדרך עלייה. כדאמרי' במס' מכות כל שבדרך ירידתו גולה דכתיב ויפל עליו עד שיפול בדרך נפילה: אלא כי אתא רבין אמר ח"מ שוגגין דכ"ע לא פליגי דפטירי פי' מדתנא דבי חזקי' כי פליגי בחייבי מלקות שוגגים וד"א ר"י אמר חייבי מיתות איתקוש [חייבי מלקות לא איתקוש] ור"ל אמר פטור בפירוש רבתה תורה חייבי מלקות כחייבי מיתות היכן ריבתה אביי אמר רשע רשע פי' נאמר בחייבי מיתות אשר הוא רשע למות ונאמר בח"מ והי' אם בן הכות הרשע. רבא אמר אתיא מכה מכה פי' דחייבי מלקות נמי איתקש למכה בהמה ולא מג"ש דח"מ ילפינן וקי"ל כר"י:

מסורת הש"ס

ס"א לפטור

ס"א לחיוב

[סנהדרין י: וש"נ]

ב"ק פג:

[ועיין לקמן תוס' לח. ד"ה אבל סימא]

גליון הש"ס

תוס' ד"ה ומי איכא וכו' א"כ מתני' סברה. כעין זה בב"מ דף ח ע"ב תוס' ד"ה מנהיג לחודיה:

ובפ' קמא דסנהדרין דקאמר מ"ט דר' ישמעאל דאמר מלקות בכ"ג אביי אמר אתיא רשע רשע רבא אמר מלקות תחת מיתה עומדת לא משום דלית ליה כו' אלא משום דלא"ל כדאמר בפ"ק דמכות גבי ואין מלקין במכות וגבי מחזירים לזכות לא בעי למימר דתחת מיתה עומדת דשמא במיתה דוקא משום דכתיב ושפטו העדה והצילו. תו"י שם"ג:

מג א מיי' פ"א מהל' נערה בתולה הל' ט סמג עשין כד טור אה"ע סי' קעז:

תורה אור

סוֹף סוֹף לָאו בַּר תַּשְׁלוּמִין הוּא! (א) לָא צְרִיכָא, דְּבַהֲדֵי דְּמַחְיֵיהּ קָרַע שִׁירָאִין דִּילֵיהּ. א"ל רַב חִיָּיא לְרָבָא: וְלִתַנָּא דְּבֵי חִזְקִיָּה, דְּאָמַר: "מַכֵּה אָדָם וּמַכֵּה בְהֵמָה" מִמַּאי דְּבַחוֹל כְּתִיב, וְלֵיכָּא לְאִיפְלוּגֵי, דִּלְמָא בְּשַׁבָּת כְּתִיב, דְּבִבְהֵמָה גּוּפָהּ אִיכָּא לְאִיפְלוּגֵי? לָא ס"ד, דִּכְתִיב: °"וּמַכֵּה בְהֵמָה יְשַׁלְּמֶנָּה וּמַכֵּה אָדָם יוּמָת". הֵיכִי דָמֵי? אִי דְּלָא אַתְרוּ בֵּיהּ — מַכֵּה אָדָם אַמַּאי יוּמַת? אֶלָּא פְּשִׁיטָא — דְּאַתְרוּ בֵּיהּ, וְאִי בְּשַׁבָּת — מַכֵּה בְהֵמָה יְשַׁלְּמֶנָּה?! אֶלָּא לָאו — בַּחוֹל. א"ל רַב פַּפָּא לְאַבַּיֵי: *לְרַבָּה, דְּאָמַר: חִידּוּשׁ הוּא שֶׁחִידְּשָׁה תּוֹרָה בִּקְנָס, וְאַף עַל גַּב דְּמִיקְטִיל מְשַׁלֵּם, מַתְנִיתִין כְּמַאן מוֹקִים לָהּ? אִי כְּר"מ — קַשְׁיָא בִּתּוֹ, אִי כְּרַבִּי נְחוּנְיָא בֶּן הַקָּנָה — קַשְׁיָא אֲחוֹתוֹ, אִי כְּר' יִצְחָק — קַשְׁיָא מַמְזֶרֶת! הָנִיחָא אִי סָבַר לָהּ כְּר' יוֹחָנָן — הוּא נַמִי מְתָרֵץ לָהּ כְּר' יוֹחָנָן, אֶלָּא אִי סָבַר כְּר"ל — הֵיכִי מְתָרֵץ לָהּ? עַל כָּרְחָךְ כְּר' יוֹחָנָן ס"ל. א"ל רַב מַתָּנָא לְאַבַּיֵי: לְר"ל, דְּאָמַר: בְּפֵירוּשׁ רִיבְּתָה תּוֹרָה חַיָּיבֵי מַלְקִיּוֹת כְּחַיָּיבֵי מִיתוֹת, מַאן תַּנָּא דִּפְלִיג עֲלֵיהּ דְּרַבִּי נְחוּנְיָא בֶּן הַקָּנָה — אִי ר"מ, אִי רַבִּי יִצְחָק.§ ת"ר: עֲרָיוֹת וּשְׁנִיּוֹת לַעֲרָיוֹת אֵין לָהֶן לֹא קְנָס וְלֹא פִּיתּוּי. אהַמְמָאֶנֶת אֵין לָהּ לֹא קְנָס וְלֹא פִּיתּוּי. אַיְילוֹנִית אֵין לָהּ לֹא קְנָס וְלֹא פִּיתּוּי, וְהַיּוֹצֵאת מִשּׁוּם שֵׁם רַע אֵין לָהּ לֹא קְנָס וְלֹא פִּיתּוּי. מַאי עֲרָיוֹת וּמַאי שְׁנִיּוֹת לַעֲרָיוֹת? אִילֵימָא עֲרָיוֹת

עֲרָיוֹת

ויקרא כד

סוף סוף. האי לא תחלוק בו לחייבו ממון, טעמא משום דאין בו כדי תשלומין, ולא משום היקישא. אבל היכא דיש בה שוה פרוטה – אימא תחלוק. לא צריכא. להכי איתקש. דבהדי דמחייה קרע שיראין וכו'. כלומר, ואשמועינן דלוקה משום חבלה, ופטור מתשלומי קריעה. לא שנא התרו בו, ולא שנא לא התרו, דלא לקי – פטור מתשלומין מהיקישא דלא תחלוק. ממאי דבחול כתיב. דפשיטא ליה דמכה בהמה בין שוגג בין מזיד חייב לשלם. דלמא בשבת כתיב. ועל כרחך אשוגג כתיב קרא, דאי במזיד – הו"ל מתחייב בנפשו, ופטור מן התשלומין. איכא לאיפלוגי. בין שוגג למזיד. לא ס"ד. דבשבת כתיב ובשוגג. ואי בשבת מכה בהמה ישלמנה. בתמיה. אלא לאו בחול. דליכא לפלוגי, ואיתקש לה מכה אדם, שלא תחלוק בו, ואפי' אינו חייב מיתה. לרבה דאמר. לרבי מאיר חדוש הוא כו'. מתניתין כמאן מוקים. לשנויי רומיא דרמינן עלה דאלו הן הלוקין, וקיימא לן דאין לוקה ומשלם. אי כר' מאיר. דאמר לוקה ומשלם, וכדשנינהו ריש לקיש. קשיא בתו. דבשלמא לריש לקיש דאוקמה להיא דגנב וטבח בשבת בטובח על ידי אחר, אבל בטובח על ידי עצמו – לא משלם, לא קשיא; דמת ומשלם לית ליה לר' מאיר אפי' בקנס. אלא לרבה קשיא בתו, דקנס הוא, וקתני מתניתין פטור. ואי כר' נחוניא בן הקנה. דאית ליה נמי לוקה ומשלם כר' מאיר, מדקאמר יום הכפורים כשבת. יוה"כ הוא דפטור מתשלומין, ומשום כרת דאית ביה, ומג"ש ד"אסון" "אסון", אבל משום לאו ומלקות דאית ביה – לא פטר. ומתניתין נמי דאית ליה לוקה ומשלם – דידיה הוא, ומת ומשלם – לית ליה, אפי' בקנס. קשיא אחותו. נהי נמי דמשום מלקות לא פטר ליה, ליפטריה משום כרת. ואי כרבי יצחק. תוקמה, דאמר במסכת מכות (דף יד.): אין חייבי כריתות בכלל מלקות מ'. ולית ליה האי ד"אלו הן הלוקין": הבא על אחותו, ומשום הכי חייבין בתשלומין. קשיא ממזרת. דהכל מודים שהוא במלקות, וקתני: אית לה קנס. הניחא אי סבר. רבה כר' יוחנן, כשלא התרו בו, דמשלם, דחייבי מלקיות שוגגין ודבר אחר חייב. איהו נמי. מוקי למתני' בשלא התרו בו, כר' יוחנן. אלא אי סבר לה. בממון ומלקות דאפי' לא התרו בו פטור מממון, ופליג אדרבי יוחנן, וכל שכן אדעולא, דאמר אפילו התרו בו משלם ממון ואינו לוקה. היכי מתריץ לה. לא כר' יוחנן ולא כעולא ולא כריש לקיש. על כרחך. אי סבירא ליה בממון ומלקות דלוקה ואינו משלם – כרבי יוחנן סבירא ליה בשוגגים דמשלם ממון, ומוקי לה בשלא התרו בו. לריש לקיש דאמר בפירוש ריבתה תורה כו'. דחייבי מלקיות שוגגין פטורין מלשלם. מאן תנא דפליג אדר' נחוניא. ומחייב תשלומין בחייבי כריתות, כגון ההיא דשבועות: ושהדליק גדיש ביוה"כ – חייבין, בפרק "שבועת העדות" (שבועות לג.), ומתני' דהכא דקנסה באחותו. ונהי נמי דלית ליה "אסון" "אסון" למיפטריה משום כרת – ליפטריה משום לאו, בין התרו בו בין לא התרו בו. דאין כרת בלא לאו חוץ מפסח ומילה. דבשלמא ר' יוחנן – מוקי לה אפילו כרבנן דפליגי עליה דרבי מאיר, דאמרי אין לוקה ומשלם, והני – בשלא התרו בו. אלא לריש לקיש כמאן מוקי לה? אי רבי מאיר. דאמר לוקה ומשלם. אי רבי יצחק. דאמר לא שייך מלקות בחייבי כריתות. וג"ש ד"אסון" "אסון" לית ליה, ובמאי ליפטר? הילכך מתניתין דהכא על כרחך ר"מ היא ולא רבי יצחק, משום דקשיא ממזרת. אבל ההיא דשבועות – בין כר"מ בין כרבי יצחק. עריות ושניות. לקמן מפרש להו. קנס. דאנוסה. פיתוי. דמפותה. הממאנת. בבעלה, כגון יתומה קטנה שהשיאתה אמה ומיאנה בבעלה. אין לה קנס. שאינה בחזקת בתולה, הואיל וניסת. איילונית. שאין לה סימני נערות לעולם, ואינה יולדת. לשון איל זכר, דוכרניתא דלא ילדה (לעיל דף יא.). אין לה קנס. לפי שאין קנס אלא לנערה, וזו שלא תביא שערות לעולם – כל כ' שנה היא בחזקת קטנה, ומשם ואילך – בוגרת. והיוצאת משום שם רע. קס"ד שלא מצא לה בעלה בתולים. ולקמן פריך: בת סקילה היא!

עריות

אם אינו ענין להכאה שיש בה שוה פרוטה. וא"ת: והא אילטריך להכי, דמהכא נפקא לן חובל בחברו לתשלומין בריש "החובל" (ב"ק פג: ושם)! וי"ל: דהך סוגיא כאידך תנאי דהתם, דמפקי החובל בחברו לתשלומין מקרא אחרינא: דלמא בשבת כתיב דבבהמה גופה כו'. וא"ת: א"כ היקישא למה לי? וי"ל: דאתיא לבין דרך ירידה לדרך עלייה, דלא שייך לפלוגי גבי שבת. אלא לאו בחול. וא"ת: בחול נמי מצינן למימר, דבהדי דמחייה לבהמה הרג את האדם, ולא אתרו ביה משום אדם! ואפי' בשבת נמי מצינן למימר דאתרו ביה משום בהמה ולא אתרו בו משום שבת! וי"ל: דמ"מ ילפינן שפיר, דמה מכה בהמה לא חלקת בין שוגג בהכאתה למזיד בהכאתה – אף אדם לא תחלוק בו בין מזיד בהכאתו לשוגג בהכאתו. א"נ: הואיל ומכה אדם איירי באתרו ביה – מכה בהמה נמי איירי בכל ענין דאתרו ביה, ולהכי לא מצי איירי בשבת, ולא בהרג אדם עמה. מתניתין כמאן מוקי לה. *תימה: תיקשי ליה לרב פפא גופיה דאיהו סבר לעיל (דף לד:) כרבה, דאמר: היתה פרה גנובה לו כו'! ועוד קשה: דלישני כעולא, דמאי דפירש בקונ' דאי סבר כריש לקיש דחייבי מלקיות שוגגין פטורין כ"ש דפליג אדעולא – זה אינו נראה, דלמא בממון אחר סבר כריש לקיש, אבל בממונא דבההוא מילתא גופיה – משלם ממון ומיפטר ממלקות מג"ש ד"תחת" "תחת"! *ונראה: דרב פפא, אפי' סבר כר"ל מצי לשנויי כדעולא, כדפרישית. אבל לאביי פריך שפיר, דלית ליה דעולא, דהא מוקי לעיל "תחת" לדרשא אחרינא. ולהכי קשיא ליה, אי ס"ל כר"ל מתני' כמאן מוקי לה. אי כר' נחוניא קשיא אחותו. לא מצי למימר קשיא ממזרת ואחותו, דע"כ כר"מ ס"ל, מדנקט: יום הכפורים כשבת, וה"ל למימר יו"ט כשבת וכ"ש יום הכפורים, אלא ודאי ס"ל או כר"מ דאמר לוקה ומשלם, או כר' יצחק דאמר אין מלקות בחייבי כריתות. הלכך לא נקט, יו"ט דמיניה לא הוה שמעינן יוה"כ שאין בו מלקות. וכיון דלא הוי כרבנן לא מוקמי ליה כרבי יצחק אלא כר"מ, ולא תיקשי ממזרת. אי כרבי יצחק קשיא ממזרת. לא הוצרך לומר אי כרבנן, דלדידהו קשיא ממזרת ואחותו. ולא מצי למימר נמי דמתני' כרבי עקיבא, דסבר עדים זוממין קנסא, ואית ליה לוקה ומשלם, ולית ליה מת ומשלם – דלרבי עקיבא מצינן למימר דלא גמר עדים זוממין ממוציא ש"ר, אע"ג דהוי קנסא מקנסא, כדפרי' לעיל (דף לג. ד"ה דאין). ואית ליה שפיר כרבנן דלוקה ואינו משלם. מאן תנא דפליג עליה דרבי נחוניא אי ר' מאיר אי רבי יצחק. תימה: דלריש לקיש בהדיא פליג ר"מ אדרבי נחוניא, דהא מוקים מתני' כר"מ, וקתני דיש קנס בחייבי כריתות! וי"ל: דידע שפיר דר"מ פליג עליה, אלא דק"ל דרבנן לא מצינן למימר דפליגי עליה, אבל לר' יוחנן – אתי שפיר: לא קנס ולא פיתוי. אית דגרס: ולא אונס, משום דפיתוי נמי קנס הוא. ואומר ר"י: דגרסי' ליה, דשייך למיקרי לאונס קנס טפי מלפיתוי, משום דאונס שותה בעציצו (לקמן דף לט.).

הממאנת אין לה לא קנס. פירש בקונט': לפי שהיא בחזקת בעולה. וקשה לר"י: דא"כ הכי דייק לקמן: הא קטנה בעלמא אית לה, דלמא ה"ק: הממאנת אין לה קנס אם בא עליה כשהיא נערה, הא נערה בעלמא – אית לה! ומיהו, אין להקשות אמאי נקט ממאנת ה"ל למינקט כל אשה שניסת ונתגרשה, דהא איכא למ"ד לקמן (דף לח.) דאפי' אם נתארסה ונתגרשה אין לה קנס! ונראה לר"י דה"פ: אין לה לא קנס ולא פיתוי – אם אנסה בעלה או פיתה אותה, כשהיתה תחתיו קודם מיאון, אע"ג דכשמיאנה איגלאי מילתא שלא היתה אשתו. והשתא דייק שפיר לקמן: הא קטנה בעלמא אית לה. אבל קשה לר"י מהא דקאמר בסמוך: וכ"ת כולה ר"מ היא, וממאנת סבר לה כרבי יהודה. והשתא, כיון דאיירי שבא עליה בעלה כשהיא נערה שוב אינה יכולה למאן, דמודה רבי יהודה כשבעל, כדאמר בפרק "בא סימן" (נדה נב. ושם)! ותירץ ר"י: דמיירי כשפירש בהדיא שאינו בועל לשם קידושין. ועוד: דפיתוי ואונס לאו לשם קידושין הוא, דבהיא לא מודה רבי יהודה.

ולא פיתוי. קשה לרשב"א: אמאי נקט פיתוי, לאי דמוקי לה בסמוך בנערה? הא כל נערה מפותה אין לה קנס, דמחלה, אפי' נערה שאינה ממאנת! ויש לומר: דנקט אין לה פיתוי אגב דנקט באידך.

אבל

[לעיל לד: לקמן לח.]

[לרב פפא לא שייך למיפרך דהא לא פריך לנפשיה משום דידע דסבר כר' יוחנן דלא דריש ג"ש דרשע ודמכה וכ"מ קא דקאמר הי מכה. ת"י]

לפי' ר"י דלעיל אתי שפיר דרשב"ל מוקי לה כר"מ אבל רבה כמאן מוקי לה אי כר' נחוניא קשיא אחותו דלדידיה אחותו לית לה קנס דחד ריבויא מוקי לחייבי לאוין וחד ליבמה לשוק אי כדפי' רשב"א לעיל קשיא אחותו דאי נוקי חד קרא לחייבי כריתות א"כ חייבי מיתות נמי ולמה שהביא מהר"מ לעיל בתוס' אתי טפי שפיר אי ר' יצחק קשיא ממזרת דלדידיה מוקמינן חד לחייבי עשה וחד לחייבי כריתות הניחא אי סבר לה כר' יוחנן אלא אי סבר כרשב"ל דחייבי מלקות שוגגין פטורין א"כ אילטריך תרי ריבויי חד לחייבי עשה וחד לחייבי לאוין והא דלא קאמר אי כרבנן קשיא אחותו משום דעיקר קושיא מכר"מ לרבנן לעיל והא קי"ל דאין לוקה ומשלם ולכך לא חזר והקשה. ת"י עפ"ג:

הגהות הב"ח

(א) גמ' תשלומין הוא (לא צריכא) תא"מ ונ"ב ס"א הא לא קשיא:

עריות ממש, שניות — מדברי סופרים, כיון דמדאורייתא חזיא ליה — אמאי אין להן קנס? אלא: עריות — [א]חייבי מיתות בית דין, שניות — חייבי כריתות, אבל חייבי לאוין — יש להן קנס, ומני — *שמעון התימני היא. איכא דאמרי: עריות — חייבי מיתות ב"ד וחייבי כריתות, שניות — חייבי לאוין, מני — *ר"ש בן מנסיא היא.§ הממאנת אין לה לא קנס ולא פיתוי. הא קטנה בעלמא — אית לה, מני — רבנן היא, דאמרי: *קטנה יש לה קנס. אימא סיפא: איילונית אין לה לא קנס ולא פיתוי. אתא לר"מ, דאמר: *קטנה אין לה קנס, והא — מקטנותה יצתה לבגר. רישא רבנן וסיפא ר"מ! וכ"ת: כולה ר"מ היא, ובממאנת סבר לה כרבי יהודה; ומי סבר לה?! והתניא: *עד מתי הבת ממאנת? [ב]עד שתביא שתי שערות, דברי ר"מ. *ר' יהודה אומר: עד שירבה שחור על הלבן! אלא ר' יהודה היא, ובקטנה סבר לה כר"מ. ומי סבר לה? והאמר רב יהודה אמר רב: *זו דברי ר"מ. ואם איתא, זו דברי ר"מ ור' יהודה מיבעי ליה! האי תנא סבר לה כר"מ בחדא, ופליג עליה בחדא. רפרם אמר: מאי ממאנת — הראויה למאן. וליתני קטנה! קשיא.§ איילונית אין לה לא קנס ולא פיתוי. ורמינהי: החרשת והשוטה והאיילונית יש להן קנס ויש להן טענת בתולים! והא מאי רומיא? הא — ר"מ, הא — רבנן. ודקארי לה מאי קארי לה? משום דאית ליה למירמא אחריתי עילויה: [ג]החרשת והשוטה והבוגרת ומוכת עץ — אין להן טענת בתולים, [ד]הסומא ואיילונית — יש להן טענת בתולים. סומכוס אומר משום ר"מ: סומא אין לה טענת בתולים! אמר רב ששת: לא קשיא; הא — *רבן גמליאל, והא — ר' יהושע. אימר דשמעת ליה לרבן גמליאל היכא דקא טענה איהי, היכא דלא קא טענה איהי מי שמעת ליה? אין, כיון דאמר ר"ג מהימנא, *כגון זו °"פתח פיך לאלם" (משלי לא) הוא.§ והבוגרת אין לה טענת בתולים.§ והאמר רב: *[ה]בוגרת נותנין לה לילה הראשון! אי

רש"י

עריות ממש. המפורש ב"אחרי מות", והן בכריתות. שניות. שגזרו חכמים על שניות להן להרחיק מן העבירה, כגון אם אמו ואם אביו, ושאר עריות השנויות בפרק ב' דיבמות (דף כא.). כיון דשניות חזיין ליה מדאורייתא. קרינן ביה "ולו תהיה לאשה". אמאי אין לה קנס. בשלמא בעריות איכא למימר כשמעון התימני, דלית ליה "נערה" "נערה" "הנערה". אלא שניות קשיא. שמעון התימני. בריש פירקין, דאמר: אשה שיש בה הויה. ר"ש בן מנסיא. דאמר: אשה הראויה לקיימה. רבנן היא. דפליגי אדר"מ, בריש פירקין. ובממאנת סבר לה כר' יהודה. דאמר נערה ממאנת. והכי תידוק מינה: נערה ממאנת אין לה קנס, הא נערה בעלמא — יש לה קנס. עד שתביא שתי שערות. ומשהביאה אינה ממאנת, ואפילו לא בעל לאחר מיכן. רבי יהודה אומר. אם לא בעל לאחר שגדלה — ממאנת. עד שירבה שחור על הלבן. ובנדה מפרש: שתי שערות שוכבות, ונראה כמו שירבה השחור. אלא ר' יהודה היא. ובממאנת נערה אשמעינן דאין לה קנס, ולא תדוק הא קטנה יש לה קנס. וגבי איילונית, דתנא נמי אין לה קנס — משום דבקטנה סבר כר"מ, וזו מקטנותה יצאת לבגר. זו דברי כו'. לקמן בפרקין (דף מ:). סבר לה כר' מאיר. דקטנה אין לה קנס, משום הכי אין קנס באיילונית. ופליג עליה. בממאנת, ואמר: עד שירבה השחור. וכי תנא הממאנת אין לה קנס, הא הראויה למאן יש לה קנס, בנערה קאמר. מאי ממאנת הראויה למאן. כלומר, כל קטנה קאמר, וכולה ר"מ היא. ויש להן טענת בתולים. להפסידה כתובתה. הא ר"מ. דאמר: קטנה אין לה קנס, ואיילונית מקטנותה יצתה לבגר. ודקארי לה מאי קארי לה. מי שהשיב תשובה זו בבית המדרש, מה עלתה על רוחו, ולא סבירא ליה דאיכא לאוקמינהו כר"מ ורבנן? משום דאית ליה למירמא אחריתא עליה. לא הביאה לבית המדרש אלא לפי שיש להשיב אחרת על זו; חרשת ושוטה אחרשת ושוטה. בוגרת. בתוליה כלים מאיליהן. הא רבן גמליאל. דאמר בפ"ק (דף יב:): היא אומרת "משאירסתני נאנסתי" — נאמנת. הכא נמי אין לה טענת בתולים להפסידה כתובתה, דאמרינן: אי הוה פקחת לטעון — הוה טענה "משאירסתני נאנסתי", ומהימנא. הא רבי יהושע. דאמר "לא מפיה אנו חיין" — הכא יש לה טענת בתולים, דאי נמי הוה טענה קמן — לא מהימנינן לה. נותנין לה לילה הראשון. ובועל כמה בעילות, ותלינן כל דמים של אותו הלילה בדם בתולים. אלמא: אית לה דם בתולים לבוגרת. דאי לא — לא הוה בעי למיתב לה אלא בעילת מצוה, וכיון דאית לה בתולים — היכא דבעל ולא מצא דם תפסיד כתובתה, דהא כנסה בחזקת בתולה ומצאה בעולה.

ה"ג

תוספות

[אבל חייבי לאוין יש להן קנס ומני שמעון התימני היא. לא הוה מצי למימר מני רבי נחוניא היא, דלדידיה לא הוה קרי להו שניות, שהרי משוה חייבי כריתות לחייבי מיתות ב"ד. והא דלא קאמר הא מני רבי עקיבא, ועריות — חייבי מיתות, ושניות — חייבי כריתות וחייבי לאוין — אלא דניחא ליה לאוקמי אפי' כרבנן, דאמרי קידושין תופסין. ועוד: משום דקאמר בלישנא קמא מני שמעון התימני היא, קאמר נמי באיכא דאמרי מני רבי שמעון בן מנסיא היא, דהוי בר פלוגתיה דשמעון התימני].

עד שירבה השחור כו'. איכא דלא גרסי "על הלבן", משום דאמרינן בפרק "בא סימן" (נדה דף נב. ושם): לא שירבה ממש, אלא כדי שיהו שתי שערות שוכבות, ונראה כמו שירבה שחור. ו"על הלבן" משמע יותר מן הלבן. ור"ח פירש: על הלבן — שהשערות סמוך לבשר הם שחורים, וברא(ש)ם לבנים*. **זו** דברי ר"מ. אמתניתין דלקמן (דף מ:) דכל מקום שיש מכר אין קנס, קאמר לה רב יהודה.

ואם איתא זו דברי ר"מ ורבי יהודה מיבעי ליה. ואע"ג דרבי יונתן ור' יאשיה סבירא להו כר"מ בס"פ "ד' מיתות" (סנהדרין סו: ושם) לפי' ר"ת, דפי': עד שיהיו שניהם שוין במיתה אחת. ואפי' לפ"ה דמפרש בני עונשין — מ"מ ר' יאשיה כר' מאיר סבירא ליה, דלית ליה הא דדרשי רבנן לקמן (דף מ:) כאן נערה כו', דהא פטר קטנה מאורסה. מ"מ לא קאמר זו דברי ר"מ ור' יאשיה, דלא פריך הכא: זו דברי ר"מ ורבי יהודה מיבעי ליה, אלא משום דרבי יהודה בר פלוגתיה דר"מ, והוי בכלל חכמים דפליגי עליה. ולהכי, אם איתא דלא פליג — ה"ל למימר זו דברי ר"מ ור' יהודה. אבל קשה: דה"ל למימר הא מני — ר' יאשיה היא, ובממאנת סבר לה כר' יהודה.

וליתני קטנה קשיא. אע"ג דהוי תני קטנה דאין לה קנס, מ"מ תני נמי אילונית. דה"א דוקא קטנה שיש לה נערות אין לה קנס. ותימה לר"י: אמאי לא משני דאגב אורחיה קמ"ל, דעד מתי הבת ממאנת — עד שתביא שתי שערות.

החרשת והשוטה כו' אין להן טענת בתולים. פי' בקונטרס: דאי הוה פקחת לטעון הוה טענה "משאירסתני נאנסתי". וקשה לר"י: דהיכי טענינן לה הכי מספק לאפוקי ממונא, כיון דאיהי לא טענה, חזקת גופה איתרעי, דהוי שור שחוט לפניך, אבל חזקת ממון לא איתרע! ומיהו, מביא ר"י ראיה לפי' הקונטרס: דאמר בפ' "המדיר" (לקמן עו: ושם): לא הוגלד פי המכה — המוציא מחבירו עליו הראיה. ומפרש דאפי' לא יהיב טבח דמי — על הטבח להביא ראיה שברשות המוכר נטרפה. והא דמפרש רב אשי למתני' ד"המדיר" דהיו בה מומין ועודה בבית אביה על האב להביא ראיה, רישא — מנה לאבא בידך, סיפא — מנה לי בידך. לא מטעם דברי ושמא ברי עדיף, כדמשמע לפום ריהטא — דא"כ הוה קשה דהיכי טענינן לה הכי? אלא כדפי' התם בקונטרס: רישא מנה לאבא בידך — דלגבי האב לא מהני חזקת הגוף דבתו, דהכתובה היא באירוסין של אב. סיפא מנה לי בידך, דלגבי דידה מהני חזקת הגוף דידה. וכן צריך לפרש, דאי מטעם ברי קאמר התם — אמאי קאמר דעודה בבית אביה על האב להביא ראיה דמשנתארסה נולדו בה מומין, אמאי צריך להביא ראיה, כיון דאמר ברי לי? דבכל ענין משמע דצריך להביא ראיה, אפילו אב אמר ברי לי. ולר"י נראה לפרש הכא: דאין להן טענת בתולים לפי שבחזקת מוכת עץ היא. ואע"ג דכולהו נמי חבוטי מחבטן — מ"מ שאר נשים יש להן טענת בתולים, מדלא קאמרי שהן מוכת עץ. אבל הנך, חרשת ושוטה, דלא מצי אמרי — בחזקת מוכת עץ נשאות. וכן נראה, דברוב ספרים ל"ג לעיל בברייתא אלא: החרשת והשוטה והאילונית יש להן קנס, ותו לא. ואין כתוב ברוב ספרים "ויש להן טענת בתולים". ולפר"י פריך שפיר, דמדקאמר יש להן קנס — אלמא לא חשבינן להו בחזקת מוכת עץ. אבל לפי' הקונטרס מאי קפריך? הכא נמי בחזקת בתולות חשבינן להו, דהא אמרינן השתא* דמשנתארסה נארסה. ורשב"א [א] הקשה לפר"י: דאמאי לא משני הא דקתני אין להן טענת בתולים כר"מ, דאמר בפ"ק (לעיל יג.): מוכת עץ, בין הכיר בה בין לא הכיר בה — מאתים. והא דקתני יש להן טענת בתולים — *כרבנן, דאמרי כתובתן מנה! וכי תימא משום דקתני חרשת דומיא דאיילונית — הא ע"כ איילונית גופה לא הפסידה כתובתה לגמרי, דהא רב ששת דמשני הא ר"ג הא ר' יהושע סבירא ליה בפ"ק (דף יא:): כנסה בחזקת בתולה ונמצאת בעולה — יש לה כתובה מנה.

[א] [נראה דלא מצי למימר הא ר"מ דהא ר"מ פליג בסיפא א"כ תנא קמא בר פלוגתיה תנא אחרינא הוא. ת"י]

עין משפט נר מצוה

מד א מיי' פ"א מהל' נערה בתולה הל' יא יג סמג עשין כד טור אה"ע סי' קעז:

מה ב מיי' פי"א מהל' גירושין הל' ז סמג עשין נ טוש"ע אה"ע סי' קנה סעי' יב:

מו ג מיי' פי"א מהל' אישות הלכה ג ד ח סמג עשין מח טוש"ע שם סי' סח סעיף ה. [וברב אלפס פ"א דמכילתין דף סו.]

מז ד מיי' שם טוש"ע שם סעי' ו:

מח ה מיי' פ"ה מהל' איסורי ביאה הל' יט סמג לאוין קיא [וברב אלפס שם]:

[וע' תוס' ב"ב קנו. ותוס' חולין כו: ד"ה עד]

תוספות רי"ד

תנו רבנן. החרשת והשוטה והבוגרת ומוכ"ע אין להם קנס וא"ל טענת בתולים פי' להפסידן כתובתן חרשת ושוטה לא דאמרי' אי הוו פקחות לטעון הוו טענו כל חדא וחדא משאירסתני נאנסתי ומהימן בוגרת נמי לא שבתולי' כלין מאליהן האיילונית והסומא יש להן ט"ב פי' א) ודוקא דקא טעין טענת פ"פ אבל אי טעין טענת דמים ל"ל דבוגרת כלין בתוליה. אבל פתח נעול יש לה (והרב אומר היפך טענות דמים יש לה טענות פ"פ אין לה):

א) הך פי' קאי אבוגרת ונראה דל"ל פי' ודווקא דקא טעין טענת דמים אבל אי טעין טענת פ"פ טענתו טענה דבוגרת כלו בתוליה וכו'.

[ולכאורה נראה דלא מצי לשנויי קמייתא כרבנן דכתובתה מנה דמ"מ תקשי אמאי יש לה קנס כיון שהיא בחזקת מוכת עץ. ת"י]

מסורת הש"ס

[לעיל כט.]

[שם]

[שם]

[לעיל כט. וש"נ]

חולין כו:

יבמות יב: ב"ב קנו: נדה נב.

[לקמן מ:]

[לעיל יב:]

[כ"ב מח. גיטין לז:]

נדה סד:

[ולמאן דמפרש התם משום כאן נמצא וכאן היה נ"ל דהכא איירי כגון שיצא קול שמשנתארסה נאנסה דאי לאו הכי הוי לן למימר כיון שבבית אביה נאנסה שמעיקרא נאנסה כדאמר התם גבי מומין. ת"י]

תורה אור

אִי דְּקָא טָעֵין טַעֲנַת דָּמִים — הָכִי נַמִי, הָכָא בְּמַאי עָסְקִינַן — דְּקָטָעֵין טַעֲנַת פֶּתַח פָּתוּחַ.§ סוּמָכוֹס אוֹמֵר מִשּׁוּם ר"מ: סוּמָא אֵין לָהּ טַעֲנַת בְּתוּלִים.§ מ"ט דְּסוּמָכוֹס? א"ר זֵירָא: מִפְּנֵי שֶׁנֶּחְבֶּטֶת עַל גַּבֵּי קַרְקַע. כּוּלְּהוּ נַמִי חַבּוּטֵי מִיחַבְּטִי! כּוּלְּהוּ רוֹאוֹת וּמַרְאוֹת לְאִמָּן, זוֹ אֵינָהּ רוֹאָה, וְאֵינָהּ מַרְאָה לְאִמָּהּ.§ וְהַיּוֹצֵאת מִשּׁוּם שֵׁם רַע אֵין לָהּ לֹא קְנָס וְלֹא פִּיתּוּי.§ הַיּוֹצֵאת מִשּׁוּם שֵׁם רַע בַּת סְקִילָה הִיא! אָמַר רַב שֵׁשֶׁת: הָכִי קָאָמַר: מִי שֶׁיָּצָא עָלֶיהָ שֵׁם רַע בְּיַלְדוּתָהּ — אֵין לָהּ לֹא קְנָס וְלֹא פִּיתּוּי. אָמַר רַב פַּפָּא: ש"מ, *הַאי שְׁטָרָא רִיעָא לָא מַגְבִּינַן בֵּיהּ. הֵיכִי דָּמֵי? אִילֵימָא דְּנָפַק קָלָא עֲלֵיהּ דִּשְׁטָרָא דְּזַיְיפָא הוּא, דִּכְוָותָהּ הָכָא — דְּנָפַק עֲלָהּ קָלָא דִּזְנַאי, וְהָא אָמַר רָבָא: *[א]יָּצָא לָהּ שֵׁם מְזַנָּה בָּעִיר — אֵין חוֹשְׁשִׁין לָהּ! אֶלָּא, [ב]דְּאָתוּ בֵּי תְּרֵי וְאָמְרִי: לְדִידְהוּ תְּבַעְתִּנְהִי בְּאִיסּוּרָא. דִּכְוָותָהּ הָכָא — [ג]דְּאָתוּ בֵּי תְּרֵי וְאָמְרִי: לְדִידְהוּ אֲמַר לְהוּ "זַיְּיפוּ לִי". בִּשְׁלָמָא הָתָם — שְׁכִיחִי פְּרוּצִין, אֶלָּא הָכָא — *אִם הוּא הוּחְזַק — כָּל יִשְׂרָאֵל מִי הוּחְזְקוּ?! הָכָא נַמִי, כֵּיוָן דְּקָא מְהַדַּר אַזִּיּוּפָא — אֵימַר זִיּוּפֵי זַיֵּיף וְכָתַב.§

מתני' [ד]וְאֵלּוּ שֶׁאֵין לָהֶן קְנָס: הַבָּא עַל הַגִּיּוֹרֶת, וְעַל הַשְּׁבוּיָה, וְעַל הַשִּׁפְחָה, שֶׁנִּפְדּוּ וְשֶׁנִּתְגַּיְּירוּ וְשֶׁנִּשְׁתַּחְרְרוּ יְתֵירוֹת עַל בְּנוֹת שָׁלֹשׁ שָׁנִים וְיוֹם אֶחָד. רַבִּי יְהוּדָה אוֹמֵר שְׁבוּיָה שֶׁנִּפְדֵּית הֲרֵי הִיא בִּקְדוּשָּׁתָהּ, אע"פ שֶׁגְּדוֹלָה. *[ה]הַבָּא עַל בִּתּוֹ, עַל בַּת בִּתּוֹ, עַל בַּת בְּנוֹ, *עַל בַּת אִשְׁתּוֹ, עַל בַּת בְּנָהּ, עַל בַּת בִּתָּהּ — אֵין לָהֶן קְנָס, מִפְּנֵי שֶׁמִּתְחַיֵּיב בְּנַפְשׁוֹ, שֶׁמִּיתָתָן בִּידֵי בֵּית דִּין, וְכָל הַמִּתְחַיֵּיב בְּנַפְשׁוֹ אֵין מְשַׁלֵּם מָמוֹן, שֶׁנֶּאֱמַר: °"וְאִם לֹא יִהְיֶה אָסוֹן עָנוֹשׁ יֵעָנֵשׁ".§ (שמות כא)

גמ' א"ר יוֹחָנָן: רַבִּי יְהוּדָה וְרַבִּי דּוֹסָא אָמְרוּ דָּבָר אֶחָד; רַבִּי יְהוּדָה — הָא דַּאֲמַרַן, רַבִּי דּוֹסָא — *דְּתַנְיָא: *שְׁבוּיָה אוֹכֶלֶת בִּתְרוּמָה, דִּבְרֵי ר' דּוֹסָא. אָמַר רַבִּי דּוֹסָא: וְכִי מָה עָשָׂה לָהּ עַרְבִי הַלָּז? וְכִי מִפְּנֵי שֶׁמִּיעֵךְ לָהּ בֵּין דַּדֶּיהָ פְּסָלָהּ מִן הַכְּהוּנָּה? אָמַר *רַבָּה: דִּלְמָא לָא הִיא; עַד כָּאן לָא קָאָמַר ר' יְהוּדָה הָכָא אֶלָּא שֶׁלֹּא יְהֵא חוֹטֵא נִשְׂכָּר, אֲבָל הָתָם — [ו]כְּרַבָּנַן סְבִירָא לֵיהּ. אִי נַמִי: עַד כָּאן לָא קָאָמַר ר' דּוֹסָא הָתָם — אֶלָּא בִּתְרוּמָה דְּרַבָּנַן, אֲבָל קְנָס דְּאוֹרַיְיתָא — כְּרַבָּנַן סְבִירָא לֵיהּ. אֲמַר לֵיהּ אַבַּיֵּי: וְטַעְמֵיהּ דְּרַבִּי יְהוּדָה הָכָא שֶׁלֹּא יְהֵא חוֹטֵא נִשְׂכָּר הוּא? וְהָא תַּנְיָא, *ר' יְהוּדָה אוֹמֵר: *שְׁבוּיָה שֶׁנִּשְׁבֵּית הֲרֵי הִיא בִּקְדוּשָּׁתָהּ, אֲפִי' בַּת עֶשֶׂר שָׁנִים כְּתוּבָּתָהּ מָאתַיִם, וְהָתָם — מַאי שֶׁלֹּא יְהֵא חוֹטֵא נִשְׂכָּר אִיכָּא? הָתָם נַמִי, דִּלְמָא מִימְנְעִי וְלָא נָסְבִי לָהּ. וְסָבַר ר"י בִּקְדוּשָּׁתָהּ קַיְימָה? וְהָתַנְיָא: *הַפּוֹדֶה אֶת הַשְּׁבוּיָה יִשָּׂאֶנָּה; מֵעִיד בָּהּ — לֹא יִשָּׂאֶנָּה. ר' יְהוּדָה אוֹמֵר: בֵּין כָּךְ וּבֵין כָּךְ — לֹא יִשָּׂאֶנָּה! הָא גּוּפָהּ קַשְׁיָא; אָמְרַתְּ: הַפּוֹדֶה אֶת הַשְּׁבוּיָה יִשָּׂאֶנָּה, וַהֲדַר תָּנָא: מֵעִיד בָּהּ — לֹא יִשָּׂאֶנָּה, מִשּׁוּם דְּמֵעִיד בָּהּ לֹא יִשָּׂאֶנָּה?! הָא לָא קַשְׁיָא; הָכִי קָאָמַר: הַפּוֹדֶה אֶת הַשְּׁבוּיָה וּמֵעִיד בָּהּ — יִשָּׂאֶנָּה, מֵעִיד בָּהּ כְּדֵי — לֹא יִשָּׂאֶנָּה. מ"מ קַשְׁיָא לְר' יְהוּדָה! אָמַר רַב פַּפָּא: אֵימָא; רַבִּי יְהוּדָה אוֹמֵר בֵּין כָּךְ וּבֵין כָּךְ — יִשָּׂאֶנָּה. רַב הוּנָא בְּרֵיהּ דְּרַב יְהוֹשֻׁעַ אוֹמֵר: לְעוֹלָם כִּדְקָתָנֵי, ר' יְהוּדָה לְדִבְרֵיהֶם דְּרַבָּנַן קָאָמַר לְהוּ: לְדִידִי — בֵּין כָּךְ וּבֵין כָּךְ יִשָּׂאֶנָּה, אֶלָּא לְדִידְכוּ — בֵּין כָּךְ וּבֵין כָּךְ לֹא יִשָּׂאֶנָּה מִבָּעֵי לֵיהּ! וְרַבָּנַן? [ז]הַפּוֹדֶה אֶת הַשְּׁבוּיָה וּמֵעִיד בָּהּ יִשָּׂאֶנָּה — לָא שָׁדֵי אִינִישׁ זוּזֵי בִּכְדִי, [ח]מֵעִיד בָּהּ כְּדֵי לֹא יִשָּׂאֶנָּה — שֶׁמָּא עֵינָיו נָתַן בָּהּ. רָמֵי לֵיהּ רַב פַּפָּא בַּר שְׁמוּאֵל לְרַב יוֹסֵף:

וְסָבַר

ה"ג: אִי דְּקָא טָעֵין טַעֲנַת דָּמִים הָכִי נַמִי. הב"ע דְּקָטָעֵין טַעֲנַת פֶּתַח פָּתוּחַ. אִי דְּקָאָמַר בָּעַלְתִּי וְלֹא מָצָאתִי דָּם — וַדַּאי טַעֲנָה מַעַלְיָיתָא הִיא. וְהָכָא דְּקָתָנֵי אֵין לָהּ טַעֲנַת בְּתוּלִים — דְּקָטָעֵין וְאָמַר פֶּתַח פָּתוּחַ מָצָאתִי, וְדָם לֹא בָּדַקְתִּי אִם נִמְצָא בָּהּ אִם לָאו. בְּנַעֲרָה וּקְטַנָּה — טַעֲנָה הִיא, כִּדְאָמְרִינַן בְּפ"ק. וְאע"פ שֶׁאֵין יָכוֹל לְבָרֵר דְּבָרָיו בְּפָנֵינוּ — אָמְרִינַן: חֲזָקָה אֵין אָדָם טוֹרֵחַ בִּסְעוּדָה וּמַפְסִידָהּ. אֲבָל מְשֻׁבֶּגֶרֶת, אֵין רַחְמָהּ צַר כְּבַתְּחִילָּה, וְדוֹמֶה לוֹ כְּאִילּוּ פֶּתַח פָּתוּחַ. שֶׁנֶּחְבֶּטֶת. וּבְתוּלֶיהָ נוֹשְׁרִין. כּוּלְּהוּ רוֹאוֹת. אִם נָשְׁרוּ בְּתוּלֵיהֶן [רוֹאוֹת דָּם]. וּמַרְאוֹת לְאִמָּן. וּפוֹסְקוֹת עֲלֵיהֶן שֶׁאֵינָן בְּתוּלוֹת, וְאִם לֹא הוֹדִיעַתּוּ — הִטְעַתּוּ. וְזוֹ אֵינָהּ רוֹאָה וְאֵינָהּ מַרְאָה לְאִמָּהּ. וְזֶה שֶׁכְּנָסָהּ — בְּחֶזְקַת נֶחְבֶּטֶת כְּנָסָהּ, וְאֵין אָדָם פּוֹסֵק עָלֶיהָ, וְלָאו טָעוּת הוּא. רִיעָא. שֶׁיָּצָא עָלָיו שֵׁם זִיּוּף. אֵין חוֹשְׁשִׁין לָהּ. אֲפִי' לִכְהוּנָּה. אֶלָּא. יָצָא עָלֶיהָ שֵׁם רָע הֵיכִי דָּמֵי — כְּגוֹן בְּעֵדִים. וְלֹא שֶׁאָמְרוּ עָלֶיהָ שֶׁנִּבְעֲלָה — דְּא"כ מַאי לְמֵימְרָא? הָא לָאו בְּתוּלָה הִיא! אֶלָּא אָמְרִי: לְדִידְהוּ תְּבַעְתִּנְהוּ לְאִיסּוּרָא, הִפְקִירָה עַצְמָהּ לְכָךְ, וְלֹא שָׁמְעוּ לָהּ. בִּשְׁלָמָא הָתָם כו'. הֵיכִי גָּמַר רַב פַּפָּא מִינָּהּ דְּלָא מַגְבִּינַן בִּשְׁטָרָא כִּי הַאי? בִּשְׁלָמָא הָתָם — שְׁכִיחִי פְּרוּצִין, וְכֵיוָן שֶׁיֵּשׁ עֵדִים שֶׁהָיְתָה מְחַזֶּרֶת אַחַר הַזְּנוּת — הַרְבֵּה מָצְאָה לָהּ, מִשּׁוּם הָכִי אֵין לָהּ קְנָס לְאַחַר זְמַן, דְּלָאו בְּחֶזְקַת בְּתוּלָה הֲוַאי. אֶלָּא. לְגַבֵּי שְׁטָר. אִם הוּא הוּחְזַק. לַחֲזוֹר אַחַר עֵדֵי שֶׁקֶר. כָּל יִשְׂרָאֵל מִי הוּחְזְקוּ. לִהְיוֹת שׁוֹמְעִין לוֹ לְזַיֵּיף. אֵימַר זִיּוּפֵי זַיֵּיף. הוּא עַצְמוֹ לָמַד לְכַוֵּין כְּתָב הַדּוֹמֶה לִכְתַב יְדֵי עֵדִים שֶׁחָתַם בּוֹ.
מתני' יְתֵירוֹת עַל בְּנוֹת שָׁלֹשׁ שָׁנִים. דְּכֵיוָן דִּרְאוּיוֹת לְבִיאָה — בְּחֶזְקַת הֶפְקֵר הֵן, וְנִבְעָלוֹת בְּגֵיוּתָן, וְהַשְּׁבוּיָה בְּשִׁבְיָיתָהּ. וְלֹא יִהְיֶה אָסוֹן עָנוֹשׁ יֵעָנֵשׁ. הָא אִם יִהְיֶה אָסוֹן — לֹא יֵעָנֵשׁ. **גמ'** שְׁבוּיָה. בַּת כֹּהֵן. אוֹכֶלֶת בִּתְרוּמָה. וְלֹא מַחְזִיקִינַן לָהּ בְּחֶזְקַת בְּעוּלָה לִפְסוֹל לָהּ הַמְחַלְּלָהּ בְּבִיאָתוֹ. מִפְּנֵי שֶׁמִּיעֵךְ לָהּ. כְּלוֹמַר, אֵין נוֹהֲגִין בָּהֶן הֶפְקֵר לְאוֹנְסָן בִּבְעִילָה, אֶלָּא לְשַׂחֵק עִמָּהֶן. [רַבָּנַן פְּלִיגֵי אַדְּרַבִּי דּוֹסָא, וְאָמְרוּ: יֵשׁ שְׁבוּיָה אוֹכֶלֶת וְיֵשׁ שֶׁאֵינָהּ אוֹכֶלֶת. כֵּיצַד? הָאִשָּׁה שֶׁאָמְרָה נִשְׁבֵּיתִי וּטְהוֹרָה אֲנִי — אוֹכֶלֶת, וְאִם יֵשׁ עֵדִים שֶׁנִּשְׁבֵּית וְהִיא אוֹמֶרֶת טְהוֹרָה אֲנִי — אֵינָהּ אוֹכֶלֶת. בְּמַסֶּכֶת עֵדֻיּוֹת]. אֶלָּא בִּתְרוּמָה בַּזְּמַן הַזֶּה דְּרַבָּנַן. דְּכֵיוָן דַּאֲפִילּוּ נִבְעֲלָה, אִיסּוּרָא דְּרַבָּנַן בְּעָלְמָא הוּא — לֹא גָּזְרוּ עַל סְפֵיקָהּ. אֲבָל קְנָס, דְּאַפּוֹקֵי מָמוֹנָא הוּא, אֵימָא לָךְ: סָפֵק בְּעוּלָה הִיא, וּמִסְּפֵיקָא לֹא מַפְּקִינַן מָמוֹנָא. דִּלְמָא מִמְּנְעִי וְלָא נָסְבִי לָהּ. אִי פָּחֲתַתְּ כְּתוּבָּתָהּ מְשַׁוֵּית לָהּ בְּחֶזְקַת בְּעוּלָה, וּמְרַחֲקֵי לָהּ אֲפִילּוּ יִשְׂרָאֵל. מֵעִיד בָּהּ. קָא סָלְקָא דַּעְתִּין דְּאַפּוֹדֶה קָאֵי, שֶׁאִם הָיָה מֵעִיד בָּהּ שֶׁלֹּא נִבְעֲלָה לְגוֹי — לֹא יִשָּׂאֶנָּה אִם כֹּהֵן הוּא. מִשּׁוּם דְּמֵעִיד בָּהּ וכו'. וְהָא אָמְרוּ: הַפּוֹדֶה אֶת הַשְּׁבוּיָה — יִשָּׂאֶנָּה. הַפּוֹדֶה אֶת הַשְּׁבוּיָה וּמֵעִיד בָּהּ יִשָּׂאֶנָּה. דְּאִי לָאו דְּקִים לֵיהּ בְּגַוָּהּ — לָא שָׁדֵי זוּזֵי בִּכְדִי, שֶׁהֲרֵי לִישָּׂאֶנָּה פְּדָאָהּ. מֵעִיד בָּהּ כְּדֵי לֹא יִשָּׂאֶנָּה. שֶׁמָּא עֵינָיו נָתַן בָּהּ.
וְרָאֲתָה

אי דקא טעין טענת דמים ה"נ כו'. כך גרס בקונטרס. ור"ת גריס איפכא, *כמו שהיה כתוב בספרים: אי דקא טעין טענת פתח פתוח — ה"נ כו'. ולעיל בפ"ק (דף ט. ד"ה האומר) פירשתי. קצת קשה לפי' ר"ת, דמפרש דמוכת עץ אין לה דמים, אבל פתחה נעול — אם כן בחנם דחק לשנויי הא ר"ג והא רבי יהושע, דה"מ לשנויי: הא — דקא טעין פתח פתוח, הא — דקא טעין טענת דמים. ושמא לית ליה חזקה דאין אדם טורח בסעודה ומפסידה, ולא מהימן בפתח פתוח להפסידה כתובתה. אע"ג דקאמר אי דקא טעין פתח פתוח הכי נמי, דמשמע דנאמן — שמא היינו לאוסרה עליו. אבל ברייתא דלעיל משמע דיש להן טענת בתולים לענין כתובה, דומיא דקנס.

כולהו רואות ומראות לאמן. פירש הקונטרס: ופוסקות עליהן שהן בעולות, ואם לא הודיעתו — הטעתו. וקשה לפירושו: דהא אליבא דר"מ קיימינן, ור' מאיר אית לי' בפ"ק (דף יג.) דמוכת עץ, בין הכיר בה בין לא הכיר בה — מאתים! ונראה לר"י דה"פ: כולהו רואות ומראות לאמן, ויודעות שהן מוכת עץ, שאמותיהן מגידות להן. ולהכי [כשהוא אומר לא מצאתי לבתך בתולים, והיא אומרת בתולה הייתי — אין לנו לתלות במוכת עץ, שא"כ היתה אומרת: מוכת עץ אני]. וכי לא אמרה מוכת עץ אני — יש לה טענת בתולים. אבל סומא — תלינן שהיא מוכת עץ אע"ג דלא אמרה, דאינה יודעת, לפי שאינה רואה ואינה מראה לאמה, ואין אמה מגדת לה.

היוצאת משום שם רע *בת סקילה היא. ופשיטא דלאו בת קנס היא, דהא בעולה ודאי היא. אבל אין לפרש הואיל ויש חיוב סקילה לבא עליה פשיטא דאין לה קנס, דקם ליה בדרבה — מיניה דהא קתני במתניתין הבא על בתו, ולעיל נמי קתני עריות בברייתא.

ואלו שאין להן קנס הגיורת והשבויה כו'. אף על גב דמדאורייתא שבויה לא הויא בחזקת בעולה, כדאמרינן בכל דוכתי דבשבויה הקילו — מ"מ אין לה קנס, דמשום גזירה שלא תינשא לכהן, עשאוה כבעולה לכל דבריה.

וכי מה עשה לה ערבי זה. נקט ערבי לפי שהם שטופים בזימה, כדאמר בקדושין (דף מט:): עשרה קבין זימה ירדו לעולם ט' נטלו ערביים.

משום דמעיד בה לא ישאנה. קס"ד: הפודה את השבויה ישאנה, בלא עדות קאמר.

מכל מקום קשיא. אליבא דרבי יוחנן פריך. וכן כל הנך פירכי דלקמן. אבל לרבה, דאמר דטעמא דרבי יהודה שלא יהא חוטא נשכר — לא קשיא מידי.

תוספות רי"ד

ת"ר יצא עליה ש"ר בילדותה אין לה לא אונס ולא פיתוי אמר ר"פ ש"מ האי שטרא ריעא לא מגבינן בי' פי' שיצא עלי' שם זיוף ה"ד אי נימא דנפיק עלי' קלא דשטר זייפא הוא דכוותה הכא נמי דנפיק עלי' קלא דזנאי והא"ר יצא עליה שם מזנה בעיר אין חוששין לה אפי' לכהונה אלא דאתי בי תרי ואמרו לדידהו תבעתנהי באיסורא פי' אלא יצא עליה ש"ר ה"ד כגון בעדים לא שאמרו נבעלה דא"כ מאי למימרא הא לאו בתולה היא אלא אמרי לדידהו וכו' פירוש והפקירה עצמה לכך ולא שמענו לה דכותה התם דאתי בי תרי ואמרו לדידהו אמר זייפו לי. בשלמא הכא שכיחי פריצות פי' היכא גמר ר"פ מינה דלא מגבי' בשטרא כי האי התם שכיחי פרוצות וכיון שיש עדים שהיתה מחזרת אחר זנות הרבה מצאה לה מ"ה אין לה קנס לאחר זמן דלאו בחזקת בתולה הואי אלא התם אם הוא מוחזק כל ישראל מי הוחזקו פי' גבי שטר אם הוא מוחזק לחזר אחר עידי שקר כ"י מי הוחזקו להיות שומעי' לו לזייף. התם נמי כיון דמהדר אזייפא אימור זיופי' זייף וכתב פי' הוא עצמו למד לכוין כתב הדומה לכת"י העדים שחתום בו. והילכך אפי' יש עדים המכירים החתימה ואומרים שחתימות יד העדים הוא [illegible] מתני' ואלו שאין להן קנס הבא על הגיורת ועל השבויה ועל השפחה שנפדו ושנתגיירו ושנשתחררו יתירות על בנות ג' שנים ויום א' [illegible] שנשבית הרי היא בקדושתה אע"פ שגדולה. הבא על בתו [illegible] אין להן קנס מפני שמתחייב בנפשו [illegible] ולא יהיה אסון ענוש יענש [illegible] וצריכי וכו' ואין הל' כר"י: ת"ר הפודה את השבויה ומעיד בה ישאנה דלא שדא איניש זוזי בכדי. מעיד בה כדי לא ישאנה פי' אם הוא כהן חיישינן שמא עיניו נתן בה [illegible] לעלמא שריא:

[וכן גירסת הערוך ערך פתח ע"ש]

מט א מיי' פי"ז מהל' איסורי ביאה הל' כא טוש"ע אה"ע סי' ו סעיף יז:

נ ב מיי' פי"א מהל' נערה בתולה הל' ט סמג עשין נד טוש"ע אה"ע סי' קעז סעיף ג בהגה"ה:

נא ג מיי' פכ"ב מהל' עדות הל' ג סמג עשין קי טוש"ע ח"מ סי' לו סעיף ז וסי' מג סעיף לג:

נב ד מיי' פ"א מהל' נערה בתולה הל' י סמג עשין נד טוש"ע אה"ע סי' קעז:

נג ה מיי' שם הל' יג יד:

נד ו מיי' פ"ו מהל' תרומות הל' יא סמג לאוין רטו:

נה ז ח מיי' פי"ח מהל' איסורי ביאה הל' כ טוש"ע אה"ע סי' ז ס"ג:

גיטין פט.

ת"י כ"י

[נ"ל דמוכח לפרש בת סקילה היא דקס ליה כדרבה מיניה ופשיטא דמרישא דברייתא שמעי' לה. ת"י]

[מקום סוגיא דמילתא דאמר ר' דוסא וכי מה עשה לה כו' שבכל הש"ס לחזק הענין שפיר גרסי' דתניא]

[תוספתא פ"ג]

[ע' היטב תוס' לקמן פט. ד"ה מרעגא והנס' לקמן לב: ד"ה דינא ותוס' שבועות מב. ד"ה אופרא ותוס' יבמות קח: ד"ה מרעגא]

[מכות ה:]

[ע' תו' לקמן לו. ד"ה הבא]

[וע' תו' שם ד"ה ועל]

גיטין פח. עדיות פ"ג מ"ו

[נ"ל רבא וע' בתוס' לעיל יח. בד"ה אביי לא אמר ועי' תוס' לקמן לו. ד"ה אמר רבה קסבר וכו' לע"ק]

[בתוספתא איתא קטנה]

[תוס' דיבמות פ"ד]

וְרָאֲתָה דָּם. בּוֹ בַּיּוֹם. דַּיָּהּ שְׁעָתָהּ. וְלֹא גָּזְרוּ בָּהּ טוּמְאַת מֵעֵת לְעֵת לְטַמֵּא טָהֳרוֹת שֶׁנָּגְעָה בָּהֶן מִשְּׁעַת טְבִילָה עַד שְׁעַת רְאִיָּיה. דְּהָא אֲפִי' יָצָא דָּם זֶה מֵאֶתְמוֹל, וְהֶעֱמִידוּהוּ כּוֹתְלֵי בֵּית הָרֶחֶם, שֶׁזֶּהוּ הַטַּעַם שֶׁל מֵעֵת לְעֵת בִּבְנוֹת יִשְׂרָאֵל – הֲלֹא דַּם גּוֹיָה כְּדַם בְּהֵמָה. וְאִם תֹּאמַר: נֵיחוּשׁ שֶׁמָּא מִשֶּׁטָּבְלָה נֶעֱקַר וְיָצָא מִיָּד? טוּמְאָה לְמַפְרֵעַ דְּרַבָּנַן הִיא, וְהֵיכָא דְּאִיכָּא לְמִיגְזַר מֵעֵת לְעֵת שָׁלֵם – גָּזוּר מִפְּקִידָה לִפְקִידָה, וְהֵיכָא דְּלָא גָּזוּר מֵעֵת לְעֵת° – לֹא גָּזוּר מִפְּקִידָה לִפְקִידָה. וּצְרִיכָה לְהַמְתִּין ג' חֳדָשִׁים. שֶׁלֹּא תִּנָּשֵׂא, לְהַבְחִין בֵּין זֶרַע הַנִּזְרָע בִּקְדוּשָּׁה לְזֶרַע הַנִּזְרָע שֶׁלֹּא בִּקְדוּשָּׁה. רַבִּי יוֹסֵי מַתִּיר. לְקַמֵּיהּ מְפָרֵשׁ טַעְמָא. צְרִיכוֹת לְהַמְתִּין. וְאַף עַל פִּי שֶׁקְּטַנָּה אֵינָהּ מִתְעַבֶּרֶת, גְּזֵירָה קְטַנָּה אַטּוּ גְּדוֹלָה. מְשַׁמֶּשֶׁת בְּמוֹךְ. נוֹתֶנֶת מוֹךְ לְאַחַר בְּעִילָה, וְשׁוֹאֶבֶת הַזֶּרַע. מִנַּטְרָא נַפְשָׁהּ. וּמַזְמֶנֶת לָהּ מוֹךְ. דְּלָא יָדְעָה הֵיכָא מִמְטוּ לַהּ. שֶׁבָּאִים לְמוֹכְרָהּ, וּסְבוּרָה דִּלְמָא מַמְטוּ לָהּ, לְגַבֵּי יִשְׂרָאֵל וּפָרְקוּ לָהּ וּמְנַטְּרָא נַפְשָׁהּ לְשַׁמֵּשׁ בְּמוֹךְ. אֶלָּא יוֹצְאָה בְּשֵׁן וָעַיִן. שִׁפְחָה שֶׁסִּימֵּא אֲדוֹנֶיהָ אֶת עֵינָהּ וְיָצְאָה לְחֵירוּת, מְנָא הֲוַת יָדְעָה מֵעִיקָּרָא דְּתֵיפּוּק לְחֵירוּת, דִּמְנַטְּרָא נַפְשָׁהּ לְזַמֵּן מוֹךְ לְשִׁימּוּשָׁהּ? כָּל מִמֵּילָא. מִידֵי דְּלֵיכָּא לְאִיזְדַּהוּרֵי בֵּיהּ מֵעִיקָּרָא דְּתֵיפּוּק לְחֵירוּת – מוֹדֶה רַבִּי יוֹסֵי. הֲרֵי אֲנוּסָה דְּמִמֵּילָא. דְּלָא הֲוַת יָדְעָה דְּלִיסְלְיק בָּהּ הָכִי, וּתְזַמֵּן לָהּ מוֹךְ. מִתְהַפֶּכֶת. שֶׁיֵּצֵא הַזֶּרַע וְלֹא יִקְלוֹט. וְהָא אֲפִילּוּ בְּמִידֵי דְּמִמֵּילָא מָצוּ לְמֶיעֱבַד, וְכוּלָּן עוֹשׂוֹת כֵּן. מִשּׁוּם דְּאִיכָּא אִיבּוּד נְשָׁמָה. יֵשׁ כָּאן עוֹנֶשׁ חָמוּר, וְדַיּוֹ בְּכָךְ אִם עֲנִשְׁתּוֹ לְאַבֵּד נְשָׁמָה, לֵיהָרֵג. אֵימָא לָא. אֵין זֶה עוֹנֶשׁ יְתֵירָה, וְלִיעֲבִיד בֵּיהּ תַּרְתֵּי. דְּלָא חֲמִיר אִיסּוּרֵיהּ. לֹא עָבַר עֲבֵירָה חֲמוּרָה, וְדַיּוֹ שֶׁתַּעַנְשֶׁנּוּ עוֹנֶשׁ אֶחָד. לֹא

תורה אור

וְסָבַר רַבִּי יְהוּדָה בִּקְדוּשָּׁתָהּ קַיְימָא? וְהָתַנְיָא: הַגִּיּוֹרֶת שֶׁנִּתְגַּיְּירָה וְרָאֲתָה דָּם, ר' יְהוּדָה אוֹמֵר דַּיָּהּ שַׁעְתָּהּ, [א]ר' יוֹסֵי אוֹמֵר: הֲרֵי הִיא כְּכָל הַנָּשִׁים, וּמְטַמְּאָה מֵעֵת לְעֵת וּמִפְּקִידָה לִפְקִידָה, וּצְרִיכָה לְהַמְתִּין ג' חֳדָשִׁים, דִּבְרֵי ר' יְהוּדָה. ר' יוֹסֵי מַתִּיר לֵיאָרֵס וְלִינָּשֵׂא מִיָּד! א"ל: גִּיּוֹרֶת אַשְׁבוּיָה קָא רָמֵית?! גִּיּוֹרֶת – לָא מְנַטְּרָא נַפְשָׁהּ, שְׁבוּיָה – מְנַטְּרָא נַפְשָׁהּ. וְרָמֵי שְׁבוּיָה אַשְׁבוּיָה; דְּתַנְיָא: *הַגִּיּוֹרֶת וְהַשְּׁבוּיָה וְהַשִּׁפְחָה שֶׁנִּפְדּוּ וְשֶׁנִּתְגַּיְּירוּ, וְשֶׁנִּשְׁתַּחְרְרוּ יְתֵירוֹת עַל בְּנוֹת ג' שָׁנִים וְיוֹם אֶחָד – [א]צְרִיכוֹת לְהַמְתִּין ג' חֳדָשִׁים, דִּבְרֵי ר' יְהוּדָה. ר' יוֹסֵי מַתִּיר לֵיאָרֵס וְלִינָּשֵׂא מִיָּד! אִשְׁתִּיק. א"ל: מִידֵי שְׁמִיעַ לָךְ בְּהָא? אֲמַר לֵיהּ, הָכִי אֲמַר רַב שֵׁשֶׁת: שֶׁרְאוּהָ שֶׁנִּבְעֲלָה. א"ה מַאי טַעְמָא דְּר' יוֹסֵי? אָמַר רַבָּה: קָסָבַר ר' יוֹסֵי אִשָּׁה מְזַנָּה מְשַׁמֶּשֶׁת בְּמוֹךְ שֶׁלֹּא תִּתְעַבֵּר. בִּשְׁלָמָא גִּיּוֹרֶת, כֵּיוָן דְּדַעְתָּהּ לְאִיגַּיּוּרֵי – מְנַטְּרָא נַפְשָׁהּ; שְׁבוּיָה נַמִי, דְּלָא יָדְעָה הֵיכָא מַמְטוּ לָהּ; שִׁפְחָה נַמִי, דְּשָׁמְעָה מִפִּי מָרָהּ; אֶלָּא יוֹצְאָה בְּשֵׁן וָעַיִן – מַאי אִיכָּא לְמֵימַר? וְכִי תֵּימָא כָּל מִמֵּילָא לָא א"ר יוֹסֵי – הֲרֵי אֲנוּסָה *וּמְפוּתָּה, דְּמִמֵּילָא, וְתַנְיָא: אֲנוּסָה וּמְפוּתָּה צְרִיכוֹת לְהַמְתִּין ג' חֳדָשִׁים, דִּבְרֵי ר' יְהוּדָה, [ב]ר' יוֹסֵי מַתִּיר לֵיאָרֵס וְלִינָּשֵׂא מִיָּד! אֶלָּא אָמַר *רַבָּה: קָסָבַר ר' יוֹסֵי: [ג]אִשָּׁה מְזַנָּה מִתְהַפֶּכֶת כְּדֵי שֶׁלֹּא תִּתְעַבֵּר. וְאִידָךְ: חָיְישִׁי' שֶׁמָּא לֹא נֶהֶפְכָה יָפֶה יָפֶה.§ שֶׁנֶּאֱ': °"וְלֹא יִהְיֶה אָסוֹן עָנוֹשׁ יֵעָנֵשׁ" וכו'.§ וְהָא מֵהָכָא נָפְקָא? מֵהָתָם נָפְקָא: °"כְּדֵי רִשְׁעָתוֹ" – *מִשּׁוּם רִשְׁעָה אַחַת אַתָּה מְחַיְּיבוֹ, וְאִי אַתָּה מְחַיְּיבוֹ מִשּׁוּם שְׁתֵּי רִשְׁעָיוֹת! חֲדָא בְּמִיתָה וּמָמוֹן, וַחֲדָא בְּמַלְקוֹת וּמָמוֹן. וּצְרִיכָא: דְּאִי אַשְׁמְעִינַן מִיתָה וּמָמוֹן – מִשּׁוּם דְּאִיכָּא אִיבּוּד נְשָׁמָה, אֲבָל מַלְקוֹת וּמָמוֹן דְּלֵיכָּא אִיבּוּד נְשָׁמָה, אֵימָא לָא. וְאִי אַשְׁמְעִינַן מַלְקוֹת וּמָמוֹן – מִשּׁוּם דְּלָא חֲמִיר אִיסּוּרֵיהּ, אֲבָל מִיתָה וּמָמוֹן דַּחֲמִיר אִיסּוּרֵיהּ אֵימָא לָא, צְרִיכָא. וּלְרַבִּי מֵאִיר, *דְּאָמַר לוֹקֶה וּמְשַׁלֵּם, תַּרְתֵּי לָמָּה לִי? חֲדָא בְּמִיתָה וּמָמוֹן וַחֲדָא

שמות כא

דברים כה

וסבר רבי יהודה בקדושתה קיימא והתניא הגיורת כו'. קשה: דהשתא דמדמה גיורת לשבויה – א"כ תיקשי ליה מתניתין גופה, דר' יהודה לא משוה גיורת לשבויה, דתנן: ר' יהודה אומר: שבויה שנפדית הרי היא בקדושתה, משמע דבהנך מודה לתנא קמא! ואמר ר"י: דמתני' אתי ליה שפיר, דמודה בגיורת שאין לה קנס, דודאי היא בחזקת בעולה, שנבעלה בעוד שלא היה דעתה להתגייר. ואפילו אם היה דעתה להתגייר משהיתה בת שלש שנים ויום אחד – מ"מ לא מנטרא נפשה, כיון דאינה ראויה להתעבר. אבל מהך דצריכה להמתין שלשה חדשים, אף על גב דדעתה לאיגיורי ומנטרא נפשה – אפילו הכי קאמר צריכה להמתין ג' חדשים, דאי אפשר לשמור עצמה מן הגוים, כ"ש שבויה שהיא מסורה בידם. **רבי** יהודה אומר דיה שעתה. פירש הקונטרס: כיון דליכא מעת לעת – מפקידה לפקידה נמי לא גזור רבנן. ורבי יוסי דקאמר ומטמאה מעת לעת – לאו דוקא מעת לעת, אלא כלומר: בתורת מעת לעת מטמאה משנתגיירה. **שבויה** מנטרא נפשה. וא"ת: והא בקטנה נמי מיירי, דלא מנטרא נפשה, דהא אינה יודעת לשמור עצמה? וקאמר ר"י דבקדושתה קיימא, דקתני במתני', יתירה מבת ג' שנים ויום אחד! וי"ל: דקטנה לגמרי אינה מוסרת עצמה לביאה, וכשהיא מוסרת עצמה לביאה, קצת היא בת דעת, ויודעת לשמור עצמה. **צריכות** להמתין שלשה חדשים דברי ר' יהודה. משמע דאפי' בקטנה שאינה ראויה להתעבר קאמר רבי יהודה דצריכה להמתין, מדקאמר: יתירות מבנות ג' ויום אחד, דגזר קטנה אטו גדולה. וקשה לר"י ולרבינו תם: דתניא ב"החולץ" (יבמות דף מב: ושם): הרי שהיתה רדופה לילך לבית אביה או קטנה כו' – צריכה להמתין ג' חדשים, דברי ר"מ. ר' יהודה מתיר ליארס ולינשא מיד. אלמא לא גזר רבי יהודה קטנה אטו גדולה! וכ"ת: דוקא בגיורת ומשוחררת ושבויה גזר טפי, כדי להבחין בין זרע שנזרע בקדושה לשנזרע שלא בקדושה – זה אין נראה, דהא לרבא דמפרש התם לעיל *טעם דצריכות להמתין גזירה שמא ישא אחותו מאביו, וייבם אשת אחיו מן אמו כו' – טפי אית לן למיגזר בקטנה בת ישראל, דשייך בה כל הנהו דמפרש התם, אבל בגיורת ושבויה ומשוחררת לא שייך שמא ישא אחותו מאביו. ועוד: דשמואל אית ליה סברא איפכא מדר' יהודה, דהא שמואל קאמר בס"פ "ד' אחין" (שם דף לד: ושם) דכולן צריכות להמתין ג' חדשים חוץ מגיורת ומשוחררת קטנה, אבל קטנה בת ישראל – צריכה להמתין. אלמא בקטנה בת ישראל גזר קטנה אטו גדולה, ובגיורת ומשוחררת לא גזר, והיינו איפכא מדרבי יהודה. ועוד: לשמואל, בשלמא בקטנה בת ישראל סבר כר"מ, אלא בגיורת כמאן? לא כרבי יהודה ולא כר' יוסי. דלרבי יהודה – בין קטנה בין גדולה צריכה להמתין, ולרבי יוסי – אפי' גדולה אינה צריכה להמתין! ומיהו, למאי דמוקי להך דהכא בשראוה שנבעלה – אתי שפיר כר' יהודה. ומצינן למימר דדוקא בראוה שנבעלה קאמר ר' יהודה, דגזרי' קטנה אטו גדולה, אבל אותה שאינה ודאי בעולה – לא. ולפי לשון אחרון דהתם לא קשה כלל, אע"ג דשמואל איפכא מדרבי יהודה, כיון דאין הטעם משום *דגזרינן קטנה אטו גדולה. דאפילו בגדולה נמי שרי, לפי שמתהפכת. ואר"י: דבס"פ "ד' אחין" (ג"ז שם לה.) מייתי הך ברייתא דהכא, ול"ג בה יתירות מבנות ג' ויום אחד. ובתוספתא נמי ל"ג ליה. ולפי זה ניחא, דמיירי בגדולה, אבל בקטנה מודה דאין צריכה להמתין, כדקאמר בברייתא דרדופה. והשתא שמואל בגיורת כר' יהודה, ובבת ישראל כרבי מאיר. ואפשר דבגיורת קטנה מודה ר' מאיר דאין צריכה להמתין. וללשון אחרון דהתם, דאמר שמואל כולם צריכות להמתין חוץ מגיורת ומשוחררת גדולה, וקטנה בת ישראל אינה צריכה להמתין בזנות, משום דזנות דקטנה לא שכיח. אבל בנשואין גזר קטנה אטו גדולה, וסבר בגיורת כרבי יוסי, ובבת ישראל כר"מ, דגזר קטנה אטו גדולה, וס"ל דדוקא בנשואין גזר ר"מ, ושמא בנשואין מודה ר' יוסי לר"מ, ומיהו, בזנות ודאי פליג, דהא שרי אנוסה ומפותה אפילו גדולה. ואית דגרסי בברייתא דרדופה ר' יוסי במקום ר' יהודה, ושם פירשנו. **אי** הכי מ"ט דר' יוסי. תימה לר"י: דמשמע דמשום דאוקימנא בראוה שנבעלה הוא דקשיא ליה מאי טעמא, בלאו הכי נמי תיקשי ליה ברייתא דרבי יוסי, דמייתי לקמן דאנוסה ומפותה, ולפי הסוגיא נראה דזה המקשה עצמו הוא דמייתי לה? ומיהו, י"ס דגרסי בסמוך: א"ל אביי: בשלמא גיורת כיון דדעתה לאיגיורי כו', ולפי גירסא זו אתי שפיר, שזה המקשה לא ידע ברייתא דמייתי לקמן, דאביי הוא דמייתי לה. וכן הוא גירסא בשילהי "ד' אחין" (ג"ז שם).

אמר רבה קסבר רבי יוסי כו'. אליבא דרבי יוחנן משני, דלדידיה דמפרש טעמא דר' יהודה שלא יהא סוטה נסכר – לא קשיא מידי [ומיהו, רבה לא קאמר אלא דלמא]. **אשה** מזנה מתהפכת. ומהשתא לא קשה אנוסה ומפותה. ומיהו, יוצאה בשן ועין מודה רבי יוסי דצריכה להמתין, דאותה למה תתהפך: *הבא על בתו. למאי דמוקי מתני' בפרק "בן סורר" (סנהדרין דף עג: ושם) במפותה – צריך לאוקמה בשבא עליה ונגרה, כדפרישית לעיל*: *ועל בת אשתו. הוה מצי למיתני אשת אביו וכלתו, דהא חשיב נמי עריות דעל ידי קדושין, אלא תנא ושייר. **חדא** במלקות וממון. לעיל* פירשתי למה לא יליף "רשע" "רשע". תימה: דבריש "החובל" (ב"ק דף פג:) פריך: הא מיבעי ליה קרא ד"לא תקחו כופר" דלא תשקול מיניה ממונא ותקטליה! ומשני: ההוא מ"כדי רשעתו" נפקא. הוה ליה למימר: ההוא מ"לא יהיה אסון" נפקא, ד"כדי רשעתו" אתא למלקות וממון! וי"ל: דהתם טעי כי היכי דטעי הכא מעיקרא לומר דמ"כדי רשעתו" נפקא מיתה וממון. [והא דלא פריך: האי במלקות וממון כתיב – לא חש להקשות משום דהוי מצי לשנויי מ"לא יהיה אסון" נפקא], אי נמי לסימנא בעלמא נקטיה התם. ומדא

נו א ב ג מיי' פי"א מהל' גירושין הל' כא כב סמג עשין נ טוש"ע אה"ע סימן יג סעיף ה ו:

יבמות לה. [כל הסוגיא ע"ש]

[שם איתא אביי]

ב"ק פג: מכות ד: יג: [לעיל לב:]

[לעיל לג: וש"נ]

[שם מב.]

[דלא גזרינן כצ"ל רש"ל]

[שייך לעיל במשנה לו:]

[דף כט. ד"ה ועל אחת]

[ג"ז שייך שם]

[לה. ד"ה רבא]

[אין לזה מובן וכן נראה מפירש"י דליתא]

גליון הש"ס

רש"י ד"ה דיה שעתה וכו' לא גזור מפקידה לפקידה. כדאיתא בנדה לו ע"א.

הגהות מהר"ב רנשבורג

א] גמ' ר' יוסי אומר הרי היא ככל הנשים. עי' נדה דף לו ע"א תוד"ה דליכא שהות וכו' והגאון מהרלרי"פ לא ציינו בתלמוד החדשים בהגהותיו:

תורה אור

וַחֲדָא בְּמִיתָה וּמַלְקוֹת. וּצְרִיכָא; דְּאִי אַשְׁמַעִינַן מִיתָה וּמָמוֹן – מִשּׁוּם דַּחֲדָא בְּגוּפֵיהּ וַחֲדָא בְּמָמוֹנֵיהּ לָא עָבְדִינַן, אֲבָל בְּמִיתָה וּמַלְקוֹת דְּאִידִי וְאִידִי בְּגוּפֵיהּ – אֵימָא מִיתָה אֲרִיכְתָּא הִיא, וְנַעֲבֵיד בֵּיהּ. וְאִי אַשְׁמַעִינַן מִיתָה וּמַלְקוֹת – דְּתַרְתֵּי בְּגוּפֵיהּ לָא עָבְדִינַן, אֲבָל מִיתָה וּמָמוֹן דַּחֲדָא בְּגוּפֵיהּ וַחֲדָא בְּמָמוֹנֵיהּ – אֵימָא נַעֲבֵיד בֵּיהּ, צְרִיכָא. °"וְלֹא תִקְחוּ כֹפֶר לְנֶפֶשׁ רֹצֵחַ" (במדבר לה) לָמָּה לִי? *דְּאָמַר רַחֲמָנָא: אלָא תִּשְׁקוֹל מָמוֹנָא מִינֵּיהּ וְתִפְטְרֵיהּ מִקְּטָלָא. °"לֹא תִקְחוּ כֹפֶר לָנוּס אֶל עִיר מִקְלָטוֹ" (שם) *לָמָּה לִי? בדְּאָמַר רַחֲמָנָא: לָא תִּשְׁקוֹל מָמוֹנָא מִינֵּיהּ וְתִפְטְרֵיהּ מִן גָּלוּת. וּתְרֵי קְרָאֵי לָמָּה לִי? חַד בְּשׁוֹגֵג וְחַד בְּמֵזִיד, וּצְרִיכִי; דְּאִי אַשְׁמַעִינַן מֵזִיד – מִשּׁוּם דַּחֲמִיר אִיסּוּרֵיהּ, אֲבָל שׁוֹגֵג דְּלָא חֲמִיר אִיסּוּרֵיהּ – אֵימָא לָא. וְאִי אַשְׁמַעִינַן שׁוֹגֵג – מִשּׁוּם דְּלֵיכָּא אִיבּוּד נְשָׁמָה, אֲבָל מֵזִיד דְּאִיכָּא אִיבּוּד נְשָׁמָה – אֵימָא לָא, צְרִיכָא. °"וְלָאָרֶץ לֹא יְכֻפַּר לַדָּם אֲשֶׁר שֻׁפַּךְ בָּהּ כִּי אִם בְּדַם שֹׁפְכוֹ" (שם) לָמָּה לִי? מִבָּעֵי לֵיהּ לְכִדְתַנְיָא: *מִנַּיִן גשֶׁאִם נִתְעָרְפָה עֶגְלָה וְאח"כ נִמְצָא הַהוֹרֵג, מִנַּיִן שֶׁאֵין פּוֹטְרִין אוֹתוֹ – שֶׁנֶּאֱמַר: "וְלָאָרֶץ לֹא יְכֻפַּר לַדָּם אֲשֶׁר שֻׁפַּךְ בָּהּ וגו'". °"וְאַתָּה תְּבַעֵר הַדָּם הַנָּקִי מִקִּרְבֶּךָ" (דברים כא) לָמָּה לִי? מִיבָּעֵי לֵיהּ לְכִדְתַנְיָא: *מִנַּיִן לַמּוּמָתִים בְּסַיִיף שֶׁהוּא מִן הַצַּוָּאר – ת"ל: "וְאַתָּה תְּבַעֵר הַדָּם הַנָּקִי מִקִּרְבֶּךָ", הוּקְשׁוּ כָּל שׁוֹפְכֵי דָמִים לְעֶגְלָה עֲרוּפָה, מַה לְּהַלָּן מִן הַצַּוָּאר – דאַף שׁוֹפְכֵי דָמִים מִן הַצַּוָּאר. אִי מַה הלְּהַלָּן בְּקוֹפִיץ, וּמִמּוּל עוֹרֶף, אַף כָּאן בְּקוֹפִיץ וּמִמּוּל עוֹרֶף? *אָמַר רַב נַחְמָן אָמַר רַבָּה בַּר אֲבוּהּ: אָמַר קְרָא °"וְאָהַבְתָּ לְרֵעֲךָ כָּמוֹךָ" (ויקרא יט) – בְּרוֹר לוֹ מִיתָה יָפָה. °"כָּל חֵרֶם אֲשֶׁר יָחֳרַם מִן הָאָדָם לֹא יִפָּדֶה" (שם כז) לָמָּה לִי? מִיבָּעֵי לֵיהּ לְכִדְתַנְיָא: *מִנַּיִן לַיּוֹצֵא לֵיהָרֵג וְאָמַר אֶחָד "עֶרְכּוֹ עָלַי", מִנַּיִן ושֶׁלֹּא אָמַר כְּלוּם – שֶׁנֶּאֱמַר: "כָּל חֵרֶם אֲשֶׁר יָחֳרַם מִן הָאָדָם לֹא יִפָּדֶה". יָכוֹל אַף קוֹדֶם שֶׁנִּגְמַר דִּינוֹ כֵּן – ת"ל: "מִן הָאָדָם" – וְלֹא כָּל הָאָדָם. *וּלְרַבִּי חֲנַנְיָא בֶּן עֲקַבְיָא, דְּאָמַר: נֶעֱרָךְ, מִפְּנֵי שֶׁדָּמָיו קְצוּבִין, הַאי "כָּל חֵרֶם" מַאי עָבֵיד לֵיהּ? מִיבָּעֵי לֵיהּ לְכִדְתַנְיָא, *רַבִּי יִשְׁמָעֵאל בְּנוֹ שֶׁל ר' יוֹחָנָן בֶּן בְּרוֹקָה אוֹמֵר: זלְפִי שֶׁמָּצִינוּ לַמּוּמָתִים בִּידֵי שָׁמַיִם שֶׁנּוֹתְנִין מָמוֹן וּמִתְכַּפֵּר לָהֶן, שֶׁנֶּאֱמַר: °"אִם כֹּפֶר יוּשַׁת עָלָיו" (שמות כא), יָכוֹל אַף בִּידֵי אָדָם כֵּן – ת"ל: "חֵרֶם מִן הָאָדָם לֹא יִפָּדֶה". וְאֵין לִי אֶלָּא מִיתוֹת חֲמוּרוֹת, שֶׁלֹּא נִיתְּנָה שִׁגְגָתָן לְכַפָּרָה, מִיתוֹת קַלּוֹת, שֶׁנִּיתְּנָה שִׁגְגָתָן לְכַפָּרָה מִנַּיִן – ת"ל: "כָּל חֵרֶם". וְלָא מִמֵּילָא, מִ"לֹּא תִקְחוּ כֹפֶר" שָׁמְעַתְּ מִינָּהּ: לָא תִּשְׁקוֹל מָמוֹנָא מִינֵּיהּ וְתִיפְטְרֵיהּ, "כָּל חֵרֶם" ל"ל? אָמַר רָמִי בַּר חָמָא: אִיצְטְרִיךְ; ס"ד אָמִינָא: הָנֵי

רש"י

לא תקחו כופר. מַשְׁמַע נַמִי: אִם תַּהַרְגֵהוּ – לֹא תַעַנְשֵׁהוּ מָמוֹן. דְּאָמַר רַחֲמָנָא. שִׁנּוּיָא הוּא דִּמְשַׁנֵּינַן: לָאו לְאַשְׁמְעִינַן דְּלָא תַּעֲבֵיד בֵּיהּ תַּרְתֵּי, אֶלָּא לְאַשְׁמוּעִינַן בְּחִיּוּב מִיתָה לְבַדָּהּ, שֶׁלֹּא יִפָּדֶה בְּמָמוֹן. לא תקחו כופר לנוס. קָא ס"ד לָא תַּעֲבֵיד בֵּיהּ תַּרְתֵּי לַהוֹרֵג בְּשׁוֹגֵג, גָּלוּת וּמָמוֹן. וּצְרִיכִי דְּאִי אַשְׁמְעִינַן מֵזִיד. דְּלָא לִיפְרוֹק נַפְשֵׁיהּ בְּמָמוֹן, הֲוָה אָמִינָא: מִשּׁוּם דַּחֲמִיר אִיסּוּרֵיהּ, אֲבָל בְּשׁוֹגֵג – לִיפְרוֹק נַפְשֵׁיהּ בְּמָמוֹן מִגָּלוּת. וְאִי אַשְׁמְעִינַן שׁוֹגֵג. דְּמִשּׁוּם דְּאֵין בְּגָלוּתוֹ אִיבּוּד נְשָׁמָה, לְהָכִי לָא לִפְטְרֵיהּ בְּמָמוֹן אֶלָּא לִיגְלֵי. אֲבָל מֵזִיד. מִשּׁוּם אִיבּוּד נְשָׁמָה אֵימוּר נִשְׁקוֹל מָמוֹנָא, וּנְקַיֵּים נֶפֶשׁ בְּיִשְׂרָאֵל. כִּי אִם בְּדַם שׁוֹפְכוֹ. וְלֹא בְּפִדְיוֹן מָמוֹן, לָמָּה לִי? מִ"לֹּא תִקְחוּ כֹפֶר" נָפְקָא. שֶׁאֵין פּוֹטְרִין אוֹתוֹ. לוֹמַר כְּבָר נִתְכַּפֵּר בְּעוֹדוֹ סָפֵק, שֶׁהָעֶגְלָה מְכַפֶּרֶת עַל הַסָּפֵק. וְאַתָּה תְּבַעֵר. בָּתַר עֲרִיפָה כְּתִיב. מִיתָה יָפָה. בְּסַיִיף, וּמִלַּד הַסִּימָנִים, שֶׁיָּמוּת מַהֵר. כָּל חֵרֶם וגו'. מַשְׁמַע לְשׁוֹן חַיָּיבֵי מִיתוֹת, כְּמוֹ "זוֹבֵחַ לָאֱלֹהִים יָחֳרָם" (שמות כב). עֶרְכּוֹ עָלַי. וְאַע"פ שֶׁעֵרֶךְ אֵינוֹ לְפִי דָמִים אֶלָּא לְפִי שָׁנִים – לֹא אָמַר כְּלוּם, דִּמְמַעֲטֵיהּ קְרָא הָכָא. וְהַאי "חֵרֶם" לְשׁוֹן הֶקְדֵּשׁ הוּא. שֶׁדָּמָיו קְצוּבִין. בַּתּוֹרָה, לְפִי שָׁנִים. וְלָא דָּמֵי לְאוֹמֵר "דָּמָיו עָלַי" – דְּדָמִים אֵין לוֹ, אֲבָל עֵרֶךְ יֵשׁ לוֹ. לַמּוּמָתִין בִּידֵי שָׁמַיִם. כְּגוֹן מִי שֶׁהָרַג שׁוֹרוֹ אֶת הַנֶּפֶשׁ, דִּכְתִיב בֵּיהּ "יוּמָת". וְלֹא מִיתַת בֵּית דִּין, דְּנָפְקָא לָן בְּסַנְהֶדְרִין (דף טו:) "מוֹת יוּמַת הַמַּכֶּה רוֹצֵחַ הוּא" – עַל רְצִיחָתוֹ אַתָּה הוֹרְגוֹ, וְאִי אַתָּה הוֹרְגוֹ עַל רְצִיחַת שׁוֹרוֹ. וְהַאי "יוּמַת" – בִּידֵי שָׁמַיִם. יָכוֹל אַף. חַיָּיבֵי מִיתוֹת ב"ד יִפָּדוּ בְּמָמוֹן. חֵרֶם מִן הָאָדָם. אָדָם שֶׁמְּחוּיָּב חֵרֶם. אֶלָּא מִיתוֹת חֲמוּרוֹת שֶׁלֹּא נִיתְּנָה שִׁגְגָתָן לְכַפָּרָה. כֵּיוָן דִּקְרָא לָא פָּרֵישׁ כָּל מִיתוֹת, מִיסְתַּיֵּיךְ אִי שָׁדֵית הָךְ חוּמְרָא דְּאֵין מָמוֹנוֹ מַצִּילוֹ אַמִּיתוֹת חֲמוּרוֹת, וּמַאי נִינְהוּ – כְּגוֹן הָעוֹשֶׂה חַבּוּרָה בְּאָבִיו, אוֹ גּוֹנֵב נֶפֶשׁ מִיִּשְׂרָאֵל, שֶׁאֵין כַּפָּרָה כְּתוּבָה בְּשִׁגְגָתוֹ, שֶׁאֵין כָּרֵת בִּזְדוֹנוֹ דְּלִיחַיֵּיב חַטָּאת בְּשִׁגְגָתוֹ. מִיתוֹת קַלּוֹת. הַיְינוּ כָּל מִיתוֹת הַחֲמוּרוֹת בָּהֶן כָּרֵת עַל זְדוֹנוֹ בְּלֹא הַתְרָאָה – יֵשׁ כַּפָּרָה בְּשִׁגְגָתָהּ בְּחַטָּאת, כְּגוֹן עֲבוֹדָה זָרָה וְשַׁבָּת וַעֲרָיוֹת. א"נ, רוֹצֵחַ – שֶׁיֵּשׁ כַּפָּרָה לְשִׁגְגָתוֹ בְּגָלוּת. וְלָא מִמֵּילָא. שָׁמְעַתְּ לָהּ מִ"לֹּא תִקְחוּ כֹפֶר" הָא גַּבֵּי רוֹצֵחַ כְּתִיבָא, וְנִיתְּנָה כַּפָּרָה לְשִׁגְגָתוֹ, וְאַשְׁמְעִינַן קְרָא שֶׁלֹּא יַצִּיל אֶת עַצְמוֹ בְּמָמוֹן. וְלָמָּה לִי תּוּ "כָּל חֵרֶם"? הָנֵי

תוספות

וחדא במיתה ומלקות. ורבנן, מלקות וממון ומיתה ומלקות תרווייהו נפקי מ"כדי רשעתו" דמשמע: אם נתחייב בהדי מלקות מיתה או ממון – משום רשעה אחת אתה מחייבו. ואע"ג דסמיך ליה "ארבעים יכנו לא יוסיף" – מ"מ אין לנו לומר דילקה ולא ימות כמו שלוקה ואינו משלם – דאתגורי איתגור?! כדפריך ב"השרפים" (סנהדרין דף פא. ושם). ואע"ג דגבי ממון ומלקות אמרינן דנדון בממון, אפילו ממונא קולא – התם משום דחס רחמנא אנחבל*. לא תשקול ממונא מיניה ותפטריה מגלות. קשה לרשב"א: דל"ל קרא? מתנא דבי חזקיה נפקא דלא חילקת בין שוגג למזיד, וכי היכי דבמזיד לא תשקול מיניה ממונא ותפטריה מקטלא – אף שוגג לא תשקול מיניה ממונא ותפטריה מגלות! ואומר ר"י: דלא שייך לאקושי שוגג למזיד כי האי גוונא, כיון שאין פדיון שניהם שוה. דפדיון של מזיד לפוטרו ממיתה, ופדיון של שוגג לפוטרו מגלות.

ואח"כ נמצא ההורג. בפירוש החומש פ"ה הך דרשה מ"ואתה תבער דם הנקי" ולא עיין כאן. ומיהו, יש לקיים פירושו דהך סוגיא דשמעתא דמוקמי' "ואתה תבער" להקיש שופכי דמים לעגלה ערופה, אתיא כמאן דאמר חנק חמור, כדמוכח בפרק "ד' מיתות" (שם דף נב:), דלמאן דאמר חנק קל – יליף סייף ברוצח מ"נקום ינקם". הלכך לדידיה אייתר "ואתה תבער" לנערפה העגלה ואח"כ נמצא ההורג. וקרא ד"ולארץ לא יכופר" דרשינן ליה לכדרבא בפ' בתרא דכריתות (דף כו.) דמייתינן עגלה ערופה אע"פ שעבר יוה"כ עליה. מה להלן בקופיץ וממול עורף. וא"ת: ממול עורף מנלן? והא "וערפו" כתיב, דמשמע עורף ממש! ויש לומר: דבפ' "עגלה ערופה" (סוטה דף מו:) גמר "עריפה" "עריפה" מחטאת העוף. הוקשו שופכי דמים כו'. הוה מצי למימר: הניחא למ"ד חנק חמור אלא למ"ד חנק קל כו'. ברור לו מיתה יפה. ומהאי טעמא לא הוה שמעינן מן הצואר, דאם יתחב סכין בלבו – הוי נמי מיתה יפה. לפי שמצינו מומתים בידי שמים. דכתיב "וגם בעליו יומת" דע"כ לא בידי אדם קאמר דכתיב "מות יומת המכה רוצח הוא" וגו' על רציחתו אתה הורגו כו'. אלא ודאי בידי שמים. ואף על גב דדרשינן מיניה בפ"ק דסנהדרין (דף טו. ושם): כמיתת בעלים כך מיתת השור – היינו מדכתיב "יומת" ולא כתיב "ימות". וכ"ת כולה להכי הוא דאתא – אם כן ליכתוב השור יסקל כבעלים, ולישתוק. אי נמי: *וגם כבעליו יומת, הלכך שמע מינה תרתי. יכול אף בידי אדם כן. יש תימה: דהיכי בעי למימר מיתה בידי אדם ממיתה בידי שמים! [ותירץ מהר"ס: כיון דאיתקש מיתת שור למיתת בעלים – נקיש נמי מיתת בעלים בידי אדם למיתת בעלים שעל ידי שור]. מיתות קלות שניתן שגגתן לכפרה מנין. פי' בקונט': כגון עבודה זרה ושבת וגילוי עריות שניתן שגגתן לכפרה ע"י קרבן, וכן רוצח ניתנה שגגתו לכפרה ע"י גלות. וקשה: דא"כ למסקנא אמאי איצטריך "חרם" ו"כל חרם" ו"לא תקחו" ג' קראי? ב"לא תקחו כופר" וב"חרם" סגי, דחד לדרך עלייה וחד לדרך ירידה שניתן שגגתו לכפרה, דהיינו מיתות קלות לפ"ה! לכך נראה: דמיתות קלות לא חשיב אלא הנהו שניתן שגגתן לכפרה ע"י ממון, או ע"י קרבן. אבל רוצח – לא ניתן שגגתו לכפרה ע"י ממון, אלא על ידי גלות. וה"פ דברייתא: אין לי אלא מיתות חמורות שלא ניתן שגגתן לכפרה ע"י קרבן, דהיינו כל מיתות שאין בהן כרת, כגון מסית ומדיח, ונביא השקר, וזקן ממרא, ומכה אביו ואמו, ומקלל אביו ואמו, וגונב נפש, ומגדף, אליבא דרבנן דאמרי בכריתות (דף ג:) דאין מביא קרבן על שגגתו, דכתיב "לעושה בשגגה" – פרט למגדף שאין בו מעשה, ורוצח. ומיתות קלות – כגון עבודה זרה ושבת ועריות, דיש בהן כרת ומביא קרבן על שגגתן. ופריך: ולא ממילא שמעת מינה מ"לא תקחו כופר", ומהתם שמעינן כל מיתות חמורות – ולמה לי קרא למיתות חמורות? אבל למיתות קלות ודאי צריך קרא. ומשני: דאיצטריך תרי קראי למיתות חמורות, חד לדרך עלייה שלא ניתן שגגתו לכפרה כלל, וחד לדרך ירידה שניתן שגגתו לכפרה על ידי גלות. קשה לרשב"א: דמאי איצטריך קרא לחייבי מיתות קלות, כגון עבודה זרה ושבת ועריות, דמה שייך שם כופר, למ"ד כופר היינו דמי ניזק? ותירץ: דרבי ישמעאל בנו של רבי יוחנן בן ברוקה לטעמיה, דאמר בפרק "שור שנגח ד' וה'" (ב"ק דף מ.): "ונתן פדיון נפשו" – דמי מזיק. הני

עין משפט נר מצוה

נז א מיי' פ"א מהל' רוצח ושמירת נפש הלכה ד סמג לאוין קסא:
נח ב מיי' פ"ה שם הל' א סמג לאוין קסב:
נט ג מיי' פ"י שם הל' ח סמג עשין עח:
ס ד מיי' פט"ו מהל' סנהדרין הלכה ד סמג עשין קג:
סא ה מיי' פ"ט מהל' רוצח הלכה ג סמג עשין עח:
סב ו מיי' פ"א מהל' ערכין הל' יג סמג עשין קכח:
סג ז מיי' פ"י מהלכות נזקי ממון הל' ד סמג עשין סז:

מסורת הש"ס

ב"ק פג.
[דנפקא לן מתנא דבי חזקיה דלא חילקת בין שוגג למזיד למאי דס"ד השתא דבעי למימר קרא לא תשקל מיניה ממונא ונחיתיה. ת"י]
סוטה מז:
סנהדרין נב:
שם דף מה. פסחים עה. [ב"ק נא. סוטה ח:]
ערכי ו:
[שם]
[שם]
[וע"ע תוס' לעיל לב. ד"ה ואין]
ס"א ליכתוב וגם בעליו יומת ותו לא.
ת"י כ"י

הני מילי. ד"לא תקחו כופר" לפטור רוצח מזיד מקטלא. היכא דהרגו. במזיד, דרך עלייה. בהנפת ידו הכהו מאחריו, דלכוונתו בשוגג לא ניתן לכפרת גלות, כדכתיב "ויפל" – דרך נפילה. מדתנא דבי חזקיה נפקא. שאין חילוק בין דרך עלייה לדרך ירידה. לחייבו ממון. והוא הדין לפדותו. ו"לא יהיה אסון" מיהא איצטריך, דאי מהיקישא, הוה אמינא: אדרבה, לאידך גיסא: מה מכה בהמה – לעולם ישלם, אף מכה אדם – ישלם. והשתא דנפקא לן פטור תשלומין למזיד מ"לא יהיה אסון", על כרחך היקישא לפטור שוגג דרך עלייה. הכי גרסינן. אלא אמר רמי בר חמא כו'. איצטריך חד מהני קראי, לאשמועינן דלא ליעביד ביה תרתי, ואף על גב דנפקא לן מ"ולא יהיה אסון". הני מילי. דלא ענשינן ליה בתרתי – היכא דסימא את עינו והרגו בה באותה מכה, ומת. בדבר אחר. במכה אחרת ובבת אחת. אימא. ניענשיה דמי עין, ומיתה בשביל ההריגה. הא. דסימא עינו והרגו בה. מאידך דבי חזקיה נפקא. דלא תיענשיה. ולא עין ונפש תחת עין. מינה קיימא לן ב"החובל", ד"עין תחת עין" לאו ממש. דאי אמרת ממש – דלמא בהדי דסמינן לעיניה מיית, והוה ליה עין ונפש תחת עין. מיהו, שמעינן מינה דלא תעביד ביה תרתי, לא שנא מת באותה מכה לא שנא לא מת. סלקא דעתך אמינא חידוש הוא שחידשה תורה. בכל תשלומי קנס, שאינו דין אלא גזרת מלך בעלמא, וכיון דחידוש הוא וגזירת חוק – אימא אע"ג דאיכא בהדיה מיתה – לשלם. קמ"ל. חד מהנך קראי יתירא שאינו ענין לממון, תניהו ענין לקנס. כתנא קמא. ודריש ליה באומר "ערכו של יוצא ליהרג עלי". מתני' שנתארסה ונתגרשה. דאילו ארוסה שלא נתגרשה חייב מיתה, ואין שם קנס. אין לה קנס. טעמא מפרש בגמרא. ורישא דקתני אשת אחיו ואשת אחי אביו דבנתארסה ונתגרשה עסקינן, וקתני יש להן קנס – ר' עקיבא היא. גמ' אלא מעתה. לר' עקיבא, הא דכתיב "נערה" למעוטי בוגרת, ו"בתולה" למעוטי בעולה. הכי נמי. דלא ממעט לגמרי, ותדרוש: נערה – לאביה, הא בוגרת – לעצמה. הא לא אשכחן דאישתמיט תנא ומתני בוגרת יש לה קנס, ונימא רבי עקיבא היא. וקנסה לאביה. ולקמן מקשינן דר"ע אדר"ע. הואיל ואביה זכאי בכסף קידושיה. שלו הוא בנערותה. ולקמן יליף לה בפרק "נערה שנתפתתה" (דף מו:). מה כסף קידושיה אף על פי שנתארסה ונתגרשה. מאחר, כשחוזרת ומתקדשת בתוך נערות. לאביה הוי. דהא כל קידושי נערות ילפינן לאביה, דגבי קידושין לא כתיב מיעוטא ד"אשר לא אורסה" כי הכא. נאמר כאן. באונס. להלן. במפתה. מה להלן במפתה, שקלים, דכתיב "ישקול". אימא

לעיל לה. ב"ק לה. סנהדרין עט: פד:

ב"ק פד.

[לעיל לד: לה:]

[לקמן ע.]

תורה אור

הני מילי היכא דהרגו דרך עלייה, [א]שלא ניתנה שגגתו לכפרה. אבל הרגו דרך ירידה, דניתנה שגגתו לכפרה, אימא נישקול ממונא מיניה וניפטריה, קמ"ל. א"ל רבא: הא – מדתנא דבי חזקיה נפקא, *דתנא דבי חזקיה: מכה אדם ומכה בהמה, מה מכה בהמה לא חלקת בו בין שוגג למזיד, בין מתכוין לשאין מתכוין, בין דרך ירידה לדרך עלייה, לפוטרו ממון אלא לחייבו ממון, אף מכה אדם לא תחלוק בו בין שוגג למזיד, °בין מתכוין לשאין מתכוין, בין דרך ירידה לדרך עלייה, לחייבו ממון אלא לפוטרו ממון! אלא אמר רמי בר חמא: איצטריך; ס"ד אמינא: ה"מ – היכא דסימא את עינו והרגו בה, אבל היכא דסימא את עינו והרגו בדבר אחר – אימא נישקול ממונא מיניה. א"ל רבא: הא נמי מאידך תנא דבי חזקיה נפקא. *דתנא דבי חזקיה: °"עין תחת עין" [ב]ולא עין ונפש תחת עין! אלא אמר רב אשי: איצטריך; ס"ד אמינא: הואיל וחידוש הוא שחידשה תורה בקנס, אע"ג דמיקטיל משלם, קמ"ל. ולרבה דאמר: *חידוש הוא שחידשה תורה בקנס, אע"ג דמיקטיל משלם, האי "כל חרם" מאי עביד ליה? סבר לה כתנא קמא דר' חנניא בן עקביא.§ **מתני'** נערה שנתארסה ונתגרשה, רבי יוסי הגלילי אומר: אין לה קנס, ר"ע אומר: *[ג]יש לה קנס, וקנסה לעצמה.§ **גמ'** מ"ט דר' יוסי הגלילי? אמר קרא: °"אשר לא אורשה", הא אורסה – אין לה קנס. ור"ע: "אשר לא אורשה" – לאביה, הא אורסה – לעצמה. אלא מעתה "נערה" ולא בוגרת, ה"נ דלעצמה? "בתולה" ולא בעולה, ה"נ דלעצמה? אלא, לגמרי – הכא נמי לגמרי! אמר לך ר"ע: האי "לא אורשה" מיבעי ליה לכדתניא: "אשר לא אורשה" – פרט לנערה שנתארסה ונתגרשה, שאין לה קנס, דברי ר' יוסי הגלילי. ר"ע אומר: יש לה קנס, וקנסה לאביה. והדין נותן: הואיל ואביה זכאי בכסף קידושיה, ואביה זכאי בכסף קנסה, [ד]מה כסף קידושיה, אע"פ שנתארסה ונתגרשה – לאביה, אף כסף קנסה, אע"פ שנתארסה ונתגרשה – לאביה. א"כ, מה ת"ל: "אשר לא אורשה" – מופנה להקיש לו, ולדון הימנו ג"ש: נאמר כאן: "אשר לא אורשה", ונאמר להלן: °"אשר לא אורשה" מה כאן נ' – אף להלן נ'; ומה להלן שקלים – אף כאן שקלים. ור"ע, מאי חזית ד"אשר לא אורשה" לג"ש, ו"בתולה" למעוטי בעולה, אימא

שמות כא

דברים כב

שמות כב

הני מילי היכא דהרגו דרך עלייה דלא ניתן שגגתו לכפרה. פירוש: לכפרה בידי אדם. אע"ג דדרך עלייה קיל טפי מדרך ירידה, כדמוכח בפרק "אלו הן הגולין" (מכות דף ט. ושם) גבי גר תושב. גולה ע"י גר תושב וכל חומרי דשמעתין לא תלי אלא במה שלא ניתן לכפרה, דאינו מקפיד התלמוד במה שסקילה ושריפה חמורין מהרג וחנק. **אבל** סימא את עינו והרגו בדבר אחר **אימא** נשקול מיניה ממונא ונקטליה. כך גרס ר"ח, דמ"לא יהיה אסון" לא נפקא לן אלא סימא את עינו והרגו בה, כי התם, שבהכאה אחת הרג את האשה וגם הולדות. אבל סימא את עינו והרגו בדבר אחר בבת אחת – לא, *להכי איצטריך "כל חרם" למיפטריה. קשה לרשב"א: דהא ר' ישמעאל בנו של ר' יוחנן בן ברוקה לא דריש קרא להכי דלא נשקול מיניה ממונא ונקטליה, אלא שלא יתן ממון ונפטריה! ושמא "אילו לא נאמר" קאמר, כדאשכחן ריש פרק "נגמר הדין" (סנהדרין דף מג. ושם) ובכמה דוכתי. ולרשב"א נראה: דהכא מסיק אליבא דתנא דבי חזקיה, אבל לרבי ישמעאל ודאי לית ליה הא דתנא דבי חזקיה. והא דאמר בריש "הנחנקין" (שם דף פד: ושם): הניחא למאן דאית ליה דתנא דבי חזקיה, אלא למאן דלית ליה – היקישא למה לי? תנא דלית ליה דבי חזקיה היינו רבי ישמעאל. ובסמוך דקאמר: ולרבה דאמר חידוש הוא שחידשה תורה בקנס כו' – סבר לה כת"ק דר' חנניא בן עקביא, הוה מצי למימר: ס"ל כרבי ישמעאל. **הא** נמי מאידך תנא דבי חזקיה נפקא. לאו מההיא דרשה גופה קאמר דנפקא לן, דהא ההיא דרשה לא שייכא כלל לסימא את עינו והרגו בדבר אחר, אלא הכי דייק: דכי היכי דדרשי' ולא עין ונפש תחת עין – ה"נ דרשינן נפש תחת נפש ולא עין ונפש תחת נפש. וסימא את עינו והרגו בד"א לא חשיב עין ונפש; אלא נפש גריד', דמה שסימא את עינו בשעת הריגה – לא חשיב כלום, דבלאו הכי היה מת, אלא שהמיתו בנער מרובה. וא"ת: *הא מילתא נמי מתנא דבי חזקיה דלעיל נפקא, דמה מכה בהמה לא חלקת בין סימא את עינה והרגה בה, להורגה בד"א כו'! וי"ל: דמכה אדם ומכה בהמה משמע ליה בהכאה אחת. וא"ת: סימא את עינו והרג בד"א, תיפוק ליה דפטור מדמי עין אפי' לא הרג, דבשעה שסימא את עינו היה רודף, וניתן להצילו בנפשו! וי"ל דמיירי בשיכול להצילו באחד מאיבריו – שלא ניתן להצילו בנפשו. **אמר** רב אשי איצטריך כו'. תימה: דמשמע דאם הרגו וקרע סיראין דידיה – דמחייב, דליכא למיפטריה לא מקרא ד"לא יהיה אסון" ולא מקרא ד"נפש תחת נפש", דהא הוי ממון ונפש תחת ממון ונפש, ולעיל (דף ל:) פטר *אביי זר שאכל תרומה משלו וקרע סיראין של חבירו! וי"ל: דלפי האמת נפקי כולהו מתנא דבי חזקיה. וה"פ: והא נמי מאידך תנא דבי חזקיה נפקא. כלומר: ע"כ לא איצטריך "כל חרס" להכי, אלא כולה נפקא לן מתנא דבי חזקיה דפטור, דאי הוה צריך קרא למפטריה בלא "כל חרס" הוה פטרינן ליה, מאידך תנא דבי חזקיה. וא"ת: וליפני דאיצטריך "כל חרס" להרג חבירו וקרע סיראין! וי"ל: ד"כל חרס לא יפדה" משמע ליה בממון שבא על ידי אותה חבלה שהמיתה באה על ידה.

סלקא דעתך אמינא חידוש הוא קמ"ל. אע"ג דבמתני' מייתי קרא ד"לא יהיה אסון" והכא מפיק קנס מ"כל חרס" – היינו משום דכייל מתניתין כל חייבי מיתות, דקתני: וכל המתחייב בנפשו כו'. אי נמי, מתניתין אתיא כתנא קמא דרבי חנניא בן עקביא.

אימא

סד א מיי' פ"ו מהלכות רוצח ושמירת נפש הל' יב יג סמג עשין עה:

סה ב מיי' פ"א מהל' חובל הלכה ב ג ד סמג עשין ע:

סו ג מיי' פ"ב מהל' נערה הל' טז סמג עשין נד טור אה"ע סימן קעז:

סז ד מיי' פ"ג מהל' אישות הל' יא סמג עשין מח טוש"ע אה"ע סימן לז סעיף א:

[וליכא למימר דהכא לא קאי אקרא דכל חרס אלא אקרא דלא תקחו כופר דהא אמרי' בסמוך ולרבה דאמר חידוש כו'. ת"י]

תוספות רי"ד

מתני' נערה שנתארסה ונתגרשה ר"י הגלילי אומר אין לה קנס ר"ע אומר יש לה קנס וקנס' לעצמה. מ"ט דר' יוסי אמר קרא אשר לא אורסה הא אורסה אין לה קנס ור"ע אומר אשר לא אורסה לאביה הא אורסה לעצמה. וקי"ל הלכה כר"ע מחבירו. ומתני' דתני הבא על בתו אין לה קנס מפני שמתחייב בנפשו כר"ע אתיא. דהיכי דמי שיתחייב בבתו השתא אילו בא עליה אחר שקיל איהו קנס. השתא שבא עליה הוא לא כ"ש ובלא מיתה נמי פשיטא דלא משלם קנס. אלא ודאי מתני' בבתו נערה שנתארסה ונתגרשה עסקינן שקנסה לעצמה כר"ע ומפני שנתחייב בנפשו פטור ותדע דסתם מתני' כר"ע אתיא דהא אשת אחיו ואשת אחי אביו דתנן לעיל יש לה קנס לא אתיא אלא כר"ע דבע"כ גירשה או נתאלמנה שאל"כ הו"ל א"א ויש בהן מיתת ב"ד:

[ולפי האמת אע"ג דמלא יהיה אסון נפקי כולהו מדתנא דבי חזקיה איצטריך עין תחת עין לכדדרשינן ולא עין ונפש תחת עין אבל לא עין ונפש תחת נפש לא איצטריך למדרשי' ולאו קרא יתירא הוא אלא מפשטיה דקרא קדריש וליכא למימר דליפתוק מלא יהיה אסון ומנפש תחת נפש נפיק כולהו מכח הקישא דתנא דבי חזקיה דאכתי לא שמעי' מיניה ממון אחר בהדי מיתה דסימא את עינו והרגו בדבר אחר לא חשיב ממון ונפש אלא נפש גרידא כדמוכח בפנים להכי איצטריך לא יהיה אסון ומהשתא שמעי' מינה אפי' הרג וקרע שיראין מהקישא דתנא דבי חזקיה. ת"י]

גליון הש"ס

גמ' בין מתכוין לשאין מתכוין. עיין לקמן מ ע"א תוס' ד"ה אחד בכלכה.

עין משפט
נר מצוה

סח א מיי' פ"א מהל' נערה הלכה טו סמג עשין נד טור אה"ע סימן קעז:

אֵימָא "בְּתוּלָה" – לִגְזֵירָה שָׁוָה וַ"אֲשֶׁר לֹא אוֹרָסָה" – פְּרָט לְנַעֲרָה שֶׁנִּתְאָרְסָה וְנִתְגָּרְשָׁה! מִסְתַּבְּרָא "אֲשֶׁר לֹא אוֹרָסָה" לִגְזֵירָה שָׁוָה, שֶׁהֲרֵי אֲנִי קוֹרֵא בָּהּ "נַעֲרָה בְּתוּלָה". אַדְּרַבָּה, "בְּתוּלָה" לִגְזֵירָה שָׁוָה, שֶׁהֲרֵי אֲנִי קוֹרֵא בָּהּ "אֲשֶׁר לֹא אוֹרָסָה"! מִסְתַּבְּרָא, *הָא – אִישְׁתַּנֵּי גּוּפָהּ, וְהָא – לָא אִישְׁתַּנֵּי גּוּפָהּ. וְרַבִּי יוֹסֵי הַגְּלִילִי הַאי סְבָרָא מְנָא לֵיהּ? נָפְקָא לֵיהּ *מִדְּתַנְיָא: °"כֶּסֶף יִשְׁקוֹל כְּמוֹהַר הַבְּתוּלוֹת" (שמות כב) – שֶׁיְּהֵא זֶה כְּמוֹהַר הַבְּתוּלוֹת, וּמוֹהַר הַבְּתוּלוֹת כָּזֶה. קַשְׁיָא דְּר"ע אַדְּר' עֲקִיבָא! תְּרֵי תַּנָּאֵי וְאַלִּיבָּא דְּר"ע. בִּשְׁלָמָא ר"ע דְּמַתְנִי' – לָא אָתְיָא ג"ש וּמַפְּקָא לֵיהּ לִקְרָא מִפְּשָׁטֵיהּ לְגַמְרֵי, אֶלָּא לְר"ע דִּבְרַיְיתָא – אָתְיָא גְּזֵירָה שָׁוָה וּמַפְּקָא מִפְּשָׁטֵיהּ לְגַמְרֵי! אָמַר רַב נַחְמָן בַּר יִצְחָק: קְרִי בֵּיהּ "אֲשֶׁר לֹא אֲרוּסָה". אֲרוּסָה בַּת סְקִילָה הִיא! ס"ד אָמִינָא: הוֹאִיל וְחִידּוּשׁ הוּא שֶׁחִידְּשָׁה תוֹרָה בִּקְנָס, אע"ג דְּמִיקְטִיל – מְשַׁלֵּם. וּלְרַבָּה, דְּאָמַר: *חִידּוּשׁ הוּא שֶׁחִידְּשָׁה תוֹרָה בִּקְנָס, אע"ג דְּמִיקְטִיל מְשַׁלֵּם – מַאי אִיכָּא לְמֵימַר? סָבַר לָהּ כְּרַבִּי עֲקִיבָא דְּמַתְנִיתִין. תָּנוּ רַבָּנַן: קְנָסָהּ לְמִי – לְאָבִיהָ, וְיֵשׁ אוֹמְרִים: לְעַצְמָהּ. לְעַצְמָהּ אַמַּאי? אָמַר רַב חִסְדָּא: הָכָא בְּנַעֲרָה שֶׁנִּתְאָרְסָה וְנִתְגָּרְשָׁה עָסְקִינַן, וְקָמִיפַּלְגִי בִּפְלוּגְתָּא דְּר"ע דְּמַתְנִיתִין וְרַבִּי עֲקִיבָא דִּבְרַיְיתָא. *אָמַר אַבַּיֵי: אבָּא עָלֶיהָ וּמֵתָה – פָּטוּר, שֶׁנֶּאֱמַר: °"וְנָתַן לַאֲבִי הַנַּעֲרָה" (דברים כב) – וְלֹא לַאֲבִי מֵתָה. מִלְּתָא דִּפְשִׁיטָא לֵיהּ לְאַבַּיֵי, מִיבַּעְיָא לֵיהּ לְרָבָא. דְּבָעֵי רָבָא: יֵשׁ בֶּגֶר בַּקֶּבֶר אוֹ אֵין בֶּגֶר בַּקֶּבֶר? יֵשׁ בֶּגֶר בַּקֶּבֶר – וְדִבְנָהּ הָוֵי, אוֹ דִּלְמָא אֵין בֶּגֶר בַּקֶּבֶר – וּדְאָבִיהָ הָוֵי?
וּמִי

רש"י

אימא בתולה לגזירה שוה. ולאו למעוטי בעולה, ויהא קנס לבעולה. מסתברא אשר לא אורסה לגזירה שוה. ואפי' אורסה אית לה קנס. שהרי אני קורא בה נערה בתולה. אע"פ שנתארסה ונתגרשה, דהא נערה בתולה היא, כדכתיב קרא. אבל בעולה שאין אני קורא בה נערה בתולה – אין לה קנס. אדרבה בתולה לגזירה שוה. ולאו למעוטי בעולה בזנות, אלא יש לה קנס לבעולה בזנות, שהרי אני קורא אותה "נערה אשר לא אורסה". מסתברא. ארוסה יש לה קנס, ובעולה אין לה. דהא אישתני גופה. ופגמה אין רב כל כך. והא. דנתארסה ונתגרשה לא נשתנה גופה. הא סברא. דחמשים כסף דאונס שקלים הן, ו"כסף ישקול" דמפתה יהו חמשים. כמוהר הבתולות. מנין המפורש אצל אונס, דהיינו חמשים. ומוהר הבתולות. יהיו שקלים. כזה. שכתוב בו "ישקול". קשיא דרבי עקיבא. דברייתא, דאמר קנסה לאביה. אדרבי עקיבא. דמתני'. לא אתיא גזירה שוה ומפקא לקרא מפשטיה לגמרי. דאתא פשטיה לאשמועינן הא ארוסה לעצמה, וחד מתרוייהו לאפנויי. אי נמי לא מופני – ליכא למיפרך מידי. אלא לרבי עקיבא דברייתא וכי אתיא גזירה שוה ומפקא מפשטיה לגמרי. דלא דריש פשטא ד"אשר לא אורסה" כלל, ומשוי אורסה כלא אורסה, ואם כן מיעקר משמעותיה! קרי ביה. בפשטיה אשר לא ארוסה – למעוטי ארוסה. בת סקילה היא. ומ"לא יהיה אסון" נפקא פטורא מתשלומין. קנסה למי. קא סלקא דעתך בסתם אנוסה קאי. בא עליה ומתה. לא הספיק האב להעמידו בדין, עד שמתה. יש בגר בקבר. אם מתה בנערותה עד שלא עמדה בדין, והגיע זמן בגרותה בקבר, מי חשיב בגר או לא? ולקמיה מפרש ואזיל למאי הלכתא. יש בגר בקבר. וכי היכי דאם לא הספיקה לעמוד בדין עד שבגרה, תנן לקמן בפרק "נערה שנתפתתה" (דף מא:) דהרי הן לעצמה ולא לאביה, והשתא נמי בגר בקבר מפקיע כח האב, ובנה ירית לה, אם יש לה בן.
ומי

תוספות

[אימא: בתולה לג"ש. ולא נמעט בעולה, כדמשמע בסמוך. נראה דר"ע דריש ג"ש מקרא דלגופיה, דהיינו בתולה קמייתא, ודקנס ודמפתה, אבל "הבתולות" דריש לכתובת בתולות, ולא שייך למידרשיה לג"ש ולא לשום רבוי, ואייתר "נער" "נערה" "הנערה" וה' ד"הבתולות" חד לחייבי לאוין ועשה, וחד לחייבי לאוין וכריתות. ואיכא ג' רבויין; ה' ד"הבתולות", ו"נער" "נערה" "הנערה". חד לכדאביי, וחד לחייבי עשה, וחד – לחייבי לאוין וכריתות. דאי איכא לר"ע חד לגופיה בלא ג"ש – א"כ נמעוט בעולה מההוא דלגופיה. ואף על גב דבקנס ליכא אלא חד בתולה דלגופיה, מגזירה שוה דמפתה יליף בתולה ולא בעולה, כי היכי דיליף מפתה מאונס לענין נערה, דלא כתיב במפתה]. (ת"י כ"י).

אימא בתולה לג"ש. תימה: דתיקשי ליה: דאימא תרוייהו לגופייהו, ולא לג"ש! ונראה דהתלמוד קים ליה דחד מינייהו לגזירה שוה, הואיל והמקראות סתומים לענין שקלים וחמשים. הלכך פריך ואימא איפכא, ולא פריך ואימא תרוייהו לגופייהו. וכי האי גוונא איכא פ"ק דסנהדרין (דף טז.) דאמר: ולא את נביא השקר אלא בב"ד של ע' ואחד. מה"מ? א"ר יוסי בר חנינא: אתיא "הזדה" "הזדה" מזקן ממרא, ופריך: הא "הזדה" כי כתיב – בקטלא הוא דכתיב, וקטלא בכ"ג! אלא אמר ריש לקיש: גמר "דבר" "דבר" מהמראתו. והשתא היכי הוה בעי למילף ולמימר רבי יוסי ברבי חנינא דאתיא "הזדה" "הזדה". אלא דהוה קים ליה דאיכא ג"ש ולא הוה ידע במאי וקאמר מסברא דאתיא הזדה הזדה. מי אתיא גזרה שוה ומפקא ליה מפשטיה לגמרי. דדיוק הא אורסה הוי שקר. וקשה: דבריש "הערל" (יבמות ד' ע.) יליף דערל אסור בתרומה מגזירה שוה דתושב ושכיר מפסח, וכתיב "תושב ושכיר לא יאכל בו" גבי פסח משום גזירה שוה, אע"פ שאינו אמת, דהא תושב ושכיר אוכלין בפסח, כדאמרינן התם דלא קני ליה רביה, ומפקי' קרא מפשטיה טפי מהכא! ואומר ר"ת: דההוא תושב ושכיר מיירי בערלים, ולהכי לא יאכל. ומוכח דלאו תושב ישראל קאמר, דהא לא קני ליה רביה, אלא ודאי בערל, ומשום הפנאה כתביה*.

ארוסה בת סקילה היא. וא"ת: מאי קשיא ליה? הא השתא לא נפיק קרא ממשמעותיה. ואי לא איצטריך לגופיה כ"ש דניחא טפי, דג"ש מופנה! ואומר ר"י, דהכי פירושו: ארוסה בת סקילה היא, וכיון דלא איצטריך למידי אלא לגזירה שוה – הוה ליה למכתב "אשר לא ארוסה" בהדיא, ואמאי שני למכתב "אשר לא ארוסה" דאיכא למטעי ולמימר הא אורסה לעצמה? דבשלמא אי הוה בארוסה שום חידוש הוה אתי שפיר במה ששינה הלשון, דאמרינן האי דשנה וכתב "אורסה" – למדרש לגזירה שוה ואתא פשטיה לחידושא, אבל השתא למה לי?

לאבי הנערה ולא לאבי מתה. וא"ת: דבפרק "נערה" לקמן (דף מה:) גבי סרחה ולבסוף בגרה תידון בסקילה, דרשינן "הנערה" – שהיתה כבר! ויש לומר: דהתם מענינא דקרא, והכא מענינא דקרא. והתם ודאי אתיא לחייבה, דאי לפוטרה – לשתוק קרא מיניה ואנא ידענא דלא הויא בסקילה, דלאו נערה היא. והכא לחיובא דקנס לא אצטריך, דמסברא מיחייב אשעת ביאה, ואי אפשר לפוטרו בולא כלום – הלכך אתא לפוטרו. יש בגר בקבר ודבנה הוי. וא"ת: היכי מצי למימר שתהא מורשת קנס לבנה? הא אין אדם מוריש קנס לבניו, כדאמרינן ריש פרק "נערה" לקמן (דף מג:), ובסמוך נמי אמר: יש בגר בקבר ופקע אב, ואי אדם מוריש קנס – כי יש בגר בקבר נמי לא פקע אב, ויהא לו מתורת ירושה! ומיהו, ההיא דבסמוך יש לדחות: דנפקא מינה אם היא חייבת לאחרים, דאם יש בגר בקבר – פקע אב, אע"ג דאדם מוריש קנס, דנוטלין בעלי חובות כלום, דלא פקע אב, והקנס הוא שלו ולא שלה. ויש לומר: *דהכא ה"מ לאקשויי והא אין מורשת קנס לבנה, אלא דעדיפא מיניה פריך. ור"י מוקי הך בעיא דהכא בבושת ופגם, דממונא הוי, ויכולה להוריש. ואע"ג דתנן בריש "נערה" (שם מא:): לא הספיקה לעמוד בדין עד שמת האב – הרי הן של עצמה, ואבושת ופגם נמי קאי, מדקתני הרי הן – משמע דאין יכול להוריש בושת ופגם! ואור"י: דלענין זה ודאי איתקוש בושת ופגם לקנס, דכתיב "תחת אשר ענה" מכלל דאיכא בושת ופגם, דלמי שזה ניתן – זה ניתן. אבל למילי אחריני – לא איתקוש. דהא בושת ופגם משלם ע"פ עצמו, וקנס אינו משלם ע"פ עצמו. אבל הקשה ריב"ס: דאמרינן ב"מרובה" (ב"ק דף עה: ושם): א"ל "חמשה בקר" אמר רחמנא, ולא חמשה חצאי בקר. איתיביה: גנב משל אביו וטבח ומכר, ואח"כ מת אביו – משלם תשלומי ד' וה'. והא הכא כיון דמת אביו זכה ליה במנתא דידיה, וקתני דמשלם תשלומי ד' וה'! ומשני: הב"ע – שעמד בדין. משמע דאי לאו משום דחמשה בקר ולא חמשה חצאי בקר – הוה אתי ליה שפיר, ולא הוה צריך לאוקומי בשעמד בדין, אלמא דאדם מוריש קנס לבניו! ומיהו, יש לדחות: דה"מ למימר וליטעמיך. אבל קשה: דמסיק לגפרא א"ל "חמשה בקר" אמר רחמנא, ואפי' חמשה חצאי בקר. א"ל מאי שנא רישא ומאי שנא סיפא? פירוש: דקתני גנב משל אביו ומת, ואח"כ טבח ומכר פטור? א"ל: רישא קרינן ביה וטבחו כולו באיסורא, סיפא לא קרינן וטבחו כולו באיסורא. משמע דאי קרינן ביה וטבחו כולו באסורא – חייב, אע"ג דלא עמד בדין, דאדם מוריש קנס לבניו. דאי בעמד בדין לא מחייב קנס, דשלו הוא טובח ומוכר! ותי' ר"י: דמיירי דעמד בדין, ואמרו: חייב אתה ליתן לו. דאם הוא טובח אחרי כן – חייב, כדאמרינן ב"הגוזל" (שם דף קו: ושם). ור"י הלבן תירץ: דההיא דפרק "נערה" איירי לענין קרבן שבועה. והכי פירושו דסוגיא דהתם: מודינא לך לענין קרבן שבועה, דרחמנא פטריה מ"וכחש בעמיתו בפקדון" וכי קאמינא דממון הוי להורישו לבניו, שאם יתבעוהו לאחר מיתת אביהן קנס שהיה חייב לאביהן שהעמידו בדין ונתחייב וכפר ונשבע והודה, הואיל וכשנפל ליורשין – כבר היה ממון, שכבר עמד בדין, ולא היה יכול להודות ולהפטר – א"כ הוי דומיא דפקדון דקרא, ומחייב קרבן שבועה. איתיביה ר"ש אומר כו' דאחין הוא. ופירוש: שאם אינו לאחין – איך מתחייב הכופר קרבן שבועה על טענותם? והא לאו בעל דברים דידהו, הוא אלא ש"מ דאחין הוא. ומסיק: כי קאמר רבה דממון הוא להורישו לבניו – בשאר קנסות, לענין חיוב קרבן שבועה. ומסיק דאצטריך "וכחש" לעמדה בדין ובגרה ואחר כך מתה, דמינה קא ירית. מכל מקום עיקרו קנס מיקרי לגבי דידה ודידיה, ולא דמי לשאר קנסות דמוריש לבניו, דלגבי בניו לא הוה קנס כלל. ומיהו, לשון להורישו לבניו – לא משמע כפירוש זה. [ועיין תוספות בבא קמא עב. ד"ה סיפא].
שלש

תוספות רי"ד

אמר אביי בא עליה ומתה פטור שנאמר ונתן לאבי הנערה ולא לאבי מתה. פי' כגון שלא הספיק האב להעמידו בדין עד שמתה. אבל אם עמד עמו בדין ונתחייב לו אע"פ שמתה [אח"כ] נותן לאביה:

מסורת הש"ס

לעיל י. [לעיל כט:]

[עי' תוס' לקמן מה. ד"ה למאי "תוס' יבמות נט. ד"ה הא]

[לעיל ל: לה:]

לעיל כב:

[ועי' תוס' יבמות עו: ד"ה אלא]

נ"ל דהכא נמי

תורה אור

ומי מעברא? והתני רב ביבי קמיה דרב נחמן: *שלש נשים משמשות במוך, אלו הן: קטנה, ומעוברת, ומניקה; קטנה – שמא תתעבר ותמות, מעוברת – שמא תעשה עוברה סנדל, מניקה – שמא תגמול את בנה. ואיזוהי קטנה – מבת אחת עשרה שנה ויום אחד עד שתים עשרה שנה ויום אחד. פחות מיכן ויתר על כן – משמשת כדרכה והולכת, דברי ר"מ. וחכמים אומרים: אחת זו ואחת זו משמשת כדרכה והולכת, ומן השמים ירחמו, משום שנאמר: (תהלים קטז) °"שומר פתאים ה'"! וכי תימא דאיעברא כשהיא נערה ואולידה כשהיא נערה, ובשיתא ירחי מי קא ילדה? והאמר שמואל: *[א]אין בין נערות לבגרות אלא ששה חדשים! וכי תימא: בציר הוא דליכא, הא טפי איכא – הא "אלא" קאמר! אלא הכי קמיבעיא ליה: יש בגר בקבר ופקע אב, או דלמא: אין בגר בקבר ולא פקע אב? מר בר רב אשי בעי לה הכי: מיתה עושה בגרות, או אין עושה בגרות? תיקו. בעי מיניה רבא מאביי: בא עליה ונתארסה מהו? א"ל: [ב]מי כתיב "ונתן לאבי הנערה אשר לא ארוסה"? ולטעמיך, הא דתניא: [ג]בא עליה ונשאת – לעצמה, מי כתיב "ונתן לאבי הנערה אשר לא נשואה"? הכי השתא?! התם, הואיל ובגרות מוציאה מרשות אב, ונישואין מוציאין מרשות אב, מה בגרות, בא עליה ובגרה – לעצמה, אף נישואין, בא עליה ונשאת – לעצמה, אלא אירוסין – מי קא מפקי מרשותא דאב לגמרי? הא תנן: *[ד]נערה המאורסה אביה ובעלה מפירין לה נדריה.§ **מתני'** *[ה]המפתה נותן שלשה דברים, והאונס ארבעה. המפתה נותן בושת ופגם וקנס, מוסיף עליו אונס שנותן את הצער. מה בין אונס למפתה? האונס – נותן את הצער, והמפתה – אינו נותן את הצער. האונס – נותן מיד, והמפתה – לכשיוציא. האונס – שותה בעציצו, והמפתה – אם רצה להוציא, מוציא. [ו]כיצד שותה בעציצו – אפילו היא חיגרת, אפי' היא סומא, ואפילו היא מוכת שחין. [ז]נמצא בה דבר ערוה, או שאינה ראויה לבא בישראל – אינו רשאי לקיימה, שנאמר: (דברים כב) °*"ולו תהיה לאשה" – אשה הראויה לו.§ **גמ'** צער דמאי? אמר אבוה דשמואל: צער שחבטה על גבי קרקע. מתקיף לה רבי זירא: אלא מעתה, חבטה על גבי שיראין הכי נמי דפטור? וכי תימא הכי נמי – והתניא, ר' שמעון בן יהודה אומר משום רבי שמעון: *אונס אינו משלם את הצער מפני

שסופה

ומי מעברא. בקטנות או בנערות כשהיא בת קנס שתלד בנערות. **משמשות במוך.** מותר להן לשמש במוך, ואינן כמשחיתות זרע. **שמא יעשה עוברה סנדל.** שאם תתעבר עובר שני, פוחת השני את צורת (א) הראשון, ודומה לסנדל שהוא דג שטוח. **שמא תגמול את בנה.** מפני שהחלב נעכר כשמתעברת, ואינו טוב ליונק, ותצטרך להעתיקו משדים, וימות. **פחות מכאן.** מבת אחת עשרה שנה משמשת כדרכה, לפי שלא תתעבר. **ויתר על כן.** על בת שתים עשרה שנה משמשת כדרכה, שאם תתעבר – לא תמות. אלמא: בקטנות לא מיעברא, שיילא לכלל לידה, דהא "ותמות" קתני. **וכי תימא.** מבת שתים עשרה ויום אחד שהגיעו ימי הנעורים נתעברה וילדה בנערות ומתה בנערות – הא נמי ליתא, דאמר שמואל: אין בין נערות לבגרות אלא ששה חדשים. משתביא שתי שערות – הויא נערה כאותן שתביא משתים עשרה שנה והלאה, ומשתביאם עד שתבגור – ששה חדשים ותו לא. ומתניתא דקתני מבת שתים עשרה ואילך אי מעברא לא מתה – בשתביאה שתי שערות קודם שתתעבר קאמר. אבל כל זמן שלא הביאה – קטנה היא. והאי דנקט מנין שנים – משום דבציר משתים עשרה ויום אחד, אפילו הביאה שערות אינו אלא שומא, כדאמרינן במסכת נדה ובקדושין. **ופקע אב.** פוקעה תביעת אב, חנה הלה במה שבידו, שאין בעל דינו קיים. וקנס לאו ממון הוא להורישו לאביה בתורת ירושה, כל כמה דלא גבתיה. **או אין בגר בקבר.** לאפקועי תביעת אב. **מר בר רב אשי.** לא בעי לה בעיא דרבא משום בגר בקבר, אלא אם מתה בנערותה מי פקעה כי בגרות דמחיים, או לא. ולהאי לישנא דמר בר רב אשי אליבא דרבא אמרו לעיל: מילתא דפשיטא ליה לאביי מיבעיא ליה לרבא. דאילו ללישנא קמא – מפשט פשיטא ליה לרבא דמיתה לא מפקעא, ודלא כאביי, כל זמן שלא בגרה. וכי קא מיבעיא ליה – בבגר בקבר קמיבעיא ליה, אבל במיתה, כל זמן שלא בגרה פליג אדאביי ואמר: לא מפקעא, וחייב. **מיתה עושה בגרות.** עושה דין בגרות, דמפקעא כח אב כי בגרות. **מהו.** מי הוי לאביה או לעצמה. **בגרות מוציאה מרשות אב.** דלא מצינו שזיכתה לו תורה בבתו אלא מכר בקטנות, ושאר שבח כגון קנסה ומעשה ידיה בנערות, כדילפינן בפרק "נערה" (לקמן דף מו:), אבל בבגרות לא אשכחן. וכיון דלא זיכתה לו תורה – אנן מהיכא תיתי לן לזכותו בשלה. **ונשואין מוציאין מרשות אב.** כדאשכחן בהפרת נדרים, דכל זמן דלא ניסת – אביה מיפר, ומשניסת – אין יכול להפר. **בא עליה.** כשהיא נערה ובגרה. **לעצמה.** דכתיב "ונתן האיש השוכב עמה לאבי הנערה", אם נערה היא בשעת נתינה. **אביה ובעלה.** ואינו מופר עד שיפרו שניהם. **מתני'** **בושת ופגם.** במתני' לקמן מפרש להו. **האונס נותן מיד.** לאביה, אע"פ שכונסה. **לכשיוציא.** בגמרא פריך: הטו אשתו היא? ומפרש לה לכשלא יכנוס. דאם כנסה – אינו נותן קנס, כדכתיב "מהר ימהרנה לו, ואם מאן ימאן וגו' כסף ישקול". אבל אונס – כתיב "ונתן חמשים כסף ולו תהיה לאשה". **שותה בעציצו.** בכלי שבחר לו לשתות בו, כלומר: על כרחו ישאנה, כדכתיב "לא יוכל לשלחה" (דברים כב). **גמ'** **שסופה**

שלש נשים משמשות במוך. פי' בקונטרס: מותרות לשמש במוך, אע"ג דשאר נשים אסורות משום השחתת זרע. ואין נראה לר"ת: *דהא קטנה ואילונית מותר לשמש בהדייהו, ולא הוי השחתת זרע, כיון שהוא דרך תשמיש, ומפרש ר"ת: "משמשות" – צריכות לשמש במוך אחר תשמיש, ועלה טובה קמ"ל. ולר"י נראה לקיים פי' הקונט', דבריש נדה (דף ג.) משמע שהמוך הוא במעיה כל שעה, והוי כמשמש על האבנים ועל העצים, ולא דמי למשמש קטנה ואילונית. ועוד: אפילו היתה נותנת מוך אחר תשמיש אסורה, °דאף על פי שאינה מצווה על פריה ורביה – מ"מ אסורה היא להשחית זרע, כדמשמע בנדה (דף יג.), דתנן: כל היד המרבה לבדוק בנשים – משובחת, באנשים – תיקצץ. ומפרש בגמרא משום דנשים לאו בנות הרגשה נינהו. משמע דאם היו בנות הרגשה – הוו אסירי. ויש לדחות: דלאו בנות איסור הרגשה נינהו קאמר. **וכי** תימא בציר הוא כו' והא בלבד קאמר. בקונטרס (בקדושין דף עט.) ל"ג ליה, דבלאו "בלבד" משמע טפי לא*. **בא** עליה ונתארסה מהו. לרבי עקיבא דמתני' קא מיבעיא ליה, דאמר נתארסה ונתגרשה קנסה לעצמה. דמי אמרינן: כיון שיצאה מרשות האב לענין קנס – יהא קנסה לעצמה, או דלמא, כיון דלענין שאר מילי לא נפקא מרשות האב – יהא קנסה לאביה. אבל לרבי עקיבא דברייתא – פשיטא דקנסה לאביה. ולר' יוסי הגלילי, נהי דאמר אין לה קנס – נמי לא מיבעיא ליה, דהא דאין לה קנס – לאו משום מיפק מרשותא דאב היא, אלא גזירת הכתוב הוא דאין לה קנס, ולא נפקא באירוסין כלל מרשות אביה, דאב זכאי בקידושיה ובמעשה ידיה אע"ג דנתארסה. והא דקא בעי לה סתם, ולא קאמר לרבי עקיבא בהדיא מהו – משום דהלכה כר' עקיבא מחבירו. **הואיל** ונישואין מוציאין מרשות אב. פי' בקונט' דילפינן מהפרת נדרים, ואע"ג דקי"ל דממונא מאיסורא לא ילפינן – ה"מ לאוקמה ברשות אב, הוא דלא ילפינן ממונא מאיסורא, אבל לאפוקי מרשות אב – ילפינן שפיר מהפרת נדרים, דבסברא מועטת יש להוציאה מרשות אב. ור"י ב"ר אברהם פי': כיון דגלי לן קרא דלאוקמה ברשות אב איסורא וממונא שוין – ה"ה לאפוקה. [ור"י מפרש: דנישואין מוציאין מרשות אב, מדדרשינן "איש אמו ואביו תיראו" איש סיפק כו' אשה אין סיפק בידה לעשות. ולא נהירא, דמעשה ידיה אינו לבעל מן התורה!]. **מה** בוגרת בא עליה ובגרה לעצמה. פירוש: דהא מצינו בוגרת שיוצאה מרשות אב לענין ממון. וקשה: דה"נ נישואין מוציאין מרשות אב לענין ממון, ואמאי צריך למילף מבוגרת? ונראה דבא עליה ובגרה לעצמה נפקא לן מ"ונתן לאבי הנערה", דדרשינן: לאבי נערה ולא לאבי בוגרת. **צער** דמאי. קשה לר"י: דמאי קא מיבעיא ליה, וכי לא ידע התלמוד שיש צער גדול לבתולה בביאה ראשונה, וכמה קטנות חולות מזה? וכ"ת דמאותו צער פשיטא ליה להתלמוד דפטור, שהרי סופה להצטער בכך תחת בעלה, והא איכא כמה תנאי ב"הכונס" (ב"ק דף נט. ושם) דלא חיישי לכחש גופנא, פירוש: דבר שסופו להיות כן. ונראה לר"י דצער בעילה משום תאות תשמיש אינו בא בשעת תשמיש אלא אחר כך, וכל צער החבלה דמחייב היינו אותו צער הבא לו בשעת חבלה, אבל מה שבא לו אחר כך מיפטר, דגרמא בעלמא הוא, הלכך בעי: צער דמאי? ורשב"א מפרש דפשיטא דצער של בתולים ליכא למימר, דע"כ תנא דמתני' חייש לכחש גופנא, מדמפתה פטור.

אי

מסורת הש"ס

יבמות יב: ק: נדה מה. נדרים לה: [תוספתא נדה פ"ב]

קדושין עט. נדה סה.

נדרים סו: עד: יבמות כט: לקמן מו: קדושין ד. לקמן מב.

[לעיל כט:]

ב"ק נט. ע"ש

הגהות הב"ח

(א) רש"י ד"ה שמא יעשה עוברה וכו' צורת השני. נ"ב ותוספות פרק המפלת הביא בשם רש"י שולד אחרון ממעך צורת הראשון ע"ש בד"ה קמ"ל בדף כה מיהו ביבמות דף יב כתב רש"י ז"ל דוחק האחד את חברו ופוחת צורתו משמע לפעמים הראשון גובר ולפעמים השני גובר ופעם פי' כך ופעם פי' כך ואין כאן טעות:

גליון הש"ס

תום' ד"ה שלש וכו' דאע"פ שאינה מצווה על פריה ורביה. עי' סנהדרין דף נט ע"ב תוד"ה והא:

עין משפט נר מצוה

[עי' תוס' יבמות יב: ותוס' נדה יג.]

סט א מיי' פ"ב מהל' אישות הל' ב טור ש"ע יו"ד סימן רלד סעיף א בהג"ה:

ע ב מיי' פ"ב מהל' נערה הל' טז סמג עשין נ טור אה"ע סימן קעז:

עא ג מיי' שם הל' טו:

עב ד מיי' פי"א מהל' נדרים הל' ט סמג לאוין רמב טוש"ע י"ד סי' רלד סעיף ה:

עג ה מיי' פ"ב מהלכות נערה הל' ז סמג עשין נ טוש"ע אה"ע סי' קעז סעיף א:

עד ו מיי' פ"א שם הל' ג סמג שם טוש"ע שם סעיף ג:

עה ז מיי' שם הל' ה טוש"ע שם סעי' ד:

[ועי' תוס' נדה סה. ד"ה וכ"ת כו' מייתבין הגירסא]

תוספות רי"ד

תניא בא עליה ונשאת לעצמה הואיל ובגרות מוציאה מרשות אב. פי' שלא מצינו שזכתה לו תורה בבתו אלא מכר בקטנותה ושאר שבח ממון כגון קנסה ומעשה ידיה בנערות כדילפי' לקמן בפ' נערה ונשואין נמי מוציאין מרשות אב. פירוש כדאשכחן בהפרת נדרים דכ"ז שלא נשאת אביה מפר נדריה ומשנשאת אין יכול להפר. מה בוגרת בא עלי' ובגרה לעצמה דכתיב ונתן האיש השוכב עמה לאבי הנערה. אם היא נערה בשעת נתינה אף נשואין בא עליה ונשאת לעצמה: **מתני'** המפתה נותן ג' דברים והאונס ד' המפתה נותן בושת ופגם וקנס מוסיף עליו אונס שנותן את הצער מה בין אונס למפתה האונס נותן את הצער והמפתה אין נותן את הצער האונס נותן מיד והמפתה לכשיוציא האונס שותה בעציצו. פי' בכלי שבחר לו לשתות בו כלומר ע"כ ישאנה דכתיב לא יוכל לשלחה כל ימיו והמפתה אם רצה להוציא מוציא. פי' האונס נותן מיד ואע"פ שכונסה שנאמר ונתן האיש השוכב עמה לאבי הנערה חמשים כסף ולו תהיה לאשה. ודרשי' תו לו אתה כופה ולא לה:

שסופה להצטער תחת בעלה, אמרו לו: אינו דומה נבעלת באונס לנבעלת ברצון! אלא אמר רב נחמן, אמר רבה בר אבוה: צער של פיסוק הרגלים. וכן הוא אומר: °"ותפשקי את רגליך לכל עובר". אי הכי מפותה נמי! אמר רב נחמן אמר רבה בר אבוה: משל דמפותה למה הדבר דומה — לאדם שאמר לחבירו: קרע שיראין שלי והפטר. שלי?! דאבוה נינהו! אלא אמר רב נחמן אמר רבה בר אבוה: פקחות שבהן אומרות: מפותה אין לה צער. והא קא חזינן דאית לה! אמר אביי, *אמרה לי אם: כמיא חמימי על רישיה דקרחא. רבא אמר: אמרה לי בת רב חסדא: כי ריבדא דכוסילתא. רב פפא אמר: אמרה לי בת אבא סוראה: כי נהמא אקושא בחינכי.§ האונס נותן מיד, המפתה לכשיוציא וכו'.§ לכשיוציא, אשתו היא?! אמר אביי: אימא לכשלא יכנוס. תניא נמי הכי: אע"פ שאמרו [א]המפתה נותן לכשלא יכנוס, בושת ופגם — נותן מיד. ואחד [ב]האונס ואחד המפתה, בין היא ובין אביה יכולין לעכב. בשלמא מפותה — כתיב: °"אם מאן ימאן אביה", *אין לי אלא אביה, היא עצמה מנין — תלמוד לומר: "ימאן", מכל מקום. אלא אונס, בשלמא איהי — כתיב: °"ולו תהיה" — מדעתה. אלא אביה מנלן? אמר אביי: *שלא יהא חוטא נשכר. רבא אמר: ק"ו: ומה מפתה שלא עבר אלא על דעת אביה בלבד, בין היא ובין אביה יכולין לעכב, אונס שעבר על דעת אביה ועל דעת עצמה — לא כל שכן. רבא לא אמר כאביי, כיון דקא משלם קנס — לאו חוטא נשכר הוא. אביי לא אמר כרבא, מפתה דאיהו מצי מעכב — אביה נמי מצי מעכב, אונס דאיהו לא מצי מעכב — אביה נמי לא מצי מעכב. תניא אידך: אע"פ שאמרו אונס נותן מיד, כשיוציא הוא — אין לה עליו כלום. כשיוציא? מי מצי מפיק לה?! אימא: כשתצא היא — אין לה עליו כלום. [ג]מת — *יצא כסף קנסה בכתובתה. רבי יוסי ברבי יהודה אומר: יש לה כתובה מנה. במאי קמיפלגי? רבנן סברי: *[ד]טעמא מאי תקינו רבנן כתובה — כדי שלא תהא קלה בעיניו להוציאה, והא לא מצי מפיק לה. ורבי יוסי ברבי יהודה סבר: הא נמי מצער לה עד דאמרה היא "לא בעינא לך".§ אונס שותה בעציצו.§ אמר ליה רבא מפרזקיא לרב אשי: מכדי, מיגמר גמרי מהדדי להא

יחזקאל טז | שמות כב | דברים כב

שסופה להצטער כו'. ואי חיבוט על גבי קרקע הוא, וכי סופה ליחבט על גבי קרקע תחת בעלה? שלי. בתמיה. דאבוה הוא. דהא כל שבח נעורים ילפינן לקמן (דף מו:) לאביה, והיאך היא יכולה למחול? ריבדא דכוסילתא. פולטוויי"א דפלמוא"ה בלע"ז. ריבדא. תורה אור ניקור. כוסילתא. כלי אומן מקיז. ואית דגרסי: כי תרפתא דסיכורי, והיא היא. אמרה לי אם. (א) אומנתו היתה. בת רב חסדא. אשתו של רבא. בת אבא סוראה. דביתהו דרב פפא. נהמא אקישא בחינכי. כלחם קשה שגורר את החיך. אשתו היא. וכי אשתו היא כבר דקאמר "לכשיוציא"? לכשלא יכנוס. שתמאן היא, או אביה, או המפתה עצמו. יכולין לעכב. שלא יכניסנה. תהיה. משמע: היא מהוה את עצמה לו. מצי מעכב. שאם רצה אינו כונס, כדאמרינן לקמן: ימהרנה לו — מדעתו. אביה נמי לא מצי מעכב. אי לאו שלא יהא חוטא נשכר. אע"פ שאמרו אונס נותן מיד כשיוציאנה אין לה עליו כלום. ולא אמרינן אין קנסה תחת כתובתה, שהרי לאביה נותן מיד. אלא כסף קנסה הוא כתובתה, וכן אם מת — יצא כסף קנסה בכתובתה. מי מצי מפיק לה. "לא יוכל לשלחה" כתיב. כשתצא היא. אם ילתה מאליה, ותבעה הימנו גט. טעמא מאי תקינו רבנן כתובה. לשאר נשים. מיגמר גמרי מהדדי. אונס ממפתה לשקלים, ומפתה מאונס לחמשים. להא

[קדושין לה. וש"נ] | קדושין מו. | [לעיל יא. וש"נ] | לקמן פ. | [לעיל לט. לקמן נד. יבמות פט.]

אי הכי מפותה נמי. יש לה לער פיסוק רגלים כמו אנוסה, ואמאי קאמר אין דומה נבעלת באונס לנבעלת ברלון? ואמר מורי הרב דודי ז"ל: *דאמתני' לא ה"מ למיפרך אמאי אונס חייב, כיון שסופה להלטער בכך תחת בעלה — דהא אפילו בעולה מלטערת בכך, ואע"ג דבא עליה עתה — סופה נמי להלטער ולא תרויח כלום. [קלת נראה דאמתני' פריך, אמאי מפותה פטור].

קרע שיראין שלי והפטר. ואע"ג דלא אמרה "על מנת לפטור" — איכא למימר דמחמת הנאת בעילה מחלה לגמרי.

[**לכשיוציא** אשתו היא. אפי' פיתה לשם אישות, מ"מ פריך: אשתו היא?! כיון דאינה לריכה גט].

בושת ופגם נותן מיד. אע"ג דאיתקש לקנס — היינו לענין שניתן זה למי שזה ניתן, אבל יש מקומות שפטור מקנס לגמרי, וחייב בבושת ופגם. **אין** לי אלא אביה היא עצמה מנין כו'. (ג) תימה לר"י: במאי מיירי? אי בקטנה או בנערה — היאך היא יכולה למאן, כיון שהאב רולה, והוא יכול לקדשה בעל כרחה למי שירלה, וה"ה לזה. ואי בשאין לה אב או שבגרה אחר כך — מה לריך קרא? תיפוק ליה שיכולה לעכב, שלא יהא חוטא נשכר, כדקאמר אביי בסמוך. וכן אביה, אמאי לריך קרא לאביי? ואומר ר"י: דנהי שאינה יכולה לעכב על אביה שלא יקדשנה לו, מ"מ מועיל מיאונה לענין שישלם קנס, וכן במיאון אביה. והא דתניא הכא המפתה לכשלא יכנוס — לריך לפרש לכשלא יכנוס מדעתה. ומיהו קשה: דהכא דרשינן מ"אם מאן ימאן" — מ"מ, שהיא יכולה לעכב. ובפרק "נערה" (לקמן מד:) דרשינן מינה לרבות יתומה לקנס! וי"ל: דליכתוב או "מאן מאן" או "ימאן ימאן" מאי "מאן ימאן" — ש"מ תרתי. ובכה"ג אמרינן ב"מרובה" (ב"ק דף סה. ושם): גבי "אם המלא תמלא" וב"החובל" (שם דף פה.): גבי "ורפא ירפא". ועוד, נראה דלאו מיתורא דקרא דריש לה התם, דאם כן מאי פריך מינה לרבי יוסי בר' חנינא דפטר מוליא שם רע על היתומה, דשאני מפתה דרבי קרא. אלא כן הוא עיקר כמו שפירש בקונטרס לקמן, דלאו מריבוי דריש, אלא ה"פ: לרבות יתומה לקנס — דדרשינן שיש קנס כשהיא מעכבת. והוא הדין דה"מ למימר לרבות בוגרת לקנס כשהיא מעכבת, דדוקא בבוגרת או ביתומה יש קנס בעיכוב שלהן. אבל כל זמן שלא בגרה — תלוי באב. והשתא דייק התם שפיר, דשמעינן דסבר האי תנא שיש קנס ביתומה, ולא ממעטינן ליה מדכתיב "לאבי הנערה" אע"ג דליכא ריבוי ליתומה כדפירשתי, דאיכא לאוקמי קרא לבוגרת.

אלא אונס בשלמא איהי כו'. תימה: כיון דאונס ומפתה מיגמר גמירי מהדדי — להא מילתא נמי ליגמרו מהדדי, כדפריך בסמוך, ומאי קאמר אלא אביה מנלן? וי"ל: דלהאי מילתא לא גמרינן מהדדי, דהא מפתה יכול לעכב ואונס שותה בעליו. וה"ה ה"נ אין אביה יכול לעכב, וה"נ קאמר אביי בסמוך. ורבא לא מסתבר ליה למימר הכי, כיון דאיכא ק"ו. וא"ת: ואיהי גבי אונס אמאי איצטריך למיכתב? נילף לאביי מסברא שלא יהא חוטא נשכר, ולרבא מק"ו! ויש לומר: ד"לו תהיה לאשה" אינו מיותר, [דאיצטריך לעשה ולדרשות דלעיל. מהר"ס. א"נ, אביי ורבא לא הוו משנו הכי אלא בתר דגלי קרא דהדיא]. **מפתה** דאיהו מצי מעכב. ואפי' פיתה לשם אישות יכול הוא לגרשה.

טעמא מאי תקינו לה רבנן כתובה שלא תהא קלה בעיניו להוציאה. אע"ג דבתולה יש לה כתובה מן התורה — זאת בעולה היא. ומיהו, תימה: דקא פסיק ותני דבכל ענין אין לה כתובה, אפילו בא עליה שלא כדרכה, ובתולה גמורה היא, ויש לה כתובה מן התורה. דהא אם בא עליה שני — יש לה קנס, ולא הוי טעמא שלא תהא קלה בעיניו להוציאה! תימה לר"י: כיון דטעמא שלא תהא קלה בעיניו להוציאה — אלמנה אמאי תקינו לה רבנן כתובה? לא היה להם לתקן אלא לגרושה בלבד! ואומר ר"י: דמתוך שהוצרכו לתקן בגרושה שלא תהא קלה בעיניו להוציאה — תקינו נמי לאלמנה, משום חינא. ומיהו, לכתחילה לא היו מתקנים משום חינא. קשה לרשב"א: הא דתניא ב"החובל" (ב"ק דף פט. ושם) וכן היא שחבלה בבעלה — לא הפסידה כתובתה. ופריך: אמאי? תזבין לכתובתה *בטובת הנאה, ותיתיב ליה בהאי חבלה! ומשני: הא מני — רבי מאיר היא, דאמר: אסור לאדם שישהא את אשתו בלא כתובה אפילו שעה אחת. והשתא כיון דטעמא שלא תהא קלה בעיניו להוציאה — תזבין כתובתה על מנת שאם תתאלמן, אבל אם יגרשנה — יהא לה כתובה, דהתם לא שייך משום חינא! ואומר ר"י: כיון דבשאר נשים שייך חינא, אף על גב דבזאת לא שייך — לא פלוג רבנן, ואסור להשהותה בלא כתובה לר"מ. וא"ת: ואמאי תני הכא יצא כסף קנסה בכתובתה? ליתני: מת — אין לה עליו כלום, דהא לא תקינו רבנן לאלמנה אלא משום גרושה, והכא מכח גרושה אין לתקן לזאת, דהא לא מצי לגרשה! ואור"י: דה"נ כיון דשייך בה חינא כמו בשאר אלמנות — אין לנו לשנותה משאר אלמנות, להכי איצטריך טעמא דיצא כסף קנסה בכתובתה, ולא חשו במה דאין לה כתובה.

מהר

[נ"ל דלמתניתא לא ה"מ כו'. מהרש"א] | [לבעלה בטובת הנאה כצ"ל. מהרש"א]

עו א מיי' פ"ב מהל' נערה הל' ז סמג עשין נד טור אה"ע סי' קעז:

עז ב מיי' פ"א שם הל' ג סמג וטור שם:

עח ג ד מיי' שם הל' ז:

ת"י כ"י

תוספות רי"ד

והמפתה לכשיוציא וכי אשתו היא. אמר אביי אימא לכשלא יכנום. פי' שתמאן הוא או היא או אבי' דדרשי' לו מדעתו. אבל אם כנסה אינו נותן כלום דכתיב גבי מפתה מהר ימהרנה לו לאשה ואם מאן ימאן אביה לתתה לו כסף ישקול. תנ"ה אע"פ שאמרו המפתה נותן לכשלא יכנום בושת ופגם נותן מיד אחד האונס ואחד המפתה בין היא ובין אביה יכולין לעכב. פי' שלא יכנסנה. בשלמא מפותה כתיב אם מאן ימאן אביה אין לי אלא אביה היא עצמה מנין ת"ל מאן ימאן מ"מ. אלא אונס בשלמא איהי דכתיב ולו תהיה לאשה מדעתה אלא אביה מנלן. אביי אמר שלא יהא חוטא נשכר. רבא אמר (קנס) [ק"ו] הוא מה מפתה שלא עבר אלא ע"ד אביה בין היא בין אביה יכולין לעכב אונס שעבר על דעתה וע"ד אביה לא כ"ש. תניא אע"פ שאמרו האונס נותן מיד לכשהיא יוצאה. פי' כגון שנתרצו שניהן בגירושין אין לה עליו כלום. מת יצא כסף קנסה בכתובתה. ר' יוסי ברבי יהודה אומר יש לה כתובה מנה וקיי"ל כת"ק והמפתה אם רצה להוציא מוציא מ"ט אמר רב אשי א"ק מהר ימהרנה לו מדעתו פירוש ומאי דתנן אם רצה להוציא יוצא מתפרש אם רצה שלא יכנום לא יכנום כדפרישנא לכשיוציא דרישא:

הגהות הב"ח

(א) רש"י ד"ה אמרה וכו' אומנתו כ"ב דילדתו אמו ומתה כפי' קדושין דף לא ע"ב: (ג) תוס' ד"ה אין לי וכו' תימה. נ"ב עי' פ' האיש מקדש דף מ ע"א וכמ"ש התוס' לשם:

לְהָא מִילְּתָא נַמִּי לִיגְמְרוּ מֵהֲדָדֵי! אָמַר קְרָא: °"מָהֹר יִמְהָרֶנָּה לּוֹ לְאִשָּׁה" לוֹ – מִדַּעְתּוֹ.§ כֵּיצַד שׁוֹתָה בַּעֲצִיצוֹ כו'.§ אָמַר רַב כָּהֲנָא, אֲמְרִיתָא לִשְׁמַעְתָּא קַמֵּיהּ דְּרַב זְבִיד מִנְּהַרְדְּעָא: נֵיתֵי עֲשֵׂה וְנִדְחֶה ל"ת! אֲמַר לִי: [א]הֵיכָא אָמְרִינַן *נֵיתֵי עֲשֵׂה וְנִידְחֵי ל"ת – כְּגוֹן מִילָה בְּצָרַעַת, דְּלָא אֶפְשָׁר לְקַיּוּמֵיהּ לַעֲשֵׂה. אֲבָל הָכָא, אִי אָמְרָה דְּלָא בָּעֵינָא מִי אִיתֵיהּ לַעֲשֵׂה כְּלָל?.§ **מתני'** יְתוֹמָה שֶׁנִּתְאָרְסָה וְנִתְגָּרְשָׁה, ר' אֶלְעָזָר אוֹמֵר: הָאוֹנֵס חַיָּיב, וְהַמְפַתֶּה פָּטוּר.§ **גמ'** אָמַר רַבָּה בַּר בַּר חָנָה אָמַר ר' יוֹחָנָן: ר"א בְּשִׁיטַּת ר"ע רַבּוֹ אֲמָרָהּ, דְּאָמַר: *יֵשׁ לָהּ קְנָס, וּקְנָסָהּ לְעַצְמָהּ. מִמַּאי – מִדְּקָתָנֵי: יְתוֹמָה, ר"א אוֹמֵר: הָאוֹנֵס חַיָּיב וְהַמְפַתֶּה פָּטוּר. יְתוֹמָה פְּשִׁיטָא! אֶלָּא הָא קמ"ל: דְּנַעֲרָה שֶׁנִּתְאָרְסָה וְנִתְגָּרְשָׁה כִּיתוֹמָה, מַה [ב]יְתוֹמָה לְעַצְמָהּ – אַף נַעֲרָה שֶׁנִּתְאָרְסָה וְנִתְגָּרְשָׁה לְעַצְמָהּ. א"ר זֵירָא אָמַר רַבָּה בַּר שֵׁילָא אָמַר רַב הַמְנוּנָא סָבָא א"ר אַדָּא בַּר אַהֲבָה אָמַר רַב: [ג]הֲלָכָה כְּר' אֶלְעָזָר. *קָרֵי רַב עֲלֵיהּ דְּרַבִּי אֶלְעָזָר: טוֹבִינָא דְּחַכִּימֵי.§ **מתני'** *אֵיזֶהוּ בּוֹשֶׁת? [ד]הַכֹּל לְפִי הַמְבַיֵּישׁ וְהַמִּתְבַּיֵּישׁ. פְּגָם – רוֹאִין אוֹתָהּ כְּאִילּוּ הִיא שִׁפְחָה נִמְכֶּרֶת בַּשּׁוּק, כַּמָּה הָיְתָה יָפָה וְכַמָּה הִיא יָפָה. [ה]קְנָס שָׁוֶה בְּכָל אָדָם. וְכָל שֶׁיֵּשׁ לוֹ קִצְבָּה מִן הַתּוֹרָה – שָׁוֶה בְּכָל אָדָם.§ **גמ'** וְאֵימָא *חֲמִשִּׁים סְלָעִים אָמַר רַחֲמָנָא, מִכָּל מִילֵּי! א"ר זֵירָא: יֹאמְרוּ בָּעַל בַּת מְלָכִים – חֲמִשִּׁים, בָּעַל בַּת הֶדְיוֹטוֹת – חֲמִשִּׁים?! א"ל אַבַּיֵי: אִי הָכִי, גַּבֵּי עֶבֶד נַמִּי יֹאמְרוּ: עֶבֶד נוֹקֵב מַרְגָּלִיּוֹת – שְׁלֹשִׁים, עֶבֶד עוֹשֶׂה מַעֲשֶׂה

שמות כב | תורה אור

רש"י

לְהָא מִילְּתָא. שֶׁיִּהְיֶה מְפַתֶּה נוֹשֵׂא עַל כָּרְחוֹ. עֲשֵׂה. "לוֹ תִהְיֶה לְאִשָּׁה". וְנִדְחֶה אֶת לֹא תַעֲשֶׂה. דְּאֵינָהּ רְאוּיָה לָבֹא בְּיִשְׂרָאֵל, כְּגוֹן מַמְזֶרֶת. מִי אִיתֵיהּ לַעֲשֵׂה כְּלָל. הַשְׁתָּא נַמִּי, מְלַמְּדִין אוֹתָהּ לוֹמַר "אֵינִי רוֹצָה". **מתני'** יְתוֹמָה שֶׁנִּתְאָרְסָה וְנִתְגָּרְשָׁה הָאוֹנֵס חַיָּיב וְהַמְפַתֶּה פָּטוּר. דְּכֵיוָן דִּיתוֹמָה הִיא, וּקְנָס שֶׁלָּהּ הִיא, וְאַחִילְתֵיהּ, דְּמִדַּעְתָּהּ נִתְפַּתְּתָה לוֹ – פָּטוּר. וּבַגְּמָרָא מְפָרֵשׁ דְּנִתְאָרְסָה וְנִתְגָּרְשָׁה מִילְּתָא אַחֲרִיתִי הִיא, וְלָא אַיְּתוֹמָה קָאֵי. **גמ'** בְּשִׁיטַּת ר"ע רַבּוֹ אֲמָרָהּ. דְּאָמַר בְּמַתְנִי': *נַעֲרָה שֶׁנִּתְאָרְסָה וְנִתְגָּרְשָׁה – קְנָסָהּ לְעַצְמָהּ. וְהָךְ נִתְאָרְסָה וְנִתְגָּרְשָׁה דְּר' אֶלְעָזָר – כְּשֶׁאָבִיהָ קַיָּים, וְקָרֵי לָהּ יְתוֹמָה מִשּׁוּם דְּפָקַע זְכוּת אָב מִינָּהּ לְגַבֵּי קְנָסָא. מִמַּאי. דִּכְר"ע סְבִירָא לֵיהּ. מִדְּקָתָנֵי אוֹנֵס חַיָּיב וּמְפַתֶּה פָּטוּר. אַלְמָא יֵשׁ לָהּ קְנָס, וּלְעַצְמָהּ. הִלְכָּךְ מְפַתֶּה פָּטוּר – דְּמִדַּעְתָּהּ עֲבַד, וְאוֹנֵס חַיָּיב. וַאֲפִילּוּ אָבִיהָ קַיָּים. דְּאִי יְתוֹמָה כִּדְקָתָנֵי – פְּשִׁיטָא דִּמְפַתֶּה פָּטוּר, אֶלָּא הָא קמ"ל כו'. יְתוֹמָה פְּשִׁיטָא. מַסְקָנָא דְּמִילְּתָא דְּר' יוֹחָנָן הִיא. טוֹבִינָא דְּחַכִּימֵי. מְאוּשָּׁר שֶׁבַּחֲכָמִים. "אַשְׁרֵי" מְתַרְגְּמִינַן טוּבַאי. ר' אֶלְעָזָר הוּא ר' אֶלְעָזָר בֶּן שַׁמּוּעַ, וְתַלְמִידוֹ שֶׁל ר"ע הָיָה, כִּדְאָמְרִינַן בִּיבָמוֹת בְּ"הַבָּא עַל יְבִמְתּוֹ" (דף סב:): וְהָיָה הָעוֹלָם שָׁמֵם עַד שֶׁבָּא ר"ע אֵצֶל רַבּוֹתֵינוּ שֶׁבַּדָּרוֹם וְשָׁנָה לָהֶם, ר"מ, וְר' יְהוּדָה, וְר' יוֹסֵי, וְר"ש, וְרַבִּי אֶלְעָזָר בֶּן שַׁמּוּעַ. **מתני'** הַכֹּל לְפִי הַמְבַיֵּישׁ. אָדָם בֵּינוֹנִי הַמְבַיֵּישׁ בּוֹשְׁתּוֹ קָשָׁה מֵאָדָם זוֹלֵל וּמֵאָדָם חָשׁוּב. וְהַמִּתְבַּיֵּישׁ. לְפִי חֲשִׁיבוּתוֹ בּוֹשְׁתּוֹ. כְּאִילּוּ הִיא שִׁפְחָה. בַּגְּמָרָא מְפָרֵשׁ מַאי גְּרִיעוּתָא מֵחֲמַת בְּעִילָה. **גמ'** יֹאמְרוּ כו'. וְהֵיכָן הוּא חִילּוּק שֶׁבֵּינֵיהֶן אֶלָּא בּוֹשֶׁת? הִלְכָּךְ יָהֵיב בּוֹשֶׁת. גַּבֵּי עֶבֶד. שֶׁנְּגָחוֹ שׁוֹר, שֶׁנָּתְנָה תּוֹרָה קִצְבָּה ל' שְׁקָלִים.

לעיל לח. | שבת קלב: ביצה ח. | לעיל לח. | גיטין כז: כריתות יג: | [ב"ק פג:] | ערכין יד:

תוספות

מהר ימהרנה לו מדעתו. וא"ת: "ולו תהיה לאשה" נידרוש נמי: "לו" – מדעתו. והא דכתיב "לא יוכל לשלחה" היינו היכא דכבר נשאה! וי"ל: דאין סברא שיהיה מדעתו, כיון שאם נשאה לא יוכל לשלחה. [ועוד "ולו תהיה" קאי אאשה, ולהכי בעינן מדעתה. אבל "מהר ימהרנה" קאי אגברא]. **ניתי** עשה ונדחה לא תעשה. לאו אנמלא בה דבר ערוה פריך, דהא אית בה לאו ועשה, כדאמרי' בפ"ק דיבמות (דף יא: ושם): "לא יוכל בעלה" וגו' – לרבות סוטה שנסתרה. והיינו לאו, ודרשינן (סוטה דף כז:): "ונטמאה" "ונטמאה" – חד לבעל וחד לבועל. אלא אשאינה ראויה לקהל פריך. וא"ת: ומאי פריך וליתי עשה ולידחי ל"ת? הא דריש מקרא בהדיא במשנה, דבעינן אשה הראויה לו! ולמאי דמשני דלא חשיב עשה – קשה, דמאי איצטריך קרא למעוטי שאינה ראויה לו? וי"ל: דלאו מיתורא דקרא מפיק ליה במתניתין, אלא ד"ולו תהיה לאשה" משמע מדעתה, ולהכי ממעט אשה שאינה ראויה לו, דהא אי אמרה לא בעינא ליה – מי איתא לעשה כלל, הלכך לא חשיב עשה, ולא דמי לא תעשה. ומ"מ ס"ד דפריך השתא היכא דאמרה בעינא ליה – ליתי עשה ולידחי ל"ת, ומסיק דאפילו אמרה בעינא ליה – לא חשיב עשה, דלא דמי למילה בצרעת. אי נמי מיתורא דקרא דריש, ופריך דליתי עשה וידחה ל"ת, ויתורא דקרא נוקי לחייבי כריתות. דאי לאו קרא – הוה שרינן אפי' חייבי כריתות, דהואיל ואיתרבו לקנס לעיל ברים פירקין, איתרבו נמי לנישואין. דקראי משתמעי שפיר דהיכא דאיכא קנס איכא נמי נישואין. אי נמי, יש לומר דהכי פריך: ניתי עשה ונידחי לא תעשה, וכי תימא שאני הכא דגלי קרא – א"כ ניגמר מהכא בכל דוכתא דלא דחי! ומשני: דלא חשיב עשה. ומ"מ איצטריך קרא, דאי לאו קרא – הוה חשבינן ליה דלא אפשר לקיים שניהם, וחשיב עשה, דעיקר מצוה היא לישא, כי היכי דאמרינן בפרק ב' דיבמות (דף כא.), דחליצה במקום יבום לאו *כלום הוא.

כגון מילה בצרעת. *אומר ר"ת: דלסימנא בעלמא נקטיה. דהא בקוצץ בהרתו איכא עשה ולא תעשה, כדאמרינן בפרק "ר' אליעזר דמילה" (שבת דף קלב:) ללשון אחד הכתוב בספרים. ומהתם לא ילפינן בעלמא דליתי עשה ודחי לא תעשה ועשה, דמה למילה שכן נכרתו עליה י"ג בריתות. אלא עיקר מילתא מכלאים בציצית. וא"ת: והא כלאים בציצית אפשר לקיים שניהם, שיעשה בטלית למר חוטין של למר! ואומר ר"י: דבטלית של פשתן אי אפשר לקיים שניהם, דלא אפשר לקיים מצות תכלת אלא ע"י כלאים, דתכלת עמרא הוא. וזה אין לנו לומר שיהא אסור ללבוש טלית של פשתן משום דאפשר בשל למר – דאין זה חשוב אפשר. והא דאמרי' בפ' "התכלת" (מנחות דף מ. ושם): כל המטיל תכלת בסדין בירושלים אינו אלא מן המתמיהין. ומפרש בגמרא גזירה משום קלא אילן. ופריך: לא יהיה אלא לבן! ומשני: אפשר במינו, כדריש לקיש, דאמר: כל מקום שאתה כו'. התם ודאי, כיון דליכא תכלת אלא הכל לבן – מצות לבן אפשר לקיים במינו. וא"ת: והא אמר התם לעיל *חוטי למר פוטרין בשל פשתן, ושל פשתן פוטרין בשל למר, ואמאי פוטרין? והא אפשר לקיים שניהם, דלבן אפשר במינו! ואור"ת: דכל ד' חוטין לבן ודאי אסור, דאפשר במינו. אבל התם קאמר דשני חוטי למר לבן פוטרים בשל פשתן, דמגו דתכלת פטרה, שכבר נעשה כלאים ע"י תכלת שבו, לבן של למר נמי פטר. ומגו דשני חוטי לבן של למר פוטרים בשל פשתן – שני חוטי לבן של פשתן נמי פוטרין בשל למר, אע"ג דלא נעשה התם כלאים ע"י תכלת שבו. וצריך עיון אם שני חוטי לבן של פשתן ושני חוטי לבן של למר מותר לתת בטלית של למר או בטלית של פשתן, דשמא לא הותרו שני חוטי לבן אלא דווקא במקום תכלת, אבל שלא במקום תכלת – לא, או דלמא לא שנא, דהא שני חוטי לבן של פשתן פוטרים בשל למר, אע"ג דהתם תכלת לא מעלה ולא מוריד, דע"י אותו תכלת לא נעשה אכתי כלאים. ואין להקשות: אי שרו שני חוטי לבן בכלאים – אפי' אין תכלת עמהן – אמאי מטיל תכלת בסדין בירושלים אינו אלא מן המתמיהין? יטילו עמו שני חוטי לבן של פשתן, דאפילו הוי ההוא תכלת קלא אילן או לבן גמור – שרי! דאיכא למיגזר שמא יטילו עמו שני חוטי לבן של למר, ויסברו שאותן שני חוטין הצבועין הן תכלת, ויהיו כל ד' חוטין לבן של למר.

[**אי** אמרה לא בעינא מי איתיה לעשה בלל. הקשה הר"ר עזרא: אמאי איצטריך קרא בפ"ק דיבמות (דף ה:) דאין עשה דכיבוד דוחה שבת? הא ליכא עשה, דאי אמר לא בעינא לכיבוד – מי איתא לעשה כלל? וי"ל: דהתם מ"מ מיד כשצוה אב – הוי עשה לעשות מצותו. ול"נ: דהכא גבי דידה ליכא עשה, דהא אי בעיא אמרה לא בעינא ליה, הלכך אין לה לעבור בלאו משום עשה דידיה, דהיא מוזהרת כמותו, והשוה הכתוב אשה לאיש, כדאמרינן ב"יש מותרות" (יבמות דף פד:). ת"י כ"ץ].

הכי גרסינן: ממאי מדקתני האונס חייב והמפתה פטור יתומה פשיטה אלא הא קמ"ל כו'. כלומר, מדקתני האונס חייב והמפתה פטור – ש"מ דיש לה קנס, וקנסה לעצמה. דאי משום יתומה נקט מפתה פטור – פשיטא דפטור, דהא מחלה. אלא ע"כ לא נקט מפתה פטור אלא משום נערה שנתארסה ונתגרשה, ולא נקט יתומה במתני' אלא ליתן טעם אמאי מפתה פטור, והלא קנסה לאביה, ואשמעי' דהרי היא כיתומה, שקנסה לעצמה. וא"ת: ומנלן הא? אדרבה, אימא דנקט יתומה למידק: טעמא דהויא נמי יתומה, הא אינה יתומה – אפילו מפתה חייב, דקנסה לאביה! וי"ל: דלית לן למימר לדיוקא אתא כל זמן דנוכל לומר דלגופיה אתא. ***אחד** כדרכה ואחד שלא כדרכה. שלא כדרכה ה"ל למינקט ברישא, אלא כן דרך התלמוד שאינו חושש, כדנקט לעיל (דף לה.) בתנא דבי חזקיה בין מתכוין לשאין מתכוין, דה"ל למינקט שאין מתכוין ברישא, כדקתני בין שוגג למזיד, אלא כן דרך התלמוד במקום שצריך לשנות הן ולאו*. **יאמרו** בעל שלימה חמשים. פירוש: הראשון שבא עליה שלא כדרכה, דמחייב קנס אפילו שלא כדרכה, כדאמרינן בפ"ק דקידושין (דף ט:): באו עליה י' ועדיין היא בתולה כו', פירוש: שלא כדרכה. וקאמר מודה רבי לענין קנס, דכולהו משלמי. ובפרק "הבא על יבמתו" (יבמות דף נט. ושם) גבי "ולו תהיה לאשה" – באשה הראויה לו, פרט לאלמנה לכ"ג כו'. ופריך: היכי דמי? אילימא כדרכה – תיפוק ליה דהויא לה בעולה, אלא לאו – שלא כדרכה. והכא הוה מצי למינקט שבאו עליה ב' שלא כדרכה, וכן בפרק "בן סורר" (סנהדרין עג:) דמוקי ההיא ד"אלו נערות שיש להן קנס" כגון שבא עליה שלא כדרכה, וחזר ובא עליה כדרכה – הוי מצי למינקט: וחזר ובא עליה שלא כדרכה. ומה שקשה על פירוש הקונטרס דהתם פירשנו ב"הבא על יבמתו" (יבמות דף נט.) ובפרק קמא דקידושין (דף ט:).

ולימא

ס"א מצוה היא | [ולספרים דלר' גרסי הכא מילה בצרעת וכלאים בציצית אלא מילה בצרעת לתודיה ...] | [דף לט:] | עי' לעיל לט. | [ועי' תוספות בפסחים פ"ה ...]

תוספות רי"ד

מתני' כיצד שותה בעציצו אפי' היא חיגרת ואפילו סומא אפי' מוכת שחין נמצא בה דבר זימה או שאינה ראויה לבוא בישראל אינו רשאי לקיימה שנאמר ולו תהיה לאשה אשה הראויה לו: וליתי עשה ולדחי את ל"ת היכא אמרי' דאתי עשה ודחי את ל"ת כגון מילה בצרעת דא"א לי' לקיומי לעשה אבל הכא אי אמרה לא בעינא ליה ליתא לעשה כלל. פי' המורה והשתא נמי מלמדים אותה לומר איני רוצה וקשה לי להאי פי' דא"כ גבי יבם אמאי אמרינן דאתי עשה ודחי ל"ת כיון דכתיב אם לא יחפוץ גלמדנו לומר איני רוצה ליבם ולא לידחי ואמאי אמרי' התם דדחי מ"ה נ"ל לפרש דמאי דאמר רחמנא גבי אונס ולו תהיה לאשה אינה אלא להפיס דעתה ואי אמרה לא בעינא לי' ליתי' לעשה כלל הלכך לאו כלום הוא עשה למדחי את ל"ת כיון שלא ציוהו הבורא אלא להפיס דעתה אבל מצות יבום רחמנא הוא דרמי עליה דאע"ג דאמרה אשה לא בעינא לא מיעקרא מצות יבום הלכך מצוה דרמי עליה רחמנא הוא ולהכי דחיא את ל"ת ואע"ג דמצי יבם למימר לא בעינא ליבומי כ"א למיחלץ הא אמרי' התם חליצה במקום יבום אינה מצוה: **מתני'** יתומה שנתארסה ונתגרשה ר"א אומר האונס חייב והמפתה פטור. פי' שתי נערות הן יתומות אע"פ שלא נתארסה שקנסה הוא לעצמה כיון שאין לה אב שאין אדם מוריש זכות בתו לבנו. וכן נערה שנתארסה ונתגרשה אע"פ שיש לה אב הוי קנסא לעצמה כר"ע. הלכך האונס חייב ליתן קנסא אבל המפתה פטור דאיהי אחילתי' גביה כיון שנתרצית לו: אמר רבה בב"ח אר"י ר"א בשיטת ר"ע אמרה דאמר נערה המאורסה יש לה קנס וקנסה לעצמה ממאי מדקתני יתומה פשיטא אלא הא קמ"ל דנערה שנתארסה ונתגרשה ה"ה כיתומה מה יתומה לעצמה אף נערה שנתארסה ונתגרשה לעצמה אמר רב הלכתא כר"א

וקרי ליה רב עליה דר"א טובינא דחכימא. פי' מאושר שבחכמים תרגום אשריך ישראל טובך ישראל: **מתני'** איזהו בושת הכל לפי המבייש והמתבייש. פי' אדם בינוני המבייש בושתו קשה מאדם זולל ומאדם חשוב והמתבייש פי' לפי חשיבותו בושתו: פגם רואים אותה כאילו היא שפחה נמכרת לשוק כמה היתה יפה וכמה היא יפה וקנס שוה בכל אדם וכל שיש לו קצבה מה"ת שוה בכל אדם: ואימא נ' כסף אמר רחמנא מכל מילי. אמר

עין משפט נר מצוה

עט א מיי' פ"ג מהל' ציצית הלכה ו:
פ ב מיי' פ"ב מהלכות נערה הלכה יד סמג עשין נד טור אה"ע סי' קעז:
פא ג מיי' פ"א שם הל' ט סמג וטור שם:
פב ד מיי' פ"ב שם הל' ד ומיי' פ"ג מהל' חובל ומזיק הל' א סמג שם ועשין ע טור שם וטוש"ע ח"מ סי' תכ סעיף כז:
פג ה מיי' פ"ב מהלכות נערה הל' ג סמג עשין נד טור אה"ע סי' קעז:

מַעֲשֵׂה מַחַט שְׁלֹשִׁים?! אֶלָּא א"ר זֵירָא: *אִילּוּ בָּאוּ עָלֶיהָ שְׁנַיִם, אֶחָד כְּדַרְכָּהּ וְאֶחָד שֶׁלֹּא כְּדַרְכָּהּ, יֹאמְרוּ: בַּעַל שְׁלֵימָה חֲמִשִּׁים, בַּעַל פְּגוּמָה — חֲמִשִּׁים?! א"ל אַבַּיֵי: אִי הָכִי, גַּבֵּי עֶבֶד נַמִי יֹאמְרוּ, עֶבֶד בָּרִיא — שְׁלֹשִׁים, עֶבֶד מוּכֵּה שְׁחִין — שְׁלֹשִׁים?! אֶלָּא *אָמַר אַבַּיֵי, אָמַר קְרָא: °"תַּחַת אֲשֶׁר עִנָּהּ", הָנֵי — תַּחַת אֲשֶׁר עִנָּהּ, מִכְּלָל דְּאִיכָּא בּוֹשֶׁת וּפְגָם. רָבָא אָמַר, אָמַר קְרָא: °"וְנָתַן הָאִישׁ הַשּׁוֹכֵב עִמָּהּ לַאֲבִי הַנַּעֲרָה חֲמִשִּׁים כָּסֶף" [א]הֲנָאַת שְׁכִיבָה — נ', מִכְּלָל דְּאִיכָּא בּוֹשֶׁת וּפְגָם. וְאֵימָא לְדִידָהּ? א"ק: °"בִּנְעוּרֶיהָ בֵּית אָבִיהָ" — [ב]כָּל שֶׁבַח נְעוּרֶיהָ לְאָבִיהָ. וְאֶלָּא הָא דְּאָמַר רַב הוּנָא אָמַר רַב: *מִנַּיִן שֶׁמַּעֲשֵׂה הַבַּת לְאָבִיהָ? שֶׁנֶּאֱמַר: °"וְכִי יִמְכּוֹר אִישׁ אֶת בִּתּוֹ לְאָמָה" מָה אָמָה מַעֲשֵׂה יָדֶיהָ לְרַבָּהּ, [ג]אַף בַּת מַעֲשֵׂה יָדֶיהָ לְאָבִיהָ — לָמָּה לִי? תֵּיפוֹק לֵיהּ מִ"בִּנְעוּרֶיהָ בֵּית אָבִיהָ"! אֶלָּא, הַהִיא בַּהֲפָרַת נְדָרִים הוּא דִּכְתִי'. וְכִי תֵּימָא: נֵילַף מִינֵּיהּ — *מָמוֹנָא מֵאִיסּוּרָא לָא יָלְפִינַן. וְכִי תֵּימָא: נֵילַף מִקְּנָסָא — מָמוֹנָא מִקְּנָסָא לָא יָלְפִינַן. אֶלָּא מִסְתַּבְּרָא דְּאָבִיהָ הָוֵי, דְּאִי בָּעֵי — מָסַר לָהּ לִמְנוּוָּל וּמוּכֵּה שְׁחִין.§ [ד]פְּגָם רוֹאִין אוֹתָהּ כְּאִילּוּ הִיא שִׁפְחָה נִמְכֶּרֶת.§ הֵיכִי שָׁיְימִינַן לָהּ? אָמַר אֲבוּהּ דִּשְׁמוּאֵל: אוֹמְדִין כַּמָּה אָדָם רוֹצֶה לִיתֵּן בֵּין שִׁפְחָה בְּתוּלָה לְשִׁפְחָה בְּעוּלָה לְשַׁמְּשׁוֹ. שִׁפְחָה בְּעוּלָה לְשַׁמְּשׁוֹ, מַאי נָפְקָא לֵיהּ מִינָּהּ? אֶלָּא: בֵּין שִׁפְחָה בְּעוּלָה לְשִׁפְחָה שֶׁאֵינָהּ בְּעוּלָה לְהַשִּׂיאָהּ לְעַבְדּוֹ. וּלְעַבְדּוֹ מַאי נָפְקָא לֵיהּ מִינָּהּ? [ה]בְּעֶבֶד שֶׁיֵּשׁ לוֹ לְרַבּוֹ קוֹרַת רוּחַ הֵימֶנּוּ.§ **מתני'** *כָּל מָקוֹם שֶׁיֵּשׁ מֶכֶר — אֵין קְנָס, וְכָל מָקוֹם שֶׁיֵּשׁ קְנָס — אֵין מֶכֶר. קְטַנָּה — יֵשׁ לָהּ מֶכֶר וְאֵין לָהּ קְנָס, נַעֲרָה — יֵשׁ לָהּ קְנָס וְאֵין לָהּ מֶכֶר. הַבּוֹגֶרֶת — אֵין לָהּ לֹא מֶכֶר וְלֹא קְנָס.§ **גמ'** *אָמַר רַב יְהוּדָה אָמַר רַב: זוֹ דִּבְרֵי ר"מ, אֲבָל חֲכָמִים אוֹמְרִים: יֵשׁ לָהּ קְנָס בִּמְקוֹם מֶכֶר. דְּתַנְיָא: *קְטַנָּה מִבַּת יוֹם אֶחָד וְעַד שֶׁתָּבִיא שְׁתֵּי שְׂעָרוֹת — יֵשׁ לָהּ מֶכֶר וְאֵין לָהּ קְנָס, מִשֶּׁתָּבִיא שְׁתֵּי שְׂעָרוֹת עַד שֶׁתִּיבָּגֵר יֵשׁ לָהּ קְנָס וְאֵין לָהּ מֶכֶר, דִּבְרֵי ר"מ, שֶׁהָיָה ר"מ אוֹמֵר: כ"מ שֶׁיֵּשׁ מֶכֶר — אֵין קְנָס, וְכ"מ שֶׁיֵּשׁ קְנָס — אֵין מֶכֶר. וַחֲכָמִים אוֹמְרִים: קְטַנָּה מִבַּת ג' שָׁנִים וְיוֹם אֶחָד וְעַד שֶׁתִּיבָּגֵר — יֵשׁ לָהּ קְנָס. קְנָס אִין, מֶכֶר לָא?! אֵימָא: אַף קְנָס בִּמְקוֹם מֶכֶר. א"ר חִסְדָּא: מ"ט דְּר"מ — א"ק: °"וְלוֹ תִהְיֶה לְאִשָּׁה" — בִּמְהַוָּה עַצְמָהּ הַכָּתוּב מְדַבֵּר. וְרַבָּנַן? אָמַר ר"ל: א"ק (א)"נַעֲרָה" — אֲפִילּוּ קְטַנָּה בְּמַשְׁמָע. שְׁמָעָהּ רַב פַּפָּא בְּרֵיהּ דְּרַב חָנָן מִבֵּי כְּלוֹחִית, אֲזַל אֲמָרָהּ קַמֵּיהּ דְּרַב שִׁימִי בַּר אַשִׁי. א"ל: אַתּוּן אַהָא מַתְנִיתוּ לָהּ, אֲנַן אַהָא מַתְנִינַן לָהּ: אָמַר ר"ל: *[ו]הַמּוֹצִיא שֵׁם רַע עַל הַקְּטַנָּה — פָּטוּר, שֶׁנֶּאֱ': °"וְנָתְנוּ לַאֲבִי הַנַּעֲרָה" — נַעֲרָה מָלֵא דִּיבֵּר הַכָּתוּב. מַתְקִיף לָהּ רַב אַדָּא בַּר אַהֲבָה: טַעֲמָא דִּכְתַב רַחֲמָנָא "נַעֲרָה", הָא לָאו הָכִי — הֲוָה אָמִינָא אֲפִילּוּ קְטַנָּה? וְהָא כְּתִיב: °"וְאִם אֱמֶת הָיָה הַדָּבָר הַזֶּה לֹא נִמְצְאוּ בְתוּלִים לַנַּעֲרָה וְהוֹצִיאוּ אֶת הַנַּעֲרָה אֶל פֶּתַח בֵּית אָבִיהָ וּסְקָלוּהָ" — וּקְטַנָּה לָאו בַּת עוֹנְשִׁין הִיא! אֶלָּא: כָּאן — נַעֲרָה, הָא כָּל מָקוֹם שֶׁנֶּאֱמַר "נַעַר" — אֲפִילּוּ קְטַנָּה בְּמַשְׁמַע.§
מתני'

מַעֲשֵׂה מַחַט. חַיָּט, תּוֹפֵר. אֶלָּא אָמַר רַבִּי זֵירָא. מֵהָכָא מִסְתַּבְּרָא שֶׁאֵין בּוֹשֶׁת בִּכְלַל חֲמִשִּׁים, דְּאִם כֵּן – אֵין הֶפְרֵשׁ בֵּין בַּעַל שְׁלֵימָה לְבַעַל פְּגוּמָה שֶׁנִּבְעֲלָה שֶׁלֹּא כְּדַרְכָּהּ, וְהֵיכָן הוּא הֶפְרֵשׁ שֶׁבֵּינֵיהֶם? ש"מ גַּבֵּי בּוֹשֶׁת, כֵּיוָן שֶׁנִּפְגְּמָה כְּבָר – אֵין בּוֹשְׁתָּהּ רַב כִּשְׁלֵימָה. תַּחַת אֲשֶׁר עִנָּהּ. גַּבֵּי "חֲמִשִּׁים כֶּסֶף" כְּתִיב. מִכְּלָל דְּבוֹשֶׁת וּפְגָם. שֶׁאֵינָם מִשּׁוּם עִינּוּי, שֶׁהֲרֵי יֶשְׁנָן בִּשְׁאָר חוֹבְלִין – אֵינוֹ בִּכְלַל זֶה. פְּגָם הוּא נֶזֶק הַנִּישּׁוֹם נַמִי בִּשְׁאָר חֲבָלוֹת. וְאֵימָא לְדִידָהּ הָוֵי. דְּבִשְׁלָמָא קְנָס כְּתִיב בֵּיהּ "וְנָתַן לַאֲבִי הַנַּעֲרָה", אֲבָל הָנֵי – לֶיהֱווּ לְדִידָהּ. בִּנְעוּרֶיהָ בֵּית אָבִיהָ. גַּבֵּי נְדָרִים כְּתִיב. וּמִיהוּ, אִיכָּא לְמִשְׁמַע מִינָּהּ דִּבִימֵי נְעוּרֶיהָ תְּלָאָהּ הַכָּתוּב בְּבֵית אָבִיהָ. בִּתּוֹ לְאָמָה. הִקִּישׁ בַּת לְאָמָה. תֵּיפוֹק לֵיהּ כו'. אֶלָּא עַל כָּרְחָךְ מֵהָתָם לָא מָצֵי לְמֵילַף, דְּהַהוּא בַּהֲפָרַת נְדָרִים כְּתִיב. נֵילַף מִקְּנָסָא. מַה קְנָסָהּ לְאָבִיהָ – אַף שְׁאָר שֶׁבַח מָמוֹן נְעוּרִים לְאָבִיהָ. אֶלָּא מִסְתַּבְּרָא. דְּבוֹשֶׁת וּפְגָם דְּאָב הָוְיָא, שֶׁהֲרֵי בְּיָדוֹ לְבַיְּישָׁהּ בְּבוֹשֶׁת בְּעִילָה, וּלְפוֹגְמָהּ בִּפְגַם בְּעִילָה. דְּאִי בָּעֵי מָסַר לָהּ. לְקַדְּשָׁהּ בְּבִיאָה. לִמְנוּוָּל וּמוּכֵּה שְׁחִין. כִּדְתְנַן לְקַמָּן, הָאָב זַכַּאי בְּבִתּוֹ בְּקִידּוּשֶׁיהָ, בְּכֶסֶף וּבִשְׁטָר וּבְבִיאָה, וְכֵיוָן דְּבְיָדוֹ לִיטּוֹל מָמוֹן לְפוֹגְמָהּ וּלְבַיְּישָׁהּ בּוּשָׁה זוֹ – הַשְׁתָּא אַפְסְדֵיהּ הַאי דְּפַגְמָהּ: [מַאי נָפְקָא לֵיהּ. לְכָל אָדָם בִּבְעִילָתָהּ, אִם בְּעוּלָה הִיא, הוֹאִיל וְלִמְלָאכָה קַיְימָא]: וּלְעַבְדּוֹ מַאי נָפְקָא לֵיהּ. לְמָרֵיהּ מִינָּהּ אִם בְּעוּלָה הִיא, מִי קָפֵיד מָרֵיהּ אֶלָּא שֶׁיְּהוּ לָהֶן וְלָדוֹת. קוֹרַת רוּחַ. שֶׁזָּהִיר בַּעֲבוֹדָתוֹ, וְאַף הוּא רוֹצֶה לַעֲשׂוֹת לוֹ נַחַת רוּחַ, לְהַטְעִימוֹ טַעַם בְּתוּלָה. **מתני'** כ"מ שֶׁיֵּשׁ מֶכֶר. לְאָב בְּבִתּוֹ, דְּהַיְינוּ בְּקַטְנוּתָהּ. אֵין לוֹ בָּהּ קְנָס. דְּאֵין קְנָס לִקְטַנָּה. כָּל מָקוֹם שֶׁיֵּשׁ קְנָס. מִשֶּׁהִיא נַעֲרָה. אֵין מֶכֶר. דְּתַנְיָא (ערכין דף כט:): יָכוֹל יִמְכּוֹר אָדָם בִּתּוֹ כְּשֶׁהִיא נַעֲרָה – אָמַרְתָּ (ב) מְכוּרָה כְּבָר יוֹצְאָה עַכְשָׁיו, שֶׁאֵינָהּ מְכוּרָה אֵינוֹ דִּין שֶׁלֹּא תִּימָּכֵר? **גמ'** זוֹ דִּבְרֵי ר"מ. דְּאָמַר אֵין קְנָס לִקְטַנָּה. מִבַּת ג' שָׁנִים. שֶׁבִּיאָתָהּ בִּיאָה, וְאֵין בְּתוּלֶיהָ חוֹזְרִין. מֶכֶר לָא. בִּתְמִיָּה. אַף קְנָס בִּמְקוֹם מֶכֶר. מִשֶּׁתְּהֵא רְאוּיָה לְבִיאָה עַד שֶׁתָּבִיא שְׁתֵּי שְׂעָרוֹת הָווּ תַּרְוַיְיהוּ, וּמִשֶּׁהֱבִיאָה שְׂעָרוֹת עַד שֶׁתִּבָּגֵר – קְנָס וְלֹא מֶכֶר. מַאי טַעְמָא דְּר"מ. דְּאָמַר קְטַנָּה אֵין לָהּ קְנָס. דְּאָמַר קְרָא. גַּבֵּי קְנָס "וְלוֹ תִהְיֶה לְאִשָּׁה". בִּמְהַוָּה עַצְמָהּ. בְּמִי שֶׁיֵּשׁ בְּיָדָהּ לְהַקְנוֹת עַצְמָהּ לְאִישׁוּת הַכָּתוּב מְדַבֵּר. אַהָא מַתְנִיתוּ לָהּ. לְהָא דְּרֵישׁ לָקִישׁ, דְּאָמַר כ"מ שֶׁנִּכְתַּב "נַעַר" בְּלֹא ה' וְקָרֵינַן נַעֲרָה – לְלַמֵּד עַל הַקְּטַנָּה בָּא. שֵׁם רַע. לֹא מָצָאתִי לְבִתְּךָ בְּתוּלִים. פָּטוּר. דְּ"וְעָנְשׁוּ אוֹתוֹ מֵאָה כֶסֶף וְנָתְנוּ לַאֲבִי הַנַּעֲרָה" מָלֵא כְּתִיב. אֶלָּא כָּאן נַעֲרָה. הַאי דִּכְתִיב "נַעֲרָה" מָלֵא, לָאו לְגַלּוּיֵי עֲלֵיהּ אָתָא, אֶלָּא עַל כָּל מָקוֹם שֶׁנֶּאֱמַר "נַעַר" חָסֵר, וְיָלֵיף הָכִי: כָּאן שֶׁאִי אֶפְשָׁר אֶלָּא בְּנַעֲרָה – כְּתִיב "נַעֲרָה" מָלֵא, וּלְלַמֶּדְךָ דְּכָל מָקוֹם שֶׁנֶּאֱמַר "נער" – אֲפִילּוּ קְטַנָּה בְּמַשְׁמַע.
מתני'

ואימא לדידה. אע"ג דפרישית לעיל (דף לח:), דבושת ופגם הוקשו לקנס, וניתן למי שקנס ניתן – היינו בתר דקים לן הכא דהוי הכל לאביה. **מסתברא** דאביה הוי דאי בעי כו'. וא"ת: אמאי לא קאמר דאביה הוי מדקא יהיב מפתה, כדאמר לקמן בריש "נערה" (דף מב.)! וי"ל: דלמא לא יהיב מפתה, דקראי דאביי ורבא באונס כתיבי. **דאי** בעי מסר לה למנוול ומוכה שחין. וממעשה ידיה ליכא למילף, דהא מיתזנא מיניה, כדאמרינן בפרק קמא דקדושין (דף ד. ושם). ולא מקדושין – דמעלמא קאתו לה. ומתרוייהו נמי לא, דחבלה דגופה שאני. תימה: דהכא לא קים לן בושת ופגם דהוי לאביה אלא מכח שיכול לקדשה למנוול ומוכה שחין, ואם כן, היכי בעי למימר בריש קדושין (דף ג:) גבי קדושי כסף: מנא לן דמיקדשה בכסף וקידושין דאביה הן? וכי תימא נילף מבושת ופגם, הא בושת ופגם גופיה לא קים לן אלא מכח שיכול לקדשה! ואומר ר"י: דאורחיה דהתלמוד דבעי לדחויי אפילו קים לן דבושת ופגם הוי דאביה ממקום אחר. *א"נ: התם בעי למילף קדושי נערה מבושת ופגם של קטנה. ומקדושי קטנה הוה יליף להו, אי לאו דהוה אמינא: הני מילי – קטנה דלית לה יד ונערה אית לה יד, כדאמרינן התם לעיל. ולהכי קאמר: וכי תימא נילף מבושת ופגם דקטנה, אע"ג דלהכי אית לה יד כדאמרינן ב"החובל" (ב"ק דף פז:): יעשה לה סגולה, ואפ"ה הוי דאביה, ה"נ קדושי נערה. ואם *היינו מפרשים דלא קאי אקדושין הא דקאמר ונילף מבושת ופגם, אלא אמעשה ידיה דאייתי התם לעיל – הוה אתי שפיר, אבל לא משמע הכי. ועוד: דא"כ הכא נמי ה"ל לאסוקי וכ"ת נילף מבושת ופגם, כיון דאמעשה ידיה קאי. וכן לקמן בפרק "נערה" (דף מו:). **כמה** אדם רוצה ליתן כו' להשיא לעבדו. תימה: דמה שומא היא זו? וכי אשה חשובה ממשפחה גדולה אינה נפסדת בפגמה אלא שוה שפחה הניסת לעבד? וי"ל: דכל אשה שמין לפי מה שהיא בענין זה, כמה אדם רוצה ליתן בין בתולה לבעולה להשיא לעבדו אשה כזאת הנפגמת. והא דנקט שפחה – אורחא דמלתא נקט, דאין דרך להשיא לעבדו בת מלכים.

הא לאו הכי ה"א אפילו קטנה והכתיב אם אמת היה וכו'. תימה לר"י: מה בכך אם קרא איירי בבת עונשין; מ"מ מלינו למימר דה"ה קטנה. דהא בא על קטנה מאורסה הוי בסקילה לרבנן, בפרק "ד' מיתות" (סנהדרין דף סו:) אע"ג דההיא פרשה דנערה המאורסה בבת עונשין כתיבא [כדכתיב "ואת הנערה על דבר אשר לא צעקה"]! ותירץ: דהתם משום דמסקינן בסמוך: כאן "נערה" – הא כל מקום שנאמר "נער" – אפילו קטנה במשמע. הלכך מחייבין ליה התם, וכולהו עריות ילפי מינה. אי נמי: דוקא במוציא שם רע סברא הוא לומר דלא מחייב קנס ומלקות אלא בגדולה, כיון דקרא איירי בבת עונשין, ולא בעלמא, משום דמוציא שם רע על הקטנה סברא הוא דפטור, דפיתוי קטנה אונס הוא*, והוי כמוציא שם רע על הנערה שנאנסה דלא מחייב. אבל אין לומר דמסתבר ליה דדוקא בבת עונשין מחייב ליה, משום שבא להורגה – דבפרק קמא דסנהדרין (דף ח:) בשמעתא דחוששין ללעז, משמע דלאו משום דקא גריס לה קטלא מיחייב.

פד א מיי' פ"ב מהל' נערה הל' א סמג עשין נד טוש"ע אה"ע סי' קעז סעיף א:
פה ב מיי' שם הל' יד:
פו ג מיי' פ"ג מהלכות אישות הל' יא סמג עשין מח טוש"ע שם סי' לז סעיף א:
פז ד ה מיי' פ"ב מהל' נערה הל' ו ופ"א מהל' חובל ומזיק הל' ב סמג עשין נד ועי' טור אה"ע סימן קעז וטור ש"ע ח"מ סימן תכ סעיף טו:
פח ו מיי' פ"ג מהלכות נערה הל' ב סמג לאוין פז ועשין נה טור אה"ע סי' קעז:

[וע"ע תוס' יומא מט: סד"ה שאני ותוס' חולין עח: סד"ה זה בנה]

[כמו שהיה סבור המקשה וה"פ שאני בושת ופגם לאביה נמי שייך פי' שמתבייש ומצטער כמותה ולא כמו שפי' שם בקונט' דאי בעי מסר לה למנוול ומוכה שחין דאכתי לא קים ליה שיכול לקדשה. ת"י עה"ג]

תוספות רי"ד

אמר אביי א"ק תחת אשר ענה הני תחת אשר ענה מכלל דאיכא בושת ופגם רבא אמר א"ק ונתן האיש השוכב עמה לאבי הנערה נ' כסף. הנאת שכיבה נ' כסף מכלל דאיכא בושת ופגם: ואימא לדידה. פי' דדוקא נ' כסף זכה רחמנא לאב אבל בושת ופגם להוי דידה. מסתברא דאבוה הוי מיגו דאי בעי מסר לה למנוול ומוכה שחין: פגם רואים אותה וכו'. היכי שיימינן לה אמר אבוה דשמואל אומדים כמה אדם רוצה ליתן בין שפחה בתולה לשפחה בעולה להשיאה לעבדו שיש לו קורת רוח ממנו: **מתני'** כל מקום שיש מכר אין קנס וכ"מ שיש קנס אין מכר קטנה יש לה מכר ואין לה קנס נערה יש לה קנס ואין לה מכר בוגרת לא קנס ולא מכר אר"י א"ר זו דברי רבי מאיר אבל חכמים אומרים יש קנס במקום מכר א"ר חסדא מ"ט דר"מ דאמר קרא ולו תהיה לאשה במהווה עצמה הכתוב מדבר ורבנן אמרי אמר קרא נערה ואפילו קטנה במשמע פי' נער כתיב וקרינן נערה מלא:

[בכלאי' יבמות לג: וסא:]

[ערכין טו.]
לעיל לג.
לקמן מו: מז. קדושין ג:
[ברכות יט: וש"נ]
נ"י כ"ש
לעיל כו. חולין כו:
[לעיל ל: חולין כו:]
לעיל כט. חולין כו: [תוספתא פ"ג ע"ש]
לקמן מד: ע"ש

הגהות הב"ח

(א) גמ' אמר ר"ל אמר קרא נגר: (ב) רש"י ד"ה אין מכר וכו' אמרת קל והומר מכורה:

וליתני

גמרא

מתני' [א]האומר: "פתיתי את בתו של פלוני" – משלם בושת ופגם על פי עצמו, ואין משלם קנס. [ב]האומר "גנבתי" – *משלם את הקרן על פי עצמו, ואין משלם תשלומי כפל ותשלומי ארבעה וחמשה. *[ג]"המית שורי את פלוני" או "שורו של פלוני" – הרי זה משלם על פי עצמו. "המית שורי עבדו של פלוני" – אין משלם ע"פ עצמו. [ד]זה הכלל: כל המשלם יתר על מה שהזיק – אינו משלם ע"פ עצמו.§ **גמ'** וליתני "אנסתי"! לא מבעיא קאמר; לא מבעיא "אנסתי" דלא קא פגים לה, דמשלם בושת ופגם על פי עצמו, אבל "פתיתי" דקא פגים לה – אימא לא משלם על פי עצמו – קא משמע לן. מתניתין דלא כי האי תנא; דתניא, רבי שמעון בן יהודה אומר משום ר' שמעון: אף בושת ופגם אינו משלם ע"פ עצמו, לא כל הימנו שיפגום בתו של פלוני. אמר ליה רב פפא לאביי: ניחא לה לדידה מאי? דלמא לא ניחא ליה לאביה. ניחא ליה לאביה מאי? דלמא לא ניחא להו לבני משפחה. ניחא להו לבני משפחה מאי? אי אפשר דליכא חד במדינת הים דלא ניחא ליה.§ האומר גנבתי משלם את הקרן וכו'.§ איתמר, פלגא ניזקא; *רב פפא אמר: פלגא ניזקא ממונא, רב הונא בריה דרב יהושע אמר: [ה]פלגא ניזקא קנסא. רב פפא אמר: פלגא ניזקא ממונא, קסבר: סתם שוורים לאו בחזקת שימור קיימי, ובדין הוא דמשלם כוליה, ורחמנא הוא דחייס עליה, דאכתי לא איעד תורא. רב הונא בריה דרב יהושע אמר: פלגא ניזקא קנסא. קסבר: סתם שוורים בחזקת שימור קיימי, ובדין הוא דלא לישלם כלל, ורחמנא הוא דקנסיה, כי היכי דנינטריה לתוריה.§ סימן: היזיק מה והמית כלל.§ תנן: *הניזק והמזיק בתשלומין. בשלמא למאן דאמר פלגא ניזקא ממונא – היינו דשייך ניזק בתשלומין. אלא למ"ד פלגא ניזקא קנסא – השתא, דלאו דידיה קא שקיל, בתשלומין איתיה?! לא נצרכא אלא לפחת נבילה. פחת נבילה תנינא: תשלומי נזק [ו]מלמד שהבעלים מטפלין בנבילה. חדא בתם וחדא במועד. וצריכא, דאי אשמועינן תם – משום דאכתי לא איעד, אבל מועד דאיעד – אימא לא. ואי אשמועינן מועד – משום דקא משלם כוליה, אבל תם – אימא לא, צריכא. ת"ש: *מה בין תם למועד? [ז]שהתם משלם חצי נזק מגופו, [ח]ומועד משלם נזק שלם מן העלייה. *ולא קתני שהתם אינו משלם ע"פ עצמו ומועד משלם ע"פ עצמו! *)תנא ושייר. מאי שייר דהאי שייר? שייר [ט]חצי כופר. אי משום חצי כופר – לאו שיורא הוא, הא

*) [סוכה נג. וש"נ]

רש"י

מתני' פתיתי. בגמ' מפרש אמאי לא תנא "אנסתי". ואינו משלם קנס. בבבא קמא* נפקא לן מודה בקנס פטור מ"אשר ירשיעון אלהים" – פרט למרשיע את עצמו. המית שורי את פלוני. והריני חייב בכופר. הרי זה משלם ע"פ עצמו. קסבר כופרא ממונא. עבדו של פלוני. והריני חייב שלשים סלע. אינו משלם. דקנס נינהו, שאפי' אין יפה דינר נותן שלשים. **גמ'** דלא פגים לה. אין לעז של אנוסה גדול כלעז של מפותה, וכיון דלאו פגם דילה הוא – מהימנינן ליה למשקל מיניה בושת ופגם על פיו. אימא לא. נהימניה להחזיק את הלעז. לא כל הימנו. שיוציא עליה לעז מזה בעיר. ניחא לה לדידה. לשאת את הלעז כדי להשתכר הממון. לא ניחא להו לבני משפחה. וב"ד אין עליהם לעשות דבר להחזיק בושתם. פלגא ניזקא. שחייבה תורה שור תם: [ממונא. ומשלם ע"פ עצמו]. לאו בחזקת שימור קיימי. אם לא ישמרום בעלים שלא יזיקו – [אינם בחזקת משתמרים מאליהם שלא יזיקו], אלא מזיקין אפי' ניזקא דלאו אורחיה, הלכך על מרייהו רמיא לנטורינהו, וזה שלא שמרו – בדין הוא דלישלם כוליה, אלא דרחמנא חס עליה. ומיהו, מה שמשלם – בדין משלם. כי היכי דנינטריה. שיוסיף שמירה על שמירתו. תנן. בבבא קמא. הניזק והמזיק בתשלומין. שניהם מפסידין בדבר. ס"ד דהכי קאמר: תרווייהו מטי להו בהאי פסידא, דניזק מפסיד פלגא, ומזיק פלגא. היינו דשייך ניזק בתשלומין. דמפסיד פלגא בממוניה. דלאו דידיה שקיל. דמה שנוטל – בחנם נוטל. בתשלומין איתיה. בתמיה. לא נצרכא אלא לפחת נבילה. הא דקתני ניזק בתשלומין, לאו בפלגא דקא שביק קאמר, אלא בההוא פלגא ניזקא נמי דקני ליה רחמנא – מפסיד כל פחת שפחתה נבילה מדמיה משעת מיתה עד שעת העמדה בדין, ששמין את הנבלה כמה היה יפה השור בחייו וכמה היתה נבילה יפה בשעת מיתה, ומשלם החצי. אבל מה שהוזלו דמי נבילה משעת מיתה עד שעת מכירה – אין המזיק משלם כלום באותו פחת. ובבבא קמא (דף י:) יליף לה מקראי, ואשמעינן האי תנא דפחת נבילה דניזק הוי. תשלומי נזק מלמד שהבעלים מטפלין בנבילה. תנא דברייתא דריש לישנא דמתניתין, דתנן בבבא קמא: משלם תשלומי נזק במיטב הארץ. ותנא עלה בברייתא, דהאי דנקט תנא דמתני' תשלומי נזק, ולא תנא משלם את הנזק – לאשמועינן הכא, שהניזק נוטל את נבילתו ומטפל בה ומוכרה, והמזיק משלים עליה מה שחייבתו תורה, אם תם – חצי, ואם מועד – הכל. ותרתי למה ליה לרבי למיתנא במתני' דבעלים מטפלין בנבילה? דקא משלם כוליה. ודיו בהפסד זה. מגופו. אינו גובה אלא מגוף השור, ואם אין בו כדי חצי נזקו – יפסיד המותר. מן העלייה. מן המיטב שבנכסי מזיק. דגבי תם כתיב (שמות כא) "וחצו את כספו", מגופו, ובמועד כתיב (שם) "שלם ישלם שור". ואם איתא דפלגא ניזקא קנסא – ניתני נמי שהתם אינו משלם על פי עצמו, ומועד משלם על פי עצמו. דמועד ודאי בדין משלם, שהרי התרו והעידו בו לשמור שורו. שייר חצי כופר. לא שנה כל החילוקים שביניהם, שהרי אף יש חילוק זה ביניהם: שהמועד שהמית את האדם משלם כופר שלם, ותם שהמית – אפילו חצי כופר, כדינו בניזקין, לא משלם. דכתיב "בעל השור נקי", ודרשינן (ב"ק דף מא:): נקי מחצי כופר. הא

תוספות

וליתני אנסתי. דהוי חדוש טפי דפטור, אע"ג דמודה שעשה פריצות. **רבי** שמעון בן יהודה אומר אף בושת ופגם אינו משלם ע"פ עצמו. אור"י: דאי קאי ר"ש בן יהודה אמתניתין דהכא, הא דמשמע בריש "נערה" לקמן (דף מב.) דלר"ש, אי דקא תבע בושת ופגם – מחייב ליה קרבן שבועה – היינו משום דהתם תבעו האב תחלה, ואין שייך לומר לאו כל הימנו כו' כדקאמר הכא. ואין צריך לומר דתרי תנאי אליבא דר' שמעון. (א) ועוד אומר רשב"א: דההיא דלקמן איכא לאוקמי בבת גרים, וניחא לה לדידה ולאביה, דליכא למימר דלמא איכא חד במדינת הים דלא ניחא ליה. ומיהו, אי קאי ר' שמעון אמתניתין דשבועות, דמייתי לקמן בריש "נערה" (ג"ז שם) – ע"כ תרי תנאי אליבא דר' שמעון.

***האומר** גנבתי כו'. מוציא ש"ר, ויוצא בשן ועין דלא תנא – איכא למימר דאתיא בזה הכלל. [שייך לעיל במתני']

***זה** הכלל כל המשלם יותר על מה שהזיק כו'. ואפילו למ"ד בפרק "שור שנגח ארבעה וחמשה" (ב"ק דף מ.) דכופר היינו דמי המזיק, לא חשיב יותר ממה שהזיק, אע"פ שפעמים שוה מזיק יותר מניזק – דפדיון נפשו הוא נותן. [ג"ז שייך לעיל]

לא נצרכא אלא לפחת נבילה. אע"ג דלאו דידיה שקיל, מ"מ כיון דזכי ליה רחמנא חצי נזק – חשבינן ליה בתשלומין מה שפחתה הנבלה. והכא לא שייך למימר קרנא דתורך קבירא ביה, כדאמרי' ב"המניח" בסופו (ב"ק דף לד.), דהתם ודאי שלא נהרג השור, שייך לומר הכי, דאין לו למכור שורו בשביל כן, שסבור שיבריא. אבל הכא, מיד כשנהרג – יש לו למוכרו, שידוע שתפחת הנבילה ותסריח.

תנינא תשלומי נזק מלמד שהבעלים מטפלים בנבילה כו'. הכי דייקא לה בבבא קמא (דף י:): חבתי בנזקו לא קתני, אלא בתשלומי נזקו כו'. **אי** משום חצי כופר לאו שיורא הוא וכו'. לאו פירכא היא, אלא שינויא הוא, דלא תיקשי למ"ד פלגא ניזקא ממונא מאי שייר – דשייר חצי כופר, ומשני: לא שייר כלום, וחצי כופר לאו שיורא הוא. וכן איכא בנזיר בפ' "ג' מינים" (דף לח: ושם) גבי אי משום "לא יחל" – לאו שיורא הוא, וכן בפרק "החליל" (סוכה דף נד. ושם). וההוא דהתם מגומגם טפי. הא

עין משפט נר מצוה

פט א מיי' פ"ב מהל' נערה הל' יב ופ"ה מהל' סנהדרין הל' יד:

צ ב מיי' פ"ג מהלכות גניבה הלכה ט סמג עשין עא טור ח"מ סי' שמח:

צא ג מיי' פ"ה מהלכות סנהדרין הלכה יד סמג עשין ע:

צב ד מיי' פ"ב מהל' נזקי ממון הל' ח.

צג ה מיי' פ"ב שם הל' ז ופ"ה מהלכות סנהדרין הלכה ט סמג עשין ע טוש"ע ח"מ סי' א סעי' א:

צד ו ז ח מיי' פ"א מהל' נזקי ממון הלכה ג סמג עשין סז טוש"ע ח"מ סי' שפט סעיף ב ג ד ט:

צה ט מיי' פ"י שם הל' ב סמג שם:

תוספות רי"ד

מתני' האומר פתיתי את בתו של פלוני משלם בושת ופגם ע"פ עצמו ואינו משלם קנס. האומר גנבתי משלם את הקרן ע"פ עצמו ואינו משלם לא תשלומי כפל ולא ד' וה'. המית שורי את פלוני או שורו של פלוני ה"ז משלם על פי עצמו. המית שורי עבדו של פלוני אינו משלם ע"פ עצמו. זה הכלל כל המשלם יתר ממה שהזיק אינו משלם ע"פ עצמו: וליתני אנסתי. לא מבעיא קאמר לא מבעיא אנסתי דלא פגים לה אבל פתיתי דפגים לה אימא לא משלם בושת ופגם ע"פ עצמו קמ"ל: ומתני' דלא כי האי תנא דתניא ר"ש בן יהודה אומר משום (רב הונא) [ר"ש] אף בושת ופגם אינו משלם ע"פ עצמו לא כל הימנו שיפגום בתו של פלוני. ואינו משלם קנס ע"פ עצמו כדנפקא לן מאשר ירשיעון אלהים פרט למרשיע את עצמו: ואי קשיא. הכא תנן דבושת הוי ממון ומשלם ע"פ עצמו ובריש פרק המניח אמרי' חסרא חסרא קנסא קמגבית בבבל וקרי התם לבושת קנס. תשובה לעולם בושת ממונא הוי לשלם ע"פ עצמו שאין בו שום יתירות אלא שמין לפי המבייש והמתבייש והתם קרי ליה קנסא לומר שאין גובין אותו בבבל דכל מידי דאית ביה חסרון כיס גבינן ליה בבבל אבל בושת דלית ביה חסרון כיס לא גבי' לי' בבבל כדאמרינן בפרק החובל: המית שורי את פלוני משלם ע"פ עצמו פי' דכופרא לאו קנסא הוא דכפי שוי' של ניזק משלם ואף למ"ד כפי שויה של מזיק כופרא ממונא הוי ומשלם ע"פ עצמו: המית שורי את עבדו וכו'. בפרק שור שנגח ד' וה' מוכיח שאפילו שויה של עבד אינו משלם ע"פ עצמו דכל ל' כסף הוו קנסא: זה הכלל וכו'. איתמר פלגא נזקא שחייבה תורה לשור תם. ר"פ אמר ממונא. פי' ומשלם ע"פ עצמו. רב הונא בריה דרב יהושע אמר פלגא נזקא קנסא רב פפא אמר ממונא סתם שוורים לאו בחזקת שימור קיימי. פי' אם לא ישמרו בעלים שלא יזיקו אינן בחזקת משתמר מאיליהן שלא יזיקו אלא מזיקין אפילו נזקא דלאו אורחיה הלכך על מריהו רמיא לנטרינהו וזה שלא שמרו בדין הוא דלשלם כוליה. ורחמנא הוא דחס עליה דאכתי לא אייעד תורא. פי' ואיהו מה שמשלם בדין משלם. ורב הונא בריה דרב יהושע אמר פלגא נזקא קנסא קסבר סתם שוורים בחזקת שימור קיימי ובדין הוא דלא לשלם כלל ורחמנא הוא דקנסיה כי היכי דנטרינהו לתורי'. פי' שיוסיף

מסורות הש"ס

[דף מב.]

ס"א טבחתי ומכרתי

ב"ק טו: מג.

שם טו. [וסם כל הסוגיא ונזכר עוד שבועות לג.]

שם יד:

שם טו:

[ואם איתא *ליתני נמי הא שהתם כו' כצ"ל רש"ל]

הגהות הב"ח

(א) תוס' ד"ה ר' שמעון וכו' דתרי תנאי אליבא דר' שמעון ומיהו אי קאי ר"ש אמתניתין וכו' ועוד אומר רשב"א וכו' דלא ניחא ליה כו' נ"ב:

הָא מַנִּי – ר' יוֹסֵי הַגְּלִילִי הִיא, דְּאָמַר: תָּם מְשַׁלֵּם חֲצִי כּוֹפֶר. *ת"ש: "הֵמִית שׁוֹרִי אֶת פְּלוֹנִי", אוֹ "שׁוֹרוֹ שֶׁל פְּלוֹנִי" – הֲרֵי זֶה מְשַׁלֵּם עַל פִּי עַצְמוֹ. מַאי לָאו בְּתָם? לָא, בְּמוּעָד. אֲבָל בְּתָם מַאי – אֵינוֹ מְשַׁלֵּם עַל פִּי עַצְמוֹ. אַדְּתָנֵי סֵיפָא: "עַבְדּוֹ שֶׁל פְּלוֹנִי" אֵינוֹ מְשַׁלֵּם ע"פ עַצְמוֹ – נִיפְלוֹג וְנִיתְנֵי בְּדִידָהּ: בַּמֶּה דְּבָרִים אֲמוּרִים – בְּמוּעָד, *אֲבָל תָּם אֵינוֹ מְשַׁלֵּם עַל פִּי עַצְמוֹ! כּוּלָּהּ בְּמוּעָד קָמַיְירֵי. ת"ש, זֶה הַכְּלָל: כָּל הַמְשַׁלֵּם יָתֵר עַל מַה שֶּׁהִזִּיק אֵינוֹ מְשַׁלֵּם ע"פ עַצְמוֹ. הָא פָּחוֹת מִמַּה שֶּׁהִזִּיק – מְשַׁלֵּם ע"פ עַצְמוֹ! לָא תֵּימָא: הָא פָּחוֹת מִמַּה שֶּׁהִזִּיק, אֶלָּא אֵימָא: הָא כְּמָה שֶּׁהִזִּיק – מְשַׁלֵּם ע"פ עַצְמוֹ. אֲבָל פָּחוֹת מַאי – אֵינוֹ מְשַׁלֵּם ע"פ עַצְמוֹ. לִיתְנֵי: זֶה הַכְּלָל: כָּל שֶׁאֵינוֹ מְשַׁלֵּם כְּמָה שֶּׁהִזִּיק – אֵינוֹ מְשַׁלֵּם עַל פִּי עַצְמוֹ, דְּמַשְׁמַע פָּחוֹת וּמַשְׁמַע יָתֵר! תְּיוּבְתָּא. וְהִלְכְתָא: פַּלְגָא נִיזְקָא קְנָסָא. *תְּיוּבְתָּא וְהִלְכְתָא?! אִין, טַעְמָא מַאי אִיתּוֹתַב – מִשּׁוּם דְּלָא קָתָנֵי כְּמָה שֶּׁהִזִּיק. לָא פְּסִיקָא לֵיהּ, כֵּיוָן דְּאִיכָּא [א]חֲצִי נֶזֶק צְרוֹרוֹת דְּהִלְכְתָא גְּמִירִי לָהּ דְּמָמוֹנָא הוּא – מִשּׁוּם הָכִי לָא קָתָנֵי. וְהַשְׁתָּא דְּאָמְרַתְּ פַּלְגָא נִיזְקָא קְנָסָא, [ב]הַאי כַּלְבָּא דַּאֲכַל אִימְּרֵי, וְשׁוּנְרָא דְּאָכֵיל תַּרְנְגוֹלֵי רַבְרְבֵי – מְשׁוּנָּה הוּא, וְלָא מַגְבִּינַן בְּבָבֶל. אֲבָל זוּטְרֵי – אוֹרְחֵיהּ הוּא, וּמַגְבִּינַן. [ג]וְאִי תָּפַס – לָא מַפְּקִינַן מִינֵּיהּ. וְאִי אָמַר: אַקְבְּעוּ לִי זִימְנָא לְאֶרֶץ יִשְׂרָאֵל, מַקְבְּעִינַן לֵיהּ, וְאִי לָא אָזֵיל, מְשַׁמְּתִינַן לֵיהּ. בֵּין כָּךְ וּבֵין כָּךְ מְשַׁמְּתִינַן לֵיהּ. דְּאָמְרִינַן לֵיהּ: סַלֵּיק הֶיזֵּיקָךְ, *מִדְּרַבִּי נָתָן. דְּתַנְיָא, ר' נָתָן אוֹמֵר: [ד]מִנַּיִן שֶׁלֹּא יְגַדֵּל אָדָם כֶּלֶב רַע בְּתוֹךְ בֵּיתוֹ וְלֹא יַעֲמִיד סוּלָּם רָעוּעַ בְּתוֹךְ בֵּיתוֹ – שֶׁנֶּאֱמַר: °"וְלֹא תָשִׂים דָּמִים בְּבֵיתֶךָ". (דברים כב)

הדרן עלך אלו נערות

הא מני רבי יוסי הגלילי היא דאמר תם משלם חצי כופר. וליכא שיורא, דאי משום דמועד משלם כופר שלם ותם אינו משלם אלא חצי כופר – הא לאו שיורא הוא, דהא תנן תם משלם חצי נזק ומועד נזק שלם, וכופר בכלל. וא"ת: אכתי ליתני דמועד אף כשהוא בסקילה משלם כופר, ותם כשהוא בסקילה אינו משלם כופר כלל, דהביאהו לב"ד וישלם לך, דהוא עצמו אינו משתלם אלא מגופו, כדאמרינן בפרק "שור שנגח ד' וה'" (ב"ק דף מב. ושם)! וי"ל: דהך נמי לא הוי שיור, דהוי בכלל הא דקתני תם מגופו ומועד מן העלייה. *ומיהו תימה: דלא אשכחן בהדיא בשום מקום שהיה אומר ר' יוסי הגלילי דתם משלם חצי כופר. ואי משום דדריש רבי יוסי הגלילי בפרק "שור שנגח ד' וה'" (ג"ז שם) "נקי" מדמי ולדות, ולא דריש "נקי" מחצי כופר, מכלל דסבר דחייב – ודלמא לעולם סבר דפטור, וטעמא משום דפטור מחצי כופר לא איצטריך קרא, דכשהשור בסקילה לא שייך כופר, דהביאהו לב"ד וישלם לך. וכשאין השור בסקילה, כגון על פי עד אחד או על פי הבעלים, פטור מדרשה, דאמר התם (דף מג.) שור שהמית בן חורין שלא בכוונה – פטור, שנאמר "השור יסקל וגם בעליו יומת" – בזמן שהשור בסקילה בעלים משלמין כופר כו'! ונראה דה"פ: הא מני ר' יוסי הגלילי היא, דאמר תם משלם חצי כופר. פי': דלא ממעט חצי כופר מ"נקי", ולאו דוקא משלם קאמר, אלא היה משלם אם היה לו ממה להשתלם. ולשום תנא לא הוה חצי כופר שיור כי אם לרבי אלעזר, דדריש "נקי" מחצי כופר, ולית ליה דרשה. וכשאין השור בסקילה – מועד משלם, ותם אינו משלם. והא דנקט רבי יוסי הגלילי טפי מרבי עקיבא, דדריש, "נקי" מדמי עבד, דלדידיה נמי דחצי כופר לא הוי שיור – דמי עבד הוי שיור*.

ואי תפס כו'. פר"ח דדוקא אי תפס את המזיק עצמו, אבל דבר אחר – לא, דלענין מזיק עצמו, סקלו חכמים, שיכול לתופסו, דאל"כ יתפוס כל אשר לו ולא נפיק מיניה, דאין דנין דיני קנסות, ואם נוטלים המותר ומשאיר כדי נזק, הרי אנו דנין דיני קנסות, ודוחק.

הדרן עלך אלו נערות

הָא מַנִּי ר' יוֹסֵי הַגְּלִילִי הִיא דְּאָמַר תָּם מְשַׁלֵּם חֲצִי כּוֹפֶר. דְּדָרֵישׁ לְהַאי "נָקִי" לִדְרָשָׁה אַחֲרִיתִי, לִדְמֵי וְלָדוֹת – אִם נָגַח אִשָּׁה וְיָצְאוּ יְלָדֶיהָ. הִלְכָּךְ לָא הֲוָה לֵיהּ לְפַלּוֹגֵי בֵּינַיְיהוּ בְּכוֹפֶר. וְכִי תֵּימָא: הֲוָה לֵיהּ לְפַלּוֹגֵי, דְּהַאי פַּלְגָא וְהַאי כּוּלֵּיהּ – הַסֵּיפָא בִּכְלַל רֵישָׁא הִיא, דְּקָתָנֵי: תָּם מְשַׁלֵּם חֲצִי נֶזֶק וּמוּעָד נֶזֶק שָׁלֵם, וְתָנָא בִּנְזִיקִין, וְהוּא הַדִּין לְכוֹפֶר. מַאי לָאו בְּתָם. וְאִי מִשּׁוּם דְּקָתָנֵי בָּהּ "הֵמִית שׁוֹרִי אֶת פְּלוֹנִי" דְּחִיּוּבוֹ כּוֹפֶר, וְתָם לָאו בַּר כּוֹפֶר הוּא – הָא מַנִּי רַבִּי יוֹסֵי הַגְּלִילִי הִיא. אַדְּתָנֵי עַבְדּוֹ שֶׁל פְּלוֹנִי כו'. דְּלָא מַשְׁכַּח פָּטוּר עַל פִּי עַצְמוֹ אֶלָּא בְּעֶבֶד. נִיפְלוֹג בְּדִידָהּ. בְּבֶן חוֹרִין. וּבִבְהֵמָה נַמִי הֲוָה מָצֵי לְשַׁנּוּיֵי חִילּוּק, וּלְמִיתְנֵי דְּאִיכָּא דְּלָא מְשַׁלֵּם עַל פִּי עַצְמוֹ. בד"א. דִּמְשַׁלֵּם ע"פ עַצְמוֹ בְּמוּעָד כו'. כּוּלָּהּ בְּמוּעָד קָמַיְירֵי. בְּמוּעָד אָתָא לְאַשְׁמוּעֵי', דְּאַף הוּא יֵשׁ בּוֹ חִילּוּק, דְּאִיכָּא בֵּיהּ מִידֵּי דְּלָא מְשַׁלֵּם עַל פִּי עַצְמוֹ, וּמַאי נִיהוּ – נְגִיחַת עֶבֶד. וְאִי הֲוָה תָּנֵי כִּדְקָאָמְרַתְּ – הֲוָה שָׁבֵיק נַמִי לְאוֹרְחֵיהּ, דְּרֵישָׁא מַיְירֵי בְּמוּעָד וְסֵיפָא נִיתְנֵי תָּם. וּמַה לִּי שְׁבַקָהּ תַּנָּא לְאוֹרְחֵיהּ גַּבֵּי נִיזָּק לְדַלֵּג מִבֶּן חוֹרִין לְעֶבֶד, מַה לִּי שְׁבַקָהּ בְּמַזִּיק וּלְדַלֵּג מִמּוּעָד לְתָם. יָתֵר עַל מַה שֶּׁהִזִּיק. כְּגוֹן נְגִיחַת עֶבֶד. וְכֵן אוֹנֵס, וּמְפַתֶּה, וּמוֹצִיא שֵׁם רַע, וְתַשְׁלוּמֵי כֶפֶל, וְתַשְׁלוּמֵי אַרְבָּעָה וַחֲמִשָּׁה. הָא פָּחוֹת מִמַּה שֶּׁהִזִּיק. כְּגוֹן חֲצִי נֶזֶק דְּתָם. הָכִי גָּרְסִינַן: לִיתְנֵי כָּל שֶׁאֵינוֹ מְשַׁלֵּם כְּמָה שֶּׁהִזִּיק אֵינוֹ מְשַׁלֵּם ע"פ עַצְמוֹ. וְהִלְכְתָא פַּלְגָא נִיזְקָא קְנָסָא. דְּהוֹאִיל וְכָל חֲצִי נֶזֶק אֵינוֹ אֶלָּא בִּנְזָקָא דְּלָאו אוֹרְחֵיהּ, לָאו עַל מָרֵיהּ הֲוָה רְמִיָא לְמִינְטְרֵיהּ בְּהָכִי, אֶלָּא קְנָסָא הוּא, כִּי הֵיכִי דְּלוֹסִיף בֵּיהּ נְטִירוּתָא. טַעְמָא מַאי אִיתּוֹתַב. כְּלוֹמַר, תְּיוּבְתָּא מַאי הִיא? מִשּׁוּם דְּלָא קָתָנֵי כָּל שֶׁאֵינוֹ מְשַׁלֵּם כְּמָה שֶּׁהִזִּיק אֵינוֹ מְשַׁלֵּם עַל פִּי עַצְמוֹ. דְּלִישְׁתַּמַּע מִינָּהּ נַמִי חֲצִי נֶזֶק – הָא לָאו תְּיוּבְתָּא הִיא. כֵּיוָן דְּאִיכָּא חֲצִי נֶזֶק. דִּמְשַׁלֵּם בְּנִזְקֵי בְּהֵמָה בְּמִתְהַלֶּכֶת וְהִתִּיזָה צְרוֹרוֹת מִתַּחַת רַגְלֶיהָ וְהִזִּיקָה, דִּתְנַן בְּבָבָא קַמָּא (דף יז.) דִּמְשַׁלֶּמֶת חֲצִי נֶזֶק. וְהַהוּא חֲצִי נֶזֶק קַיְימָא לַן בְּב"ק דְּהִלְכְתָא גְּמִירִי לָהּ מִסִּינַי שֶׁהוּא תּוֹלָדָה שֶׁל רֶגֶל, וּפְטוּרָה בִּרְה"ר כִּי רֶגֶל. וְנִזְקֵי רֶגֶל לָאו קְנָסָא נִינְהוּ אֶלָּא מָמוֹנָא, שֶׁהֲרֵי מוּעֶדֶת מִתְּחִילָּתָהּ, וְגַבֵּי צְרוֹרוֹת הוּא דְּאַקֵּיל רַחֲמָנָא. וְכֵיוָן דְּמָמוֹנָא הוּא, מְשַׁלֵּם ע"פ עַצְמוֹ, מִשּׁוּם הָכִי לָא פְּסִיקָא לֵיהּ לְמִיתְנֵי כָּל שֶׁאֵינוֹ מְשַׁלֵּם כְּמָה שֶּׁהִזִּיק, דְּהָא אִיכָּא הַאי. דַּאֲכַל אִימְּרֵי. שֶׁתָּנַק טְלָאִים חַיִּים וַאֲכָלָם. מְשׁוּנָּה הוּא. אֵין דַּרְכּוֹ בְּכָךְ, וְכָל נֶזֶק מְשׁוּנֶּה בִּבְהֵמָה הָוֵי תּוֹלָדָה דְּקֶרֶן תַּמָּה, שֶׁאַף הִיא מְשׁוּנָּה, שֶׁאֵין דַּרְכָּהּ בְּכָךְ, וַחֲצִי נֶזֶק הוּא דִּמְשַׁלֵּם. וְכֵיוָן דִּקְנָסָא הוּא – לָא מַגְבִּינַן לֵיהּ בְּדַיָּינֵי בָבֶל, שֶׁאֵין שָׁם סְמִיכָה בִּזְקֵנִים וְלָא מִקְּרוּ מוּמְחִים, וְגַבֵּי קְנָס כְּתִיב (שמות כב) "יַרְשִׁיעֻן אֱלֹהִים". אוֹרְחֵיהּ הוּא. וַהֲווּ לְהוּ נִזְקֵי דְּשֵׁן, וְשֵׁן מְשַׁלֶּמֶת נֶזֶק שָׁלֵם, וּמָמוֹנָא הוּא וְגוֹבִין אוֹתוֹ בְּבָבֶל. וְאִי תָּפַס. נִיזָּק מָמוֹנָא דְּמַזִּיק גַּבֵּי קְנָסָא דַּחֲצִי נִזְקוֹ, דְּאֵין צָרִיךְ לַעֲסוֹק לְפָנֵינוּ. לָא מַפְּקִינַן מִינֵּיהּ. וְגַבֵּי פַּלְגָא נִזְקֵיהּ. וְאִי לָא תָּפַס, וְאָמַר הַמַּזִּיק: קִבְעוּ לִי זְמַנָּא בְּאַרְעָא דְּיִשְׂרָאֵל, הַשִּׂיאוּהוּ לֵילֵךְ עִמִּי לָדוּן לִפְנֵי דַּיָּינֵי אֶרֶץ יִשְׂרָאֵל – קָבְעִינַן לֵיהּ. בֵּין כָּךְ וּבֵין כָּךְ. בֵּין שֶׁרוֹצֶה נִיזָּק לֵילֵךְ לְאֶרֶץ יִשְׂרָאֵל, בֵּין שֶׁאֵינוֹ רוֹצֶה. מְשַׁמְּתִינַן לֵיהּ. לַמַּזִּיק, מִיהָא לַהֲרוֹג אוֹתוֹ כֶּלֶב וּלְסַלֵּק הֶיזֵּיקֵיהּ.

הדרן עלך אלו נערות

תוספות רי"ד

שיוסיף שמירה על שמירתו ת"ש כל המשלם יתר ממה שהזיק אינו משלם ע"פ עצמו. פי' כגון נגיחת העבד וכן אונס ומפתה ומוציא שם רע ותשלומי כפל ותשלומי ד' וה' הא פחות משלם פי' כגון חצי נזק דתם. לא תימא פחות ממה שהזיק אלא אימא הא כמה שהזיק משלם ע"פ עצמו א"ה ליתני זה הכלל כל שאינו משלם כל מה שהזיק משלם ע"פ עצמו דמשמע פחות ומשמע יותר תיובתא. ופסיק תלמודא והלכתא פלגא נזקא קנסא. פי' דהואיל וכל חצי נזק אינו אלא היזקא דלאו אורחיה לאו על מרא רמיא לנטורי בהכי אלא קנסא הוא כי היכי דלוסיף ביה נטירותא תיובתא והלכתא אין טעמא מאי איתותב. פי' תיובתיה מאי הוא משום דלא תני הכי פי' לא קתני כל שאינו משלם (כלו) [כמה שהזיק] ש"מ (נמי) חצי נזק [ממונא] הא לאו תיובתא הוא כיון דאיכא חצי נזק צרורות דהל' גמירי לה דממונא הוא ומשלם ע"פ עצמו שהן תולדה דרגל מש"ה לא קתני פי' משום כיון (דאין) [דאיכא] חצי נזק המשתלם [ע"פ עצמו] (כנזק) [כגון] בהמה המהלכת והתיזה צרורות מתחת רגליה והזיקו דתנן בבבא קמא דמשלם חצי נזק והאי חצי נזק קי"ל דהל' גמירי לה דממונא הוא ומשלם ע"פ עצמו שהן תולדה דרגל ופטורים בר"ה כרגל ונזקי רגל לאו קנסא נינהו אלא ממונא שהרי מועדת בתחילתה ובגבי צרורות הוא דאקיל רחמנא. וכיון דממונא הוא משלם ע"פ עצמו מ"ה לא פסיקא ליה למיתני כל שאינו משלם דהא איכא האי. והשתא דאמרת פ"נ קנסא האי כלבא דאכיל אימרא ושונרא דאכיל תרנגולא רברבא משונה הוא. פי' אין דרכו בכך וכל נזק משונה בבהמה הוי תולדה דקרן תמה שאין דרכה בכך וחצי נזק הוא שמשלם. וכיון דקנסא הוא לא מגבי' בבבל. פי' בדייני בבל שאין שם סמיכה בזקנים ולא מיקרי אלהים מומחים ולגבי קנס כתיב אשר ירשיען אלהים. ואי תפיש ניזק ממונו של מזיק גבי קנסא דחצי נזקו ולא מפקי' מיניה. ואי אמר אומניה בהדי לדינא בא"י מזמינן לי'. פי' ואי לאו תפיש ואמר קבען קבעו לי זמנא בא"י קבעי' לי' ואי לא אזיל משמתנן לי': בין כך ובין כך. פי' בין שרצה ניזק לילך בא"י בין לא. משמתנן ליה עד דמסלק היזקה מביתיה מר' נתן דתניא אר"נ מנין שלא יגדל אדם כלב רע בתוך ביתו ולא יעמיד סולם רעוע שנאמר ולא תשים דמים בביתך. ופי' וה"ה נמי דלקנס דאונס ומפתה אע"ג דלא מגבי' ליה בבבל אי תפיש לא מפקי' מיניה אבל להזמינו לדין לא"י לא מזמנן ליה שאין עתה ישיבות קבועות שם כאשר היה אז. וראיתי בתשובות רב צמח גאון ז"ל אלו נערות שיש להן קנס ששאלת מהו להגבות שלא יהא חוטא נשכר כיוצא בזה אמרו חכמים אין מגבין קנס בבבל שלח לי' חסרא חסרא קנס קמגבית בבבל אלמא הלכתא רווחת היא שאין מגבין קנסות אלא בירושלים ובסנהדרין של כ"ג ותו קאמרי' א"ר נזקי שור בשור ונזקי שור באדם גובין אותן בבבל אבל אדם באדם ואדם בשור אין מגבין אותו בבבל (ולא) [אך] משום שלא יהא חוטא נשכר ושלא יהו [בני אדם] פרוצים בניזקין שכיון שהם יודעים שאין מגבין קנסות בבבל שלוחים יד זה בזה נהגו חכמים האחרונים לנדותו עד שהוא מפייסו בממון או שירבה עליו רעים ויפייסו בדברים. ומעשה בא' שהפיל שינו של חבירו ובא לפני מר רב צמח גאון ז"ל וא"ל דבר קצוב אני חותך עליך ופייסהו או בממון או בדברים ועכשיו כל דיני קנסות בזמן הזה שהנהיג אדונינו מר רב צמח גאון ז"ל אנו נוהגים בו היום בכל קהלות הקודש:

גליון הש"ס

תוס' ד"ה הא מני וכו' ומיהו תימה. עי' תשובת מהרלב"ח סי' קי"ב:

תלמוד בבלי

הוצאת קורן ירושלים

— מהדורת נאה —

מסכת כתובות
דף כט. עד דף מא:

COMMENTARY BY

Rabbi Adin Even-Israel
Steinsaltz

EDITOR-IN-CHIEF

Rabbi Dr Tzvi Hersh Weinreb

EXECUTIVE EDITOR

Rabbi Joshua Schreier

•

STEINSALTZ CENTER
KOREN PUBLISHERS JERUSALEM

Please note that the number ranges that appear at the bottom of each daf of the Vilna pages indicate the corresponding pages of the Koren Talmud Bavli translation and commentary.

תלמוד בבלי

— מהדורת נאה —

כתובות חלק ג

Steinsaltz Center

ירושלים

KOREN